The Past in Perspective

The Past in Perspective

AN INTRODUCTION TO HUMAN PREHISTORY

Kenneth L. Feder
Central Connecticut State University

Mayfield Publishing Company
Mountain View, California
London • Toronto

For Josh and Jacob

Library of Congress Cataloging-in-Publication Data
Feder, Kenneth L.
    The past in perspective : an introduction to human prehistory /
Kenneth L. Feder.
      p.   cm.
    Includes bibliographical references and index.
    ISBN 1-55934-384-2
     1. Man, Prehistoric. 2. Human evolution. 3. Fossil man.
4. Human remains (Archaeology)   I. Title.
GN766.F43   1995
573.3—dc20   95-23783
                                     CIP

Manufactured in the United States of America
10 9 8 7 6 5 4 3 2

Mayfield Publishing Company
1280 Villa Street
Mountain View, California 94041

Sponsoring editor, Janet M. Beatty; production editor, Lynn Rabin Bauer; manuscript editor, Elliot Simon; text and cover designer, Jeanne M. Schreiber; art manager, Jean Mailander; illustrators, Academy Artworks, Joan Carol, Patti Isaacs, and Judith Ogus; cover photograph © Tom Till; manufacturing manager, Randy Hurst. The text was set in 10.5/12.5 Minion by Thompson Type and printed on 45# Optimatte, PMS 1595, by Banta Company. Photograph on pp. 450–451 by the Food and Agriculture Organization, United Nations, photo by H. Null.

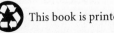 This book is printed on recycled paper.

Preface

"The past is a bucket of ashes," said the poet Carl Sandburg. Surely he was wrong. The past is not cold, dead, and spent. It is alive in everything we are and will be. We live in a universe filled with its traces. The stars in the night sky shine with a light that began its journey millions of years ago. The fossilized remnants of creatures that once walked the earth lie entombed in the soil beneath our feet. Cooking hearths and food scraps, pyramids and pottery, stone tools and bone awls, cave paintings and ivory sculptures—all date to the ancient human past yet exist in the present. They are not ashes; they represent comprehensible evidence of species and cultures whose time is past, but that nonetheless deserve our attention.

The Past in Perspective: An Introduction to Human Prehistory focuses on this evidence of the past in an accessible chronicle of human physical and cultural evolution. The audience for this text is undergraduates who have had no previous coursework in archaeology; for many, it will be their only academic exposure to our prehistoric past. Rather than overwhelm beginning students with an all-inclusive, detailed survey of the human past, this text looks at the major themes of the human evolutionary story. It begins with the evolution of our earliest hominid ancestors, traces the evolution of the modern human species, and follows the various pathways our ancestors took in the development of food-producing societies and complex civilizations. My goal throughout was to instill in readers an appreciation for the long chronicle of humanity and the ongoing processes we use to construct and assess that story.

HOW THE TEXT IS ORGANIZED

Chapters 1–4 provide context and background for the discussion of human prehistory. Chapter 1 places the study of the human past in the context of science, using genealogy as a metaphor for the study of human prehistory. Chapter 2 focuses on how a scientific approach to the study of prehistory developed and the role biblical literalism played. Chapter 3 is a brief overview of key methodologies employed by archaeologists and paleoanthropologists. Chapter 4 presents a geological and biological context for the evolution of humanity; this summary of the geology and paleontology of the earth focuses on the evolution of the Miocene apes.

Following these introductory chapters with their contextual purpose, Chapters 5–15 present a chronological survey of the human past. Each chapter follows a consistent format with these headings: **Chapter Overview, Prelude, Chronicle, Issues and Debates, Case Study Close-Up, Visiting the Past, Summary,** and **To Learn More.** My belief is that a consistent format provides a pedagogical advantage; the trajectory of human physical and cultural evolution becomes far more apparent and connected. What we know, what we don't know, and what are still topics of vigorous debate will be clear to the reader.

The CHAPTER OVERVIEW introduces the primary topic of the chapter in several brief paragraphs.

The PRELUDE represents a conscious attempt on my part to provide a pedagogical "hook" for each chapter. Personal anecdotes or fascinating historical incidents, for example, immediately engage students in the key issue or issues of the chapter, whether it is upright locomotion, the origins of artistic expression, or the power of ancient civilizations.

The CHRONICLE presents in narrative form a consensus view of that part of the human past that is the chapter's focus. It represents the heart of each chapter, providing our current understanding of the time period covered, the hominids discussed, and the cultural evolutionary developments reflected in the time period.

ISSUES AND DEBATES sections discuss the answers we have been able to provide for key questions about human physical and cultural evolution as well as the unresolved issues that remain and the ongoing debates. These sections provide differing—and sometimes competing—perspectives. Students are thus exposed to the sometimes messy process of science fraught with disagreements, shifting paradigms, and only hard-won consensus.

The CASE STUDY CLOSE-UP is a detailed examination of one or more sites considered diagnostic or emblematic of the time period or primary issue of the chapter.

VISITING THE PAST sections direct readers to key sites mentioned in the chapter that are open to the public, suggest museums where the materials from important sites discussed in the chapter are displayed, and point out computer software "virtual visits" that provide detailed discussions, photographs, videos, and animations related to the chapter topic.

Each chapter SUMMARY provides a brief recapitulation of the key issues in the chapter.

TO LEARN MORE presents a short list of books, magazine articles, and additional CD-ROM titles that focus on the central topics and issues of the chapter.

ADDITIONAL FEATURES

In addition to a consistent chapter format, I've included a number of additional features that I hope will make this text a more useful learning tool.

- A **timeline** opens every chapter and helps place the key events and sites mentioned in the body of the chapter within a global historical context. The timeline in Chapter 1 shows at a glance the chronological focus of each chapter in the text.
- To help students better orient themselves on the world stage, I've included abundant maps throughout the book. In addition, for Chapters 5–15, I've provided at the beginning of each chapter a **list of sites,** broken out by country, discussed therein.
- A list of **Key Terms** at the ends of chapters identifies important terms that appear in boldfaced type within the chapters; definitions can be found in the end-of-book glossary.
- The text's **visual appeal** enhances its readability. Detailed, colorful charts and drawings, as well as abundant photographs, underscore significant points in the text. Captions of the artwork add information rather than simply label the pictures.
- Full-color photographs that are cross-referenced to pertinent text discussions appear in a thematically organized **Color Portfolio.** The five thematic groupings offer close looks at the Ice Man, apes, the Paleolithic, the Neolithic, and civilization.
- The **Glossary, References,** and a comprehensive **Index** make information readily accessible.

SUPPLEMENTARY MATERIAL

The **Instructor's Manual** includes a test bank of multiple choice and short answer/essay questions, as well as chapter overviews, lists of key words, and suggested sources for videos, CD-ROMS, and Internet sites.

A **computerized Test Bank** is available free of charge to qualifying adopters. It is a powerful, easy-to-use test generation system that provides all test items on computer disk for IBM-compatible or Macintosh computers. You can select, add, or edit questions, randomize them, and print tests appropriate to your individual classes.

ACKNOWLEDGMENTS

I want to begin by thanking the many colleagues whose research has inspired this book and those who have provided specific help in the form of telephone conversations, letters, photographs, and artwork. I would especially like to note the kind and generous assistance of James Adovasio, Alison Brooks, Jeff Dahlberg, Tom Dillehay, James Dyer, Dan Early, John Fleagle, George Frison, Diane Gifford-Gonzalez, Michael Gramly, Fred Grine, Frank Hole, Bill Iseminger, John McCamant, Dolores Piperno, William Powers, John Shea, Pat Shipman, Fred Smith, Robert Tague, Krystyna Wasylikowa, and Melinda Zeder. Also, many thanks to the American Museum of Natural History, the Institute of Human Origins, and the Food and Agriculture Organization of the United Nations (especially to Ms. Giuditta Dolci-Favi) for the fine photographs they supplied.

Reviewers of this manuscript provided invaluable help; I'm particularly grateful to Douglas B. Bamforth, University of Colorado at Boulder; Peter Bleed, University of Nebraska, Lincoln; Christopher R. DeCorse, Syracuse University; Richard Effland, Jr., Mesa Community College; Douglas R. Givens, Saint Louis Community College; Nicholas Honerkamp, University of Tennessee at Chattanooga; and Paul D. Welch, Queens College, CUNY.

At Central Connecticut, my colleague Michael Park has been, as always, a terrific help. He has answered graciously every late-night phone call, acting as my sounding board, as well as being an unending source of figures, references, and information. I must thank two administrators, as well, for their assistance in providing release time to work on this book: Karen Beyard, Vice President of Academic Affairs, and George Clarke, Dean of Arts and Sciences. Also, many thanks to June Wellwood of Interlibrary Loan for all her good work on my behalf.

The folks at Mayfield have been, as usual, terrific. Thanks to Pam Trainer, who I hope has already forgiven me for all those permission letters I asked her to send; to Jeanne Schreiber for working her artistic magic in producing a thoroughly beautiful design; and to Jan Beatty, my sponsoring editor, who suggested this book in the first place. I especially want to thank my production editor, Lynn Rabin Bauer, who served as an ever-patient guide in the challenging task of bringing this book into the world.

My family's role in this book has been substantial. I'd like to thank Murray H. Feder, my globe-trotting father, for the wonderful photographs he supplied me. As you can readily see from the chapters herein, my sons Josh and Jacob have been genuine inspirations to me in thinking about the human past. A special thanks goes to Josh, who, though only nine years old, found a source for photos of Chauvet Cave after I was told that no photos were available. As is true with every undertaking in our charmed lives, my wife Melissa has made the entire process of writing this book fun. And, of course, thanks are due to Harpo for occasionally lifting his paws from my arms long enough for me to type a sentence or two and to Randolph for keeping the manuscript warm—and for those narrow-eyed glances that speak volumes. Surely my cats are what evolution has been aiming for all along.

Contents

6 The Human Lineage   116

7 Our Immediate Ancestors

9 Expanding Intellectual Horizons
ART AND IDEAS IN THE UPPER PALEOLITHIC   214

13   An Explosion of Complexity
THE FLOWERING OF CIVILIZATION IN THE OLD WORLD   356

14 An Explosion of Complexity
THE FLOWERING OF CIVILIZATION IN THE NEW WORLD   404

15 Chiefs and Kings in Recent Prehistory   428

The Past in Perspective

1

Prologue to the Past

CHAPTER OVERVIEW

Like genealogists who study the roots of individual families, paleoanthropologists and archaeologists study the roots of the human species. With evolution as the guiding principle, these scientists investigate humanity's biological and cultural past. This book focuses on the work of paleoanthropology and archaeology, viewing the story of humanity through the lens of evolution.

Some people decry the evolutionary perspective, believing it degrades the sanctity of human life. However, the evolutionary perspective views each life and each culture as precious. Each individual life has great dignity and enormous value when it is perceived as the unique product of 3.5 billion years of evolution. In the evolutionary view, we are each part of a grand work-in-progress. We and our societies are unique evolutionary experiments. This view generates a philosophy in which each of us is invaluable and irreplaceable.

CHRONOLOGICAL FOCUS OF THE CHAPTERS				
	15 billion	20,000,000	10,000,000	5,000,000
Chapter 1				
Chapter 2				
Chapter 3				
Chapter 4				
Chapter 5				
Chapter 6				
Chapter 7				
Chapter 8				
Chapter 9				
Chapter 10				
Chapter 11				
Chapter 12				
Chapter 13				
Chapter 14				
Chapter 15				
Chapter 16				

Years ago

4,000,000   3,000,000   2,000,000   1,000,000   500,000   250,000   100,000   50,000   10,000   Present

PROLOGUE

INTELLECTUAL HISTORY

METHODOLOGY

You can see them almost any day in town and county halls, court houses, libraries, and church basements. Often, they are older, retired people; but they also are young business people and middle-aged housewives, scientists and college students, computer programmers, writers, and carpenters. They all have one interest in common, an all-consuming avocation that occupies their time—the search for their genealogical roots. Crouched over dusty volumes of old birth records, death certificates, tax lists and marriage enumerations, deeds and wills, treaties and court cases, school lists and plantation records, immigration files and ship manifests, these amateur genealogists seem to be looking for their own place in history, searching for evidence of their own beginnings, pieces of their own past. They are looking for the names and records of their ancestors, reaching back across the chasm of time to connect with their roots (Figure 1.1).

Genealogical research is infectious and fascinating. Somehow, it puts your own life in a firmer context when you can view it as one link in a great chain of ancestors stretching back across generations and centuries. An awareness of your family history changes your perspective drastically, allowing you to view your life as not just an ephemeral thing of the here and now, but as part of a story that flows through time.

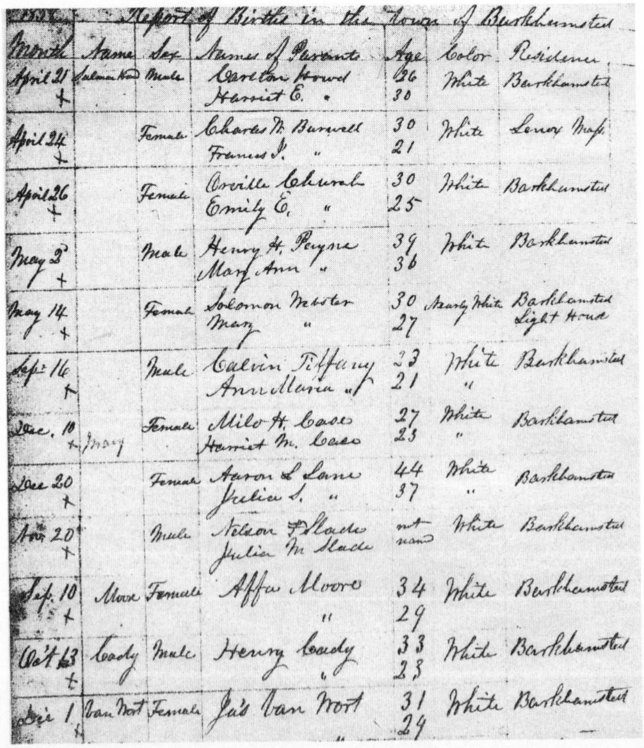

1858 Report of Births in the Town of Barkhamsted

Month	Name	Sex	Names of Parents	Age	Color	Residence
April 21 +	Salmon Howd	Male	Carleton Howd Harriet E.	26 30	White	Barkhamsted
April 24 +		Female	Charles M. Burwell Frances J. "	30 21	White	Lenox Mass.
April 26 +		Female	Orville Church Emily E. "	30 25	White	Barkhamsted
May 2 +		Male	Henry H. Payne Mary Ann "	39 36	White	Barkhamsted
May 14 +		Female	Solomon Webster Mary "	30 27	Nearly White	Barkhamsted Light House
Sept 16 +		Male	Calvin Tiffany Ann Maria "	23 21	White "	Barkhamsted
Dec. 10 + Mary		Female	Milo H. Case Harriet M. Case	27 23	White "	Barkhamsted
Dec 20 +		Female	Aaron L Lane Julia S. "	44 37	White "	Barkhamsted
Nov 20 +		Male	Nelson F. Slade Julia M Slade	not known	White	Barkhamsted
Sep. 10 +	Moore	Female	Affa Moore "	34 29	White	Barkhamsted
Oct 23 +	Cady	Male	Henry Cady "	33 23	White	Barkhamsted
Dec 1	Van Nort	Female	Ja's Van Nort "	31 29	White	Barkhamsted

FIGURE 1.1

This page from the records of the town of Barkhamsted, Connecticut, listing births for 1858, is an example of the written records that genealogists rely on to trace individuals and their families. (Barkhamsted, Connecticut, Town Records)

AN ARCHAEOLOGICAL GENEALOGY

In a sense, this book is about genealogical research, but of a much broader, deeper sort than that conducted by people looking for their relatives in centuries past. This book is about the genealogy of the human species, focusing on the ultimate biological and cultural roots of humanity. Our techniques, by necessity, differ from those of standard genealogy. Our raw data consist not of documents, photos, and records, but of bones, tools, pots, and pyramids. The time periods on which we focus are far different as well. The longest-lived families commonly can be traced back only hundreds of years, but the human family can be traced back millions of years. And our journey of discovery takes us not to local town halls and libraries, but to the sun-soaked savannas of Africa, the frigid caves of Ice Age Europe, the humid rain forests of Mesoamerica, and the fertile flood plains of the Tigris and Euphrates rivers in southwest Asia (Figure 1.2).

FIGURE 1.2

While genealogists may focus on local town records to trace an individual family through time, paleo-anthropologists and archaeologists often must journey farther afield in their attempt to trace the history of the entire human family. Here are two such places: the American Arctic, home to the first humans to settle in the New World (top: *see Chapter 10*), *and the forest of the central Yucatan Peninsula in Mexico, homeland of one of the world's ancient civilizations* (bottom: *see Chapter 14*). (*Top:* courtesy Marc Banks; *bottom:* K. L. Feder)

Though our methods and scales are very different, we "genealogists" of all sorts are pursuing the same thing; we are searching for our past in order to understand ourselves better. Where do we come from? How did we become who we are? What challenges confronted our ancestors along the way, and how did they respond to them? Just as genealogists investigate such issues as they apply to themselves and their own families, **paleoanthropologists** and **archaeologists** confront these same questions as they relate to the human species as a whole. They go beyond issues of their own personal sagas and focus on the grand sweep of human evolution and history to produce the genealogy of the whole human family. This book will focus on our human genealogy—what we currently know and understand about the roots of us all.

AN EVOLUTIONARY PHILOSOPHY

Evolution is the organizing theme of this book. The term itself evokes so much emotion and misunderstanding, it is important first to put it in context. I'll begin with the story of a confrontation I had with someone for whom evolution was an obscene concept.

Creationism

I had just attended a lecture given by a sincere but horribly misinformed gentleman who described himself as a **creationist;** he believed that God had created the universe and everything in it exactly as it now appears (Gish 1972; Morris 1974). He rejected completely the theory of evolution, in which the world and life are viewed as the result of entirely natural processes of change over enormous periods of time. He also categorically rejected the idea that evolution might be the process by which God created and continues to create life. Furthermore, he objected especially strenuously when the theory of evolution, in any form, was applied to the human species.

For the lecturer, the only acceptable explanation for the origin of life in general and human life in particular was the one in the Bible, in the Book of Genesis. An all-powerful, all-knowing God, he asserted, created humankind a mere 6,000 years ago. In this view, the history of the universe, including all human history and cultural development, had to be wedged into this incredibly narrow span of time.

It seemed to me that the lecturer based his arguments against evolution on a misinterpretation of evolution as well as his own unfamiliarity with the evidence. Nevertheless, his concern about the implications of evolution—what it signified about the value and importance of human life *if* we had been the product of a natural process rather than the ultimate creation of God—was obviously heartfelt. "What is the value of an individual human life—of *your* life," he asked, "if you are not the personal creation of a divine being but, instead, merely the result of a series of highly improbable chemical and biological accidents?"

These were reasonable concerns articulated by a deeply concerned person, issues we should all perhaps consider. Why should we help to protect or preserve the environment, endangered species, or even the lives of other people if we are just natural creatures living in a cruel world rather than the children of God? According to the theory of evolution, we are not so special, we are not the "crown of creation." Evolution, in the speaker's opinion, was responsible for a view of humanity that led to the seemingly complete devaluation of life and the deification of the self that we have witnessed in the twentieth century.

An Evolutionary View

I could not have disagreed more vehemently then or now with such a characterization of the theory of evolution and its implications. Biological evolution simply implies a process of systematic change through time. The natural world is vast and diverse, and many living things are born into it. Some of those living things possess, by chance, characteristics that increase the likelihood of their survival and of their having descendants who share those advantageous characteristics. An individual may be born that is faster, stronger, more dexterous, or able to move more efficiently through its habitat. It may be better camouflaged, have better visual acuity, be better at attracting a mate, or possess greater intelligence. These advantages may make it more likely to survive and more likely, therefore, to pass those characteristics on to subsequent generations.

Over vast spans of time an entire species can be moved toward these advantageous characteristics, since those who lack them tend to die more quickly—often, before becoming old enough to mate and produce descendants who also lack them. Through the slow and steady accumulation of advantageous characteristics, or as a result of the rapid appearance of a dramatically different and advantageous feature, a species can become so different that it no longer is even the same kind of animal. It has become a new and different species: It has evolved.

The varied and changing natural world provides the context in which an organism must live and to which it must adjust. Biological evolution is not directed; species do not actively develop strategies for survival—called **adaptations.** And biological evolution has no direction; species do not necessarily become bigger, stronger, or faster. In fact, the fossil record shows that most species become extinct. Those that survive do so because at least some individual members are lucky enough to possess physical or behavioral adaptations that allow them to.

For some species, the means of adjustment go beyond the solely biological. Such species are able, as a result of their great intelligence, to develop new adaptations virtually instantly. They can invent new ways of surviving and teach these new ways to other members of their species and to their offspring. These survival methods are not biological; they are cultural. **Culture** represents the nonbiological strategies for survival. Modern human beings rely, as did our ancient human ancestors, on cultural adaptations for survival. A discussion of these adaptations and how they, too, have systematically changed through time makes up a large portion of this book.

With all this in mind, I spoke to the lecturer afterwards, not hoping to change his fundamental view, but to point out a basic fallacy in his argument about what the theory of evolution means about the value of life itself. It is true, I admitted, that most evolutionists considered the processes that led to humans as undirected and accidental. But that most definitely did not lead us to denigrate the value of an individual life, I tried to assure him. There is great dignity and enormous value in each individual life when it is perceived as the unique product of 3.5 billion years of evolution, for we are each part of a grand work-in-progress. From an evolutionary perspective, each life, each person, and each human society is a unique experiment with enormous potential for success. As a result, I maintained, one could argue that the life of the individual was even more precious within a worldview that perceives each of us as the unlikely result of a series of improbable events spread out across such a very long time rather than as the very recent result of a supernatural creation.

I doubt I made much of an impression on the speaker, but I hope this book can make an impression on you. It may seem paradoxical, but it is true: The evolutionary perspective, which essentially has little place for the actions of a divinity, and that is often attacked as being "godless," nonetheless provides a view of life in which all living things are sacred, the product of so special a chain of contingent events as to impart great value and significance to all life—and to all ways of life.

OUR HUMAN GENEALOGY

The saga of human biological and cultural evolution ultimately is a genealogy written not in words but in things—in fragmentary skeletons, shattered stone tools, broken pots, charred seeds, elaborate burials, stone carvings, cave paintings, and monumental ruins. Paleoanthropologists and archaeologists, using the methods to be outlined briefly in Chapter 3, study the genealogy of humanity that was "written" in the language of material remains.

This book will chronicle the story of the human past, focusing on the period before the development of writing and describing an ongoing journey that began in the furthest reaches of antiquity and continues to the present. We rely on the physical evidence as it has been revealed through the work of paleoanthropologists and archaeologists. The organizing theme of this treatment of the human past will be evolution, here encompassing the physical evolution of our species as well as the evolution of human culture.

We will begin by seeing how our understanding of evolution did not burst spontaneously into our collective consciousness. Like the creatures whose existence and natures it attempts to explain, the evolutionary view itself "evolved." Chapter 2 will focus on the evolution of our scientific perception of the past.

KEY TERMS

paleoanthropologist	evolution	adaptation
archaeologist	creationist	culture

2

Perceiving the Past

AN INTELLECTUAL HISTORY

CHAPTER OVERVIEW

In the seventeenth century, the Reverend John Ray hoped to glorify God by the study of His works. Although some declared that the pursuit of knowledge was unpleasing to God, Ray paved the way for scientists to observe and understand the universe as well as ourselves.

Some scientists studied the world and saw evidence of physical upheavals characterizing the earth's history. Others viewed the earth as the product of slow-acting causes still operating and saw the world as ancient and ever-changing. This notion provided the time and context necessary for Charles Darwin's evolutionary view of life.

	1640	1650	1660	1670	1680	1690	1700	1710
GEOLOGY		Bishop Ussher determines that creation took place in 4004 B.C., 1650				*The Wisdom of God* by John Ray is published, 1691 William Whiston proposes that a collision between earth and a comet caused Noah's flood, 1696		
BIOLOGY								
ARCHAEOLOGY								

10

1720	1730	1740	1750	1760	1770	1780	1790	1800	1810	1820	1830	1840	1850	1860	1870	1880

Theory of the Earth by James Hutton published, 1788

William Smith's stratigraphic tables first circulated, 1799

William Smith's stratigraphic tables published, 1815

Principles of Geology by Charles Lyell published, 1830

Linnaeus publishes his taxonomy for all living things, 1758

Philosophie Zoologique by Jean-Baptiste Lamarck published, 1809

Darwin begins his voyage on the *Beagle*, 1831

Darwin writes a synopsis of his theory of evolution, 1844

The Origin of Species by Charles Darwin published, 1859

The Descent of Man by Charles Darwin published, 1872

John Frere finds flint tools in soil layer deep in quarry in Hoxne, England, 1797

Flint tools and bones of extinct animals found in Kent's Cavern, England, 1824

Human bones found with bones of extinct animals in French cave, 1828

C. J. Thomsen publishes museum guide and introduces three-age system, 1836

Boucher de Perthes finds ancient flint axes, 1837

Primitive skull found in Neander Valley, Germany, 1856

Geological Evidences of the Antiquity of Man by Charles Lyell published, 1863

Researches in the Early History of Mankind by Edward Tyler published, 1865

Ancient Society by Lewis Henry Morgan published, 1877

It may seem obvious to most of us in the late twentieth century that the world is an ancient place. Material evidence of the distant past is all around us in the form of old rocks, plant and animal fossils, the skeletal remains of ancient people, and the physical traces of the things they made and used (see Chapter 3). We read about such fossil discoveries in books, see important new finds trumpeted on the television news, and visit museums where ancient geological, paleontological, and archaeological specimens are on display. An abundance of science programming on television focuses on the modern disciplines that devote their energies to illuminating antiquity. Discussion about the ancient past—of woolly mammoths and prehistoric cave paintings, of pyramids and ancient volcanic eruptions—is all around us.

But the fact that the world is old was neither self-evident nor obvious to thinkers in past centuries. To most of them, the earth was a relatively recent creation of God, as were plants, animals, and human beings. Though humanity possessed a history, most thought this history reflected a short period of time, adding up to no more than several thousand years. By the same token, the idea that the history of the planet, the story of life, or the chronicle of humanity could be investigated through the analysis of the material traces of past times was far from obvious to them. What was gone was gone, they assumed, and without written records from the periods in question, that information could never be recovered and reviewed; as a result, the past could never be understood.

Only after an intellectual journey that was both long and difficult did scholars realize that evidence of the past still existed and could be studied. Through its study they came to realize that the earth, life, and humanity were ancient and had changed dramatically during their lengthy existence. This chapter looks at that intellectual journey.

The individuals discussed here are arguably among the most historically significant in the development of the modern sciences that investigate the past. Though most were not specifically paleoanthropologists or archaeologists, their work was central to the development of the disciplines that are the focus of this book. The human story could not have been told without what archaeologist Donald Grayson (1983) calls "the establishment of human antiquity." Proving the great antiquity of our species was necessarily preceded by confirming the great antiquity of the planet. This chapter is about the establishment by scientists of the seventeenth through nineteenth centuries of the great antiquity of earth and later of humanity.

The thinkers discussed here, however, were far from being the only ones who contributed to the growth of our scientific understanding of the past. There were many others who, though steeped in a particular worldview and religious perspective, also were dedicated to the objective and scientific understanding of the world around them. It was not easy—for some it surely was agonizing—to come to grips with the realization that what they considered their God-given intellectual abilities were leading them to question their assumptions about how God had created the world. To all these thinkers we owe a great debt. They created the intellectual climate that allowed for the illumination of the human past.

JOHN RAY: NATURAL SCIENTIST

John Ray was a man of God, a man of science, and a man of conscience (Figure 2.1). He was born in England in 1627 to a blacksmith father and a mother we know little about except for her great piety. Even as a child, Ray possessed a keen mind, and he developed an early interest in the local plants and animals that abounded in and around his village of Black Notley (Green 1959; Raven 1950). Ray was a devout Christian and also a dedicated **empiricist;** he based his reasoning on observation and rejected such popular beliefs as astrology and occultism. His innate brilliance led to training at some of England's finest schools—including Cambridge University.

Though natural science was Ray's hobby, his vocation was the Church. Ordained in the Church of England (the Anglican Church) in 1660, Ray was expelled from the church in 1662 when he, along with 2,000 fellow churchmen, refused to sign a statement opposing Puritanism.

Ray's expulsion from the church to which he had proposed to devote his life set in motion a new trajectory for the young theologian from Cambridge University. Without a church or a flock, he began a lifelong devotion to worshipping God through the study of God's creations. Emblematic of Ray's scientific perspective and approach, the title of his most far-reaching work is: *The Wisdom of God as Manifested in the Works of the Creation* (first published in 1691). If Ray could not devote his life to preaching the words of God, he could still devote his life to studying the works of God.

FIGURE 2.1

John Ray, a seventeenth-century natural scientist who believed that scientists could illuminate the "wisdom of God" through the study of the natural world.

How to Study the Wisdom of God

Ray's studious approach to worshipping God was not commonly accepted in the seventeenth century. Many believed that the nature of the universe and life was unfathomable to mere humans. As Ray notes (in the preface to his 1690 work *Synopsis Methodica Stirpium Britannicarum,* as translated in Raven 1950:251): "There are those who condemn the study of Experimental Philosophy [what today we call natural history] as mere inquisitiveness and denounce the passion for knowledge as a pursuit unpleasing to God."

For these thinkers, the search for explanations of "small" mysteries about the world (Why is the sky blue? How does the moon shine? Why do people walk on two feet?) was doomed to failure. Such attempts were viewed as little more than the pitiful undertakings of human beings, with their imperfect capabilities, to comprehend the work of God.

Ray disagreed thoroughly with this sentiment. The bulk of *The Wisdom of God* is not a religious treatise or a discussion of the Bible, but a reflection of his "passion for knowledge." His book is a detailed exposition on nature by a scientist who had dedicated his life to its study as a way of serving his God.

A Perfect World

Forged in the crucible of observation rather than revelation, Ray's knowledge of nature yielded great insights into the workings of the world around him. Some of his conclusions sound remarkably modern. For instance, when Ray points out how each creature possesses the precise blend of characteristics necessary for its survival in a particular environment, he is building the framework for the modern concept of adaptation. The great diversity of life, so important in Charles Darwin's formulation of his theory of evolution (discussed later in this chapter), plays an important role in Ray's argument for the existence of God. For Ray, the diversity of life shows the brilliance of a creator who endowed all the animals with very different physical attributes and behavioral characteristics, enabling each to survive in its own particular way, in its own unique niche.

In one remarkable passage, Ray even presages some very modern arguments about one of humanity's most significant features—upright posture (see Chapters 5 and 6): "The wisdom and goodness of God appears in the erect posture of the body of man which is a privilege and advantage given to man, above other animals" (Ray 1974:151).

Not content merely to point this out, Ray goes on to suggest what those "advantages" might be. He cites the fact that erect posture is "most convenient for prospect and looking about one" (p. 153), therefore allowing humans to spot resources as well as dangers. He also asserts that upright posture frees human hands from the task of locomotion, so they can make and use implements. Ray's two explanations for the advantages of upright posture conferred on humanity by God have long been favorite explanations of anthropologists for the adaptive advantages of upright posture conferred through evolution (see Chapter 5).

Though Ray surely was precocious in his scientific approach to the study of nature, his conclusions always were the same regarding the source of the complexity, beauty, and harmony he saw there: that the universe, the world, and life were a reflection not of the complex workings of inherent natural processes, but instead of the wisdom and genius of God.

No Place for Amendments: An Unchanging World

Ray's fundamental approach to the study of creation was to focus on what he perceived to be its perfection and to maintain that such perfection was proof positive that the universe was the product of an infinitely wise and powerful creator. With this as his central assumption, it should come as no surprise that Ray argued that the universe, the earth, and life itself were basically unchanging, having been "fixed" in their perfection at creation. In other words, if the harmony, complexity, and perfection of the world in 1691 was evidence of God's work, then the world seen in that year must have been, for the most part, indistinguishable from the world as God created it. In fact, in *The Wisdom of God* and in the rest of his career as a naturalist and scientist, Ray was perhaps the most eloquent seventeenth-century proponent of the hypothesis of a fixed creation—the idea that the universe was set during the Genesis creation week and had not changed in any fundamental way since that time. As Ray (1974:164) put it: "Man is always mending and altering his works: But nature observes the same tenor because her works are so perfect that there is no place for amendments."

Ray admitted that the world around us is not completely static. He allowed for minor changes from the original state of things as God had produced them. There were cyclical changes like seasons, completely random alterations in the world due to accidents or cataclysms, and general change, in the sense of a decline from the original perfection of God's creation. But the concept of fundamental change was not permissible in Ray's natural theology. In his view (1974: Preface), the world around him reflected "the works created by God at first and by him conserved to this day in the same state and condition in which they were first made."

A WRECK OF A WORLD

Even in Ray's own time, there were those who, though agreeing that the study of the natural world was a valid way of glorifying nature's author, disagreed with his interpretation of the fixed nature of God's creation. These thinkers believed that the earth had changed radically from the original creation and that this change had been decidedly for the worse. They agreed with Ray that the world God created had been perfect and that some of that perfection could still be seen and used as an argument for God's existence, but they also viewed the modern world as a pale reflection of the perfect place God had created. Reverend Thomas Burnet in his book *Sacred Theory of the Earth* (1680) called the modern world "the dirty little planet." Benjamin Franklin summed up this perspective best when he characterized the earth of his time as "this wreck of a world we live on" (Greene 1959:39).

These thinkers believed that the world God had created was, indeed, perfect, but had been decaying since the time of the creation. They also believed that through the careful, objective study of nature, scientists could reveal the processes God had employed to set the universe in motion, including those that were causing the world to fall apart.

FIGURE 2.2

*Following Edmund Halley,
William Whiston suggested
that a comet striking the
earth had been the cause
of Noah's flood. In this illustration, a comet passes
by the earth, deforming
the planet into an oblong
shape. According to
Whiston, the flood resulted
from water in the comet's
tail (shown here on the
right) as well as water
gushing up from the earth's
interior when the surface
cracked because of its defor-
mation.* (William Whiston,
New Theory of the Earth, 1696)

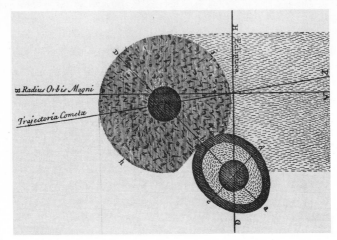

Noah's Flood

The Bible states that God decided to destroy the world and all its living things through a great, universal deluge, saving only the family of Noah and representatives of each kind of animal. The Bible does not provide the details of how God proposed to accomplish this destruction. And for most believers it was enough to know simply that God wished it to happen, and it did.

For others, curiosity led them to study nature and to propose the possible natural processes God might have employed for effecting such a destruction. Edmund Halley (after whom the famous comet is named) proposed in 1694 that a comet crashing into the earth (sent, of course, by God) might have initiated the great flood. Halley feared the reaction if he published such a seemingly mechanical or naturalistic explanation for divine retribution for human depravity, so he circulated his idea only among friends. In 1696, however, another writer, William Whiston, published precisely this hypothesis in his *A New Theory of the Earth* (Figure 2.2). To accommodate this physical explanation to theology, Whiston suggested that God had known during the creation week that the human species would descend into a depraved state, and immediately set in motion the comet, preordained to encounter the earth at just the right time! Some thinkers began to view Noah's flood as one in a series of catastrophes that had afflicted earth since creation. This argument was based in part on their perception of earth as a "wreck," but not a particularly old one.

The Age of the Earth

It was commonly believed in the sixteenth and seventeenth centuries that the world was only a few thousand years old. For example, in Shakespeare's play *As You Like It*, written in about 1600, one of the characters states, "The poor

world is almost six thousand years old." In 1642, John Lightfoot calculated creation's date at 3928 B.C., making the world 5,570 years old at that time (Brice 1982:19). There were other, similar estimates.

Ultimately, most people came to accept the determination of Irish Archbishop James Ussher that the earth had been created in 4004 B.C. and that God had begun the work "upon the entrance of the night preceding the twenty-third day of October" (from Archbishop Ussher's *Annales* in Brice 1982:18). This date later became widely accepted, since, beginning in 1701, it was printed as a marginal note in all English Bibles. Though Ussher's precise figure is often maligned by modern scientists and writers, he arrived at it in 1650 through rather detailed historical research, analysis of astronomical cycles, and reference to Biblical genealogies (Gould 1991).

If Ussher's figure were true, then the earth in 1690 was less than 5,700 years old. Unless a series of cataclysms had occurred, this was quite a short period of time to progress from the perfect place God had created to our imperfect world—with its cracks and crevices (canyons and valleys), its imperfect drainage (meandering, rather than straight, rivers), its irregular topography (hills and mountains), and its assorted other wrinkles and wounds. This is precisely what **catastrophists** proposed.

The Catastrophists

Most naturalists in the late seventeenth through the eighteenth centuries followed John Ray in his belief that the world could be understood through science, but they moved away from the notion that scientific observation showed the world to be perfect and static. Instead, they believed that the world changed through catastrophic, natural, physical processes that had been set in motion by God at creation and which could be understood through careful study (Figure 2.3).

FIGURE 2.3

Catastrophists believed that during its history, earth had suffered numerous cataclysms, most the result of floods and volcanic eruptions. Clearly such natural catastrophes occur. Here are two recent examples: the 1980 eruption of Mt. Saint Helens in Washington state and the Mississippi River floods of 1993. Even natural disasters on this scale are far too small, however, to support the catastrophist perspective. (Mt. Saint Helens: AP/Wide World Photos; Mississippi River: James A. Finley, AP/Wide World Photos)

Catastrophists argued amongst themselves not about whether catastrophes had occurred, but about what specific, natural processes God had employed. However, catastrophists faced the problem of scale. For example, though flooding was a common natural phenomenon that often wrought great destruction, and volcanoes were understood as capable of incredible devastation, the power of these processes seemed far too limited to produce, in the accepted time frame provided by Bishop Ussher, the kinds of planetary decay catastrophists believed characterized the earth. Though enormous on a human scale, great floods and powerful volcanic eruptions seemed trifling on a planetary scale. Catastrophists had to posit that calamities—the likes of which human history had never witnessed or recorded—had occurred in the past in order to produce the degree of degeneration they perceived in the physical world.

EQUABLE AND STEADY CHANGE

Clearly, scientists in the seventeenth and eighteenth centuries were wrestling with the issue of the character of God and the essence of nature. Virtually all believed in an all-powerful creative force that used natural processes as tools. These scientists were empiricists and spent their professional lives examining those tools that God used. They were firm believers in the notion that through careful observation and the use of logic—intellectual tools granted by God only to humans—they could solve the mysteries of God's creation.

But therein lay a great paradox. For earth to be as young as theologians believed it to be, the scientists who based their intellectual arguments on observation were forced to accept the existence of catastrophic processes that they simply could not observe since they were no longer occurring. But most were unwilling to risk arguing in direct opposition to theology.

James Hutton and the Radical View of Uniformitarianism

Scottish scientist James Hutton became one of the first proponents of a hypothesis that stood in opposition to catastrophism (Figure 2.4). In his view, first espoused in 1788 in his seminal and revolutionary work *Theory of the Earth*, "The operations of nature are equable and steady," not unpredictable and catastrophic (1959:19). This viewpoint of Hutton and others gave rise to the new perspective of **uniformitarianism.**

Hutton viewed the world as a marvelously constructed, perfectly synchronized machine—not one merely switched on at creation and destined to run down, but a machine brilliantly conceived to readjust and recreate itself continually. Certainly Hutton believed in God, but not one who would create a perfect world programmed to begin to disintegrate immediately after its creation. Hutton proposed a world designed by a creator so clever that slow

FIGURE 2.4

Eighteenth-century Scottish geologist James Hutton, one of the first and most persuasive proponents of uniformitarianism.
(James Hutton, *Theory of the Earth*, 1795)

and steady processes of decay were eternally offset by slow and steady processes of rejuvenation.

For example, catastrophists interpreted the discovery of the fossil remains of marine organisms at locations hundreds or even thousands of miles from the coast and at elevations of several thousand feet above sea level as evidence for a universal flood as described in the Bible. Hutton viewed these data quite differently. He believed that the presence of fossilized marine organisms on dry land indicated that these places had at one time been under the ocean. He suggested that during earth's history the hardest mountains erode, producing fresh soil in which plants can grow and on which humans can subsist. These soils are continually washed out across the land into rivers and ultimately flow into the oceans, where they become part of the seabed. Marine organisms live and die on these surfaces, depositing their shells. All of the loose materials at the bottom of the sea—including those fossil remains—eventually are consolidated through heat and pressure back into rock again, and through volcanic action the rock is slowly raised up to become mountains once more. Eventually, these mountains also will erode back into soil, the soil will be washed back into the sea, and so on, ad infinitum. Because of this endless cycle, any investigation of the history of the earth reveals "no vestige of a beginning—no prospect of an end" (Hutton 1959:200).

In Hutton's view, it was unnecessary to propose rare, irregularly occurring catastrophes to explain the appearance of the modern world. We could best understand the history of the earth, Hutton suggested, if we study those regular, uniform, natural processes of destruction and renewal that operate and are observable in the present, and then extrapolate their impacts backward through time. As he put it, "In examining things present, we have data from which to reason with regard to what has been" (1959:19). Processes like **erosion** and **weathering**—seen every day in rivers cutting their channels, in tides resculpting the shore, or in wind carving canyons—could have produced the present appearance of the earth, if afforded sufficient time. In a conceivably indirect criticism of Bishop Ussher's calculation, Hutton maintained that "time, which means everything in our ideas and is often deficient in our schemes, is to nature, endless" (1959:15). Hutton argued that once it was accepted that these ordinary processes were responsible for earth's alteration since creation, earth's actual age could be deduced. Through the careful scientific study of the rates and patterns of ordinary processes of erosion and weathering, "we find . . . means for concluding a certain portion of time to have necessarily elapsed, in the production of those events of which we see the effects" (1959:19).

For the earth to have attained its appearance, modern observable phenomena must have been operating for a sufficiently long time to have produced such things as mountain chains, meandering rivers, great canyons, and eroded valleys. Because the rates of erosion and weathering could be measured, one needed only to ask how long such processes must have been operating in order for modern features to have formed.

ANCIENT HUMANS?

In 1797, only two years after the publication of Hutton's expanded version of *Theory of the Earth,* John Frere, a young Englishman, found some curious stone tools in a brick-earth quarry in the small English village of Hoxne (Figure 2.5). He wrote a letter describing the artifacts to the London Society of Antiquaries that was read before the group in the same year and printed in their journal in 1800 (Frere 1800).

Some of the objects Frere reported on were finely made, as were other stone tools of sharp flint previously found throughout England and elsewhere in Europe. With Hutton's concept of an ancient earth still quite controversial, however, all of human history—including previous cultures that apparently made stone tools instead of metal ones—had to be shoe-horned into a very short period of time.

This resulted in some rather remarkable suggestions about the primitive-looking stone objects that had been found. Some proposed that they had been fashioned, not by ancient people, but by modern elves and fairies! In the mid-1600s, in a more naturalistic but equally improbable explanation, Ullisses Aldrovandi suggested that such objects were produced by nature through "the admixture of a certain exhalation of thunder and lightning with metallic matter . . . which is coagulated by the circumfused moisture and conglutinated into a mass" (Daniel and Renfrew 1988:29–30).

Other scientists in the seventeenth century were not quite so enamored of explanations that relied on fairies and elves or thunder and lightning. They suggested that these flint objects were made by people in the past. But this explanation still was hampered by the restriction that a previous race of stone-tool-using humans could be no more than about 6,000 years old because that was the age of the earth and the universe that God had created. Some scientists suggested that the tools were made by pre-Adamites (literally, people "before Adam," created by God in a previous construction of the world not mentioned in the Bible). Another approach that conformed better to the 6,000-year restriction and a more standard biblical view was to credit the manufacture of the implements to a race of barbaric people who had lived after Adam and before Noah's flood.

FIGURE 2.5

Two views of one of the flint implements discovered and reported on in 1797 by John Frere. Frere believed that the great depth at which the implements were found, as well as their position in a soil layer beneath one in which the bones of extinct animals had been located, indicated great antiquity for the makers of such tools. (From John Frere's "Account of Flint Weapons Discovered in Hoxne, Suffolk," *Archaeologia,* 1800.)

The Implications of Frere's Discovery

What made Frere's discovery so significant was that for perhaps the first time, primitive stone tools could be shown to have originated at great depth (in this case, ten feet below the surface) and that the bones of extinct animals were found *above* the tools, in more recent soil layers. Frere recognized that from a uniformitarian perspective, this implied a great age for the tools and, in turn, a significant age for the humans who made them.

Frere's argument for the antiquity of the artifacts he found was based on their **stratigraphic** position in the quarry. Frere and members of the society may have been aware of the work of surveyor William Smith, who a few years earlier had recognized that the soil beneath the earth's surface occurred in layers and that the layers produced ordered and regular groups of fossils. Smith showed that the layers could be identified and distinguished by their population of fossil species, with sequentially lower layers representing increasingly ancient time periods. In 1799 Smith circulated a handwritten table showing the order of strata he had encountered, but he did not publish a detailed report until 1815, laying the groundwork for the analysis of **stratigraphy** (see Chapter 3; Grayson 1983).

Frere's excursion to Hoxne may have put him at the right place to add to the mounting evidence for the uniformitarian perspective of an ancient earth—and to show that the human species was a part of that story—but he surely had made his discovery at the wrong time. Smith's stratigraphic work was quite new, and Hutton and his supporters were in the midst of the first skirmishes of a battle to defend uniformitarianism against the attacks of a hostile scientific and religious community. Hutton and his followers were more interested in evidence related directly to the age of the earth rather than other, somewhat incidental, and even more controversial evidence confirming a human presence on an ancient earth. As scholar A. Bowdoin Van Riper (1993) points out, even many ardent uniformitarianists continued to maintain that humans were a recent addition to an ancient earth that had passed through a series of stages leading up to the modern world. Sadly, Frere's letter to the society about the stone tools and their apparent great age was promptly forgotten.

More Stone Tools . . . and Bones

Additional evidence discovered in the early 1800s also failed to convince most scientists of the great antiquity of the human species. For example, in 1828, in the town of Narbonne, France, a museum curator reported the discovery of human bones together in the same cave deposit with the bones of extinct animals. The gentleman who made the discovery, however, elected not to make any connection between the human and animal remains, suggesting that their co-occurrence was a result of chance (Daniel and Renfrew 1988:33).

At about the same time, Father J. MacEnery announced the discovery of flint tools and the bones of extinct animals in Kent's Cavern in Torquay in southern England. MacEnery's evidence, gathered between 1824 and 1829, was strong that the tools and animal remains were of equal age; they were found together, sealed beneath a stalagmite in the cavern. MacEnery's writings show him initially to have been quite excited about the implications of his discovery as it related to the antiquity of humanity. Nevertheless,

MacEnery ultimately backed off from any claim of association between the tools and the bones of extinct animals (Grayson 1983). Most believed, despite the lack of evidence, that the stone tools had gotten under the stalagmites only recently, when humans dug out ovens in the cave floor (Daniel and Renfrew 1988: 33–34).

These and other discoveries made in the early years of the nineteenth century implied a greater antiquity of the human species than allowed for in Bishop Ussher's biblically based chronology. The unearthing of tools and bones seemed to place our species deep in time in Hutton's uniformly changing, ancient earth. Yet none of these discoveries separately or together were viewed as compelling by most scientists.

The denial of great human antiquity might be ascribed to pressure applied by the church or simply to a stubborn refusal to accept the evidence. But, as Donald Grayson (1983) shows, this is an unfair assumption. Certainly, there was a desire to reject the claim of great age for our species, but until about 1859 the evidence supporting this claim just wasn't that strong. Stratigraphy was a new approach, and archaeological excavation methods were not well developed. In the court of scientific opinion, the physical association between artifacts and the bones of extinct animals could not be proven beyond a reasonable doubt.

THE SLOW AGENCY OF EXISTING CAUSES

FIGURE 2.6

Nineteenth-century English geologist Charles Lyell. Lyell was the most eloquent and thorough of the uniformitarianists.
(Charles Lyell, *Principles of Geology*, 1830)

Hutton had fired the first salvos in a revolution in thinking about the processes responsible for the physical features of the earth and the age of the planet. But in the intellectual battle that ensued, Hutton barely was able to hold his position. The human place in time could not be established when time itself was still a point of such great contention. It became the task of the brilliant British geologist Charles Lyell (Figure 2.6) to continue this revolution in thinking about the past and to provide time enough for an ancient humanity. The subtitle of Lyell's seminal work, *Principles of Geology,* first published in 1830, conveys the essence of his approach: "An attempt to explain the former changes of the earth's surface by reference to causes now in operation" (Lyell 1990).

To come to a rational understanding of the earth, Lyell felt it necessary to dispense entirely with "imaginary pictures of catastrophes and confusion such as haunted the imagination of the early cosmogonists" (1990:72). His fundamental assertion was that "all past changes on the globe had been brought about by the slow agency of existing causes" (1990:63).

Perhaps the most revolutionary and problematic deduction from such a hypothesis concerned the time necessary to produce the kinds of geological features seen on the earth if only the "slow agency of existing causes" was considered. Lyell himself admitted, "The imagination was first fatigued and overpowered by endeavoring to conceive the immensity of time required for the annihilation of whole continents by so insensible a process" (1990:63). But he went on to apply his fundamental axiom of uniformitarianism to estimate the ages of significant geological features. In a work published in 1863, for example, Lyell calibrated the modern rate at which the Mississippi delta was growing, and concluded that at its current rate of growth it must have taken 100,000 years to have attained its size.

Needless to say, such an estimated age for the Mississippi delta was shocking to those who accepted Bishop Ussher's determination for the age of the entire earth. Lyell was viciously attacked in print and charged with heresy, but such allegations rang hollow. Though the Bible measures the period of creation as six days, it does not place that creation week in time; nowhere does the Bible actually record the age of the universe, earth, or life. Hutton's and Lyell's view and that of uniformitarianism may have contradicted the interpretation of an archbishop, but it did not disclaim the word of God.

Lyell was a great scientist and a persuasive proponent of the uniformitarian perspective. His work resonated in the minds of many geologists, biologists, and archaeologists, and freed them from the prison of the perspective of a recent earth into whose chronology all of their observations and deductions had to be crammed. Charles Darwin later was to state, without too much exaggeration, "The science of geology is enormously indebted to Lyell—more so, as I believe, than to any other man who ever lived" (Barlow 1958).

ANCIENT HUMANS REVISITED

With Lyell, uniformitarianism was to become the orthodox perspective in geology. The earth was old, and its story could be read in its ancient layers. Discoverers of primitive-looking stone artifacts found at a great depth began to suggest great antiquity for humanity as well—how old was still a matter of conjecture, but certainly far greater than Bishop Ussher's calculation of 5,700 years. With the discovery of clusters of such stone tools and with no evidence of the use of metals found alongside, it became increasingly obvious that human cultures had changed dramatically since the time of the makers of stone tools.

Cultures Ancient and Changing

Just six years after the initial publication of Lyell's *Principles of Geology,* a guidebook was published describing the artifacts that could be seen in the Danish National Museum in Copenhagen. Written by Christian Jurgensen Thomsen, the guidebook organized the museum's collection chronologically into three prehistoric ages—stone, bronze, and iron—based on the most-favored raw materials used to make tools during each of the three epochs.

Inherent in Thomsen's **three-age system** was the notion that culture had changed through time, in a predictable sequence. The three ages were developmental as well as chronological. There was an implied succession of increasing technological sophistication, an evolution toward tools that were better (more effective, more durable) but also more difficult to manufacture.

That culture has been undergoing great change during the human tenure on the planet was no more evident in the nineteenth century than was the notion of an ancient earth. In fact, it was surprising to some thinkers that the very oldest traces of human culture did not include metal tools. They assumed that metallurgy had simply always been around. Thomsen deserves credit for recognizing, and making explicit in his guidebook, that the archaeological record clearly shows great changes in human technological abilities.

More Stone Tools

In 1837 a French customs official, Jacques Boucher de Perthes, initiated a long and detailed search for flint axes. In 1839 he began publishing volumes about the tools he had found, concluding that they represented an ancient and culturally primitive period of human history from long before Noah's flood. Boucher de Perthes was not taken seriously by most scientists. Another two decades would pass before mounting evidence would lead to a fundamental shift in the view of those studying human antiquity. This shift would accompany one of the most momentous events in the history of science: the 1859 publication of Charles Darwin's great work, *The Origin of Species by Means of Natural Selection.*

FIGURE 2.7

Charles Darwin, the father of modern biological evolutionary theory. (Negative no. 108781, courtesy of Department of Library Services, American Museum of Natural History)

CHARLES DARWIN AND THE ANTIQUITY OF LIFE

In 1828, less than two centuries after the Reverend John Ray entered Cambridge University to pursue a degree in theology, another bright, young Englishman entered those "hallowed halls," in pursuit of the same degree. His name was Charles Darwin (Figure 2.7).

Unlike Ray, Darwin had no great desire to become a man of the cloth. In fact, at the age of nineteen, the young Darwin had no great predilection for much of anything and had not shown any particular aptitude, much to his physician father's consternation. At least initially while at Cambridge, Darwin was essentially aimless. Though quite bright, he was not a top student and even needed tutoring in mathematics. His "major" of theology had been selected by default, and his primary interests did not include coursework, but, instead, shooting, fox hunting, and taking long walks.

Darwin took a natural science course at Cambridge under a brilliant scientist and charismatic professor, John Stephens Henslow, a remarkable teacher who became a mentor to many of his students. Henslow regularly took his students on long geological tours and on botanical and zoological field trips, and he often invited his students to parties attended by some of the most brilliant scientists of the time, where discussions of astronomy, geology, and biology continued long into the evening. It was in the heady atmosphere of Henslow's world that the young theology student Charles Darwin began to reconsider the course mapped out for his life as a simple country parson.

At the same time, like John Ray, Darwin began to question one of the requirements of ordination in the Church of England: signing a statement subscribing to the church's "Thirty-nine Articles," some of which had been devised to keep Roman Catholics and Anabaptists out of the church. Darwin felt that his conscience might prevent him from signing, thereby indicating his agreement with such statements (Bowlby 1990:102). Darwin confided his reservations to Henslow, a devoutly religious man himself, who nevertheless encouraged him to continue his theological as well as his scientific studies.

Henslow genuinely liked Darwin and felt that he had a real knack for observing nature. Though not his first choice, he recommended his young student to the post of naturalist aboard a British government survey ship, the *Beagle,* which was to produce detailed sailing charts of the coast of South America and then circumnavigate the world. The voyage was to begin in 1831 when Darwin was just twenty-two years old. The task of the ship's naturalist was to collect geological, botanical, and zoological specimens in all areas visited by the ship. Despite some initial misgivings on the part of his father, who was still supporting him financially, Darwin agreed to the position and began a mission that was supposed to last two years but actually lasted closer to five. Thus, events had conspired to push the young theology student to collect the data that would, twenty-eight years later, lead to one of the most important books ever published in the name of science.

The Voyage of the Beagle

Darwin kept a detailed journal of all that he saw during that remarkable five-year expedition (Darwin 1845)—arguably the most significant travelog ever kept. During frequent port stops and landfalls, Darwin walked or rode on horseback across some 3,000 miles, collecting thousands of specimens that he sent back to England for further study by experts in botany, zoology, and geology. Indeed, Darwin's collection and investigation of the plants and animals of these previously unexplored territories (unexplored by a Western naturalist, anyway) opened the eyes of many Europeans to the immense and often unrecognized diversity of life present in the world.

A Paradigm for Life

Darwin had brought with him a copy of Lyell's recently published *Principles of Geology,* and he read it during the trip, becoming a committed convert to uniformitarianism. He recognized that Lyell had provided an overarching theoretical framework for interpreting the geological history of the earth—a **paradigm** for how the earth changes through time. Darwin also recognized that for the grand expanse of living things there was no such overarching perspective, no scientific paradigm that could explain the great diversity of life he saw during his five-year voyage.

This is not to say that there was no commonly accepted reason for life's diversity, commonalities, and interrelationships, but they were explained as simply resulting from the will of God, just as John Ray had maintained nearly 150 years previously. Life was seen as having been "fixed" (or set) at creation. In fact, Karl von Linné, the well-known eighteenth-century Swedish biologist better known as Carolus Linnaeus, had developed a **taxonomy** of living things that we still use today (dividing all life into branching categories of kingdom, phylum, class, order, family, genus, and species—see Chapter 4). This taxonomy assumed that each species was immutable and had been fixed at creation. Similarities and differences among various species were explained by Linnaeus as simply reflecting the way God made them in the beginning. As a popular saying maintained, "God created and Linnaeus arranged."

Darwin was certainly aware of the Linnaean taxonomic system, but his observations during the voyage made it increasingly difficult for him to accept the tenet of the immutability (or "fixity") of species. Darwin was not the first to question this concept. In fact, his grandfather, Erasmus Darwin, had written about the evolution of life, and a French naturalist, Jean-Baptiste Lamarck, had developed a detailed explanation of how organisms evolved by sensing a change in their environment, acting in some new way in response to that change, and then passing those changes down to subsequent generations. Darwin, ever the empiricist, was not all that interested in his grandfather's largely speculative approach. He also felt that Lamarck's mechanism was simply unsupported by real data. Though he came to no definite conclusions of his own during the voyage (at least not in anything he wrote), Darwin collected some provocative information on this subject that set the stage for the evolutionary drama he ultimately was to unfold.

The Mutability of Species

Though he didn't think it was important at the time, Darwin recognized that animals he encountered on islands off the coast of South America resembled, but were not identical to, animals found on the mainland, where they must have originated. The island descendants of mainland species seemed to have altered from their original state after migrating. The descendants must have

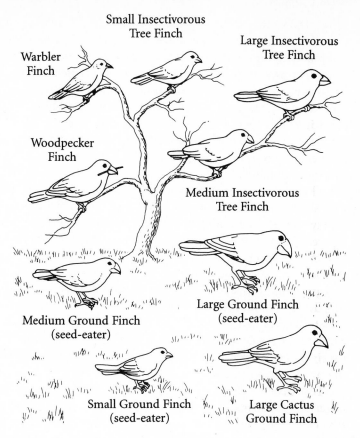

Small Insectivorous
Tree Finch

Large Insectivorous
Tree Finch

Warbler
Finch

Woodpecker
Finch

Medium Insectivorous
Tree Finch

Medium Ground Finch
(seed-eater)

Large Ground Finch
(seed-eater)

Small Ground Finch
(seed-eater)

Large Cactus
Ground Finch

FIGURE 2.8

Schematic drawings of several of the various finch species found in the Galapagos Islands. Darwin noted the exquisitely precise adaptations of each of the species to the particular habitats offered by each different island. Ultimately, he suggested that these unique adaptations had been the result of natural selection. (From E. Peter Volpe, *Understanding Evolution,* 5th ed. Copyright © 1985 Wm. C. Brown Communication, Inc., Dubuque, Iowa. All Rights Reserved. Reprinted by permission.)

become better adjusted, or **adapted,** to the different environmental conditions in their new habitats. Even on different islands within island chains, individual kinds of animals resembled each other, though differing in significant attributes from island to island.

For example, on the Falkland Islands, off the southeast coast of South America, foxes were recognizably different from one island to the next. All these island foxes must have come from the mainland, so why were they different from mainland foxes, why did they vary from island to island, and how could this have happened? On the Galapagos Islands, 500 miles west of the northwestern coast of South America, Darwin found that tortoises living on each of the dozen large islands could be differentiated, and so could finches—small birds whose source was certainly the mainland. The finches did not look precisely like any other South American finch, and they differed in form and behavior among islands (Figure 2.8). How had each type of finch become uniquely adjusted to the particular features of its island, if the finch species (like all species in the Linnaean view) was immutable and fixed at creation? This mystery simply could not be explained within the accepted paradigm of the fixity of species.

In 1836, after a long and successful voyage, Darwin and the *Beagle* returned triumphantly to England. Many of Darwin's reports and specimens had preceded him, and he returned to find his work roundly praised by the scientific community. Darwin met and was befriended by geologist Charles Lyell, who was extremely grateful that Darwin's geological observations matched precisely his uniformitarian view of the evolution of the earth.

Darwin's Conversion to Evolution: "Like Confessing a Murder"

As early as the late 1830s, Darwin began building a new paradigm for biology, one based on the notion of the mutability of species. In 1844 Darwin wrote fellow scientist and dear friend Joseph Hooker: "At last gleams of light have come, and I am almost convinced (quite contrary to the opinion I started with) that species are not (it is like confessing a murder) immutable" (Bowlby 1990:254).

Darwin's theoretical edifice was to be constructed with the brick and mortar of his own scientific observations and those of his colleagues. Lyell supplied the uniformitarian perspective, which provided eons of time. Economist Thomas Malthus in his *Essay on the Principle of Population* (1798; which Darwin read in 1838) provided the raw numbers when he pointed out the ability of animals to reproduce at a rate far greater than that necessary to maintain a steady population. Darwin's own observations of the incredible diversity within and among species provided evidence of the extreme range of variation of life on the planet. And Darwin's growing understanding of **artificial selection** in agriculture and animal breeding—where people decide which individual animals or plants will be allowed to live and reproduce in order to pass down traits viewed as preferable by the human breeders—provided an analogous mechanism for how change within a species might be wrought without human intervention. With this information as his foundation, Darwin began building his theory of **descent with modification,** based on the process he called **natural selection.**

In 1844, the same year he "confessed" to Hooker about his shift to a theory of mutability of species, Darwin wrote a synopsis of his new theory, explaining "the simple way by which species become exquisitely adapted to various ends" (Bowlby 1990:254).

But Darwin was not ready to go public with his revolutionary idea. First, he felt he needed an enormous data set to support his radically new perspective. He also wished to answer all possible criticisms before they were posed. Further, throughout his life he was subject to horrible attacks of nausea, heart palpitations, and other symptoms that seem to have been brought on by unpleasant events in his life. As a result, Darwin was not ready to submit for publication the discussion of his theory, or to submit himself to the intense controversy and personal criticism it was certain to generate. This reluctance to go public changed only in 1858 on learning that Alfred Russel Wallace, a younger man who was not a trained scientist but a professional collector of botanical and zoological specimens, was circulating a paper he had written in which he proposed almost precisely the same mechanism for change as Darwin.

THE ORIGIN OF SPECIES

So, in 1859, twenty-eight years after Darwin set sail on the *Beagle,* more than twenty years after he began setting down the first drafts of his theory, and fifteen years after outlining its major themes in an unpublished paper, Darwin's masterpiece, *The Origin of Species by Means of Natural Selection,* at last was published. In the introduction to the book, Darwin succinctly articulates the essence of his theory:

> As many more individuals of each species are born than can survive; and as, consequently, there is a frequently recurring struggle for existence, it follows that any being, if it vary, however slightly in any manner profitable to itself, under the complex and sometimes varying conditions of life, will have a better chance of surviving, and thus be *naturally selected.* From the strong principle of inheritance, any selected variety will tend to propagate its new and modified form. (Darwin 1952:7)

As Darwin saw it, variation within a species provided some individuals with characteristics that allowed them a better chance for survival under the conditions established by nature. Those individuals were "selected" by nature to survive and pass along their advantageous characteristics to their offspring. Given the time allowed for by Lyell, the vast numbers of organisms that pass through this world as calculated by Malthus, and the huge amount of variation seen by Darwin, a process of selection analogous to that maintained in breeding programs could produce not just a new, improved version of the same species, but a new species!

In this way, for example, finches of a single species might lose their way in a storm and get blown to an island where conditions were quite different from their mainland home. Many of the finches would die, unable to survive in their new circumstances, but a few might, by chance, possess characteristics that would enable them to endure. They would pass those features on to their offspring; and over many generations, birds with those qualities would continue to be selected for, that is, to survive. After a time, the island finches would no longer resemble the mainland finches. Given sufficient time, they might become so different they would be a different species entirely.

Human Evolution

As astounding as Darwin's suggestions were, perhaps what bothered people most was the deduction that this process could be applied to the evolution of human beings. An ape with a slightly larger brain and greater intelligence might be more apt to survive than his or her slower cousins. Over time, through natural selection, large brains would be increasingly selected for, and eventually the ape would become human. The implication so shocked Charles Lyell that, though by and large a supporter of Darwin and a close personal friend, he never quite accepted that human intellect could be produced via such a mechanism.

Darwin knew how delicate the subject of human evolution might be. In 1857 he wrote Wallace: "You ask whether I shall discuss 'man.' I think I shall avoid the whole subject, as so surrounded with prejudices; though I fully admit that it is the highest and most interesting problem for the naturalist" (Bowlby 1990:325). He hinted at the applicability of natural selection to humanity in *Origin* when he concluded that, by the application of the theory, "Much light will be thrown on the origins of man and his history" (Darwin 1952:243). As will be seen throughout this book, Darwin was right.

The Human Factor

In 1856, the year before Darwin indicated to Wallace his desire to steer clear of any mention of humanity in his discussion of evolution, a partial fossil skull was found in the Neander Valley in Germany (see Figure 7.9). At least two similar skulls had been found previously in Europe (in Belgium and on Gibraltar), but these largely were ignored. The Neander Valley skull, like those found previously, was as large as a modern human skull, though it looked quite different. As we will see in Chapter 7, while some scientists declared as a pathological oddity the large, flat skull with great ridges of bone above where the eyes had been, others saw it as representative of an ancient race of humans.

Discoveries related to the question of human antiquity accelerated in the late 1850s. A few months before the November 1859 publication of Darwin's *The Origin of Species,* the respected geologist John Prestwich delivered an address to the Royal Society of London announcing his belief that flint tools he had seen in France that had been excavated by Boucher de Perthes provided convincing evidence of the great antiquity of humanity. The archaeologist John Evans had accompanied Prestwich to France and had come to the same conclusion. The week after Prestwich's speech, Evans delivered a speech to the Society of Antiquaries—the same society John Frere had written to sixty-two years earlier—in which he asserted that Frere had been right after all. The sites he saw in France convinced him of the great age of the flint artifacts he saw there—and they looked just like the artifacts Frere had discovered, and they were in a similar stratigraphic position. Evans concluded: "This much appears to be established beyond doubt, that in a period of antiquity remote beyond any of which we have hitherto found traces, this portion of the globe was peopled by man" (Daniel and Renfrew 1988:37).

With the notion of a uniformly changing, very ancient earth in place, the new artifactual and skeletal evidence was convincing many people of the great antiquity of the human species. There still was substantial debate over what "great antiquity" meant on any kind of a fixed time scale. No date could be fixed to the early humans who had made the stone tools, nor could any age be assigned to the German skull. But opinion clearly was shifting in the scientific community away from a less-than-6,000-year-old earth and human species to one far more ancient than that.

Also in 1859, the venerable Charles Lyell announced that he was now convinced of the chronological length of the human presence on the earth, which he knew to be ancient (Daniel and Renfrew 1988:37). His publication of the *Geological Evidences of the Antiquity of Man* would come four years later (1863), providing a massive compendium of the evidence for ancient human traces. Lyell's initial statement of support for great age for humanity, and especially the publication of *Geological Evidences,* meant the previous heresy of a greatly ancient human species now bore "the stamp of scientific orthodoxy" (Van Riper 1993:9).

CULTURES EVOLVING

Led first by Hutton and then Lyell, the uniformitarianists had shown that the earth was old; the pages of its ancient history were the strata that lay beneath our feet. Archaeologists had placed human-made objects on those ancient pages, proving the great antiquity of humanity within the stratigraphic history of the planet.

Darwin had gone on to show that within the lengthy history of the earth, plants and animals had changed dramatically; they had, in fact, evolved. And now, the ancient human-made objects found by the early archaeologists— the stone tools—provided clear evidence that human culture had evolved as well. As Charles Lyell himself pointed out (1863:379), if culture had remained constant throughout human history, then archaeologists should be finding "buried railways or electrical telegraphs" along with other scientifically advanced artifacts in ancient stratigraphic layers. Instead, archaeologists were finding stone tools, admittedly finely made but essentially and fundamentally primitive, associated with the bones of extinct animals in ancient stratigraphic levels. Clearly, this was evidence of great change from the culture of the earliest humans to those of the modern (nineteenth-century) world. As surely as geologists had shown that the earth had sustained enormous change over a vast expanse of time and as surely as biologists now were showing that life itself had experienced great change, so archaeologists were showing that human behavior had also changed greatly during our species' history on earth.

The recognition of great cultural changes from earliest times to the present lent support for the three-age system and its identification of all that had happened in between. What Christian Thomsen understood and made concrete others now began to build on in constructing broad theories of cultural evolution. For example, Edward Tyler's *Researches into the Early History of Mankind and the Development of Civilization* (1865) expanded on Thomsen's chronology, subdividing his stone age into an "unground stone" phase (in which tools were produced by the presumably more primitive method of flaking or striking) and a "ground stone" phase (in which tools were produced by the presumably more advanced method of grinding and polishing).

For most thinkers in the nineteenth century, the cultural evolution they perceived in the archaeological record was synonymous with cultural progress. Tyler (1871:198) characterized culture change as "in the main, an upward development." Thus, it is understandable: If the world and even human beings were not the stable, safe, reassuring entities they had once been presumed to be, at least it could be assumed that the human past was a story of continual, if slow, improvement. And not surprisingly, nineteenth-century European scientists assumed that the pinnacle of cultural development was nineteenth-century Europe. To them, the archaeological record presented a long and remarkable tale of a species hoisting itself up from its original primitive state to an ever-increasing level of civilization.

Some scholars suggested specific sequences of culture change that most of humanity had passed through in the long ascent toward modern civilization. For example, Lewis Henry Morgan (1877:8) theorized that "the experience of mankind has run in nearly uniform channels." In Morgan's view, cultures evolve through stages he labeled savagery, barbarism, and civilization (with each stage involving substages) and marked by increasingly complex material culture and greater sophistication in how people feed themselves. Where Thomsen's sequence dealt only with the advancement in the raw materials used to make tools, Morgan's included the invention of fire and pottery, the development of farming and animal husbandry, the use of iron tools, and, finally, the invention of a written, alphabetic language. In Morgan's view, virtually all cultures in human history had passed through his various stages, and those that were still in one of the more primitive levels by the nineteenth century had simply become "stuck" at some stage in this universal sequence as the result of something lacking in their society, for example, an important invention like metal or an alphabet.

We now view culture as adaptation, as the fundamental way in which people adjust to their surroundings. Cultures change as conditions change, and there is no necessary "upward" movement or progress. Cultures survive not because they become better, but because they become better adapted to their world. Nevertheless, thinkers like Thomsen, Tyler, and Morgan made the important observation, not self-evident in the nineteenth century, that human behavior has vastly changed through time. This behavior became translated into the material record, which provided the data the early archaeologists used to frame their cultural evolutionary constructs. That same material record—now much expanded—continues to provide much of the data on which this book is based. The methods by which data gathering is accomplished are the focus of the next chapter.

JOHN RAY GETS THE FINAL WORD

There is an irony in discussing the work of John Ray in a book about the human past, a book whose underlying theme is one of evolution and change. Ray's work was a watershed, with enormous impact on Western scientific thought for close to 200 years. One could argue, in fact, that the enormous impact of Ray's work was a key factor in holding back acceptance of a completely natural explanation for the universe and life, as well as the concept of evolution.

Ultimately, though Ray was surely wrong in his conclusions, we owe him a tremendous debt for his basic proposition that questions concerning the processes and functioning of the world around us are both suitable to ask and approachable through scientific study. Ray is largely responsible for starting us down a path with whose ultimate direction he would vehemently have disagreed, but one that has led us to a more complete understanding of the universe, life, and the human species.

We began our historical discussion with a belief in an unchanging universe that was created less than 6,000 years ago by an omnipotent God, and was populated by plants, animals, and people whose forms and qualities were forever fixed at creation. That universe was simple, predictable, and reassuring.

We now hold the modern scientific view of the universe and life, initially espoused by Lyell and Darwin, as ancient and dynamic, unpredictable and serendipitous, awesome and awful. It is no wonder, therefore, that so many people are terrified by the modern scientific perspective and retreat to pseudoscience. Even today, more than 130 years after the publication of *The Origin of Species,* Darwin is excoriated by people calling themselves "scientific creationists" (see Chapter 1) who assert that Darwin and his theory are evil, that one of the most brilliant scientists who ever lived was an agent of the devil. Many of these same people demand that the teaching of evolution be banished from the classroom.

Such opinions are the result of little more than fear. But what we have lost in terms of a pleasant and comforting view of the world and the human species' place in it is more than made up for in the infinitely fascinating story we can now tell of the evolution of our species. And, as John Ray stated, "Those who scorn and decry knowledge should remember that it is knowledge that makes us men, superior to the animals and lower than the angels, that makes us capable of virtue and happiness such as animals and the irrational cannot attain" (Raven 1950:251).

SUMMARY

We began this chapter with a discussion of the life and work of theologian and natural scientist John Ray. Ray believed that God's creation could be studied, and that in so doing we were glorifying that creation. He believed that the world and all life within it had been established during the creation week and that the world today is just as God had made it, and reflects the perfection of creation.

Natural scientists who followed Ray saw the world as a "wreck," having decayed since the time of creation. Viewing the world as quite young, perhaps no more than 6,000 years old, these thinkers suggested that the history of the earth was marked by a string of catastrophes.

James Hutton and Charles Lyell were spokesmen for a different perspective. Rejecting claims of hypothetical catastrophes, they explained the appearance of the earth on the basis of observable, slow, steady, and uniform natural processes. They asserted that such observable natural phenomena could produce the current state of the earth if afforded sufficient time. They measured the age of the earth not in thousands of years but in hundreds of thousands and even millions of years. Especially during the nineteenth century, researchers began uncovering tantalizing bits of evidence—in the form of flint implements together with the bones of extinct animals and even those of human beings—that suggested this ancient earth had been populated by early forms of humanity.

Charles Darwin viewed the biological world as the result of natural processes of change. His theory of natural selection allowed for an overarching explanation for the diversity of life on the planet. With the amount of time provided by Hutton's and Lyell's perspective of earth history, the process of natural selection could have produced the great diversity of life seen on the planet, it could explain differences and similarities among different kinds of organisms, and it even could explain the evolution of humanity.

TO LEARN MORE

If you are interested in a detailed discussion of the life of John Ray, Charles Raven's (1950) biography, *John Ray, Naturalist: His Life and Works,* is your best choice. For Charles Darwin, John Bowlby's 1990 monograph, *Charles Darwin: A New Life* and *The Autobiography of Charles Darwin* (Barlow 1958) are recommended. Of course, if you want a first-hand glimpse of how the thinkers discussed in this chapter, as well as their contemporaries, worked out the problems presented by the study of the origins of life and the planet, consult their works cited in the text. Two fine sources on the history of archaeological thought are Glyn Daniel and Colin Renfrew's (1988), *The Idea of Prehistory,* and William H. Stiebing, Jr.'s (1993), *Uncovering the Past: A History of Archaeology.* For more detailed coverage of the early history of the discipline, see Donald Grayson's (1983), *The Establishment of Human Antiquity,* and A. Bowdoin Van Riper's (1993), *Men Among the Mammoths: Victorian Science and the Discovery of Human Prehistory.*

KEY TERMS

empiricist

catastrophist

uniformitarianism

erosion

weathering

stratigraphic

stratigraphy

three-age system

paradigm

taxonomy

adapted

artificial selection

descent with

    modification

natural selection

3

Probing the Past

CHAPTER OVERVIEW

Paleoanthropology and archaeology are sub-disciplines within the field of anthropology. While other anthropologists study living groups of people, primates, language, or behaviors across cultural boundaries, paleo-anthropologists and archaeologists focus on the biological and cultural evolution of our species.

Paleoanthropologists and archaeologists study the physical remains of human beings and our evolutionary ancestors. These scientists also examine the material remains of these ancient ancestors: the things they made and used and then lost or discarded. By the analysis of the bones of humans and human ancestors as well as their artifacts, paleoanthropologists and archaeologists hope to better understand how our ancestors evolved and adapted. This chapter summarizes some particular techniques used by scientists to paint a picture of the human past.

APPLICABLE RANGE OF MAJOR DATING TECHNIQUES

1 million   900,000

Radiocarbon
Radioactive decay

Archaeomagnetism
Alignment with changes in location of the earth's magnetic pole

Dendrochronology
Counting of annual growth rings

Uranium series
Radioactive decay

Obsidian hydration
Chemical process: accumulation of weathering rind on artifact

Fission track
Radioactive decay leaves microscopic tracks in crystals at known rate

Thermoluminescence (TL)
Radiation damage: accumulation of TL in crystals

Electron spin resonance
Radiation damage: accumulation of unpaired electrons in crystals

Potassium argon (K/Ar)
Radioactive decay

Paleomagnetism
Alignment of particles with pole reversals

800,000	700,000	600,000	500,000	400,000	300,000	200,000	100,000	Present

T he work of many of the thinkers discussed in Chapter 2—along with the investigations of many other scientists—laid the foundation for the science of the human past. However, it was geology and biology, not the study of ancient humanity, that were preeminent in the minds of men like John Ray, Charles Lyell, and Charles Darwin. The study of artifacts and human physical remains was secondary to the primary data needed to establish the antiquity of the earth and the nature of life.

With the recognition that the world was both ancient and changing, the study of humanity's place in that world could become the scientific discipline known as **anthropology.** This book presents the prehistoric journey of humanity across an evolutionary landscape as revealed by modern anthropology, focusing on the data of many of that field's subdisciplines (Figure 3.1).

AN ANTHROPOLOGICAL PERSPECTIVE

Contemporary anthropology is the study of people. Of course, the other social sciences—economics, political science, psychology, sociology—also study people, but from very particular perspectives, focusing on specific aspects of human behavior. Anthropology, on the other hand, attempts to be more holistic and integrative in its approach. If other social scientists specialize in the workings of specific systems within human society, anthropologists tend to be generalists who want to know how human society, with all its interrelated parts, works as a whole, and how it came into existence.

Some anthropologists—called **ethnographers**—study humans by residing in particular societies and observing the behaviors of the people living in them. Margaret Mead, who spent many years among the Samoans (people inhabiting an island chain in the Pacific Ocean) is probably the most famous ethnographer (Figure 3.2). In the past, many ethnographers, most of whom were members of Western societies, chose to focus on exotic, non-Western

FIGURE 3.1

The major subdivisions of the field of anthropology, including the two that are the focus of this book: paleoanthropology and archaeology. While these subdivisions represent distinct approaches, there are numerous connections among them. Moreover, each can be further subdivided into subspecialties.

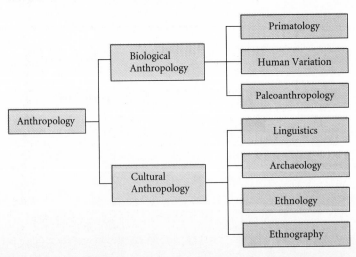

people. Today, ethnographers study inner-city youth gangs, rural farming communities, factory workers, and even the community of academic anthropologists. Each group, in its own way, represents a society—or a part of a larger society—the study of which can tell us something about the human condition.

Researchers who go beyond examining a particular group of people to compare the behaviors of different cultures are said to be conducting **ethnology.** An ethnologist might take the work of several ethnographers who have conducted detailed studies of specific human groups and investigate, for example, how those various peoples deal with death, discipline their children, choose a mate, or build their houses. A highly specialized subfield of anthropology is **anthropological linguistics.** Here, the focus is language—how it evolved and the historical relationships among the known languages.

Primatologists are another kind of anthropologist who lives with the groups they study (Figure 3.3). Instead of living among and studying people,

FIGURE 3.2

Margaret Mead, in native dress (on the left), poses with a native Polynesian woman. (Courtesy of the Institute for Intercultural Studies, Inc., New York. Photo from the Library of Congress)

FIGURE 3.3

Jane Goodall's work among the chimpanzees has provided enormous insight into the lives of chimps, and, indirectly, into the lives of our ancient ancestors (see Chapter 4). (Courtesy of the Jane Goodall Institute. Photo by Ken Regan)

Don Johanson, whose work in east Africa has revealed the remains of some of our most ancient hominid ancestors, is shown here at Hadar, a fossil locality that has provided the remains of Lucy and other members of the species Australopithecus afarensis *(see Chapter 5). (Courtesy of the Institute of Human Origins)*

these anthropologists focus their attention on the group of animals called the nonhuman **primates.** Prosimians, monkeys, apes, as well as people are all primates (see Chapter 4). Primatologists aim to better understand our nearest living relatives. Believing that all primates share a common evolutionary heritage, primatologists hope to gain insights into our ancestral line. Jane Goodall is perhaps the best-known primatologist, having devoted much of her life to living among and learning about chimpanzees in the wild. Dian Fossey was another primatologist; she lived and worked with gorillas in the African nation of Rwanda. Her life and work was the subject of a biography by Farley Mowat, *Woman in the Mists* (1987), and the Hollywood movie *Gorillas in the Mist.*

Other anthropologists focus their attention more specifically on the human past, examining human origins and biological development. These **paleoanthropologists** have as their database the early biological history of our species, focusing on the skeletal remains of our human ancestors (Figure 3.4). **Archaeologists,** on the other hand, rely on the material, cultural remains left behind by past people, including those same varieties of human beings whose bones the paleoanthropologists unearth (Figure 3.5). Material remains may include the tools and other objects people made and used, from simple stone-cutting tools to complex monuments. While archaeology is often perceived as being a romantic enterprise, it is perhaps more like the study of "other people's garbage," as a PBS TV documentary called it (PBS 1980).

Paleoanthropologists and archaeologists investigate the evolutionary history of humanity, both the biological evolution of our species and its cultural evolution. Humans are not only biological organisms whose **adaptation** is rooted in our genes; we are cultural organisms whose uniquely great intelligence allows us to invent much of our strategy for survival. As researchers first recognized in the eighteenth century (see Chapter 2), these invented adaptations—our **cultures**—have evolved just as surely as have our bodies

Archaeologist Melinda Zeder of the Smithsonian Institution has worked extensively in the Middle East, exploring some of the world's most ancient Neolithic sites (see Chapter 12, especially the section "Case Study Close-Up"). (Courtesy of Melinda Zeder)

and brains. Not only did our human ancestors leave behind their physical remains, which reflected their biological adaptation, but they also left behind the material objects they made and used as part of their cultural adaptation. The study of these two sources of information—their bones and artifacts—allows us to paint a picture of the lives of our ancient human ancestors.

EPISTEMOLOGY: HOW WE KNOW WHAT WE KNOW

This book focuses on the results of the paleoanthropological and archaeological study of the human past. There are many fine texts whose focus is the methodology of those disciplines—how paleoanthropologists and archaeologists go about recovering and analyzing evidence (see "To Learn More," at chapter's end). It is not my intent here to discuss in detail the **epistemology** of those disciplines—how the information presented in this book about human biological and cultural evolution was obtained. Where appropriate and necessary, particular methods or processes will be covered along with a specific site, issue, or time period.

Still, there are a number of important, general issues regarding method that should be covered. Just as geologists and biologists employ specific methods to investigate the earth and life, paleoanthropologists and archaeologists use specific methods to investigate the human past. What follows is a brief introduction to those methods.

The "Science" in the Study of the Past

Science is a method for explaining the world around us. It begins with the objective observation of that world. Biologists focus on living things, astronomers focus on other planets, stars, and galaxies, and geologists observe the earth itself. Anthropologists, however, concentrate on humanity, and paleoanthropologists and archaeologists focus more specifically on the human past.

All scientists observe the world and look for patterns, correlations, cause-and-effect relationships, and trends, in the hope of describing the way the world works—how the earth was formed, how rivers flow, how life originated, or how humanity evolved. From the things observed and the patterns perceived, scientists come up with general explanations, or **hypotheses,** for those observations and patterns.

Scientists are not content, however, just to generalize about the world. They need also to deduce predictions about what other data should be found if their hypotheses are valid, if they explain accurately how things work. In paleoanthropology and archaeology this is accomplished through the procedures outlined in this chapter and by a rigorous adherence to the scientific method.

Science is a process as much as a result, and it rarely provides absolute answers. Usually all we can hope for are increasingly better descriptions of how things are—or were. Certainty in science is rare.

Paleoanthropologists and archaeologists face an added obstacle to maintaining scientific objectivity: The conclusions we reach relate directly to how we view ourselves. We are not bacteria or stars or rocks, and conclusions about how those things work do not have the same kind of impact as conclusions about who we are and where we have come from. Thus, we must not only emphasize an objective scientific approach to the past, but also recognize the special problems presented when, as scientists, we look at our own species.

Paleoanthropology and prehistory, therefore, are always works in progress. This book will share with you the certainties as well as the uncertainties of these fields. The consensus views presented in each chapter's "Chronicle" section almost certainly will change, sometimes radically. This is not an indictment of science, but a recognition of how science works. Scientists, being human, may not always be happy when their neatly conceived constructs are overturned. But their allegiance must be to truth and not to how they would prefer the truth to be.

Let us now go on to explain briefly the methods of paleoanthropology and archaeology.

PALEOANTHROPOLOGICAL AND ARCHAEOLOGICAL SITES

Paleoanthropological and archaeological **sites** are places where physical evidence of a past human presence can be recovered. Such evidence consists of: (1) the skeletal remains of human beings or human ancestors, (2) **artifacts**—objects made and used by past peoples (Figure 3.6), and (3) **ecofacts**—

FIGURE 3.6

Artifacts are objects that human beings manufactured. These long, stone blades are part of a cluster of thirty such artifacts found in an ancient site in southern New England.
(K. L. Feder)

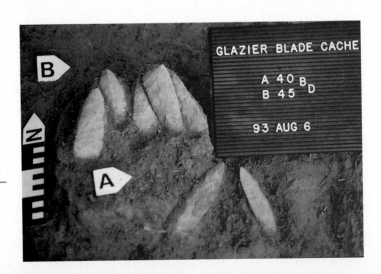

environmental elements that exhibit traces of human use or activity, such as the bones of butchered animals (see Figure 10.17, for example).

Wherever people have lived or worked, they have used material from the surrounding environment: stone, clay, metal, wood, bone, plant fibers, seeds, antler, animal hides, and so on. These materials ultimately are lost, used up and discarded, or hidden away for future use. Where conditions in the soil allow for their preservation, these items can be found and recovered for analysis by scientists who study the human past. Together, these physical remnants make up the archaeological site.

Sites are defined not only by the recovered objects themselves, but also by the physical arrangement of the remains. The preserved spatial context of archaeological remains—where things were used and left by an ancient people—allows us to reconstruct the activities that took place at a site. Most reconstructions of past times are based on analysis of human remains, artifacts, and ecofacts, as well as their spatial arrangement at sites where people lived or performed special tasks. Sites can be small and short-term, like hunting camps, or large and permanent, like the sites of the world's first cities in Mesopotamia (see Chapter 13).

How Sites Are Formed

Sites come into existence through a series of site formation processes: Tools can be discarded or lost, food remains can be thrown in a trash pit or pile, dead bodies may be intentionally and ceremonially buried, valuable objects may be "cached," or hidden away, for a future retrieval that never comes, human ancestors may be killed by animals and their remains dragged into a lair, etc. The study of how the paleontological remains in a particular place ended up there is called **taphonomy;** we can also apply this term to the study of how a paleoanthropological or archaeological remain came to rest in its place of discovery. Recognition of how an item became part of the paleoanthropological or archaeological record provides insights into the behavior of the human beings who left those items behind.

How Sites Are Preserved

Once material objects are laid on or in the earth, natural processes may serve to cover, protect, and preserve them. Volcanic ash or lava, silt from a flooding river, sand blown by the wind, a collapsed cave roof, or an avalanche, all may cover the objects left behind by people, preserving them until nature or anthropologists uncover them many years later. Some of the materials used by people, especially stone tools and pottery, preserve very well under most circumstances. Other materials, like bone and plant remains, require special

FIGURE 3.7

At Skara Brae, in the Orkney Islands north of Scotland, an ancient site a few thousand years old was exposed by the winds and waves of a North Atlantic storm. (Courtesy of James Dyer)

conditions for preservation. When archaeologists and paleoanthropologists are lucky, an archaeological site is itself like a fossil, a preserved physical representation of a past people and way of life.

How Sites Are Found

Archaeological sites are found in a number of ways. While some natural processes may preserve sites, other such processes may expose them. Rivers cutting into their banks, wind blowing sand away from an area, or waves eroding a beach may bring to light ancient, buried remains (Figure 3.7). Many of the sites related to the earliest history of humanity have been exposed by these processes of erosion. Places like Olduvai Gorge in Tanzania and the Hadar region of Ethiopia (see Chapters 5 and 6) present naturally exposed layers of ancient geological deposits (Figure 3.8). By walking over these places systematically, paleoanthropologists and archaeologists have found many of the important ancestral human fossils discussed in this book.

In other cases, archaeologists do not have the luxury of naturally exposed ancient layers in which to search for artifacts, ecofacts, or human skeletons. In these areas, sites can be searched for through a process of subsurface sampling, where **test pits** are placed at regular intervals in an attempt to locate ancient material buried by natural processes (Figure 3.9). In some cases, sophisticated **remote-sensing** devices—ground-penetrating radar, proton magnetometers, electrical resistivity meters—can help in the search for sites by

FIGURE 3.8

The ancient soil levels and many sites of Hadar have been revealed through the slow-acting process of erosion. Much of Don Johanson's work on the fossil species Australo-pithecus afarensis *(see Chapter 5) has been conducted at Hadar (see also Figure 3.4).* (Institute of Human Origins)

FIGURE 3.9

In areas of the world where natural processes have not exposed ancient sites, archaeologists must dig to reveal buried cultural deposits. Test pits are often excavated to explore an area for buried archaeological material. (K. L. Feder)

probing for anomalous readings under the surface that may indicate the presence of buried cultural material or soil disturbance by ancient people. Aerial photography can help identify large-scale land modifications or buried remains that affect the growth of vegetation.

How Data Are Recovered from a Site

Once a site has been found, the arduous task of extracting the physical evidence from the ground begins. Paleoanthropological and archaeological evi-

FIGURE 3.10

Excavation in square units by slowly peeling away soil layers aids in maintaining the spatial relationships among the materials found at a site. (K. L. Feder)

FIGURE 3.11

The stones lining the bottom of a 4,000-year-old earth oven demarcate this archaeological feature. The stones were heated in a fire, then placed in the bottom of a pit, where the heat radiated by the stones was used for cooking. (K. L. Feder)

dence is rare, precious, and often fragile, so the methods used to unearth it have been designed accordingly.

We must recover our data with great care. Though power equipment and picks and shovels may be used to remove the culturally sterile overburden, once within the zone of a site, hand-held trowels, dental picks, and brushes ordinarily are relied on to remove the soil enclosing site materials (Figure 3.10). Material may be left exactly where found in order to expose the possible **associations** among the remains. For example, a single stone, found and then tossed in a bag, is not nearly as informative as a series of stones, each one left in place, that together denote an earth oven (Figure 3.11).

As careful as we are in excavating a site, small fragmentary remains can be missed. All excavated soil ordinarily is sifted through wire screening of ¼-inch, ⅛-inch, or even smaller mesh, to ensure 100% recovery. In some cases, the soil matrix may be taken to an on- or off-site lab, where standing water may be used to help in separating artifacts, ecofacts, or human bone from the surrounding soil.

ANALYZING ARCHAEOLOGICAL DATA

How Artifacts Are Analyzed

In analyzing artifacts, at minimum we want to know where the raw materials for the objects came from, how the items were manufactured, and how they were used.

The Sources of Raw Materials.   Raw material sources—where a particular rock type for making stone tools or clay for making pots was obtained—can be traced by analyzing small amounts of impurities in those raw materials. The percentages of particular impurities often are unique and diagnostic of specific sources and can serve as a fingerprint for a raw material's place of origin through the application of a number of techniques that fall under the heading **trace element analysis.** Artifacts can be examined for their particular percentages of these trace elements. Possible sources for the raw material from which the artifact was made also can be examined for their trace element percentages. In many cases where a raw material source and the artifact have matching trace element profiles, it can be suggested that the raw material for the artifact was derived from that source.

Tool Manufacture and Use.   How an item was made can be assessed through **experimental replication,** the process of attempting to make an authentic recreation of an ancient artifact. Also useful is the examination of historically described groups that possessed a technology analogous to that of the ancient people being studied. The use an artifact served can be deduced from its **morphology**—its form, what it looked like—and by the evidence of **wear patterns.** Different actions (piercing, cutting, scraping, engraving, chopping) performed by different tools on different raw materials (stone, wood, leather, bone, antler) leave distinctive and diagnostic wear traces (striations, polish, scars) that can be assessed through replication (J. J. Shea 1992). In an experiment conducted by archaeologist Lawrence Keeley (1980), replicated tools were utilized in various ways and on various raw materials. These tools can serve as models of different wear patterns for comparison with archaeologically found tools. If the wear traces on an archaeological specimen are similar to those on an experimental specimen—where the action performed and the material used are known—then conclusions can be reached concerning how the archaeologically recovered tool was used.

Some artifacts even possess traces of the materials on which they were used; archaeologists have found microscopic plant remains and even blood from animals killed with a tool. Recent advances in blood residue analysis have allowed for the recovery of animal blood from stone tools and even the identification of the animal species involved.

Social Patterns.   Along with providing insights into technology and use, artifacts can sometimes help illuminate other, less concrete aspects of ancient lifeways. The particular style of an artifact made by an individual is often a reflection of who taught the maker. How people learn to make objects within a culture is a social decision. For example, they may learn from a parent who is passing down a family tradition of spearpoint or ceramic styles. The style seen in the archaeological remains, therefore, reflects this aspect of an ancient social system.

Some archaeological **features** reflect even more directly on nonmaterial practices of a people. Most obvious here are burials, which often are a direct reflection of a group's religious ideology as it relates to its recognition of the significance of death as well as possible belief in an afterlife. Neandertals (see Chapter 7) interred their dead with tools and food 60,000 years ago, and what is uncovered may inform us of their perspective on life and death. Egyptian pharaohs were laid to rest in sumptuous splendor (see Chapter 13), and what is unearthed in their pyramids informs us of their beliefs about the meaning of death and provides insights into their minds.

How Ecofacts Are Analyzed

Animal bones, charred seeds, nut fragments, the shells of marine organisms, and fruit pits recovered at sites may represent the food remains of past people. Since diet is an important part of a culture, scientists would like to reconstruct the subsistence practices of prehistoric people.

Since the skeletons of different animal species are usually distinctive, and where remains are not too fragmented, the kinds of animals present in an archaeological deposit can often be identified. Cut marks on bone and charring from a fire are good indicators that the animal was used for food. Many archaeology labs possess **osteological comparative collections,** or bone libraries, where ancient specimens can be compared to known, labeled specimens to help identify the species recovered in excavation.

The minimum number of animals represented in the **faunal assemblage** at a site can also be reconstructed. Since most animals exhibit two distinct forms on the basis of sex—that is, **sexual dimorphism**—scientists often can distinguish male from female animals. Also, as animals go through a number of **osteological** developmental stages—changes in their bones as they grow and mature—the age at death of an animal hunted, killed, cooked, and eaten by a prehistoric people can often be determined. In addition, the bones of wild animals can be differentiated from those of domesticated animals: Domesticated animals frequently are smaller than their wild ancestors, the teeth of domesticated dogs are more crowded than those of their wolf progenitors, and the bones of wild animals are often denser than those of their domesticated descendants. Knowing the species of an animal, its sex and age, whether the people were hunting only older animals, and whether they were avoiding killing females or killing off most of the young males but allowing females to survive to adulthood (a common pattern among domesticated animals) can provide insights into the subsistence strategies of an ancient people.

Plant remains, including seeds, nuts, and wood, can be recovered and analyzed and the contribution of plant foods to the diet can be assessed. Since plants are available seasonally, the yearly schedule of a people can be reconstructed based on which plant foods are present at a site and which are absent. We usually can differentiate the seeds, grains, or fruits of wild species from those that have been altered by humans through **artificial selection** (see Chapter 12) in the process of domestication.

How Human and Prehuman Skeletal Remains Are Analyzed

The bones of human ancestors are an invaluable resource to paleoanthropologists and archaeologists. To begin with, the fact that archaic forms of human beings existed is shown most clearly by the presence of their bones, which are different from those of either apes or modern humans. (See the many photographs in Chapters 5–7 of creatures who were ancestral to us but, at the same time, were not quite us.) These bones can inform us about how human ancestors walked, the kinds of climates to which they were adapted, the foods they ate, their general level of nutrition, and the diseases and traumas from which they suffered. Comparing the bones of ancient human ancestors to those of modern people can help us place these specimens accurately in the human evolutionary line.

The Sex of a Skeleton.   Throughout, this book will refer to specific fossils as being male or female. This is possible because of the recognition of sexual dimorphism. Human and ape males, for example, have skeletons that often are readily distinguishable from females of the same species: Males tend to be larger, with heavier, rougher bones, and have larger bony ridges above their eye orbits (sockets) than do females of the same primate species. In some primate species, males have a bony crest on the top of their skulls, while females lack this feature. The human pelvis is differently configured in females than in males, since it serves as part of the birth canal in women. With enough skeletal elements recovered, we often can be quite sure of the sex of the individual.

AGES OF TOOTH ERUPTION

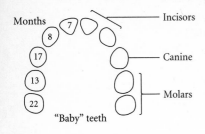

AGES OF EPIPHYSEAL UNION

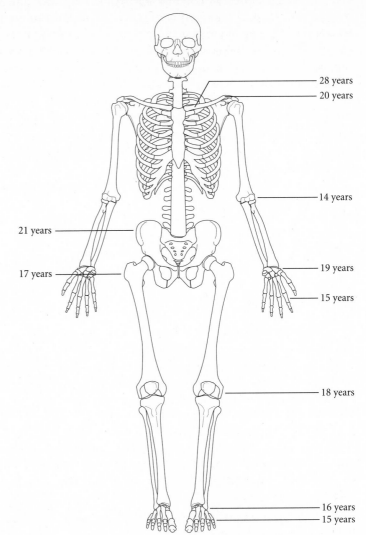

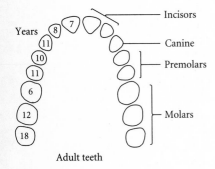

FIGURE 3.12

These diagrams show the age order of tooth eruption and of epiphyseal fusion for human beings. Careful analysis of skeletal remains can reveal species, sex, age at death, nutritional status, cause of death, and geographic origin of the individual.

Age at which the epiphyses in the indicated area fuse to the shafts.

Age at Death.   Our discussion of human fossils will occasionally mention the approximate age at death of an individual. As with animals, the bones of human children go through a series of developmental changes during the course of their lives. Tooth eruption and replacement provide developmental markers of human maturation, as does **epiphyseal fusion** (Figure 3.12). When you are born, each of the long bones in your arms, legs, hands, and feet is in three sections: a shaft, or **diaphysis,** and two endcaps, or **epiphyses** (singular, *epiphysis*). The shafts and endcaps fuse during growth at more or less set times during our teen years, marking maturity and full growth. Later changes in **cranial sutures**—the places where the different cranial plates come together—as well as in the region where the pubic bones come together—the **pubic symphysis**—can be used to estimate an individual's age at death.

Geographic Origin.   We all recognize that people's physical features differ based on the geography of their origins; humans from different parts of the world possess a constellation of physical traits—skin color, nose shape, hair texture, body proportions—that distinguish them from people from other parts of the world. Skeletal traits also vary geographically, so, in some instances, the skeletal remains of an individual can be traced to the part of the world from which they came. For example, one reason we know that Native Americans originated in Asia is that the oldest skeletal remains in North America share a group of skeletal characteristics with Asian people (see Chapter 10).

Pathology and Disease.   The bones in a human body are like a book on which some of that human's life experiences are written. Healed bone breaks, episodes of malnourishment during growth, specific dietary deficiencies, the ingestion of certain poisons, arthritis, tuberculosis, syphilis, cancers, and many other conditions leave recognizable traces on bones. These marks can be read by the specialist in **paleopathology.** Even the primary vegetal foods in a diet can be detected in bones, under certain circumstances [see the discussion in "Issues and Debates" in Chapter 4 on the $^{13}C:^{12}C$ ratio ("What Replaced the Forests?")]. The paleopathological evidence on the bones of European Neandertals will be discussed in Chapter 7; the higher level of malnutrition evident on their bones may explain why the Neandertals became extinct.

Preserved Bodies.   Human skeletal remains are poignant reminders of our own mortality, along with being valuable sources of information about the lives of ancient people. It is not so hard to imagine flesh on the bone and to consider that the dry, hard "specimen" analyzed by the archaeologist was once part of a living human being. But on rare occasions, the human being behind the osteological remains does not have to be imagined. Some complete—or nearly complete—bodies of ancient humans have been remarkably preserved. These rare discoveries present to the archaeologist a uniquely clear window on the past.

Nearly intact bodies 2,000, 3,000, even 4,000 years old have been recovered from Danish peat bogs (Glob 1969). The anaerobic character of the bogs—the complete lack of oxygen—prevents the survival of bacteria that eat flesh. Several partially complete bodies have been removed from the bogs, with internal organs intact, the skin—including fingerprints and body markings such as tattoos—fully preserved, facial expressions clearly discernible, even the hair on their heads and eyebrows and eyelashes preserved virtually completely. The equivalent of autopsies conducted on the modern deceased can be performed on these ancient corpses. Diseases, traumas, parasites, and even the immediate cause of death can be diagnosed. Some of the bog bodies were the remains of people who had been executed by strangulation; in at least one case, the rope used was preserved along with its victim, and was discovered intact and in place around the deceased's neck.

Even the final meal of a person can be ascertained. In one well-known case, that of the so-called Lindow Man found in a bog in England, the stomach contents revealed a final meal that was known to be a ceremonial offering ingested by sacrifice victims in an ancient Druid ceremony some 2,000 years ago (A. Ross and Robins 1989). Lindow Man, a probable Druid prince, ate a ceremonial charred cake before he was garroted and then interred in that peat bog.

Recently, another well-preserved ancient body was found (Color Plate 1). This so-called "Ice Man" was essentially freeze-dried beneath a glacier in the Italian Alps (D. Roberts 1993; Sjøvold 1992; Spindler 1994). When discovered accidentally by two German hikers, his body was just peeking out from the ice; they first thought it was a doll. When officials arrived on the scene, they presumed the body was the remains of one of the many recent hikers who had died in unexpected blizzards. Only when the body was removed from the ice and the surrounding area searched for evidence were ancient tools and clothing found: grass-lined shoes, a hafted copper axe, an ash-handled flint knife and woven grass sheath, an antler-tipped stick for sharpening the flint tool, twelve unfinished arrows, an unfinished bow, and a deerskin quiver (Color Plate 2). Radiocarbon dating (see the next section) indicates that the Ice Man lived about 5,000 years ago, yet his organs are intact and his flesh preserved; you can still make out enigmatic tattoos consisting of a series of parallel lines on his body.

A detailed analysis of the Ice Man's body currently is under way. Preliminary results show that he probably was in his thirties or forties when he died. X-rays show clearly that he suffered from arthritis in the neck as well as in the lower back and right hip. His body also displays evidence of a number of traumas sustained during his life: Eight ribs show evidence of healed or healing fractures; the bones of at least one toe exhibit evidence typical of frostbite; the single preserved fingernail shows furrows that probably represent periods of reduced nail growth attributable to malnutrition or other bodily stress. Much more analysis remains to be done. The remarkable preservation of the Ice Man is enabling scientists to conduct a postmortem more than 5,000 years after his death.

DETERMINING THE AGE OF A SITE OR SPECIMEN

Until fairly recently in the history of paleoanthropology and archaeology, dating fossils and sites depended on relative sequences based on **stratigraphic** layering of the earth's surface—and a lot of guesswork. The fundamental technique had changed little since William Smith recognized its applicability in the late eighteenth and early nineteenth centuries (see Chapter 2). Fossil specimens and archaeological sites were assigned to particular stratigraphic layers. Dates were derived based on assumed rates of formation of the layers above and below, on the guessed ages of fossils of extinct species found in association with human remains, and on a bit of intuition.

Dating Techniques Based on Radioactive Decay

Stratigraphic sequences, fossil associations, and even intuition are still used by paleoanthropologists and archaeologists in dating specimens, but these are no longer the only or primary methods of dating. Researchers can now rely on **radiometric** dating techniques based on the known rates of decay of several radioactive (unstable) **isotopes** (varieties) of common elements like carbon (^{14}C dating), uranium (uranium series dating), potassium (potassium/argon, or K/Ar, dating), and argon (^{40}Ar/^{39}Ar dating). These techniques provide **absolute dates** rather than **relative dates.** This does not necessarily mean they are accurate. The term *absolute* means only that we can associate a year or range of years with an object or site rather than place the sites or objects only in chronological order, as is the case in relative dating.

    K/Ar dating has been particularly useful when applied to early human ancestors (Dalrymple and Lanphere 1969). It is based on the decay of a radioactive form of potassium, a common element found in volcanic deposits, into argon gas. When a volcanic layer is deposited, all of the argon already present from previous potassium decay bubbles off into the atmosphere. In a sense, the atomic clock in the ash or lava is set to zero and there is no argon left in the deposit. When the volcanic rock solidifies, the unstable potassium continues its slow decay to argon, which is trapped in the rock. Because we know the rate at which potassium decays to argon—its **half-life** is 1.31 billion years—then by measuring how much argon has accumulated in the rock, we can determine how long the argon has been building up since the rock was last liquefied (that is, since the volcanic eruption that deposited the lava) and, therefore, when that rock was deposited.

    This dates the rock and, usually, not the fossil, unless the creature was actually found within a lava flow. In the case of the Laetoli footprints featured in the "Prelude" in Chapter 5, dating the ash layer directly dates the footprints and, hence, the creature that made the prints. Ordinarily, however, human fossils are found above or below a dateable layer. When a fossil is found above a dated layer, the fossil must be younger than that layer; that is, the creature was alive at some point after the volcanic layer was deposited. When a fossil is found beneath a dated layer, we can be sure it is older than that deposit; that is, the creature was living in the area before the dated layer was deposited. Under the best of circumstances, the fossils can be associated with layers both above and below them, enabling us to bracket their age.

For more recent sites, especially those dating to within the last 50,000 years, **radiocarbon dating,** or **carbon dating,** is extremely useful. Based on the known decay rate of a radioactive form of carbon, ^{14}C, carbon dating can date anything containing carbon. Since all living and once-living things contain this element, carbon dating can be applied to plant and animal remains such as wood, bone, seeds, and antler. Even human remains can be dated via radiocarbon dating. Because the half-life of ^{14}C is relatively short—5,730 years—radiocarbon dating has a fairly narrow temporal range of application. In a specimen that is too young, not enough of the ^{14}C has decayed to measure statistically with confidence; in a specimen that is too old, not enough ^{14}C is left. Carbon dating is best applied to remains less than 50,000 years old and more than a few hundred years old.

Dating Techniques Based on Radiation Damage

Electron spin resonance dating (ESR) is one of a number of techniques that dates materials through the measurement of radiation damage—in this case, the buildup of electrons trapped in crystalline materials at a site (Grün 1989, 1993; Grün and Stringer 1991). When, for example, a tooth is formed, the electrons in the atoms of that tooth are technically in an unexcited state, or "ground state." As a result of natural radioactivity in the tooth itself, as well as in the soil in which the tooth is deposited, some of those electrons get transferred to higher energy levels and get "trapped" there. The number of trapped electrons is a function of characteristics of the material (in this case, tooth enamel), the amount of background radiation, and time—how long since the tooth formed. Because the trapping characteristics of different materials as well as background radiation levels can be measured and accounted for, the number of electrons trapped in a sample can be used to determine the age of the sample. ESR can date teeth that are more than a few thousand years old, but its key contribution is in dating sites that are too old for radiocarbon dating—in other words, sites more than 50,000 years old. The upper limit for ESR is unknown; it has been estimated at somewhere between 10 million and 100 million years (Grün and Stringer 1991:165). Even the younger limit renders the technique applicable to sites directly related to human evolution. Greatest success has been achieved on mollusk shells, speleothems (cave deposits), corals, volcanic rock, and tooth enamel. It does not, however, work well on bone (Grün and Stringer 1991:155).

Thermoluminescence, like ESR, measures the amount of energy trapped in material recovered at archaeological sites from natural radioactive decay in the surrounding soil. Again, such energy is released at a set rate in a given soil, so the amount captured in site materials is a reflection of their age.

Thermoluminescence has been applied successfully to fired clay objects, especially pottery, as well as to stone that has been heated to a high temperature—for example, the rocks lining a fireplace. In both cases, the application of heat—the firing of the pot or the heating of the stone in a fire—releases all of the energy previously trapped in the material. This effectively sets the trapped-charge clock to zero. Then, once the pot or stone is returned to the earth, it again begins to accumulate energy at the set rate produced by the natural radioactivity of the surrounding soil. Knowing that rate allows calculation of how much time has elapsed since the object was heated and, hence, when people were present at the site making pots or banking their hearths with stones.

Fission-track dating, another radiation-damage measurement, bases age estimates on the number of visible "tracks" left by radioactive decay in site materials; these microscopic tracks build up at a regular rate.

Dating by Measuring Chemical Processes

Obsidian hydration measures the regular buildup of a "hydration layer" on freshly exposed volcanic glass; a fresh surface is exposed when a human hammers off a stone flake while making obsidian tools. The exposed surface immediately begins to combine chemically with water in the air around it or in the soil in which it is deposited. The thickness of the layer on an exposed obsidian surface is a function of time, the moisture level and temperature of its environment of deposition, as well as characteristics of the particular obsidian. Where that moisture level can be measured and controlled for, the age of the flake can be determined. Where the rate of hydration-layer development can be determined, an absolute date can be derived for the artifact. In other cases, only relative dates can be determined; we can figure out which objects are older than others on the basis of their thicker hydration layer.

Dating by Measuring Paleomagnetism

Paleomagnetic dating is based on the fact that the position of magnetic north has fluctuated over time. The orientation of naturally magnetic particles in a lava flow is measured to determine the direction of magnetic north when the flow was hot. Since the location of magnetic north has been determined for long periods of time, volcanic layers that preserve evidence of the location of north when the deposits were laid down can be dated (Kappelman 1993).

SUMMARY

Archaeologists and paleoanthropologists apply a broad array of techniques in their investigation of the human past. This chapter has briefly surveyed some of the more important procedures for recovering and analyzing the data on which the rest of this book is based.

How sites are formed, how they become preserved, and how they are discovered are key questions for archaeologists and paleoanthropologists. Once found, data can be analyzed to determine the following: the age of the materials, how tools were made and used, the subsistence base of the people, and aspects of their social and even religious lives. Past people can also be investigated directly through analysis of their physical remains, which determines the age, sex, health status, and geographic origin of an ancient individual. The evolutionary relationship between a prehistoric person and modern human beings can therefore be determined.

Using the general procedures outlined in this chapter, and many other very specific analytical techniques mentioned throughout this book, archaeologists and paleoanthropologists can reveal the chronicle of the human past. We begin that chronicle in Chapter 4.

TO LEARN MORE

There are many fine textbooks describing the methods of archaeology and paleoanthropology; see especially: Wendy Ashmore and Robert Sharer's (1996) brief introduction, *Discovering Our Past,* Second Edition, and their longer *Archaeology: Discovering Our Past* (Sharer and Ashmore 1993); Brian Fagan's *Archaeology: A Brief Introduction* (1991b) and his longer *In the Beginning: An Introduction to Archaeology* (1991c); Colin Renfrew and Paul Bahn's *Archaeology: Theories, Methods, and Practice* (1991); and David Hurst Thomas' short work *Archaeology: Down to Earth* (1991) and his longer *Archaeology* (1989). For the analysis of human skeletal material, a classical treatment has been provided by Wilton Marion Krogman (1962) in his *The Human Skeleton in Forensic Medicine.* There is probably no better recent source than Tim White and Pieter Folkens' (1991) *Human Osteology.*

KEY TERMS

anthropology	primatologist	culture
ethnographer	primate	epistemology
ethnology	paleoanthropologist	hypothesis
anthropological	archaeologist	site
linguistics	adaptation	artifact

ecofact

taphonomy

test pit

remote sensing

association

trace element analysis

experimental replication

morphology

wear patterns

feature

osteological comparative
collection

faunal assemblage

sexual dimorphism

osteological

artificial selection

epiphyseal fusion

diaphysis

epiphysis

cranial suture

pubic symphysis

paleopathology

stratigraphic

radiometric

isotope

absolute date

relative date

K/Ar dating

half-life

radiocarbon dating

carbon dating

electron spin resonance
dating

thermoluminescence

fission-track dating

obsidian hydration

paleomagnetic dating

4

Genesis

Human prehistory and history represent little more than 4 million years in a 15 billion year story. The 3.5 billion year history of life on earth is characterized by the evolution and extinction of countless species. Ironically, it was the massive wave of extinction at the end of the Miocene Epoch, approximately 7 million years ago, that paved the way for the evolution of the first hominids.

When the forests contracted at the end of the Miocene, many ape species became extinct. Some, such as the ancestors of modern chimps, bonobos, gorillas, orangutans, gibbons, and siamangs, possessed adaptational advantages and were able to survive. Another ape species was unable to compete successfully in the forests and was pushed out onto the savanna. But because this species possessed the unique ability to walk upright, they were able to survive and, in fact, thrive. These were the first hominids.

Years ago	
6,000	Beginning of urban life, the evolution of the state, and the invention of writing
12,000	Beginning of the domestication of plants and animals
30,000	Explosion of art in the form of painting and sculpture
80,000	Hominids are burying their dead
150,000	Approximate time of the appearance of modern-looking human beings
500,000	Hominids have mastered the use of fire
1.5 million	Hominids have expanded geographically into Asia by this time
1.8 million	Hominids with brains two-thirds of modern size appear in Africa
2.5 million	Tool-using hominids are found in Africa
5 million	Most ape species have become extinct; the first upright primates — the hominids — appear soon after this time
25 million	Beginning of the florescence of the apes
65 million	Dinosaurs become extinct; the first primates appear on earth
190 million	The first warm-blooded animals — mammals — appear on earth
225 million	Beginning of the period of dinosaur dominance on earth
425 million	The first terrestrial life forms appear on earth after this time
600 million	Time of the so-called Cambrian Explosion of life: a great proliferation of life forms, all living in the ancient seas of the earth
1 billion	The first multi-cellular life forms appear on earth a little after this time
3.5 billion	The first single-celled organisms appear on earth
5 billion	Formation of our solar system; the earth has become a solid planetary body by 4.5 billion years ago
12 billion	First stars
15 billion	Beginning of everything — the Big Bang

Imagine that you are sitting in a darkened movie theater in front of a giant screen like those in some larger science centers or museums. The screen is black except for a single point of light. You are about to view a two-hour history of the universe in which everything happens proportional to when it actually happened in time. It is absolutely quiet as the film begins. You are looking back in time 15 billion years at our own universe. But there are no stars, no planets, no life, no people. Everything in the universe as we know it—the millions of galaxies, the trillions of stars, everything that ever is to be in the universe, including the raw material of our world and even the components of our own bodies—is condensed into that tiny dot of light at the center of the screen.

Suddenly, the bright speck begins to swell in a remarkable inflation. All the matter and energy that had been concentrated in that point of light expands to fill the center of the screen as it arches outward, piercing the surrounding darkness. You have just witnessed what astrophysicists and cosmologists call the "Big Bang." (Fifteen billion years later, scientists can still measure its faint echo in the form of microwave radiation.) This was the birth of the universe, the birth of time and space. This was Genesis.

The energy from the initial explosion dissipates as light ripples across the screen. Twenty-five minutes into the movie, the debris from that paroxysmal first explosion begins to congeal into the first stars. It is 12 billion years ago. You watch as these stars pass through patterned stages of development, burning brightly for a time, then cooling down and darkening. Some explode cataclysmically as supernovae, spewing forth atoms produced in their nuclear furnaces (Figure 4.1).

Two-thirds of the way through the movie, about an hour and twenty minutes into it, the camera zooms in on one corner of the screen, where one

FIGURE 4.1

The Orion Nebula is an interstellar cloud where stars are forming much as they did in the early years of the universe.
(National Optical Astronomy Observatories)

star and nine planets are beginning to crystallize from the debris ejected by the stellar explosions seen previously. It is our own sun and solar system, and it is 5 billion years ago.

The camera zooms in on the third planet orbiting the yellow star. Though you do not yet see the familiar blue and green image, clearly this is our own earth in its infancy, around 4.5 billion years ago.

The camera now pans across a primeval ocean, then dives into the sea. It is a little more than an hour and a half into the movie—3.5 billion years ago in real time—and you are looking at the first living creatures to appear on the planet, single-celled organisms that left their fossil impressions on the ancient strata of Australia, Africa, and Greenland, where paleontologists have studied them. It is not until 112 minutes into the 120-minute film that more complex, multicelled organisms begin leaving their marks on rocks dating in real time to a little after a billion years ago.

At 115 minutes and forty-five seconds into the movie, you witness an explosion of life; within two-and-a-half seconds, living things are nearly everywhere. It is around 525 million years ago, and all of the major modern taxonomical groups have come into existence (Bowring et al. 1993). You have just viewed the so-called **Cambrian Explosion.** Soon, the vast ocean on the screen is filled with fish; it is 116 minutes and thirty seconds into the movie—about 450 million years ago. Just a few seconds later, the camera swings around to view dry land, where you see the first terrestrial animal life moving around. One minute later, small reptiles begin scurrying across the planet's surface. After another half minute, the camera reveals an astounding array of impressively large land animals. With less than two minutes left in the two-hour movie, the screen is filled with dinosaurs, who began their dominance of the earth 235 million years ago. Unless you watch very carefully you might miss the first appearance of groups of small, furry creatures—the mammals. They show up in the movie with only about one minute forty seconds left, and in the fossil record slightly more than 200 million years ago. With a little more than thirty seconds to go in the movie (65 million years ago), the dinosaurs disappear and some of the small mammals climb into the trees, to become the ancestors of monkeys and, eventually, apes (R. Martin 1993).

Don't blink, or you will miss what happens next. With just a bit more than two seconds left in the movie, the first upright-walking human ancestors flash across the screen for a second, their brains the size of an ape's. Then another ancestor appears, with a brain larger than any ape's, standing upright and making tools. From this point, everything that humanity has accomplished on earth—the manufacture of stone tools, the taming of fire, the invention of agriculture, the development of cities, the industrial revolution, walking on the moon, and right up to you and your life at this instant—all of this bursts across the screen in the last second of the movie [Nigel Calder's (1983) *Timescale* is the source for the temporal framework of the account just given].

CHRONICLE

Paleoanthropologists and archaeologists devote their studies to the period of time represented by not even two seconds in the imaginary movie just described. Though this period may not be terribly significant from a universal perspective, in human terms we are talking about more than 4 million years, or 200,000 generations of ancestors, a very long time, indeed.

Before we get to these final two seconds, beginning in the next chapter, let us go back to about two minutes before the end of the movie, to the earth of 25 million years ago, a world far different from our own. It is during this period, called the **Miocene Epoch,** that the evolutionary stage was being set for the dramatic entry of our earliest human ancestors.

MIOCENE PREFACE

The world of the Miocene Epoch (from about 25 million to 5 million years ago; see Figure 4.2) is one we can scarcely imagine. Large areas of the earth could best be characterized by the title of an Ursula K. LeGuin (1972) novel: *The Word for World Is Forest.*

LeGuin, a superb science fiction writer, is well-known for creating imaginatively alien cultures. (Probably not coincidentally, her father was Alfred

FIGURE 4.2

Humans appear extremely late on this standard time scale for earth history. The earliest hominids date no further back in time than the Pliocene Epoch.

ERA	PERIOD	EPOCH	MILLION YEARS AGO
Cenozoic	Quaternary	Holocene	0.01
		Pleistocene	1.7
	Tertiary	Pliocene	5
		Miocene	25
		Oligocene	38
		Eocene	55
		Paleocene	65
Mesozoic	Cretaceous		135
	Jurassic		190
	Triassic		225
Paleozoic	Permian		270
	Carboniferous		345
	Devonian		400
	Silurian		425
	Ordovician		500
	Cambrian		600
Precambrian	Proterozoic		1,000
	Archeozoic		3,000
	Azoic		4,600

Kroeber, one of the founders of American anthropology.) In *The Word for World Is Forest,* LeGuin created a place called Athshe, a planet covered entirely by lush, ancient, forest and populated by a gentle, intelligent ape species that worshipped the wooded world in which it lived.

Much of the earth of the Miocene was like the imaginary world of Athshe. Large stretches of Africa, Asia, and North and South America were thickly forested (Pearson 1978). Places that today are covered with grassland, prairie, and agricultural crops were then fertile forests, populated by an astounding bestiary of tree-loving species [see Donald E. Savage and Donald E. Russell's (1983) *Mammalian Paleofaunas of the World* for a listing (with maps) of Miocene fossil species].

Unlike the fictional planet Athshe, however, there was no single, dominant ape species on the real world of the Miocene earth. During this epoch, our planet was quite remarkable; it was a matchless place for forest-dwelling creatures like apes, and many species evolved to fill the varied **niches** offered by this rich world. Paleontologists today count as many as thirty-nine distinct ape species in the incomplete fossil record of the Miocene (Peter Andrews 1985; Fleagle 1988; R. Martin 1990). Undoubtedly, more species will be found as research continues.

THE SURVIVORS

For comparison, consider what you might find in a modern zoo: small populations representing most of the current ape species, which, depending on how you count them, number as few as eight and no more than thirteen (Ape Portfolio—Color Plates 3, 4, 5).

The Context of Classification

Recall the taxonomic system mentioned in Chapter 2 that was developed by eighteenth-century natural scientist Carolus Linnaeus to categorize all living things. Biologists still use that system, in a somewhat expanded format, and nonscientists use it in a casual way all the time. When we talk about the "animal kingdom" or refer to our own species as "*Homo sapiens,*" we are using the Linnaean taxonomic system.

The Linnaean system begins by assigning living things to their appropriate "kingdom." In Linnaeus' time there were only two known kingdoms: plant and animal. Today, a number of additional kingdoms have been conceptualized to account for different forms of microscopic life. Linnaean kingdoms are then divided into phyla (singular, **phylum**), phyla are divided into classes,

FIGURE 4.3

The basic categories of the Linnaean taxonomic system.

HUMAN TAXONOMY

Kingdom: Anamalia
Phylum: Chordata
Class: Mammalia
Order: Primates
Suborder: Anthropoidea
Superfamily: Hominoidea
Family: Hominidae
Genus: *Homo*
Species: *sapiens*
Subspecies: *sapiens*

and classes are divided into orders. Orders are further divided into families, families into genera (singular, genus), and genera into species (Figure 4.3). Modern applications add categories like suborder, subspecies, and superfamily to help classify plants and animals more precisely.

The position of an organism in this system is analogous to your home address. If someone in Paris, France, asked where you were from, you might begin with the most general part of your address, saying you are an American. In the same way, the Linnaean divisions begin along the most general lines possible; the broadest way of dividing life is on the basis of how organisms obtain food—plants manufacture it through the biochemical process of photosynthesis, while animals need to ingest it. After informing your Parisian friend that you are an American, she might ask where in America you are from. So you break it down a little more specifically, saying you are from the New England area or the southern or northwest region of the country. Next, you might get a little more specific and tell her which state you are from, then which town, and, ultimately, your street address. Similarly, each subsequent division in the Linnaean taxonomy is based on increasingly specific details—in this case, physical and behavioral characteristics.

THE ORDER PRIMATES

We can divide members of the animal kingdom into various phyla based on the presence or absence of a backbone. We can divide animals with backbones into classes by examining more specific features, such as how they regulate body temperature, whether they give birth to live young or lay eggs, and whether they have fur, fins, scales, or feathers. The class Mammalia, for example, includes fur-bearing, warm-blooded animals with backbones who give birth to live young; we humans are, of course, mammals.

The mammals can be further sectioned into various orders based on more specific characteristics of body form, tooth configuration, brain-size, and so on. The apes, monkeys, and humans are placed within the order Primates, one of the orders within the class Mammalia. In distinction to animals placed in other orders within the mammal class, like Carnivora (which includes bears, seals, wolves, dogs, and lions) or Rodentia (mice, rats, squirrels, and beavers), **primates** differ in that they have larger brains in proportion to their body size, grasping hands and feet instead of paws or hoofs, fingernails instead of claws, eyes positioned on the front of their heads instead of on the sides (which affords stereoscopic vision), and single births instead of multiple-birth litters.

The primate order is further subdivided into two suborders, Prosimii and Anthropoidea. Anthropoidea includes monkeys in the Old and New World, apes, and human beings. Prosimii includes the lemurs of the island of Madagascar and a few other species in Africa and Asia.

The suborder Anthropoidea is next divided into two infraorders that include the New World monkeys, with their broad, flat noses and widely spaced nostrils (the Platyrrhini), and the Old World monkeys, with their narrow, more humanlike noses (the Catarrhini). The Platyrrhini infraorder is placed in a single superfamily called Ceboidea; the Catarrhini is divided into two superfamilies called Cercopithecoidea (Old World monkeys) and Hominoidea (apes and humans). Apes and humans are separated from monkeys at this point in the taxonomic breakdown on the basis of their relatively larger brains and their lack of tails. Figure 4.4 presents a Linnaean taxonomic chart for the primates.

MODERN APES

Apes belong to the superfamily Hominoidea (see the Ape Portfolio—Color Plates 3–5). Among the living ape species, there is in Africa the gorilla (*Gorilla gorilla*), with three varieties or subspecies (eastern lowland, western lowland, and mountain gorilla). Also in Africa is the common chimpanzee (*Pan troglodytes*) and the pygmy chimpanzee, now called the bonobo (*Pan paniscus*). The last of the so-called "great apes" is the orangutan (*Pongo pygmaeus*), with two regional varieties, one on the island of Borneo and one on Sumatra.

Beyond these large apes are the smaller apes, or "lesser apes." These are the variously enumerated species of gibbons in Asia [*Hylobates* species, with between four and nine recognized species, including the siamang (*Hylobates syndactylus*)]. The gibbons live in a wide arc across southern Asia, from northeast India to Borneo, into Sumatra and Malaysia.

Ape Adaptations

The apes are **arboreal** creatures, meaning they are forest dwellers, physically and behaviorally adapted to life in and among the trees. Their arms are made

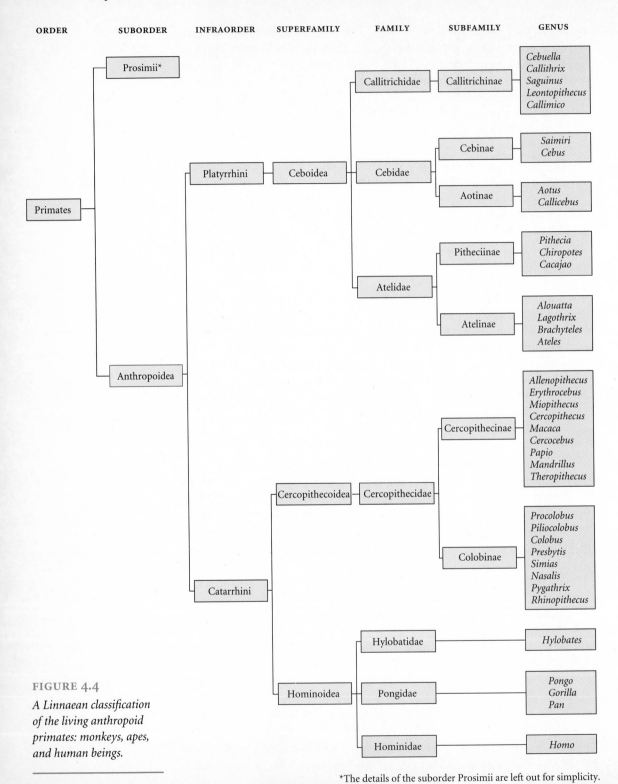

FIGURE 4.4

*A Linnaean classification
of the living anthropoid
primates: monkeys, apes,
and human beings.*

*The details of the suborder Prosimii are left out for simplicity.

FIGURE 4.5
A chimp exhibits its characteristic knuckle-walking ability. (K. L. Feder)

for climbing and swinging. Though gorillas are simply too large to spend much time in the trees, and though all apes spend some time on the ground, apes for the most part spend much of their day climbing, gathering food, sleeping, and playing in trees. Chimps, bonobos, and especially gibbons and siamangs are expert **brachiators. Brachiation** is the act of swinging, arm over arm, through the trees. More than one writer has described gibbons and siamangs as the trapeze artists of the ape family. Orangs, on the other hand, are too big and slow to swing through the trees, but they are expert climbers.

All of the great apes share a unique mode of ground locomotion called **knuckle walking.** When apes move around on the ground they habitually and preferentially do so on all fours. They are **quadrupeds** who, instead of using the palms of their hands the way monkeys do, balance on the middle bones of their fingers (Figure 4.5).

Ape Taxonomy

Ape taxonomy is based on gross morphological characteristics—in essence, what the various kinds of apes look like. In recent years, molecular biology has enabled science to assess the relationships among species more precisely by looking within the organisms to compare the actual genetic blueprint, the **DNA,** for various kinds of animals. For apes and humans, a measurement can be derived for degrees of similarity among them. Once we measure how much difference there is between the DNA of two species, and assuming more or less fixed rates of change in the DNA through time, dates can be suggested for how long ago modern species diverged from a common ancestor (Sibley and Ahlquist 1984).

FIGURE 4.6

FIGURE 4.6

Analysis of the similarities and differences in the ge-netic codes—DNA—among various modern primates has produced this evolutionary phylogeny of the taxonomic order that includes monkeys, apes, and human beings. (From Sibley and Ahlquist 1984)

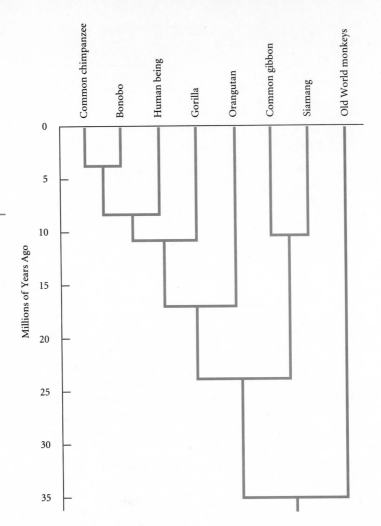

Figure 4.6 shows a reconstruction, based on this technique, of ancestral relationships—a **phylogeny**—for the apes and humans. On the basis of such DNA comparisons, most researchers believe that chimps are our nearest living relatives—and we theirs (Gibbons 1992). In other words, chimps have more in common with us than they do with gorillas. Remarkably, with all of the obvious differences between chimps and humans, our DNA sequences—the biological blueprints that define a chimp and a human—are 98–99% identical.

This level of genetic similarity has led some scientists to propose a fundamental change in how we classify apes and human beings. Instead of dividing the superfamily Anthropoidea into the pongids (including gibbons, orangs, gorillas, chimps, and bonobos), as done here, and the hominids (in-

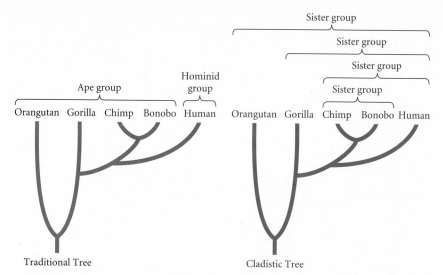

FIGURE 4.7
*The taxonomic approach
of cladistics is based on
evolutionary branching.
This phylogeny for
primates is based on
cladistics. Compare this
phylogeny to the one in
Figure 4.6.*

cluding only human beings), it has been suggested that the family Pongidae should include only gibbons and orangs, with the family Hominidae to include gorillas, chimps, bonobos, and human beings. Such a taxonomy reflects the much closer relationship now recognized between these apes and humans.

In an approach to classification that differs from the Linnaean taxonomy, with its emphasis on the current appearance of species, the method of **cladistics** uses charts called cladograms to define **sister groups**—species whose degree of similarity supports the notion that they may have evolved directly from a common ancestor (Figure 4.7). In the cladistic approach, chimps and bonobos form a first-level sister group; they are so similar as to indicate that they share a very recent common ancestor. At the next level, chimps and bonobos together form a sister group with human beings. This means that while we are not as similar to chimps and bonobos as they are to each other, we are more similar to them than we are to any other living creatures.

Though there is some disagreement among scientists on which are the most pertinent variables to measure—morphological or genetic—and whether the best approach is Linnaean or cladistic, there is unanimity on the most important issue: The creatures we label as apes and humans (some cladists even reject these as actual categories) are remarkably similar in their morphology and in their DNA, implying a relatively recent divergence from a common ancestor.

Why the Study of Apes Is Relevant to the Study of Humanity

We are not descended from chimps, bonobos, gorillas, or orangutans; they have been evolving separately from us as long as we have been evolving separately from them. But we share with them a common ancestor, as yet unrec-

FIGURE 4.8

Population statistics for the modern apes. The number of living mountain gorillas is tragically small, but even those with substantially larger populations are still seriously threatened with extinction. (Data from Linden 1992 and the World Wildlife Fund)

	Estimated Population
Gorilla	
Mountain	650
Eastern lowland	3,000–4,000
Western lowland	30,000–50,000
Chimpanzee	200,000
Bonobo	10,000–20,000
Orangutan	5,000–20,000
Gibbon	? (all species are endangered)
Siamang	? (endangered)

ognized in the paleontological record, but almost certainly dating to no more than 5–7 million years ago—just a few frames of the imaginary movie with which this chapter began. By studying their conduct in a natural setting, we can catch glimpses of behaviors we share: A chimp infant runs to its mother when frightened; adults embrace and pat each other's backs; chimps live in tightly knit social groups, make and use tools, and occasionally walk on two feet while carrying objects in their hands. It is likely we inherited these shared behaviors from a common ancestor who lived more than 5 million years ago and from whom both chimps and humans descended. By studying modern apes, primatologists are able to get a glimpse of our own distant past.

We will discuss a number of fossil ape species, not because these species are individually important to our discussion of human evolution, but because their number and diversity typify the world just before the appearance of our first hominid ancestors. To comprehend the environmental and evolutionary context of our earliest ancestors, we have to understand what preceded them, where they came from.

For a broad presentation about the modern apes, see J. R. Napier and P. H. Napier's (1967) *A Handbook of Living Primates*. It is sad to report that all of these unique and beautiful creatures are gravely endangered as a result of habitat destruction; the current best estimates for the remaining populations of each of the ape species are provided in Figure 4.8. But even if these populations were not threatened with extinction, the modern era would still be impoverished in the number of existing ape species when compared to that of the Miocene, when "the word for world was 'forest.'"

FOSSIL APES OF THE MIOCENE

Primatologist John Fleagle (1988) lists thirty-nine distinct species of extinct fossil apes, all of whose remains date to the Miocene. The many Miocene apes

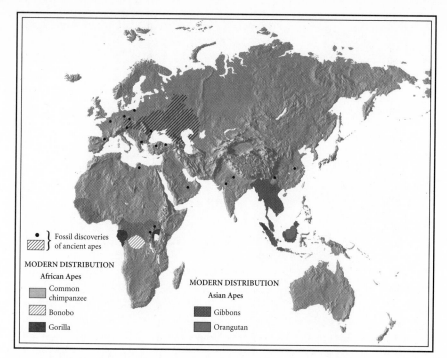

MAP 4.1

*Miocene fossil ape and
modern ape distributions.*

flourished in a far broader area of the world than apes of the current period
(Map 4.1), and their fossil remains are spread throughout much of Europe
and Asia as well as Africa. Fossil apes dating to the Miocene Epoch have been
discovered in Spain, France, Italy, Greece, Turkey, Hungary, India, Pakistan,
and China, far from where we find apes today (Peter Andrews 1985; Peter
Andrews and Stringer 1989). Like their modern counterparts, many of these
extinct fossil apes are found in areas that were tropical forests during the
Miocene; but some also inhabited cooler, drier, temperate woodlands where
apes do not reside currently.

The range in size of the Miocene apes was greater than that of modern
ape species. For example, *Micropithecus clarki* was the size of a small monkey,
weighing just a bit more than 4.5 kg (7.5 lb), smaller than even the smallest
of the living lesser apes. On the other hand, the aptly named *Gigantopithecus
blacki* has been estimated at having weighed 300 kg (660 lb), quite a bit larger
even than the mean weight of an adult male gorilla [they average only about
180 kg (400 lb) in the wild]. The other many species of Miocene apes, categorized as *Dryopithecus, Oreopithecus, Pliopithecus, Laccopithecus, Sivapithecus,*
and so on, all fall somewhere between these extremes of size (Figure 4.9).

Based on reconstruction from skeletal and dental remains, the many
Miocene apes also exhibit a very broad range in their anatomical features.
Several articles in *New Interpretations of Ape and Human Ancestry,* edited by
Russell L. Ciochon and Robert S. Corruccini (1983) (including those by S. C.

FIGURE 4.9

An artist's conception of a small segment of the diversity of Miocene apes.
(Courtesy of John G. Fleagle/ Academic Press; drawn by Stephen Nash)

Ward and D. R. Pilbeam; D. Falk; A. C. Walker and M. Pickford; and M. D. Rose), present detailed discussions of the skeletal anatomy of several of the Miocene apes. During the Miocene, apes attained their highest level of diversity in morphology, habitat, and adaptation, ranging far more broadly than modern apes in their form, where they lived, and what they ate. *Dendropithecus macinnesi,* for example, was small, with long, thin arms, ideal for brachiating (Peter Andrews 1985). Its skeletal anatomy suggests that members of

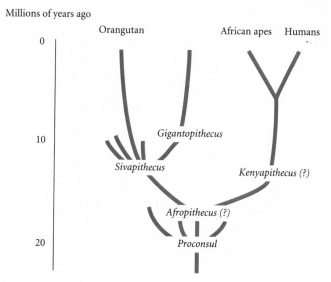

Millions of years ago

FIGURE 4.10

Phylogeny for apes and humans, based on the fossil record.

this species were capable climbers and leapers in their east African tropical forest. Their teeth indicate they subsisted on a diet primarily of fruits. On the other hand, *Proconsul nyanzae* was chimplike in appearance, but had rather short arms and squatter proportions, indicating it was probably more at home on the ground than in the trees of its dry forest habitat (Walker and Pickford 1983). *Oreopithecus,* found in Italy, was probably a leaf-feeder in the swamp-forest it inhabited. Its long arms and hooklike hands enabled it to move around in the forest canopy in a manner similar to tree sloths and un-like any of the living apes (Peter Andrews and Stringer 1989). *Dryopithecus* was adapted to the temperate woodlands of Europe—recent paleontological research has suggested that *Dryopithecus* may have shared a common ances-tor with the gorilla (Begun 1992). *Kenyapithecus* was adapted to the subtropi-cal forest of east Africa. And *Sivapithecus,* which appears to be ancestral to the modern orangutan, was at home in the seasonal woodlands of southeast-ern Europe and south-central Asia (Fleagle 1988).

Figure 4.10 presents a general phylogeny for the fossil and modern apes, showing current conceptions of their evolutionary relationships. This figure also shows how the human position on this phylogeny is viewed. It is on that branch our energies will focus.

Today, there is commonly a single ape species (rarely more than one) and never more than three different ape species occupying a single habitat (Peter Andrews 1985:197). In comparison, broadly contemporaneous Miocene fos-sil ape species commonly occurred four and five to a habitat. This indicates that these apes were probably close neighbors that coexisted by residing in different levels of the forest canopy, where they subsisted on different foods. This is another reflection of the greater diversity of Miocene apes as com-

FIGURE 4.11

The change through time in the number of ape species as a percentage of the number of Old World primate species, from 20 million years ago to the present, including the precipitous decrease in the number of ape species through the Miocene.

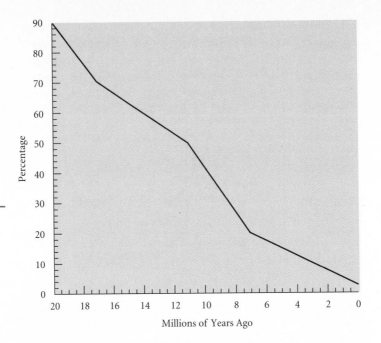

pared to modern species. Figure 4.11 shows the decreasing numbers through time of ape species as a percentage of all Old World primates.

Though only a small sample of Miocene apes has been discussed here, it should be clear that apes were varied and widespread during the Miocene, much more so than today. See Peter Andrews and Stringer's (1989) *Human Evolution: An Illustrated Guide* for paintings of a broad sample of reconstructed Miocene ape species and see John Fleagle's (1988) *Primate Adaptation and Evolution* and F. Szalay and Eric Delson's (1979) *Evolutionary History of the Primates* for detailed discussions of the Miocene fossil apes.

ISSUES AND DEBATES

WHAT HAPPENED TO THE APES AT THE END OF THE MIOCENE?

As already stated, the surviving ape species are threatened with extinction as a result of habitat destruction at the hand of humanity. As the tropical forests of Africa and Asia that are home to the apes are cleared for agriculture to support the burgeoning human population, the apes are pushed into smaller and smaller enclaves. Without a concerted effort by our species, the same species that is responsible for their current precarious position, our nearest living evolutionary relatives may become extinct except in zoos and animal parks.

At the end of the Miocene, the many species of apes that are represented in the fossil record also faced extinction, but not by any human agency; our direct ancestors had not yet evolved. Instead, a natural environmental change began to shrink the rich forest world. Though paleoclimatologists and paleobotanists disagree about how and why this change took place, almost all agree that large areas of the extensive forest lands began to contract sometime during the middle or late Miocene, to be replaced largely by grasslands, or **savannas,** by the beginning of the next epoch, the Pliocene, about 5 million years ago. And with the contraction of the forest, most of the ape species that had thrived there became extinct.

WHAT CAUSED THE SPREAD OF THE SAVANNA?

The reasons for the climatic shift at the end of the Miocene are complex. Part of the cause, at least in southern Europe and northern Africa, may have to do with continental drift. It was during the Miocene that Australia and South America shifted northward, changing the flow of cold ocean currents, and isolating Antarctica at the south pole. As a result, its ice covering experienced a period of dramatic growth. This growth in Antarctic ice caused a substantial drop in worldwide sea level, since water was tied up as ice at the south pole and did not melt back into the surrounding ocean.

Sea depth at the Straits of Gibraltar, at the western margin of the Mediterranean Sea, is less than the amount by which the ocean level dropped [40–70 m, or 130–230 ft (Boaz 1992:40)] when the Antarctic ice grew rapidly. When sea level dropped sufficiently, therefore, the Mediterranean Sea became cut off from the Atlantic Ocean. Without the inflow from the Atlantic, the Mediterranean actually dried up entirely. Known as the **Messinian Event,** the drying up of the Mediterranean produced an enormous, dry salt flat; deep-sea drilling cores in the Mediterranean basin show substantial deposits of salt dating to this period. The drying up of such a substantial body of water would have resulted in a marked decrease in rainfall across a wide expanse of Europe, western Asia, and northern Africa. The Miocene forests in the area around the Mediterranean would have soon been replaced by arid grasslands.

WHAT REPLACED THE FORESTS?

Whatever the cause of the growth of the savannas at the expense of the forests at the end of the Miocene, a number of avenues of research show that it occurred and that more than the area around the Mediterranean was involved. For example, geologists Thure Cerling, Yang Wang, and Jay Quade (1993) have shown that soils and fossil teeth in south-central Asia (Pakistan) and North America (the western United States) exhibit a simultaneous, dramatic increase between 7 million and 5 million years ago in their concentration of

FIGURE 4.12

This graph shows the dramatic proportional increase of ^{13}C in fossil teeth and soils at the end of the Miocene. (From Cerling, Yang, and Quade 1993)

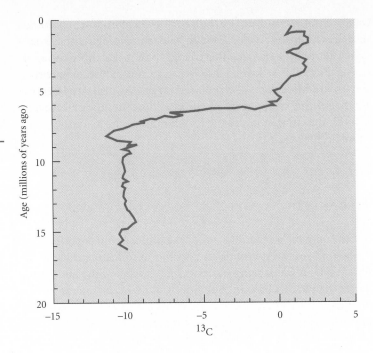

the ^{13}C **isotope** (variety) of the element carbon (Figure 4.12). The common and stable isotope of carbon is ^{12}C. There is, however, another carbon isotope, ^{13}C. The ^{13}C found in carbon dioxide in the atmosphere is involved far more readily in the particular photosynthesis process used by many grasses and sedges (those following the so-called **C4 pathway**) than it is in trees, virtually all of which follow a different photosynthesis pathway (**C3 pathway**) or in succulents, which follow the so-called **CAM pathway.** As a result, most grasses have a higher concentration of ^{13}C than trees or succulents. The ^{13}C concentration in the plants growing in an area becomes reflected in local soils as that vegetation decays, as well as in the bones and teeth of the herbivorous animals ingesting those plants. Since we know the relative concentrations of ^{13}C in most trees (C3 pathway) and succulents (CAM pathway) as opposed to many grasses (C4 pathway), then by measuring the concentration of that isotope in soil and fossil bones and teeth in an area, we can deduce which kind of plants (in simplest terms here, trees, succulents, or grasses) were most abundant in that area.

Cerling and co-workers interpret the overall and dramatic increase in ^{13}C concentration at the end of the Miocene as an indication of "a rapid expansion of C4 biomass [that is, grasses] in both the Old and the New World starting 7 to 5 million years ago" (1993:334). They further point out that the "synchronous expansion of C4 ecosystems in both the New and Old World suggests a change in global conditions rather than local development" (p. 345). More recent research (M. Morgan et al. 1994) in Pakistan and Kenya

questions the rapid rate the previous study suggested for the expansion of savannas and contraction of the forests worldwide, but still supports the general contention that this was a significant, worldwide phenomenon. As
Morgan and colleagues have been quoted: "We agree that significant environmental changes occurred around 7 million years ago, near the time when the
first hominids [members of the human evolutionary family] appeared"
(Bower 1994d:38).

THE IRONY OF EXTINCTION

Evolution and extinction are serendipitous and unpredictable. Extinction is,
in fact, the norm; it is estimated that 99% of the plant and animal species
that have existed during the 3.5-billion-year history of life on earth are extinct. The role of extinction in evolution also is sadly ironic. Sometimes it is
the extinction of one species, genus, or family of animals that opens up the
evolutionary field to another. In fact, it was the extinction of the dinosaurs
that allowed a previously insignificant class of animals, the mammals—of
which we are one—to explode into prominence. Just as surely, the massive
wave of ape extinctions resulting from the great climatic and habitat changes
that accompanied the end of the Miocene provided the catalyst for the florescence of the small number of ape species that were able to adapt, adjust, and
survive (Gingerich 1986; Pickford 1983).

Remember, environmental change does not cause evolution, and evolution is not progressive or directional. Changing environmental conditions
simply set up situations in which some physical or behavioral characteristics,
previously of little use to their possessors, become highly advantageous.
Through natural selection, as suggested by Darwin (see Chapter 2), these advantageous features allow those members of a species that possess them a
better chance at surviving under the new environmental regime.

This appears to be precisely what happened at the Miocene/Pliocene
boundary. Unfortunately, the fossil record is so poor for this period of upheaval that we cannot be sure in our reconstruction of what transpired. Almost
certainly, those species that survived the terminal Miocene possessed some
characteristics that, by chance, gave them an advantage in the very different
world that was establishing itself. Perhaps it was their remarkable ability for
brachiation that ensured the survival of the ancestors of today's gibbons and
siamangs when forests were shrinking and competition for remaining space
was fierce. Maybe it was the strength, size, intelligence, and social systems of
the ancestors of modern gorillas that allowed for their survival. The intelligence and behavioral flexibility of the ancestors of chimps and bonobos
probably provided them with an advantage as the myriad Miocene ape
species vied for space in the diminishing forests of 7 million years ago.

The modern apes, therefore, can be viewed as the descendants of the winners of this evolutionary struggle. The losers were those who, at the end of the Miocene, found themselves in an alien habitat in which their physical and behavioral characteristics, honed by millions of years of evolution to life in a thick, humid forest, were useless and who could not survive on the savannas.

One ape species at the end of the Miocene possessed a different, uniquely advantageous characteristic, ironically one that would not have been all that beneficial for life in the forest: the ability to walk on two legs, which all living apes can do with varying degrees of success. But this is inefficient and tiring for them; the bones and muscles of their hips and legs simply are not compatible with that form of locomotion (see Chapter 5). This was probably much the same for the apes of the Miocene.

But one Miocene species could stand up and walk on two legs better than the others. While providing no great advantage in the forests, this ability was valuable in the expanding grasslands that replaced the Miocene woodlands. Natural selection, as discussed in Chapter 2, feeds on variability. The nascent ability for upright locomotion within one Miocene ape species provided natural selection with the raw material needed to produce a creature fully capable of **bipedal locomotion,** one that habitually and efficiently walked on two feet. Ironically, this successful species shared something in common with those species that lost the evolutionary struggle at the end of the Miocene and became extinct: It could not compete successfully for space in the diminishing forests. It also was pushed out onto the growing savanna. In this new habitat its idiosyncratic ability for bipedal locomotion meant survival. This species was the first human ancestor.

CASE STUDY CLOSE-UP

As Takayoshi Kano (1990), who has studied bonobos in the wild since 1974, tells it, the Mongandu people of Zaire, in Africa, believe that the ancestors of human beings and of the bonobos once lived side by side in the forest, not as hunter and hunted, but as brothers. This recognition of the great similarity between bonobos and people is now being adopted by science.

Though called "pygmy chimpanzees," bonobos are not just a smaller version of the chimp. A recent study (Doran 1993) shows that their hands are more hooklike and their shoulder blades longer and narrower, giving them an enhanced capability at suspensory behavior (essentially, hanging from tree branches) when compared to common chimps. Also, bonobos commonly use their palms when walking on all fours on large tree branches; common chimps almost always knuckle walk.

Kano's wild bonobo studies (carried out with primatologist Randall Susman) are giving science a first-hand look at this intriguing species. Kano has shown that bonobos differ from chimps behaviorally as well as physically; they walk upright more often and are more willing to share food.

Also, bonobos have generated interest as a result of being about the most indiscriminatingly sexual of the primates, having frenzied bouts of group sex (heterosexual—including face-to-face positioning—as well as homosexual) whenever the mood strikes them, usually as a result of fear or general excitement. While dominant males may mount and force copulation with subordinate males, forced copulation between males and females is unknown.

The chimpanzee studies of Jane Goodall (1971, 1986, 1990; see Figure 3.3) have provided a wealth of sometimes surprising information about the common chimp. Her work demonstrated, for example, that chimps make tools by stripping twigs of the bark, to serve as "fishing poles" for termites (which they like to eat). She has also shown chimps to engage in occasional cooperative hunts; the meat from the kill is the only food chimps will generally share with one another. Her work has even revealed the dark side of the species: Groups of chimps have been known to hunt down and kill chimps from another group.

It is not surprising that some of the best-known and most important primatological studies were inspired and supported by a paleoanthropologist. The well-known scientist Louis Leakey played a key role in helping establish the research programs of Jane Goodall with the chimps and Dian Fossey with the mountain gorillas. Their work, as well as that of a broad array of other primatologists, provides us with a unique approach to questions regarding our own past.

The paleontological sites that formed the basis of our discussion of the Miocene apes are located in Africa, Asia, and Europe, and most are not particularly appropriate places to visit. There really isn't much to see. Observing living primates in the wild is also problem-

VISITING THE PAST

atical. For a time, the government of Rwanda in Africa was allowing a small number of tours to visit gorilla habitat. Now that nation is in complete disarray because of its civil war, and there is no knowing when such tours will again become feasible.

However, living primates can be observed at most large American zoos. There is an ongoing debate about the ethics of placing highly intelligent animals like chimps and gorillas in zoos in the first place. However, zoos may one day be the only places where such animals still exist—extinction is that real a possibility in the wild for many of the primates. There are relatively good zoos where apes are given ample room, a healthful diet, trees to swing in, rocks to climb on, pools to swim in, and so on. Most importantly, these very social creatures are allowed to live in social groups. If this is your only opportunity for seeing apes in a quasi-natural setting, as it is for most of us, take advantage of it. Examine their mode of locomotion. See their social interactions. Watch them play. And consider that the very small distance provided by these zoos between the "visitor" and the "specimen" is an unintended metaphor for the narrow biological distance that separates us from them.

SUMMARY

On a universal time scale, the human story is little more than a recent after-thought. We are but one species among many within the taxonomic order Primates, a category we share with monkeys and apes. The living apes represent the survivors of a much larger cohort that flourished during the Miocene Epoch, from 25 million to 5 million years ago. Many of the Miocene ape species became extinct as a result of a significant climate change that caused forests to shrink worldwide between 7 million and 5 million years ago. One of the Miocene apes that was pushed out of the diminishing forest possessed a characteristic that enabled it to survive on the growing grassland: It could walk on two feet better than its competitors. This ape species is the first member of the human family.

TO LEARN MORE

If you are interested in reading more about our present understanding of the history of the universe and life on the planet, see Nigel Calder's (1983) *Timescale*. John G. Fleagle's (1988) *Primate Adaptation and Evolution* is a splendid textbook, with just about everything you might want to know about the taxonomic order we share with monkeys and apes. Jane Goodall's (1971, 1986, 1990) three books on her experiences among the chimps are marvelously written works, filled with remarkable data and personal observations about the meaning of her work. Dian Fossey chronicled her work among the gorillas in her book *Gorillas in the Mist* (1983). The movie *Gorillas in the Mist* presents a dramatic telling of her story and how she literally gave her life to the study and protection of the endangered primates she came to love.

KEY TERMS

Cambrian Explosion	primates	knuckle walking
Miocene Epoch	arboreal	quadrupeds
niche	brachiator	DNA
phylum	brachiation	phylogeny

cladistics
sister group
savanna

Messinian Event
isotope
C4 pathway

C3 pathway
CAM pathway
bipedal locomotion

5

African Roots

Human beings are distinguished by large brains, great intelligence, and reliance on culture, but fossil evidence shows our earliest ancestors did not share these characteristics. The first steps of the hominids were literal first steps; upright locomotion differentiated them from the other apes.

The oldest hominids—the australopithecines—date to more than 4 million years ago. Several different species with varying brain sizes and body configurations have been identified, but they all share an anatomy suited to walking on two feet.

About 2.5 million years ago, a new hominid form appears in the fossil record. *Homo habilis* had a larger brain than the apes and exhibited a greater reliance on culture. *Homo habilis* and some of the australopithecines were contemporaries. The latter were highly specialized and became extinct, and the former are direct ancestors of modern humans.

82

Millions of years ago

	5	4	3	2	1
Ardipithecus ramidus		▪			
Australopithecus anamensis		▬			
Australopithecus afarensis			▬▬▬		
Australopithecus africanus				▬▬	
Australopithecus robustus					▬▬▬
Australopithecus boisei					▬▬▬
Australopithecus aethiopicus				▪	
Homo habilis				▬▬	

One summer afternoon, my six-year-old son, Josh, and I were walking barefoot on the sandy shore that surrounds Cape Cod Bay in Massachusetts. The piercing blue sky and the blue-green sea seemed magnified on this perfect New England summer beach day. The sun was warm and pleasant on our faces as we paced the edge of a strand of small shells and pebbles.

CHAPTER SITES

AFRICA
Allia Bay
Aramis
Chemeron
Hadar
Kanapoi
Koobi Fora
Laetoli
Lothagam
Maka
Olduvai
Tabarin
West Turkana

With each step, our feet sank into the soft, damp sand. Wearing shoes most of the time, we don't often think about the mechanics of walking. Ordinarily, we wear footwear with stiff, hard soles and walk on hard pavement. Walking barefoot on soft sand, however, reminds us of how the process actually works. Walking is more than just two slabs of leather alternately clomping down on pavement. Instead, our feet interact with the earth, gripping the soil beneath and pushing us forward in our effort to get from here to there. When my younger son, Jacob, began to walk, I could see clearly the interaction between his feet and the surface on which he was walking, even when it was wood flooring or carpeting. He tried to increase his stability by curling his toes to grip the ground as best he could. Once we learn to walk, we go back to that mode only when we walk on sand or loose soil.

That afternoon on the beach, the sensations of walking were readily apparent. With each step, the heel struck first, leaving deep, moist impressions as the sand compressed beneath our weight, all of which was focused on that small point at the heel. Then, each foot rolled forward, the arch lightly curving over the sand as the sides of the sole left thin, sharp indentations. Next, all in a fraction of a second, we rocked up onto the ball of the foot, thrusting our center of gravity forward as we pushed our other leg before us. Finally, our toes pushed down, gripping the earth, with sand squishing up between and around them as we continued to push our bodies forward, ready to catch ourselves in the next step with the other foot. Behind us on the Cape Cod sand was the unmistakable trail of two human beings—one big, one small—walking together.

After a while, Josh looked up at me and asked: "Where do people come from?" I remember thinking how easy it would be just to tell him the story of Adam and Eve or one of a thousand other **creation stories.** Instead, I began to explain about evolution, and how, before the first people, there were creatures like apes that began, over a long time, to look more and more like people, first walking on two legs, then using tools, and with ever-expanding brains. The discussion got especially interesting when Josh, who easily grasped the ape connection, wanted to know where the first ape came from, and then the first mammal, and so on.

Soon, however, Josh tired of my explanation and ran off to skip stones, leaving me to gaze back at the footprints that marked our journey to this point. The waves lapped at the impressions of our feet, beginning to erase them from the sand, eliminating all trace of our presence. I looked down at the trail of footprints and saw in the path we walked a metaphor for the lives of my young son and me. Two people, one big, one small, bonded in blood

FIGURE 5.1

On the left is the Laetoli pathway, the fossilized footprints of at least two human ancestors who walked in a remarkably modern fashion. On the right is the recent pathway of a father and his six-year-old son. Though separated in time by more than 3.5 million years, the two sets of footprints clearly show the continuity of bipedal locomotion in the hominid family. (Left: Peter Jones; right: K. L. Feder)

and deed, sharing a journey together, but with trails destined, inevitably, to diverge, each making his own pathway and then, each pathway, in time, to be washed away and forgotten, as if it had never been. I thought of all the quiet walks taken by fathers and sons and mothers and daughters. I wondered about their conversations, their explanations, their accommodations with life, and with each other.

Our disappearing trail of footprints reminded me of another such trail, made in a far distant time by two people who passed together across a landscape. Those footprints, however, were not washed away by the tide or blown away by the wind. Those prints, left in a fine volcanic ash on an east African plain in a place called Laetoli, in the modern nation of Tanzania, were preserved because of a rare ash type known as carbonatite that was spewed out by a nearby volcano (Hay and Leakey 1982; M. Leakey and Hay 1979; White and Suwa 1987).

The conditions and sequence of events had to be perfect for those footprints to be preserved. First, a thin ash layer had to be deposited. Soon after, a mild rain had to fall, turning the ash into the consistency of wet cement. Immediately following this, and before the ash had hardened, the two people (and, perhaps, another) had to walk across its surface, leaving their footprints in the still-damp ash. Then the sun needed to come out to dry the ash bed to the hardness of rock before another rainfall might wash it all away. Finally, another ash layer had to be deposited, covering the footprint trail and protecting it from the natural erosion that might otherwise have destroyed it. Even stolid scientists have characterized the preservation of the Laetoli footprint trails as "miraculous" (Johanson and Edey 1982).

Those footprints were found more than 3.5 million years after the two people, possibly a child and an adult, and perhaps a third person, strode across its surface (R. Leakey and Lewin 1992; Figure 5.1). We will never know their names or why they were walking, apparently in cadence and, perhaps,

MAP 5.1

Fossil localities of early hominids.

Mediterranean Sea

Hadar
Aramis Maka

Allia Bay
Chemeron
Kanapoi   Koobi Fora
Lothagam   Tabarin

Olduvai
Laetoli

ATLANTIC OCEAN

Makapansgat
Sterkfontein   Swartkrans
Kromdraai

△ *Ardipithecus*
◆ Australopithecine
● Australopithecine and *Homo habilis*

Taung   *INDIAN OCEAN*

giving our imagination free reign, hand in hand across the ash bed. Yet in taking those steps, they achieved a kind of immortality. Perhaps most remarkably, their footprints show that those anonymous folk, whose life journey occurred so many years ago, walked in a fashion that is nearly indistinguishable from how my son and I walked on the Cape Cod beach (Charteris, Wall, and Nottrodt 1981; Day and Wickens 1980; T. White 1980; T. White and Suwa 1987; and see Figure 5.1). Those people were among the earliest **hominids,** with whom all living people share a temporally distant but biologically intimate connection. This chapter is about the first people and the world in which they lived.

CHRONICLE

We ended the last chapter with a discussion of an extinct ape species, as yet unidentified in the fossil record, that had been pushed out of the shrinking forest onto the growing grassland at the end of the Miocene Epoch and the beginning of the Pliocene. This species was able to survive when so many of its contemporaries could not because its members had a unique advantage: They could walk on two feet more proficiently than other apes of the time. Though this Miocene ape species is, as yet, hypothetical, its evolutionary descendants are most decidedly not; they left the very real footprints at Laetoli as well as indisputable skeletal evidence at a large number of sites in Africa (Map 5.1).

THE FIRST HOMINID

The earliest hominids are classified by most researchers as belonging to the genus *Australopithecus* (Figure 5.2). Because they were upright walkers, we no longer include them in the ape, or **pongid,** taxonomic family (technically, the family **Pongidae**), which includes all apes, living and extinct. Instead, we place them in the hominid taxonomic family (the family **Hominidae**), which includes all modern and fossil human beings. All people today are hominids; so were the creatures who left the Laetoli footprints 3.5 million years ago.

The Genus Australopithecus

The very earliest specimens that have been labeled as **australopithecines** are also the most fragmentary. A few broken-up fossils may date to between 4 million and 6 million years ago, pushing the genus back to about the time of the ape/hominid split at the Miocene/Pliocene boundary. For instance, the Lothagam lower jaw, found in Kenya, has been classified as *Australopithecus* and is potentially more than 5.6 million years old (Hill and Ward 1988; Hill, Ward, and Brown 1992). Another *Australopithecus* mandible, from the Tabarin site, also in Kenya, is dated to 4.9 million years ago, and an upper arm bone from the Chemeron site in the same country is more than 4.2 million years old (Chamberlain 1991).

A series of fossils dated to more than 4 million years ago has been recovered at Aramis in the Afar region of Ethiopia. The discovery includes a number of teeth, a child's lower jaw, a few fragments of the base of an adult's **cranium** (the skull minus the lower jaw), and sections of an upper and lower left arm (T. White, Suwa, and Asfaw 1994).

Though in some ways similar to *Australopithecus,* this find is now called *Ardipithecus ramidus* and seems to represent an evolutionary line separate from that of the hominids. Cranial fragments indicate a very chimp-like skull. Paleo-environmental evidence suggests the presence of a closed woodland when the ape-like *ramidus* was alive.

Also dating to about 4 million years ago are the exciting new discoveries made in Kanapoi and Allia Bay, Kenya (M. G. Leakey, et al. 1995). The 12 specimens from Allia Bay and the 9 from Kanapoi, including teeth, cranial fragments, and some bones below the skull, have been assigned the species name *Australopithecus anamensis.*

The *anamensis* jaw fragments and fossil teeth are ape-like. An upper arm bone found 30 years ago—now assigned to this species based on its stratigraphic position—exhibits many human-like features. In addition, and more significantly, both ends of a tibia (shin bone) that were recovered are very human-like; its discoverers identify this bone as clearly indicating bipedal locomotion nearly half a million years before the Laetoli footprints. The environment in which *Australopithecus anamensis* lived was characterized by open woodland or bushland conditions.

FIGURE 5.2

From these drawings of the skeletons of a modern chimpanzee, Australopithecus afarensis, africanus, *and* robustus, *and a modern human being, the skeleton of* afarensis, *with its chimplike skull, can safely be characterized as that of an upright ape.*

Three Members of the Genus *Australopithecus*

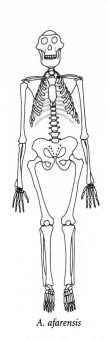

A. afarensis

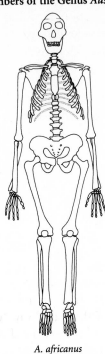

A. africanus

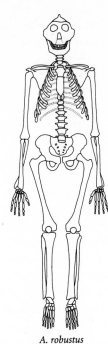

A. robustus

Modern human being

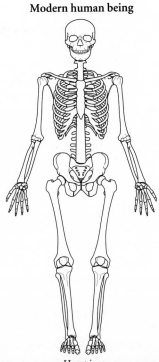

H. sapiens

Modern ape

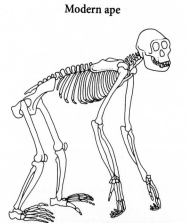

(Pan troglodyles—chimpanzee)

The discoverers of *anamensis* suggest that it provides the clearest picture of a human ancestor dating to about 4 million years ago. As such, this recently discovered fossil may represent the species ancestral to all of the other hominids to be discussed here.

Australopithecus afarensis

Far better known and with a far larger sample of remains is a later, somewhat less apelike form of the same genus, *Australopithecus afarensis*. Along with its being the creature that probably left the footprint trail described earlier in this chapter's Chronicle section, a significant number of *afarensis* fossils has been discovered. The great majority of *afarensis* fossils date to the period from 4 million to 3 million years ago. The most significant of these were found in the Afar geographical region of Ethiopia, where the first and most complete specimens were discovered at the site of Hadar (Figure 5.3), highlighted in this chapter's Case Study Close-Up section.

Some individuals are critical of the evolutionary conclusions of paleoanthropology because they believe the data always to be quite scanty and equivocal. As paleoanthropologist Richard Leakey (R. Leakey and Lewin 1992:81) points out, however, the fragmentary remains of close to 1,000 individuals have been recovered that date to the early period of hominid evolution. *Afarensis* alone has produced more than 300 individual specimens. Among the key elements of the *afarensis* skeleton that have been found and used to define the species are the pelvis, vertebrae, leg bones, fingers, feet, jaws, skull fragments, a nearly complete cranium, and teeth. Together, these skeletal elements allow us to paint a reliable picture of a creature that, beginning about 4 million years ago, was not becoming bipedal but already was fully upright (see Figure 5.2 and this chapter's Issues and Debates section).

The **postcranial** skeleton (everything below the skull) of *afarensis* is diagnostic of a creature far more like a human than like an ape. The feet of *afarensis* were quite modern, lacking the divergent big toe of the apes. The ape big toe is positioned on its foot just like our thumbs are positioned on our hands, allowing the ape to grasp objects with its feet (for example, grasping tree branches when climbing) far better than we can. *Afarensis* possessed the foot of a walker, not that of a climber. Also, the pelvis was quite similar to ours, and is easily distinguished from an ape's (see Figure 5.16); the configuration of the pelvis is an accurate indicator of a creature's mode of locomotion (see this chapter's Issues and Debates section).

On the other hand, *afarensis* had not left its ape heritage behind entirely. In some specimens, the arms were relatively long and the finger bones were long and curved, like an ape's (Susman, Stern, and Jungers 1984). This may mean that *afarensis* retained some of the arboreal ability of its ape ancestors at the same time that it walked bipedally on the ground.

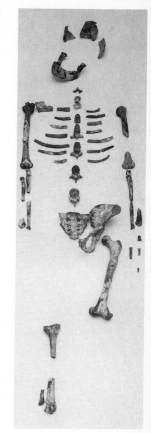

FIGURE 5.3

This 45% complete skeleton of the fossil known as Lucy plus a series of thirteen other Australopithecus afarensis *specimens have been dated to 3.18 million years ago.* (© 1995 John Reader, Science Source/Photo Researchers)

FIGURE 5.4

The most complete skull yet found of Australopithecus afarensis, *designated A.L. 444-2, shows it to be chimplike in appearance, lending further support to the notion that the hominid line began with upright posture, not big brains.*
(Institute of Human Origins)

Though *afarensis* may have been a proficient climber, recent evidence shows clearly that this first hominid species had moved away from the heavily arboreal adaptation of apes. Paleoanthropologist Tim White (see Bower 1993a) excavated fragments of an upper and lower arm from a deposit dated to 3.4 million years ago at the site of Maka in Ethiopia. The upper arm bone (**humerus**) is proportionally short, like a modern human's and unlike the relatively long arm of the ape, with its adaptation for life in the trees. The recent discovery of one of the lower arm bones (**ulna**) of an *afarensis* specimen lends further support to the notion that the arms were more like a human's than an ape's. The specimen exhibits some apelike characteristics, but in general pattern is more like that of a modern human (Kimbel, Johanson, and Rak 1994; Aiello 1994).

All of the essentially human qualities of the postcranial skeleton of *Australopithecus afarensis* must be contrasted with the almost entirely apelike features of its skull. The nearly complete cranium recently discovered at Hadar shows this clearly (Kimbel, Johanson, and Rak 1994). This cranium, labeled A.L. 444-2 by its excavators, is the most complete *afarensis* skull yet found (Figure 5.4). It dates to about 3 million years ago, making this specimen one of the youngest yet identified in the *afarensis* fossil species. Its discovery is quite recent, and a detailed description has not yet been published. Nevertheless, it is apparent that, in its overall form, A.L. 444-2 is certainly more apelike than any subsequent human ancestor, including other, later versions of *Australopithecus* to be discussed. Cranial capacity is apelike, in the range of 400–500 ml—like a modern chimpanzee, about one-third the human mean for brain size (see Figure 5.15). The upper portion of the face is small when compared to the lower part (as in apes), which is the opposite of the pattern seen in modern human beings. The jaws jut out and are snoutlike—they are said to be **prognathous**—just like in an adult ape, and again quite different from the relatively flat face of a modern human being.

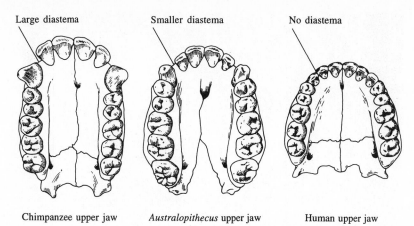

Large diastema   Smaller diastema   No diastema

Chimpanzee upper jaw   *Australopithecus* upper jaw   Human upper jaw

FIGURE 5.5

From this comparison of the maxillae (upper jaws) of chimps, Australopithecus, *and modern human beings, it is clear that the teeth in a chimp's mandible are arranged in a boxlike pattern, like those of* Australopithecus. *Modern human teeth form a curve or arch.* (Adapted from drawings by Luba Dmytryk Gudz from *Lucy: The Beginnings of Humankind.* © 1981, Donald C. Johanson and Maitland A. Edey)

The *afarensis* jaw also is apelike in overall appearance (Figure 5.5). Humans and apes have the same numbers and kinds of teeth: two incisors, one canine, two premolars, and three molars in each quadrant of the adult mouth. Human teeth, however, in both the upper jaw—the **maxilla**—and the lower jaw—the **mandible**—are positioned in a curving arch that expands to the rear of the mouth; ape teeth present a more boxlike appearance, with the premolars and molars set in nearly parallel rows perpendicular to the incisors. Also, apes have proportionally much larger canine teeth and a gap in the teeth of the opposing jaw to allow room for the large canines when the mouth is closed. This gap, or **diastema,** is not present in the human jaw; our canines are much smaller, and so no gap in the opposing jaw is needed. The *afarensis* jaw is not quite like an ape jaw but not quite like a human jaw either. The configuration of the teeth is more like a box than an arch; there is a small diastema; and tooth size, including that of the canines, is more apelike than human.

The evidence, then, is quite clear: *Australopithecus afarensis* seems to have been a bipedal ape living between 4 million and 3 million years ago. It looked like a chimpanzee standing on two short, but otherwise humanlike legs, with no diverging big toe (Figure 5.6). What we share with *afarensis* is a mode of locomotion, but not a level of intelligence or a reliance on culture.

A FORK IN THE HOMINID ROAD

In the consensus view presented here, *afarensis* was the only representative of the hominid line from perhaps more than 4 million years ago and until about 3 million years ago (for another, quite different view, see R. Leakey and Lewin 1992). At about 3 million years ago, *afarensis* seems to have evolved into a somewhat different form of hominid. We call these new fossils by the taxonomic name *Australopithecus africanus*. Like its evolutionary progenitor, *africanus* was bipedal and still walked in an essentially modern human fash-

FIGURE 5.6

This artist's conception of Australopithecus afarensis *shows the ability of this ancestral hominid to walk on two feet and also to climb trees.* (Courtesy of John Fleagle; drawn by Stephen Nash)

FIGURE 5.7

The cranium of Australopithecus africanus, *a lightly built, or "gracile," australopithecine form that followed* afarensis *in southern Africa.* Africanus *flourished after 3 million years ago, and appears to have become extinct by 2.2 million years ago.* (Transvaal Museum, D. C. Panagos)

ion. It also retained a basically apelike skull and brain (Figure 5.7). There are a number of fairly well-preserved *africanus* crania, all apelike, with a sloping forehead and large ridges of bone above the eyes. On the other hand, the jaw is a bit more humanlike and the face not quite so prognathous as *afarensis,* so in some ways it seems a little more human in appearance. Nevertheless, its brain size still falls into the range of the great apes (see Figure 5.15).

Africanus dates to no more than 3 million years ago and seems to fade out of the picture by about 2.2 million years ago. At that point, a larger bipedal form seems to have taken its place (Figure 5.8). Called *Australopithe-*

FIGURE 5.8

The cranium of Austra-lopithecus robustus. Robustus *appears to have been a highly specialized hominid, with extremely powerful jaws adapted to processing a diet of hard, gritty foods.* Robustus, *which may have replaced* africanus, *became extinct around 1 million years ago.* (Transvaal Museum, D. C. Panagos)

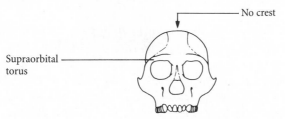

Australopithecus africanus

FIGURE 5.9

The cranial anatomy of the gracile and robust australopithecines.

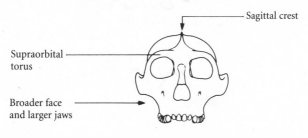

*Australopithecus robustus
(Paranthropus robustus)*

cus robustus by most paleoanthropologists (though a growing minority, based on the rather substantial morphological difference between *africanus* and *robustus,* place the latter in a different genus, *Paranthropus*), it was a biped, and its brain size was a bit greater than in *africanus.* More significant is the difference in the cranial architecture of *robustus:* Where the top of the *africanus* skull is round and smooth, the top of the *robustus* skull sports a thin ridge of bone called a **sagittal crest** (Figure 5.9). Such a crest allows for a much larger,

FIGURE 5.10

Teeth tell the story of a significant difference in the diets of the gracile and robust australopithecines. A photomicrograph of an africanus *molar* (top) *provides evidence of a diet of soft foods, perhaps roots and meat. A photomicrograph of a* robustus *molar* (bottom) *shows clear evidence of a diet rich in such foods as hard seeds and nuts.* (Courtesy of F. E. Grine)

stronger temporalis muscle, which powers the movement of the mandible while chewing.

This feature of the *robustus* skull, along with its much larger-surfaced molars and microscopic evidence of wear on the molar surfaces (Figure 5.10), is a pretty good indication of a shift in dietary emphasis in *robustus,* when compared to *africanus,* toward a diet of hard foods such as seeds and nuts rather than roots, fruits, or leaves (Grine 1987). Recent analysis of the mineral content of their bones indicates that the *robustus* diet may have included meat as well (Bower 1992a). *Robustus* fossils disappear from the paleontological record by about 1 million years ago.

The *robustus* pattern of powerful cranial architecture is even more pronounced in another fossil hominid, *Australopithecus boisei* (Figure 5.11), whose specimens date from 2 million years ago to 1 million years ago, making it partially contemporaneous with *robustus. Boisei* is different enough from *robustus* to warrant separate species status. In other words, there was more than one distinct hominid species living in Africa during the same period, a situation similar to the modern situation for pongids, in which there are two extant species of chimp (the common chimp and the bonobo; see Chapter 4).

To complicate matters further, there is a well-preserved, virtually intact cranium (specimen designation KNM WT-17000), called "the Black Skull" for its darkly stained appearance, that is even more robust than *boisei* but older than either *robustus* or *boisei.* Dating to about 2.5 million years ago, the Black Skull has a smaller cranial capacity than even *afarensis* (Walker et al. 1986; Johanson 1993). Because of its extreme robusticity, its small cranial capacity, and its early date, no one is quite sure how to interpret the Black Skull, though it might represent a form ancestral to *boisei,* or, perhaps, to both *boisei* and *robustus.* Some paleoanthropologists label the Black Skull *Australopithecus aethiopicus.*

A FOREST OF HOMINIDS

Don't let the proliferation of names throw you off; it can be daunting even to paleoanthropologists. It becomes even more difficult when trying to suggest how these different-named fossil species are related in evolutionary terms. Remember, it often isn't easy even among living creatures to define relationships and to differentiate species. There is no agreement, for example, on the number of distinct gibbon species and how all the living varieties are related (Chapter 4). A species is ordinarily defined on the basis of the ability of its members to mate and produce fertile offspring; but this is not a useful yardstick when dealing with fossil bones.

Nevertheless, based on the dating of the specimens, detailed comparative analysis of the fossils themselves, and some guesswork, a number of models have been constructed to express how the various early fossil hominids relate

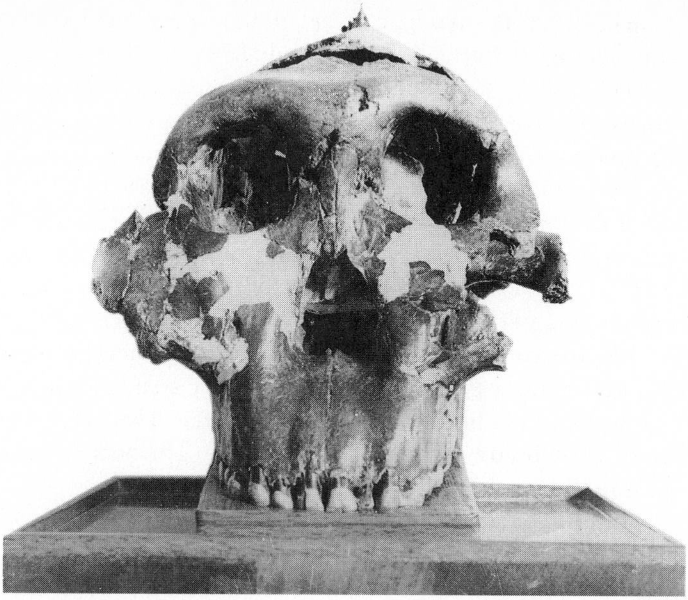

FIGURE 5.11
This skull of one of the so-called hyperrobust australopithecines, Australopithecus boisei, *exhibits an enormous crest of bone on the top, where powerful chewing muscles would have attached. The australopithecines seem to have followed an evolutionary pathway that led to hominids with a highly specialized diet.*
(© Bob Campbell)

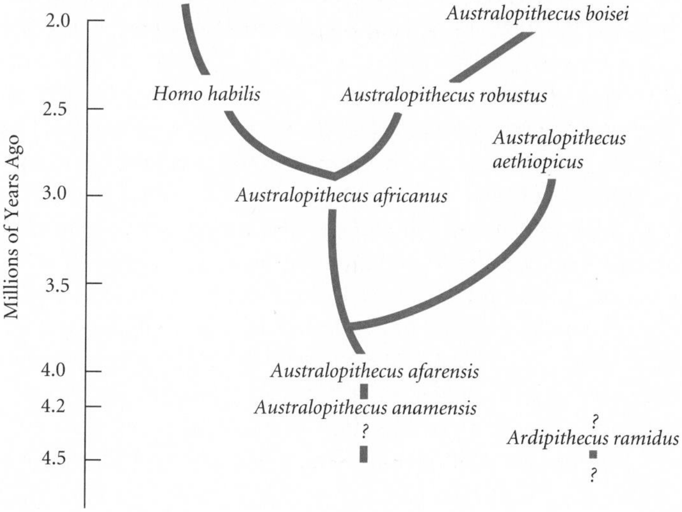

FIGURE 5.12
This phylogeny shows the evolutionary relationships among the fossil hominids discussed in this chapter.

in terms of evolutionary connections: which are ancestral, which are descendant forms, which are contemporaries, which are evolutionary offshoots that became extinct, and which led more directly to the modern human species. Though no general consensus exists, Figure 5.12 presents a common view of how the australopithecines are related in evolutionary terms (Grine 1993; Skelton and McHenry 1992).

In the view favored here, based on the highly detailed analysis by paleo-anthropologists Randall Skelton and Henry McHenry (1992) of seventy-seven skeletal traits and on new information discovered since their analysis, *Australopithecus anamensis* may be the ancestral form, having produced the oldest dates. The far-better-known *Australopithecus afarensis* descended from *anamensis* and was the sole hominid species for about 1 million years. *Australopithecus africanus* represents a population descendant from *afarensis*, with both the diet-specialized *robustus* and *boisei*, in turn, splitting off from its line. The Black Skull—*Australopithecus aethiopicus*—here represents another australopithecine evolutionary pathway branching off from *afarensis*. At about the same time that the robust australopithecines start to head down their evolutionary pathway with their physical adaptation to a highly specialized diet, another line emerges from *africanus*. That line is different, with a far greater reliance on culture for survival. (The next section will focus on this evolutionary line.)

New discoveries will no doubt force us to revise our models. But some facts almost certainly will not be amended: The six named species subsumed within the genus *Australopithecus* shared the fundamental, original hominid adaptation—they walked on two feet.

Ultimately, no matter which view you subscribe to, what the fossil record shows is change through time within the *Australopithecus* genus, with a burst of change and a proliferation of types occurring after 2.5 million years ago. This burst of change is the source of much of our confusion, since it resulted in a host of new hominid types whose evolutionary relationships are proving difficult to resolve. But how we resolve the confusion is, at least for our purposes here, not nearly as interesting as the fact that there was the proliferation in the first place. We will be discussing a possible explanation for this evolutionary burst in this chapter's Issues and Debates section.

Finally, how we divide up the various kinds of australopithecines—and whether we call them *Australopithecus* or *Paranthropus*—is not vital to the rest of our discussion. Most of the australopithecines were evolutionary deadends. Today, we simply do not see any bipedal, sagittally crested, apelike creatures walking around with brains slightly larger than one-third of our brain size. Any arguing we might do about them remains a debate about extinct species.

A DIFFERENT PATH

Soon after 2.5 million years ago, and just as the australopithecines were experiencing great changes in their evolutionary pathway, another hominid seems to have branched off from the main line of the *Australopithecus* genus (see Figure 5.12). This breakaway group followed a different evolutionary route, one in which its survival on the African savanna was not the result of an increasingly specialized diet, but, instead, was due to an increase in intelligence

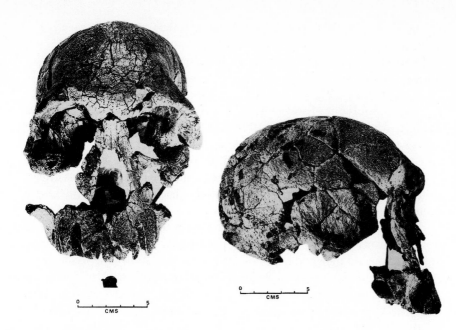

FIGURE 5.13

The cranial capacity of this fragmentary cranium of Homo habilis *shows that* habilis *possessed a brain larger than any ape. Dated at 2.4 million years ago,* habilis *represents the first hominid with an expanded brain.* (National Museum of Kenya)

made possible by an expanding brain. This creature first appears in the fossil record about 2.4 million years ago (Bower 1993b,c; Hill et al. 1992; Schrenk et al. 1993), a little before *africanus* became extinct, which makes it a contemporary of *Australopithecus robustus* and *aethiopicus.* But this new form cannot be mistaken for any variety or form of *Australopithecus.* With a much flatter face, a steeper forehead, and a larger brain—a mean size close to 700 ml, larger than any ape brain and just about one-half the modern human mean—this clearly is a new and different hominid. It is called *Homo habilis.*

Sharing the same genus as modern humans means that *habilis* was much more like us than were any of the australopithecines. Following the analogy used in Chapter 4: Whereas taxonomically *Homo sapiens* might live in the same neighborhood as the australopithecines, we live on the same street as *Homo habilis.*

The skull of *Homo habilis* was not just larger than that of the australopithecines, it was larger in proportion (Figure 5.13). The shape was different as well, with significantly less prognathism, a taller, steeper forehead, and a more rounded profile. All of these features seem to presage modern human beings.

Once again, however, this "new and improved" hominid retained some pongid features in its postcranial skeleton. Though postcranial remains of *habilis* are scanty, what has been found shows that, like the australopithecines, from the neck down they can be safely characterized as upright apes. The arms are still long and the legs short in proportion to each other, much like an ape but unlike a human's short arms and long legs (Johanson et al. 1987).

HOMO HABILIS, THE TOOLMAKER

The species we label *Homo habilis* on the basis of its skeletal characteristics exhibits another key feature not previously seen in the archaeological record: They made stone tools. We do not know whether any of the australopithecines made tools out of soft material like wood or animal hide that would have decayed long ago. As mentioned in Chapter 4, modern chimps are known to manufacture tools by stripping the bark off of twigs, which they then poke into termite mounds (Goodall 1986). The termites get stuck in the sticky residue on the stripped wood. The chimps pull out the twigs after a suitable wait, and then feast on fresh termites. The australopithecines were probably capable of similar work.

It also seems possible that at least some of the later australopithecines were physically capable of making stone tools. Researcher Randall Susman (1994) compared the hand bones of specimens of *Australopithecus afarensis, Australopithecus robustus* (he calls them *Paranthropus robustus*), *Homo erectus* (see Chapter 6), *Homo sapiens neanderthalensis* (see Chapter 7), and modern humans. While the *afarensis* hand Susman examined was similar to that of a chimp, all of the other specimens examined, including *robustus*, were more similar to a modern human's hand. So the evidence does not show that *robustus* was physically incapable of making tools.

However, the first appearance of the oldest stone tools closely coincides with the earliest appearance of *Homo habilis*. As archaeologists Kathy Schick and Nicholas Toth (1993:103) point out, the relatively small brain of the robust australopithecines and the small number of presumed stone tools found at their sites argue against their being tool makers. Robust australopithecines' massive cranial architecture further suggests to these researchers that they didn't need a cultural assist in the form of stone tools to process food in the first place. Although the question of who exactly made the first stone tools—and who did not—is still open to debate, it is certain that *Homo habilis* possessed both the hand anatomy and the increased intelligence needed to carry out the sophisticated process of forethought and action in the production of permanent tools.

Oldowan Technology

These oldest stone tools date back to about 2.5 million years ago and were first recognized, defined, and described by the famous paleoanthropologist team of Louis and Mary Leakey (M. Leakey 1971). They called the tools **Oldowan,** after the place where they were first found and where the Leakeys had devoted so much of their research energy, Olduvai Gorge in Tanzania.

The Leakeys originally defined Oldowan tools as a series of specifically shaped, sharpened rocks that served as chopping tools. Mary Leakey (1971) classified Oldowan choppers into a number of types based on shape and inferred function—cutting, chopping, scraping, and so forth. More recent

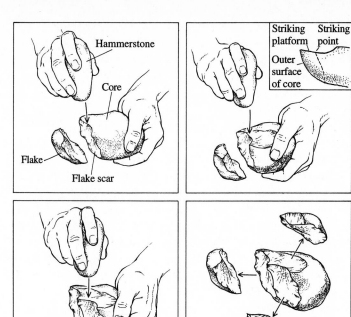

work, however, by Nicholas Toth (1985) and Kathy Schick (Schick and Toth 1993) shows clearly that, though some of the "Oldowan choppers" may have been used as tools, the vast majority functioned as **cores** from which **flake** tools were produced.

The maker of the tool, or the **knapper,** begins with a more or less spherical nodule of stone. Holding this **object piece** in one hand, the knapper strikes it with a **hammerstone,** usually a fortuitously shaped harder rock (or just one less likely to break as a result of its particular geometry). Without much trouble, the knapper can knock a flake off the stone (Figure 5.14). He or she then turns the object piece around in his or her hand so the interior surface of the rock that was just exposed with the first hammerstone blow is facing up. Next, using that surface as a **striking platform,** the knapper strikes down on it with the hammerstone, thereby removing a stone flake from the opposite side of the object piece. Repeating this several times can produce a number of sharp, relatively straight-edged flakes useful for cutting, scraping, sawing, chopping, and the like. Microscopic analysis of a large collection of Oldowan flakes shows that many were used for these purposes (Keeley and Toth 1981; Toth 1985). The flakes exhibited a polish on their edges that is typically caused by cutting plant material, butchering animals, and woodworking.

Stone flakes are sharper, stronger, and more durable than the teeth or nails nature provided our ancestors. While you don't need to be a genius to figure out how to make stone tools, it does take what researcher John Gowlett calls an "appreciation of the properties of stone" (1986:251). The production of Oldowan tools took some knowledge of the characteristics of different rocks, an understanding of their breakage patterns, forethought in planning the sequence of blows, a bit of hand–eye coordination, and flexibility to change the planned sequence when problems cropped up. More fundamentally, this process takes enough intelligence to recognize that a round, dull rock can be transformed into a large number of straight, thin, sharp pieces of rock suitable for many different uses. Clearly, this is the thought process of an intelligent being.

To Schick and Toth (1993), the archaeological record at *Homo habilis* sites suggests quite a bit of forethought and planning in the manufacture of stone tools. In their view, Oldowan was not a simple and "expedient" technology in which tools were made only to fill an immediate need from whatever happened to be available. If this had been the case, then flakes and the cores from which they originated would all be found together where they were made and used, and they would have been produced from raw materials found nearby.

Instead, the archaeological record shows that cores were transported, sometimes several kilometers from their point of origin. *Homo habilis* was willing to travel some distance for a source of stone known to be superior for the production of sharp, durable tools. The cores themselves appear to have been moved around to wherever flakes were needed; it is common to find flakes, but not their source cores, at a site. The cores, apparently, were carried to the next place tools might be needed. This shows a high level of planning and intelligence. As Schick and Toth (1993:128) maintain: "This is a much more complicated pattern than many would have suspected from this remote period of time. It bespeaks to us an elevated degree of planning among these early hominids than is presently seen among modern non-human primates."

THE FATE OF *HOMO HABILIS*

The existence of *Homo habilis* was rather short in evolutionary terms: Occurring first in deposits that are about 2.4 million years old, their remains disappear entirely sometime after about 1.8 million years ago. But the evidence does not imply that *Homo habilis* simply became extinct, leaving no evolutionary descendants. In fact, *habilis* appears to have evolved into another hominid species. This evolutionary jump and the new species that resulted is the focus of the next chapter.

ISSUES AND DEBATES

WHAT WERE THE FIRST STEPS IN HOMINID EVOLUTION?

The evidence regarding how the hominid family began is unequivocal. The first hominids were, fundamentally, bipedal apes; the first steps of our evolution were literally "first steps." The physical evidence shows that creatures dating to at least 4.2 million years ago had a skeletal anatomy suitable for walking on two feet, in a manner similar, if not identical to, modern human beings. At the same time, these creatures possessed brains of a size and configuration virtually indistinguishable from those of some species of fossil and modern apes (Figure 5.15). The consensus on this is clear.

This scenario of the origin of the human line, based on locomotor patterns rather than growth in brain size and intelligence, was not what most nineteenth-century evolutionary scientists expected, and may seem to contradict common sense even today. After all, the hallmark of our species, the characteristic that seems to distinguish us the most from other animals, including the apes, is our great intelligence. Chimps and bonobos, for all their great intelligence, inventiveness, and even their capacity for communication, have brains less than one-third the size of the modern human brain (about 450 ml compared to about 1,450 ml). In other words, our brains are a quantum leap larger in volume, more than three times larger than those of chimps and bonobos.

We might expect, therefore, that our brain has been evolving the longest and was the first characteristic that differentiated us from the other primates— and that its growth is what initiated the split between the pongid and hominid families. In fact, many scientists held this view in the late nineteenth and early twentieth centuries. For example, Grafton Elliot Smith, a renowned British scientist who published extensively on human evolution, expressed the perspective of many others when he characterized the then-hypothetical earliest human ancestor as "merely an ape with an overgrown brain"

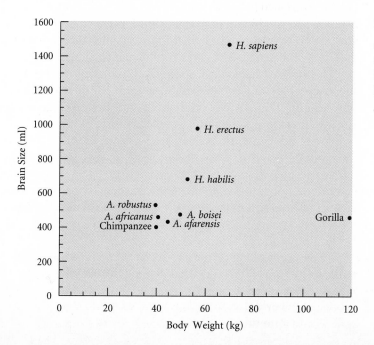

FIGURE 5.15

A comparison of brain size and body weight in a number of different ape and hominid species.

(1927:105–106). The belief that the fossil record should provide specimens that looked like apes with "overgrown" brains made many people susceptible to a hoax. The famous fossil found at Piltdown in Southern England seemed to be that big-brained early ancestor. Many scientists suspended their usual skepticism and accepted the Piltdown finding. But the fossil turned out to be a modern human skull planted with an ape jaw that was doctored so as to appear to belong to the skull (see Feder 1996).

WHAT CAUSED THE PROLIFERATION OF HOMINID SPECIES?

An environmental change at the end of the Miocene served as a catalyst for the evolution of the hominids. A substantial and growing body of evidence now points to another significant worldwide environmental shift that precipitated the split in the hominid evolutionary pathway at 2.5 million years ago to 2.4 million years ago (Johanson and Shreeve 1989; Prentice and Denton 1988; Shackleton et al. 1984; Shackleton and Opdyke 1977; Vrba 1985, 1988, 1993).

Deep-sea cores (based on oxygen isotope calibrations; see Chapter 6) suggest that beginning about 3.2 million years ago and greatly accelerating after 2.5 million years ago, the polar ice caps and continental glaciers in the northern hemisphere experienced rapid growth. Expanding ice sheets usually suggest a cooling of the planet, and with cooler temperatures the world gets drier. This deduction is supported by the pollen record, which shows a series of worldwide shifts from woodlands to grasslands that cut back further on the forests, already depleted after the Miocene. The worldwide decrease in temperature and the growth of permanent ice fields intensified at about 1.6 million years ago, marking the beginning of the **Pleistocene Epoch,** often called the "Ice Age" but actually a period of fluctuating climate (see Chapter 6).

The work of paleoanthropologist Elisabeth Vrba (1985, 1988, 1993) shows a proliferation of new grassland animal species after 2.5 million years ago, including arid-adapted creatures like gazelles, antelopes, and wildebeests. She interprets this as the result of an expansion of savanna habitats and the creation of new grassland niches because of the overall cooling of the planet. As commonly happens when new niches open up (new ways to make a living in an environment), evolution moves quickly to fill those niches with life. Since natural selection is fueled by environmental conditions, when those conditions diversify, selection accelerates for species with characteristics advantageous for the newly created conditions. Vrba calls this process a **turnover-pulse** (1993:50).

So our hominid ancestors, both direct and indirect—whose adaptation to life on the grasslands was what defined the taxonomic family in the first place—experienced disruption, change, and expansion as the savannas expanded and changed after 2.5 million years ago. One important change was a split within *Australopithecus* along perhaps two separate lines (see Figure

5.12). In other words, a single ancestral hominid species, *afarensis,* evolved into a number of different species. One of those lines, increasingly adapted to a diet of nuts and seeds, represent an evolutionary deadend; we are the current representatives of the other line.

HOW DO WE KNOW THE HOMINIDS WERE UPRIGHT?

The configuration of the skeleton is quite different for creatures who walk quadrupedally and those who are habitual bipeds. The most important part of the skeleton in this regard is the pelvis, made up of a left and a right **innominate** bone (Figure 5.16). The innominate bones of a primate quadruped—for example, a chimpanzee—have a long and narrow top blade (the **ilium**) that connects to the base of the pelvic bone (the **ischium**), creating a flat plane. A human innominate, on the other hand, has an ilium that is short and broad and, when compared to a chimp's, flares out at the top and seems

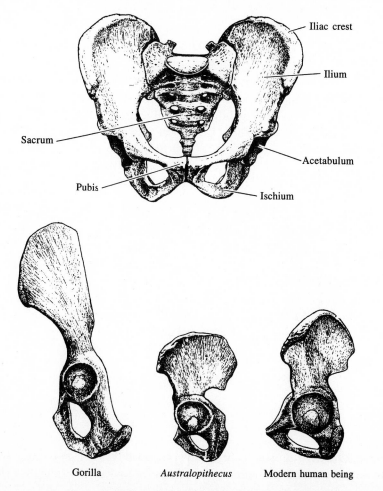

Gorilla   *Australopithecus*   Modern human being

FIGURE 5.16

A comparison of the pelvis of a gorilla, an Australopithecus, *and a modern human. Despite some differences, the pelvises of the extinct and the modern hominid are far more similar to each other than either is to that of the ape. This is because the pelvis determines the configuration of the muscles that attach to the upper leg, which, in turn, determines how an animal walks: Apes are quadrupeds;* Australopithecus *and modern human beings are bipeds.* (From "The Antiquity of Human Walking" by John Napier. Copyright © April 1967 by *Scientific American,* Inc. All rights reserved.)

twisted to the side, producing a complex curve away from the plane of its ischium (Lovejoy 1988).

The configuration of the innominate bone in an animal determines the position of the large gluteal muscles, which in turn determines how the creature could most easily get around. Thus, the position of the ilium on the innominate bone of an extinct animal allows us, with some accuracy, to deduce how that creature walked—in other words, whether it got around on four legs or two.

There really is very little argument about the pelvis of *Australopithecus afarensis* as well as of the other australopithecines; they have an innominate bone very similar to that of a modern human being (Lovejoy 1988; Lovejoy, Heiple, and Burnstein 1973; see Figure 5.16). Though scientists who have examined the bones disagree about whether *afarensis* differed in some of the particulars of walking [for example, Stern and Susman (1983) suggest that, though bipedal on the ground, *afarensis* shuffled more like a chimp], most of them maintain that afarensis walked remarkably like we do (Lovejoy 1988).

IS THERE OTHER EVIDENCE FOR BIPEDALITY?

Though the pelvis is the best place to look for evidence of locomotion, other parts of *afarensis* anatomy further support bipedality. The Laetoli footprints (see Figure 5.1) are virtually indistinguishable from footprints of a modern human; individually they exhibit the typical pattern of a human foot, and together they match the human stride (Charteris, Wall, and Nottrodt 1981; Day and Wickens 1980; T. White 1980; T. White and Suwa 1987). The prints display a humanlike arch and lack any hint of the divergent big toe that characterizes the apes.

Other skeletal evidence of upright locomotion includes the bones around the knee. Fragments of the **femur** (upper leg) and **tibia** (lower leg) of *afarensis* have been found that show clearly that its upper and lower leg joined at an angle more like modern human beings than apes (Johanson and Shreeve 1989). The preserved foot bones of *afarensis* are longer and more curved than the modern human form, but, like the footprints, they exhibit a modern arrangement of the big toe. In fact, when the large, well-preserved foot from the site of Hadar (see the Case Study Close-Up section in this chapter) is scaled down to the size of the Laetoli prints, it is a perfect match (Johanson and Shreeve 1989:197).

WHY BIPEDALISM?

Though the environmental change hypothesized by Vrba shows how evolution in general, and for hominids in particular, may have accelerated on the grasslands as new niches opened up, it does not address the fundamental question of what advantages a bipedal ape might have had over its quadrupedal cousins.

As anatomist Owen Lovejoy (1984) points out, we can't explain the success of bipedalism on the basis of its current utility. The question must be asked in an evolutionary framework and placed within the context of natural selection: If you are an ape, what is it about walking on two feet in the savanna that increases your likelihood of survival and, in turn, the probability that you will reproduce and pass on the genetic disposition for bipedal locomotion to another generation, for whom greater proficiency for that mode can be further acted on by natural selection?

Seventeenth-century natural historian John Ray, featured in Chapter 2, believed that upright walking was an endowment from God, giving human beings a unique advantage, enabling them to see for greater distances—to spot resources as well as dangers—and to carry objects.

Modern explanations of why this ability was the key selective factor in early hominid evolution are a bit more complex, though they often build on Ray's assertions. Modern hypotheses elaborate on how the ability to walk on two feet allowed our ancestors to survive at the end of the Miocene while so many other ape species became extinct, and why it continued to be the central adaptive trait of the hominids until brain expansion took over more than 1.5 million years later.

The Upright Provider

Consider the hypothesis proposed by anatomist Owen Lovejoy (1981, 1984), who suggests that the key advantage to bipedal locomotion was that it freed the hands to carry things. Specifically, it freed the hands of males to carry food back to a camp or village where females and their offspring could be provisioned.

Among modern primates, chimp females raise and provide for their children. They are often quite good mothers, devoting much time and energy to the health and well-being of their offspring. From an evolutionary perspective, they are doing all they can to ensure that these children—individuals carrying half their genes—will survive to reproduce and pass on those genes. Male chimps, on the other hand, generally have little to do with infants. Since chimp society is sexually promiscuous, they don't know which, if any, infants they have sired. So, from an evolutionary perspective, why should they waste time providing for offspring that probably do not carry their genes?

Obviously, for a female the more offspring she gives birth to, the greater the likelihood that one or more will survive to adulthood and continue passing on her genes. But there's a tradeoff in a species like chimps (and especially humans), where offspring are dependent on their mothers for extended periods (chimps commonly stay with their mothers for eight to ten years). With each new baby, the female can spend less and less time caring for older children, which may lower their chances for survival. Any help she can get, especially if she has more than one young child, will improve the likelihood of survival of all of her children. It makes sense for her to solicit assistance from a concerned adult male, thereby allowing her to be a full-time mother to her youngest child and not have to collect food for herself or her other children.

But how can she convince a male to do this? In Lovejoy's view, she must assure him that the offspring are his and that, by helping them, he ensures that half his genes get passed along as well. Only a pattern of sexual fidelity—in other words, monogamy—can do this. Basically, it's a trade: Females increase the likelihood their children will survive by remaining sexually faithful to one male. The male receives exclusive sexual access to a female and an increased probability that he will father offspring. All he has to do is faithfully provision the female and the children he has sired with her. This ability to bring food and other resources back to the female and the young is made feasible, in Lovejoy's view, by the freeing of the hands which, in turn, is made possible by walking on two feet.

Remember, individual animals are not making a conscious choice to enhance their contribution to the evolutionary gene pool. Females merely are choosing to associate with males who help them care for their children, and males help females who provide them with sex. These behaviors increase the probability that offspring survive to adulthood. In terms of natural selection, it should be apparent that those late Miocene apes who were pushed out onto the savanna and who acted in a way that increased the likelihood of their offspring's survival were more successful than those who did not: Their population increased while other groups became extinct. Since the provisioning behavior was made possible by upright walking, that ability would be strongly selected for.

Lovejoy's hypothesis explains bipedality, sexuality, and the development of monogamous family structure all at the same time. However, it has not gone uncriticized for being male-oriented and generally mistaken about modern primate behavior and the prevalence (or actual lack) of monogamy in modern human foraging societies (Tanner 1981; Zihlman 1979). There is at least one glaring problem here: When a male is away gathering food, what is to prevent a female from copulating with other males? In fact, such behavior may be to her advantage, by increasing the number of males willing to provision her and her offspring. Sex is used in many of the social primates to make alliances and maintain friendships. In such a scenario, sexual fidelity might even be disadvantageous, particularly if the male doesn't do a good job of provisioning. Ultimately, it is difficult to understand how a more rigid pattern demanding sexual fidelity actually could be maintained in ancient hominid societies.

The Upright Scavenger

Anthropologist Pat Shipman (1984, 1986) has proposed another hypothesis. Using the scanning electron microscope, Shipman has examined the remains of animal bones recovered at early hominid sites. She found microscopic evidence of tooth marks from predators and scavengers, as well as cut marks from stone tools, made when hominids removed the meat (Figure 5.17). In some instances she found carnivore and stone tool marks on the same bones, either with the tool marks superimposed on the carnivore tooth marks or with the tool marks made first. In other words, sometimes the hominids got at the bones after carnivores had already chewed on them (indicating hominid scavenging behavior), and sometimes carnivores had access to the bones only after the hominids had processed them (indicating hominid hunting behavior). There are too few marks, however, to come to any conclusion regarding the relative contribution of hunted versus scavenged meat.

As we will discuss later in the Issues and Debates section in this chapter, archaeologist Lewis Binford (1987a) has shown that the animal bones found at ancient hominid sites usually are from meat-poor parts of the carcass. This suggests to Binford, as well as to Shipman, that the early hominids largely were scavengers of meat, chasing off large carnivores after a kill or simply waiting for them to leave after they had filled their stomachs.

Walking on two feet is highly advantageous to hominids who were opportunistic scavengers rather than habitual hunters. Hunters need to run, and an animal can run faster on four feet than on two. Scavengers, however, don't need to run; their prey isn't going anywhere. But scavengers still need to find their quarry, and that means walking great distances and scanning a broad territory for evidence of a predator kill. Bipedalism is highly energy efficient, in part because it involves only two limbs, and yields greater endurance for walking long distances. It also is advantageous in the treeless and shadeless savanna; wandering, upright scavengers reduce the surface area of skin exposed to the burning African sun (Wheeler 1991).

On top of this, since scavengers always need to be wary of the return of the predator who did the killing in the first place, as well as of other large, aggressive scavengers—like hyenas or jackals, who might compete for the same kill—it is wise to get in and out quickly: Cut the meat off the bone as fast as possible, and carry it back to a safe place to eat. The free hands of a bipedal hominid can both carry the tools for extracting the meat from the carcass and carry the meat home.

The Efficient Walker

Primatologist Peter Rodman and anthropologist Henry McHenry (Johanson, Johanson, and Edgar 1994) have proposed what may be the simplest and most elegant hypothesis of all. After analyzing the energy expended by

FIGURE 5.17

This micrograph of fossil bone from FLK Zinj at Olduvai Gorge shows tool marks on the bone (the horizontal lines and the diagonal line beginning at the top of the photo) and a carnivore tooth mark (beginning on the right side and angled toward the center). The carnivore mark overlies the tool mark, indicating that the hominids sliced meat off of this part of the bone before a scavenger began eating. (Photo by Pat Shipman)

chimps when they walk quadrupedally and by humans with their upright gait, Rodman and McHenry determined that human locomotion was simply more efficient than chimp locomotion, meaning we expend less energy to accomplish the same task. As the Miocene forest shrunk and ape species were pushed out onto the growing savanna, where food resources were more dispersed, a more efficient way of moving across increasing distances in the search for food became adaptively advantageous.

All of the accumulated evidence of twentieth-century paleoanthropology basically brings us back to John Ray's seventeenth-century suggestions for the advantages of bipedalism. Though the modern hypotheses are more elaborate, they all suggest that the abilities to carry things, to move around in a more energy-efficient way, and perhaps to see across greater distances were crucial in the selection process. Hominids, who could walk upright, had the advantages that afforded them a better chance of survival in their grassland habitat.

WHAT ABOUT THE HOMINID BRAIN?

Under the very best of circumstances, paleoanthropologists are limited to the direct study of the hard parts of a hominid's anatomy that lend themselves to preservation: teeth (which are the hardest parts of our bodies and so the most abundantly preserved ancient hominid remains) and bones (which, though not as hard as teeth, under the right circumstances will fossilize and be preserved for millions of years). But if we want to know about early hominid intelligence, we are usually limited to hypothesizing on the basis of brain size as determined from the volume of the preserved skull. The brain itself is soft tissue and quickly decays, usually leaving no trace. However, under rare circumstances a cast of the brain, showing features of its exterior surface, can survive when minerals replace the brain as it decays, filling the skull like jello in a mold. Called **endocasts,** these natural models of ancient brains can show us what the exterior surface of an ancient brain looked like.

Anthropologist Dean Falk (1984) has examined the seven known cranial endocasts of *Australopithecus africanus*. The exterior surface of all these casts are virtually indistinguishable from the brains of modern apes. They display none of the characteristics of the exterior of the human brain that distinguish it from that of an ape's brain. Specifically, the brains of the australopithecines are symmetrical: The left and right halves appear to be mirror images of each other. Modern human brains are decidedly asymmetrical: The left and right halves look different and actually are associated with different functions. Since we view the australopithecines as a series of bipedal apes, that they lack this feature of the human brain is to be expected.

Where nature has not provided endocasts, they can be manufactured by coating the inside of a fossil skull with liquid latex or a similar material that, when dry, can be peeled off. This artificial endocast reflects the form of the interior surface of the skull and, it is hoped, shows features of the exterior of the brain with which it was in constant contact for an individual's lifetime. The artificial endocast of a *Homo habilis* specimen (ER 1470) shows a far more humanlike asymmetrical morphology, providing further evidence of the ancestral connection they share with us.

WERE THE EARLY HOMINIDS HUNTERS?

From the physical remains of ancient hominid skeletons, we can reconstruct what they looked like and how they walked. We also know about their stone tools. These artifacts are quite durable and show in a direct way the technological abilities of the first tool-making hominids. Every stone tool is a fossil of a series of actions, and we can fairly accurately reconstruct those actions and, hence, a technology.

When dealing with ancient sites and fossils, however, more detailed questions of lifestyle are often extremely difficult to answer. For example, the nature of their **social systems**—how they related to each other within groups, how they defined "family," who they considered suitable mates—is, perhaps, forever out of reach. We are relegated to using living primates or hunting-and-gathering groups of human beings, neither of whom should be considered all that reliable as models for prehistoric hominid behavior. Using modern primate models, R. A. Foley and P. C. Lee (1989) make an interesting attempt to construct early hominid social systems. They suggest that savannas encourage relatively large group size because of the greater risk of predators in a grassland environment. They maintain that large groups based on male kin alliances are adaptive under these circumstances. Applying this scenario specifically to *afarensis,* they see a social organization consisting of related males who interacted with females and their offspring and for whom they provide protection from predators. Of course, it is extremely difficult to find data to test such a hypothesis.

Subsistence, that part of a culture's economic system that supplies the necessities for survival, is something that archaeological research can often illuminate more directly. For instance, as shown in Chapter 3, the dietary pattern leaves physical remains in the form of bones, seeds, nuts, and so on that can be studied. So the diet of the earliest members of the human family is, at least potentially, reconstructable.

In the past, many paleoanthropologists assumed that the first humans were hunters and that any tools found would relate to a hunting adaptation. Actually, there is very little evidence to support this view. Neither the Oldowan choppers nor the used flakes would have been all that handy as spearpoints. Moreover, a detailed **taphonomic** analysis conducted by archaeologist Lewis Binford (1987a) has shown that animal bones found at early hominid sites typically are not those we would expect to find at the hunting camps of proficient hunters. The animal skeletal elements found are not those that would have been associated with the best cuts of meat, like upper limbs. Binford determined that the excavated animal bones were mostly lower limbs and parts of skulls and mandibles, among the least meaty of animal parts. Moreover, many of the tools found at *habilis* sites would have been more suitable for extracting marrow than for removing meat from bones; marrow inside the shafts of long bones, typically left behind by carnivores, is a staple for many scavengers. This indicated to Binford that early hominids were probably not proficient hunters at all but, instead, opportunistic scavengers of the carcasses of animals killed by large carnivores.

The electron microscope analysis conducted by Pat Shipman (1983, 1984, 1986) along with Richard Potts (Potts and Shipman 1981) (discussed earlier with the origins of bipedality) further supports the hypothesis that scavenging played a major role in the diet of early hominids. For example, the cut marks on animal bones Shipman examined from *habilis* sites in Olduvai Gorge tend to be near the midshaft of the bones (Shipman 1983). For later groups known to be butchering entire carcasses rather than just scavenging them, the cut marks are almost always located near the joints, where the best meat is available. The location of the cut marks on the Olduvai animal bones seems to conform better to a scavenging rather than a hunting mode of subsistence.

Though scavenging might seem an unreliable mode of subsistence, under certain circumstances it is a reasonably low-risk strategy that yields an abundance of food. Using as a model modern ecosystems broadly similar to those in which the early hominids found themselves, a number of analyses have shown scavenging to be a productive subsistence strategy (Blumenschine 1989; Blumenschine and Masao 1991). Where large, social scavengers such as hyenas are in small numbers [a decrease in the number of hyenas seems to coincide with the appearance of *Homo habilis* (Blumenschine 1987)], it may have made sense for hominids to allow other, larger predators to expend their energy in the kill, and then take advantage of what they left behind, or even run them off and "steal" the meat in what is called "confrontational scavenging."

Though scavenging clearly was important in the early hominid quest for food, other research shows that hunting also was a part of early hominid subsistence. Henry Bunn and Ellen Kroll (1986), analyzing stone flakes and bones from the 1.8-million-year-old FLK site in Olduvai Gorge in Tanzania, found substantial evidence for reliance on meat based on the presence of bones representing the meatiest parts of animals that bore ample evidence of stone-tool cut marks. The evidence for hunting seems a bit stronger for small animals, with a pattern of scavenging but also some hunting of larger animals.

If animals are being scavenged, the scavenger grabs whatever portion of the killed animal can be obtained and takes it to a secure place. The archaeological sites that develop in such secure places produce lots of small portions of animals, bones reflecting whatever pieces of the animals the scavenger was able to grab. In the case of hunting, on the other hand, the hunters are carrying most if not all of an animal back to a place where the food can be shared; they have complete control of the animal from the time of its killing to the time of its being eaten. At FLK, large sections of animals were found, suggesting that hunting was a primary mode of subsistence there.

We needn't be too concerned about the finer points of the nature of early hominid subsistence. All researchers would probably agree that hunting was not predominant in the subsistence base of the australopithecines or in *Homo habilis.* Though we have to be careful when generalizing from nonhuman primates, we do know that chimpanzees in the wild occasionally engage in cooperative hunts (Goodall 1986). In questioning the hunting abilities of early hominids, many archaeologists and paleoanthropologists are reacting to previous, overly romantic versions of a human past populated by killer apes [see Robert Ardrey's (1961) *African Genesis* for his now-discounted view that the killer instinct is what allowed our ancestors to thrive]. But, in reacting to the killer-ape hypothesis, as paleoanthropologist Daniel Stiles (1991) has pointed out, there is no reason to believe our hominid ancestors were less capable than chimps in their ability to plan, coordinate, and carry out a hunt. The first hominids were not born killers, but they probably did rely on meat to a certain degree, some of it scavenged, some from hunting. The early hominids probably were opportunistic foragers, taking whatever food they could, whenever the opportunity presented itself.

SINGLE OR MULTIPLE SPECIES?

All living human beings are members of the same species, *Homo sapiens,* which means fertile males and females can mate and produce viable, fertile offspring, despite wide variability within the species. Would a paleoanthropologist from another planet, confronted with the fragmentary skeletal remains of a number of different kinds of modern human beings, recognize that the small, light skeletons of Mbuti pygmies, for example, and the large, heavy bones of Athapaskan Indians belong to the same species?

Real paleoanthropologists have been faced with a similar dilemma as they have tried to define the boundaries of fossil species. For a long time, especially when samples were quite small, virtually every new discovery gave birth to a new species name. Each new species consisted of a population of one. Each **hypodigm**—the list of fossil specimens hypothesized to belong to the same species—contained only the original specimen. A great proliferation of names ensued, with even small differences used to justify separate species status for new finds.

More recently, this situation has changed as paleoanthropologists have recognized the morphological variability possible within a single species. As a result, species names have been dropped as increasing numbers of individual cases have been subsumed under the same species names, and hypodigms have grown in size as well as variability.

For some scientists, the shift to a smaller number of species has gone too far. In the case of *Homo habilis,* for example, Bernard Wood (1992a,b) suggests that the current hypodigm reflects too much variability to represent a single species. Since a rather large number of contemporary, different species of *Australopithecus* are recognized, might not such complexity characterize the first representatives of the genus *Homo?* Specifically, Wood agrees that all of the specimens from Olduvai Gorge currently assigned to the taxon *Homo habilis* should remain as members of the hypodigm along with some, but not all, of the specimens from Koobi Fora (see Map 5.1). These fossils have in common a larger cranial capacity than any of the australopithecines (and smaller than the species *Homo erectus,* to be discussed in the next chapter) but a postcranial skeleton that is similar if not identical to *Australopithecus.* The rest of the Koobi Fora specimens currently contained in the *Homo habilis* hypodigm, according to Wood, should be placed in a separate species and called *Homo rudolfensis.* Like *Homo habilis, Homo rudolfensis* has a larger brain than *Australopithecus,* but its postcranial skeleton is more modern in appearance.

Most researchers still adhere to the single-species model, including paleoanthropologist Philip Tobias, who helped define *habilis* more than 25 years ago (L. Leakey, Tobias, and Napier 1964; Tobias 1991). A recent analysis of brain size differences within the known *Homo habilis* specimens shows a range similar to other fossil species and even within modern ape species, supporting the one-species model (J. Miller 1991). But the sample size for early *Homo* is quite small, so this issue cannot be decided with any confidence. Only more research and larger sample sizes will help solve this problem.

RATES OF CHANGE IN EVOLUTION

As paleontologist Stephen Jay Gould (1994) points out, most people think that evolution proceeds along a steady, even course, with small, incremental changes leading to large changes across the vast expanse of time. Yet, when we look at the evidence for the fossil species *Australopithecus afarensis,* we see something quite different. The oldest commonly accepted *afarensis* specimen is the Belohdelie frontal bone from a skull dated to 3.9 million years ago. The youngest is the nearly complete Hadar cranium, A.L. 444-2, dated to 3 million years ago. Separated by nearly 1 million years, these two specimens are remarkably similar, where comparisons can be made. They imply fundamental stability in the species during this period, not accretional change.

Gould and his colleague Niles Eldredge proposed a perspective on evolution called **punctuated equilibrium** (Eldredge and Gould 1972). In this view, species tend to remain stable for long periods of time before undergoing—perhaps in response to a dramatic change in their environment—a period of relatively rapid change ("rapid" in geological time is still rather slow by human standards). Long periods of stability—"equilibrium"—marked by rapid bursts of change—"punctuations"—seem to characterize the history of many species, including our own. If Gould is right, and if Elisabeth Vrba is right in her conclusion of a period of rapid and dramatic environmental change, then the extinction of *afarensis* and the proliferation of a number of new hominid forms after 3 million years ago are directly connected.

Hadar, located in the Afar triangle of northeastern Ethiopia, is one of the most spectacular fossil hominid sites ever excavated. All by itself, the Hadar site disproves the notion that the pronouncements of paleontologists are based on a tiny handful of unrecognizable bone fragments or indistinguishable teeth. This one site produced 250 hominid fossil bones representing fourteen individual members of the species *Australopithecus afarensis* (Johanson and Shreeve 1989:21). Perhaps most significantly, Hadar produced Lucy.

CASE STUDY
CLOSE-UP

The remains of the fossil that her discoverers named Lucy were found in 1974. Close to one-half of her skeleton was recovered, including parts of the skull, the lower jaw, ribs, vertebrae, arm bones, left innominate, left femur (upper leg), and parts of the lower right leg (see Figure 5.3). The following year, fragmentary remains of thirteen more individuals were found, including nine adults and four children. Dubbed "the First Family," all these individuals were deposited at the same time and seem to have died together.

The Hadar fossils provided the name for this hominid species, *Australopithecus afarensis,* after the Afar region of Ethiopia where the site is located. Lucy and the First Family fossils constitute solid support for the interpretation presented in this chapter: Dating to more than 3.18 million years ago, the first hominids were, essentially, bipedal apes.

Lucy has received most of the attention as a result of her remarkable degree of preservation, but her size is not typical of the group found at Hadar. Lucy, an adult, was tiny by modern standards, standing only a little over 110 cm (3½ ft) tall, with an estimated weight of about 30 kg (65 lb), small even by *afarensis* standards. But Lucy is a female in a species that exhibits a large measure of **sexual dimorphism,** that is, a big difference between males and females. For example, among gorillas—a species with strong dimorphism—males are commonly twice the size of females. A recent analysis shows that sexual dimorphism among the known *afarensis* specimens is less than that exhibited by gorillas and orangutans but more than in chimpanzees and much more than in modern human beings (McHenry 1991). Lucy falls within the broad range of sizes represented in the First Family fossils. Though she is a small female, she is clearly a female.

The Hadar specimens show what these ancient hominids looked like: They were bipedal. Their arms were proportionally longer than in modern humans, with hands quite modern in appearance except for fingers that curled more like an ape's fingers. Their jaws were an amalgam of ape and human. They had ape-sized brains housed in skulls that exhibited large, apelike bony ridges above the eyes, and a highly prognathous profile.

Hadar presents an astonishing picture of more than a dozen individuals who probably knew each other and perished together in the dim mists of our own beginnings. Like the footprints at Laetoli, they have achieved a kind of immortality as a result of the lucky accident of the preservation of their bones. And like the Laetoli prints, that lucky accident affords us, 150,000 generations later, the luxury to contemplate where and how we began.

VISITING THE PAST

Unfortunately, most of you reading this book will probably not be able to visit Africa anytime soon, so you won't be visiting any of the fossil localities discussed here or shown in Map 5.1. Even if you were able to, most of the sites are nondescript, without any on-site museum or display. The Laetoli footprints, for example, were left in place and, after casts of the individual hominid prints were made, were covered up in an attempt to preserve the site for the future when, perhaps, a museum can be built over and around them. Some of the sites are in currently rather dangerous areas where tourists are not welcome. For example, Donald Johanson, Lucy's excavator, was unable to return to Hadar for some time because of political turmoil in that part of Ethiopia (Johanson and Shreeve 1989).

Most of the significant early hominid fossils are housed in museums, particularly the National Museum of Tanzania in Dar es Salaam, the National Museum of Kenya in Nairobi, eastern Africa, and in various museums in southern Africa. However, very few of the actual original specimens are on display. Almost all are locked away, to preserve them for future research as new techniques of analysis are developed—for example, the extraction and analysis of minute quantities of DNA left in fossil bone.

The good news is that many natural history and science museums, especially those in big cities in the United States and Canada, have displays showing casts of some of the original fossils, replicas of the Laetoli pathway, dioramas showing artists' reconstructions of ancient hominids, and even some actual stone tools. Many of these exhibits are quite well done and certainly worth a visit. Recently, the American Museum of Natural History in New York City refurbished their human evolution exhibit, relying extensively on fossil casts, computers, holograms, and other high-tech tools.

SUMMARY

Humanity began its evolutionary journey more than 4 million years ago as an "upright ape." It was bipedal locomotion and not brain size or intelligence that first distinguished us from the apes. Our first upright ancestor is *Australopithecus*, known from a number of fossil localities in eastern and southern Africa. Its ability to walk on two feet was advantageous in many ways: It could travel more energy efficiently, which assisted in scavenging. With the hands freed, it could carry tools to where they were needed and bring back food to provision the young and possibly the females with children.

Around 2.5 million years ago, an environmental change in Africa, sparked by worldwide cooling, induced a burst of evolution in the hominid family. A number of varied species branched off from *Australopithecus afarensis* after this time. One branch, *Homo habilis,* had a brain size larger than any ape. With its larger brain, *habilis* was able to produce the first stone tools—simple, but revealing a level of planning and forethought that reflects the great intelligence of this first member of our genus.

TO LEARN MORE

You can research many of the specific technical issues dealt with in this chapter by tracking down the sources cited in the text. For well-written, less technical, and broader discussions of the paleoanthropology and archaeology of the first hominids, books co-authored by two of the best-known scientists in the field are terrific choices, specifically: Donald Johanson and Maitland Edey's (1982) *Lucy: The Beginnings of Humankind;* Don Johanson and James Shreeve's (1989) *Lucy's Child: The Discovery of a Human Ancestor;* and Richard Leakey and Roger Lewin's (1992) *Origins Reconsidered: In Search of What Makes Us Human.* Donald Johanson's latest book, co-authored by Lenora Johanson, his wife, and Blake Edgar (1994), *Ancestors: In Search of Human Origins,* brings the reader up to date on the latest discoveries in Africa and beyond, and covers the entire story of human evolution. The book was a companion to a PBS-TV series of the same name. The videos are available at many libraries and anthropology departments.

For books written by authors outside of paleoanthropology that chronicle the search for and analysis of the earliest hominids—and that expose the humanity behind the scientists involved in the search—see Delta Willis' (1989) *The Hominid Gang: Behind the Scenes in the Search for Human Origins* and noted science writer Roger Lewin's (1987) *Bones of Contention: Controversies in the Search for Human Origins.*

KEY TERMS

creation story	mandible	innominate
hominid	diastema	ilium
pongid	sagittal crest	ischium
Pongidae	Oldowan	femur
Hominidae	core	tibia
Australopithecine	flake	endocast
cranium	knapper	social system
postcranial	object piece	subsistence
humerus	hammerstone	taphonomic
ulna	striking platform	hypodigm
prognathous	Pleistocene Epoch	punctuated equilibrium
maxilla	turnover-pulse	sexual dimorphism

6

The Human Lineage

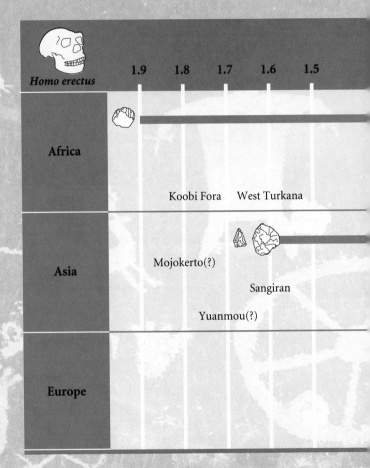

Homo erectus	1.9	1.8	1.7	1.6	1.5
Africa					
			Koobi Fora	West Turkana	
Asia					
		Mojokerto(?)			
				Sangiran	
		Yuanmou(?)			
Europe					

CHAPTER OVERVIEW

According to the fossil record of Africa, close to 1.8 million years ago a new hominid made its appearance on the evolutionary stage—*Homo erectus*. It possessed a brain larger than that of *Homo habilis* from which it evolved; the *Homo erectus* brain was two-thirds of the size of modern human brains.

Homo erectus exhibited increasing intelligence as well as an increased reliance on cultural adaptations. Though its anatomy was best suited to life in the tropics, *Homo erectus* expanded into other regions by at least 1 million years ago, and as much as 1.5 million years ago. A sophisticated stone tool technology, cooperative hunting, the controlled use of fire, clothing, and the possible construction of shelters were all a part of the *Homo erectus* adaptation. A reliance on culture is the hallmark of this human ancestor.

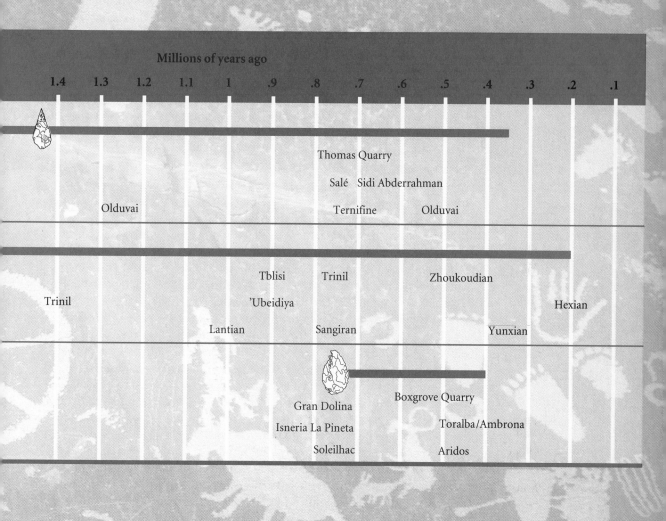

Millions of years ago

1.4 1.3 1.2 1.1 1 .9 .8 .7 .6 .5 .4 .3 .2 .1

Thomas Quarry

Salé   Sidi Abderrahman

Olduvai   Ternifine   Olduvai

Tblisi   Trinil   Zhoukoudian

Trinil   'Ubeidiya   Hexian

Lantian   Sangiran   Yunxian

Gran Dolina   Boxgrove Quarry

Isneria La Pineta   Toralba/Ambrona

Soleilhac   Aridos

PRELUDE

Woody Allen once remarked: "Some hope to achieve immortality through their works. I'd like to achieve it by not dying." How nice if such a thing were possible. Paleoanthropologists and archaeologists face the certainty of human mortality all the time—philosophically, theoretically, and personally. Our allotted life span of "three-score and ten" seems unjustly short and insignificant when compared to the millions of years of the human saga. Ironically, archaeologists continually deal with the remains of individuals who, paradoxically and contrary to Woody's wish, have achieved immortality, of a sort, precisely *by* dying.

As famed paleoanthropologist Richard Leakey (R. Leakey and Lewin 1992) admits, it sometimes is easy to forget that the bits and fragments, shards and slivers of fossilized bone we paleoanthropologists hold in our hands, place under our microscopes, and mount in museum displays were connected to actual, thinking, feeling beings. This may be partly because we're dealing with such small fragments. But sometimes we get lucky and recover the nearly complete skeleton of an individual—then it becomes impossible to forget we are looking at the remains of once-living creatures. The remains of the boy from Nariokotome, west of Lake Turkana, in Kenya, is one of those cases (R. Leakey and Walker 1985; Walker and Leakey 1993; Figure 6.1).

This boy was only eleven or twelve years old at the time of his death. Ironically, the age of the West Turkana boy is estimated the same way today's parents gauge the physical development of their own children: My older son, Josh, seven years old as I write this, has begun to lose his **deciduous dentition**—his baby teeth, shed like the leaves of deciduous trees—to be replaced by his **permanent dentition.** His twenty baby teeth will be replaced by his adult teeth, and, at the same time, permanent molars—the "six-year molars"—have now broken through the gum line in the back of his jaw, where there were no teeth previously. By adulthood, a total of 32 permanent teeth will fill his upper and lower jaws. The loss of the deciduous teeth and the appearance of the permanent teeth occur at fairly set times during an individual's life, so we can gauge our children's level of maturation by the timed loss of baby teeth and the fixed appearance of their six-year molars, their twelve-year molars, and their eighteen-year molars (the "wisdom teeth").

By the time of the Nariokotome boy's death, his first (six-year) and second (twelve-year) permanent molar teeth had already erupted; that is, they were above where the gum line would have been and, therefore, must have been exposed in his mouth. Both of his upper deciduous canines were still in place, and his permanent upper canine on the right side was just erupting (F. Brown et al. 1985:789; B. H. Smith 1993). None of his third molars had yet broken through. Thus, by using the rate of dental maturation for modern humans as a guide (Moorrees, Fanning, and Hunt 1963), we can conclude that the Turkana boy was probably about twelve years old at the time of his death (B. H. Smith 1993).

The cause of death of the West Turkana boy is a sad mystery. What we do know is that he was struck down in his youth, leaving a remarkably well pre-

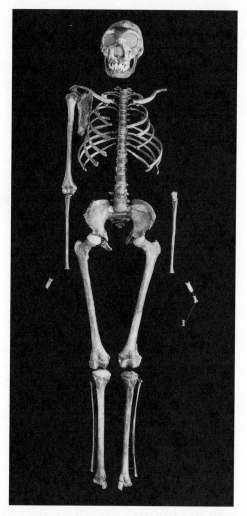

served, nearly complete skeleton that shows little except great health and vigor. Alan Walker, one of the fossil's excavators, describes him as a "strapping youth" and estimates his height at between 5 feet 4 inches and 5 feet 8 inches (R. Leakey and Lewin 1992). Except for some evidence of infection where he had lost a deciduous tooth, there is no sign of pathology on the skeleton, no evidence of disease, and no indication of trauma.

The West Turkana boy died on the edge of a lagoon near a lake. The position of his bones indicates that his body floated face down in the shallow water after he died. Fortunately, no scavengers picked at his corpse as it decayed, so most of the body remained pretty much in place, if not intact. Animals coming to the lagoon for a drink may have walked on the body, breaking one of the legs and scattering the rest of the bones as the flesh, muscle, and tissue that had once been a boy were washed away. After the soft parts had

FIGURE 6.2

This fossil cranium designated ER 3733, at nearly 1.8 million years of age, is the oldest known specimen of the fossil species Homo erectus. (National Museums of Kenya)

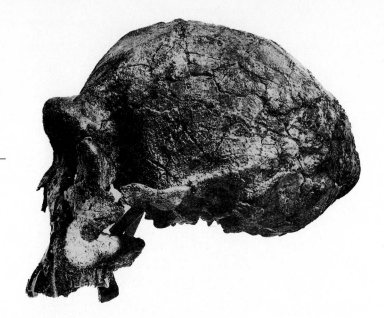

decayed, a gentle current dispersed the bones across a linear distance of about 7 m (slightly more than 21 ft). The bones were then covered in the mucky lake bottom by waterborne silt and ash from a nearby volcano, where they rested for close to 1.6 million years.

In August 1984, Kenyan paleontologist Kamoya Kimeu was scouting for fossils in Nariokotome, in an area that is now a dry lake bed. Kimeu was looking for fossils on his day off before the camp of paleontologists planned to move to another locality because so little of importance had been found in the area. Within a short time, he spotted a skull fragment, and an excavation was initiated. Soon the nearly complete skeletal remains of a boy were uncovered, revealing, with unprecedented clarity, an enormously ancient ancestor.

It is ironic that by dying in the right place at the right time, a young boy has achieved an immortality that none of us will probably attain. Even 1.6 million years after he lived, in a time and world we can barely imagine, people still ponder his life. We place him in the taxonomic category *Homo erectus,* and his people are the focus of this chapter.

CHRONICLE

Soon after 1.8 million years ago, a new form of hominid appears in the fossil record of eastern Africa. Potassium/argon dating has placed the oldest specimen—a skull labeled ER 3733 (Figure 6.2) from a rich fossil locality called Koobi Fora, east of Lake Turkana (R. Leakey and Walker 1985)—at about 1.78 million years ago (Feibel, Brown, and McDougal 1989). The species is given the name *Homo erectus*. Physically and culturally, *Homo erectus* is recognizably human, yet it is intriguingly different from us.

COLOR PORTFOLIO

COLOR PLATE 1
The so-called Ice Man of the Italian Alps was found by two German hikers in 1991. Entombed in the ice for 5,000 years, the Ice Man is perhaps the most dramatic example of a preserved ancient body now providing anthropologists with information about the lives of prehistoric people. (Chapter 3) © *Paul Hanny/Gamma Liaison*

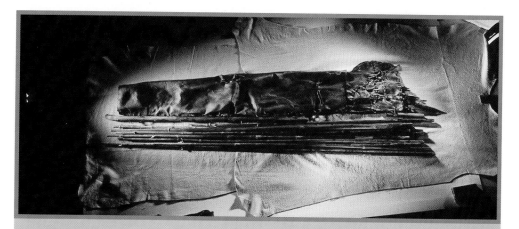

COLOR PLATE 2
The remarkable state of preservation of the Ice Man's equipment is exemplified by the leather quiver and arrow shafts found in the excavation immediately following the discovery. (Chapter 3) *Kenneth Garrett/National Geographic Image Collection*

COLOR PLATE 3
Chimpanzees are our nearest living relatives. A female (center) holds on to her offspring while being groomed from behind. (Chapter 4) © *Steve Turner/Animals, Animals*

APES
Insights on the Human Past

COLOR PLATE 4

A very impressive adult male silverback gorilla in his prime stands in a quadrupedal pose in his natural habitat in Zaire, Africa. (Chapter 4) © *B. G. Murray/Animals, Animals*

COLOR PLATE 5

Exhibiting the remarkable flexibility and climbing abilities of the Asian great ape species, this orangutan is holding onto a vine with its toes and the fingers of one hand while dipping the other hand in water for a drink. (Chapter 4) © *Konrad Wothe/Animals, Animals*

COLOR PLATE 6

A finely chipped, symmetrical Lower Paleolithic handaxe. Beginning nearly 1.5 million years ago, handaxes were sophisticated, multi-purpose tools made by the species *Homo erectus* in Africa, Europe, and western Asia. (Chapter 6) © *David L. Brill, Atlanta*

THE PALEOLITHIC
Technology and Art of Our Most Ancient Ancestors

Katanda 16   Katanda 9

COLOR PLATE 7

Barbed bone artifacts found in Katanda, Zaire in Africa. These sophisticated implements date to more than 90,000 years ago and may reflect the greater intelligence and technological sophistication of the first anatomically modern *Homo sapiens* when compared with archaic members of our species. (Chapter 8) *Alison Brooks, George Washington University*

COLOR PLATE 8

This fragment of a spear-thrower shows two ibexes wrestling. The fine carving of this artifact is characteristic of the Upper Paleolithic and is an example of the great skill and artistic abilities found during this period. (Chapter 9) *Musée de l'Homme; D. Destable*

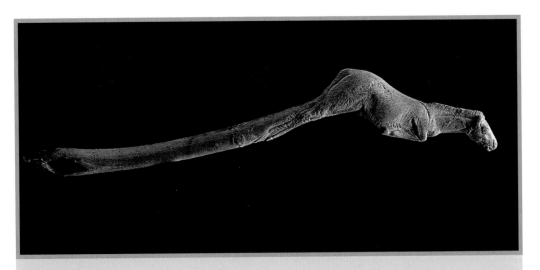

COLOR PLATE 9

This spear-thrower is a splendid example of the ability of Upper Paleolithic people to combine form and function. It comes from France and dates to the Magdalenian period. (Chapter 9) © *David L. Brill, Atlanta*

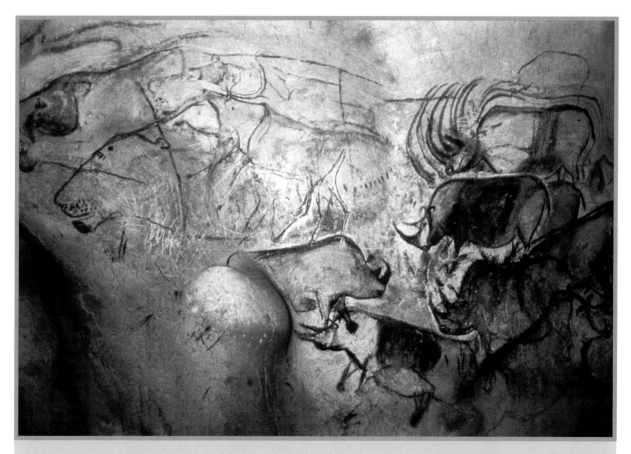

COLOR PLATE 10

Dating to earlier than 20,000 years ago, Upper Paleolithic artists painted more than 300 animals on this wall in Chauvet Cave in southern France. The paintings include these wonderful depictions of rhinoceroses and lions—animals that inhabited France during the Pleistocene Epoch. (Chapter 9) *AP/Wide World Photos*

COLOR PLATE 11

Carnivores have only rarely been found depicted in the cave art of the Upper Paleolithic; Chauvet Cave is a stunning exception. The large spotted bear and the smaller panther are only two of a large sample of bears, lions, and panthers on the walls of this cave found in December, 1994. (Chapter 9) *AP/Wide World Photos; Jean Clottes*

COLOR PLATE 12

An array of finely flaked fluted points from the Richey Clovis Cache were discovered in Washington state and are dated to 11,200 years ago. (Chapter 10) *Great Lakes Artifact Repository; Michael Gramly*

COLOR PLATE 13

A sample of the many varieties of maize grown today. The variability of maize was a key factor in the ability of agriculturalists to select for characteristics that would be advantageous in their particular region throughout the ancient Americas. (Chapter 12) © *David Cavagnaro/ Peter Arnold, Inc.*

COLOR PLATE 14

Built more than 4,000 years ago, the ziggurat at the Mesopotamian city of Ur is a testament to the ability of early state societies to conscript the labor of a large population to produce monumental public works. (Chapter 13) © *1994 Comstock*

COLOR PLATE 15

From the 4,000-year-old tomb of Puabi in ancient Sumeria, this gold bull-head harp exemplifies a number of elements unique to state societies. Clearly the product of a specialist, this object, made from rare and precious materials, served to symbolize the standing of a member of the ruling class in a stratified society. Full-time specialists and social stratification are hallmarks of the state. (Chapter 13) © *Boltin Picture Library; Lee Boltin*

COLOR PLATE 16

Crafted from gold and lapis lazuli (dark blue stone), the coffin lid of Egyptian pharaoh Tutankhamun is among the many splendid objects recovered from his tomb. The tomb symbolizes the wealth and power of the leaders of the world's ancient civilizations. (Chapter 13) *Boltin Picture Library; Lee Boltin*

COLOR PLATE 17

The sphinx of ancient Egypt was constructed more than 4,500 years ago and is an integral part of the Giza Necropolis that includes the largest pyramids built by the ancient Egyptians. (Chapter 13) *M. H. Feder*

COLOR PLATE 18

Two pyramids of the Giza Necropolis, including the burial chamber of the pharaoh Cheops (Khufu), behind the sphinx. Cheops's pyramid contains more than 2.5 million blocks of stone and stands 150 m (nearly 500 ft) high. (Chapter 13) *M. H. Feder*

COLOR PLATE 19

The citadel of Mohenjo-daro (background) looms over the remnants of neatly gridded streets lined with the houses of the Indus Valley civilization's elite social class. (Chapter 13)
© P. Agee/Anthro-Photo

COLOR PLATE 20

Bronze metallurgy played a significant role in the development of ancient Chinese civilization. This charming casting of a baby elephant perched atop an adult elephant was found at An-yang, a capital city of the Shang civilization. (Chapter 13) *Ceremonial covered vessel of the type* huo, *in the form of an elephant. Chinese, Shang, late An-yang, 11th century* B.C. *Wooden stand. Surface: a light green patina. Courtesy of the Freer Gallery of Art, Smithsonian Institution, Washington, D.C.*

COLOR PLATE 21

Olmec jade carving of a human figure found in the Mexican Gulf Coast state of Vera Cruz. Jade figurines played an important role in Olmec religious expression in a broad geographical area in Mesoamerica. (Chapter 14) *Transparency #K9857; courtesy Department of Library Services, © American Museum of Natural History*

COLOR PLATE 22

The "Kunz Axe" is an Olmec ceremonial jade carving of an axe with a human-like face. (Chapter 14) *Transparency #K9849; courtesy Department of Library Services, © American Museum of Natural History*

COLOR PLATE 23

The impressive Temple I (Temple of the Giant Jaguar) at the Maya site of Tikal in Guatemala, a pre-Columbian city of some 50,000 people. Built around A.D. 700, Temple I towers 45 m (145 ft) above the Great Plaza. (Chapter 14) *Courtesy Michael Alan Park*

COLOR PLATE 24

The "Nunnery" Quadrangle and the Pyramid of the Magician at the Maya site of Uxmal in the central Yucatán Peninsula. Uxmal reached its peak in the so-called Post-Classic period, after the fall of Maya cities to the south. (Chapter 14) *K. L. Feder*

COLOR PLATE 25

An exquisite gold object from one of the very impressive elite Moche culture burials at Sípan, Peru in South America. (Chapter 14) © *UCLA Fowler Museum of Cultural History; Susan Einstein*

COLOR PLATE 26:

The Pyramid of the Sun at the ancient city of Teotihuacán in central Mexico. This pyramid, with a volume of more than 1 million cubic meters (more than 10 million cubic feet), was the centerpiece of a city whose population ultimately exceeded 125,000 by its peak at A.D. 600. (Chapter 14) *M. H. Feder*

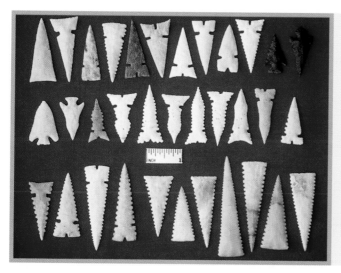

COLOR PLATE 27

A sample of finely chipped projectile points from a grouping of more than 1000 that were recovered from the burial of a member of the ruling elite at Cahokia in Illinois. (Chapter 15) *Cahokia Mounds State Historic Site*

COLOR PLATE 28

The Square Tower House ruin is nestled in a niche at the base of a cliff in Mesa Verde in Colorado. With names like "Cliff Palace," "Balcony House," and "Spruce Tree House," the cliff dwellings of Mesa Verde were the products of a sophisticated chiefdom society that flourished more than 500 years ago in the American Southwest. (Chapter 15) *K. L. Feder*

COLOR PLATE 29

The temple/palace of Angkor Wat represents the culmination of architectural complexity of the ancient Khmer civilization of Southeast Asia. (Chapter 15) © *J. Halpern/ Anthro-Photo*

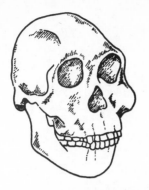 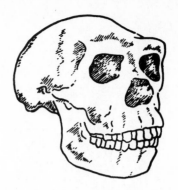

FIGURE 6.3

In this comparison of the skulls of Homo habilis *and* Homo erectus, *the skull of* erectus *is seen to be larger and more modern (less ape-like) than that of* habilis.

Homo habilis   *Homo erectus*

THE APPEARANCE OF *HOMO ERECTUS*

The cranium of this new member of the human lineage was quite different from that of its evolutionary antecedent, *Homo habilis* [Figure 6.3; and see Rightmire (1990) for a detailed, technical discussion of the anatomy of *erectus*]. To begin with, its skull, and by implication its brain, was significantly larger. Most specimens have cranial volumes in excess of 800 ml, and the species as a whole has a mean cranial capacity of close to 1,000 ml (see Table 6.1). The Nariokotome boy's cranial capacity was 880 ml; it is estimated that his brain size, had he lived to adulthood, would have been a little over 900 ml (Begun and Walker 1993:346). The largest members of the hypodigm have skulls with volumes over 1,200 ml. This places the brain size of the species far above that of *Homo habilis* and within the lower range of modern human beings.

The skull of *erectus* was not just larger than that of *habilis,* it was differently configured and differently proportioned in ways that signify a shift toward a more modern human appearance. For example, the forehead of *erectus* is somewhat flatter and less sloping than that of *habilis,* a bit more similar to the modern, virtually vertical, human forehead. The back, or **occipital,** portion of the *erectus* skull is rounder than that of *habilis,* with a much larger area for muscle attachment. Larger and stronger muscles were needed to support its much larger, heavier skull.

Analysis of cranial endocasts (see Chapter 5) of a number of *Homo erectus* specimens (Holloway 1980, 1981) shows intriguing similarities to the modern human brain. Most significantly, anthropologist Ralph Holloway discovered hemispheric asymmetry in the *erectus* brain, similar to that seen in modern human beings. The different halves, or hemispheres of the human brain regulate different tasks; in particular, human speech is ordinarily controlled by the left hemisphere. As a result, the two halves of a human brain are of slightly different shape, proportion, and size. Whether the asymmetry in the endocasts of the *erectus* brain means they were capable of humanlike speech cannot be determined. But the configuration of the *erectus* brain was

TABLE 6.1

Major Homo erectus Fossils Discussed in Chapter 6

COUNTRY	LOCALITY	FOSSILS	CRANIA	AGE	BRAIN SIZE (ML)
Java	Trinil	Skull cap, femur	"Java Man"	<1 million yrs	940
	Sangiran	Cranial and postcranial fragments from approx. 40 individuals	S-2	0.7–1.6 million yrs	800
			S-4	0.7–1.6 million yrs	900
			S-10	0.7–1.6 million yrs	850
			S-12	0.7–1.6 million yrs	1,050
			S-17	0.7–1.6 million yrs	1,000
			1993 Cranium	1.1–1.4 million yrs	856
	Ngandong	Cranial and postcranial fragments from over a dozen individuals	N-1	<1 million yrs	1,170
			N-6	<1 million yrs	1,250
			N-11	<1 million yrs	1,230
			N-12	<1 million yrs	1,090
	Sambungmachan		Sambungmachan	<1 million yrs	1,000
	Modjokerto	Child's cranium		1.8 million years?	
China	Zhoukoudian	Cranial and postcranial remains of over 40 individuals	II	<0.46 million yrs	1,030
			III	<0.46 million yrs	915
			VI	<0.46 million yrs	850
			X	<0.46 million yrs	1,225
			XI	<0.46 million yrs	1,015
			XII	<0.46 million yrs	1,030
			Locality 13	0.7 million yrs	
	Hexian (Longtandong)	Partial skull	"Hexian Man"	0.27 million yrs?	1,000

COUNTRY	LOCALITY	FOSSILS	CRANIA	AGE	BRAIN SIZE (ML)
China (cont.)	Lantian (Gongwangling)	Cranial fragments, mandible	"Lantian Man"	0.7–0.8 million yrs	800
	Yunxian	Two crania		>0.35 million yrs	
Tanzania	Olduvai	Cranial and postcranial fragments, including mandibles and pelvis and long-bone fragments	OH 9	1.25 million yrs	1,060
			OH 12	0.6–0.8 million yrs	800
Kenya	East Turkana	Cranial and postcranial fragments including mandibles and pelvis and long-bone fragments	KNM-ER 3733	1.78 million yrs	850
			KNM-ER 3883	1.57 million yrs	800
	West Turkana	Nearly complete juvenile individual	KNM-WT 15000	1.5 million yrs	880
Algeria	Ternifine	Three mandibles and a skull fragment		0.5–0.7 million yrs	
Morocco	Thomas Quarries	Mandible and skull fragments		0.5 million yrs	
	Sidi Abderrahman	Two mandible fragments			
	Salé	Skull fragments	Salé	0.4 million yrs	880
	Tbilisi	Mandible fragment, 16 teeth		0.9–1.6 million yrs	
England	Boxgrove Quarry	Tibia		0.48–0.51 million yrs	
				Mean	971.96
				Standard Deviation	116.50

Data from: Walker and Leakey (1993); Feibel et al. (1989); Holloway (1980, 1981); Rightmire (1990).

definitely more like that of modern human beings, and different from that of the chimp, gorilla, orangutan, australopithecine, and *habilis* specimens to which Holloway compared them.

On the issue of speech capability, researchers Jeffrey Laitman and R. C. Heimbuch (1984) concluded that the base of the *erectus* cranium—the **basicranium**—is far more like that of modern humans than of *Homo habilis* or apes. Because the muscles involved in the production of speech are connected to the basicranium, this may indicate that the physical capability for human or humanlike speech production was present in *Homo erectus*. From this, Laitman has concluded (Bower 1989:25) that *Homo erectus* could produce human speech at the level of a modern six-year-old. (Ask any first-grade teacher how fast and loud that is, and you can see that *Homo erectus* was probably not limited physically in the ability to speak.)

Beneath the intriguingly humanlike brain, the *erectus* face itself is somewhat flatter, projecting less than the *habilis* face, though it still is far more prognathous than that of a modern human. Above the eye orbits, *Homo erectus* crania display a massive ridge of bone called a **supraorbital torus.** This "brow ridge" is present in the skulls of all ape species and is generally absent in the modern human form, though some people, especially males, exhibit relatively smaller but discernible ridges above their eyes.

From the front, the *erectus* skull presents a flattened trapezoidal shape as opposed to the corresponding, very round appearance of a modern human skull. The sides of the *erectus* skull begin nearly parallel at the base, then angle inward toward the top. This provides a keel, but not a bony crest, at the apex of the skull. Also, preserved nasal bones indicate that *erectus* was the first of our ancestors to possess the modern human form of a projecting nose, rather than the inset nostrils that characterize the living apes and earlier hominids (Franciscus and Trinkaus 1988).

Below the skull, the bones of *Homo erectus* bear witness to a creature that indisputably walked upright, in a manner similar, if not identical, to that of modern human beings. To be sure, the West Turkana boy and other, more fragmentary postcranial remains exhibit a skeletal architecture indicative of great muscularity and strength, probably outside the range of modern human beings. Nonetheless, as more than one paleoanthropologist has stated, you would not be alarmed if a *Homo erectus,* with a cap pulled down low over his or her forehead and face and appropriately dressed, were to sit down next to you in class (and he, or she, might appear to be an ideal candidate for the football team!).

It had long been assumed that nonmodern hominids were smaller in stature than modern humans. Certainly, Lucy was tiny (see Chapter 5), and many of the Neandertal fossils indicate a short, stout body shape for these extinct hominids (see Chapter 7). The Nariokotome boy, however, shows that relatively short stature was not universal among our ancient ancestors. At about 5½ ft in height at only twelve years of age, he was tall, even by modern standards. Since he was still developing (see the Issues and Debates section in this chapter), he certainly would have grown even taller; at full growth he may have been a six-footer.

THE EVOLUTIONARY POSITION OF *HOMO ERECTUS*

Current consensus is that *Homo erectus* is the direct evolutionary descendant of the African hominid species *Homo habilis.* The oldest *erectus* fossils are found in Africa, often in the same areas where *habilis* remains have been recovered (Map 6.1). Fossils like the Nariokotome boy (officially designated KNM-WT 15000), ER 3733, ER 3833, and OH 9 share the standard suite of *erectus* cranial characteristics and date to between 1.78 million years ago and 1.25 million years ago (Figure 6.4; Rightmire 1979a, 1990). Later African *erectus* remains, dating from between 500,000–800,000 years ago, include the OH 12 calvarium from Olduvai Gorge in Tanzania, a skull fragment and three mandibles from Ternifine (now called Tighenif) in Algeria, and skull and mandible fragments at Thomas Quarries, a braincase from Salé, and two mandibles from Sidi Abderrahman, all in Morocco. These later fossils are quite similar, where comparisons can be made, to the older African material.

In terms of cranial capacity and morphology, all of the African *erectus*

MAP 6.1

Fossil localities of Homo erectus.

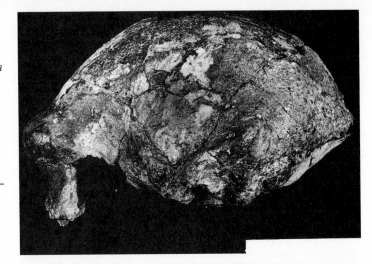

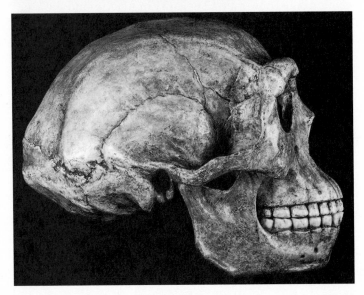

fossils reflect a position midway between *Homo habilis* and anatomically modern human beings. *Erectus* is interpreted as representing, therefore, an "evolved" *Homo habilis.* In this construct, evolution within the *Homo* line is actually far simpler than that seen within the australopithecine line, with its multiple contemporaneous species. However, notice that the oldest *erectus* fossil is very close in time, and perhaps even overlaps slightly, with the youngest *habilis* fossils. This may mean that the situation is a bit more complex than the current consensus view would have it. We will deal with this issue in greater detail in the Issues and Debates section in this chapter.

WORLD CONQUERORS

A comparison of Maps 5.1 and 6.1 should show a significant difference. Whereas all the australopithecine and *Homo habilis* sites were located within the boundaries of Africa, sites producing *Homo erectus* fossils or artifacts dated to the period of *Homo erectus* are far more widespread, with localities in Europe and Asia as well as Africa (Rightmire 1991b). This reflects one of the most important characteristics of *erectus:* Though originating in Africa from *habilis* roots, this new species soon spread throughout much of the Old World. If a major theme of the previous chapter was that our ancestors were first distinguished from the apes by the ability to walk on two feet, then a major focus of this chapter is where that ability took them.

Asia: The Middle East

When charting the movement of *Homo erectus* out of Africa and into Asia, it is clear that populations of the hominid must have traveled through northeast Africa and into southwest Asia before moving further east. Though the fossil record for later periods is quite rich for the area we now call the Middle East (see Chapter 7), this is not true for the time period in question here, around 1.5 million years ago or more. As a result, there are very few sites that may be associated with *Homo erectus* in southwest Asia. Perhaps the oldest and most important site is 'Ubeidiya in the Jordan Valley (Bar-Yosef 1980). There are no hominid remains at the site, but there is a recognizable *Homo erectus* tool assemblage consisting of stone choppers, picks, and bifaces (see the discussion of *Homo erectus* toolmaking later in this chapter). 'Ubeidiya is estimated to be close to 1.4 million years old.

Asia: Java

Ironically, some of the most important, well-known, and earliest discoveries of *Homo erectus* fossils were made not in Africa, but in east Asia, at the geographic end point of their expansion. Newly applied dating procedures place some of the Java specimens at about the same antiquity as the oldest African *erectus* fossils.

In a remarkable instance of intuition, Dutch physician Eugene Dubois (1894) traveled to the island of Java in the western Pacific in the late nineteenth century expressly to seek out evidence of human origins in the Asian tropics. In 1891, along the Solo River in the vicinity of the town of Trinil, he came upon a **calvarium**—the top part of the cranium, minus the facial bones and the base of the skull—that looked not quite human but not quite apelike

(Figure 6.5). It possessed large brow ridges like those of apes. But the cranial capacity, as best as could be judged at the time, was far larger than an ape's while still smaller than a modern human's. Dubois labeled the find *Pithecanthropus erectus,* meaning "upright ape-man." Still popularly referred to as "Java Man," we now include Dubois' discovery in the *Homo erectus* hypodigm. Its 940-ml estimated cranial capacity and its age (still uncertain but probably about 1 million years old) place it firmly in the *erectus* species.

Also along the Solo River, northeast of Trinil, is the site of Ngandong. About a dozen crania were found here in the 1930s (Santa Luca 1980; Bartstra, Soegondho, and Wijk 1988). Though their skulls are quite large when compared to the other *Homo erectus* specimens contained in the hypodigm, Philip Rightmire (1990) in his summary monograph on the species provides a detailed analysis that indicates that the Ngandong fossils belong in the same taxonomic group.

Just 40 miles east of Trinil, another important fossil locality, called Sangiran, was found in 1937. The cranial remains of about 40 individuals have been recovered (see Figure 6.4). Some of the crania are more complete than the Trinil calvarium and share its form and size (Holloway 1981).

Most of the Javanese hominid remains were found more than fifty years ago—primarily by local farmers and other workers, and not in controlled archaeological excavations. This has rendered dating the specimens a bit problematical, for it is difficult to be certain which geological deposit, and precisely where in the deposit, the material originated. Scientists are pretty sure of the geological formation from which they were recovered—called the **Kabuh Formation;** its estimated age is about 700,000–800,000 years, so the hominids are presumed to be about this old.

A recent discovery may change this assumption. Paleoanthropologist Donald Tyler has identified another skull unearthed by farmers at Sangiran (Mark Rose 1993). It is clearly a *Homo erectus,* with a cranial capacity of 856 ml. In this case, however, Tyler has been able to associate the skull with a specific geological deposit more precisely than was possible with the earlier Sangiran discoveries. He has dated the age of the deposit to between 1.1 million years ago and 1.4 million years ago. Either of these dates would push back the

Homo erectus expansion out of Africa fairly significantly. Tyler is excavating at the site in hopes of finding additional evidence of the *Homo erectus* occupation and to date more confidently the newly found specimen. The possibility that some of the Java material may date back even further is discussed in the Issues and Debates section in this chapter.

Asia: China

One of the most important *Homo erectus* sites ever discovered is in the village of Zhoukoudian, about 50 km (35 mi) southwest of Beijing. The cave at the site and the surrounding area produced the remains of about 45 *Homo erectus* individuals in a region possessing a continental climate, then and now, not unlike the northern United States—obviously a far cry from tropical Africa, where the species originated. Occupation of the main site (Locality 1) by "Peking Man" has been dated through thermoluminescence, electron spin resonance, uranium series, and fission track dating to between about 600,000 and 230,000 years ago, though a maximum date of 462,000 years is considered more accurate for the earliest occupation of the site (Pope 1992). Another site, located about 1 km south of the original Peking Man cave site, Locality 13, has been dated to 700,000 years ago (Jia and Huang 1990).

Of great importance is the evidence in the cave site that *Homo erectus*, at least toward the end of its occupation of the area, had mastered the use of fire. The issue of the controlled use of fire by *Homo erectus* is dealt with in the Issues and Debates section in this chapter. More details concerning the site, its discovery, and its significance—and the tragic mystery of the disappearance of the fossils more than fifty years ago—are provided in this chapter's Case Study Close-Up.

Chinese paleoanthropology has produced a number of other, important *Homo erectus* discoveries. The Lantian skull from Gongwangling Hill of Shensi Province in east-central China has been dated to at least 500,000 years ago; new dating indicates it may be a bit more than 1 million years old (Chen and Zhang 1991). The Lantian cranium had a capacity of about 800 ml (Woo 1966). Its large brow ridges and broad face are very close in appearance to that of the Zhoukoudian fossils.

The remains of at least three individuals, including the nearly complete calvarium of a young male, were found near the village of Longtandong in Hexian County, Anhui Province, in eastern China. It has an estimated cranial capacity of about 1,000 ml (Wu and Xingren 1982; Wu 1985). The Hexian material seems to be the youngest *Homo erectus* specimens yet discovered; thermoluminescence and uranium series dating place the specimen at somewhere between 150,000 and 270,000 years ago (Pope 1992). This late date, if it holds up, indicates that late populations of *Homo erectus* were contemporary with early groups of *Homo sapiens* in China (see Chapter 7).

The latest discoveries of *Homo erectus* in China are the crania of two individuals found in Yunxian in Hubei Province in the east-central part of the country (Li and Etler 1992). These are quite large and complete, though very distorted. The researchers estimate a minimum age of 350,000 years for the two crania, which present an interesting mix of features similar to both the Zhoukoudian material and later, more modern-looking human ancestors. Much work needs to be done restoring these very important fossils before their significance can be fully assessed.

Asia: Siberia

Recent work at a site on the Lena River in Siberia in Russia may represent the farthest east extent of *Homo erectus,* and their adaptation to the coldest climate (Bower 1994b). Called the Diring site, it may date to about 500,000 years ago (claims of a 2-million-year age have been roundly rejected, and even the 500,000-year age is doubted by many). No hominid fossils have been found here, but a large assemblage of stone tools has been recovered. Since the climate in and around Diring is far colder than anything previously known for *Homo erectus* and since no other sites in Siberia are known to date to before 35,000 years ago, most paleoanthropologists are skeptical about the site and its association with *erectus.*

Europe

We have seen how *Homo erectus* appeared first in Africa nearly 1.8 million years ago and spread to east Asia by at least 1 million years ago, and perhaps even substantially earlier. Europe, on the other hand, seems to have been settled fairly late by the species. In the early 1980s, paleoanthropologist Christopher B. Stringer (1981:12) could reasonably state: "I do not accept as yet proven that *H. erectus* existed in Europe during the middle and later parts of the middle Pleistocene." In their review of the paleontological record of Europe, Cook et al. (1982:54) concluded that "[p]rior to about 350 ky [thousand years], evidence for human activity in Europe is extremely scarce." Even Philip Rightmire's (1990) broad review of the species does not cite a single European example of *Homo erectus.*

Those few European sites that date to soon after the inception of *Homo erectus* expansion beyond Africa at about 1 million years ago include Gran Dolina in Spain, Isneria La Pineta in central Italy, Vallonet Cave and Soleilhac in France, and Kärlich in Germany. All of these sites date to after 1 million years ago; Gran Dolina dates to 780,000 years ago (Carbonell et al. 1995), Isneria La Pineta to 730,000 years ago (Coltorti et al. 1982), and Soleilhac to 800,000 years ago (Weaver 1985). The most recently excavated site, Gran Dolina, has produced the oldest hominid skeletal evidence in western Europe: 36 bone fragments representing 4 individuals.

Nevertheless, the dearth of evidence for *Homo erectus* in Europe before 500,000 years ago may reflect the fact that despite attempts by African hominids to move north by or before about 1 million years ago, conditions did not allow for the successful expansion of hominids into that continent. Researcher Alan Turner (1992) cites as a possible explanation the extremely rich faunal record in Europe for the period 1.5–0.5 million years ago related to large carnivore species adapted for scavenging. Some of these European fossil carnivores exhibit teeth and jaws adapted for crushing bones and devouring virtually an entire carcass after it had been abandoned by the large flesh-eating cats that killed the prey in the first place. In such a setting, *Homo erectus* might have been faced with extremely heavy competition for animal carcasses to scavenge. If scavenging was a major part of the *Homo erectus* subsistence strategy (see the Issues and Debates section), then this may be a viable explanation for the apparent lack of success of the species in Europe during this period.

By 500,000 years ago, the predator and scavenger populations in Europe had become similar to those in Africa, where hominids had been thriving for close to 3.5 million years. In fact, it is after about 500,000 years ago that stone tools become common in the archaeological record, and it is clear that *Homo erectus* was present in some numbers. Unfortunately, their fossil remains have not been forthcoming; just a few years ago, Philip Rightmire correctly characterized European *Homo erectus* remains so far recovered as little more than "a few bits of human bone" (1991b:183). Recent, encouraging discoveries include a fragment of a fossilized tibia, or shinbone, recovered from Boxgrove quarry in West Sussex, England, together with typical *Homo erectus* tools (see the later discussion). The specimen has been dated to between 515,000 and 485,000 years ago (Bahn 1994).

THE AGE OF ICE

In 1991, one of the largest volcanic eruptions of the twentieth century occurred on Mt. Pinatubo in the Philippines. The eruption had an impact on worldwide climate as tons of fine ash wafted into the upper atmosphere and circled the globe. The ash cloud actually blocked out sufficient sunlight to drop the earth's temperature by a few degrees, enough to be the probable cause of the long, cold winter experienced in the northern hemisphere after the eruption.

As significant as the eruption of Mt. Pinatubo was, and as serious as its climatic impact may have been, it pales in comparison to the change in worldwide climate whose first impacts were felt about 3.2 million years ago (see Chapter 5), and which accelerated after 2.5 million and then again at about 1.6 million or 1.7 million years ago (Shackleton et al. 1984). For reasons that are still uncertain, beginning at this time the earth became a significantly colder place, particularly after about 900,000 years ago, with northern latitudes and higher elevations becoming covered by huge, expanding ice fields

FIGURE 6.6

Worldwide glacial coverage during the peak periods of glaciation in the Pleistocene Epoch.

called **glaciers** (Shackleton and Opdyke 1973, 1976; Figure 6.6). One of the proposed explanations, in fact, is that the earth entered a period of intense volcanic activity—like Mt. Pinatubo except hundreds or even thousands of times over. Other hypotheses blame the descent into colder temperatures on a decrease in solar output, interplanetary dust, or a change in the earth's orbit.

This colder period of time is called the **Pleistocene Epoch** (see Figure 4.2 for a time chart placing the Pleistocene chronologically in the history of the earth). By convention, its inception is marked at 1.7–1.6 million years ago, though some push it back to the sharp worldwide temperature decrease that occurred 2.5 million years ago (Stipp, Chappell, and McDougall 1967). Researchers mark the end of the Pleistocene at 10,000 years ago, when worldwide temperature rose and glaciers shrunk. The modern period is called the **Holocene Epoch.** Some researchers believe the Holocene truly demarcates the end of the cold temperatures of the Pleistocene. Others disagree, holding that we are currently in a relatively warm period that is destined to end in only a few thousand years.

Though initially conceptualized and still commonly thought of as an "Ice Age" of unremitting cold, the Pleistocene actually was an epoch of fluctuating climate, with periods called **glacials** much colder than the present. These glacials were characterized by widespread ice and snow cover—imagine most of the central and northern United States and Canada and much of northern Europe looking and feeling like Greenland. But within the glacials themselves were colder and warmer periods, with attendant glacial advances (**stadials**) and retreats (**interstadials**). Between the glacials were relatively long **interglacial** periods during which temperature often approached, sometimes equaled, and rarely may even have exceeded the modern level. If the ice age is, in fact, not over, then we are probably currently in an interglacial.

The pattern of temperature fluctuation and glacial advance and retreat can be studied in a number of ways. Glaciers leave significant and recognizable features as they cover the land. If you live in the northern third of the United States or virtually anywhere in Canada, then you can still see the effects of the huge, moving continental sheets and rivers of ice, some a few kilometers thick, as they rode over everything in their path. Glacial geologists can read a landscape for its glacial deposits, which can then be dated to develop a chronology of glaciation, as each subsequent expansion of ice overrode the previous one [see Richard Foster Flint's (1971) *Glacial and Quaternary Geology* for the classic work on the New World Pleistocene].

The Oxygen Isotope Curve

The worldwide sequence of glacial advances and retreats can also be studied indirectly, via the ratio of two isotopes (varieties) of oxygen (^{16}O:^{18}O) present in the preserved, dateable shells of ancient marine microorganisms called **foraminifera.** The foram shells reflect the ^{16}O:^{18}O ratio in seawater when they were alive. That ratio changes depending on how much of the ocean's seawater evaporates, falls on the land as snow, and then does *not* melt back into the ocean as worldwide temperature declines. Because ^{16}O is lighter than ^{18}O, water (H_2O) molecules containing ^{16}O are lighter and, therefore, evaporate more readily than water molecules with ^{18}O. During cold periods, water evaporates from the oceans and falls as snow in higher elevations and upper latitudes, and less of the snow melts off in the spring. The ocean, therefore, becomes somewhat depleted of ^{16}O relative to ^{18}O. The curve representing the relative proportion of ^{16}O:^{18}O has been determined by Shackleton and Opdyke (1973, 1976). Their results are presented in Figure 6.7. Covering the last 780,000 years, a bit less than the last half of the Pleistocene, the Shackleton and Opdyke chronology exhibits ten periods of drops in ^{16}O and, therefore, significantly colder temperatures and greater ice cover on the earth's surface. Further research has indicated at least ten additional such periods in the first half of the Pleistocene.

All of this climatic instability must have affected our hominid ancestors. Chapter 5 discussed the possibly key role the climate change, which dated to around 2.5 million years ago, may have had in the evolution of *Homo habilis*. Though *Homo erectus* did not penetrate into areas where there were large continental ice sheets after 1.7 million years ago, all of the earth was influenced during the Pleistocene. Sea level dropped substantially, perhaps by as much as 125 m (more than 400 ft), during glacial maxima. Such a drop altered the configuration of most of the world's coasts, exposing as dry land

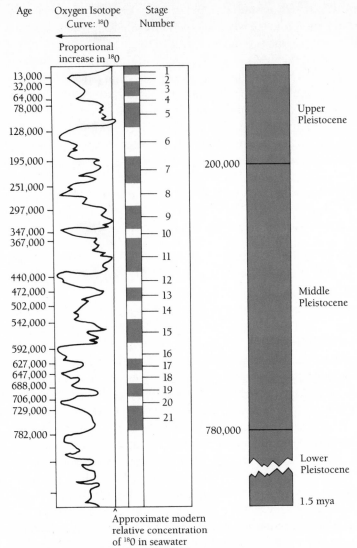

FIGURE 6.7

The Shackleton and Opdyke curve of ^{18}O concentration in fossil foraminifera is an indirect reflection of glacial expansion and contraction during the last 780,000 years.

Odd numbered stages (in color) = warmer periods, less glacial ice cover
Even-numbered stages = colder periods, more glacial ice cover

thousands of square kilometers that previously and presently are under water. The climate of areas even far south of the furthest extent of the glaciers changed, as low-pressure systems altered their usual flow patterns. These changes certainly altered the conditions to which *Homo erectus* needed to adapt. Adaptive flexibility seems to have been a hallmark of the members of this species. Their ability to inhabit new regions with environmental conditions far different from their tropical source, as well as their ability to change as their surroundings altered, bear witness to their great intelligence and, in fact, their humanity (see the Issues and Debates section).

FIGURE 6.8

The Acheulean handaxe, a tool of Homo erectus *in Europe and Africa. These two examples were found in France.* (K. L. Feder)

HOMO ERECTUS: THE TOOLMAKER

The great advance in toolmaking represented by *Homo erectus* as compared to *Homo habilis* is made clear by the following anecdote.

In a class I teach called "Experimental Archaeology," we spend a lot of time trying to replicate, as authentically as possible, various stone tools made by prehistoric people. We follow a chronological, evolutionary sequence, first replicating the Oldowan tools of *Homo habilis,* then making copies of the **Acheulean handaxe** (named for the French site of St. Acheul, where they were first identified) that typifies *Homo erectus,* at least in Africa and Europe (Figure 6.8). The earliest and simplest handaxes have been found in Africa and can be dated to about 1.4 million years ago. Earlier tools (prior to 1.4 million years ago) made by *Homo erectus* give the appearance of advanced Oldowan choppers. There seems to have been a slow development of the far more complex handaxe from the simpler Oldowan chopper after the first appearance of *erectus* in Africa sometime after 1.8 million years ago. Interestingly, the handaxe is found nearly exclusively in Africa and Europe. It is rarely—some claim never—found at eastern Asian *Homo erectus* sites. *Homo erectus* probably spread out of Africa and into Asia before its invention in Africa, which would explain why the early *Homo erectus* sites in eastern Asia lack that tool. It is still a mystery why the tool didn't make it into Asia later on.

Students generally have little trouble making impressive versions of Oldowan choppers and flake tools—with a little elbow grease, and after mastering the proper striking angle of hammerstone on core. This is not the case, however, for the *Homo erectus* handaxe, which is not easy to make, at least

FIGURE 6.9

Through a process of bifacial flaking, a symmetrical, finely made handaxe was produced. Compare this to the process for producing Oldowan tools (see Figure 5.14). (Noel G. Coonce)

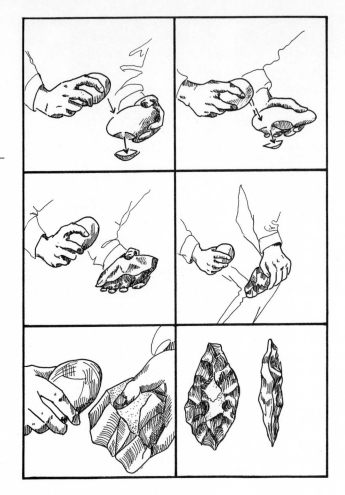

not without lots of practice, knowledge, and time. Very few of my students ever develop proficiency in handaxe production.

This comes as no surprise. To produce an Oldowan tool takes very few steps, and the process affords wide latitude for variation: With only three or four blows from a hammerstone, and little precision in placing the blows, you can make such a tool. A handaxe is another thing entirely. Handaxes are symmetrical, finely flaked, and often aesthetically exquisite (see Figure 6.8 and the Paleolithic Portfolio, Color Plate 6). Dozens of flakes are removed from the core, not just a few (Figure 6.9). Even quite simple handaxes, such as the earliest known examples, from the site of Konso-Gardula in Ethiopia (Asfaw et al. 1992) and dated to 1.4 million years ago, can take 25 individual hammer strikes. The best-made examples, which date to after 1 million years ago in Africa and more recently in Europe, took nearly three times that number (Constable 1973:128). Each flake blow must be located precisely in order to allow for the proper positioning of the next strike. The stone must be turned over again and again between hammer strikes, to maintain symmetry and to keep the edge of the tool straight. All or, at least, most of the exterior rind, or **cortex,** of the object piece was removed in order to keep the tool relatively thin and light, so flakes needed to shoot across the face of the axe at the same time that the edge was being maintained. This takes great skill, precision, and strength.

Experimental archaeologist Mark Newcomer (1971) has replicated hand-axes, determining that at least some were made in three separate steps. First, a blank, or **preform,** was roughed out with a stone hammer into the general shape of the desired end product. Then, the preform was refined via a second stage of percussion with another, softer stone or even a piece of antler used in thinning the tool. Finally, the edges were straightened and sharpened in one last application of percussion. All the work was worth it: For the same mass of stone, a handaxe produces about four times more cutting edge than an Oldowan chopper and, at the same time, yields far more usable, sharp flakes. Newcomer (1971), during the production of a single handaxe, produced more than fifty flakes usable as is for cutting or scraping.

The handaxe appears to have been an all-purpose tool (a colleague of mine calls them the "Swiss Army rocks" of the Pleistocene). Its sharp tip was used for piercing, the thin edges for cutting, and the steeper-angled edges toward the butt of the tool for scraping or chopping. Archaeologist Patricia O'Brien (1984) even suggests that it may have been used as a projectile, thrown like a discus at fleeing game animals. The flakes removed during manufacture were used on the basis of their form and thickness.

SUBSISTENCE

Remember the major issue concerning the subsistence base of *Homo habilis:* Were they hunters of big game, or merely scavengers of remnants of kills left by carnivores? As a whole, the evidence supports the view that *Homo habilis* had a broad and opportunistic subsistence strategy: Big-game hunting was probably not preeminent, but hunting, scavenging, and gathering wild plants together provided subsistence for *Homo habilis.*

The evidence regarding *Homo erectus* as a big-game hunter is not much stronger than for *Homo habilis.* For example, the sites of Torralba and Ambrona in Spain, which date to about 350,000 years ago, are located on two hills overlooking a valley that served as a natural pass for large game animals on their seasonal migrations during the Pleistocene. Though no *Homo erectus* remains were found at the site, lots of tools and the remains of 55 elephants, 26 horses, 25 deer, 10 wild cattle, and 6 rhinoceroses were recovered (Freeman 1973).

It seems clear from the evidence of tools as well as cut marks on the bones

(Shipman and Rose 1983) that *Homo erectus* was present at the site and cut some meat off the animal carcasses. However, because the bones themselves were so badly weathered, it cannot be concluded that the animals were hunted, killed, and then systematically butchered by the hominids (Binford 1987b). In fact, the faunal and lithic remains at both Torralba and Ambrona are better evidence for opportunistic scavenging of animals already dead than for big-game hunting by *Homo erectus* (Binford 1987b; Klein 1987).

Better evidence, at least of butchery, comes from the nearby sites of Aridos 1 and 2, 18 km southeast of Madrid, Spain (Villa 1990). Both sites produced a single, apparently butchered elephant, dating to probably about 350,000 years ago. Mixed in with the bones were the tools used to cut off the meat, as well as the waste flakes produced in sharpening the cutting and scraping tools.

While there is no evidence of hunting at either Aridos site—no spearpoints were found, for example—there also is no evidence that *Homo erectus* gained access to the carcasses after carnivores had their fill—there are no tooth or gnaw marks on the bones.

That the flint that served as the raw material for the tools at Aridos came from deposits at 3 km distance, and that much of the toolmaking occurred away from the butchery site, with mostly sharpening conducted on-site, exhibits what researcher Paola Villa calls "planning depth." This indicates that the hominids who butchered the elephant carcasses at Aridos knew that elephants roamed the area and that there was always a chance one or more of them might die at any given time—the Aridos 1 elephant was a juvenile and Aridos 2 was an old male, both subpopulations with a high natural mortality rate. The *Homo erectus* population in the area seems to have planned for the lucky occasions when a carcass became available by collecting the raw material and making the tools in advance. Planning ahead for a future eventuality is a human behavior, and the evidence at Aridos suggests that *Homo erectus* was capable of this.

ISSUES AND DEBATES

DID THE PLEISTOCENE CAUSE THE EVOLUTION OF *HOMO ERECTUS*?

We saw in the case of the earliest split between pongid and hominid at the end of the Miocene, between 5 million years ago and 7 million years ago, as well as with the initiation of the *Homo* line 2.5 million years ago, that a significant change in climate predated and may have inspired the evolution of our ancestors. It is tempting to suggest that the changes produced by the Pleistocene are at the root of the apparently rapid divergence of *Homo erectus* from *Homo habilis*. However, the timing of the climate changes during the Pleistocene seems to rule out this possibility. Though the first appearance of *erectus* and the accepted beginning of the Pleistocene Epoch are roughly contemporaneous, significant global cooling and the growth of continental ice sheets predate this as well as their expansion into Asia and Europe. This conclusion may change if older specimens of *Homo erectus* are found (see the discussion later in this chapter).

Even if the Pleistocene is not at the root of the development of *erectus* as a new species of hominid, it remains an important consideration in our reconstruction of *Homo erectus* intelligence and cultural capability. *Homo erectus* was able to thrive and expand geographically despite the unsettled climatic and geographic conditions produced by the Pleistocene. Their adaptability and flexibility are hallmarks of the human cultural adaptation and show how similar to us members of this different species must have been.

WHAT ENABLED THE GEOGRAPHIC EXPANSION OF *HOMO ERECTUS*?

The spread of *erectus* out of Africa into new habitats with different climates, resources, and challenges was not made possible by or accompanied by any change in their physical adaptation. Natural selection for a cold-adapted version of *erectus,* for example, was not what made possible their spread into climates colder and more seasonal than those of their tropical African birthplace.

Intelligence

It seems clear that what enabled *Homo erectus* to survive where human ancestors had not previously been able to penetrate was intelligence and the ability to invent new adaptations as needed. While *Homo habilis* was a cultural creature, as shown by their invention, manufacture, and use of stone tools, it is *Homo erectus* who seems to be the first human ancestor to rely for survival on the invented, learned, and passed-down adaptations of culture. In the use of sophisticated tools and in the taming of fire (see the next section), *Homo erectus* exhibits how similar the species was to us. Their reliance on culture was an adaptive strategy that would define forever what it means to be a human being, and it is the most important thing we modern humans share with them.

Control of Fire

There is something very compelling, even to us twentieth-century humans, about a simple open flame: the smell of wood smoke, the crackling and popping of dry tinder, the warmth of the fire. For countless generations of our human ancestors, fire was more than just a diversion; it meant warmth and light, power and strength—in fact, survival itself. When did the first human ancestors make the great leap from fear of this elemental natural force to understanding and controlling it?

The best available evidence indicates that *Homo erectus* was our first ancestor able to control fire. The timing of their earliest use of controlled fire, however, is a point of contention within paleoanthropology [see James (1989) for a skeptic's perspective].

An analysis performed by Andrew Sillen and C. K. Brain (1990) at the site of Swartkrans in South Africa, for example, shows that controlled fire may have been present as much as 1.3 million years ago. That there was fire at Swartkrans is indisputable: There is evidence of burned bones, though there are no hearths. But fire can be produced naturally, by lightning or by extremely hot, dry conditions. Sillen and Brain have shown, through experimentally burning bone to different temperatures and then comparing the results to the archaeological assemblage at Swartkrans, that the latter were heated to a temperature of perhaps 800°C, far higher than expected for a natural grass fire and more in keeping with an artificially produced and maintained flame. The jury is still out on their conclusion, though the possibility is intriguing.

Some of the best evidence for the use of fire dates to much later, from Zhoukoudian 460,000 years ago in northeast China, which was characterized then and now by long, cold, snowy winters. Other, somewhat less certain evidence comes from sites of similar age in France (l'Escale) and Hungary (Vértesszölös; see Chapter 7). The controlled use of fire may have been the key cultural adaptation that enabled members of this tropically derived and adapted species to survive outside the tropics. Fire gives warmth and protection from animals, and enables cooking, which renders meat more digestible and makes it safer by killing bacteria. Fire also produces light and, therefore, probably played an important role in extending the usable part of the day for members of a species who, like us and most other primates, relied primarily on vision for their sensory input but who, also like us, did not see well in the dark.

Although there are no remains of actual hearths at Zhoukoudian, there is evidence in the form of ash and cinders as well as burned bone and stone. While recent reanalysis of the Zhoukoudian material calls into question some of the more imaginative reconstructions of fire use at the site [L. Binford and Chuan (1985) and L. Binford and Stone (1986) are skeptical of most, though not all, of the evidence], it seems clear that fire was part of the cultural repertoire of *Homo erectus;* it probably had to be for members of this species to survive in the cold climate of northern China.

THE "ART" OF MAKING TOOLS

An important point should be made about the handaxes we discussed previously: They were better made than they had to be. That is to say, the Acheulean handaxes—at least many of the later ones—have a symmetry, balance, precision, and beauty that took a lot of work, but work that was not absolutely necessary from a utilitarian perspective (see the Paleolithic Portfolio, Color

Plate 6). Within sites, there appears to have been a high level of consistency in handaxe form, as if the makers were adhering to a particular standard. For example, paleoanthropologist John Gowlett (1984) found a remarkable consistency and uniformity in the ratios among length, width, and thickness of the handaxes he studied from the 700,000-year-old Kilombe site in Kenya.

That such extra care was taken in their production implies that their makers were interested in more than simple utility. *Homo erectus* toolmakers must have been producing beautiful objects for the sake of displaying their great skill or for the pleasure of producing a thing of beauty. Though the first true art is usually associated with anatomically modern humans of a much later period—the cave paintings of the European Upper Paleolithic (see Chapter 9) are clearly recognizable as art—for producing stone tools more artfully than they needed to, some of our much earlier ancestors may well deserve the credit for being the first true artists (Gowlett 1984).

RAISING *HOMO ERECTUS*

My understanding of the care necessary for raising human babies as compared to the young of other species has been forged on the anvil of experience: I've got two kids and two cats, and there simply is no comparison. We adopted the cats when they were seven-week-old kittens, ready to leave their mothers. They could walk, could feed themselves, were litter-box trained, knew how to manipulate human beings to get anything they wanted, and were fierce hunters of blowing leaves and dust bunnies. My kids, like all baby humans, are another story. Immediately following birth, and for an extended period thereafter, my kids were capable of crying, filling their diapers, sleeping, and little else.

Whereas after just several weeks of life animals such as cats attain a reasonable level of competence at moving around, eating, and defending themselves, human children are utterly dependent on adults to satisfy all their needs for a very long time—usually years, even decades. Some specialists characterize even full-term human babies (nine months of gestation) as inherently premature and little more than embryos living outside the womb. The term **altricial,** which is used to characterize baby birds who are completely dependent on their parents for fulfilling their needs, applies also to human babies.

There are a number of reasons why evolution would have selected for a seemingly dangerous situation in which human children are born at an early stage of development. A reconfiguration of the human pelvis was necessary to allow our first hominid ancestors to stand up. This change in pelvic form provided for a change in muscle positioning and shape necessary for bipedal locomotion. It also had an incidental effect: It greatly narrowed the pelvic outlet in females, making it far more difficult for a baby's body to pass through the birth canal [see Rosenberg (1992) for an informative discussion

FIGURE **6.10**

The birth canals of apes and modern human beings, and the fossil pelvises of extinct hominids allow for a comparison in the birth process of these three kinds of creatures. (Courtesy of Robert Tague)

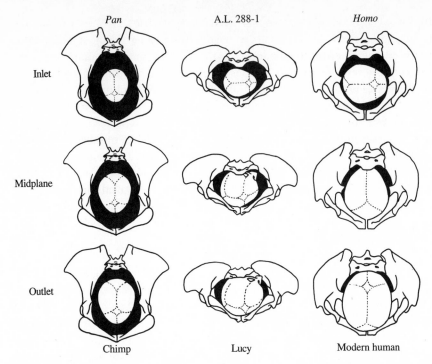

Pan   A.L. 288-1   Homo

Inlet

Midplane

Outlet

Chimp   Lucy   Modern human

of the evolution of human childbirth]. This can be shown by a simple statistic: Average birth labor time for a chimpanzee is about two hours; for a human mother it is more than fourteen hours (Rosenberg 1992:99).

A detailed comparison by Robert Tague and Owen Lovejoy (1986) of the reconstructed pelvis of the fossil Lucy (*Australopithecus afarensis*) with the pelvises of a chimpanzee and a modern human female indicates that, though bipedality probably complicated birth for *Australopithecus* females, it still was not as problematical as it is for modern human women (Figure 6.10). The brains of the various *Australopithecus* species were still quite small, so while there may have been a tighter fit at birth, this probably presented little problem since their heads were still no bigger than those of chimp babies.

However, as natural selection began to favor greater intelligence in the hominids—made possible by an increase in brain and, therefore, head size—a problem did develop: A smaller pelvic outlet was forced to accommodate an increasingly large head at birth. Nature's solution, still hardly perfect, as witnessed by the often difficult time women have in birthing children, was twofold. The first strategy was to maximize pelvic outlet size in females by fine-tuning the configuration of the pelvis. Male and female human pelvises became readily distinguishable because the pelvis exhibits **sexual dimorphism.**

The second strategy of natural selection was timing the birth of human babies at an earlier stage in fetal development, when the head, though large, was still small enough to pass through the birth canal. Today, this is reflected in the fact that the human newborn has a smaller head, proportional to its ultimate adult size, than any of the living apes. A human newborn's brain is less than 25% of its ultimate adult size (Jordaan 1976:274). Compare this to the great apes, in whom a newborn's brain is more than 40% of its adult size. Most human brain growth occurs outside the womb, after birth. This is fundamentally different from the situation for all the apes. For example, while the rate of brain growth declines dramatically in chimpanzees immediately after birth, human babies maintain what is essentially a relatively fast fetal rate of brain growth for an entire year after they are born (Rosenberg 1992:106; R. Martin 1989). The proportionally small size of the human baby's head at birth is what enables the baby to be born at all, given the constraints of pelvic outlet size necessitated by upright walking. But this situation presents problems, for the less developed a newborn of any species is, the more susceptible it is to trauma, infection, cold, and death.

Birth at an early stage of development for an organism with a large and complex brain has some advantages. Stimulation and learning begin earlier, while the brain is still experiencing rapid growth, and bonding between parents and children is, of necessity, stronger. This can be advantageous in a species that depends for its survival so thoroughly on learned behavior and social relations. It is beneficial for humans to be born at an immature stage of development and to have an extended childhood; the learning curve is simply a lot steeper and longer for us than it is for cows, cats, or even other primates.

An additional hypothesis holds that one of the key changes that characterized ancient hominids from *Homo habilis* onward is **neotony,** or the "holding on" to features that are typical of newborn apes (Gould 1977). And modern human adults resemble baby chimps more than they resemble adult chimpanzees. Our lack of body hair, rounded skulls, flat faces, and even the point of articulation between the base of our skull and backbone are all things we share with fetal or newborn, but not adult, chimpanzees.

This brings us back to the boy from West Turkana. Based on the size of his skull, we can say that hominid **encephalization,** or brain expansion, was already well under way 1.6 million years ago and probably earlier. As an infant, the Nariokotome boy's head size surely challenged the size of his mother's birth canal. Almost certainly, natural selection was already at work, favoring survival of infants born at an earlier stage of fetal development. This selective process, however, would work only if adults—particularly mothers, but potentially fathers and other adults—could spend an enormous amount of time caring for the newborns. This must have been the case for the West Turkana boy.

The altricial nature of a *Homo erectus* child at birth can be added to another human characteristic exhibited by the West Turkana boy: an extended period of physical development and delayed maturation. A twelve-year-old cat is an older adult, and even a twelve-year-old chimp is a fully mature adult. But the twelve-year-old West Turkana boy was still physically immature, as evidenced by his dental development and the development of the bones of his arms, legs, hands, and feet—none of the **epiphyses** (see Chapter 3) of the West Turkana boy had yet fused at the time of his death. He was just a boy.

As F. Brown et al. (1985) point out, the West Turkana boy shows clear evidence of an extended period of immaturity that is characteristic of modern human beings. This long period of childhood allowed them, 1.6 million years ago for the boy from West Turkana and for all *Homo erectus* children, to learn what they needed to know. A long period of learning is emblematic of the human species.

IS *HOMO ERECTUS* OLDER THAN WE THINK?

A number of enigmatically old sites in Asia and Europe need to be considered when assessing the consensus on *Homo erectus* presented in this chapter's Chronicle. For example, redating of three *Homo erectus* crania from Java, one found in 1936 (the Mojokerto child) and two found at Sangiran in 1974, has excited and perplexed virtually everyone in the field. The new dating technique measures the decay of a radioactive isotope of argon into a stable form (^{40}Ar to ^{39}Ar). The dates derived are 1.8 million years for the Mojokerto child's skull and 1.6 million years for the Sangiran crania (Bower 1994a; Swisher et al. 1994). The first date, if valid, puts *Homo erectus* in Asia not only substantially earlier than expected, but also earlier than in Africa.

A few sites in China seem to lend support to the notion of the great antiquity of *Homo erectus* outside of Africa. The Yuanmou Man site, consisting of some hominid teeth, possibly *Homo erectus,* found near Upper Nabang Village in Yunnan Province in south China, may date to as much as 1.7 million years ago (Jia and Huang 1990:209).

We can add to this list of anomalously old *Homo erectus* fossils outside of Africa the recent find in the former Soviet republic of Georgia of a mandibular fragment with sixteen teeth that appears to belong in the hypodigm. G. Philip Rightmire indicated that it "could well be a *Homo erectus* mandible," when he saw it displayed for the first time (Shreeve 1993:28). The volcanic deposit that underlies the fossil may be 1.6 million years old. Though the fossils surely are younger than this, if they are anywhere close to this age, they would be not only the oldest hominid remains in Europe, but also older than most of the *erectus* finds inside Africa. The Tblisi volcanic deposit, however, may also be much younger, "only" about 900,000 years old. The dating was determined through paleomagnetism of the volcanic deposit. The problem is that magnetic north was in the same direction from the site at two possible times: 1.6 million and 0.9 million years ago. The **faunal assemblage,** or list of animal remains, found with the hominid mandible seems to match the assemblage from other sites in the region that are more firmly dated to 1.6 million years.

While most paleoanthropologists are reserving judgment on the age of the Tblisi mandible, it is another intriguing bit of evidence for an older radiation of *Homo erectus* out of Africa.

Does all this mean that the consensus view presented in this chapter's Chronicle is backwards and that *erectus* appeared first in Asia and migrated to Europe and Africa, rather than the other way around? This is difficult to believe, since no older, more primitive hominid from which *erectus* could have evolved has ever been found outside of Africa. Could the very early appearance of the species in Java or Europe signify that even older specimens will be found in Africa, considering that all other evidence indicates they evolved there? Possibly, but as we push *erectus* further back, it becomes increasingly difficult to accept the consensus scenario that it evolved from *Homo habilis;* they would have been contemporaries.

Paleoanthropologist R. J. Clarke (1990) has suggested the intriguing alternative that *Homo habilis* may have expanded out of Africa before the evolution of *erectus*. In a more complicated scenario than the one presented here, Clarke suggests that the Asian *habilis* migrants from Africa (which, he admits, are as yet undetected in the paleoanthropological record) later evolved into the Asian *Homo erectus,* while the original African *habilis* evolved into a different, contemporaneous *Homo* species. He calls it *Homo leakeyi,* including all of the African specimens we have here labeled simply as African representatives of the species *Homo erectus*. As we will see, the notion of separating *Homo erectus* into two separate species, one in Africa and one in Asia, has also been suggested by Bernard Wood.

Before we rewrite the story of *Homo erectus,* we need to deal with a few unanswered questions. As is typical in paleoanthropology, the dates for the extremely old Java crania are derived not from the skulls themselves, but from the deposits from which they were recovered. It is possible that the deposits are older than the skulls, the hominid remains having settled into a lower stratum than their original place of deposit. It probably will take an ***in situ*** discovery—found in place—by a trained excavator before such an old date will become broadly accepted. Until direct evidence of *Homo habilis* is found in Asia, Clarke's suggestion of an earlier hominid migration out of Africa remains speculation.

WAS THERE ONLY ONE SPECIES?

As mentioned previously, there is some controversy concerning the issue of variability within fossil species (see the Issues and Debates section in Chapter 5). While most paleoanthropologists maintain there was a single hominid species between 1.78 and 0.4 million years ago and that all hominids that date to this time period belong to the taxon *Homo erectus,* there is a minority opinion that because of so much variability within the accepted hypodigm it should

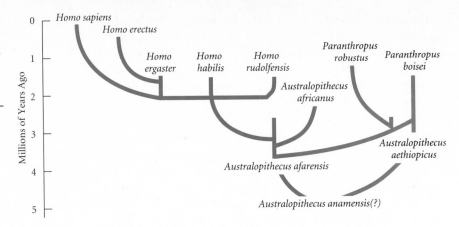

FIGURE 6.11

One alternative phylogeny proposed for the fossil hominids. (From Bernard Wood 1992a,b)

be split into at least two separate species (Philip Andrews 1984). (Part of the rationale for this presages the bitter argument to be dealt with in Chapter 7 concerning the origin of modern humanity.)

Bernard Wood (1992a,b) has suggested, as mentioned in Chapter 5, that the currently accepted hypodigm making up *Homo habilis* would be better divided into two species: *H. habilis* and *H. rudolfensis.* Wood goes on to suggest that another *Homo* species, which he labels *Homo ergaster,* was at least partially contemporary with these two species in east Africa. Into *Homo ergaster* Wood places the very early African fossils (including the West Turkana boy and ER 3733) we have labeled here simply as the first representatives of *Homo erectus.* In Wood's view, *Homo ergaster* later splits, with one line leading to *Homo erectus* and another to *Homo sapiens* (Figure 6.11).

Wood's view is attractive for a couple of reasons. As the *erectus* fossils have been pushed back in time, we are beginning to see some temporal overlap between *erectus* and *habilis.* As a result, it has become increasingly difficult to view *erectus* as simply and directly descendant from *habilis;* it would have to be descendant from some population of *habilis* while the species as a whole continued for a time before becoming extinct. Later on, we see a lot of temporal overlap between the most recent Asian *erectus* fossils and the earliest representatives of the species *sapiens* in Africa and Europe. As we will see in Chapter 7, in one view, *Homo erectus* in China represents an extinct offshoot of the main line of human evolution. Wood's view accommodates this by creating a separate line, *Homo ergaster,* which he views as partially contemporaneous with *erectus* (which was destined for extinction) and directly ancestral to *sapiens.*

On the other hand, Philip Rightmire, who has written perhaps most extensively on *erectus,* continues to maintain that all of the members of the hypodigm, from Africa to eastern Asia, from 1.78 million years ago to 0.4 million years ago and conceivably later, are from a single species (1990; Bower 1992b). He believes that *Homo sapiens* evolved from *erectus* populations in Africa or

Europe that expanded later to replace contemporary populations of *erectus* in Asia.

The previously mentioned recent discoveries in Yunxian, China, complicate matters further. Though admitting that the skulls are quite distorted and much work needs to be done to reconstruct them carefully, their excavators, Li Tianyuan and Dennis Etler (1992), believe that the two crania exhibit a mosaic of primitive (that is, *erectus*) traits and modern (that is, *sapiens*) traits. This leads them to conclude that *Homo sapiens* evolved from *erectus* roots in several parts of the world. Though they do not state this explicitly, they probably accept the proposition that all of the current residents of the hypodigm belong to the single *erectus* species as currently constituted.

An important rule in science, **Occam's razor,** states that when there are multiple ways to explain the same data, choose the simplest explanation until the evidence is overwhelming that it is otherwise. Let us follow that rule here. A number of researchers, comparing the African and Asian specimens currently labeled *Homo erectus,* conclude that they belong together in the same species (Bräuer and Mbua 1992; Turner and Chamberlain 1989). Andrew Kramer's (1993) analysis of the amount of variation within our current construct of the species shows no more variability within the *erectus* hypodigm than within the single extant species of modern human beings. In other words, *Homo erectus* fossils from Africa and Asia across a time span of nearly 1.4 million years are no more different from each other than are the skeletons of modern people from different parts of the globe and who are all acknowledged to belong to a single species. This is very strong support for the single-species theory as applied to *erectus.* Still, we must be ready to modify this position if new data support a more complex scenario like that of Bernard Wood's.

STABILITY OR CHANGE?

How much change is exhibited in *Homo erectus* fossils included in the hypodigm but separated by an extraordinarily long time span? Lasting from 1.78 million years ago to 0.4 million years ago, *Homo erectus* is one of the longest-lived of the hominid species. If evolution is thought of as a gradual, steady process (see the discussion of punctuated equilibrium in Chapter 5 and the Issues and Debates section in Chapter 7), then we might expect *erectus,* if it was the direct ancestor of humanity, to exhibit such steady evolution toward the anatomically modern condition over its lengthy existence on the planet. As evidence for this view, some researchers point to certain changes through time within the *Homo erectus* species: The back teeth get smaller, and the anatomical structure of the face and lower jaw decrease (Wolpoff 1984).

On the other hand, Philip Rightmire (1981, 1985, 1990) argues that such changes are extremely minor and that, especially when considering the enormous amount of time involved and the geographical breadth of *Homo erectus,* the evidence is overwhelming for great stability within the species over

This graph of the trend in Homo erectus *brain size through time shows a rather remarkable stability from the first appearance of the species some 1.8 million years ago to the most recent specimens, dating to 400,000 years ago.*

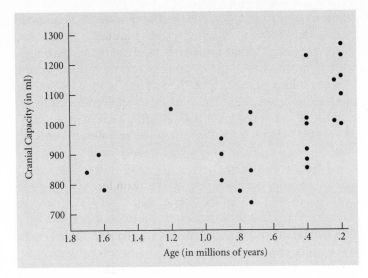

its entire existence. As Rightmire points out, all of the *Homo erectus* specimens, from the very oldest to the most recent, are "built on a common plan" (1990:190).

Even brain size within the species can be shown to be fundamentally stable through time: There is no significant increase in cranial capacity within *erectus* from its earliest appearance in Africa 1.78 million years ago until it is replaced by *Homo sapiens* sometime after 400,000 years ago (Figure 6.12). Rightmire (1981, 1990) applies the statistical procedure of regression analysis to the data and finds no statistically significant temporal trend in brain size. Though researcher Steven Leigh (1992) disputes this result, maintaining that, at least within the Asian subsample of *erectus,* the increase in brain size through time is statistically significant, that increase is extremely small. As Figure 6.12 shows, statistical significance issues aside, there appears to be little change in cranial capacity through time until about 400,000 years ago.

Interestingly, this period of relative stability in brain size is also a period of great cultural stability regarding stone tools. The handaxes made by *Homo erectus* change only slightly from 1.4 million to 400,000 years ago. One million years of relatively little change in a technology is in stark contrast to the modern situation, in which technologies change virtually overnight. That stability lends further support to the notion of *Homo erectus* as a fundamentally unchanging species representing a long period of evolutionary equilibrium. At about 400,000 years ago, however, a steep increase in brain size over a short interval is seen. This jump in brain size, in fact, is how the earliest appearance of members of our species is identified.

So it seems that *Homo erectus,* like *Australopithecus afarensis* (see Chapter 5), was a stable, long-lived species. The fossil evidence again supports the evolutionary model of punctuated equilibrium—with *Homo erectus* representing a long period of equilibrium in the hominid line. Major changes in brain size and cranial morphology did not occur until around 400,000 years ago. Those changes produced and defined the first *Homo sapiens* in what is seen here as being a punctuational event (see Chapter 7).

CASE STUDY CLOSE-UP

In 1918, a fossil locality southwest of Beijing, China, was explored by Swedish geologist Johan Gunnar Andersson. Andersson took advantage of a local Chinese belief that fossil bones were actually the remnants of dragons and that powder made from ground-up "dragon bones" was a cure-all. Many local druggists collected such bones for use in their medicines. Even today, paleontologists rely on local druggists for leads in their search for fossil ("dragon") bones (Jian and Rice 1990).

In 1918, Andersson was directed by a druggist to a hill called Jigushan (Chicken Bone Hill) near the village of Zhoukoudian (Jia and Huang 1990). Convinced there was a rich array of fossil bones in the surrounding region, he began excavating on another hill, called Longgoshan—Dragon Bone Hill. In 1926, two humanlike teeth were recovered; in 1929, with the dig now led by British scientist Davidson Black, a nearly intact skull was encountered in a cave at the top of the hill (Locality 1). The fossil was recognizably different from almost everything that had been found previously, with the possible exception of Java Man. A new species was named and defined: *Sinanthropus pekinensis.* The specimens from Zhoukoudian are now included in the species *Homo erectus,* but in the popular mind both then and now, it may forever be known as "Peking Man."

The cave at Dragon Bone Hill was spectacularly productive by any standards. By the time excavations were finished at Zhoukoudian, the expedition had recovered, along with thousands of specimens of ancient animals, 15 fragmentary skulls, six more complete crania, 13 fragmentary mandibles, 3 upper jaws, some postcranial bones (including pieces of femur, upper arms, toe bones, numerous teeth), and a single vertebra of Peking Man (Jia and Huang 1990:161–162). All told, the remains of more than forty hominid individuals were recovered from deposits in the cave dated to between 462,000 and 200,000 years ago (according to fission-track dating as reported by Jia and Huang 1990:111). Being so numerous and discovered so early in our thinking about human evolution, the Peking Man fossils played an important historical role in the scientific conceptualization of human evolution and in interpretations of the culture of ancient human beings.

Tragically, the Zhoukoudian hominid assemblage was lost during World War II when they were being removed from China by U.S. Marines in an attempt to keep them away from Japanese invaders, coincidentally on the same day that Pearl Harbor was attacked. The Marines were captured and imprisoned, and to this day no one knows what became of their precious fossil cargo. (It may have been destroyed by Japanese troops or simply lost, or they may have been found later by Chinese druggists who ground them up for medicine. There even is a very slight possibility that some are still hidden away in China, Japan, or the United States.) Paleoanthropologist Harry Shapiro (1974) provides a riveting account of the discovery and loss of Peking Man. See Janus and Brashler (1975) for an interesting, if unreliable, account of an attempt to track down the present whereabouts of the bones, replete with stories of clandestine meetings atop the Empire State Building and multimillion-dollar ransom demands. Also, see Jia and Huang (1990) for a detailed telling of the story of Peking Man by one of its excavators (Jia Lanpo).

VISITING THE PAST

Just as with the fossils and sites related to *Australopithecus* and *Homo habilis* discussed in the previous chapter, you need to travel a great distance to visit the *Homo erectus* sites discussed here. Even then, the important fossil remains usually are unavailable for viewing by all but researchers in the field. Again, however, most large museums in major American cities have displays on human evolution that cover some of the important discoveries and issues dealt with in this chapter.

China has a fine museum display at Zhoukoudian. Upgraded in 1979, the museum is devoted to the finds made at the Peking Man site as well as the area surrounding Zhoukoudian. On display are casts of the now-lost original hominid fossils, tools, the bones of animals killed and eaten by the ancient inhabitants of the locality, as well as a general display on human evolution. Zhoukoudian, being close to Beijing, is reasonably accessible to tourists.

In Kenya, Africa, the Olorgesailie sites containing a number of excavated localities are open to tourists. The sites date to after 400,000 years ago, and numerous, sometimes finely made handaxes have been left exactly where they were found by the excavators (including Louis and Mary Leakey) and, presumably, where they were left by *Homo erectus*. The monograph by Glynn Isaac (1977) provides details on the excavation and analysis of the Olorgesailie sites.

One of the most interesting of the Olorgesailie localities is Site B. The remains of many stone tools and the smashed bones of an extinct species of baboon were found there; some have been left in place for viewing. The bones appear to have been broken for marrow extraction. Because so much has been left in place, the visitor can gain a unique insight into the appearance of a 400,000-year-old *Homo erectus* site as it was discovered by the archaeologists who excavated it.

SUMMARY

Sometime after 1.8 million years ago, *Homo habilis* was replaced by a new hominid species, *Homo erectus*. *Erectus* possessed a larger brain than *habilis*; its mean brain size of about 1,000 ml is two-thirds the modern human mean. With its larger brain and attendant greater intelligence, *Homo erectus* was able to adapt to the changing environmental conditions posed by the Pleistocene Epoch. Its greater intelligence is evidenced by its more sophisticated stone tools as well as its controlled use of fire. Reliance on a cultural rather than a physical adaptation enabled members of this species to expand into new habitats in Asia and, later, Europe, and to adjust to environmental conditions far different from those presented in its African birthplace.

Homo erectus was a stable and long-lived species. Fossils from Africa to east Asia show a consistent morphology from close to 1.8 million to 400,000 years ago. After 400,000 years ago, brain size, relatively stable during the existence of *erectus,* exhibits a rapid increase, signifying the evolution of the first *Homo sapiens* from an *erectus* base.

TO LEARN MORE

Richard Leakey and Roger Lewin's (1992) *Origins Reconsidered: In Search of What Makes Us Human* provides a nice discussion on the discovery, excavation, and interpretation of the Nariokotome boy. A more technical and detailed work on the Nariokotome skeleton, edited by two of its excavators, Alan Walker and Richard Leakey (1993), is now available. The best general technical work on *Homo erectus* is G. Philip Rightmire's (1990) *The Evolution of* Homo erectus: *Comparative Anatomical Studies of an Extinct Human Species.* A very informative treatment of *Homo erectus* can be found in *Ancestors: In Search of Human Origins* by Don Johanson, Lenora Johanson, and Blake Edgar (1994). The November 1985 issue of *National Geographic,* though a little out of date, presents a well-written discussion of *Homo erectus.*

KEY TERMS

deciduous dentition	Holocene Epoch	altricial
permanent dentition	glacial	sexual dimorphism
occipital	stadial	neotony
basicranium	interstadial	encephalization
supraorbital torus	interglacial	epiphysis
calvarium	foraminifera	faunal assemblage
Kabuh Formation	Acheulean handaxe	in situ
glacier	cortex	Occam's razor
Pleistocene Epoch	preform	

7

Our Immediate Ancestors

THE ARCHAIC HUMANS

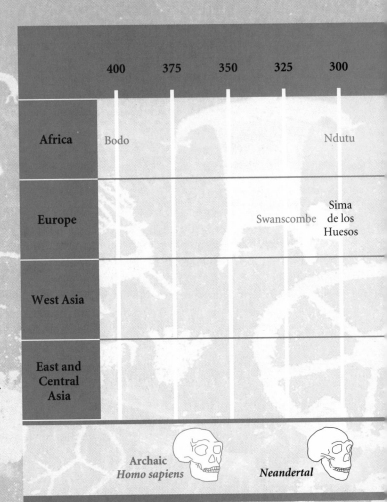

	400	375	350	325	300
Africa	Bodo				Ndutu
Europe				Swanscombe	Sima de los Huesos
West Asia					
East and Central Asia					

Archaic *Homo sapiens*

Neandertal

CHAPTER OVERVIEW

Beginning about 400,000 years ago, a great change appeared in the fossil hominid record. Brain size expanded and the fossils began to look so much more modern that they are categorized as *Homo sapiens,* though of a type called "archaic" or "pre-modern."

The best known of the archaic *Homo sapiens* are the Neandertals. Represented by the skeletons of hundreds of individuals, the Neandertals seem to have been highly specialized physically to life in the arctic-cold of Pleistocene (Ice Age) Europe and western Asia. They may have been too specialized; the last Neandertals died out about 33,000 years ago.

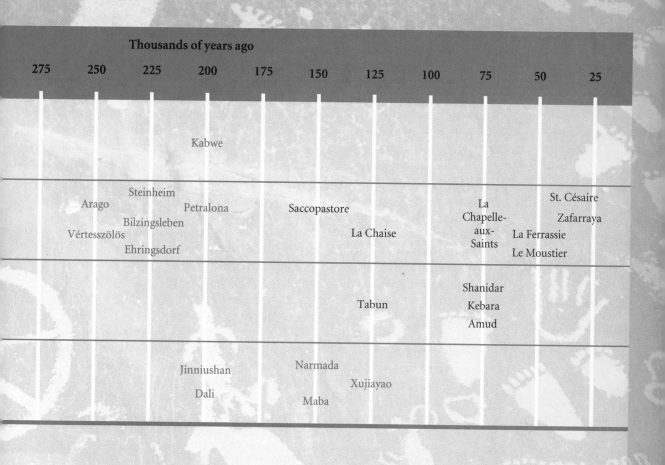

Thousands of years ago

| 275 | 250 | 225 | 200 | 175 | 150 | 125 | 100 | 75 | 50 | 25 |

Kabwe

Steinheim

Arago
Petralona
Saccopastore
La Chapelle-aux-Saints
St. Césaire
Zafarraya

Bilzingsleben

Vértesszölös
La Chaise
La Ferrassie

Ehringsdorf
Le Moustier

Shanidar

Tabun
Kebara

Amud

Jinniushan
Narmada

Xujiayao

Dali
Maba

What would have happened if not one, but two separate and unequal species of human beings had somehow survived to the present? This fascinating concept is the basis for a novel by French author Jean Bruller [pen name Vercors (1953)]. In it, a group of explorers investigates a secluded, pristine valley in the highlands of New Guinea in the mid-twentieth century.* The explorers discover a population of a presumedly extinct variety of human being—*living* hominids, more advanced than Peking Man (*Homo erectus*) yet less advanced than modern human beings. Called "tropis," these creatures make stone tools, speak a simple language, have fire, and bury their dead.

In actuality, of course, all modern human beings belong to a single species, *Homo sapiens sapiens,* and all of us are more alike than different in our physical appearance, intellect, and emotion, no matter what our geographic origin or family heritage. But it didn't have to turn out this way. There could today have been different, coexisting species of human beings with different physical and intellectual capacities, just as there are different species of bear, antelope, elephant, and camel—and just as there were different, contemporaneous, and coexisting species of hominids in the past (see Chapter 5).

In Vercors' novel, the primitive people discovered in New Guinea are treated quite badly. They are essentially enslaved. On the one hand, they are not true "people," so there is no law preventing their exploitation (just as there is no law against harnessing a horse to a plow). On the other hand, they are far more intelligent than any other nonhuman animal and can be trained to do things modern humans can do but find degrading, boring, or dangerous.

Considering the amount of mistrust and hatred that exists today among the empirically minimally different individuals of our single species, it is frightening to consider what the world would be like if there were truly different, coexisting species of human beings. In a broad sense, this almost happened.

The Neandertals to be discussed in this chapter are an extinct variety of human beings that come chronologically closer to the modern era than any other nonmodern hominid, having become extinct only a little more than 30,000 years ago, a mere tick on the evolutionary clock. As we will show here and in Chapter 8, there may well have been an overlap of tens of millennia during the waning years of the Neandertals and the ascendance of the earliest anatomically modern human beings.

As will be shown, the Neandertals were not only similar to us in many ways, but also quite different. Though often depicted as apelike or subhuman, they managed to survive during an extremely harsh period of the Pleistocene, or Ice Age. They did so through their great intelligence, inventing

---

*As late as the 1930s such places existed on New Guinea, completely unknown to Europeans. Perhaps 1 million people lived there, people who were truly the last substantial aboriginal population on the planet, untouched by European disease, missionaries, exploitation, or plain cultural hegemony. Their story is chronicled in a PBS documentary and companion book, both titled *First Contact* (Connolly and Anderson 1987).

sophisticated stone tools for hunting, producing clothing and shelter, and using fire. Neandertals are also noted for another behavior that contradicts their modern stereotype: They buried their dead. In recognizing the enormity of death and in ceremonially disposing of the mortal remains of their comrades, they were exhibiting a behavior that shows their close kinship to us. Despite their intelligence, Neandertals were surely quite different from us. Considering how badly we humans treat one another—and that we are more similar to each other in how we look and how we think than we would be to living Neandertals—the Neandertals probably would have ended up like the primitive hominids in Vercors' book, doomed by us to lives of confinement, drudgery, and pain (Gould 1988).

The Neandertals, however, did not survive to the present. Who they were, how they were related to other nonmodern human beings, why and how they became extinct, and what place, if any, they had in the evolution of anatomically modern human beings are questions addressed in this chapter.

CHAPTER SITES

EAST ASIA
Chaohu
Dali
Jinniushan
Maba
Narmada
Xujiayao

Throughout much of Europe, Africa, and parts of Asia beginning about 400,000 years ago, *Homo erectus* was being replaced with creatures similar though not identical to what is formally called **anatomically modern *Homo sapiens.*** The hominid tree appears to have sprouted a number of diverging branches at this time, collectively called **archaic *Homo sapiens*** or sometimes simply **premodern *Homo sapiens.*** This

CHRONICLE

MAP 7.1

Fossil localities of "archaic" Homo sapiens.

name recognizes their affinity to us—they are members of our species. It also recognizes their differences: They are archaic, or older and extinct versions of human beings.

With the exception of the Neandertals, whose fossil population numbers in the hundreds, there is only a small, but growing, sample of archaics (Map 7.1), and great variation within this group. As a result, again with the exception of the Neandertals, who are generally labeled *Homo sapiens neanderthalensis,* there is no agreed-on name applied to premodern humans, no

TABLE 7.1
Major Archaic Homo sapiens *Fossils (Exclusive of the Neandertals)*

COUNTRY	LOCALITY	FOSSILS	AGE (YEARS)	BRAIN SIZE (ML)
Germany	Steinheim	Cranium	200,000–240,000	1,200
	Bilzingsleben	Cranial fragments	228,000	
	Ehringsdorf	Cranial fragment	225,000	
	Mauer	Mandible	<450,000	
England	Swanscombe	Occipital cranium	225,000	1,325
Greece	Petralona	Cranium	160,000–240,000	1,400
France	Arago	Cranium and fragmentary remains of 7 individuals	250,000	1,200
Hungary	Vértesszölös	Occipital fragment	200,000	1,250
Zambia	Kabwe (Broken Hill)	Cranium, additional cranial and postcranial remains of several individuals	>125,000	1,280
Tanzania	Ndutu (Olduvai)	Cranium	200,000–400,000	1,100
Ethiopia	Bodo	Cranium	200,000–400,000	
South Africa	Elandsfontein	Cranium		
India	Narmada	Cranium	150,000 ?	1,300
China	Jinniushan	Nearly complete skeleton	200,000	1,350
	Dali	Cranium	200,000	1,120
	Maba	Cranium	130,000–170,000	
	Xujiayao	Fragments of 11 individuals	100,000–125,000	
			Mean	1,252.50
			Standard Deviation	78.50

Data from: Day (1986); Pope (1992); Rightmire (1990).

subspecies designation. Lumping all non-Neandertals in the category "archaic *Homo sapiens*" does not imply that they all belonged to the same subspecies; rather, it reflects our lack of information about them. Some scientists (for example, Stringer 1994) have applied the name *Homo heidelbergensis* to the non-Neandertal European archaics, but there presently is no consensus on this issue.

What all archaics share is a bigger, more modern-size brain than *Homo erectus*. The mean cranial capacity of the archaics, excluding the Neandertals with their very large skulls, is a little over 1,200 ml—more than 20% larger than their evolutionary antecedents (Table 7.1). Most of the premodern specimens also possess large brow ridges, like *erectus*. But more like the modern form, they also exhibit steeper foreheads, generally (though not universally) thinner cranial bones, and flatter faces than *erectus*. However, there is a lot of variation among the premodern *sapiens* specimens: Some have relatively thin cranial bones, others thick; some have nearly vertical foreheads, others' foreheads slope back more severely.

PREMODERN HUMANS: FOSSIL EVIDENCE

Versions of archaic *Homo sapiens* are known from Europe, Africa, and Asia, where they appear to have evolved in place from previous populations of *Homo erectus*.

Europe

The Steinheim cranium from Germany, for example, exhibits the typical mix of archaic and modern morphology of the premodern humans (Figure 7.1).

FIGURE 7.1

The Steinheim cranium from Germany, one of the most complete archaic Homo sapiens *specimens found in Europe, falls within the lower range of cranial capacity of modern humans. The form of the skull, however, is far from modern in appearance.*
(State Museum for Nature, Stuttgart, Germany)

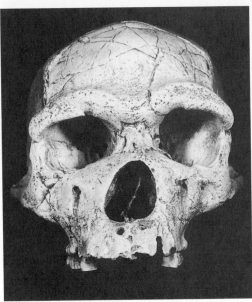

FIGURE 7.2

These nearly complete pre-modern human European crania come from Petralona in Greece (left) *and Arago in France* (right). (*Left:* Courtesy Christopher B. Stringer; *right:* The Institute of Human Paleontology, Paris. H. de Lumley)

The skull is round in profile, like that of a modern human being, and the face is flat, but the brow ridges are huge by any standards; no modern human being has such an enormous ridge of bone above the eye sockets. Brain size is around 1,200 ml. Electron spin resonance dates the deposit from which the skull was recovered to between 200,000 and 240,000 years ago (Ikeya 1982). The fragmentary remains of the Swanscombe cranium come from England, and the nearly complete Petralona skull from Greece (Figure 7.2); skull fragments from Bilzingsleben and Ehringsdorf and a mandible from Mauer all come from Germany; a large, fragmentary sample of bones comes from Vértesszölös in Hungary; and the remains of four adult and three juvenile archaics derive from the Arago site in France. Swanscombe dates to around 325,000 years ago (Ovey 1964; Szabo and Collins 1975), Petralona to 160,000–240,000 (Poulianos 1971–72; Henning et al. 1981), Bilzingsleben and Ehringsdorf to about 225,000 (Cook et al. 1982), Vértesszölös from between 250,000 and 475,000, and Arago to 250,000 years ago (Cook et al. 1982; Gamble 1986).

Africa

Africa also has a grouping of archaic *Homo sapiens,* including the Kabwe (also known as Broken Hill), Ndutu, and Bodo skulls. The Kabwe specimen

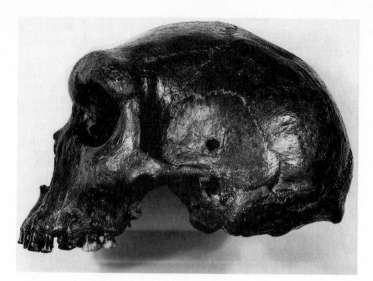

FIGURE 7.3

Premodern Homo sapiens *from Africa include the Kabwe (formerly called Broken Hill) specimen, one of the best-known examples.* (The Natural History Museum, London)

(Bräuer 1984) is a large, very robust skull with enormous brow ridges (Figure 7.3). Its cranial capacity is just under 1,300 ml. The age of Kabwe is uncertain, but it is probably at least 125,000 years old and may be twice that. The Ndutu skull (Clarke 1990) is dated to between 200,000 and 400,000 years ago. It is generally smaller and less robust than the Kabwe cranium. Ndutu cranial capacity has been estimated at about 1,100 ml. Bodo may be as much as 400,000 years old.

Asia

In Asia, a number of fossils can be placed within the archaic category. From central India comes the Narmada hominid, with its cranial capacity of 1,200–1,400 ml and a morphology reminiscent of the African and European archaics (Kennedy et al. 1991). Dating is unclear, though artifacts associated with the skull are probably no more than 150,000 years old. The Narmada cranium, though distinctive, has more in common with other examples of European and African archaic *Homo sapiens* than it does with *Homo erectus.*

A substantial and growing list of sites in eastern Asia is providing testimony for the presence there of archaic *Homo sapiens* (Brooks and Wood 1990; Chen and Zhang 1991; Pope 1992). Perhaps of greatest interest because of its antiquity and the relative completeness of the skeleton is the so-called Jinniushan Man from Yingkou County, Liaoning Province (Figure 7.4; Lu 1987). The cranial capacity, estimated at about 1,330–1,390 ml, is large for an archaic *Homo sapiens,* and the cranial bones are very thin, like a modern human's and unlike the thick cranial bones of other archaics. Its general shape

FIGURE 7.4

Archaic Homo sapiens *from Asia include this specimen from Yingkou in the Jinniushan Mountains, one of the most complete archaic human fossils outside of Europe.* (China Pictorial Photo Service)

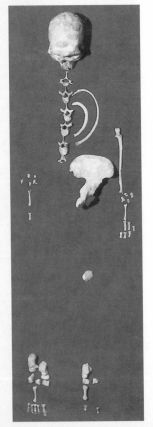

and form, however, is a mixture of primitive and modern; it doesn't look quite like anything from anywhere else. Animal teeth found in the same cave and from the same layer as the hominid have been dated by electron spin resonance to about 165,000–195,000 years ago and by uranium series to 200,000 years ago (Chen, Yang, and Wu 1994).

These dates for Jinniushan suggest that early archaic *Homo sapiens* were contemporaries of late *Homo erectus* in China; the Jinniushan dates overlap the final dates at Zhoukoudian and Hexian (Chen and Zhang 1991; and see Chapter 6). Additional fragmentary remains at Chaohu, located just 50 km from Hexian, appear to represent premodern *Homo sapiens*. Chaohu is the same age as the *Homo erectus* remains at Hexian, further evidence of the two species' partial contemporaneity in east Asia. The implication is that while one or more *Homo erectus* populations in east Asia crossed an evolutionary rubicon and evolved into a more modern form, other populations remained static, retaining their more primitive morphology.

Other archaic or premodern *Homo sapiens* from China include the Dali cranium from northern Shaanxi Province (Figure 7.5). Its cranial capacity has been estimated at 1,120 ml; its form has been described as intermediate between that of *erectus* and that of modern *sapiens* (Pope 1992). The site has produced a uranium series date of about 200,000 years old. In southern China, the Maba specimen, a partial skullcap, is reminiscent of the European Neandertals. It has been dated to 130,000–170,000 years ago. Xujiayao in Shanxi Province has produced hominid remains that seem to belong with the archaic *Homo sapiens*. Dating from about 100,000–125,000 years ago, the 11 individuals in the fossil record exhibit a form midway between that of Chinese *Homo erectus* specimens from Zhoukoudian and that of modern *Homo sapiens* (Pope 1992).

PREMODERN HUMANS: CULTURAL EVIDENCE

There is no great cultural break or jump seen in the archaeological record of the archaic humans. Handaxes similar to those manufactured by *Homo erectus* are common at archaic *Homo sapiens* sites in Europe and Africa; east Asia shows continuity in the stone toolmaking tradition as well. In fact, it is not until about 200,000 years ago that a new and more efficient industry develops.

Called **Levallois**, the new industry involves a shift in emphasis from the production of core tools to the production of flake tools. Instead of sculpting a large, multipurpose tool from a stone nodule and using only the waste flakes that fortuitously fit a given need, emphasis now shifts to the flakes themselves, whose form and size are controlled by careful preparation of the core (Figure 7.6). The stone nodule, or core, is no longer the object to be shaped into a tool, but, instead, becomes the source from which flakes of given sizes and shapes are produced. The flakes are used as blanks to be refined into tools

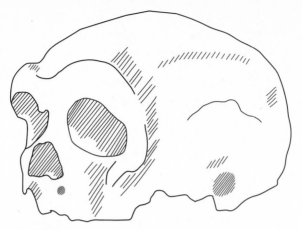

FIGURE 7.5
This nearly complete cranium from Dali is another well-known premodern human from Asia.

1 2 3 4 5cm

Side views

Top views

FIGURE 7.6

In the toolmaking technology called Levallois, a stone core was prepared so as to produce flakes of a consistent size and form.
(After J. Bordaz. 1970. *Tools of the Old and New Stone Age.* New York: Natural History Press.)

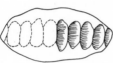

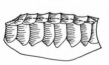

Flake

Core

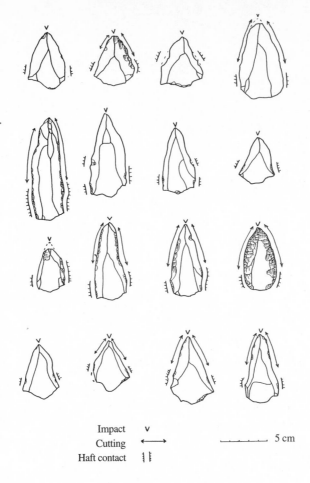

Impact	v
Cutting	←——→
Haft contact	⌡ ⌡

——— 5 cm

intended for specific tasks. The Levallois technique enabled flakes of predetermined size and form to be produced (Figure 7.7).

Modern experts in stone-tool replication often perform the following remarkable feat: They take a stone nodule in hand, draw an outline on it in the precise shape of the flake they want to remove by striking the core with a hammerstone. A good knapper can remove a flake whose edges closely approximate the drawn outline. The key is knowing how a particular rock type breaks and preparing the rock beforehand in order to control how it will break when struck. The Levallois technique involves this kind of careful preparation of the stone core for patterned and predictable flake removal.

Preparing the core allowed archaic humans finer control of flake removal than was previously possible. The right shape for tools with particular functions like cutting, piercing, or perforating could be ensured. The technique is also far more efficient in its use of stone than either Oldowan or Acheulean. A greater amount of sharp, useable edge is produced per unit weight of core.

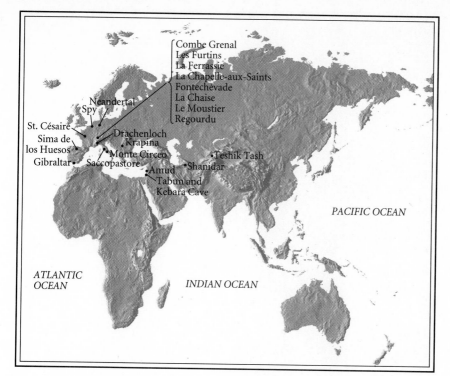

MAP 7.2
Fossil localities of Neandertals.

A replicative study by Bruce Bradley (Gamble 1986) showed that four or five predictable flakes could be removed from a single Levallois core.

THE NEANDERTALS

In one sense, the Neandertals are just another group of archaic *Homo sapiens*. They happen to be better known because of a number of historical accidents (Map 7.2). For example, they were abundant in Europe, where most early paleoanthropological research was undertaken, since most of the world's paleoanthropologists have come from Europe. Also, Neandertals used caves extensively, which preserves archaeological remains better. Thus, the Neandertals deserve a more in-depth look, if only because so much is known about them by both paleoanthropologists and the general public.

There are numerous misconceptions about the Neandertals. In popular parlance, a "Neandertal" is an individual who is stupid, crude, boorish, animalistic, a real "throwback." For many people, the Neandertals represent all of our human ancestors, icons of our primitive and brutal past. The first artistic reconstruction of a Neandertal in a natural setting, ostensibly based on a Neandertal skeleton, appeared in 1909 in the French magazine *L'Illustration* [see the discussion of the meaning of artistic representations of Neandertals in Moser (1992)]. The image is a grotesque caricature of a hairy ape-man

This original Neandertal diorama at the Field Museum of Natural History in Chicago emphasizes the supposedly primitive and apelike character of the Neandertals. (The Field Museum, negative #66702, Chicago)

beast. Neandertals have been the archetype of "cavemen" ever since: ugly, apelike, violent, brutish, and stupid (Hager 1994). A famous diorama at the Field Museum of Natural History in Chicago, now maintained for its historical significance but not its scientific accuracy, depicts the Neandertals as hairy, dirty creatures with crudely sewn animal pelts for clothing, barely standing upright, with knees bent, heads thrust forward, and a vacant expression on their faces (Figure 7.8). Misleading images of Neandertals have, until fairly recently, shown up in newspapers, books, and magazines, and unintelligent, animalistic Neandertals have been depicted in movies as villains out to kill modern human beings. For a detailed and lively discussion of the history of scientific—and not so scientific—thinking about the Neandertals, see paleoanthropologists Erik Trinkaus and Pat Shipman's (1993) *The Neandertals: Changing the Image of Mankind.*

SO WHO WERE THE NEANDERTALS, REALLY?

In truth, the Neandertals are a riddle. In many ways they were similar to us. Their brain size was equal to or even larger than our own (Table 7.2). But

TABLE 7.2
Major Neandertal Specimens Discussed in Chapter 7

COUNTRY	LOCALITY	FOSSILS	CRANIA	AGE (YEARS)	BRAIN SIZE (ML)
Spain	Atapuerca	Remains of at least 24 individuals	Adult	>300,000	1,125
			Adult	>300,000	1,390
			Juvenile	>300,000	1,100
Germany	Neandertal	Skullcap			1,250
France	La Chappelle	Skeleton	"Old man"		1,620
	Fontéchevade	Cranial fragments of several individuals		100,000	1,500
	La Ferrassie	8 Skeletons	LF-1	>38,000	1,680
	La Chaise	Cranium		126,000	
	St. Césaire	Skeleton		36,000	
Belgium	Spy	Cranium			
Italy	Mt. Circeo	Cranium			
	Saccopastore	Cranium			1,350
Yugoslavia	Krapina	Cranial and postcranial fragments of >45 individuals		Isotope stage 5	1,300
Israel	Tabun	Skeleton, mandible, postcranial fragments	T-1	60,000	1,270
	Amud	Skeleton	A-1	70,000	1,740
	Kebara	Postcranial skeleton		60,000	
Iraq	Shanidar	Nine partial skeletons	S-1	70,000	1,600

With Atapuerca

Mean 1,410.42

Standard Deviation 181.34

Without Atapuerca

Mean 1,478.89

Standard Deviation 165.68

Data from: Day 1986; Arsuaga et al. 1993.

FIGURE 7.9

This skullcap of the specimen that gave the Neandertals their name was discovered in the Neander Valley in Germany in 1856. (Rheinisches Landesmuseum, Bonn, Germany)

their brain configuration was different from ours, with less of their brain in the front and more to the rear. Their skulls were marked with huge brow ridges like older hominid species, their faces protruded in an ape-like fashion, and there was an enormous mass of bone at the rear (occipital) portion of the skull, where large muscles were attached that enabled the Neandertals to balance their large, heavy heads. They were physically far more powerful than modern human beings, and their pelvises were configured differently.

The Neandertal* name comes from the Neander Valley in Germany, where, in 1856, not the first such fossil was found, but the one that first caught the attention of the scientific community (see Chapter 2 and Figure 7.9). The recovered skull exhibited both modern human and primitive, nonhuman features. Though it was big, indicating a brain size at least as large as that of a modern human being, the shape was all wrong, with protruding, apelike bony ridges above the eyes, a face that projected forward like that of an ape, and a flattened profile rather than the rounded profile of a modern human skull.

Researchers of the time had difficulty explaining the Neandertal skull. (One scholar even suggested that its peculiar appearance was the result of "stupendous blows" with a heavy instrument sustained during the individual's lifetime.) However, as more Neandertal specimens—as all such similar fossils were labeled—were discovered in Europe, it became clear that the Neandertal skull form represented a distinct and extinct variety of humanity.

---

*You will sometimes find *Neandertal* spelled *Neanderthal*. The original German spelling included an *h*, though it was (and is) pronounced as if no *h* were present. Modern German spelling has removed the *h*, so it is not used in this text. To complicate matters further, according to the rules of biological nomenclature, under most circumstances the original name given to a species cannot be changed. Since the Neandertals were originally given the species name *neanderthalensis*, with the *h*, we are obliged to leave the *h* when using the taxonomic name.

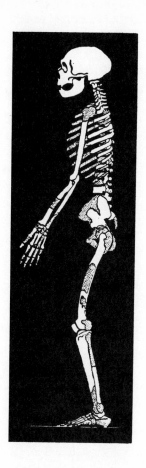

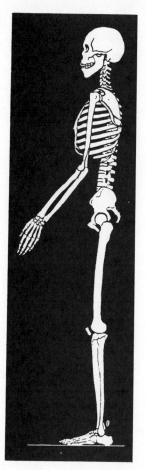

FIGURE 7.10

In Marcellin Boule's comparison between the skeleton of a Neandertal (left) *and that of a modern human being* (right), *the bent knees, curved spine, and thrust-forward head were inaccuracies that contributed to the impression that Neandertals were primitive and apelike.*
(From *Fossil Men* by Marcellin Boule and Henri Vallois, Dryden Press)

In the attempt to assess the precise relationship between the Neandertals and modern humans, a major error crept into the discussion. In 1913, French scientist Marcellin Boule produced a reconstruction of the entire Neandertal skeleton that was rife with error (Boule and Vallois 1923). Assuming, on the basis of the form of the skull, that the Neandertals were apelike, Boule's reconstruction showed a bent-over, splayed-toe, apelike creature (Figure 7.10).

It probably didn't help that the specimen Boule chose to focus on had had a bad case of arthritis that may have caused the individual to bend over when walking. As Erik Trinkaus (1985) points out, however, Boule had two other, perfectly normal Neandertal specimens in his lab at the time, and the disease present in the one he chose to work on did not justify the apelike appearance Boule imparted. Most likely, Boule made the reconstruction apelike from the neck down because it fit his preconception of what it would have looked like based on its appearance from the neck up. Later, when Boule helped the French artist produce his drawing and when others, like the designers of the diorama at the Field Museum of Natural History, put flesh on

Boule's skeletal creation, they compounded the error by giving the Neandertals an open-mouthed, dazed expression that could not even have been implied by the bones. It is from this incorrect reconstruction that our modern, insulting use of the name derives.

But who were the Neandertals, really? The evidence now is quite extensive that they were not club-toting caricatures; neither, as Erik Trinkaus and Pat Shipman put it, were they "simply funny-looking humans" (1993:385). They were a distinctive, now-extinct variety of human beings, in some ways like us and in some ways very different (Figure 7.11). Most paleoanthropologists apply the taxonomic label *Homo sapiens neanderthalensis* to them, though some want to place them in a species separate from modern human beings: *Homo neanderthalensis* (Gould 1988). Their roots in Europe can now be traced back to more than 300,000 years ago, an age equivalent to that of some of the other European archaics already mentioned (Arsuaga et al. 1993;

FIGURE 7.11

In this more recent comparison of the skeletons of a modern human being and a Neandertal, the so-called "musculoskeletal hypertrophy" of the Neandertals is readily apparent.
(After Stringer and Gamble 1993)

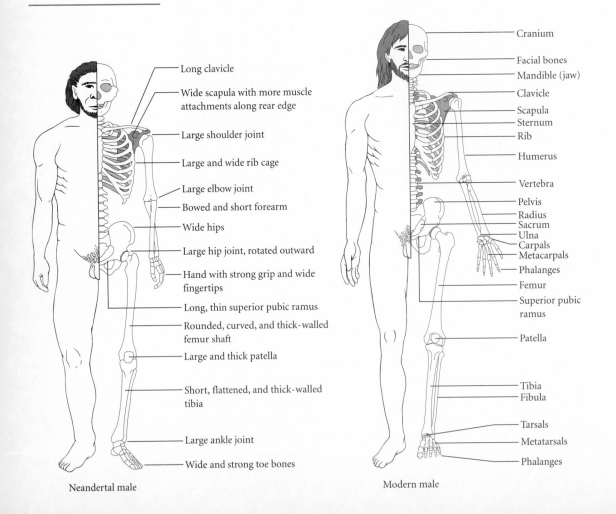

Long clavicle

Wide scapula with more muscle attachments along rear edge

Large shoulder joint

Large and wide rib cage

Large elbow joint

Bowed and short forearm

Wide hips

Large hip joint, rotated outward

Hand with strong grip and wide fingertips

Long, thin superior pubic ramus

Rounded, curved, and thick-walled femur shaft

Large and thick patella

Short, flattened, and thick-walled tibia

Large ankle joint

Wide and strong toe bones

Cranium

Facial bones

Mandible (jaw)

Clavicle

Scapula

Sternum

Rib

Humerus

Vertebra

Pelvis

Radius

Sacrum

Ulna

Carpals

Metacarpals

Phalanges

Femur

Superior pubic ramus

Patella

Tibia

Fibula

Tarsals

Metatarsals

Phalanges

Neandertal male

Modern male

Stringer 1993). However, true, or "classic," Neandertals possessing all the typical traits (to be discussed) were confined to Europe and west Asia and date from about 130,000–33,000 years ago.

Morphological Evidence

Though we now recognize the Neandertals as being closely related to modern humanity, controversy persists concerning the precise place of the Neandertals in the human family: Were they our evolutionary grandparents, or just distant cousins? (See Trinkaus 1983a,b, 1986, 1989; Trinkaus and Shipman 1993; Wolpoff 1989b; and especially F. Smith 1991.) On this issue, paleoanthropologists seem to suffer from the ironic disadvantage of a wealth of data: Whereas other fossil species are represented by samples of just a few to a dozen or so, it has been estimated that more than 400 separate Neandertal individuals have been excavated, and are represented by thousands of bones. A limited database presents less to argue about than a more substantial body of evidence.

Cranial Morphology. Neandertal brain size often surpassed that of modern human beings. Skull sizes range from about 1,300 ml to more than 1,600 ml, with a mean of nearly 1,480 ml (see Table 7.2); modern human mean cranial capacity is about 1,450 ml. However, the configuration of the Neandertal cranium—long and low in profile, with a steeply sloping forehead—is far different from the round, high profile of a modern human with its virtually vertical forehead. The Neandertal face was large, with the lower portion far forward of the eyes and brows. Also, Neandertals lacked the thin, pointy chin that typifies modern human beings. The robust features of the Neandertal head and face can be seen even in young Neandertals, including a three-year-old Neandertal child from Gibraltar (Dean, Stringer, and Bromage 1986) and a ten-month-old infant from Amud Cave in Israel (Bower 1994b).

From the Neck Down: Designed for Cold. Contrary to Boule's reconstruction, below the head the Neandertal skeleton is essentially modern in appearance, but with some crucial differences. One morphological pattern is consistent with a physical adaptation to cold: Neandertals were big—relatively wide with broad, squat torsos and short extremities (see Figure 7.11; Trinkaus 1983a; Ruff et al. 1993), a body form associated in modern humans with cold environments because it retains heat better than a body with a small torso and long limbs. Christopher Ruff (1993) compares the Neandertal body to that of a modern Inuit (Eskimo). This adaptation probably reflects the fact that the Neandertals first appeared in Europe during Pleistocene isotope stage 6 and flourished there during isotope stage 4 (see Figure 6.7), both glacial maxima in Ice Age Europe. Another likely adaptation to cold was the Neandertal's large, projecting nose, beyond the size range of modern humans, valuable in cold, dry climates for conserving moisture during vigorous physical activity (Trinkaus 1989). That recovered skeletons of Neandertal children are quite large relative to modern human skeletons of similar age could be another case of a modern human pattern being reflected in the extreme by Neandertals—the tendency for women living in colder climates to give birth to larger babies (Dean, Stringer, and Bromage 1986; F. Smith 1991).

From the Neck Down: Built for Strength.   Not all skeletal features of the Neandertals are related directly to their adaptation to life in a cold climate. A suite of characteristics seems to reflect the enormous strength and endurance of the Neandertals. Some of these features are so striking, they differentiate Neandertals absolutely from modern humans.

In about every area on the skeleton, the Neandertals exhibit what is called **musculoskeletal hypertrophy.** Paleoanthropologist Erik Trinkaus and a number of his co-workers have produced a detailed body of evidence on this point. For example, Neandertal lower legs, when exposed to a test of twisting and bending strength, were twice as strong as the bones of modern humans who had lived a vigorous lifestyle (Lovejoy and Trinkaus 1980). The breadth of their scapulae (shoulder blades) and the length of their clavicles (collar bones), along with the robusticity of areas of muscle attachment on those bones, is indicative of broad, powerful shoulders (Churchill and Trinkaus 1990). This, plus the great size and robusticity of their upper arm bones (Ben-Itzhak, Smith, and Bloom 1988) and the large areas for muscle attachment on their forearms (Trinkaus 1983a) indicate clearly that the Neandertals had tremendous upper body strength. Even in their ribs, vertebrae, and fingers, Neandertal bones show areas for muscle attachment far larger than what is seen in modern humans. The bones of the Neandertal hand indicate an extremely powerful grip (Trinkaus and Villemeur 1991). Paleoanthropologist Fred Smith put it most succinctly: "Neandertals seem to represent the high-water mark for the genus *Homo* in favoring the brawn approach to environmental adaptation" (1991:225). In other words, a spear-wielding Neandertal would have made an imposing adversary.

While the Neandertals certainly were capable of upright posture and bipedal locomotion, evidence exists that they may have walked somewhat differently from modern humans. The nearly complete right half of a Neandertal pelvis from Kebara Cave in Israel is very different from that of a modern human, which has been interpreted as signifying differences in posture and locomotion (Rak 1990; see this chapter's Case Study Close-Up section).

Fossil Evidence

Neandertal Origins.   The remains of at least 24 individual hominids have thus far been recovered from a spectacular site in a cave called Sima de los Huesos in the Atapuerca Mountains of northern Spain. The layer in the cave lying above that from which the bones have been recovered has been dated to more than 300,000 years in age, making the bones at least that old. Though the bones are more than twice as old as those of the so-called "classic" Neandertals, researchers characterize the morphology of the crania of the two adults and one child thus far recovered as "Neanderthal-like" and as anticipating the Neandertal cranial form (Arsuaga et al. 1993:535). Cranial capacities have been measured at 1,125 ml and 1,390 ml for the two adults and 1,100 ml for the juvenile. Preliminary analysis indicates that the Atapuerca hominids exhibit ten out of fifteen (two-thirds) typically Neandertal cranial and postcranial characteristics (Stringer 1993). They have less in common with either *Homo erectus* or modern *Homo sapiens.*

These very early (or "pre-") Neandertals from northern Spain have some features in common with the other archaic *Homo sapiens* from Europe already listed. Christopher Stringer (1993) proposes that the Atapuerca Neandertals and most if not all of the other European archaics represent a single, variable group of hominids whose differences are the result of geographic distance and time. The excavators propose that the morphology of the Atapuerca fossils implies a gradual evolution of Neandertals in Europe.

"Classic" Neandertals. While these oldest Neandertal-like fossils can now be dated to more than 300,000 years ago, "classic" Neandertals are less than half that age. The site of La Chaise, France, has produced typically Neandertal remains dating to 126,000 years ago (Cook et al. 1982), and the site of Fontéchevade, also in France, is probably more than 100,000 years old (Gamble 1986). Because the earliest Neandertal sites are in Europe, and because their physical characteristics originated in an environment marked by the ice and cold of the Pleistocene, it seems clear this marks their origin. They spread into southwest Asia only later, retaining their unsuitable (for the Middle East) physical adaptation to a cold climate.

The great florescence of the Neandertals in Europe and southwest Asia occurred between 80,000 and 40,000 years ago. Sites that have produced important Neandertal remains that are closely similar in morphology (Figure 7.12)

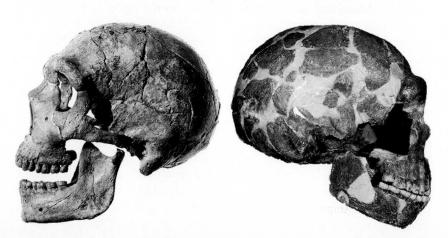

FIGURE 7.12

These typical Neandertal skulls are from (left) *Amud, Israel, and* (right) *Tabun, Israel.* (*Left:* Israel Antiquities Authority; *right:* The Natural History Museum, London)

include Le Moustier, La Chappelle-aux-Saints, and La Ferrassie in France; Spy in Belgium; Saccopastore and Mt. Circeo in Italy; Krapina in Yugoslavia; Amud, Kebara, and Tabun in Israel; and Shanidar in Iraq.

NEANDERTAL CULTURE

Stone Tools

FIGURE 7.13

These typical Mousterian tools are produced by a core-and-flake technology practiced by the Neandertals. (Reprinted with permission from F. Bordes. 1961. Mousterian cultures in France. *Science* 134:803–810. Copyright 1961 American Association for the Advancement of Science)

Without guidance, many people attempting to replicate stone tools rely on brawn. They take one rock in each hand, close their eyes, smash the stones together, and hope that useful flakes wind up in the rubble at their feet. Though Neandertals were brawny, their toolmaking relied at least as much on brain power as on physical prowess.

Named for the French Neandertal site of Le Moustier, the **Mousterian** toolmaking tradition of the Neandertals represents not a replacement of the Levallois technique, but a refinement. The Mousterian is a **Middle Paleolithic** industry; it is more sophisticated than the Oldowan (Chapter 5) or Acheulian (Chapter 6) industries of the **Lower Paleolithic** and less so than the Aurignacian industry of the **Upper Paleolithic** (Chapter 8).

Mousterian flakes were smaller and more precisely made than the earlier Levallois flakes. This meant that the Neandertals were capable of producing flakes whose size and shape matched more precisely the form needed for a predesignated purpose. Instead of a single, all-purpose tool like a handaxe, or a few particular kinds of tools like the earlier Levallois industry, dozens of different task-specific, standardized Mousterian tool types are recognized. French archaeologist François Bordes (1972) defined 63 specific Mousterian tool types for cutting, slicing, piercing, scraping, sawing, and pounding (Figure 7.13). Archaeologists disagree about how to interpret these types. Bordes broke them down into five groupings that he interpreted as representing five separate, coexisting European Neandertal cultures. Lewis Binford and Sally Binford (1966; S. Binford 1968) viewed the five groupings of tools as five different sets of **tool kits** made and used at different sites by the same, not different groups. Harold Dibble (1987) considers both of these views incorrect, suggesting that Bordes' groupings represent only different stages in the use-life of the tools; that is, they look different as they wear out and are resharpened. Whatever the case, the complexity of the Neandertal stone-tool assemblage clearly is the result of the complexity of what they were doing with those tools.

Each Mousterian flake received more precise treatment once it was removed from the core. Whereas an Acheulian handaxe may have required as many as 65 blows of a hammerstone, in the production of a highly specialized Mousterian tool an additional hundred or more blows were needed to shape and sharpen the edge once the flake was removed from its core (Constable 1973).

Subsistence

Archaeologist Lewis Binford has been an important researcher in the field of **ethnoarchaeology,** in which anthropologists residing with living groups of people study them from an archaeological perspective. One focus of ethnoarchaeology is to examine how behavior is transformed into what we find in the archaeological record. By investigating the data's journey from behavior to archaeological evidence, it is hoped that insights will be gained on how to interpret back from archaeological evidence to behavior.

Lewis Binford's (1978) classic study among the Nunamiut, a living Inuit (Eskimo) group in Alaska, focused on their pattern of hunting, butchering, preparing, and disposing of animal resources. Binford has used what he learned among the Nunamiut to interpret the archaeological record at the Neandertal site of Combe Grenal in France (L. Binford 1987b). In examining the remains of animals processed by the Neandertal inhabitants of the site, he recognized butchering patterns in the cut marks preserved on the bones he had seen in the fresh kills of the Nunamiut. Cut marks similar to those made by the Nunamiut on caribou jaws to extract the tongue, for example, were seen by Binford on the mandibles of horse, reindeer, and aurochs (wild cattle) at Combe Grenal. From this he concluded that the Neandertals had a similar pattern of behavior designed to extract the tasty delicacy of tongue meat.

Based on his analysis of the animal bones at Combe Grenal, Binford is unconvinced that the Neandertals were great hunters. He did not find an abundance of butchering marks on those parts of the bones of animals at the site reflecting the best cuts of meat. Binford understood this to mean that the Neandertals were probably opportunistic scavengers, subsisting on the poorer meat left over by carnivores. If so, it was a successful strategy, allowing Neandertals to flourish during extremely cold periods of the Pleistocene, when meat may have been the only reliably available source of food.

On the other hand, investigators at Kebara Cave in Israel (Bar-Yosef et al. 1992) found evidence of an abundance of gazelle and fallow deer in the Neandertal diet. Evidence of burning and cut marks on those bones, as well as on elephant, horse, and several other mammalian species, shows the breadth of the animal subsistence base of the cave inhabitants. An abundance of carbonized seeds of wild peas found in the fireplaces is a direct indicator that the Kebara Neandertals also ate locally available vegetal foods.

The occurrence of numerous triangular, pointed artifacts in the tool assemblage at Kebara seems to indicate that hunting was a significant part of the Neandertal subsistence quest (see Figure 7.7). Archaeologist John Shea (1988, 1993, 1994) has noted the presence of a set of diagnostic patterns of damage he calls **impact wear** on some Mousterian triangular points found in southwest Asia, including those recovered at Kebara Cave. This damage is represented by clusters of small fractures on the point and nearby edge of the tool. Shea has shown experimentally that this is the probable result of using these tools as projectiles—as in a hunting spear. When the stone-tipped spear enters an animal's body—by thrusting or throwing—it will often strike a bone. That impact removes the kinds of damage flake Shea has recognized. Shea has found these damage flakes to be fairly common on Mousterian points in southwest Asian Neandertal sites.

While the precise importance of hunting to the diet at Neandertal Mousterian sites at Kebara and elsewhere is not measurable, it is almost certain that there was some hunting. The extent of the faunal deposit in Kebara Cave clearly indicates that the Neandertal inhabitants were proficient at obtaining meat. This is not surprising considering that their enormous skeletal and muscular strength would have provided the stamina needed to walk great distances in tracking animals—and in Pleistocene Europe, in the snow and cold. And once they had tracked down the animals, their great physical strength, along with their sophisticated tool kit, would have made them formidable hunters.

Compassion

It is often said that a society can be judged by how it treats its sick or injured. Ironically, evidence shows that the Neandertals, whose intelligence is so often maligned and who are used as a symbol for brutality, may actually have been compassionate and caring. This suggestion stems from evidence of survival of Neandertal individuals who had significant health problems or who had suffered severe trauma sometime during their lives. Some of these individuals had been in such bad shape that they probably could have survived only with the help of comrades.

The best, though not only, example comes from the skeleton of an adult male (Shanidar I) found in Shanidar Cave in Iraq (Solecki 1971; Trinkaus 1983b). This Neandertal had lived a rather eventful life, to judge by his skeleton, which showed several serious, but healed, bone fractures. There was evidence of severe trauma to the left side of the head: The left eye orbit had been fractured so badly that it is likely the blow blinded his eye. His right arm had been so severely smashed, that the lower part had been amputated (perhaps by the blow, perhaps intentionally in an early example of surgical amputation). The right leg showed signs of disease and possible trauma.

It is clear this individual had sustained a heavy trauma at some time in his life, and that, rather remarkably, he had survived. Such survival would have been a virtual impossibility without the help and care of his companions. As K. A. Dettwyler (1991) points out, he still could have made a significant contribution to his society, so we should not interpret his and other remains as indicating absolutely selfless acts of compassion; he was not an individual who, once healed, necessarily would have been a physical "burden" to society. Nevertheless, the survival of Shanidar I does show a level of care, at least during the healing process, that is usually associated only with mod-

FIGURE 7.14

This intentional burial site found at La Ferassie in France shows the Neandertals' affinity with the modern human practice of burying their dead. (Musée de l'Homme, Paris, M. Lucas, Photographer)

ern human beings. That the Neandertals may have been caring for the sick and wounded merely shows how similar they may have been to us.

Burial of the Dead

In at least one essential area, Neandertals behaved much as we do: They buried their dead. At sites such as Le Moustier, La Chapelle-aux-Saints, and La Ferrassie in France; Teshik-Tash in Uzbekistan; Shanidar in Iraq; and Amud, Tabun, and Kebara in Israel, the evidence indicates that Neandertals interred their dead in the ground, most often in an intentionally flexed position, knees drawn up toward the chest, and even with some simple items such as stone or bone implements, ochre, or unmodified animal bone (Figure 7.14; Harrold 1980).

Archaeologists Anna Belfer-Cohen and Erella Hovers (1992) surveyed burial data for the Middle Paleolithic period of the Neandertals and counted fifty-nine intentional burials. They point out that these burials make no sense as a mere hygienic way to dispose of a dead body. Why put that much time into digging a hole if a dead body can be far more unceremoniously dumped in the woods, allowing scavengers to do the work? They conclude that the Neandertals were burying their dead in recognition of the significance of death.

More than that is difficult to tell. It is impossible to know, for example, if Neandertals intended the tightly flexed position of many of the bodies the way some modern people have, as mimicking a fetus in the womb. Did the Neandertals use the fetal position [14 of 20 Neandertal burials (70%) examined by archaeologist Frank Harrold (1980:200) were so positioned] to symbolize death as the end of the circle of life? Were the bodies tied into this flexed position to confine the spirit to the grave? Or was such a position simply most convenient because it minimized the size of the hole that had to be dug? Were grave goods intended for use in a perceived afterlife? Or were they simply remembrances for a dead friend? We simply do not know the answers.

We should not conclude that Neandertals were just like us—had funerals, memorial services, and formalized cemeteries [see L. Binford (1987a) and Gargett (1989) for a debunking of some of the more fanciful reconstructions of Neandertal burial ceremonialism]. But the questions raised by the intentional disposal of the dead practiced by the Neandertals are more important than the answers we might suggest. Clearly, Neandertals understood the significance of death and recognized it through burial. Here again, these very different human ancestors exhibit their kinship to us.

ISSUES AND DEBATES

WHY ARE THE NEANDERTALS EXTINCT?

The Neandertals and other archaic humans are extinct, having been replaced by anatomically modern human beings. In the consensus view presented in this book, the Neandertals were not the immediate ancestors of modern people, but a side branch of human evolution, at least partially overlapping in time with anatomically modern human beings (see Chapter 8). What significant advantages did the early anatomically modern humans have over the archaics that led to the survival of the modern humans and the extinction of the archaics? The European fossil record may shed light on this question.

Some evidence indicates that the Neandertals were having a rough time in Pleistocene Europe. For one thing, the Neandertals were rather short-lived as compared to even ancient anatomically modern humans. Erik Trinkaus and D. D. Thompson (1987:126) have shown that, in a sample of 246 Neandertals, four out of ten died before reaching adulthood. And of those that survived childhood, less than 10% were more than 40 years old at death

(1987:127). Paleoanthropologist Olga Soffer (1992:252, 1994:103–104) has shown that, in her Neandertal sample of about 200, 43% died at less than 12 years of age, while under 30% of early modern humans in a similar-size skeletal sample (about 150) died that early in life.

As alluded to in Chapter 3, the human skeleton preserves a record of dietary deficiencies suffered during its developmental years. For example, **Harris lines** [cracks on the ends of long bones (arm and leg) that result from dietary deficiency during the developing years] and **enamel hypoplasia** (zones of thin tooth enamel that result from unmet nutritional needs during early childhood) are present to a far greater degree in Neandertal remains than in the remains of early anatomically modern human beings. Marsha Oglivie, Bryan Curran, and Erik Trinkaus (1989), for example, found evidence of hypoplasia in the enamel of 36% of 669 Neandertal teeth, reflecting an estimated incidence of 75% of the individuals represented. This is more than double the incidence in nutritionally stressed recent human samples (Oglivie, Curran, and Trinkaus 1989:30). Other studies have produced similar results (Molnar and Molnar 1985; M. Brennan 1991). As Olga Soffer (1994) points out, this paleopathological evidence indicates that Neandertal children suffered far more physical stress than their anatomically modern contemporaries.

Finally, Erik Trinkaus (1989) points to a notable decrease in evidence of trauma when early anatomically modern fossils are compared to Neandertals: fewer broken bones among the early moderns than in Neandertal skeletons.

Together this evidence has been interpreted as indicating that the Neandertals were, perhaps, too highly specialized in their physical, genetically determined adaptations to the harsh climates of the Ice Age and in their great size and strength. As Erik Trinkaus (1983a) points out, massive and heavily built individuals like the Neandertals incur a higher energy cost than those more lightly built. Where Neandertals needed to burn more calories by ingesting greater amounts of food to keep their heavily built bodies warm, anatomically modern humans could get by with less, simply because they were smaller and more lightly built. The paleopathological evidence cited may have resulted from the Neandertal inability to procure enough food under the harsh conditions of Ice Age Europe.

Moreover, anatomically modern humans may have possessed better cultural buffers against the climate of the Pleistocene. According to archaeologist Richard Klein (1994), when compared to the cultures of Middle Paleolithic Neandertals, anatomically modern humans produced more complex tools with a greater number of types, obtained better raw materials from greater distances to make those tools, used bone as a source of raw material for tool manufacture, built more complex structures, buried their dead in more complex graves, and produced indisputable works of art. As Klein puts it, a "very substantial behavioral gulf" separates the Neandertals from anatomically modern humans (1994:11) (see Chapter 8).

Of great importance in this discussion is the fact that rather than having to burn calories to keep warm, anatomically modern humans could more efficiently burn wood than their Neandertal cousins. As pointed out by Klein (1994), the archaeological evidence shows that Neandertal hearths were simple and do not exhibit the more sophisticated design and better heat retention of fireplaces constructed by anatomically modern human beings. At Kebara Cave, for instance, Neandertal hearths are round or oval and show no use of stone and, therefore, no banking of the heat as is typically found in the hearths of early modern humans. Additionally, Arthur Jelinek (1994) suggests that some of the artifacts made by modern human beings—but not by Neandertals—were part of a tool kit for the manufacture of more effectively tailored cold-weather clothing; Jelinek calls this clothing "personal insulation" (1994:83). Because cultural adaptations are faster, more flexible, and often less energy expensive than physical adaptations that accomplish the same thing, anatomically modern humans would have an enormous advantage over the Neandertals.

Based on these probable advantages, statistical models have been produced that indicate just how easily the extinction of the Neandertal could have been accomplished. Ezra Zubrow (1989), a mathematician turned archaeologist, has determined that under certain circumstances, when Neandertal mortality exceeds that of anatomically modern humans by between only 1% and 2%, the complete extinction of the Neandertals can occur in only thirty generations—less than a thousand years. So it is ironic: The very physical features that allowed Neandertals to survive and even thrive for a time under the harsh conditions of Pleistocene Europe ultimately led to their extinction. They appear to have become too massively built, too specialized for life in the cold. This put them at a distinct disadvantage when conditions changed and food became harder to obtain.

COULD NEANDERTALS TALK?

This may appear to be a question almost impossible to answer. After all, sound does not fossilize and the next best source of information about oral communication—the muscles and tissues that make up the human vocal tract—leave no direct physical trace. Fortunately, however, such muscles and tissues are connected to bone, in particular at the base of a hominid's cranium. Analysis of the basicranium (as mentioned previously for *Homo erectus*) may inform us concerning an extinct hominid's ability to speak.

The work of Philip Lieberman (1984; Lieberman et al. 1992) and Edmund Crelin (1987), both separately and together (Lieberman et al. 1972), has served as a lightning rod in the debate about Neandertal speech. Based on their analysis of the basicranium of Neandertal, they reconstructed the soft parts of Neandertal vocal anatomy and then used a computer to simulate the sounds a Neandertal might have been capable of making and the speed with which they could be made. In their reconstruction of Neandertal vocal tract anatomy as implied by the morphology of the base of the skull, the larynx was positioned high up in the throat, and the pharynx lacked the sharp bend that typifies modern humans. In fact, the reconstructed Neandertal vocal tract resembled more a chimpanzee or a newborn human than an adult human being. They concluded that, while the Neandertals could make sounds, they were incapable of producing anything close to the range of sounds that characterizes human speech. Lieberman (1992) has gone so far as to suggest that the great differences he postulates between the speech of Neandertals and early anatomically modern humans may have served as one of the key factors to keep these groups apart. This might explain how Neandertals and modern humans maintained separate evolutionary trajectories, though they were contemporaries and, in some cases, living in close proximity to each other (see Chapter 8).

Many, if not most, paleoanthropologists are highly critical of Lieberman and Crelin's conclusions. Even if the Neandertals were physically incapable of producing the complete range of sounds we are capable of making, no modern human language requires all those sounds anyway. Neandertal brains are so large and their culture so complex, it is difficult to believe that their linguistic abilities were as elementary as some researchers have suggested. In addition, the recent discovery of a very modern-looking hyoid bone (a horseshoe-shaped bone in the throat) at Kebara Cave (Arensburg et al. 1990) has led some researchers to conclude that the Neandertals were physically capable of fully human speech. There this debate stands.

DID NEANDERTALS WORSHIP CAVE BEARS?

You may still find in popular literature the claim that the archaeological record shows that the Neandertals regularly killed the large species of European Ice Age bear, *Ursus spelaeus,* and then built shrines for the skulls of these huge beasts.

Unfortunately, the notion of bear-worshipping Neandertals simply doesn't hold up under careful taphonomic analysis. As shown by paleontologist and cave bear expert Björn Kurtén (1976), the supposed archaeological features used to support this notion—a stone chest filled with bear skulls at the site of Drachenloch, Switzerland, a stone cubicle with 20 skulls at Regourdu in France, and other accumulations of cave bear skulls at Les Furtins and Saone-et-Loire—were more in the minds of the excavators than in reality. Kurtén has shown in these and other cases that key data concerning the positioning of the bones are contradictory in the various sketches made by the excavators and further contradict some of their notes on the discoveries. Moreover, if Neandertals cut up the bear carcasses with stone tools, they were very neat about it; no stone tools have been found in association with the bear remains, and no cut marks have been found on the bear bones.

The bears likely died natural deaths in the caves, where there is clear evidence of their having lived. Scavengers then came in, removing some of the body along with some of the bones. Commonly in such a situation, the large skull is left in place. Any other bear who subsequently moves into the cave simply pushes the skull against a wall, out of the way. After a time, a group of skulls can accumulate. It might appear to be intentional and cultural, but it is not. It can be explained as the result of taphonomic processes that involve no human agency. And the stone chests the researchers reported were nothing more than piled-up rock, fallen from the roof of the caves, covering the bones of the bears who lived and died there. The image of the lone hunter, with nothing more than a spear in hand, facing off against an angry bear well over ten feet tall when on its hind legs, hoping to claim its cave home and then to propitiate its dead spirit, is evocative indeed. The extant evidence, however, simply does not support this romantic image.

DID NEANDERTALS PRODUCE ART?

The creative impulse and the desire to use symbols, realistic or not, to express this impulse—to produce art—seems a uniquely human trait. Certainly, the art of the Upper Paleolithic to be discussed in Chapter 9 is recognizable as the product of a thoroughly modern human intelligence. So, in assessing their relationship to us, we might well consider whether the Neandertals produced art.

The answer is a qualified maybe. Although there is nothing like the cave paintings or figurines of Upper Paleolithic Europe discussed in Chapter 9 associated with the Neandertals, some examples of crudely incised bones, perforated bones, and polished ivory have been found at Neandertal sites that are possible evidence of artistic expression by the Neandertals (Chase and Dibble 1987; Simek 1992). Though the objects are clearly less sophisticated than the art seen later in Europe, in the desire to scratch symbols on a stone or to polish a bit of ivory, the Neandertals were exhibiting a fundamental similarity to us.

WERE NEANDERTAL BABIES LESS ALTRICIAL THAN MODERN BABIES?

As shown in Chapter 6, the configuration of the female pelvis can be used to estimate the degree of development of a hominid newborn. For some time, no intact Neandertal pelvis had been found, and the available fragments seemed to indicate a Neandertal pelvic inlet that was quite a bit larger than in modern human females. This led Erik Trinkaus to suggest that Neandertal babies were born at a more developed fetal stage than modern humans. He postulated that a larger birth canal would have allowed the birth of Neandertal babies of a year or more gestation, significantly more than the nine-month gestational period of modern humans (Trinkaus 1983a, 1984). This implied that Neandertal babies would have been less altricial than modern human newborns. This would be another, highly significant difference between them and us.

While no well-preserved female Neandertal pelvis has yet been found, the recent discovery and analysis of a complete right pelvis of a Neandertal male at Kebara Cave has caused Trinkaus to withdraw his suggestion of a longer gestation for Neandertals (Bar-Yosef et al. 1992). Analysis of the pelvis by researcher Yoel Rak (1990) shows some significant differences from that of modern human beings, but has also shown that the Neandertal pelvic inlet would have been no different in size from that of modern human females. Robert Tague (1992) concludes that, based on the Kebara pelvis, Neandertal babies could have been proportionally no larger than those of modern humans without making birth even more difficult than it is among modern human females. So the relatively large size of Neandertal children when compared to anatomically modern children of the same age is probably related to accelerated development after birth, not faster or longer prenatal development (Dean et al. 1986).

Kebara Cave is located on Mt. Carmel in Israel, in a region rich in Middle Paleolithic sites in general and Neandertal fossils in particular. The first excavation in the cave occurred in 1927, and researchers have returned intermittently in the ensuing years. Most recently, between 1982 and 1990, previously unexcavated parts of the cave were meticulously excavated [a detailed summary of all of the work conducted in the cave can be found in Bar-Yosef et al. (1992)].

CASE STUDY CLOSE-UP

The extensive artifact and faunal assemblages recovered from the cave provide a detailed picture of life in southwest Asia in the Middle Paleolithic. As mentioned previously, the Neandertal inhabitants of the cave subsisted on the meat of a wide range of animals, especially gazelle and fallow deer. They also collected and ate plant foods that abounded near the cave.

The artifact assemblage is typically Mousterian. Most of the lithic raw materials for tool production were obtained locally, from no more than 5 km away from the cave. All stages of the reduction sequence, from core preparation to final flake sharpening, were found in the cave. Wear pattern analysis carried out by archaeologist John Shea (1989) shows that the tools were used for various activities, including woodworking, butchering animals, bone and antler carving, and hideworking.

The skeleton of a Neandertal male was excavated at Kebara in 1983. He was 25–35 years old when he died some 60,000 years ago. We do not know how he died—there is no sign of significant disease or trauma on his skeleton, though it does display some enamel hypoplasia, so common among the Neandertals, as discussed earlier. We do know that he was intentionally buried, having been laid on his back in an east–west orientation, his head facing west. Based on the positioning of his bones, the excavators concluded that in his grave, his right arm had been laid across his chest, with his hand on his left breast. His left arm and hand had been placed on his stomach. Though the vast majority of animal bones in the cave bore evidence of gnawing by carnivores and scavengers, there were no gnaw marks on the Neandertal's bones. His body had been placed in a trench by his comrades, leaning up against the north wall of the grave. This leaning of the body against a wall of earth, and the infilling of the trench after placement, served to preserve much of the skeleton in correct anatomical sequence.

In a most unfortunate but equally intriguing turn of events, the otherwise largely intact skeleton was missing the head; no cranial fragments whatsoever were found in the thorough excavation of the burial. The mandible was in place, which seems to rule out animal disturbance as the cause of the head's disappearance. The researchers suggest that the head was intentionally removed by the deceased's cohorts after sufficient decay, to render the task minimally disruptive to the rest of his remains (Bar-Yosef et al. 1992:529). Why this would be done is a mystery, though some ceremonial treatment of the skull of a dead comrade is a reasonable possibility.

As mentioned previously, the Kebara skeleton has provided significant information concerning the Neandertal ability to speak, in the recovery in anatomical position of the hyoid bone of the throat (Arensburg et al. 1990). It has also cleared up the question of Neandertal pelvic inlet size (Rak 1990), showing a pelvic form different from anatomically modern humans, but not larger. For many researchers, the image of nearly mute Neandertals giving birth to large, relatively mature babies at twelve or more months' gestation has been put to rest by the Kebara adult burial.

VISITING THE PAST

Among the museums that display the most significant array of archaic and, in particular, Neandertal material is the Musée de l'Homme (Museum of Man) in Paris. Even if you are not planning to visit France, virtually any large natural history museum in the United States or Canada has displays on the Neandertals. It would be an interesting project to see how many of these museums continue to present old and inaccurate depictions of Neandertal life.

SUMMARY

Beginning some 400,000 years ago, *Homo erectus* gave way to a more modern-looking hominid form. Their fossils look enough like us to be granted the taxonomic label *Homo sapiens,* albeit of a premodern or archaic form. With a mean cranial capacity reaching past 1,220 ml, their brain size falls well within the modern human range.

One sort of archaic human, the Neandertals, is the best known of the premodern humans. Present in large numbers in Europe and southwest Asia, they were a successful and intelligent hominid. Their tool technology, called Mousterian, was far more efficient and sophisticated than the Acheulian technology of *Homo erectus*. There also is evidence that they cared for their sick, buried their dead, and were the first human ancestor to use symbols.

In some interpretations, the Neandertals are directly ancestral to at least some modern humans. The preponderance of evidence seems to indicate that the Neandertals were physically specialized to life in Ice Age Europe and represent an extinct side-branch of human evolution. This interpretation, however, leaves us in a bit of a quandary. If the Neandertals were a side-branch off the main evolutionary line, which, if any, of the other, non-Neandertal archaic humans were directly ancestral to us? That question is the focus of the next chapter.

TO LEARN MORE

Erik Trinkaus and Pat Shipman's (1993) *The Neandertals: Changing Images of Mankind* is an enormously informative and well-written history of the discovery and interpretation of the Neandertals. Paleoanthropologist Christopher Stringer and archaeologist Clive Gamble (1993) have written a terrific book, *In Search of the Neanderthals,* on the modern arguments and consensus about the significance of the Neandertals and their place in the evolution of anatomically modern people. *Discover* magazine has published a valuable summary of the various controversies surrounding the Neandertals (Fischman 1992).

KEY TERMS

anatomically modern
   Homo sapiens
archaic *Homo sapiens*
premodern *Homo*
   sapiens
Levallois

musculoskeletal
   hypertrophy
Mousterian
Middle Paleolithic
Lower Paleolithic
Upper Paleolithic

tool kit
ethnoarchaeology
impact wear
Harris lines
enamel hypoplasia

8

The Evolution of Us

THE ORIGINS OF MODERN HUMANS

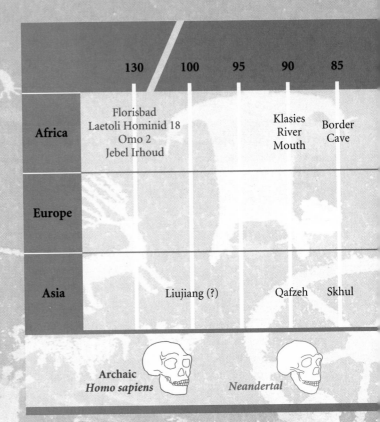

	130	100	95	90	85
Africa	Florisbad Laetoli Hominid 18 Omo 2 Jebel Irhoud			Klasies River Mouth	Border Cave
Europe					
Asia		Liujiang (?)		Qafzeh	Skhul

Archaic *Homo sapiens*   *Neandertal*

CHAPTER OVERVIEW

Anatomically modern human beings appear in the fossil record about 100,000 years ago. Two competing models—the replacement hypothesis and the multiregional approach—have been proposed to explain their evolution. In the former model, modern humans evolved once in one place—probably southern Africa—and spread out from there. Anatomically modern human beings replaced archaic humans wherever the two came in contact. In the latter model, modern human beings evolved from their archaic antecedents in various world areas more or less simultaneously. A deductive test of the evidence lends some support to the replacement model.

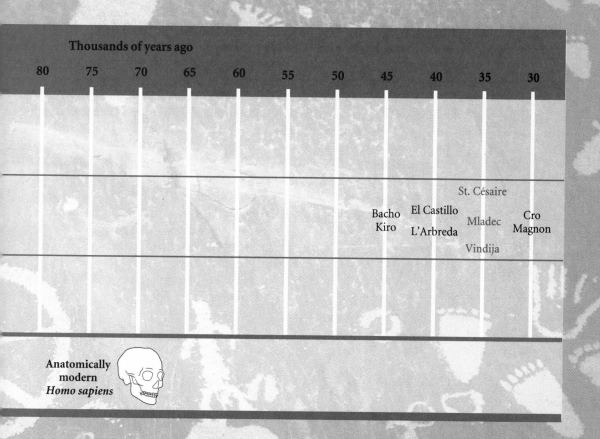

Thousands of years ago

| 80 | 75 | 70 | 65 | 60 | 55 | 50 | 45 | 40 | 35 | 30 |

Bacho Kiro   El Castillo   St. Césaire
             L'Arbreda   Mladec   Cro Magnon
                           Vindija

Anatomically modern *Homo sapiens*

The last quagga died in an Amsterdam zoo in 1883. The zoo animal was the final representative of a beautiful species of striped wild equine—members of the horse family—that lived in southern Africa until the late 1800s. Nineteenth-century paintings of African wildlife show it as a fascinating mixture of horse and zebra, with stripes only on the forequarters, neck, and head (Figure 8.1). The zebralike stripes faded to the rear, where its coat turned a solid chestnut brown. Its uniquely patterned hide was precisely what spelled its doom: The quagga was hunted relentlessly and to ultimate extinction by those who felt its skin was more suitably hung on a wall than left on a living, breathing animal.

Zoologists have long wondered about the place of the quagga in the animal kingdom. Was it a horse, a wild ass, a zebra, or something else entirely? Taxonomists from Linnaeus' time (see Chapter 2) to the present have relied largely on observation of form and behavior to classify plants and animals, and evolutionists have used these resulting classifications to suggest the biological relationships among living species. But with no living examples to study and no behavior to observe, conclusions concerning where the quagga fit into the living world were necessarily based on fading black-and-white photographs, paintings, written descriptions, and preserved museum specimens. This all changed in 1984.

MITOCHONDRIAL DNA AND MOLECULAR ARCHAEOLOGY

The quagga was one of the first extinct animals to have its actual **DNA** extracted from a preserved piece of the creature (Higuchi et al. 1984). Researchers Svante Pääbo, Russell Higuchi, and Allan Wilson (1989) have called the process employed in the quagga DNA retrieval and analysis "molecular archaeology."

Nuclear DNA, the so-called double helix of two parallel, connected strands of chemicals, looking much like a twisted ladder, serves as the blueprint for an individual and a species, and is present in most of the cells of an organism. Most cells also contain another kind of DNA, called **mitochondrial DNA (mtDNA).** Mitochondria (singular, *mitochondrion*) are usually referred to as the cells' energy factories.

There are major advantages to using mtDNA instead of nuclear DNA to trace the evolutionary connections among organisms. To begin with, mitochondrial DNA consists of a much shorter set of genetic instructions than nuclear DNA. Instead of the human nuclear DNA's double helix, which codes for more than 100,000 genes, human mitochondrial DNA comes in small, two-strand rings and codes for only 37 genes that control the mitochondrion (Wilson and Cann 1992). The human mitochondrial genome (the entire mitochondrial DNA sequence for humanity) is already completely known (Stoneking 1993); at the current rate of research our nuclear genome will not be entirely known until the beginning of the next century.

Also, while the DNA contained within the mitochondria of an organism's cells is unique to that individual and species, it plays little if any role in coding for the characteristics of the individual. Though some mutations in an organism's mtDNA are known to cause major neurological problems, many mutations in mtDNA have no effect on the organism (Wilson and Cann 1992:69). These mutations are adaptively neutral; they are neither selected for nor screened out in an evolutionary sense. So the appearance of the mtDNA within a population is largely the result of accumulated accidents that otherwise have little impact.

When compared to nuclear DNA, mtDNA observation indicates that mutations, or errors, build up at a relatively rapid and constant rate. It can be viewed, therefore, as a clock, and the number of changes (mutations) from a previous state is primarily a function of time. This aspect of mitochondrial DNA has enabled its use in the investigation of the nature and timing of the evolution of modern human beings (see the discussion later in this chapter).

Another advantage of using mtDNA in assessing evolutionary connections is that it is inherited only in the female line and so is less complicated to use as an evolutionary marker. The mtDNA of two different individuals in each generation do not mix, so it is much easier to trace back through generations than is ever-recombining nuclear DNA. Mitochondrial DNA evolutionary analysis is analogous to the genealogical tracing of a family name that remains pretty much the same as far back as you go, with only occasional random, regular changes in the spelling. Using nuclear DNA for the same purpose would be like trying to trace a lineage of people where in each generation the family name changed to a random combination of letters in the mother's and the father's names.

FIGURE 8.1

Although the quagga (bottom) became extinct in 1864, DNA extracted from its preserved hide has allowed for a precise analysis of its place in a taxonomy of living things. (George Bernard/Animals, Animals)

RESURRECTING THE QUAGGA

A 140-year-old quagga skin had been preserved in a German museum. Russell Higuchi and his co-workers isolated and then chemically extracted DNA from the hide. Next, using a genetic engineering technique called **polymerase chain reaction (PCR),** which greatly increases the quantity of mtDNA in a sample from even a single preserved DNA molecule, the scientists were able to produce copies of preserved quagga mtDNA for study.

Finally, a procedure called **DNA hybridization** was applied. In this procedure the double helix strands replicated by PCR are broken apart by the application of heat, and divided strands of DNA from other species are then mixed together with DNA from the species in question. The chemical bonds—the "rungs" in the DNA "ladder"—attempt to reestablish themselves, and strands from different animals attempt to bond chemically to each other if they are reasonably similar. How well the strands from two different species connect— as measured by how difficult they are to break apart by the subsequent addition of heat—is a reflection of how similar the species are and, by inference, how long ago they may have diverged from a common evolutionary ancestor. When DNA hybridization is performed on human beings and chimpanzees, for example, we see a remarkable concordance: The DNA strands connect amazingly well, showing close to 99% identity.

When the mtDNA of the extinct quagga was compared to that of modern species, its place relative to them was ascertained: Its mtDNA was much more similar, and bonded more completely, to that of a particular kind of zebra (the Burchell Zebra) than to that of a horse or a wild ass.

Other studies have extracted DNA from an extinct Siberian woolly mammoth whose 40,000-year-old remains were preserved in ice. Its DNA was quite similar to that of modern elephants (Pääbo et al. 1989). A 14,000-year-old saber-toothed tiger, recovered from the La Brea tar pits in Los Angeles, produced DNA similar, but not identical, to living species of large wild cats (Grimaldi 1993).

And yes, one key element in the plot of the book and movie *Jurassic Park* is actually true: DNA has been successfully retrieved from insects caught in amber dating to more than 25 million years ago (Grimaldi 1993). This DNA has been used to assess accurately the evolutionary relationships of extinct bees and termites. But no dinosaur DNA has yet been recovered from the guts of biting insects dating to the Jurassic period, so you won't be visiting a real *Jurassic Park* anytime soon. On the other hand, the first small fragment of dinosaur DNA has recently been retrieved from a bone found deep in a coal seam in eastern Utah (Monastersky 1994c). Still, using such fragmentarily preserved genetic instructions to grow a living version of a beast may never be possible.

MOLECULAR ARCHAEOLOGY AND THE EVOLUTION OF HUMAN BEINGS

DNA has also been recovered from human remains. Ancient human DNA that can be compared to modern human DNA has been extracted from a 2,400-year-old Egyptian mummy (Pääbo 1985), 500–800-year-old Chilean mummies (Rogan and Salvo 1990), some well-preserved 7,000-year-old human brains [found in waterlogged conditions at archaeological sites in Florida (Pääbo, Gifford, and Wilson 1988)], and human bones from Illinois dated to A.D. 1300 (Stone and Stoneking 1993). When the genetic makeup of an ancient person can be compared directly to that of modern individuals, his or her relationship to modern people can be assessed. And that is precisely where this discussion is leading.

Suppose we could recover DNA from an ancient fossilized hominid bone? One set of fossils from which we might want to recover DNA would certainly be the Neandertals, discussed in the previous chapter. If we could figure out where and how the Neandertals and other extinct varieties of near-modern people fit into the human evolutionary story—which known specimens were members of a group immediately ancestral to us and which (if any) were merely side branches doomed to extinction—much of the maddening confusion surrounding the question of modern human evolution (the focus of this chapter) would be resolved.

But in asking these questions, we are in a position similar to twentieth-century scientists who wished to understand better the relationship of the quagga to modern, living groups of equines. To classify the Neandertals and other archaic humans accurately and to assess their evolutionary relationships to each other—and to us—we would like to have living examples to examine directly their morphology and behavior. But, like the quagga, all of the archaic varieties of *Homo sapiens* are extinct. All modern human beings and all historically recorded humans are members of the same species and subspecies: *Homo sapiens sapiens.* Paleoanthropologists are in an even less enviable position than the quagga researchers. Zoologists at least had photographs, paintings, and preserved quagga specimens at their disposal. Paleoanthropologists have only the direct evidence of the bones of our immediate evolutionary forebears and the indirect evidence of modern human genetic variation.

Today it is unclear whether ancient hominid fossil bone contains any intact nuclear or mitochondrial DNA strands; time and fossilization may have destroyed all of the genetic material. But suppose "molecular archaeology" conducted on fossil hominid bones [or, as geneticist Mark Stoneking (1993) suggests, on ancient blood residue] were possible.

Currently, an attempt is under way to extract mtDNA from a vertebra from the Neandertal site of Shanidar Cave (see Chapter 7; Johanson, Johanson, and Edgar 1994:285). If (let's be optimistic) minute, intact strands of ancient hominid mtDNA are actually present in fossil bone, then scientists will be able to extract it and compare it to the DNA of modern humans and to DNA sequences recovered from fossil bones representing other hominid species. By comparing DNA directly among various human ancestors, our evolutionary trees will no longer have to be based on gross morphological characteristics as reconstructed from fragmentary fossil remains. Instead, our evolutionary models could be based on the actual genetic instructions that determine what we are, whether it's *Homo sapiens, Homo erectus,* or *Homo habilis.* And, perhaps, at last we would be able to resolve one of the most vexing riddles about human evolution: How did anatomically modern *Homo sapiens* evolve? Let's hope that researchers Rebecca Cann, Olga Richards, and J. Koji Lum are right when they state that "new technology for extracting DNA from bone will eventually resolve many mysteries, including exactly what became of Neandertal populations in Western Europe" (1994:137).

But until this becomes a reality, we must rely on the complex and sometimes contradictory conclusions drawn from analysis of the morphology of fossilized bone, the artifacts made by the people who now are nothing more than those bones, and the current genetic makeup of humanity—the kinds of evidence this chapter will examine.

CHRONICLE

Whereas previous chapters' Chronicle sections have presented the consensus opinion on each chapter's topic, there is, unfortunately, no consensus on the origins of anatomically modern *Homo sapiens*. Instead, there are two competing models for explaining the source and timing of the evolution of modern human beings, and numerous approaches somewhere between the two opposing explanations. One explanation is called, variously, the "out of Africa," "Noah's Ark," or "replacement" model. The other is the "multiregional" or "regional continuity" view (Figure 8.2).

THE REPLACEMENT MODEL

In the replacement model, whose chief proponent is British paleoanthropologist Christopher B. Stringer (1990, 1992a,b, 1994; Stringer and Andrews 1988), nearly all of the fossils of archaic *Homo sapiens* described in Chapter 7 (at least those from Europe and Asia) represent extinct forms of human beings that contributed nothing to the evolution of modern humanity. Instead, the evolution of anatomically modern human beings is considered to have occurred just once, in one place—currently believed to be Africa, perhaps in the south of that continent—and fairly recently—between 100,000 and 200,000 years ago.

In this view, the first anatomically modern human beings spread out from their African homeland, first into southwest Asia, then east to the rest of Asia and north and west to Europe (Figure 8.3). There, these African-originating modern humans encountered populations of archaic humans—

FIGURE 8.2

The replacement model and the multiregional model predict different patterns for the evolution of modern human beings.

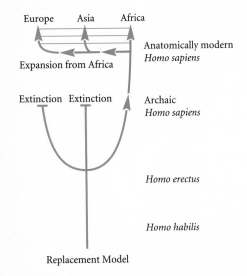

Replacement Model

There is no (or limited) contact (represented by the horizontal lines) until the evolution of anatomically modern humans.

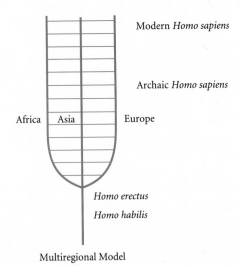

Multiregional Model

Horizontal lines represent contact and gene flow among the three continents.

the premodern people discussed in Chapter 7—and possibly even remnant groups of *Homo erectus.* For a time they were contemporaries, perhaps living virtually next door to each other. Though they belonged to the same species —both the modern and archaics were *Homo sapiens* and can be traced back to earlier *Homo erectus* populations in Africa—they did not interbreed. The anatomically modern humans possessed some fundamental advantage, as yet poorly understood, over their archaic neighbors—perhaps they were smarter or could communicate more effectively. The modern humans replaced archaics wherever they came into contact. Archaics could not successfully compete for resources with the modern humans and so became extinct, leaving no genetic endowment to modern humanity.

THE MULTIREGIONAL MODEL

In the multiregional (or regional continuity) model, whose champion is American paleoanthropologist Milford Wolpoff (Frayer et al. 1993; Thorne and Wolpoff 1992; Wolpoff 1989a, 1992; Wolpoff, Wu, and Thorne 1984; Wolpoff et al. 1994), the evolution of modern human beings was a geographically broad process, not an event restricted to a single place. Various geographically separated groups of archaic humans—representing many regions—

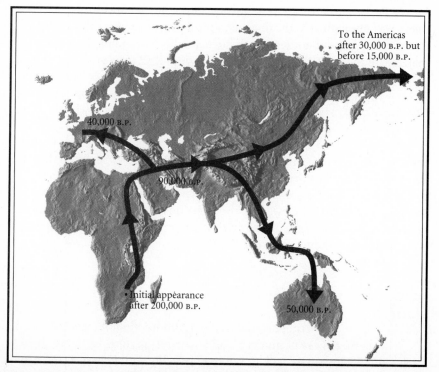

FIGURE 8.3

The geography of the evolution of modern humans implied by the replacement model.

together evolved toward the modern form. Enough contact between groups in Africa, Europe, and Asia was maintained to allow for **gene flow** among them. This gene flow was sufficient to keep the archaics as a single, variable species. Through migration and intermarriage among the different groups, new, advantageous modern traits, originating in various places and among different archaic groups, rippled through the population of premodern humans (Wolpoff et al. 1994:178). Together and simultaneously, not separately and independently, all these groups evolved into the modern form while still maintaining some relatively minor regional traits traceable back to their *Homo erectus* ancestors. Gene flow among groups was not so great as to wipe out such local, regional, or "racial" characteristics. So *Homo erectus* and archaic *Homo sapiens* in east Asia evolved into the modern people of Asia; the Neandertals of Europe and west Asia evolved into modern Europeans and west Asians; and the archaic humans of Africa evolved into the modern people of Africa. All groups remained part of the human species, yet all maintained their own unique physical features.

THE MIDDLE GROUND

The pure replacement and multiregional views have been tempered by scholars searching for a middle ground in this debate. Günter Bräuer (1992), for example, agrees with Stringer that Africa was the source of modern humanity at a fairly late date, but does not accept the notion of complete replacement. He believes that as the first anatomically modern human beings spread from Africa, they did not replace the archaics they encountered; instead, they mated with them, producing hybrid populations that, ultimately, were pulled along to modernity. Also falling somewhere in between is Fred Smith (1991, 1992), who holds that modern human traits developed in a single population (maybe Africa, maybe someplace else) and then spread primarily through gene flow (as opposed to migration) into archaic groups.

Since there is so much debate on the issue of the evolution of modern human beings, this Chronicle must end here. Because virtually all data are interpreted differently depending on which model is being used, the evidence for each model will be presented in the Issues and Debates section. But as yet there are no definitive answers to the questions to be raised. The issues are complex and the debate is unresolved, which makes this part of the human story both exasperating and exciting.

ISSUES AND DEBATES

REPLACEMENT OR CONTINUITY?

As both Christopher Stringer and Milford Wolpoff agree, the competing views of modern human evolution must be tested deductively, with data. Here we will lay out the predictions of the replacement and multiregional models—those things we expect to find in the fossil and genetic records if one or the other hypothesis is correct—and then examine the record to see how well it matches those predictions. The predictions are taken largely from Stringer and Andrews (1988), Wolpoff (1992), and Wolpoff et al. (1994).

What We Would Expect on the Basis of the Replacement Model

If the replacement model is correct—if early anatomically modern humans evolved in Africa from earlier archaic roots and then spread from there, replacing indigenous hominids in Europe and Asia—then the fossil record should show the following:

1. The oldest anatomically modern human fossils should be found in Africa and nowhere else.
2. There should be continuity only in Africa. That is to say, fossil forms intermediate between archaics and moderns should be found only in Africa.
3. Outside of Africa, the emigrant moderns should be contemporaries of indigenous archaics until the nonmodern humans became extinct.
4. There should be a distinct break in the form of archaic and modern human fossils outside of Africa as African moderns replaced indigenous archaics. The first anatomically modern humans in Europe and Asia should look like the early anatomically modern humans in Africa, since that is where they originated. The earliest modern-looking humans in Europe and Asia should exhibit no specific skeletal continuities with the premodern human fossils of their regions.
5. The archaeological record is expected to show the sudden appearance of nonlocal, African-originating artifact types in Europe and Asia as the early anatomically modern African population spread from its place of origin.

What We Would Expect on the Basis of the Regional Continuity Model

If the multiregional hypothesis is to be upheld, then the following, quite different predictions can be made about the fossil record:

1. Early versions of anatomically modern *Homo sapiens* should be found in many different regions. No one region should have anatomically modern fossils substantially older than any other region.
2. Intermediate forms—advanced archaics—should be found in each region, since evolution from premodern to modern occurred everywhere.
3. Because local archaics are everywhere ancestral to modern humans in their regions, there should be no or very little chronological overlap between them.

MAP 8.1

*Fossil localities of early
anatomically modern
Homo sapiens.*

4. Local skeletal traits should show continuity between archaic and modern
   humans because in each region local archaics evolved into modern people.
5. The archaeological record should show a continuity in regional artifact
   types, since as local premodern humans evolved physically into modern
   humans, their archaic toolmaking traditions evolved into more sophisticated modern traditions.

We can now briefly check out these predictions.

Testing the Implications of Replacement and Continuity

*1. Are the oldest anatomically modern human fossils found in Africa and no-
where else, or are early versions of anatomically modern* Homo sapiens *found
in many different regions?*

Those who support replacement view a number of fossil sites in Africa as
supporting their hypothesis. They see the hominid fossils from these sites as
being the earliest anatomically modern human beings yet found and demonstrably older than the earliest moderns found in Europe or Asia. Key sites in this
interpretation are Border Cave and Klasies River Mouth in South Africa, Omo
in Ethiopia, and Singa in the Sudan (Map 8.1).

The Border Cave site, for example, produced the remains of four hominids
from different layers in the cave deposit: a complete mandible, a partial

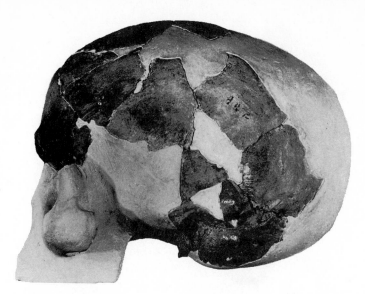

FIGURE 8.4

This nearly complete skull from Border Cave in South Africa has a suggested date of 100,000 B.P. If this is correct, the Border Cave hominid is an early anatomically modern human being. (Courtesy Professor P. V. Tobias, University of the Witwatersrand, Johannesburg, South Africa)

mandible, a fragmentary infant skeleton, and a fairly complete cranium (Figure 8.4). The cranium looks quite modern (Rightmire 1979b): It has a modern cranial capacity and no appreciable brow ridges, it is round in profile, and the face is flat (Beaumont, de Villiers, and Vogel 1978; Bräuer 1984). Recent electron spin resonance dates on animal teeth found in association with the hominid remains indicate that the cranium and partial mandible are probably more than 70,000–80,000 and less than 90,000 years old, the complete mandible is 50,000–65,000 years old, and the infant skeleton is 70,000–80,000 years old (Grün, Beaumont, and Stringer 1990). Unfortunately, the cranium was not excavated professionally, so precisely where it came from in the cave is not certain and therefore the date may not apply.

At Klasies River Mouth (KRM; see Figure 8.12), the hominid material can be assigned more confidently to a stratigraphic layer and, therefore, to a date, but the bones are more broken up and, as a result, more difficult to assign to a particular taxonomic category. The site itself was meticulously excavated in 1966–68 and produced thousands of artifacts and several fragmentary human remains (Figure 8.5; Singer and Wymer 1982). The bones, including several lower jaws and some cranial fragments, were analyzed by their excavators as well as by paleoanthropologist Philip Rightmire (1984) (whose work on *Homo erectus* was discussed in Chapter 6). They agreed that the Klasies River Mouth fossils were essentially modern in appearance. A modern human chin was clearly apparent in at least one of the mandibles, and the bits of cranial bones, though large and robust by modern standards, nevertheless looked more modern than archaic. For example, there is no evidence of a brow ridge. The hominid remains were firmly dated to about 100,000 years ago by reference to stratigraphy.

FIGURE 8.5

This mandible from Klasies River Mouth, though fragmentary, is rather lightly built and, therefore, relatively modern in appearance. The hominids found at this site are firmly dated to around 100,000 years ago. (From *The Middle Stone Age at Klasies River Mouth, South Africa,* by Ronald Singer and John Wymer, University of Chicago Press)

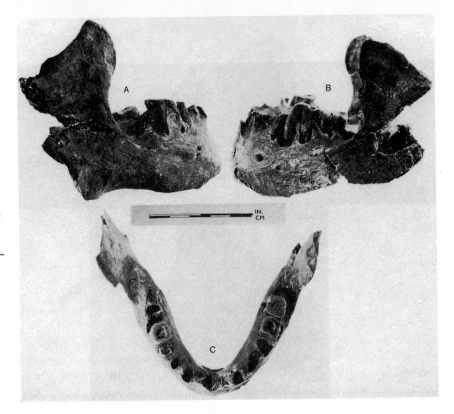

Recent research has served to confirm both the identification of the hominid material at KRM as modern and the great antiquity of the site. Fragments of two upper jaws, some individual teeth, and a broken lower arm bone (ulna) were recovered in 1984–89. Detailed analyses of the upper jaws indicate that they are quite modern (Bräuer, Deacon, and Zipfel 1992). Additional analyses of these newer finds and the original discoveries at KRM provide further confirmation of the modern aspects of the material (Deacon and Shuurman 1992; Rightmire 1991a). Philip Rightmire and Hilary Deacon compared the KRM material directly to European Neandertal specimens and noted fundamental differences. Finally, recent ESR dating of animal teeth found in the same layer as the hominid fossils places the age of the specimens at about 90,000 years (Grün, Shackleton, and Deacon 1990).

Supporters of regional continuity contest the age of the Border Cave specimen and the identification of the KRM specimens as anatomically modern. As already stated, the Border Cave cranium was not professionally excavated and its association with any firm date is admittedly problematical. The KRM fossils are rather robust for modern humans and only one of the mandibles has a diagnostically modern chin. The KRM hominids are interpreted by some scholars as representing an archaic form of humanity (Caspari and Wolpoff 1991; Frayer et al. 1993; Wolpoff and Caspari 1991).

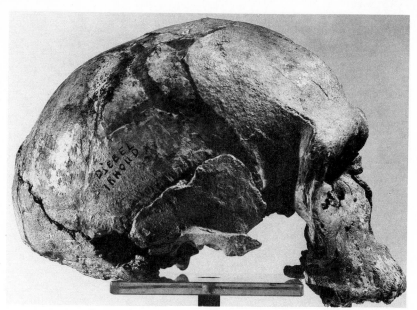

FIGURE 8.6

This cranium from Jebel Irhoud in north Africa has been interpreted as representing a form intermediate between archaic and modern Homo sapiens. *Some researchers contend that such intermediate forms are found only in Africa, lending support to the replacement model (see Figure 8.2).* (Musée de l'Homme, Paris)

In addition, Geoffrey Pope (1992), an expert on Chinese paleoanthropology, has suggested that the well-preserved and absolutely modern hominid specimen from Liujiang, China, may be as old as some of the African specimens mentioned; it has been uranium series dated to more than 100,000 years ago (Pope 1992:275). This supports the multiregional view that anatomically modern humans appeared in several places more or less simultaneously.

Altogether, the preponderance of evidence seems to support the view that the first anatomically modern human beings have been found only in Africa. It should be clear, however, that a definitive answer is not yet possible.

2. Is there continuity only in Africa, or are forms intermediate between archaic and modern humans found in many regions?

Supporters of the replacement model maintain that Africa is the only continent that has produced fossils intermediate in form between its earliest modern specimens and older archaic humans. Multiregionalists, on the other hand, see intermediate forms in many places.

As mentioned in Chapter 7, African fossils such as Kabwe, Ndutu, and Bodo are clearly archaic in appearance and generally have been dated to before 200,000 years ago (see Figure 7.3; again, Kabwe's dating has been a problem). Another set of African fossils, however, seems to be less archaic but not quite modern either, and appears to fit the morphological gap between purely archaic and anatomically modern forms. The Florisbad, Ngaloba (Laetoli hominid 18), Omo 2, and Jebel Irhoud crania all appear to represent forms transitional between archaic and modern humans (Figure 8.6; F. Smith, Falsetti, and Donnelly 1989). Supporters of the replacement model contend

FIGURE 8.7

The Mladeč cranium from western Europe shows traits that may link European Neandertals and anatomically modern human beings, supporting the multi-regional model or, perhaps, the idea that Neandertals and modern humans mated. (Courtesy of Fred Smith)

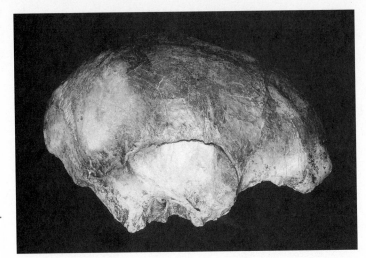

that such intermediate forms are not found outside of Africa, which is precisely what this view predicts, because it assumes that archaic humans outside of Africa did not evolve into modern humans but instead became extinct and were replaced by moderns who had evolved in Africa and then spread from there (see Figure 8.3).

Supporters of regional continuity point to other regions of the world where they perceive fossil forms intermediate between archaic and modern humans, a veritable mosaic of premodern and modern traits in crania from all over the world. In east Asia, for example, the 350,000-year-old Yunxian crania (Li and Etler 1992), discussed in Chapter 6, are seen as exhibiting several traits intermediate between older Asian *Homo erectus* populations and more recent modern-looking hominid fossils from Asia.

Perhaps of greatest significance are the fossil remains from several eastern European sites, including Mladeč, Kůlna, Sipka, and Vindija (F. Smith 1994; Figure 8.7). In many cranial and mandibular features, the Vindija remains appear to be transitional between the classic Neandertal pattern and the anatomically modern human form. Their crania are lighter and less robust than typical Neandertals. As Fred Smith states, while the Vindija remains are "clearly still Neandertals, it is difficult not to recognize Vindija as a transitional sample between most Neandertals and early modern Europeans" (1994:232).

On the other hand, as Erik Trinkaus (1983a) points out, there is little evidence of Neandertals' slowly evolving, postcranially, into the modern form. While brow ridges in some populations, like that of Vindija and Mladeč, are smaller, the crania more rounded, and the face less prognathous, the bones below the head retain the standard suite of robust Neandertal features. It is therefore rather difficult to conclude that some Neandertals represent an overall transition to the modern form. Günter Bräuer (1992) suggests that populations like those of Vindija represent hybrids between local Neandertals and immigrant (from southwest Asia) anatomical moderns; this may be the most reasonable explanation.

3. Were archaic and anatomically modern human beings contemporaries?

The replacement model predicts that outside of Africa, fossil evidence will show the contemporaneity of locally evolved archaic humans and immigrant groups of African moderns; southwest Asia is pointed to as verification. There, in caves that are sometimes in quite close proximity to each other, the remains of Neandertals and fundamentally modern humans have been found (though this is a point of contention, as discussed later in the chapter). Dating techniques place the archaic and modern humans in their respective caves during the same periods, and may even indicate that the modern humans are *older* than some of the Neandertals.

For example, classic Neandertals have been excavated at Kebara Cave, featured in Chapter 7's Case Study Close-Up section, as well as at the sites of Amud and Tabun (see Figure 7.12), in Israel. With their large, heavy skulls, large brow ridges, flattened occipitals, sloping foreheads, and prognathism, their form is unmistakably Neandertal. The Kebara site dates to 60,000, Amud is closer to 70,000, and Tabun has now been dated to about 100,000 years ago (McDermott et al. 1993).

Quite robust but otherwise rather modern-looking specimens have been excavated at the sites of Skhul and Qafzeh, also in Israel. Skhul, on Mount Carmel, is not even 100 m from Tabun, with its Neandertal fossils, and Qafzeh is less than 30 km east of those two cave sites. Kebara Cave is also close by, about 10 km south of Mount Carmel. It is remarkable that such different-looking, generally contemporaneous hominids have been found in such a restricted area (see Maps 7.2 and 8.1).

The ten or so individuals represented in the fossil record at Skhul and the twenty hominids at Qafzeh are generally (but not universally) categorized as anatomically modern or near modern. The crania present round profiles, nearly vertical foreheads, and flatter faces·than do the Neandertals, though their brow ridges, small by Neandertal standards, are quite marked when compared to most modern humans (Figure 8.8). A detailed comparison of 82 fossil hominids from Africa, southwest Asia, and Europe, including Neandertals as well as the Skhul and Qafzeh materials, showed that the latter were primarily anatomically modern, with certain specimens from these sites showing some similarities to Neandertals (Bräuer and Rimbach 1990:805).

The Skhul and Qafzeh sites are now judged to be broadly contemporaneous with the new date for Tabun. Thermoluminescence conducted on burned flints at Qafzeh has produced a date of 92,000 years ago (Valladas et al. 1988), ESR produced an age of more than 90,000 years (Stringer 1988), and a uranium series date further confirms this with a range of 85,000–110,000 years (McDermott et al. 1993). Skhul has been dated with ESR to between 81,000

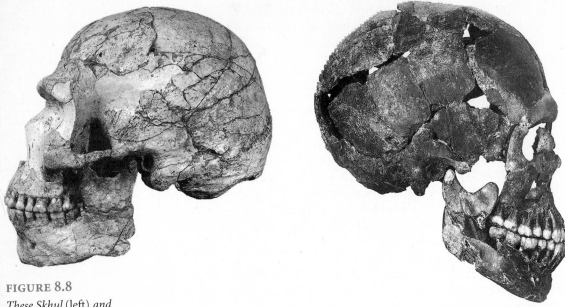

FIGURE 8.8

These Skhul (left) and Qafzeh (right) skulls from Israel are quite modern in appearance and are clearly dated to the period of around 100,000 years ago. Neandertals lived in Israel at the same time, further supporting the replacement model. (Left: Peabody Museum, Harvard University, photograph by Hillel Burger; *right:* Laboratory of Vertebrate and Human Paleontology, Paris, Bernard Vandermeersch)

years ago and 101,000 years ago (Stringer et al. 1989) and more recently by uranium series to about 80,000 years ago (McDermott et al. 1993).

The issue of the contemporaneity of archaic and modern forms outside of Africa comes up again in the European fossil record. The Neandertal fossil from the site of St. Césaire (Figure 8.9) in France is dated to 36,000 B.P. (Mercier et al. 1991; Stringer and Grün 1991) and the Neandertal mandible from Zafarraya, Spain, is 33,400 years old (Rose 1995). The earliest anatomically modern human fossils from Europe are those from the French site of Cro-Magnon, dated to after 30,000 years ago. However, artifacts of a tradition called **Aurignacian** (see Chapter 9) and associated only with modern humans and never with Neandertals have been found in western Europe; they are contemporary with or even predate the St. Césaire and Zafarraya Neandertals (Klein 1994). For example, Aurignacian tools have been recovered at the El Castillo and L'Arbreda sites in Spain from levels dated to 38,000 years ago (Bischoff et al. 1989; Valdes and Bischoff 1989; and see the discussion later in this chapter).

Overall, the data from Africa, the Middle East, and Europe confirm the replacement model. Neandertals seem too different to be directly ancestral to modern humans in Europe or southwest Asia and certainly cannot be ancestral to modern humans if they are contemporary with them, living in nearby caves or adjacent valleys in the Middle East and Europe.

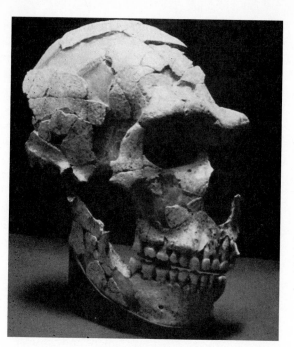

FIGURE 8.9
This Neandertal skull from St. Césaire, France, is among the most recent of the Neandertal specimens, dating to about 36,000 years ago, which is long after anatomically modern Homo sapiens *evolved, making problematic any hypothesis that modern humans evolved from the Neandertals.* (Transparency A11, Courtesy Department of Library Services, American Museum of Natural History)

    4. Is there a break in the form of archaic and modern human fossils outside of Africa, or do local skeletal traits show continuity between archaic and modern humans in each region?

    If anatomically modern humans evolved in Africa and spread from there, replacing archaics in all regions, locally derived, region-specific traits should disappear in each area as the indigenous archaics became extinct. The modern in-migrants in Europe and Asia should look like the earliest anatomically modern Africans, and not at all like the local archaics they are replacing. Local traits presently seen among modern people (skeletal features that are the equivalent of "racial" characteristics) would have evolved only very recently, after the replacement occurred.

    Obviously, if, instead, there was regional continuity in Africa, Europe, and Asia, then region-specific traits of the skeleton might be expected to be maintained within populations evolving from archaic to modern. In other words, skeletal traits specific to a particular region would show continuity from *Homo erectus* through archaic *Homo sapiens,* through the earliest anatomically modern humans, right up to the population of human beings living in an area today (at least among those individuals who can trace their ancestry back deeply in the area).

    Paleoanthropologist David Frayer (1992) lists specific Neandertal skeletal features found (admittedly in lower numbers) in anatomically modern human fossils in Europe. For the most part, however, the first anatomically modern humans in Europe—the so-called Cro-Magnon people from France dating to between 25,000 years ago and 30,000 years ago—are proportioned entirely differently from the Neandertals. Tall and thin, with long extremities, they look, as Christopher Stringer has said, "as if they walked straight out of Africa" (P. Ross 1991:47).

But there is one area in which the evidence seems most strongly to support the multiregional view, since continuity, at least in a number of traits, is the rule. Even the strongest proponents of the replacement model agree there is evidence for continuity of traits, at least in east Asia (Stringer 1994). More than fifty years ago, physical anthropologist Franz Weidenreich (1943) listed twelve very specific features of *Homo erectus* skeletons found in Asia and dating from about 500,000 years ago that matched those seen among modern, twentieth-century Asians. More recently, as Wolpoff et al. (1994) point out, general traits present in modern Asians, including overall cranial robusticity and detailed features of the face, can be seen in east Asian fossils dating all the way back to Java Man. Paleoanthropologist Andrew Kramer (1991), in comparing the mandibles of the Sangiran *Homo erectus* specimens and the lower jaws of modern Australians and Africans, found evidence for continuity between Javanese *erectus* specimens and those of local modern humans. Specific traits like a shovel shape in the maxillary (upper jaw) incisors, which is found throughout modern Asian populations, is exhibited in every east Asian fossil hominid where those teeth are preserved (Wolpoff et al. 1994:187).

This evidence for continuity, however, does not convince everyone. Lahr and Foley (1992) point out that some of the supposed continuities in form between premodern and modern Asian humans are simply the result of the size of their crania and teeth. Stringer (1992a) sees many of the supposedly regionally diagnostic traits as far more widespread in ancient times. In other words, many of the east Asian traits that show continuity between *Homo erectus* and the modern residents of Asia were also present in other archaic populations in Africa and Europe. In a recent statistical comparison of archaic and modern humans performed by Christopher Stringer (1992b), little continuity could be seen between fossil archaic and modern populations in Asia. Stringer went on to show high levels of skeletal traits, putatively restricted to European, Asian, and Australian populations, present in a Late Pleistocene sample of African crania.

Colin Groves (1989) and Phillip Habgood (1992) have analyzed the claim of morphological continuity from *Homo erectus* to modern Asians. In their view, many (though not all) of the features that show continuity in Asia are merely primitive retentions—features seen in many ancient hominids in Asia, Africa, and Europe that coincidentally have been maintained to a higher degree in modern Asians. Even the presumably diagnostic Asian trait of shovel-shaped incisors turns out not to be so diagnostic; Habgood (1992:279) provides an extensive list of European and African fossils exhibiting shovel-shaped in-

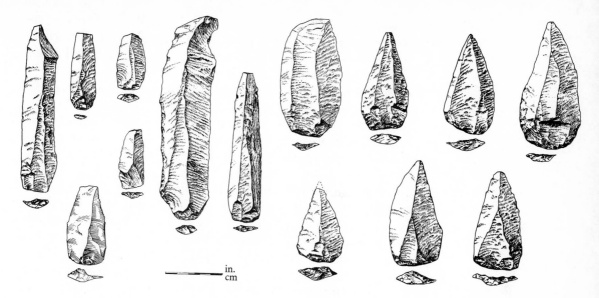

FIGURE 8.10

These long blade tools dating to close to 100,000 years ago from the site of Klasies River Mouth, South Africa, were associated with fragmentary remains of anatomically modern human beings (see Figure 8.5). (From *The Middle Stone Age at Klasies River Mouth, South Africa,* by Ronald Singer and John Wymer, University of Chicago Press)

cisors (including australopithecines, *Homo erectus*, Neandertal, and early and relatively late anatomically modern humans from Europe and Africa).

If these claimed Asian traits are not uniquely Asian traits at all, but were features once widespread, the case for regional continuity is seriously weakened. It would be entirely possible, in this view, for those supposedly regionally restricted traits to have been present in the earliest anatomically modern African migrants to Asia and Europe. Based on the work of Stringer and especially of Groves and Habgood, the case for regional continuity of traits seems only weakly supported by the Asian evidence and even less strongly by the European evidence.

5. Does the archaeological record show the sudden appearance of nonlocal, African-originating artifact types in Europe and Asia as the early anatomically modern African population spread out from its place of origin, or is there continuity in regional artifact types as local premodern humans evolved into modern ones?

While the European Neandertals were making their Mousterian tools, anatomically modern humans in Africa were producing assemblages categorized as Middle Stone Age. Though the makers of Middle Stone Age tools are supposed to have been anatomically modern human beings, there is little in these assemblages to indicate greater technological sophistication or intelligence on their part when compared to European Neandertals. There is evidence for somewhat more sophisticated stone tools at Klasies River Mouth (Figure 8.10 and see this chapter's Case Study Close-Up section), including long stone blades. (Blades generally require more preparation of the stone core from which they are produced and represent a more efficient use of the stone, which produces proportionally more sharp cutting edge than in the Mousterian technology.) But, by and large, African Middle Stone Age lithic assemblages do not clearly reflect any great technological leap forward coinciding with the evolution of modern humans.

Recently, however, compelling evidence—not in stone, but in bone—for increased technological complexity associated with early anatomically modern human beings in Africa has been found at three sites at Katanda in eastern Zaire. Dating to about 90,000 years ago, the lithics recovered at these sites reflect a fairly typical Middle Stone Age assemblage and, as such, are similar to European Mousterian industries (Yellen et al. 1995). The excavators of these sites also recovered very sophisticated bone tools, including barbed and unbarbed points and a dagger-shaped object of unknown function (Paleolithic Portfolio, Color Plate 7). They suggest that the technological sophistication of these bone tools indicates "modern behavioral capabilities" of the early anatomically modern inhabitants of Africa, distinct from the capabilities of contemporaneous archaic humans of Europe (Yellen et al. 1995:555). This is the first clear artifactual support for the notion that human beings possessing a modern level of intelligence evolved in Africa first, as much as 90,000 years ago.

Unfortunately for the replacement model, these Middle Paleolithic African blade and bone tools do not appear to have accompanied their makers on their migration to Asia. In fact, there is no archaeological evidence in the form of an alien or invasive tool technology in Asia dating to the Middle Paleolithic that might mark the arrival of immigrant, anatomically modern Africans. The earliest modern-looking hominids in southwest and east Asia practiced the same stone-toolmaking tradition as the local, indigenous archaic-looking people. The stone-tool assemblages from Skhul and Qafzeh, with their modern-looking fossils, and nearby Tabun, with its contemporary, archaic-looking fossils, exhibit the same stone-tool tradition: They were all making Mousterian tools (Shea 1990; Thorne and Wolpoff 1992).

It would bolster the replacement model if there was some evidence of an African-looking tool assemblage accompanying the supposedly immigrant anatomically modern humans in Asia. In other archaeological cases where migration is claimed, the confirming evidence of the sudden appearance of a new and exotic way of making tools, traceable to the source of the immigrants, is demanded (Feder 1994a, 1996); when such evidence is lacking, the hypothesized immigration is usually rejected.

The situation in Europe, on the other hand, is quite different. Though African blades are not found at the earliest modern human sites, there is, as archaeologist Francis Harrold (1992) points out, a close correspondence between different-looking hominids and tool traditions on that continent: Neandertals in Europe are almost always associated with tools of the Mousterian tradition (described in Chapter 7) while the first anatomically modern humans in Europe are associated with the more sophisticated Aurignacian tradition (to be described in detail in Chapter 9).

The earliest sites exhibiting the Aurignacian tradition in Europe include l'Arbreda Cave in eastern Spain, El Castillo Cave in northern Spain, Istallöskö in Hungary, and Bacho Kiro Cave in Bulgaria (Straus 1989). As mentioned previously, the Spanish sites date to about 38,000 years ago (Bischoff et al. 1989; Valdes and Bischoff 1989); the Hungarian and Bulgarian sites date to about 43,000 years ago. James Bischoff and his colleagues, who analyzed the Spanish sites, characterize the appearance of Aurignacian tools in the Spanish caves, as well as the other European sites mentioned, as "abrupt" (Bischoff et al. 1989:573). The Mousterian and Aurignacian technologies are quite different and, in the case of the Spanish sites, the raw materials used are different: The Mousterian flakes are almost all made of locally available quartz and quartzite, whereas the Aurignacian tools are almost all made of a more distantly available flint. There is no evidence there of a slow, steady transition from a Mousterian to an Aurignacian tradition, no sign of an evolution of the simpler Mousterian tradition of the Neandertals to the more sophisticated Aurignacian tradition of the first anatomically modern humans in Europe. Bischoff and his colleagues take this to support the replacement model; when a new toolmaking tradition appears abruptly in the archaeological record, with no evidence of its having evolved from an earlier way of doing things, it is often concluded that the new tradition arrived from the outside, the product of a new group's migration into the area.

To be sure, the oldest European sites with Aurignacian tools, as previously mentioned, have produced no hominid remains. To date, Neandertals have never been found with such tools, and few expect that they will be. Unless such a surprising discovery is made, there seems to be a good correspondence between the appearance of physically modern people and a new tool tradition in Europe: Both the people and their toolmaking tradition show up rather suddenly, about 40,000 years ago.

Certain data complicate this conclusion. Just as there is support for the notion of biological hybridization between Neandertal and anatomically modern humans in Europe, there also is support for a melding of their different tool traditions. The so-called **Châtelperronian** tradition had been thought to have been produced by anatomically modern human beings because of the presence of long, narrow stone blades, a hallmark of the modern humans in Europe (Figure 8.11). But this was only an assumption, since Châtelperronian tools had not been found in direct association with the bones of the people who made and used them. The tradition was a bit mysterious because, aside from the blade component, it looked rather like Mousterian. Châtelperronian tools were finally found in firm association with skeletal remains of a Neandertal, not of a modern human being: the St. Césaire Neandertal, dated to 36,000 years ago (see Figure 8.9). This has led to a dramatic reassessment of the significance of the Châtelperronian. If, as seems to be the case, the tradition is fundamentally Mousterian, with elements of the Aurignacian grafted on (Harrold 1989), then it would appear that an indigenous Mousterian flake industry in Europe produced by Neandertals added blade-

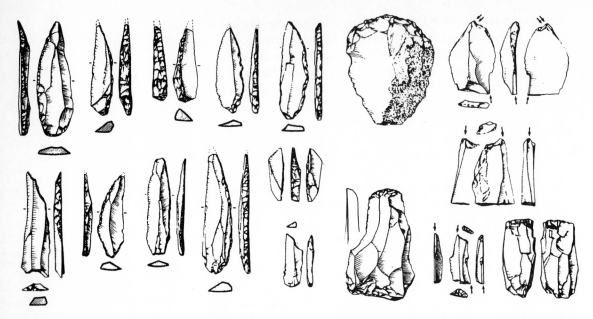

FIGURE 8.11

Tools of the Châtelperronian tradition, such as these, were found with the St. Césaire Neandertal. This tradition may represent a cultural blending of the Neandertal Mousterian and the anatomically modern human tradition called Aurignacian. (Adapted from Bordes and Labrot 1967)

like tools beginning sometime after 40,000 years ago, just when anatomically modern humans show up in the fossil record. Since the timing is right and the Aurignacian industry of anatomically modern humans has a major component of blade tools, it may be the source. In other words, flake-tool–manufacturing Neandertals may have shifted, at least in part, to blade tools as a result of contact with anatomically modern people who were making such tools. Neandertals living side by side with anatomically modern human beings, and even borrowing the idea behind some of their more effective tools, supports the replacement model.

Châtelperronian is rather short-lived, dated between about 36,000–33,000 years ago. Châtelperronian artifacts are sometimes found in the same sites as Aurignacian but separated stratigraphically; they are sometimes even interdigitated, with Châtelperronian tools in layers sometimes above Aurignacian tools, sometimes below (and sometimes both), for example, at the Le Piage site in France (Simek 1992). This indicates fairly clearly that they were produced by separate groups who inhabited these sites at different times. The Châtelperronian, therefore, can be interpreted as supporting the replacement model in Europe.

On a related matter, paleoanthropologist Geoffrey Pope (1992), who strongly supports regional continuity in human evolution, has wondered how, if the replacement model is valid, newcomers to a region who were highly intelligent but with no experience in a new and alien habitat could outcompete and cause the extinction of local, indigenous hominids, who had developed a cultural adaptation to that territory over millennia? It would help the replacement case if a new and much advanced tool assemblage accompanied the newcomers, one so far superior to that of the less intelligent and less capable archaics that it enabled the newcomers to displace the indigenous group. It can be argued that the European evidence supports this scenario exactly, with anatomically modern humans and their more sophisticated Aurignacian tools replacing Neandertals with their simpler Mousterian technology. Clearly, however, such a claim cannot be made for the archaeological record of Asia, where continuity in the stone-toolmaking tradition is the rule.

HOW CAN MODERN HUMAN GENETICS INFORM US ABOUT THE ANCIENT ORIGINS OF HUMANITY?

Though we cannot yet extract DNA from fossil hominid bone, DNA analysis can still be of value when addressing the question of modern human origins. By investigating the mitochondrial DNA of living humans, we are looking at the latest point on an evolutionary continuum. Since we are pretty sure when and how that continuum began—we split off from the apes some 5–7 million years ago (see Chapter 4)—we can suggest how the modern condition most likely developed.

The use of modern mitochondrial DNA to illuminate the question of human origins has been reported in the popular media since 1988, even getting a cover story in *Newsweek,* headlined "The Search for Adam and Eve" (Tierney, Wright, and Springer 1988). The media attention initially was generated by the work of geneticists Rebecca Cann, Mark Stoneking, and Allan Wilson (1987), who examined the mitochondrial DNA of a sample of living human females (as mentioned in the Prelude section of this chapter, we all inherit our mtDNA from our mothers—the mtDNA present in sperm is jettisoned at conception and so is not passed down).

Given that mtDNA accumulates mutations relatively faster than nuclear DNA, Cann, Stoneking, and Wilson were struck by the fact that the modern human mtDNA they analyzed was quite homogeneous across populations from different regions and even among people who had no genetic admixture with individuals from other areas. The population that exhibited the relatively highest degree of diversity within its mtDNA was the African sample. The researchers drew two main conclusions.

First, since the mtDNA showed so little overall diversity, modern human beings must have evolved relatively recently. Diversity in mtDNA develops as a result of mutations that build up quickly relative to nuclear DNA. A lack of diversity across widely separated populations indicates a lack of time for this diversity to develop. Humans have only a small fraction of the mtDNA diversity of that seen, for example, among modern chimpanzees. If chimps have been a separate species for 5–7 million years, and assuming that mutations accumulate in the human mtDNA genome at the same rate as in chimps [in fact, the rate has been shown to be the same for a wide variety of animals, including apes, monkeys, rats, birds, and rhinoceroses (Cann, Stoneking, and Wilson 1987:34)], then human beings must have been a separate species for only a much shorter span of time.

Second, the oldest modern human mtDNA and, therefore, the source of the rest of the world's mtDNA, was African. The African mtDNA had accumulated more mutations and so exhibited greater diversity and looked different from the rest of the world's mtDNA. Mutation accumulation is a factor of time, so the African mtDNA must have been the oldest.

From here, Cann and her co-workers got more specific. Using the known age of the establishment of a number of human populations as a standard, they derived what was effectively an mtDNA clock, a measurement of the rate of mtDNA accumulation. For example, knowing that New Guinea and Australia had first been settled between 50,000 years ago and 60,000 years ago (see Chapter 10), they measured the amount of mtDNA mutation accumulation among modern New Guineans and aboriginal Australians during those years. Then they compared modern African mtDNA to that from New Guinea and Australia and discovered about three times more mutations in the mtDNA from Africa. This means that about 150,000–180,000 years have passed since the African mtDNA began accumulating mutations; this they interpreted as the age of the first anatomically modern *Homo sapiens* (Wilson and Cann 1992). Cann and her colleagues even argued that all modern mtDNA could be traced statistically back to a single female living in Africa about that time. The news media and some skeptical paleoanthropologists dubbed this woman "Eve."

Clearly, this interpretation supports the replacement model. It seems to indicate that modern humans evolved first in Africa after about 200,000 years ago, and only later were populations established in Europe and Asia.

Unfortunately, Cann, Stoneking, and Wilson's methodology had major problems. Their initial sample was very small, only 147 women. The "African" sample consisted of African Americans and not actual Africans, so the possibility of the admixture of mtDNA from Asians, Native Americans, and Europeans existed. Finally, a reanalysis has shown that their results were affected by the order in which the data were input by the researchers; a different order would have yielded a different geographical center for the origin of modern mtDNA (Templeton 1992).

In reanalyzing the same data, biologist Alan Templeton (1993) comes to conclusions in direct opposition to those of Cann, Stoneking, and Wilson. He views the mtDNA of modern humans as indicating an equal age in Europe, Asia, and Africa, as well as low levels of consistent genetic contact between groups in those areas. In other words, Templeton's interpretation of the mtDNA of modern humans supports the multiregional model. Research by French geneticists Laurent Excoffier and André Langaney (1989) using a much larger sample than Cann and her co-workers found that modern African mtDNA exhibits less, not more, diversity than Asian and European DNA.

In a different approach, the work of geneticist Tom Kocher (as cited in Cann, Richards, and Lum 1994:144–145) has shown that the diversity within a sample of chimpanzee mtDNA is forty to fifty times greater than that seen within the human sample. Again, applying some simple mathematics, if the chimp and human evolutionary lines diverged some 5–7 million years ago (see Chapter 4), then mtDNA variation within the chimps has been accumulating for that long. Because modern human mtDNA exhibits only $\frac{1}{40}$ to $\frac{1}{50}$ the variation seen among chimps, modern humans must have been accumulating that variation for $\frac{1}{40}$ to $\frac{1}{50}$ as long as the chimps have. This places the origin of the modern human line at somewhere between 100,000 years ago and 175,000 years ago.

Altogether, genetic research into the origins of modern humanity, which was intended to solve the problems presented by the vicissitudes of fossil bones, has merely added to the muddle. Rebecca Cann and others have recognized some of the mistakes made in the original research and have gone on to conduct additional work on the mtDNA of living humans. This new work, now based on a combined sample of more than 5,000 women, including Africans in Africa, seems to lend support, though admittedly not very much, for an African source for modern human beings (Cann 1992; Cann, Richards, and Lum 1994; J. Long et al. 1990; Stoneking 1993; Vigilant et al. 1991). However, the various mtDNA arguments are still being sorted out (Hedges et al. 1992); the mitochondrial DNA research of Cann and her colleagues alone can no longer be viewed as strong support for the replacement model.

Recently, scientists analyzed a section of the Y chromosome of 38 human males representing a broad geographic sample of the species (Dorit, Akashi, and Gilbert 1995). Mutations accumulate in genes over time and, therefore, the greater the differences at a particular section of a gene between two species that originated from a common ancestor, the greater the deduced amount of time since their evolutionary divergence. At the genetic locus examined in this research, chimps were most similar to human beings, with gorillas, orangs, and baboons showing increasingly greater differences, indicating proportionally longer periods of evolutionary separation.

It was expected that even within our single human species, some discernible differences would still be found among human beings from different regions, indicating random changes during the time people in different parts of the world have been separated. The researchers, however, saw no differences at all at the genetic locus examined among the 38 men sampled. They concluded that modern human beings (specifically males) could have been evolving separately for no more than 270,000 years—and perhaps for substantially less than this. The researchers conclude that their small sample of individuals provides further support for the replacement model of human evolution: For the section of the Y chromosome that was sampled to be identical in males from all over the world, we all must have originated from a common source relatively recently.

Additional modern genetic support for the replacement model has been provided recently, when a research team led by geneticist David Goldstein compared segments of nuclear DNA called "microsatellites" from 148 individuals representing 14 native populations from around the world (Bower 1995). The evolutionary tree based on geographic similarities and differences at the microsatellite sites and rates of change at those genetic locations indicate that all humans originated in Africa and then spread from there at about 150,000 years ago.

WHICH EVIDENCE IS BETTER: GENES OR BONES?

In assessing the origins of modern humans, it is reasonable to ask which kind of evidence ultimately will be more important in the debate between those who support the replacement model and those who stand behind the multiregional model. Milford Wolpoff et al. (1994) maintain that the genetic evidence of modern humans can only suggest ways that human evolution may have occurred, while the paleontological record provides the hard data to test those suggestions. Allan Wilson and Rebecca Cann, on the other hand, believe that genetic interpretation will inform us more precisely about modern human origins than any analysis of bones, since "paleontologists cannot be sure that the fossils they examine do not lead down an evolutionary blind alley" (1992:68). Ultimately, we can hope that one day soon, the genetic information preserved in the bones themselves will enable us to answer directly the vexing questions raised here.

CASE STUDY CLOSE-UP

Looking out from the Klasies River Mouth caves, you can see the huge expanse of the Indian Ocean. Inside the cave, looking with the mind's eye back through the ancient layers deposited at your feet, you can see the story of the earliest beginnings of modern humanity (Figure 8.12).

The caves near where the Klasies River empties into the Indian Ocean may have been first explored scientifically in 1923 during a survey of caves and rock shelters along the South African coast. The geological, paleontological, paleoanthropological, and archaeological work accomplished at the cave in the major excavations of 1966–68 are reported in Ronald Singer and John Wymer's (1982) *The Middle Stone Age at Klasies River Mouth in South Africa.* Because of the caves' significance to questions of the origins of anatomically modern human beings, additional excavations were carried out there in 1984–89. The human remains recovered at Klasies River Mouth (KRM) have been discussed previously in this chapter, so the focus here will be on the stone-tool assemblage and the faunal remains.

An extensive array of stone tools was recovered at KRM. The vast majority of the tools were made from locally available beach cobble quartzite. Cobbles used by the cave's inhabitants to make tools were available virtually at

FIGURE 8.12

The area around the caves at Klasies River Mouth, South Africa. (From *The Middle Stone Age at Klasies River Mouth, South Africa,* by Ronald Singer and John Wymer, University of Chicago Press)

the doorstep of the Klasies River Mouth caves.

The technology represented at KRM is, in the vernacular of African archaeology, a Middle Stone Age (MSA) industry, which means that it is essentially Mousterian in its technology. For the duration of the Late Middle Paleolithic occupation of the caves, the inhabitants were removing flakes of various shapes and sizes from carefully prepared nodules of stone, in a manner not unlike that of their European contemporaries.

Compared to European Mousterian industries, however, KRM exhibits a number of more finely made long flakes, called **blades,** with parallel or slightly subparallel (gently converging) sides (see Figure 8.10). Some blades with converging edges had been further flaked, after removal from their cores, into apparent spear points. Some of these tools seem, in a general way, to anticipate later, more advanced Late Stone Age industries in Africa and even the Aurignacian industry of the European Upper Paleolithic, to be discussed in Chapter 9. It is probably not coincidental that these more advanced-looking tools are found associated with modern-looking humans.

Faunal analysis of the bone assemblage at KRM supports the notion that hunting played a major role in the inhabitants' subsistence. We know that the inhabitants of KRM and other Middle Paleolithic sites in coastal South Africa were among the first people in the world to exploit aquatic resources, including shellfish, seals, penguins, fish, and sea birds (Klein 1977).

Archaeologist Richard G. Klein (1976, 1982, 1983) has examined the **age-mortality** profiles of the animal remains at Klasies and compared them to profiles from animal populations for which mortality was the result of natural attrition and not hunting. The profile is constructed from the percentages of animals in each age group—in other words, the percentage of animals that died or were killed within each established age span.

At KRM, the age-mortality profile produced from the bones of Cape buffalo is quite similar to that seen in **attritional profiles** of modern members of this species from east African game parks, where the animals are not hunted (Klein 1983:39). Attritional profiles reflect the percentages of animals in each age grouping that die of natural causes, with high percentages occurring among the old and the young, and lower percentages occurring in the middle or prime years of life.

The Cape buffalo is large (700–900 kg, or 1,500–2,000 lb), gregarious (herding), and very aggressive. Its typical response when threatened is to charge its attacker, making it challenging and downright dangerous to hunt with a rifle, much less with a stone-tipped spear point. The age-mortality profile of Cape buffalo at KRM seems a good indicator that they were not hunted but, rather, were scavenged by the human inhabitants of the cave; that is, the animals died of natural causes and were brought back to the cave.

The age-mortality profile for the eland remains at the cave is quite different. Eland are large antelope, similar in size to Cape buffalo. Behaviorally they are quite different, however, being relatively docile. When threatened, they tend to run together, making them easier to drive and kill than buffalo. The eland produce a **catastrophic profile,** which has percentages for each age category equal to those of a living population—as if a catastrophe were to occur and all members of a group were wiped out at the same time. A catastrophic profile for eland at KRM is a good indication that the animals were not simply dying natural deaths and then being dragged into the caves; they were being killed in percentages relative to their ages equal to those percentages in the population.

VISITING THE PAST

Virtually any large natural history museum will have displays on the origin of anatomically modern human beings. Some may be out of date, having been made when the French site of Cro Magnon was presumed to represent the oldest evidence of anatomically modern human beings anywhere in the world. But many others, including the American Museum of Natural History in New York City, present an updated display where the vexing question of modern human origins is touched on. The important sites discussed here are located all across the face of the earth. The key fossils are housed in various museums and research facilities.

SUMMARY

Two opposing models have been proposed to explain the evolution of anatomically modern human beings. The replacement model maintains that modern humans evolved once, in Africa, sometime between 100,000 years ago and 200,000 years ago. From there they spread throughout the rest of the world, replacing indigenous groups of archaic *Homo sapiens* and even, possibly, *Homo erectus*. The multiregional model hypothesizes that anatomically modern humans evolved across all of Africa, Europe, and Asia, together and simultaneously. Gene flow resulting from mating was sufficient to move newly evolved, modern traits throughout the many premodern populations. This gene flow, however, was not sufficient to swamp, or wipe out, local physical features, which are maintained even into the present era as so-called "racial" characteristics.

Hypotheses intermediate to the more extreme formulations of the replacement and multiregional models have been proposed. The data discussed in this chapter, consisting of skeletal evidence, artifacts, and modern genetics, provide only ambiguous support for either extreme or for any intermediate formulation. The question of modern human origins continues to be a source of often-bitter debate among paleoanthropologists and geneticists.

TO LEARN MORE

Obviously, the debate over the issues of this chapter has been summarized only briefly. If you wish to know more about current thinking on the origins of anatomically modern people, the following citations are a good place to start. A fascinating book on the mitochondrial DNA evidence, revealing the personalities of many of the scientists involved in the ensuing debate, is Michael Brown's (1990) *The Search for Eve.* For technical summaries of the debate over modern human origins from the multiregional perspective, see Vol. 95, No. 1, of the journal *American Anthropologist* [articles by Frayer et al. (1993) and Templeton (1993) as well as a more replacement-oriented position by Leslie Aiello (1993)]. Another nice summary favoring replacement is an article by Richard Klein (1992) in the journal *Evolutionary Anthropology.* And, of course, see any of the articles by Christopher Stringer, especially his 1994 summary "Out of Africa: A Personal History," for a strong presentation of the replacement model. There even is a wonderful and dramatic piece of speculative fiction, *Dance of the Tiger,* by paleontologist Björn Kurtén (1980), focusing on the shared world of Neandertals and anatomically modern human beings.

KEY TERMS

DNA
nuclear DNA
mitochondrial DNA
    (mtDNA)
polymerase chain
    reaction (PCR)

DNA hybridization
gene flow
Aurignacian
Châtelperronian
blade
age-mortality profiles

attritional profile
catastrophic profile

9

Expanding Intellectual Horizons

ART AND IDEAS IN THE UPPER PALEOLITHIC

CHAPTER OVERVIEW

The Upper Paleolithic is marked by dramatic changes in human culture the world over. Beginning after 50,000 years ago, we see a shift toward a lithic technology based on the production of blade tools; an expansion in the subsistence quest; an increase in site size; use of raw materials such as bone, shell, and antler; the production of nonutilitarian objects; the use of exotic materials; the elaboration of burials; and the production of true art in the form of cave paintings and portable sculptures.

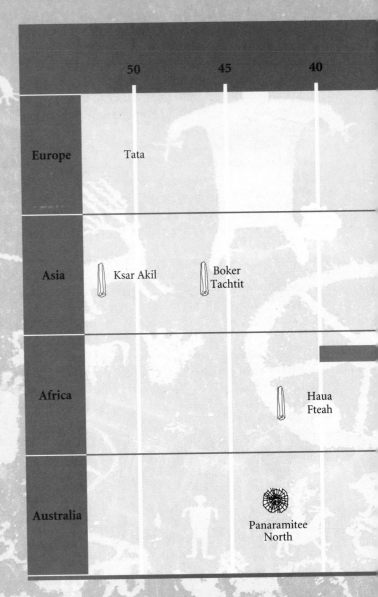

	50	45	40
Europe	Tata		
Asia	Ksar Akil	Boker Tachtit	
Africa			Haua Fteah
Australia		Panaramitee North	

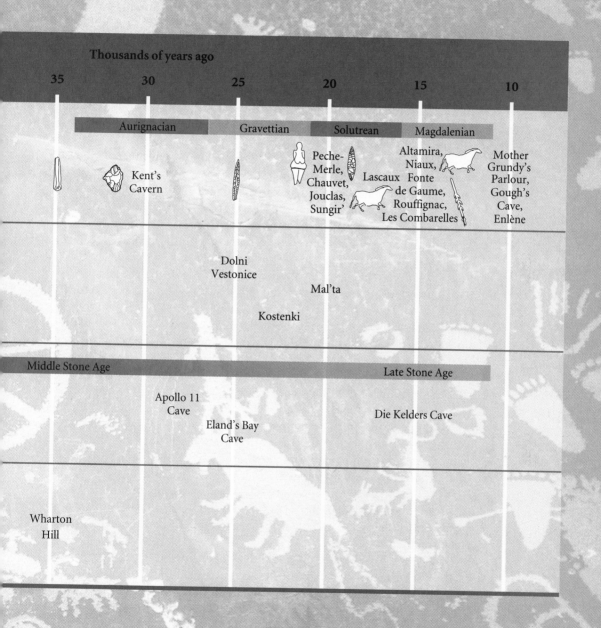

Thousands of years ago

35   30   25   20   15   10

Aurignacian   Gravettian   Solutrean   Magdalenian

Kent's Cavern

Peche-Merle, Chauvet, Jouclas, Sungir'   Lascaux   Altamira, Niaux, Fonte de Gaume, Rouffignac, Les Combarelles   Mother Grundy's Parlour, Gough's Cave, Enlène

Dolni Vestonice

Mal'ta

Kostenki

Middle Stone Age   Late Stone Age

Apollo 11 Cave   Die Kelders Cave

Eland's Bay Cave

Wharton Hill

PRELUDE

Ushered into this world several hours after the fireworks of July 4, 1993, my younger son, Jacob, turned one-year-old on July 5, 1994. Coincidentally, on that day he exhibited what is a uniquely human ability: He began creating works of "art." With a series of magic markers, he scribbled colors onto the page, stopping after each flourish to look up and smile at his proud father.

I will admit that he seemed more interested in uncapping and capping the markers, and that he got as much ink on the table and on his hands as on the paper. But who could deny his obvious talent?

More to the point, who could deny his humanity? While there have been some silly attempts to get zoo animals to produce works of art (chimpanzees and elephants, at last count), which then sell for ridiculous sums (at least it raises money for financially strapped zoos), it is only human beings who possess the desire, ability, and even the *need* to produce art.

Educational psychologists have long pondered the significance of the universal and unique human behavior of producing art, which seems to manifest itself even while we are still quite young (DiLeo 1970; Gardner 1980; G. Thomas and Silk 1991). For Freud (1976), a child's drawings represent a safety valve, allowing him or her to express deep, largely unconscious fears by safely reliving them on paper. For Freud, art also provides a way for children to express unconscious wishes. For the best-known child development researcher, Jean Piaget (Piaget and Inhelder 1969), drawings reflect the developmental stages a child's intellect passes through on the road to adulthood. Jacob's scribblings fall within Piaget's early stage in which "pure play" represents a significant activity.

Other researchers have emphasized the sensory pleasure (both motor and visual) of producing a picture; still others (Arnheim 1956) have suggested that drawing or painting are simply "universally satisfying." Ultimately, however, as psychologists Glyn V. Thomas and Angèle M. J. Silk (1990:70) point out: "It is not easy to give a totally convincing answer to the question of why children draw. . . . While all these proposed motivations [those just listed] seem plausible, it is rare to find independent evidence for their validity."

Jacob has been passing through the well-established stages of symbolic/artistic achievement, unaware of the arguments among psychologists over the significance of his accomplishments. He is only one link in a long chain of human beings—first as children, later as adults—who have applied pigment to metaphorical canvases and produced something that was initially just in their heads but now resides outside them. This chain begins perhaps 50,000 years ago with our anatomically modern ancestors and continues to the present. The period when we see the initial appearance of uniquely modern human capacities like artistic, symbolic expression—the Upper Paleolithic—is the focus of this chapter.

Though the earliest anatomically modern human beings date to more than 100,000 years ago, they do not become culturally differentiable from their archaic contemporaries for a long time (as discussed in Chapter 8, and see the Issues and Debates section in this chapter). In fact, it is not until after 50,000 years ago and perhaps as late as 40,000 years ago that the archaeological record begins to exhibit the remnants of a material culture—and, by inference, a spiritual, artistic, and intellectual culture—previously unknown and recognizably modern (Chase and Dibble 1987; Chase 1991). Prehistorians call the period when modern behavior becomes manifested in the archaeological record the Upper Paleolithic. The behavior of Upper Paleolithic people can be distinguished absolutely from the behavior of their Middle Paleolithic predecessors. As archaeologist Anthony Marks (1990:56) characterizes it, the evidence from the Upper Paleolithic indicates "at least dramatic and, at most, a profound and fundamental change in both behavior and human potentials."

CHRONICLE

THE UPPER PALEOLITHIC
GREAT LEAP FORWARD

Archaeologist Randall White (1982) has contrasted the cultures of the Middle and Upper Paleolithic. Using as guides his list and the lists of archaeologist Richard Klein (1989) and of Heidi Knecht, Anne Pike-Tay, and Randall White (1993), we can examine the following cultural evolutionary "disconformities," or breaks, between the Middle and Upper Paleolithic:

- A dramatic shift in stone-tool technology, from a reliance on flake tools to the production of stone blades
- A broadening of the subsistence base to include a greater range of animal and plant species in the quest for subsistence
- Much larger sites
- A dramatic increase in the production of bone, antler, ivory, and shell tools
- A shift from very few non-utilitarian items to an abundance of them
- A greater use of imported, "exotic" goods—raw materials obtainable only from great distances away from habitation sites
- Much more elaborate burials
- A shift from virtually no works of art to the highly characteristic use of symbol and the production of art

We will now discuss in detail each of these changes from Middle Paleolithic life to Upper Paleolithic culture.

FIGURE 9.1

These stone blades from the site of Ksar Akil in Lebanon date back to before 40,000 years ago and may be as old as 52,000 years. (Reprinted from Paul Mellars, ed.: *The Emergence of Modern Humans: An Archaeological Perspective.* Copyright © Edinburgh University Press. Used by permission of the publisher, Cornell University Press.)

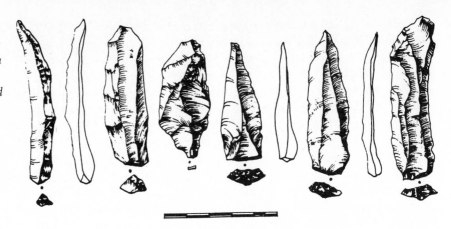

Stone Blades of the Upper Paleolithic

Blades are commonly defined as flakes that are at least twice as long as they are wide. The regular and efficient production of blades from a prepared stone core is a fundamental characteristic of the stone-tool industries of the Upper Paleolithic. This advance in tool manufacture represents a far more efficient use of stone, with more than five times the amount of usable edge generated from the same quantity of stone than when regular flakes were being produced.

Sites exhibiting a blade technology date back to before 40,000 years ago (Figure 9.1). In the Near East, for example, at the sites of Boker Tachtit in Israel (Marks 1990, 1993) and Ksar Akil in Lebanon (Ohnuma and Bergman 1990), the shift from a Levallois prepared–core-and-flake technology (see Chapter 7) to a stone-tool technology based on the production of elongated blades occurred by at least 45,000 years ago at Boker Tachtit and perhaps as much as 52,000 years ago at Ksar Akil (Marks 1993:12). In Africa, sites like Haua Fteah Cave show this shift to have occurred by about 40,000 years before the present, or B.P. (Van Peer and Vermeersch 1990). In central and southeastern Europe, the shift from Mousterian flake to Upper Paleolithic blade production occurred before 40,000 B.P. (Svoboda 1993); in western Europe, the shift seems to have occurred a bit later, about 38,000 B.P. (Allsworth-Jones 1990).

In reconstructing stone-core reduction sequences at these and other sites, researchers have concluded that, where Levallois cores became exhausted after the removal of just a few flakes, many more blades could be removed from the same core, producing far more cutting edge from the same mass of stone.

Unlike earlier stone-tool manufacturing systems, the blade technologies of the Upper Paleolithic are short-lived, and change is greatly accelerated (Figure 9.2). In western Europe, for example, the **Aurignacian** tradition, which

FIGURE 9.2

Tools from the Aurignacian tradition (left), *a blade-based industry of the European Upper Paleolithic dating from 34,000 B.P. to 27,000 B.P. The long spear-points of the descendant Solutrean tradition* (right), *dating from 21,000 B.P. to 16,000 B.P., are beautifully crafted and were highly effective.* (Transparencies 610, *left,* and 609, *right,* courtesy Department of Library Services, American Museum of Natural History)

consisted of a specific set of tools that included retouched blades, engraving tools called burins, and stone scrapers, is dated to between 34,000 years ago and 27,000 years ago. From 27,000 B.P. to 21,000 B.P., the **Gravettian** tradition develops, with its emphasis on smaller blades and denticulate knives. The **Solutrean** tradition, dated from 21,000 years ago to 16,000 years ago, is the most striking of all, characterized by finely made, bifacially flaked, symmetrical, leaf-shaped projectile points. Solutrean points are among the most finely made stone tools ever found. The Solutrean was followed by the **Magdelanian,** from 16,000 B.P. to 11,000 B.P., where the emphasis was not on stone tools at all, but, rather, on bone and antler, with the attendant production of microblades.

Together, these various industries of the Upper Paleolithic show us two very important things. First, lithic technology has jumped forward, with a number of different manufacturing techniques that used stone more efficiently; produced more effective tools for cutting, scraping, piercing, and so on; and that yielded objects far more symmetrical and balanced than those of the Middle Paleolithic. From our twentieth-century Western vantage point (or, perhaps, bias), European Upper Paleolithic industries produced tools that are more aesthetically pleasing, more artfully rendered, than those of earlier traditions.

Second, and equally as important, the profusion of specific tool-tradition names points to one of the most salient differences between the Middle and Upper Paleolithic: Whereas Middle Paleolithic technology is marked by relative homogeneity temporally and geographically, Upper Paleolithic technology is marked by relatively rapid change and far greater geographic variability.

Broadening the Subsistence Base

Undeniably, the hunting of big game—**megafauna**—made a significant contribution to the subsistence of Upper Paleolithic people. In central and eastern Europe, for example, sites dating between 28,000 B.P. and 10,000 B.P. reflect the major role of the woolly mammoth in the subsistence base of Upper Paleolithic people. At a single site, Dolni Vestonice I, the remains of more than 100 mammoths butchered by the inhabitants have been identified (Soffer 1993). At this same site, butchering marks have been located on the remains of horse and reindeer as well. Also in Europe are the Kostenki-Borshevo sites located along the Don River in the eastern part of European Russia. The list of game animals present at these Upper Paleolithic sites is extensive; included in archaeologist Richard Klein's (1969:64) enumeration are mammoth, woolly rhinoceros, horse, cattle, musk ox, red deer, elk, reindeer, and saiga antelope, among others. Klein also points out the extensive presence of the butchered bones of carnivores such as brown bear, arctic fox, lynx, and wolf, and suggests their significance, not so much for food, but for the rich, warm fur they would have provided for people living in a cold, tundra environment.

The situation is much the same in Africa and western Europe, where Upper Paleolithic inhabitants exploited local large game animals. In Siberia, the site of Mal'ta near Irkutsk shows extensive hunting of woolly mammoth and reindeer. In South Africa, at Late Stone Age sites such as Die Kelders Cave and Eland's Bay Cave, remains of eland (a large antelope) are abundant, and there is evidence of the hunting of the Cape buffalo, a far more dangerous animal and one avoided during the Middle Paleolithic (Klein 1983). In the Upper Paleolithic of western Europe, at sites such as Abri Pataud in France, the bones of reindeer, elephant, horse, and wild cattle were found (White 1982). At Mother Grundy's Parlour, a cave occupation site in Great Britain dating to about 12,000 B.P., the remains of woolly rhinoceros and mammoth, reindeer, and wild horse were found (C. Smith 1992). Also in Great Britain, Gough's Cave shows extensive use of wild horse and red deer more than 12,200 years ago (C. Smith 1992).

The faunal remains of fish and bird food species, virtually absent in Middle Paleolithic contexts, are far more common at Upper Paleolithic sites. The same South African sites just mentioned, for example, show evidence of the extensive reliance on seals, penguins, mollusks, and flying shore birds (Klein 1983:43). The bones or shells of these organisms have been found, along with grooved-stone net weights used in fishing and possible early fishhooks (called "gorges") that were baited and attached to lines. This expansion of the food base to include small game, aquatic resources, and fowl is diagnostic of the Upper Paleolithic.

Larger Sites of Aggregation

Middle Paleolithic sites tend to be small, representative of the encampments of nomadic, **opportunistic foragers,** taking advantage of whatever resources they could wherever they became available, without much planning in advance (L. Binford 1984). Though Upper Paleolithic sites include similarly small foraging camps, there are much larger sites dating to the Upper Paleolithic. Randall White (1982) interprets these as places of aggregation, localities where numerous small bands of people would come together seasonally. The site of Mal'ta, in Siberia, for example, covers an area of some 600 square meters (about 7,500 square feet) (Chard 1974:20), with the remains of numerous dwellings whose frames were made from the large bones of woolly mammoth (Figures 9.3 and 9.4). This size is far larger than the standard Middle Paleolithic site.

The **settlement pattern** of the Middle Paleolithic reflects a strategy of opportunistic foraging within a pattern of unrestricted wandering. Here, the nomadic band moves in no particular pattern, following resources wherever they might become available. The pattern of subsistence in the Upper Paleolithic appears to be different, at least in part. During the Upper Paleolithic, the settlement pattern seems to indicate a shift to a fixed seasonal round as part of a strategy of **logistical collecting** (L. Binford 1984). People still lived in nomadic bands, but the movement of the band was no longer unrestricted, instead following a fixed yearly pattern where at least some seasonally occupied sites were returned to each year, perhaps by members of other bands. Subsistence and movements were planned out in advance as people gained a detailed knowledge of their territory, seasonality, and the behavior and shifting locations of the plants and animals on which they subsisted.

FIGURE 9.3

This reconstruction of a dwelling made of mammoth bone is evidence that in the Upper Paleolithic in Siberia, trees were not generally available for construction but the bones of large game animals were. (Department of Library Services, American Museum of Natural History, Negative #69368fr15)

FIGURE 9.4

This hide-covered structure with a superstructure of wood, bone, and antler from the site of Mal'ta is another example of the use of animal bone in Upper Paleolithic construction.

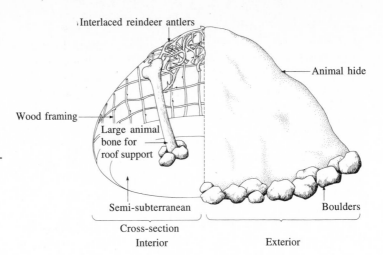

Interlaced reindeer antlers

Animal hide

Wood framing

Large animal bone for roof support

Semi-subterranean

Boulders

Cross-section
Interior

Exterior

Some sites were continually visited by aggregations of related people during fixed and known times of the year when resources may have been particularly abundant at these places—for example, at a topographic bottleneck on a migration route for large animals. Some of these sites, perhaps, became ritually sanctified through the use of artwork to denote the significance of a particular place to the members of the group. This possibility will be discussed in the section on the appearance of artwork in the Upper Paleolithic and in the Issues and Debates section.

Branching Out in Raw Materials

Expanding their raw material base beyond stone, Upper Paleolithic toolmakers also used bone, antler, shell, and ivory for such tools as sewing equipment (awls, punches, and needles) and hunting equipment (projectile points). Along the Dnestr River in Russia, Upper Paleolithic sites have produced slotted daggers of reindeer antler. At the Kosoutsy site in this same region, reindeer antler was also used as a raw material for the manufacture of spearpoints for use in the hunt, and thin slivers of reindeer bone were used in the production of eyed needles (Borziyak 1993).

Eyed needles are indirect evidence of sewing and the inferred manufacture of sewn clothing during the Upper Paleolithic. More direct evidence of the production of tailored clothing comes from the 22,000-year-old site of Sungir', just north of Moscow, in Russia. Beads used for fastening were found in a pattern in the ground, outlining what appears to have been pants, a shirt or jacket, a cap, and shoes (Klein 1989; R. White 1993).

Ivory eyed needles have been found at Jouclas, in France, dating to 21,000 years ago (Dennell 1986). Long, pointed bone spearpoints with inserts of small, sharp flint blades have been reconstructed at the Amvrosievka sites in eastern Europe (Krotova and Belan 1993). Barbed bone harpoons (like those from Kent's Cavern in Great Britain) (C. Smith 1992), antler hammers, wrench-like bone "shaft-straighteners" (like the one recovered at Gough's Cave in Great Britain and often called *bâtons de commandement*), and bone awls all have been found in Upper Paleolithic sites from western Europe to east Asia.

The **spear-thrower** was an innovation of the Upper Paleolithic. This tool is an elongated, hooked handle that attaches to the butt of a spear and effectively increases the length of the arm of the person throwing the spear. A longer arm increases the contact time between the inception of the throw and the release, allowing for greater accuracy, speed, and distance; it works for the same reason a baseball pitcher with a long arm can often throw the ball harder and faster than one with a shorter pitching arm. A 13,000-year-old spear-thrower from Enlène Cave, France, was carved from reindeer antler (Dennell 1986). Along with being a useful tool, this spear-thrower is far more beautiful than it had to be; the handle was finely carved into the image of two ibexes (mountain goats) locked in combat (see the Paleolithic Portfolio, Color Plates 8 and 9).

Clearly, the Upper Paleolithic represents a period when our human ancestors perfected technologies that previously they had barely experimented with, branching out into the use of raw materials other than stone for the unique benefits and special qualities afforded by bone, ivory, and antler.

Abundance of Nonutilitarian Objects

In my classes I see many students, men and women, wearing nonutilitarian items of personal adornment: necklaces, earrings, nose rings, ear cuffs, finger rings, bracelets, anklets, hair pins. Some have gold and silver draping every extremity and dangling from a multitude of pierced body parts.

All our bodies look basically the same, built along one of two fundamental models: male or female. But we have invented numerous ways of decorating ourselves—defining, identifying, and distinguishing ourselves—with objects of adornment. Such artifacts interpretable as items of personal ornamentation are virtually absent from Middle Paleolithic contexts. Upper Paleolithic sites, however, are replete with them. Stone, bone, antler, shell, and ivory jewelry is common, often found as grave goods. Other Upper Paleolithic nonutilitarian objects include engraved animal bones that may have served as objects of personal or group identity (Conkey 1980) and even as items for keeping track of lunar phases (Marshack 1972).

One site where such items are abundant is Mal'ta in central Asia (Chard 1974). Dated to sometime after 15,000 B.P., the site has produced a wealth of items of adornment. A small child was found buried at Mal'ta with a necklace made of bone and antler beads. Also found were schematic carvings of birds, a carved bone plaque with designs consisting of dots and wavy lines etched

FIGURE 9.5

This figurine is one of some thirty such figurines carved from the bone of woolly mammoth found at the site of Mal'ta, in Siberia. (Musée de l'Homme. J. Oster)

or punched into the surface of the bone, and depictions of human beings (Figure 9.5).

A spectacular necklace was recovered from Rocher de la Peine in France. There, 13,000 years ago, an Upper Paleolithic jewelry-maker strung together beads of dentalium shell, three large bear teeth, and one tooth from a Late Pleistocene European lion (Figure 9.6; Dennell 1986). The shells came from the coast, about 100 miles from the site.

As Randall White (1982) points out, the appearance of items of personal adornment that were often painstakingly made, frequently out of exotic material that must have been difficult to obtain—and therefore "expensive" in terms of time and effort to obtain it—is significant. In White's view, such objects imply increasing awareness and importance of individual identity in Upper Paleolithic society.

Archaeologists Heidi Knecht and Anne Pike-Tay, writing along with Randall White (1993:3), have suggested that the use of personalized ornaments may signify the existence of hierarchical social systems in the Upper Paleolithic, with such ornamentation symbolizing the social position and role of the wearer. Whatever the significance of the development of items of personal adornment, it seems clear that people in the Upper Paleolithic were much like ourselves.

Use of Exotic Raw Materials

The ability to obtain raw materials and manufactured goods from great distances might seem to be a strictly modern feature. Look around your house and try counting up the goods that originated in other countries—stereo equipment and camera manufactured in Japan, clothing made in China or the Philippines, car from Germany, sneakers from Great Britain, backpack from India, wristwatch from Switzerland, calculator from Singapore, and on and on.

But the expansion of economic systems to connect places at great distances from each other actually has a long history. Recent research found that the majority of the dishes used by a group of outcasts living in the wilderness of northwestern Connecticut from 1740 to 1860 originated in England (Feder 1994b). And even in the Upper Paleolithic the expansion of the geography of economies can be seen, as raw materials and manufactured goods began traveling far greater distances than in the Lower or Middle Paleolithic.

Whereas Middle Paleolithic people relied on raw materials whose source was close to their habitations, in the Upper Paleolithic we see far more extensive use of raw materials available only at great distances from living sites. For example, at the Kostenki-Borshevo sites in Russia, some local lithic materials (quartzite and brown and yellow flint) were used in making stone tools. Also used, however, was a black flint that possessed superior chipping qualities (it chipped more regularly) but was not available in the Kostenki-Borshevo

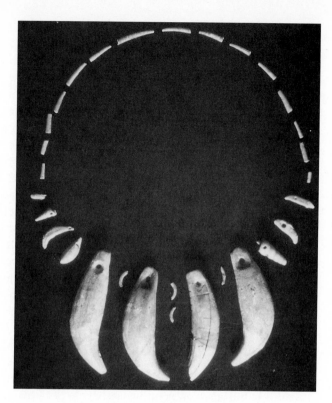

region. Its nearest possible source was about 150 km (97 mi) away. Analysis of the raw materials recovered at the site suggests that the flint obtained by the inhabitants of the Kostenki-Borshevo region for their artifacts actually came from a source 300 km (176 mi) distant (Klein 1969:227).

The situation is much the same throughout the geographical extent of Upper Paleolithic cultures. For example, in Moravia, in south-central Europe, flint commonly was moved across distances of 100 km (65 mi) from its source (Oliva 1993:52). In rare instances, apparently highly valued material like obsidian (volcanic glass) from Hungary is found in Paleolithic sites up to 500 km (325 mi) away (Oliva 1993:52). Even where quite serviceable stone was available locally, material obtainable only from great distances was often used. Archaeologist Martin Oliva (1993) suggests that maintaining long-distance contacts through trade seems to have been more important than the specific qualities of the lithics themselves and that the stone and its trade took on more of a ritual meaning than just a utilitarian meaning.

Using raw materials from great distances away in the Upper Paleolithic implies a greater reliance on trade with distant groups and, perhaps, also implies broader social networks (hypothetically maintained by seasonal get-togethers evidenced at the aggregation sites) than anything seen in Middle Paleolithic contexts.

More Elaborate Burials

When Duane Allman, slide guitarist in the Allman Brothers southern rock band, was killed in a motorcycle accident, he was buried with his famous guitar in his hands and his steel slide on his left ring finger. If the modern folk tale is true, a woman in California (sometimes the story has it in Florida) was buried in a nightgown, seated at the wheel of her brand new Jaguar (or Porsche, take your pick). Other modern examples include the burying of married people wearing their wedding bands or the burying of devout Christians with a cross around their neck. Burying the dead with treasured personal items is a longstanding human tradition. Egyptian pharaohs were buried with food, jewelry, furniture—even other people (see Chapter 13). The emperors of imperial China were buried with chariots and entire life-sized ceramic armies of soldiers and horses. It is a pattern we see repeated over and over. Whether because it is believed that the deceased will need such items in the afterlife or simply because of the desire to place with a departed friend some items of personal identification, the practice of burying the dead with objects that were meaningful to them and their loved ones seems near universal.

Clearly, the first human burials are associated with Middle Paleolithic archaic humans, that is, European and southwest Asian Neandertals (see Chapter 7). However, fundamental differences exist between Middle and Upper Paleolithic burials. For example, archaeologist Frank Harrold (1980) has compared a series of thirty-six Middle Paleolithic Neandertal burials with ninety-six Upper Paleolithic burials of anatomically modern humans. Only about 40% of the Neandertal burials included **grave goods,** objects intentionally buried with the dead (as objects of remembrance or, perhaps, as needed in an afterlife). Virtually all such objects were simple tools or animal bones. On the other hand, about 90% of the Upper Paleolithic burials contained grave goods, and these items were far more elaborate than the material included with the Middle Paleolithic interments. Upper Paleolithic burials included some of the same items of personal adornment mentioned previously: necklaces, bracelets, stone and bone artifacts (see the Case Study Close-Up section).

Production of Art

There are many compelling images of the human past that we can imagine, for example, australopithecines walking side by side on an African ash bed (Chapter 5), or beetle-browed Neandertals mourning over the remains of a fallen comrade placed in a crudely dug grave (Chapter 7). But perhaps none of these is more evocative than my own imagined scene of two cave painters from the Upper Paleolithic.

In the dark recesses of a narrow cave, a flickering oil lamp smears dancing shadows on a flat rock wall. A young woman, tall and lithe, her muscular

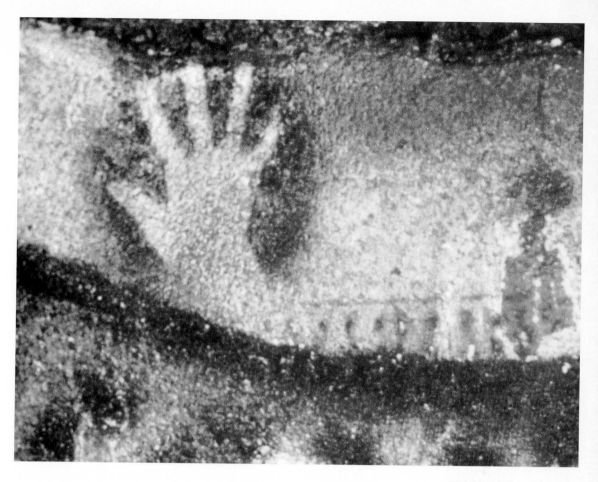

FIGURE 9.7

This image of a human handprint from the cave wall of Peche-Merle in France is an eternal signature of a human being who lived more than 20,000 years ago. (Musée de l'Homme. B. G. Dellue)

arms coated with a thin layer of grime and sweat, carefully places a dark slurry in her mouth. With one hand, she picks up a hollow reed and holds it to her lips. Her other, she lays on the rock face. Aiming the reed at the area around her hand, she sprays a fine mist of pigment out the end of the reed. After a few puffs, she removes her hand from the wall to reveal a remarkable artistic creation: a negative image of her hand, a signature some 20,000 years old (Figure 9.7).

By her side, a young man, tall and broad and with a deeply lined face belying his youth, dips a frayed twig into a thick red paste. Using skills of observation and artistry developed during his short life, he conjures up a vision held in a part of his memory as deep as where he now labors breathlessly in the cave: A galloping horse, wild and free, is making a desperate but doomed attempt to flee from her hunters. A red gash on her belly leaks blood where a stone-tipped spear pierced her hide. Soon she falls, and the hunters are thrusting their spears deep into her viscera, until at last she is quiet.

Today, though long dead, the mare lives again in a creation of pigment, memory, awe, and sorcery. Once a creature of blood and bone, sinew and muscle, she is now a creature of color and binder. No longer running across the plains of western Europe, she appears on a flat wall of rock, straining against her fate and bleeding eternally in the deep recesses of a dark cave. In this incarnation she has lived for 20,000 years now, and in her life of pigment and memory and magic, she will live forever (see the Paleolithic Portfolio, Color Plates 10 and 11).

THE MEANING OF UPPER PALEOLITHIC ART

Applying a very broad but explicit definition of the kind of symbolism that characterizes human art—the use of two-dimensional realistic or abstract images representing real objects or phenomena—archaeologist Philip Chase (1991) concludes that there is no evidence of the use of symbols in the Lower or Middle Paleolithic, no symbolic representations of the real world.

Others have disagreed with this conclusion. For example, at the Mousterian site of Tata, in Hungary, a carved, polished fragment of a woolly mammoth molar, dated to more than 50,000 years ago and associated with Mousterian tools, was stained with red ochre pigment (Marshak 1976). Researcher Alexander Marshak maintains that the object could have served no utilitarian purpose. Though carefully worked, it has no sharp edge and exhibits no evidence of use. Did the object signify membership in a group, did the ochre symbolize blood? Though possibly representing Neandertal art and their use of symbol, precisely what this artifact signifies is still unclear.

When we look at the record for anatomically modern human beings from after 50,000 years ago, all ambiguity disappears. It is abundantly clear that it is in the Upper Paleolithic that humanity experienced what more than one author has likened to an "explosion" of artistic and symbolic creativity (Conkey 1978:74; Pfeiffer 1982, who titles his book *The Creative Explosion*). From incised bone to carved statues to cave paintings, the Upper Paleolithic is marked by the beginning of human artistic and symbolic expression. The roots of such expression may be traced back to the Middle Paleolithic, but only dimly. It is in the Upper Paleolithic (and not just in Europe) that we see the uniquely human capacity—and perhaps need—to mark our existence through the creation of permanent, symbolic works of art.

The Earliest Art: Australia and Africa

Though we may not know what the images and objects mean, many artifacts dated to the period beginning about 40,000 years ago clearly denote the use

of symbol and the production of art. For example, at Wharton Hill in Australia (Map 9.1), more than 36,000 years ago, an aborigine etched an oval shape into the abutting rock face (Bednarik 1993:5; see Chapter 10 for a discussion of the human presence in Australia). A radiocarbon date was derived from organic material recovered from inside the groove and encased in the rock varnish (a weathering rind of rock that builds up on an exposed surface) of the **petroglyph** (literally, "rock-writing"). The organic deposit could have gotten into the groove only after the groove was made, providing, therefore, a minimum possible age for the carved oval shape. At the nearby site of Panaramitee North, a curvilinear petroglyph has been dated via the same technique, to 43,000 B.P. (Bednarik 1993:6). These dates, if correct, render the Australian petroglyphs the earliest evidence of art in the world.

The first African art has been dated to as much as 28,000 years ago (Phillipson 1993). Stone slabs with painted and engraved images of animals have been excavated from deposits dating to this time at the Apollo 11 cave site in southern Namibia (Map 9.1; Wendt 1976). The animals are natural renderings of the fauna of southern Africa for the time period of their production.

Upper Paleolithic Art in Europe

The artwork of Late Pleistocene Europe is far better known than the Australian or the African artwork, partly as a result of geography—it is found in an area where extensive archaeology has been conducted—and partly because of placement—its location in caves has kept it better preserved. In the cave paintings (**parietal art**) and in carved statues and inscribed bone, antler, and ivory (**mobiliary art**), Upper Paleolithic Europeans produced an astounding amount of art (Map 9.1). Some of the paintings and inscribed artifacts incorporate geometric designs and abstract images whose meanings are difficult to interpret. In many of the paintings and carvings, though we may never be certain of the artist's intent (see the Issues and Debates section), we cannot help but recognize the images they were producing. Cave walls in France and Spain especially, but also those scattered throughout Europe, are adorned with realistic depictions of the animals of the Upper Paleolithic. Images of prehistoric horse and bison, woolly mammoth and rhinoceros, reindeer and wild cattle flow across cave-wall canvases at places like Lascaux and Altamira, Les Combarelles, Niaux, Les Trois-Frères, Peche-Merle, and Fonte-de-Gaume (see the Paleolithic Portfolio, Color Plates 10 and 11; Leroi-Gourhan 1982).

Southwestern Europe alone has some 200 caves with Paleolithic artwork, and more caves are found fairly regularly. The most exciting recent find was Chauvet cave (Hughes 1995). This cave near Avignon, France, contains an amazing array of paintings. Most people who have seen them consider them some of the most beautiful examples of Paleolithic artwork ever discovered. The dates derived for the artwork at Chauvet are stunning: The two oldest dates of the eight derived from carbon samples taken from the paintings were greater than 30,000 B.P., making the Chauvet artwork the oldest cave paintings yet discovered in Europe.

In their paintings, produced from about 30,000 years ago to 10,000 years ago, the artists of the Upper Paleolithic have willed to us evocative images of their natural surroundings and, at the same time, whispered to us of their intellectual world. At Niaux, France, a detailed image of a bison includes two spears penetrating its body. At Rouffignac, also in France, two outlined woolly mammoths appear to confront each other in an apparent dance for dominance. At Chauvet, a group of overlapping, stiff-maned horses rendered in shades of gray seems to be relaxing on the cave wall surface. At Lascaux, a badly wounded bison, its viscera hanging from its wounded belly, is confronting its attacker, knocking over an outlined hunter.

Upper Paleolithic artists also depicted themselves, though commonly more schematically and less realistically (Figure 9.8). Researchers Patricia Rice and Ann Paterson (1988) analyzed more than 100 human images from 32 caves in western Europe. Their statistics are provocative: More than three-quarters of the images are men, who tend to be depicted singly, in an active mode—running, walking, spear-throwing. Females tend to be portrayed at rest, and in close proximity to other females. What does this mean in terms of the roles of males and females in Paleolithic society? This glimpse into the sexual division of labor in societies that existed more than 15,000 years ago simply is not enough to draw any conclusion.

Though largely enigmatic in their meaning, these caves were clearly not art galleries. In the more than 150 mostly western European caves where significant numbers of paintings have been found, some images overlap, and the strange juxtapositioning of the animals—some floating above others, some upside down in relation to others—shows quite clearly that individual paintings and panels were not intended as part of a single tableau.

The relative frequency of species depicted and their locations are not random. Carnivores, for example, are often placed in the least accessible parts of the caves, and the herbivores seem to be depicted in proportion to their significance in the diet of the people who painted them (see the Issues and Debates section). While at some caves animal species that served as food for Paleolithic hunters predominate, the newly discovered Chauvet cave has quite a few paintings of carnivores: three cave lions, a panther, and a bear. Chauvet also presents us with the single largest concentration of paintings of woolly rhinoceroses—fifty of them.

FIGURE 9.8

The cave walls are haunted by the cryptic images of the people who produced the remarkable artistic legacy of the Upper Paleolithic. This image appears at the site of Le Portel in France.

The Venus Figurines

Then there are the so-called **Venus figurines.** Most of them, across much of Europe, date to the period between 25,000 and 23,000 years ago (some were made nearly 27,000 years ago and a few date to 20,000 years ago) (Gamble 1986). One group, but by no means all, of these statuettes depicts obese females, usually without faces but with enlarged breasts and buttocks (Figure 9.9). This particular variety of the female figurines has become the stereotype of this class of artifacts, perhaps, as archaeologist Patricia Rice (1981) points out, because these are the ones most often depicted in books on prehistoric art. Many researchers have suggested that they were fertility symbols, realistic depictions of pregnant females, or portrayals of women with various medical conditions.

However, these suggestions are difficult to support when large samples are examined. Patricia Rice (1981) looked at a group of 188 Venus figurines and found their shape, size, and form to be quite varied. There were depictions of thin and fat women, women with large breasts and women with small breasts, pregnant and not pregnant women, and women who were, by Rice's estimation, old, middle-aged, and young (based on the depiction of physical appearance, especially the presence or absence of lines in their faces and in how flat or saggy breasts, stomachs, hips, and buttocks looked).

Rice (1981:408) proposes that the deduced age spread of the Upper Paleolithic female figurines in her large sample was remarkably similar to the actual age distribution in historical hunter-gatherer populations. So in her view, the Venus figurines depict women of all shapes and sizes, all ages, and all

FIGURE 9.9

These two examples of the so-called Venus figurines—the famous Venus of Willendorf (left) and a relief carving from a cave in France (right)—fit the common stereotype of such figurines: broad hips, large breasts, fat bellies, and vague faces. (Left: Neg. no. 326474, photographer Lee Boltin. Courtesy Department of Library Services, American Museum of Natural History; right: Musée de l'Homme. D. Ponsard)

states of fertility. More recently, Jean-Pierre Duhard (1993) has examined Upper Paleolithic depictions of human beings. While he questions some of Rice's methodology, he agrees with her most general conclusion: "The women depicted display every variation and accurately reproduce the forms encountered among living people" (Duhard 1993:87). Duhard also points out that some males are depicted among the figurines, although most are female and many of the females are pregnant.

The precise meaning of the cave paintings as well as of the figurines is elusive. But what is key here is that in painting their images in caves, in engraving designs on antler, and in sculpting depictions of women, the artists of the Upper Paleolithic were doing something that we recognize as human behavior. They were creating images from their memory, filtered through the lens of their imagination. In doing this they left us wonderful works to ponder.

ISSUES AND DEBATES

WHY IS THERE NO CORRELATION BETWEEN ANATOMICAL AND BEHAVIORAL MODERNITY?

At the chronological boundary between the Middle and Upper Paleolithic, prehistorians are faced with a riddle. As we have seen in Chapter 8, anatomically modern human beings with presumably physically modern brains encased within demonstrably modern crania perched atop modern postcranial skeletons appear in the archaeological record more than 100,000 years ago. But though these first human beings represent a jump to modern morphology from their physically archaic roots, the archaeological record shows no such great leap in their behavior at this time. The Katanda bone artifacts from Zaire, discussed in Chapter 8, are quite sophisticated and date to 90,000 years ago. But these materials are still exceptional. Generally speaking, in virtually every other instance, though minor differences exist in the kinds of tools made, the way fireplaces were constructed, and so forth, the material culture of Middle Paleolithic archaic *Homo sapiens* is quite similar—in some cases, virtually identical—to the material culture of the earliest anatomically modern humans living at the same time.

In fact, the great leap forward to a more modern culture does not appear to have occurred until sometime after 50,000 years ago—more than 50,000 years after the first appearance of humans whose cranial morphologies suggest they had brains capable of modern adaptations right from the start.

We still do not understand why this extended temporal gap exists between the first appearance of ostensibly modern humans and the first appearance of a modern-looking material culture. Archaeologist Richard Klein (1989, 1994) even suggests that, though we call them anatomically modern *Homo sapiens* on the basis of skeletal features, perhaps the hominids represented at Border Cave, Klasies River Mouth, Skuhl, and Qafzeh (see Chapter 8) were only superficially modern, retaining a fundamentally archaic neuroanatomy. In other words, though we can't prove it archaeologically, perhaps their modern-looking skulls housed brains that were not yet modern and so they were not yet intellectually capable of producing the material culture that characterizes the Upper Paleolithic. Klein suggests that what amounts to a rewiring of the human brain occurred sometime between 40,000 years ago and 50,000 years ago, allowing for a great leap to modern intelligence. As of now, this remains an untested—perhaps untestable—hypothesis.

WHAT DOES THE ART OF THE UPPER PALEOLITHIC MEAN?

It is difficult not to be moved by the images that adorn the cave walls of ancient Europe and elsewhere. With twentieth-century-A.D. eyes we can appreciate the visual beauty and movement of the artwork. But what did these works mean to the twentieth-millennium-B.P. eyes of their creators? And why did they do it?

There are as many answers to these questions as researchers who have contemplated them. Some have argued that the art of the Upper Paleolithic explains itself: It is (and was) beautiful and was produced for the simple joy of creating something of beauty and power, just as modern artists do. It was "art for art's sake" (Halvorson 1987).

Most researchers, though, eschew such an explanation as no explanation at all and have sought deeper meaning in the art. There has long been a "just-so" explanation, proposing that when a hunting people depict animals in their artwork, they are necessarily practicing what is called sympathetic magic. The hunters paint the animals and show them being speared or captured in the magical, symbolic realm, to ensure their capture and slaughter in the real world.

French researcher André Leroi-Gourhan (1968) championed a popular hypothesis that the cave art was filled with sexual symbolism, with phallic spears piercing vulva-like wounds on the animals. So the animal depictions of the Upper Paleolithic were not about animals or hunting at all; instead, they were about sex and gender.

Other researchers have suggested that cave paintings depicted actual historical events, hunts symbolically and artistically recorded for posterity. And still others have likened the paintings to mounted animal-head trophies hung on the walls of their modern hunters.

Recent researchers have tried to delve more deeply, seeing the artwork as part of a system of communication of ideas through the use of animals and geometric patterns as symbols, the specific meaning of which may be lost forever. Archaeologist Meg Conkey (1980) views the 1,200 bones engraved with abstract geometric patterns at Altamira Cave, Spain, as the identifying symbols—the "flags"—of different groups of people who came together at the cave during periods of population aggregation. Michael Jochim views the cave paintings of northern Spain and southern France—the so-called Franco-Cantabrian region—as symbols marking territory. Social stresses that accompanied population influx into the region during the period after 25,000 B.P. may have resulted in the need to mark territory with symbols of ownership. Painting animals—probably the most important resources of a territory—within a sacred place in the territory like a cave might have served to announce to all interlopers the rightful ownership of the surrounding lands. Clive Gamble (1982, 1986) views the Venus figurines as a symbolic social glue, helping to maintain social connections between geographically distant groups through a common religion and art style.

More recently, researchers Patricia Rice and Ann Paterson (1985, 1986) have returned to a more economic perspective. Their statistical analysis of the numbers and kinds of animals seen on cave walls in the European Upper Paleolithic shows interesting correlations with the faunal assemblages of habitation sites in Spain and France. Small, nonaggressive animals like reindeer and red deer were important in the diet of the cave painters and seem to have been depicted on cave walls in proportion to their economic importance. On the other hand, animals less often seen in faunal assemblages, but impressive, dangerous, and productive of large quantities of meat when they were successfully procured, also were commonly included in the artwork. However, the newly discovered Chauvet Cave contradicts this pattern, with its stunning depictions of animals not known to have been exploited for food by Paleolithic Europeans, including carnivores like lions, bears, and panthers as well as woolly rhinoceroses.

The art of the Upper Paleolithic has been depressingly resistant to any comprehensive explanation for its existence. That we cannot even fathom the reason for our own children's scribblings (see this chapter's Prelude section) does not bode well for our attempt to illuminate the motives for and meanings of the artwork of our Upper Paleolithic ancestors. Perhaps we are destined merely to enjoy the cave paintings and Venus figurines, much as we delight in those crayon, pencil, and paint images we attach with magnets to our refrigerators. That would not be so terrible, so great is the aesthetic enjoyment we might derive from them. Then again, it is undeniable that there are insights yet to be extracted from these beautiful puzzles which, when solved, will tell us much about what it means to be a human being.

DOES THE PALEOLITHIC HAVE A GENDER?

On many levels, gender issues are part of our ideas about human behavior, both in the past and in the present (Gero and Conkey 1990; Spencer-Wood 1991). For example, the discussion of the origins of upright walking in Chapter 5's Issues and Debates section presented the hypothesis of Owen Lovejoy that bipedalism arose to enable males to provision females. Issues of sex roles, monogamy, and paternity—for *Australopithecus* as well as their modern descendants—are bound up in his hypothesis.

Gender issues are just as pertinent to our discussion of the Upper Paleolithic. Consider cave art. I intentionally tried to surprise you in the Prelude's vignette of two Paleolithic artists: One of them was female. Many people think, on the basis of virtually no data, that men were the ancient artists of the Paleolithic. But why?

Archaeologist Diane Gifford-Gonzalez (1993) points out that in most popular reconstructions of ancient life, virtually all of the important and exciting behaviors reflected in the archaeological record have been ascribed only to ancient males. Surveying the work of eighty-eight modern artists, Gifford-Gonzalez determined the proportions of males and females depicted performing a number of different tasks (Figure 9.10). Her results are truly amazing. For example, in her sample of 331 images of individual ancient people, all of the individuals depicted performing a ritual, hunting, or carrying game were males. And 90% of those depicted producing Paleolithic artwork were males. In the same sample, not one male was shown holding a baby or touching a child.

From illustrations in coffee-table books to diorama kits for kids to professionally produced museum dioramas, images abound of ancient men hunting, creating art, and performing ceremonies, while women are shown in the background with children, performing drudge work like scraping hides or cooking. So it is not surprising that many people assume that the role of ancient women focused on cooking food, making clothing, and, of course, bearing and raising children. These same people assume it was men who, by wit, sinew, and intelligence, fed their families by tracking, killing, and bringing animals back to the cave. Then, though exhausted from providing sustenance for their families, they worked the evenings away, producing great works of art, as fresh and vibrant today as they must have been 25,000 years ago when they were painted. In this view, men were involved in all of the exciting, intellectually stimulating, and physically challenging activities, while women got to clean up.

FIGURE 9.10

In this graph, archaeologist Diane Gifford-Gonzalez shows the kind of sex role stereotyping modern artists have engaged in when depicting Paleolithic people. Women are commonly shown caring for children and working animal hides; men are shown hunting, using tools, carrying game, performing rituals, and producing art. (Adapted with permission from Diane Gifford-Gonzalez)

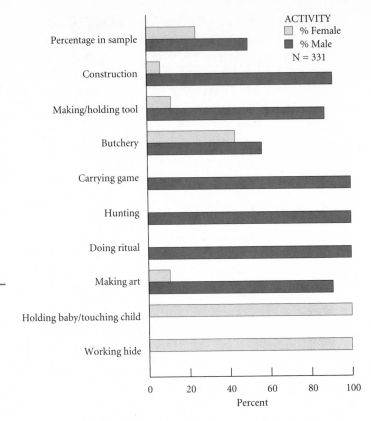

In truth, we must admit our ignorance; we don't know who produced the cave art in the Upper Paleolithic or who performed rituals. We must not allow our twentieth-century preconceptions about the sexual division of labor to bias our view of the ancient past. It could have been women as easily as men who applied those remarkable images onto the cave walls, carved the figurines, and held positions of ritual importance. At the same time, we should not presume that Paleolithic men played out a 1950s-style fatherhood: stiff, distant, and uninvolved. It is far more likely that survival during the Pleistocene required all members of a group to contribute in many different ways; Paleolithic people probably could not have afforded to restrict the contributions of individuals on the basis of sex. Perhaps at some point we might recognize the same thing.

**CASE STUDY
CLOSE-UP**

The site of Sungir' is located about 150 km (100 mi) northeast of Moscow, in Russia (R. White 1993). Dating to at least 25,000–30,000 years ago (and possibly as much as 38,000 B.P.), five burials (an older male, an adult female, a young girl, a teenage boy, and an individual of undetermined sex) have been excavated at the site.

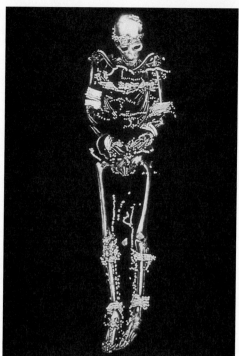

FIGURE 9.11

This skeleton of an older man who lived more than 25,000 years ago is one of five burials excavated at the Upper Paleolithic site of Sungir' near Moscow. More than 3,000 ivory beads were sewn into his burial garments. (Musée de l'Homme. O. Bader)

    The Sungir' graves are loaded with grave goods, primarily items of adornment (all data on the Sungir' graves taken from R. White 1993:287–296). The older male was adorned with nearly 3,000 finely worked ivory beads; some apparently were part of a beaded cap and the rest were positioned in strands around his body (Figure 9.11). A flat stone pendant was located on his neck. On his arms were twenty-five finely carved bracelets made from the ivory of a woolly mammoth. The young boy's body was surrounded with more than 4,900 ivory beads. A carved ivory pendant had been placed on his chest. He wore a belt decorated with 250 polar fox teeth. There was an ivory pin at his throat, an ivory lance and carved ivory disk at his side, an ivory sculpture of a woolly mammoth under his shoulder, and by his left side a human femur (not his own), with a cavity filled with red ochre. Next to the adolescent boy lay the young girl, buried with more than 5,200 strung beads, an ivory pin at her throat (perhaps a clasp for a garment long since decayed away), small ivory lances, and three ivory disks carved with intricate latticework.

    An enormous amount of time must have been invested in preparing these items for burial. Replication of the beads has indicated that forty-five minutes were needed to make just *one* of the ivory beads in the Sungir' burials (R. White 1993:296). If this estimate is accurate, then 2,000 hours of work were needed just for the beads in the older man's burial, and more than 3,500 hours per child were needed for their beadwork.

We cannot say why such items turn up in Upper Paleolithic burials, nor what such items meant to the people of that period. Nevertheless, that such labor, care, and—yes—love was invested in remembrances for the dead means that the emotional and spiritual world of the Upper Paleolithic must have been remarkably similar to our own, more than 30,000 years later.

VISITING THE PAST

Of all the site visits suggested so far in this book, none are as dramatic as the painted caves of Paleolithic Europe. Unfortunately, some of the best-known sites are now closed to the public. Years of tourist visits have taken their toll on the artwork. Lights and especially the increased humidity produced by breathing and perspiring has harmed many of the precious painted images.

Spain and France have come up with an innovative solution to this problem: Replicas of some image groups from Altamira and Lascaux Caves have been produced. The actual contours of the ceiling of Altamira Cave were measured and copied in an artificial material. The cave paintings were then copied on this surface. The artificial cave with its replica artwork is on display at the Archaeological Museum in Madrid.

A more ambitious project is ongoing at Lascaux, where so-called Lascaux II is partially complete (Ruspoli 1986). Here, in a concrete blockhouse about 200 m from the actual cave, a new cave is being constructed to the exact measurements of the original. Modeled concrete is replicating precisely the cave surfaces, and teams of artists are producing near-perfect copies of the originals. Hundreds of thousands of tourists have visited Lascaux II since it opened in 1984, providing a wonderful opportunity to visit the past, even when the original is off-limits.

SUMMARY

For 50,000 years—from 100,000 years ago to 50,000 years ago (virtually half the duration of the existence of the modern species *Homo sapiens sapiens*)—the material culture of human beings as reflected in the archaeological record was indistinguishable from that of our archaic contemporaries. Then, sometime after 50,000 years ago, a remarkable transformation occurred that resulted in cultural systems with a decidedly modern cast. This period of intellectual upheaval is called the Upper Paleolithic. The cultures of the period are characterized by: the production of blade tools; a broadening of the subsistence base; an increase in the size of some sites (implying a practice of temporary population aggregation); the use of bone, antler, ivory, and shell in toolmaking; the manufacture of nonutilitarian items, some of which served as items of personal adornment; the extensive use of nonlocal, exotic raw materials; the regular placement of elaborate grave goods in burials—including items of personal adornment; and the first appearance of artwork, in the form of naturalistic paintings, fanciful sculptures, and engraved bone and antler. In the material culture of the Upper Paleolithic we see a recognizably "modern" human pattern.

TO LEARN MORE

There are many useful works that detail the significant changes seen at the boundary between the Middle and Upper Paleolithic. For technical reports, see many of the individual articles in the edited volume *The Emergence of Modern Humans: An Archaeological Perspective* (Mellars 1990). For splendid photographs of cave paintings from a variety of caves there is André Leroi-Gourhan's (1982) *The Dawn of European Art*. For a detailed photographic treatment of Lascaux, don't miss Mario Ruspoli's (1986) *The Cave of Lascaux: The Final Photographs*. It is a magnificent coffee-table book, but also much more, with lengthy discussions of the painted images. Another book with terrific photographic images of cave art, but one that also has much to say about the significance of the art itself, is *Dark Caves, Bright Visions* by Randall White (1986), the archaeologist whose work on the Middle/Upper Paleolithic transition provided a framework for part of this chapter's Chronicle section. For thoughtful discussions of the meaning of Upper Paleolithic artwork, there is no better place to start than John Pfeiffer's (1982) *The Creative Explosion: An Inquiry into the Origins of Art and Religion*. Though a bit dated, Pfeiffer is always a good read. For a more recent and more technical book-length treatment, see the thought-provoking *The Dawn of Belief: Religion in the Upper Paleolithic of Southwestern Europe* by Bruce Dickson (1990). For a more popularly oriented, article-length piece, one of the best and most succinct is archaeologist Pat Shipman's (1990) "Old Masters" in the magazine *Discover*. For another popularly oriented article, by one of the most thoughtful researchers in the field of Paleolithic art, see Margaret Conkey's (1981) "A Century of Paleolithic Cave Art" in *Archaeology* magazine.

KEY TERMS

Aurignacian	opportunistic foragers	petroglyph
Gravettian	settlement pattern	parietal art
Solutrean	logistical collecting	mobiliary art
Magdelanian	spear-thrower	Venus figurines
megafauna	grave goods	

10

Expanding Geographical Horizons

NEW WORLDS

CHAPTER OVERVIEW

Beginning after 60,000 years ago, human population expanded into much of the rest of the habitable world. Sahul (Australia/New Guinea/Tasmania) exhibits evidence of human occupation by 50,000 years ago. Western Melanesia was populated by 30,000 years ago.

Northeast Asians crossed the Bering Land Bridge at least 13,000 years ago, passing into Alaska and northwest Canada. By close to 12,000 years ago, human populations had passed south of the ice to populate North and South America. Some evidence points to a possible earlier migration: 15,000 years ago, 20,000 years ago, or even more than 30,000 years ago. The islands of Micronesia and Polynesia also show evidence of occupation after 3,500 years ago.

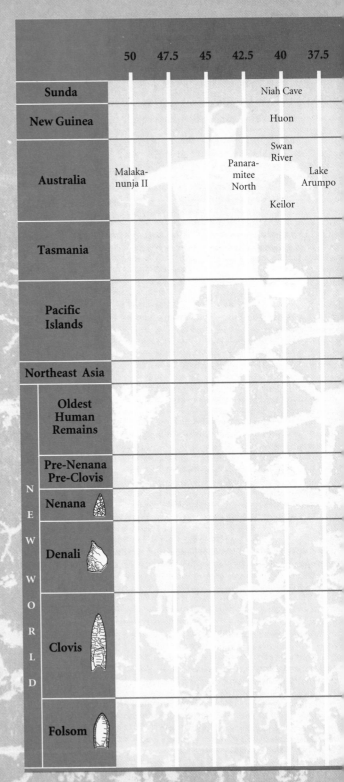

		50	47.5	45	42.5	40	37.5
Sunda						Niah Cave	
New Guinea						Huon	
Australia		Malaka-nunja II			Panara-mitee North	Swan River / Keilor	Lake Arumpo
Tasmania							
Pacific Islands							
Northeast Asia							
N E W W O R L D	Oldest Human Remains						
	Pre-Nenana Pre-Clovis						
	Nenana						
	Denali						
	Clovis						
	Folsom						

Thousands of years ago — archaeological sites timeline chart

Thousands of years ago	35	32.5	30	27.5	25	22.5	20	17.5	15	12.5	10	7.5	5	2.5	Present
			Leang Burung					Timor							
			Kuk		Nombe / Kosipe										
	Mammoth Cave / Devil's Lair / Wharton Hill	Lake Mungo	Willandra Lakes 50		Mandu Mandu / Hamersley / Koonalda	Nullarbor / Puritjarra									
	Wareen Cave		ORS7, Acheron, Bone, Nunamira		Cave Bay Cave	Kutikina, Beginner's Luck									
			Solomon Islands										Fiji / Society, Cook, Samoa	Hawaii / Easter Island / New Zealand	
	Ikhine						Dyuktai	Ushki							
										Midland					
										Tepexpan, Marmes, Arlington, Pelican Rapids					
										Meadowcroft / Monte Verde					
										Dry Creek I / Moose Creek / Walker Road					
										Dry Creek II / Usibelli, Slate Creek, Donnelly Ridge, Campus Site, Healy Lake, Teklanika River, Panguingue Creek II					
										6LF21 / Debert / Murray Springs, Dent, Lehner, Anzick / Clovis, Richey, Colby, Domebo, Vail					
											Casper / Olsen-Chubbuck / Folsom / Lindenmeier				

Sunday, July 20, 1969, was a momentous day in human history: For the first time in the existence of our species, a human being walked on the soil of another world. On that day, American astronaut Neil Armstrong left the relative safety of the lunar lander, climbed down the ladder, took a final step off, and became the citizen—if only temporarily—of another world.

NASA, leaving nothing to chance, had scripted a weighty but succinct statement to be intoned by the first human to walk on the moon. But wouldn't you know it, he blew his lines. As Armstrong made his first contact with the lunar surface, he uttered the following words: "That's one small step for man, one giant leap for mankind." But this statement is redundant and basically meaningless; "man" and "mankind" are synonymous in this context. He meant to say, "That's one small step for *a* man, one giant leap for mankind." In other words, though the step off the lunar lander was literally a "small step" for an individual, it represented a giant figurative leap forward for the human species.

The literal and figurative step Armstrong took that day was a significant one, but really just one stride in the great march of human history, a history marked by uncounted steps, both small and big, and leaps, both modest and great. From our literal first steps onto the African savanna to Armstrong's first step onto the lunar surface, human history has been filled with small steps that collectively have added up to giant leaps. One thing that surely characterizes our species is the desire to take those steps and to explore both new vistas of the imagination and actual vistas of new lands. This chapter focuses on the exploration of such new horizons by our anatomically modern ancestors as they spread into the new worlds of Australia and the Americas.

CHRONICLE

When British explorer Captain James Cook's ship made landfall on the east coast of Australia in 1770, he had no professional speech writers to help commemorate the occasion. The record of his first impressions on encountering native Australians is more mundane than Neil Armstrong's remarks: "Sunday 29th April. Saw as we came in on both points of the bay Several of the natives and a few hutts [*sic*]. Men, women and children on the south shore abreast of the Ship, to which place I went in the boats in hopes of speaking with them" (A. Price 1971:65).

When the first British settlement of the Australian continent was established at Sydney harbor in 1778, the colonists also arrived by ocean-going vessels, as did Cook. Cook and those who followed found a land populated by more than a quarter-million people, and perhaps as many as 1 million. Those natives were the descendants of settlers who had also arrived by sea. Lacking a written language, the original settlers left no record of their reaction to their "giant leap" to a new continent. Only the archaeological record speaks to us about how they survived as a people in their new world.

THE SETTLEMENT OF GREATER AUSTRALIA

The original Australians, called Aborigines, were an enigma to the European colonizers (Figure 10.1). In the Europeans' biased view, the Aborigines seemed primitive in their material culture, a Stone Age people with few material advances, throwbacks to a distant time in human history. Yet what these people lacked in things, they more than made up for in ideas. They possessed a range of sophisticated social systems; the individual Aborigine had a far denser web of relations and was far more knowledgeable of his or her social connections than was the average European. These supposedly primitive people also had a richly detailed mythology and oral history, and a sophisticated knowledge of their natural surroundings.

As different as they were from the European settlers, these native Australians shared at least one thing with the newcomers; as already mentioned, they had arrived by watercraft (Birdsell 1977; Jones 1989, 1992; J. White and O'Connell 1982). Their voyages of exploration and migration—a series of small steps adding up to one giant leap to a new world—occurred some 50,000 years before the arrival of the Europeans.

Paleogeography in the Western Pacific

During the height of the Pleistocene, ice covered much of the northern latitudes and higher elevations of the world, locking up a prodigious quantity of the earth's water in permanent ice fields, so much water that sea level was lowered by at least 100 m (325 ft) and perhaps as much as 150 m (500 ft). During glacial maxima, the islands of Java, Sumatra, Bali, and Borneo were connected to each other in a single land mass called **Sunda** (or **Sundaland**) (Figure 10.2). Sunda, in turn, was connected to mainland southeast Asia. The oceans separating these islands from each other, as well as from Asia proper, are not as deep as the amount by which sea level was depressed during glacial maxima. Wide swaths of land connecting these territories, now many meters under the ocean's surface, were exposed during periods of lowered sea level.

During these same periods of depressed sea levels, Australia, New Guinea, and Tasmania were similarly connected as a single land mass, called **Sahul,** or "Greater Australia" (see Figure 10.2). Unlike Sunda, however, Sahul was never connected to mainland Asia. Even when the Pleistocene glaciers were at their most extensive and sea level was at its lowest, Sahul was still separated from Asia by a water barrier. In fact, Greater Australia has been separated from Asia since the two were separated through continental drift more than 100 million years ago. This long-standing isolation of Australia has resulted in that continent's unique native fauna of kangaroos, wallabies, wombats, and koala bears—the marsupials (primitive mammals that give birth to very immature young who complete their gestation in pouches)—and platypuses, echidnas, and spiny anteaters—the monotremes (egg-laying mammals). Only a very

FIGURE 10.1

Today's aboriginal people of Australia are the descendants of the first migrants, who arrived about 50,000 years ago. (© Irven DeVore/ Anthro-Photo)

FIGURE 10.2

The current coastlines of Australia, New Guinea, and southeast Asia, as well as the coastline during glacial maxima. Arrows show proposed migration routes from Sunda (the combined land mass of the islands of southeast Asia) to Sahul (Greater Australia).

small number of Asian mammals, including some rodents (rats and mice) and bats, were able to cross the gap and populate Australia in prehistory (Diamond 1987a). Bats flew across the water, and rodents were probably washed out to sea from Asia on matted vegetation, which fortuitously washed up on the shores of Sahul.

The **Wallace Trench,** located between New Guinea/Australia and Java/ Borneo, is an enormous undersea chasm, nearly 7,500 m (25,000 ft) deep. Though the lands of Sunda and Sahul crept toward each other during glacial maxima at 65,000 years ago, then 53,000 years ago, and again at 35,000 years ago, they never coalesced, kept apart by the deep waters of **Wallacea,** the sea over the Wallace Trench (Glover 1993).

The Road to Sahul

Oceanic islands in Wallacea, like Timor and Sulawesi (formerly called the Celebes), would have served as stepping stones between Asia and Australia during the Pleistocene. Anthropologist Joseph Birdsell (1977) has suggested a series of possible routes from Sunda to Sahul during periods of lowered sea level (see Figure 10.2). During glacial maxima and the concomitant lowering of sea level, one viable route starts on the eastern shore of contemporary Borneo, continues east through Sulawesi, and includes several island hops to northwest New Guinea. The longest inter-island gap would have been about 70 km (43 mi); the mean of the eight gaps in this route is only about 28 km (17 mi) (Birdsell 1977:127). An alternate route suggested by Birdsell is more southerly, beginning in Java, traversing the Indonesian archipelago, crossing south to Timor and then south to Australia proper. This route also contains eight ocean crossings, with a maximum of 87 km (54 mi) and a mean of a little more than 19 km (12 mi) between landfalls (Birdsell 1977:127). When sea level was not as low as the proposed maximum, the distances become greater and the trip more difficult.

   As Birdsell points out, this voyage likely did not take place all at once, but transpired, perhaps, over several generations, as people with a marine adaptation explored the islands in their vicinity and discovered more distant islands accidentally by being blown off course during storms. These people might then have settled on some of the islands, and the process would have been repeated, pushing the limits of their world ever farther out along its edges.

The Discovery of Greater Australia

The timing of the original human discovery and settlement of Greater Australia has long been disputed. It cannot have preceded a human presence on coastal southeast Asia (which is the most logical source for the native Australian population), and it must have followed the development of a coastal adaptation and the invention of seaworthy watercraft.

   The archaeology of tropical southeast Asia, unfortunately, is not well known enough for us to trace with confidence the aboriginal inhabitants of Sahul to their Sunda source. Only a few early sites have been found in the most logical source areas, and these are all too late to represent a population

MAP 10.1

Sites representing the earliest occupation of Greater Australia.

ancestral to Greater Australia's first settlers—they are, in fact, much younger than the oldest sites now known from Sahul (Map 10.1).

For example, one of the older sites in southeast Asia is located in Niah Cave on the island of Borneo. The lowest levels in the cave produced stone flakes, bone tools, and the remains of several animal species, including tapir, pig, monkey, deer, and porcupine (Jones 1989). One of the larger stone tools recovered at the site exhibits a distinct notching or grooving around its middle—in essence, a "waist." This form turns up again on the other side of Wallacea, in New Guinea and Australia, and may indicate a genealogical connection between the peoples who made this tool form on both sides of the Wallace Trench. Radiocarbon dates place the earliest occupation of Niah Cave at around 40,000 years ago. A fully modern, lightly constructed human skull was recovered from this same level in the cave.

The oceanic island of Sulawesi in Wallacea has produced archaeological evidence of human occupation dating to 31,000 years ago at the Leang Burung cave site (Jones 1992). The oldest occupation of Timor is more recent still, dating to within the last 15,000 years. As indicated, these islands may have been used as stepping stones from Sunda to Sahul. But again, the archaeological record has not provided sites old enough to represent the earliest migrants in transit.

THE EARLIEST OCCUPATION OF GREATER AUSTRALIA

Evidence in Greater Australia is accumulating that the process of colonization began at least 50,000 years ago and possibly earlier. Archaeologists simply have not found—and may never find—the sites of the people in Sunda before they migrated to Australia. As a coastally adapted people, their habitations were probably near the coast. But the coast of 50,000+ years ago, which was during a glacial maximum, was farther out as a result of lowered sea level. The ancient coast and the human habitations located there today are many kilometers out from the modern Asian shoreline and many meters below the ocean's surface.

The Archaeology of Sahul

The earliest-known settlement of New Guinea, then a part of Greater Australia, was located on an ancient, exposed coral reef on Bobongara Hill on the north coast of Papua New Guinea, at the southeastern terminus of the Huon Peninsula. The site has been dated by thermoluminescence to 40,000 B.P. (Groube et al. 1986). Recovered from the site were a number of axe heads with a distinct narrowing or notching toward their middles (thus the name "waisted axes" and the similarity to the waisted tool found at Niah Cave in Borneo), a couple of stone cores for making flake tools, and a small number of flakes. Waisted axes have been found in archaeological contexts elsewhere in New Guinea, most notably at the Kosipe site, dating to 26,000 years ago, and at Nombe dating to 25,000 years ago (J. White and O'Connell 1982). The waist was probably produced to aid in hafting the stone axe onto a wooden handle. Groube et al. (1986) suggest that these axes were used in forest clearing, which, according to Rhys Jones (1989:764), would have encouraged the growth of wild foods like yams, taro, and sugarcane by opening up the thick forest canopy and allowing more sunlight to reach the ground. The Kuk site in the New Guinea highlands, consisting of some carbon and **fire-cracked rocks,** is dated to a little before Kosipe and Nombe and may be as old as 30,000 years.

The modern continent of Australia has produced evidence of human habitation substantially older even than the New Guinea sites. Archaeologists Richard Roberts, Rhys Jones, and M. A. Smith (1990) have excavated at the Malakunanja II site in Arnhem Land in northern Australia. The excavators recovered more than 1,500 artifacts, including stone flakes, a grindstone, and pieces of ground hematite and ochre (used in producing yellow and red pigments for paints). Thermoluminescence dates of 61,000, 52,000, and 45,000 years ago were obtained from the deposit in which the artifacts were found (Roberts, Jones, and Smith 1990:154).

Other relatively old sites in Australia include Swan River (the Upper Swan Bridge site) in the southwestern part of the country, which has produced radiocarbon dates of 39,500 B.P., 37,100 B.P., and 35,000 B.P. in association with about 200 artifacts, including stone chips, worked flakes, and flakes with edges exhibiting wear patterns (Jones 1992). The chert used to make some of the Swan River artifacts was available only during the Pleistocene, when sea level was low enough to allow access to the source. Also in southwest Australia is Devil's Lair, with a series of hearths, stone and bone artifacts, and the remains of kangaroos that had been killed, butchered, and eaten by the cave's human inhabitants. Radiocarbon dates place occupation of the cave at before 32,000 years ago, and perhaps as much as 38,000 years ago (Jones 1992). Eleven km (7 mi) northwest of Devil's Lair is Mammoth Cave, where burned bones, possible stone artifacts, and charcoal have been dated to between 31,000 years ago and 37,000 years ago. The Keilor site, near the city of Melbourne in southeastern Australia, has produced some quartzite flakes that were intentionally struck off a core. The soil layer in which the artifacts were recovered is estimated to be more than 36,000 years old and less than 45,000 years old (J. White and O'Connell 1982).

Willandra Lakes

The Willandra Lakes region in western New South Wales in the southeastern section of the country, characterized by a succession of ancient Pleistocene lakes that were dry for perhaps as much as 10,000 years, has produced a number of important aboriginal sites (Figure 10.3). At Lake Arumpo, for example, a midden of freshwater mussel shells has been dated to 37,000 years ago.

Perhaps the archaeologically richest of the Willandra Lakes is Lake Mungo, occupied as early as 32,000 years ago. Five discrete sites were identified around the now-dry lake bed (Barbetti and Allen 1972). Archaeologists located numerous ancient fireplaces, some stone cores and flakes, steep-edged scraping tools, an earth oven, and the burned eggs of emu (large, flightless birds indigenous to Australia). Charcoal from the fireplaces produced radiocarbon ages ranging from 24,020 to 32,750 years old (Barbetti and Allen 1972:48).

One of the Lake Mungo localities produced the remains of a cremated human female dated to 26,000 years ago (the "Mungo I" skeleton; Bowler,

FIGURE 10.3
Willandra Lakes, the fossil lake region of southeast Australia, have produced some of the oldest skeletal evidence of a human presence on the continent.
(Institute of Human Origins. Donald Johanson, photographer)

Thorne, and Polach 1972). After her death, her body was burned and the bones were pulverized and then interred. About 25% of the Mungo I skeleton was recovered and enough recognizable cranial fragments were found to reconstruct the skull partially; the young woman was fully anatomically modern and rather **gracile,** physiologically, lacking the large brow ridges or heavy buttressing bone typical of modern Australian natives (Bowler et al. 1970). Mungo II consists of thirty small fragments, and not much can be determined about its morphology. The more complete Mungo III skeleton, dated to between 28,000 and 30,000 years ago, looks quite similar to Mungo I (J. White and O'Connell 1982:37). Buried in an extended position and not cremated, Mungo III was an adult male, again showing a cranial architecture far lighter than that of modern natives.

Just north of Lake Mungo, the Willandra Lakes skeleton was recovered. Dating to between 20,000 and 30,000 years ago (and, therefore, conceivably more recent than the Lake Mungo remains) Willandra Lakes 50 (as the skeletal remains are designated) is far different in appearance, exhibiting enormously thick cranial bones (some seven times thicker than the Lake Mungo remains). As Australian archaeologist Rhys Jones (1992) has pointed out, in these three specimens (Mungo I and III and the Willandra Lakes 50 cranium) from sites just a few miles apart, there is a greater difference in cranial bone thickness than within and among all modern human populations! For Jones, such a difference is not possible within a single population. He sees two biologically distinct populations inhabiting the same region of Australia at different times (see the Issues and Debates section in this chapter).

THE SPREAD THROUGH AUSTRALIA

The Australian sites discussed so far are located in a ring around the perimeter of the continent (see Map 10.1). As archaeologist Sandra Bowdler (1977, 1990) points out, the initial human population entered Australia from the north and then spread primarily east and to a lesser degree west along the coast, focusing on those areas with tropical coastal environments most like those of the source areas from which they migrated. When they moved inland, it was always along major river systems, enabling a shift in their subsistence foods from marine to riverine resources.

This makes sense when you consider that the first inhabitants of Australia were almost certainly a coastally adapted people. This coastal adaptation, including the use of watercraft, enabled their discovery of Sahul and their migration onto its land mass in the first place. People with a coastal subsistence focus would have been wise to spread along the coast of their newly found home. And, as shown, the oldest human sites in Australia are located along the modern coastal rim or in formerly wetter interiors drained by rivers or dotted with lakes (the Lake Mungo area, for example).

But today's coastal sites are located some distance—in some cases, more than 150 km (93 mi; Bowdler 1990)—from the shoreline of Pleistocene Australia. Just as with the sites of the Asian ancestors of those who migrated to Sahul, the Australian coast of 30,000–50,000 years ago is now located many kilometers off shore, is currently under many meters of water, and is well hidden from twentieth-century archaeologists. In fact, sites along the modern Australian coastline actually represent the seasonal, *interior* encampments of people whose coastal habitations have all been inundated by rising Holocene sea level. Just a few of the ancient sites near the modern coast— for example, the Mandu Mandu Rockshelter of North-West Cape dating to 20,000–25,000 years ago—exhibit a faunal assemblage reflecting a truly marine subsistence base. There, the remains of fish, crabs, and mussels were recovered (Jones 1989).

Archaeologist Arthur Jelinek (1992:346) suggests that the earliest occupation of Australia substantially predates even the oldest of the known Australian sites—dating perhaps to between 60,000 and 75,000 years ago and coinciding with the glacial maximum of oxygen isotope stage 4 (see Figure 6.7). Those sites are located on the ancient Australian coast and may never be found. Barring a new glacial period with lowered sea level, the sites in Sunda of the ancestors of the first migrants to Sahul are probably forever out of reach, as are the sites of the first migrants once they got to Australia.

The Australian Interior

The earliest inhabitants of Australia seemed to have avoided, at least initially, the vast, harsh, dry interior of the continent (J. White 1993). It is not until

20,000–25,000 years ago that human groups began to penetrate the dry core of central Australia. Evidence from the Puritjarra Rockshelter in the Cleland Hills of central Australia shows that the cave was occupied intermittently between 22,000 and 12,000 years ago (M. A. Smith 1987). The stone tool assemblage included primarily large flake tools but also some small flakes and cores. Other interior sites of similar antiquity include two rockshelter sites from the Hamersley Plateau in western Australia—dated at 21,000 B.P. and 26,000 B.P., respectively—and evidence of flint mining in the Nullarbor Plain dated to 20,000 years ago (Jones 1987).

TASMANIA

Tasmania is the last "new world" in Sahul to be occupied by human beings. A human population first entered what is today the island of Tasmania when it was still connected to the Australian continent. The earliest people of Tasmania lived farther south, and closer to Antarctica, than any other human group to that point. The environment was entirely different from any faced previously by Australian Aborigines—a frozen tundra not unlike that of Upper Paleolithic Europe (see Chapter 9).

Tasmania shows archaeological evidence of occupation as early as 35,000 years ago at Wareen Cave and 30,000 years ago at the ORS7 site as well as at Acheron, Bone, and Nunamira Caves in south-central Tasmania (Cosgrove, Allen, and Marshall 1990). Archaeologists Richard Cosgrove, Jim Allen, and Brendan Marshall (1990) conducted a survey of south-central Tasmania, locating 41 sites occupied between 30,000 and 11,000 years ago. Sites like Cave Bay Cave, located on Hunter Island off the northwest coast of Tasmania, date to about 23,000 B.P. (Bowdler 1974). On Tasmania proper there is Beginner's Luck Cave and Kutikina Cave (formerly Fraser Cave), both initially occupied at 20,000 years ago. Kutikina is extraordinarily rich, with over 75,000 stone flakes and tools recovered from less than a 1% sample of the site (Kiernan et al. 1983). Most of the tools are steep-edged scrapers, similar in appearance to those recovered at Lake Mungo. The faunal assemblage is dominated by the remains of the large wallaby (a member of the kangaroo family) and the wombat (a sizable, heavyset, burrowing marsupial) (Kiernan, Jones, and Ranson 1983:30). Interestingly, there are no remains of the larger, now-extinct animals that typified the Pleistocene of Australia. This Australian Pleistocene megafauna probably was already extinct by the time humans first penetrated Tasmania.

GREATER AUSTRALIA: A BROAD RANGE OF ADAPTATIONS

In the stereotype, the Australian Aborigines were a homogeneous group, possessed of a simple technology, barely eking out a living in the great arid desert of central Australia. In this view, they had become stuck in time, holdovers from a primitive Stone Age society, forever limited by their harsh environment. But the archaeological record shows clearly that such a stereotype is inadequate to characterize Aboriginal culture. Rather, the ancestors of the native people of Australia arrived by watercraft 50,000 years ago in what had to have been, at least in part, a planned, intentional migration. Beginning with an adaptation to a tropical, coastal environment, they managed by 30,000 years ago to have adapted to the myriad habitats of Greater Australia. There were coastal people who maintained many of their original maritime adaptations, but there also were people who had adjusted to the temperate regions of the interior as well as some who had developed cultural strategies for coping with environments as diverse as the Great Sandy Desert in the interior—one of the hottest, driest places on earth—and the sub-Antarctic tundra of south-central Tasmania. And the lives of these people extended far beyond the quest for subsistence. In Koonalda Cave, located near Australia's south-central coast, is preserved some of the world's oldest artwork, a series of meandering lines made by human fingers as much as 24,000 years ago—a sort of finger painting in the soft limestone of the cave's ceiling (Johanson, Johanson, and Edgar 1994). As mentioned in Chapter 9, potentially even older art has been dated at Wharton Hill and Panaramitee North, where microscopic vegetable matter recovered from within the grooves of petroglyphs of geometric figures has been dated to 36,000 B.P. and 43,000 B.P., respectively (Bednarik 1993). If these dates hold up (and the methodology is a bit controversial), this Australian aboriginal art will be the oldest known from anywhere in the world.

The lesson of the earliest settlement of Australia is not one of the persistence of a primitive, backward people, but of the nearly infinite capacity of human groups for adaptive flexibility. It is a lesson we will see repeated in the initial discovery of and migration to the Americas.

COMING TO AMERICA

On Thursday, October 11, 1492, a sea voyager had an encounter that forever affected the trajectory of human history—another of those small steps that became a giant leap. Documenting the ship's arrival, the journal of the captain of that momentous voyage reads: "When we stepped ashore we saw fine green trees, streams everywhere and different kinds of fruit. . . . Soon many of the islanders gathered around us. I could see that they were people who would be more easily converted to our Holy Faith by love than by coercion" (Cummins 1992:94). Thus begins Christopher Columbus's narrative of the first contact between Europeans and American natives since the series of short-lived, brutal incidents on Newfoundland in Canada and recorded in the Viking sagas at the beginning of the eleventh century A.D. (Magnusson and Paulsson 1965).

Thinking he had discovered a series of islands off the coast of Asia, Columbus called the people he encountered *los Indios,* or Indians. After his initial voyage, Columbus returned three more times, always expecting that the Asian continent lay just beyond the limits of his previous exploration. Though Columbus never accepted it, most European scholars concluded that he had happened on, not a cluster of islands immediately off the coast of south Asia, but, as Amerigo Vespucci was to characterize it in 1503, a "New World," populated by peoples unknown to and not even conceived of by Europeans.

This New World consisted of two entire continents that make up almost 28.5% of the world's land surface, with a native population estimated to have been in the tens of millions and speaking more than 1,500 different languages and dialects. Individual groups had adapted to nearly all of the countless habitats of the Western Hemisphere, from frigid arctic tundra to arid sandy deserts, from luxuriant tropical rain forests to temperate woodlands, from seacoasts to mountains, from river valleys to plateaus. And they lived ways of life as varied as did people inhabiting the "known" continents: hunters and gatherers in small, nomadic bands foraging for food in a seasonal round; fisherfolk in established villages, harvesting the plentiful natural resources of river and shore; farmers in huge adobe apartment complexes, tending the kinds of crops that even today feed the population of the planet. There were great kingdoms with impressive cities, splendid monuments of pyramids and palaces, and powerful hereditary rulers, not unlike King Ferdinand and Queen Isabella of Spain, the monarchs who had funded Columbus's expedition.

THE SOURCE OF *LOS INDIOS*

Almost as soon as it was recognized that Columbus had "discovered" a new world with people unknown to his benefactors, questions were raised concerning the origins of those "new" people. True to the spirit of the period, the answers had to conform to biblical interpretation: American natives had to be derived, ultimately, from Adam and Eve, and then more recently, from those few people who had survived Noah's flood.

Despite broad speculation concerning the source of the Native American population (see Feder 1996 and Williams 1991), quite early on some scholars recognized a connection between the natives of the New World and the people of Asia. In 1555, for example, the Portuguese traveler Antonio Galvão noted physical similarities between Asians and Native Americans in their eyes, noses, and general body shape.

Jesuit missionary Friar Joseph de Acosta (Huddleston 1967) used the Bible to come up with a precociously accurate hypothesis concerning the geographic origins of Native Americans. Acosta pointed out in 1590 that all animals on earth except those on board Noah's ark had been killed in the great flood. After the flood, he reasoned, the many animals present in the New World

FIGURE 10.4

The modern coastlines of northeast Asia and north-west North America as well as the projected coastline of Beringia during glacial maxima.

must have descended from the animals saved on board Noah's ark. That is, animals native to the New World must have arrived after the flood by walking into the Americas from the landing place of Noah's ark—according to the Bible, someplace in southwest Asia on "the mountains of Ararat." Acosta argued that what animals could accomplish, people could have done as well.

Thus, there must have been a land connection between the Old and the New Worlds to allow animals descended from those saved on the ark to walk into the Western Hemisphere, Acosta argued. He knew where such a connection could *not* have been, based on sixteenth-century exploration of the American coastline. By a process of elimination, he suggested that the Old World and the New World were probably joined somewhere in northwestern North America and northeastern Asia. That is, the first Americans must have come from Asia, having walked into the New World from the Old World at a point where they were joined. It was not until about 150 years later that Russian explorer Vitus Bering verified what the native people of northeastern Siberia and northwestern North America had long known: The Old World and the New World are separated by only about 90 km (55 mi) of sea, called the Bering Strait (Figure 10.4).

Today the Bering Strait is only 30–50 m deep (100–165 ft). But during periods of glacial maxima in the Pleistocene, sea level was depressed by far more than this, exposing a wide platform of land connecting Russia and Alaska that was as wide, perhaps, as 1,500 km (1,000 mi) from north to south. During long periods in the Pleistocene, people in northeast Asia could have walked into the New World across the body of land today called the **Bering Land Bridge** (see Figure 10.4).

Early thinkers like Galvão and Acosta were correct. Geographically, a northeastern Asian origin for Native Americans makes sense. Gross anatomical characteristics like those cited by Galvão have long shown the biological connection between Asians and Native Americans. Modern analysis of the mitochondrial DNA of Native Americans also supports the idea that the aboriginal human population of the New World was derived wholly from Asia (Gibbons 1993; Stone and Stoneking 1993; D. Wallace, Garrison, and Knowler 1985).

WHEN DID THE FIRST MIGRANTS ARRIVE?

Though anthropologists agree on the geographic and genetic sources of Native American populations, there is still great controversy over the timing of the arrival of the first settlers of the New World. To find out when people first entered the Americas from Siberia we need to know three things:

1. When was the Bering Land Bridge exposed and open for travel?
2. When was eastern Siberia first inhabited (the source population for New World migrants)?
3. What is the age of the earliest sites in the New World?

When Was the Bering Land Bridge Exposed and Open for Travel?

Actually, the land bridge idea might not be necessary to explain aboriginal migration patterns. If Australia's first settlers could have populated that "new world" as early as 50,000 years ago (remember, there was no land bridge between Sunda and Sahul; they had no choice but to arrive by boat), then northeast Asians might have done the same thing during periods when no land bridge was present between Asia and North America. And even without a land bridge, during periods of extreme cold the Bering Strait could have frozen, producing an ice bridge between the two hemispheres.

Nonetheless, a wide land connection between the two continents would have facilitated the movement of animals and people. Anthropologists know that the Bering Land Bridge was exposed several times during the Pleistocene (Müller-Beck 1967) and continuously from 35,000–14,000 years ago (Hopkins 1982:12; Meltzer 1989:474). This may represent the key interval for migration into the Americas, based on what little is known about the timing of the earliest human presence in Siberia, people who would have served as the population source for the first settlers of the Americas.

When Was Eastern Siberia First Inhabited?

As with the earliest populating of Greater Australia, the archaeology of eastern Siberia is poorly known. Eastern Siberia is a difficult place to do archaeology,

TABLE 10.1

Sample of Sites in Eastern Russia Occupied at Times of Possible Human Population Movement into North America

SITE NAME	LOCATION	AGE	ARTIFACTS
Dyuktai Cave	Central Siberia	After 18,000 B.P.	Wedge-shaped cores, simple bifaces
Ust'-Mil II	Central Siberia	11,500–35,000 B.P.	Wedge-shaped cores
Ikhine	Southern Siberia	31,000–34,000 B.P.	Burins, cores
Ezhantsy	Central Siberia	35,000 B.P.	Wedge-shaped cores, biface fragments
Berelekh	Lower Indigirka Valley	12,000–13,000 B.P.	Bifaces
Ushki Lake	Kamchatka	13,000–15,000 B.P.	Bifaces, burins, microblades, unifaces

Data from F. H. West (1981).

and relatively little work has been done there. Archaeologist David Meltzer (1989) points out that we simply do not know when it was first inhabited.

Archaeologist Frederick Hadleigh West (1981:107–111) lists twenty important Siberian sites dating from as recently as 8,000 years ago and as much as 35,000 years ago, scattered through what he labels "western Beringia" (Table 10.1). Unfortunately, many of the dates derived from these sites are only estimates. Radiocarbon dates indicate a human presence in central Siberia by at least 20,000 years ago and possibly as much as 34,000 years ago (the latter at the Ikhine site on the lower Aldan River). Recent work at the Diring site in eastern Siberia (mentioned in Chapter 6) may lead us to revise this construct radically. Though highly questionable, dates for the occupation of that site have been proposed by its excavator, Yuri Mochanov, from between 500,000 and 2 million years ago (Bower 1994c). The cultural designation of the materials as well as the dates have been called into question.

On the question of the earliest settlement of the Americas, one of the most important sites on the west side of Beringia is Dyuktai Cave, on the Aldan River in central Siberia (Yi and Clark 1985). The site radiocarbon-dates to about 18,000 B.P. Though some distance from Beringia itself, the site is important for the artifact assemblage it has produced. There are some striking similarities between the small, **wedge-shaped cores** and **microblades**

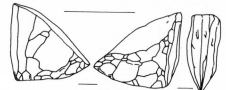

0   5 cm

FIGURE 10.5

These stone tools from the Dyuktai culture, eastern Russia (about 18,000 B.P.), exhibit a preponderance of so-called wedge-shaped cores, small stone cores of the implied shape from which sharp microblades were removed. (From Seon-bonk Yi and Geoffrey Clark, in "The 'Dyuktai Culture' and New World Origins," *Current Anthropology*)

struck off those cores at Dyuktai—and at a number of similar, more or less contemporaneous sites in central Siberia—and tools found in Alaska several thousand years later as part of a complex known as the **Paleo-Arctic tradition** (Figure 10.5). Microblades can be set into bone, antler, or wooden handles, producing very sharp, highly effective cutting tools.

Though the area of the earliest Siberian sites is still only poorly known, there appears to be no substantial evidence for human occupation much before 30,000 B.P.; even evidence much before 20,000 B.P. is weak (Meltzer 1993:161). Jelinek (1992) may be correct that until about 25,000 years ago, prehistoric people simply had not yet developed an adaptation for life in the arctic, so they could not have survived in Siberia. And without adapting to Siberia, they could not have had access to the Bering Land Bridge and the two continents that lay on the other side.

What Is the Age of the Earliest New World Sites?

The dating of the earliest human settlement of the Americas is a point of contention among archaeologists. Some believe there was an early migration from Asia more than 15,000 years ago and perhaps as much as 40,000 years ago (Map 10.2). A number of sites—in particular Meadowcroft Rockshelter in western Pennsylvania and Monte Verde in Chile—have been meticulously excavated and dated and suggest an initial entry via Beringia more than 15,000 years ago (see the Issues and Debates section). Others are more conservative, suggesting a more recent date of about 12,000 B.P., for which date the evidence of human presence in the New World is abundant and indisputable.

To put these divergent claims in chronological and cultural perspective, we need to return to our discussion of Dyuktai. As archaeologists William Powers and John Hoffecker (1989) point out, it is now clear that there was a

MAP 10.2

*Sites representing the
earliest occupation of
North America and
South America.*

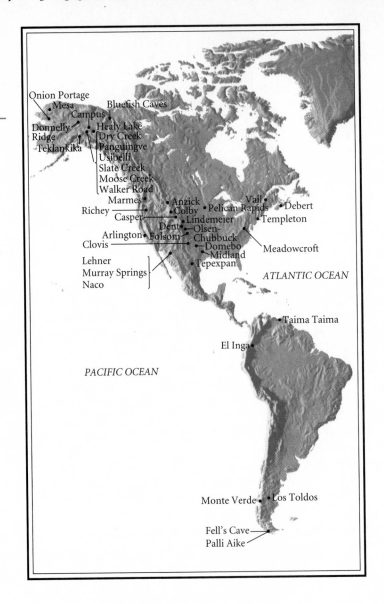

widespread tradition of producing small blades from wedge-shaped cores in
northeast Asia and northwest North America at the end of the Pleistocene.
Sites with wedge-shaped cores and microblades have been excavated in
Siberia, China, Japan, and Mongolia, as well as in Alaska and northwestern
Canada (Morlan 1970). These sites are older in the Old World than in the
New World, and a "genetic" connection between the industries of western
and eastern Beringia seems clear.

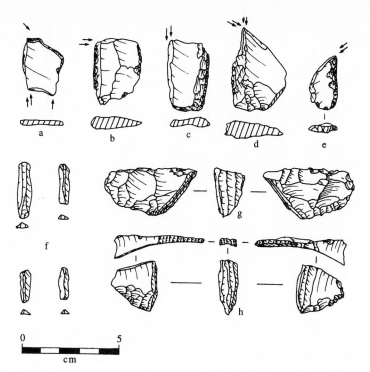

FIGURE 10.6

These stone tools from the Denali Complex of Alaska, dating to after 11,000 B.P., include some wedge-shaped cores (g and h), suggesting a derivation from the older wedge-shaped cores in Asia (see Figure 10.5). (Courtesy William Powers)

DENALI AND NENANA

In Alaska, sites exhibiting tools of the locally designated **Denali Complex** of wedge-shaped cores, microblades, bifacial knives, and **burins** have been excavated in the Nenana Valley, about 100 km (62.5 mi) southwest of Fairbanks, in east-central Alaska (Figure 10.6; Powers and Hoffecker 1989). Sites like Dry Creek (Component II), Panguingue Creek (Component II), Usibelli, and Slate Creek in the Nenana Valley are assigned to the Denali Complex; Dry Creek has produced a radiocarbon date of about 10,700 B.P. (Powers and Hamilton 1978). Denali Complex sites outside of the Nenana Valley include Donnelly Ridge in central Alaska, the Campus Site near Fairbanks, the Teklanika River sites in Mt. McKinley National Park, and Healy Lake (West 1967). These all date to around 10,000 years ago (West 1975). A very different-looking industry of microblades and cores has been found in the earliest levels at the Onion Portage site (Akmak) in western Alaska, also dating to around 10,000 B.P. (D. Anderson 1968, 1970).

All this seems to provide a very neat and simple answer to questions surrounding the first human settlement of the Americas: Beginning some 18,000 years ago, microblade-making northeast Asians slowly made their way across Beringia, ending up in Alaska by about 10,700 years ago or a few hundred years earlier. The problem is, Denali Complex sites are not the oldest in the

FIGURE 10.7

In these stone tools from the Nenana Complex of Alaska, dating to 11,800 B.P., the lack of wedge-shaped cores, the presence of bifacially flaked tools, and dates that are older than those associated with the Denali Complex suggest a different and older migration of northeast Asians into the New World. (Courtesy William Powers)

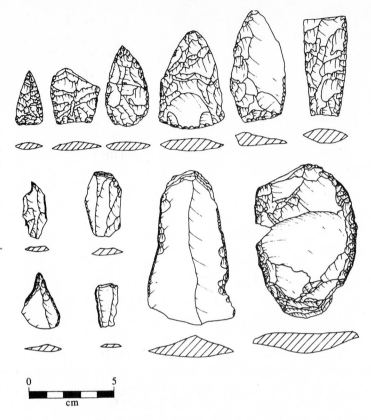

New World; they're not even the oldest in Alaska. There is a cultural level at Dry Creek (Component I), earlier than the Denali level at the same site, and the sites of Moose Creek and Walker Road have produced radiocarbon dates ranging between 11,000 B.P. and 11,800 B.P. in their lowest levels. The stone-tool assemblages at these sites—classified as the **Nenana Complex**—show no evidence of Denali Complex wedge-shaped cores and look very little like the stone tool assemblage at Dyuktai. Instead, these assemblages include bifacially flaked spear points (Figure 10.7). Interestingly, an assemblage consisting of a broad array of bifacial spear points has been identified at a series of sites around Ushki Lake in the central Kamchatka peninsula in eastern Russia. Ushki is dated to about 14,000 years ago (Dikov 1978; Dikov and Titov 1984).

The Nenana Complex may be derived from the industry seen at Ushki in Kamchatka, representing an early movement of Asians (about 12,000 B.P.) across the Bering Land Bridge into the New World. Following the hypothesis of West (1981), Powers and Hoffecker (1989) suggest that the Siberian microblade industry seen at sites like Dyuktai may be at least indirectly ancestral to the later Denali Complex (dated to about 11,000 B.P.) and other early New World microblade industries. Denali, in this view, represents a migration subsequent to an earlier movement of Siberians with a bifacial industry like that seen at the Ushki and Nenana Complex sites.

As Powers and Hoffecker see it, the Denali Complex was restricted to the far north. However, in their view, possessors of the earlier Nenana stone tool tradition were able to expand to the south. As archaeologists Ted Goebel, Roger Powers, and Nancy Bigelow (1991) point out, with the exception of Clovis spearpoints (to be discussed shortly), the Nenana stone-tool assemblage is virtually identical to that seen to the south and associated with Clovis points. It was descendants of these people, Powers and Hoffecker argue, who made a small technological step in spearpoint form—the so-called **fluted point**—that allowed for an enormous adaptive leap, and the successful occupation of two continents.

THE MARCH SOUTH

Before we can discuss bringing the transplanted Asians in Alaska south into the rest of the New World, we must consider an additional environmental issue. The Pleistocene saw two primary centers of glacial expansion: the **Laurentide** ice sheet in northeastern North America, which spread south, east, and west and covered much of the northern latitudes of this continent, and the **Cordilleran** ice sheet, whose center was in the Rocky Mountains. During glacial maxima, when sea level was at its lowest and the land bridge at its largest, the Laurentide continental glacier spread farthest west and the Cordilleran mountain glacier spread farthest east. Though the two major ice bodies did not wax and wane in synchrony (Catto and Mandryk 1990), it is likely that they coalesced, at least in some places, for periods of time, as they expanded simultaneously (Figure 10.8). For example, at about 18,000 B.P. the two major ice fields coalesced near the present border of British Columbia and Alberta, Canada, across a linear distance of 1,200 km (715 mi) (H. Wright 1991).

In other words, the periods when it was easiest for human groups to migrate into Alaska from northeast Asia may have coincided with the periods when it was impossible for them to spread farther south because their way was blocked by an insurmountable ice barrier a few kilometers high. The overall timing and extent of this barrier is still uncertain. Even where and when coalescence did not occur, the so-called **ice-free corridor** (or **McKenzie corridor**) may have been inhospitable for large game animals and therefore of little interest to human hunters; much before 14,000 B.P. the corridor was probably a place to avoid rather than enter (H. Wright 1991). For example, pollen studies indicate that when an ice-free corridor was available for travel, vegetation was too poor to support large populations of animals (Mandryk 1990)—and without animals, there would have been no reason for humans to be there. And there is no archaeological evidence of an early human presence in the corridor until about 11,000 years ago (Burns 1990).

Knut Fladmark (1979, 1986) has suggested a possible coastal route as an alternative to an interior route through an ice-free corridor. Such a route,

FIGURE 10.8

Map showing the proposed boundaries of the Cordilleran and Laurentide ice sheets of North America. Though the two may have coalesced in some localized areas during glacial maxima, for long periods an ice-free corridor may have existed by which people south of Alaska could have migrated into North America south of the ice sheets.
(Courtesy David Meltzer)

however, would have been even more difficult, since huge ice fields flowing into the Pacific would have blocked passage south for many miles. The presence of an ice-free corridor ultimately may still be a crucial factor in the movement of people south of Alaska at the end of the Pleistocene, a valve controlling the timing of population movement south. Evidence points to the existence of an inhabitable corridor before 20,000 years ago and after 14,000 years ago.

EVIDENCE SOUTH OF ALASKA

As already stated, in Powers and Hoffecker's view, the Nenana Complex, derived from industries originating in Siberia, including a heavy component of bifacially flaked spearpoints, is the ultimate source for the most widespread and successful of the Late Pleistocene cultures of the New World. Sometimes called **Clovis,** for the site in New Mexico where the distinctive spearpoints that characterize the tool assemblage were first recognized, these **Paleoindian** sites number in the hundreds and are found throughout the continental United States. Where dates have been derived through ^{14}C, Clovis sites fit into a narrow range, between 11,500 B.P. and 11,000 B.P., appearing virtually simultaneously across much of the New World (Haynes 1982, 1987, 1992).

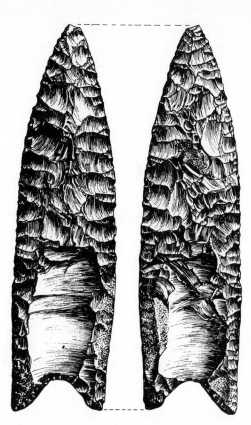

FIGURE 10.9

The flutes, or channels, on both faces of this Paleoindian Clovis projectile point from the Lamb site in western New York State extend less than halfway up the point. Clovis dates to between 11,500 and 11,000 B.P. (Courtesy Michael Gramly, Great Lakes Artifact Repository. Drawn by Val Waldorf)

The oldest human skeletons yet found in the New World date to approximately this same Paleoindian period. The female skeleton from Midland, Texas (originally called "Midland Man" but now known to have been a female), long thought to have been one of the oldest human skeletons from the New World, has recently been dated by uranium series to 11,600 years ago (Hoppe 1992). A small number of other human remains have been dated, with varying degrees of certainty, to the period between 11,500 years ago and 10,500 years ago: the Tepexpan skeleton from Mexico, the Pelican Rapids find (known as "Minnesota Man," another misidentified female), the Marmes skull from Washington state, "Arlington Man" from Santa Rosa Island in California (Owen 1984), Wilsall (Anzick) in Montana, and the Mostin site in northern California (Stafford 1990; Taylor 1991).

Clovis Technology

Clovis spearpoints are distinctive in having a channel, or flute, on both faces (Figure 10.9; Paleolithic Portfolio, Color Plate 12). The channel, made by removing (usually) a single broad flake from both faces of the point, originating at the base and ordinarily extending one-quarter to one-third of the way toward the tip, is assumed to have been an aid in hafting the stone point onto a wooden shaft. As mentioned previously, this small technological step seems to have resulted in an adaptive leap that allowed for the rapid expansion of human groups across the New World. This great leap forward is strictly an American invention. It was not part of any western Beringian technology, nor is it present in the Nenana Complex in Alaska. So-called "fluted" points are unknown in northeast Asia and are, in fact, older in the American southwest than in Alaska. The recently excavated Mesa site in northern Alaska has produced about 50 bifacially flaked spearpoints, none of which possesses a channel. The Mesa site's thirteen radiocarbon dates range from 9,700 B.P. to 11,700 B.P. (Bower 1993a) and may be contemporary with fluted points farther south. Michael Kunz, the excavator of the Mesa site, maintains that the points there are not directly related to fluted points and represent yet another separate and distinct early stone tool industry in northwestern North America (Bower 1993a:215).

The rapid, almost simultaneous appearance of fluted points throughout much of the New World is striking. Whereas there are either no sites or, at best, very few sites in America dated to before 12,000 years ago (see the Issues and Debates section), there is a virtual explosion of Clovis sites in the American southwest and beyond, dating from between 11,500 and 11,000 years ago (Haynes 1992). Stratified sites such as Clovis, Lehner, Murray Springs, Dent, Colby, and Domebo, all in the southwest, produced fluted spearpoints and dates in that time range (Haynes 1982).

But Clovis points are also found throughout Canada, the continental United States, and Mexico. In the northwest, the spectacular Richey Clovis Cache in central Washington State (Paleolithic Portfolio, Color Plate 12), an apparent ceremonial interment of huge fluted points as much as 23.25 cm (a bit more than 9 in.) in length, has been dated at 11,200 B.P. (Gramly 1993; Mehringer and Foit 1990). In the American northeast and southeast, thousands of fluted points have been recovered from hundreds of sites (David Anderson 1990). Sites may be younger in the east—but not much: The Vail site in Maine has produced radiocarbon dates of 10,300 B.P. and 11,120 B.P. (Gramly 1982); the mean radiocarbon age of the Debert fluted-point site in Nova Scotia is 10,600 B.P. (MacDonald 1985); and Templeton (6LF21) in Connecticut has been dated to 10,190 B.P. (Moeller 1980).

Even at the most distant New World spot imaginable from Beringia, Fell's Cave at the southern tip of South America (Tierra del Fuego), a fluted point in association with the bones of extinct horse and sloth has been recovered from a site dated to 10,000 years ago (Bruhns 1994). Nonfluted fishtail points were also found in Fell's Cave and in other sites dating to this time in South America at sites such as Palli Aike, also in Tierra del Fuego, Los Toldos in Patagonia, and El Inga in northern Ecuador. Long, leaf-shaped El Jobo points were found at Taima Taima in Venezuela, also dating to the Late Pleistocene.

The Clovis Advantage

It is not entirely clear what it was about the Clovis adaptation that allowed its bearers to spread so quickly across two continents. The Americas south of the ice sheets must have been a treasure trove for a people whose subsistence depended, at least in part, on hunting (Haynes 1964, 1980). Ecologist Paul S. Martin (1987) has jokingly referred to the New World, with its abundant big-game resources, as "Clovisia, the Beautiful." Imagine a continent teeming with animals—animals that had never seen a human hunter, with no fear of this puny, two-legged beast. There were mammoths, mastodons, bison, horse, caribou, musk ox, ground sloths, giant beavers, tapirs, and more, all ripe for the taking by efficient hunters who had very little competition (P. Martin and Guilday 1967). A new hunting technology like the fluted spear may have been a key factor in the success of the culture. Even a small initial population, given a reasonably high birth rate, could have moved out in a rapid wave of population expansion, resulting in the narrow range of the Clovis radiocarbon dates (P. Martin 1973; Mosimann and Martin 1975).

Clovis Subsistence

The megafauna (big-game) hunting component of Paleoindian subsistence has been exaggerated in the past. Kill sites tend to be highly visible archaeologically, with their large complement of bones, broken weapons, and butchering equipment (see the Case Study Close-Up section). Though the image of Paleoindians risking life and limb to track down and kill a two-ton, hairy elephant is more romantic, they most probably relied on root grubbing, seed gathering, and small-mammal trapping, at least some of the time (Meltzer 1993; Johnson 1991). Still, some Paleoindians, in a manner similar to the Inuit people (Eskimos), must have relied on hunting, since little else was available in their territories. During some parts of the year, most Paleoindian groups relied on hunting for survival. But once past the glacial and periglacial north and onto the American plains, they could find and exploit many other foods, including seeds, nuts, berries, fish, and small mammals. Away from the glacial front, where animals may have been the only consistent source of food—for example, the woodlands of eastern North America—Paleoindians were probably "generalist foragers" who not only took big game when the opportunity presented itself but also exploited smaller game and plant foods in their territories (Dincauze 1993).

Nonetheless, large game animals played a part in their economy. C. Vance Haynes points out that the remains of the extinct North American elephants, woolly mammoth or mastodon, have been recovered from the majority of Clovis sites in the American west, where animal bones have been preserved (1982:390). When these elephants became extinct around 11,000 years ago,

FIGURE 10.10

Folsom points are younger and generally smaller than Clovis points, and the flute extends nearly the entire length of the point. This is a Paleoindian fluted Folsom point from the Johnson site, Colorado. (Courtesy Michael Gramly, Great Lakes Artifact Repository. Drawn by Val Waldorf)

the Paleoindians in the western United States shifted their hunting focus to bison. The technology changed, producing shorter spearpoints, but with channels extending almost to the tip. These so-called **Folsom** points (Figure 10.10) are of the culture that bears the same name and includes sites such as Lindenmeier in Colorado (Wilmsen 1974), Olsen-Chubbuck in Colorado (Wheat 1972), and Casper in Wyoming (see the Case Study Close-Up section; Frison 1974a,b).

Although Clovis represents the first *successful* cultural adaptation to the Americas south of the glaciers, were the fluted-point-making Paleoindians truly the first Americans, or were they merely hugely successful, archaeologically visible relative latecomers? This is perhaps the most contentious issue of all and will be covered in this chapter's Issues and Debates section.

INTO THE PACIFIC

The Pacific Ocean, the last great frontier on the planet that humans have explored and settled (with the exception of the modern investigation of Antarctica), covers one-third of the earth's surface. It stretches 15,500 km (9,600 mi) from north to south and 20,000 km (more than 12,000 mi) from east to west. Its total area is about 180 million km² (70 million mi²).

Europeans, considered relative latecomers, did not cross the Pacific until Ferdinand Magellan's circumnavigation of the globe in A.D. 1519–1522. Close to a thousand of the 25,000 islands scattered across the ocean were already inhabited—and had been for a few thousand years—by the time of Magellan's voyage.

A Pacific Islander "Age of Exploration"

The fascinating story of the initial exploration and settlement of the Pacific belies the cultural conceit that the "age of exploration" began and ended in the European Renaissance. The successful exploration and colonization of Pacific islands by a people without some of the technological advantages of European explorers (such as quadrants, sextants, compasses) is all the more remarkable when you consider the following: The total land mass of the 25,000 Pacific islands represents only 0.7% of the total area of the ocean, and average island size is only about 10 km by 6 km (6 mi by 4 mi) (Terrell 1986:14). Some of the inhabited islands are far smaller. Though many of these islands are geographically clustered and "intervisible" (visible one from the other), the individual clusters are often separated by hundreds, even thousands, of kilometers. Simply finding such island clusters while sailing a small canoe was a remarkable feat. Settling them successfully was nothing short of miraculous.

FIGURE 10.11

Modern Polynesians use traditional navigational techniques to travel hundreds of miles across the open ocean, much as their ancestors did when they initially explored and settled the Pacific islands.
(Courtesy Department of Library Services, American Museum of Natural History, transparency no. K6306)

Yet, discover, explore, and colonize many of those islands is precisely what settlers from southeast Asia and New Guinea did. And they accomplished this largely as the result of intentional geographic expansion. Certainly serendipity played a role in the peopling of the Pacific. Though countless sailors must have been blown off course and died before making it to safe haven, some lucky ones may have made accidental landfall on uninhabited islands and become their permanent settlers. But this cannot be the primary way in which Pacific islands were colonized. Just as Europeans in the fifteenth century began deliberately to explore the oceans, the southeast Asians and New Guineans must have been doing the same many years before. As archaeologist Geoffrey Irwin (1993:7) points out, "We know colonisation was deliberate, because explorers took with them the plants and animals, women and men necessary to establish viable settlements." In other words, colonization of the Pacific was largely planned, and colonists brought with them the people and things necessary for the successful establishment of new communities (Figure 10.11).

Geoffrey Irwin (1993) has, with his colleagues S. H. Bickler and P. Quirke (1990), conducted computer simulations of exploration and colonization strategies in the Pacific. They have shown that, under the right conditions and when the right search strategies are applied, even Pacific islands at great distance from each other can be safely and successfully explored and colonized, with return trips possible to the original homes of the migrants. They have shown graphically and mathematically that, as archaeologist John Terrell (1986:72) has suggested, to the highly skilled navigators and sailors of ancient Polynesia, "the sea must have been more an enticing highway than an encompassing barrier."

Pacific Geography

The Pacific Islands are usually divided into three groupings (see Map 10.1): **Melanesia**—the so-called "black islands" of New Guinea and smaller islands to the east, including the Solomon Islands, the Bismarck Archipelago, Santa Cruz, New Caledonia, Vanuatu, and Fiji; **Micronesia**—the "small islands" north of Melanesia; and **Polynesia**—"many islands," including a broad triangle of islands demarcated at its points by Hawaii to the north, Easter Island to the southeast, and New Zealand to the southwest.

Pacific Archaeology

The larger islands of Melanesia, including those of the Bismarck Archipelago and the Solomons, have produced archaeological evidence of occupation by 30,000 years ago. These islands were explored and settled by inhabitants of New Guinea, which, as previously mentioned, was settled prior to this. The Melanesian islands farther to the east and in deeper water, as well as all the islands of Micronesia and Polynesia, were settled much later in a second wave of exploration and migration beginning probably little more than 3,500 years ago (Irwin 1993).

The spread of people through east Melanesia and Polynesia was accompanied by a common culture. Being a maritime people, fishing played a significant role in their food quest. They also were food producers, bringing non-native agricultural staples with them as they colonized islands, including pig, as a major source of animal protein, and domesticated root crops, especially yams. They also brought a common pottery style, called **Lapita** (Figure 10.12). In fact, the earliest occurrence of a human population on the inhabited islands of Polynesia is invariably marked by the appearance of Lapita pottery. The Lapita designation is now applied to the entire cultural complex of Polynesia, and includes a maritime adaptation, the raising of pigs, the growing of certain root crops and fruit trees, the use of shell in producing tools and ornaments, and the manufacture of Lapita pottery.

The Lapita complex is absent from Australia or the islands of Micronesia. It appears first in the archaeological record of the Bismarck Archipelago and, perhaps, Fiji a little more than 3,500 years ago (Irwin 1993:39). Expansion proceeded eastward, with large island groups like Samoa, the Cook Islands, and the Society Islands being settled in turn, after about 2,500 years ago. The Hawaiian Islands, far to the north, were settled by about 1,600 B.P. (about A.D. 400); Easter Island, at the eastern limit of Polynesia, was settled at about the same time. New Zealand, though much closer to the Australian coast, was settled not by natives of that continent, but by Polynesians. The earliest evidence for a human presence on New Zealand dates to about A.D. 1000.

FIGURE 10.12

Lapita pottery is found virtually everywhere Polynesians explored and settled after 3,500 B.P. (Courtesy of Dr. Richard Shutler, Jr., and Dr. Mary Elizabeth Shutler)

Why the Pacific Islands Were Settled

Irwin (1993:211–212) lists some of the possible motives for the expansion into the vast and previously uncharted Pacific: curiosity about what lay beyond the horizon, a desire to find areas suitable for habitation and rich in resources, and the need to find new land as a result of overpopulation or warfare. As Irwin points out, motives are not testable archaeologically. And, as Terrell (1986) indicates, the motives to move out into the Pacific were likely as mixed and as varied as those of Europeans in their own age of exploration.

Whatever the reasons, the many inhabited islands of the Pacific, populated initially by people possessing very few, rather homogenous cultures, produced a wide array of adaptations once they were settled. Settlers exploited the most valuable resources, developing their own unique adapta-

tions to each island or island chain. On New Zealand, the moa—a large flightless bird unique to that nation—became a major component in the diet of a hunting society. Powerful and complex agricultural societies arose on Hawaii and Tonga (Kirch 1984). The fascinating people of Easter Island developed great skills at organizing their own labor, which enabled the quarrying, carving, transportation, and erection of the hundreds of enormous sculpted stone heads that have generated such interest and speculation (Figure 10.13). All of today's enormous diversity developed from those first courageous voyages across the vast Pacific Ocean a few thousand years ago.

ISSUES AND DEBATES

HOW MANY ABORIGINAL MIGRATIONS TO AUSTRALIA WERE THERE?

The question of the number of distinct migrations to Australia arises for the simple reason that two very different skeletal morphologies seem to be reflected in the archaeological record. One is the lightly constructed cranial form present in the ancient Lake Mungo skeletons, dating to 30,000 years ago. The other is the very robust form of the Willandra Lakes cranium, dating to probably less than 30,000 years ago, and the more recent (though still ancient) similarly robust crania like those from Kow Swamp.

The Kow Swamp sample of forty individuals is radiocarbon-dated to between 9,000 B.P. and 13,000 B.P. The large brow ridges, receding foreheads, and large, rugged mandibles are unlike the Lake Mungo remains, and much more similar to Willandra Lakes 50. In fact, Willandra Lakes 50 and the Kow Swamp remains are so ruggedly built they have even been compared to *Homo erectus* remains from east Asia, in particular, Javanese fossils from Trinil and Sangiran (Frayer et al. 1993; Kramer 1991; see Chapter 8).

The differences in cranial form have led physical anthropologist Alan Thorne (1977) to conclude that two separate human populations with different cranial forms moved into Australia before 20,000 years ago. However, as J. Peter White and James O'Connell (1982) point out, this conclusion is difficult to support with such a small sample of crania for an entire continent and with so many differing habitats that people adapted to over such an extensive period of time. In their view, variations in cranial form merely reflect regional differentiation among native Australians, who can be derived from a single population wave from Asia more than 50,000 years ago.

WHO REALLY DISCOVERED AMERICA?

There have been many claims of a pre-Clovis occupation of the New World south of the glaciers (see Bryan 1978 and Shutler 1983). Yet, the analytical histories of these sites seem to exhibit a common pattern: Discovery (or rediscovery) is followed by great scholarly commotion on the claim of their great antiquity. Then the media proclaim the "Clovis first" hypothesis dead, and the site fades into obscurity as problems arise in the dating method used, the association of the dates with the cultural material cannot be supported, and even the identification of the chipped stone or broken bones as artifactual (as opposed to naturally occurring items, or "geofacts") is shown to be problematical (Dincauze 1984; Meltzer 1989, 1993a,b,c; Owen 1984). Few (some would argue none) of these purportedly ancient sites seem to be able to live up to the following standards of evidence set by geologist and Paleo-indian scholar C. Vance Haynes (1969):

- Any pre-Clovis site must possess either a human skeleton or artifacts indisputably made by human beings.
- The archaeological remains must have been found in place, in the original geological stratigraphic position.
- The site must have a reliable date associated with it.

More recently, archaeologist Nicholas Toth (1991:69–70) has produced a more detailed set of criteria for judging pre-Clovis sites. Like Haynes, Toth (1991:70) suggests that "no excavated American prehistoric site has been

FIGURE 10.14

Stone tools from the earliest indisputable cultural layer at the Meadowcroft Rockshelter in western Pennsylvania. The layer in which these tools were found dates to more than 12,800 years ago. (Courtesy James Adovasio)

proven to be, beyond a reasonable doubt, an antiquity of over 15,000 years (and valid claims of sites over 12,000 years old seem few and far between)." However, once the questionable sites have been eliminated, a few sites do exceed Clovis in date, and may represent early, far less successful incursions into the New World.

Meadowcroft

Meadowcroft Rockshelter in western Pennsylvania is one of the most deeply stratified archaeological sites ever excavated in the New World. Within the natural rock enclosure, human beings made tools, cooked food, and threw away trash, taking advantage of the natural protection afforded by the small cave. The excavators of Meadowcroft have chronicled the human occupation of western Pennsylvania back thousands of years (Adovasio et al. 1979–80a,b; Adovasio, Donahue, and Stuckenrath 1990; Carlisle and Adovasio 1984). And at the base of the sequence brought to light by these researchers may be the oldest radiocarbon dates associated with human-made material in the New World. Six dates earlier than 12,800 B.P. have been associated with stone tools near the base of the Meadowcroft sequence. Sealed beneath a rockfall from the roof of the shelter dated to 12,000 B.P. were 400 lithic artifacts, including blades, knives with retouched edges, and an unfluted bifacial projectile point (Figure 10.14).

Monte Verde

Monte Verde, in Chile, is another potentially pre-Clovis site, impressive for both its degree of archaeological preservation and the care with which it was

FIGURE 10.15

These stone tools from Monte Verde, in Chile, date to as early as 13,500 B.P. (Courtesy Tom Dillehay)

excavated (Dillehay 1987, 1989; Dillehay and Collins 1988). The major cultural level has produced unfluted bifacial spearpoints and other stone tools. Because of the anaerobic conditions of the wet peat bog that encapsulates the site, organic preservation is stunning: Pieces of mastodon meat, wooden foundations of ten huts, and bits of plants used by the inhabitants have been recovered (Figure 10.15). Nine of the ^{14}C dates for the main occupation range from 11,800 B.P. to 13,500 B.P. Another, deeper layer was excavated a short distance from the site, and possible artifacts were recovered. The date for this level exceeds 33,000 years, but again, the association of the date with human-made implements is problematical. Another South American site, Alice Boër in Brazil, is nearly as old as the main occupation at Monte Verde.

Both Meadowcroft and Monte Verde have their share of problems and detractors. The Meadowcroft dates are questioned on the basis of possible contamination of the charcoal used in dating and the completely modern plant and animal assemblage from the bottom of the cultural sequence (Dincauze 1981; Tankersley and Munson 1992, but see Adovasio, Donahue, and Stuckenrath 1992); the Monte Verde dates and cultural affiliations have also been questioned (Lynch 1990).

Was Clovis the First?

A well-reasoned argument presented by archaeologists David Whitley and Ronald Dorn (1993) leads them to conclude that evidence supports a pre-Clovis occupation of the Americas. They cite the accepted dates for Clovis sites in the North American southwest. Then they suggest rather generous rates of population growth and geographic expansion for these Clovis hunters. Remember, Paleoindians were not rushing to South America; they got there as they expanded their territory as necessitated by population growth. And it must have taken additional time to adapt to new territories, which would have slowed down growth and expansion. But even at a fixed and probably unrealistically swift rate of movement south (about 6.4 km, or 4 mi, per year), it is impossible to get the Clovis people to accepted South American sites on time. For a number of ancient sites in South America—Monte Verde among them—even the most conservative interpretation of their post-Clovis carbon dates still places the occupations too long ago to be derived from Clovis migrants from the north (Whitley and Dorn 1993:630). This would seem to indicate that these ancient South American sites were produced by a people who inhabited North America before the invention of Clovis technology.

Neither Meadowcroft nor Monte Verde is close to Beringia: Monte Verde is 16,000 km (10,000 mi) distant. The implication is that there should be an extensive archaeological trail of sites, successively older still, leading from Chile and Pennsylvania back to Beringia, reflecting this earlier, pre-Clovis movement of people south of the glaciers. Such a trail is apparent for the Clovis Paleoindians but not for any pre-Clovis migration. It has been suggested that patterns of erosion and deposition in the Late Pleistocene in North America were not conducive to site preservation, so the discovery of undisturbed early sites in stratigraphic context is unlikely (Butzer 1991). Perhaps we haven't looked in the right places or the sites are barely visible archaeologically. The other possibility, of course, is that we have found no trail of sites because there is none.

The "first" or the "oldest" of anything draws attention far more than whoever or whatever comes in second. This is certainly true regarding the debate surrounding the earliest migration to the New World. However, the debate may be much ado about, not nothing, but not very much. Ultimately, if any of the contenders for the title of "first Americans" unseats Clovis and its immediate Nenana predecessor, one thing is clear: There weren't many of them, their sites are few and far between, and they were not terribly successful. Clovis sites are ubiquitous; pre-Clovis sites are extremely rare.

THE FIRST AMERICANS: WORDS, TEETH, AND GENES

Linguists, physical anthropologists, and geneticists have weighed into the debate surrounding the arrival in America of the first migrants from northeast Asia. The data used by Joseph Greenberg, Christy Turner, and Steven Zegura (1986) to calculate how long Native Americans have been separated from their Asian counterparts are: (1) the rate of linguistic change through time from a particular source, (2) the degree of morphological change seen in human teeth once a descendant group has become isolated from a parent population, and (3) the rate at which genetic change builds up in the descendant population. Their conclusion supports the "Clovis first" model. They envision three major movements of people into the New World: an original, Clovis movement after 14,000 B.P., a secondary incursion of Na-Dene speakers (northwest coast Indians), and a third and final grouping of Eskimo-Aleut.

However, other researchers, looking at different data sets, have come to very different conclusions. Linguist Johanna Nichols (1990) is critical of Greenberg's linguistics, suggesting that the enormous diversity seen in Amerindian languages must have taken more on the order of 37,500 years to develop. Ultimately, only archaeological sites will resolve this issue. When sites are found that conform to Haynes' standards, we will be able to conclude that there were migrations into the New World before Clovis. Until then, this will remain a major point of contention in New World prehistory.

WHAT—OR WHO—KILLED THE AMERICAN MEGAFAUNA?

Ecologist Paul S. Martin's "Pleistocene overkill" hypothesis (Martin 1967; and see P. Martin and Wright 1967) involves a compelling scenario: The first human migrants to the American heartland find a flourishing bestiary that would put any modern African game park to shame. The seemingly limitless food source allows these paleohunters to expand their population at a rapid rate, ultimately filling two continents. Yet the seeds of their destruction are planted in the magnitude of their success. Large game animals, their populations already stressed by the changing climate at the end of the Pleistocene, are overhunted and ultimately suffer extinction. The human hunters at the root cause of this go on to shift their adaptive strategies to other resources, having little choice but to restructure drastically their subsistence and their culture.

This scenario would be remarkable if it were true. We in the late twentieth century are well aware of our role in the destruction of habitat and the endangering of species—all wrought by our technologically sophisticated hand. Could ancient people with little more than stone spears similarly have caused the extinction of numerous species of animals? Thirty-five genera (and many species) suffered extinction in North America around 11,000 B.P., soon after the appearance and expansion of Paleoindians throughout the Americas (twenty-seven genera disappeared completely, another eight became locally extinct, surviving only outside of North America; Grayson 1987:8).

Although climate changed at the end of the Pleistocene, warming trends had happened before (see Figure 6.7). A period of massive extinction of large mammals like that seen about 11,000 years ago had not occurred during the previous 400,000 years, despite those changes (Guthrie 1990). The only apparently significant difference in the Americas 11,000 years ago was the presence of human hunters of these large mammals. Was this coincidence, or cause and effect?

We do not know. Ecologist Paul S. Martin has championed the model that associates the extinction of large mammals at the end of the Pleistocene with human predation. He has co-authored a work (Mosimann and Martin 1975) in which a computer simulation showed that in around 300 years, given the right conditions, a small influx of hunters into eastern Beringia 12,000 years ago could have spread across the New World in a wave and wiped out game animals in a "blitzkrieg" (their term) to feed their burgeoning population.

The researchers ran the simulation several ways, always beginning with a population of 100 humans in Edmonton, Alberta, Canada, at 11,500 years ago. Assuming different initial North American big-game-animal populations (75–150 million animals) and different population growth rates for the human settlers (0.65%–3.5%), and varying kill rates, Mosimann and Martin (1975:314) derived figures of between 279 and 1,157 years from initial contact to big-game extinction.

Many scholars continue to support this scenario. For example, geologist Larry Agenbroad (1988) has mapped the locations of dated Clovis sites alongside the distribution of dated sites where the remains of woolly mammoth have been found (in both archaeological and purely paleontological contexts). These distributions show remarkable synchronicity (Agenbroad 1988:71).

There are, however, many problems with this model. Significantly, though a few sites are quite impressive (see the Case Study Close-Up section), there really is very little archaeological evidence to support it. Writing in 1982, Martin himself admitted to the paucity of evidence; for example, at that point, the butchered remains of only 38 individual mammoths had been found at Clovis sites (P. Martin 1982:403). In the years since, few additional mammoths have been added to the list; there still are fewer than 20 Clovis sites where the remains of one or more butchered mammoths have been recovered (Agenbroad 1988:66), a miniscule proportion of the millions that necessarily would have to have been slaughtered within the overkill scenario.

Though Martin claims the lack of evidence actually supports his model (the evidence is sparse because the spread of humans and extinction of animals occurred so quickly), this seems like a weak argument. And how could we ever disprove it? As archaeologist Donald Grayson (1987) points out, in other cases where extinction resulted from the quick spread of human hunters—for example, the extinction of the moa, the large flightless bird of New Zealand mentioned earlier—archaeological evidence in the form of butchered remains is abundant. Grayson (1991) has also shown that the evidence is not so clear that all or even most of the large herbivores in Late Pleistocene America became extinct after the appearance of Clovis. Of the 35 extinct genera, only 8 can be confidently assigned an extinction date of between 12,000 and 10,000 years ago (Grayson 1991:209). Many of the other genera, Grayson argues, may have succumbed before 12,000 B.P., at least half a century *before* Clovis shows up in the American west.

Ultimately, environmental change at the end of the Pleistocene may have played a more significant role in the widespread extinctions that occurred at this time among large game animals. Biologist R. Dale Guthrie (1990) suggests that the Pleistocene/Holocene boundary was unlike previous periods of warming, and resulted in far more drastic consequences for large herbivores hunted by humans and also for small rodents and other species not part of Clovis subsistence. Geologist Ernest Lundelius (1988) proposes that the end of the Pleistocene produced climates that displayed greater seasonality—more seasonal differences in temperature and precipitation. As climate became more seasonal, biotic diversity decreased as extreme seasonal conditions made large areas uninhabitable for many species. This, Lundelius maintains, was the primary cause of Late Pleistocene extinction.

As of this moment, which factors were key and which were incidental in the extinction of large American mammals at the end of the Pleistocene is unclear. As most researchers admit, it will take years of research to solve this puzzle.

At the Naco site in Arizona, a single mammoth was slaughtered by Paleoindian hunters more than 11,000 years ago. Eight large fluted points were found resting in the skeleton of the dead prehistoric elephant.

CASE STUDY CLOSE-UP

At the Lehner site, also in Arizona, thirteen elephants were killed by Clovis hunters brandishing spears tipped with fluted points (Haury, Sales, and Wasley 1959). The age profile of the Lehner mammoths is catastrophic (see discussion in Chapter 8). In other words, the age spread of the mammoths killed at the site (from 2 to 30 years) is similar to the age spread in a living group of elephants. This suggests to archaeologist J. Saunders (1977) that the Lehner mammoths do not represent thirteen individual, random kills of elephants in nearly the same spot over an extended period. Instead, it suggests that an entire small family group of adult, adolescent, and juvenile elephants was killed at the same time. Though some have questioned whether Clovis hunters equipped with only stone-tipped spears could kill so many elephants at one time (Haynes 1982), the age profile is significant.

The hunting skills of the Paleoindian hunters at the Casper site in Wyoming have been questioned by no one (Frison 1974a,b). Though they ordinarily lived in small hunting bands for much of the year, several bands coalesced in a larger encampment during the late summer and fall, when the bison were traveling in larger groups and were relatively easy to herd. The bringing together of small bands for communal hunts also allowed for the reinforcement of social connections and trade, and gave young people an opportunity to find suitable mates in other bands.

A bit more than 10,000 years ago, a small group of bison approached the dune field at what is today the Casper archaeological site. Using whatever natural cover was available, perhaps camouflaging themselves with brush and even smearing themselves with bison dung to mask their human smell, the hunters quietly surrounded the beasts—members of an extinct subspecies (*Bison bison antiquus*) of today's American buffalo (*Bison bison bison*). As the bison approached the edge of the sand dune, the hunters burst from their hiding places, creating an enormous amount of noise and commotion.

Heeding their instinct to flee when threatened, the beasts rushed headlong into what appeared to be the only safe avenue where no hunters were in their

FIGURE 10.16

These projectile points from the Casper site in Wyoming were probably used to kill bison who were stampeded into the leeward side of a parabolic sand dune about 10,000 years ago. (Courtesy George Frison)

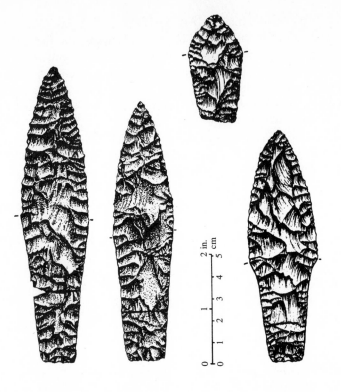

way. But instead of escape, the bison found a natural trap as they stampeded into the sandy hollow on the leeward side of the parabolic dune, precisely where the hunters had intended them to go. The animals quickly became mired in the soft sand. They panicked as they dimly perceived their predicament, and then quickly exhausted themselves, trying helplessly to extricate their huge bulks on hooves intended for long treks across the hard ground of the plains, not the soft footing of sand. They became easy targets for human hunters wielding stone-tipped spears (both fluted Folsom points and an unfluted variety called "Hell Gap"; Figure 10.16). Nearly eighty bison were caught, killed, butchered, and eaten by the Paleoindians at Casper (Figure 10.17). Having eaten their fill and then drying and preserving the huge quantity of meat leftover, the various bands went their separate ways, perhaps to meet again in another year and another place where the bison could be hunted yet again.

 **VISITING THE PAST**

Most larger natural history and university museums in the United States have displays on the earliest human settlement of the New World and information regarding Paleoindians. For example, the Denver Museum of Natural History devotes space to the Dent site Paleoindian mammoth kill as well as the Folsom site, showing the original points in situ, between the ribs of an ancient bison. The University of Colorado Museum has an informative display on the Olsen-Chubbuck Paleoindian

FIGURE 10.17

This is part of the bison bone bed at the 10,000-year-old Casper site in Wyoming. The animals were trapped in the sand by the ancient hunters and then killed with projectile points like those shown in Figure 10.16. (Courtesy George Frison)

bison kill site. In the east, the Thunderbird Museum and Archaeological Park in Front Royal, Virginia, has displays on the Thunderbird Paleoindian site. Excavations conducted by the museum in the Shenandoah Valley are open to visitors interested in witnessing archaeological excavation. In the southwest, the Blackwater Draw Museum, located between Clovis and Portales, New Mexico, devotes part of its display to the nearby Blackwater Draw Paleoindian site.

SUMMARY

In the Late Pleistocene, expanding human populations intruded into new territories and, ultimately, migrated into three previously uninhabited continents: Australia, North America, and South America. Australia was populated by coastally adapted southeast Asians. Using watercraft, by accident and perhaps through intentional exploration, they moved out into the western Pacific, inhabiting the oceanic islands of Borneo, Sulawesi, and Timor, and eventually made landfall on Greater Australia: New Guinea, Tasmania, and Australia proper. Archaeological evidence shows this happened 50,000 years ago—possibly more—during a period of lowered sea level, when the trip by watercraft would have been easier than it is today. The first settlers maintained a tropical/coastal orientation to their economy, initially turning inland only along major rivers. The dry interior of the continent was settled more than 20,000 years later.

During the Late Pleistocene, the New World was intermittently connected to the Old World by a vast land bridge, making possible passage by land from northeast Asia to northwest North America. This certainly occurred by 12,000 years ago. At this time, eastern Siberia was populated and the Bering Land Bridge was exposed. Several early sites in Alaska and the Canadian Yukon date to the period immediately after 12,000 years ago, and bear lithic industries analogous to those in Siberia. Some of these early settlers moved south, perhaps through an ice-free corridor, into the American west, where they invented a new projectile-point technology. The projectile's fluted points allowed these settlers to expand across two continents. These Clovis people may not have been the first arrivals; some sites in both North and South America may be older. But Clovis represents the first broadly successful occupation of the New World.

TO LEARN MORE

Though published more than a decade ago, J. Peter White and James F. O'Connell's (1982) *A Prehistory of Australia, New Guinea, and Sahul* is still the best synthesis of the archaeology of Greater Australia. Another very useful book is Josephine Flood's *Archaeology of the Dreamtime: The Story of Prehistoric Australia and Its People* (1990). Frederick Hadleigh West's (1981) *The Archaeology of Beringia* is still a useful source on the connection between Siberia and the first settlement of the New World. For an even-handed treatment of the controversy over the earliest settlement of the Americas, read David Meltzer (1993b) "Pleistocene peopling of the Americas" in the journal *Evolutionary Anthropology*. For detailed information about the Paleoindian adaptation to the Americas, see the numerous articles in *Clovis: Origins and Adaptations*, edited by Rob Bonnichsen and K. L. Turnmire (1991). A recent, popularly oriented book by David Meltzer (1993c), *Search for the First Americans*, provides a helpful summary of the current consensus and arguments over the earliest settlement of the New World. Two excellent sources on the colonization of the Pacific are John Terrell's (1986) *Prehistory in the Pacific Islands* and Geoffrey Irwin's (1993) *The Prehistoric Exploration and Colonisation of the Pacific.*

KEY TERMS

Sunda (or Sundaland)
Sahul
Wallace Trench
Wallacea
fire-cracked rock
gracile
Bering Land Bridge
wedge-shaped cores
microblade

Paleo-Arctic tradition
Denali Complex
burin
Nenana Complex
fluted point
Laurentide
Cordilleran
ice-free corridor (or
    McKenzie corridor)

Clovis
Paleoindian
Folsom
Melanesia
Micronesia
Polynesia
Lapita

11

After the Ice

CULTURAL CHANGE IN THE POST-PLEISTOCENE

CHAPTER OVERVIEW

The end of the Pleistocene was marked by massive, long-term climate change. Human beings throughout the world were faced with the challenge of adapting to the new environments being established in the early Holocene. Different societies responded in different ways. In many areas subsistence shifted necessarily as plant and animal species became locally extinct. Small mammals and plant foods increased in importance in certain regions. Some societies intensified the subsistence quest, focusing on particularly rich resources, and, as a result, became more sedentary. Most areas were marked by increasing cultural diversity.

	11.5	11	10.5	10	9.5	9
Europe			Younger Dryas Stadial		Star Carr	Mount Sandel
North America						Early Archaic
East Asia						
Australia						
South America			Vegas Phase	Pachamachy Cave	Vicuña hunting	
Africa			Capsian			

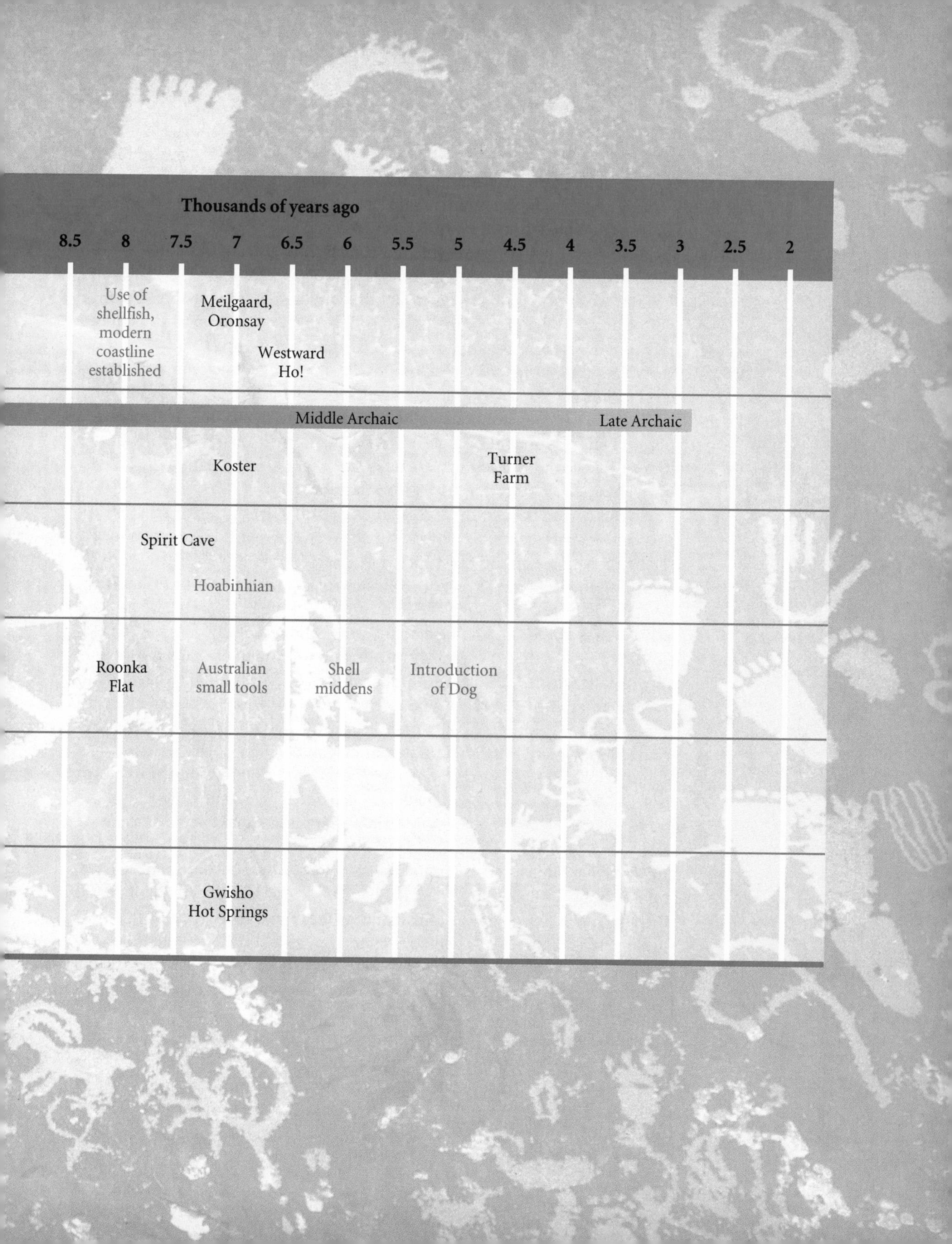

Thousands of years ago

8.5	8	7.5	7	6.5	6	5.5	5	4.5	4	3.5	3	2.5	2

Use of shellfish, modern coastline established

Meilgaard, Oronsay

Westward Ho!

Middle Archaic

Late Archaic

Koster

Turner Farm

Spirit Cave

Hoabinhian

Roonka Flat

Australian small tools

Shell middens

Introduction of Dog

Gwisho Hot Springs

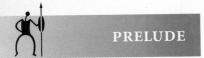
We tend to think of the Pleistocene as enormously distant in time from us. The Ice Age isn't *our* age; it's a past time, when conditions were much colder and glaciers covered large portions of the earth that today are home to tens of millions of people. We blithely refer to the period after 10,000 years ago as the Holocene (recent) Epoch, as if giving it a separate name ensures that our time is different and our climate more pleasant and constant than that of times past.

But we don't know that for a fact. In actuality, most available evidence points to a very different conclusion. In Figure 6.7 we saw variations in the ^{18}O content of seawater and, by inference, the amount of glacial coverage on land. That figure shows a series of other breaks from cold climate—long **interglacials** and shorter **interstadials**—other remissions from glaciation during the Pleistocene. How can we be sure that the current, relatively ice-free period isn't just another break in Arctic-like conditions over much of the higher elevations and higher latitudes, an interglacial inevitably to be followed by another descent into glacial conditions?

Deep cores taken in the Greenland ice cap, where ice formed in strata that can be analyzed for air temperature during each period of formation, indicate that we are in the most recent of a series of relatively warm periods spanning the last 90,000 years (Monastersky 1994a). But without knowing what might have precipitated the cold episodes of the Pleistocene, we have no way of knowing whether those conditions fundamentally changed 10,000 years ago or whether they are almost certain to return, perhaps in the not-too-distant future. The last interglacial lasted about 20,000 years (from 135,000 to 115,000 years ago), and at least one of the ice cores taken in Greenland indicates wild swings of climate even within that relatively warmer period (Monastersky 1994b). With that as our guide, then, perhaps we are only about halfway into an interglacial, and glacial conditions are poised to return in 10,000 years. Overall, the data do not provide much comfort to those who want to believe that the glacial conditions that punctuated the Pleistocene are really over.

Even when we look back into the recent past, we see relatively short-lived, minor "blips" in the warm trend that has characterized the earth's climate for the last 10,000 years. In fact, the climate from the mid-twelfth to the mid-nineteenth centuries has been characterized as a "Little Ice Age," or Neo-Borea. Historical records make it clear that this short relapse into glacial conditions had a significant impact on the agricultural patterns and lives of millions of Europeans and Americans (Grove 1988).

For example, historical records as well as paleoclimatological data indicate a significant, though brief, cooling trend between A.D. 1150 and 1400. The Vikings were forced to abandon their western Greenland colony by A.D. 1345 as expanding pack ice and a sharp increase in the number of North Atlantic icebergs made the voyage between the colony and Scandinavia treacherous and as life on Greenland became increasingly harsh.

Things warmed up between A.D. 1400 and 1550, but then cooled off again for another three centuries. In the mid-nineteenth century, when another warming trend commenced—a trend we probably are still in (but for how long?)—people were once again forced to respond and readapt to the new climatic conditions.

But any adaptations developed in response to such short-term, small-scale environmental changes pale in comparison to what it must have been like between 12,000 and 10,000 years ago when massive, long-term climate changes occurred. From the cave painters of Upper Paleolithic Europe to the mammoth hunters of central Asia, from the Paleoindian hunters of Pleistocene megafauna in the New World to the reindeer hunters of northern Europe, from the lakeside dwellers of southeast Australia to the lake dwellers of central Africa—people were faced with slow but cumulatively massive changes in their accustomed environments. Temperatures rose, ice sheets melted, coastlines were inundated and reconfigured, large herbivores became extinct, new game and unfamiliar plant life invaded home territories, lakes dried up, and weather patterns changed. The old ways of living no longer meshed with changed climates, altered habitats, and different floral and faunal populations.

Human beings had little choice but to adapt, move, or die. Where they could, some shifted territories, trying to follow conditions with which they were most familiar. Some may have seen their cultures wither and die as conditions changed more rapidly than they could or were willing to respond to. Many groups, however, changed their ways of life by adapting to the new conditions of the Holocene. Their cultural response to the changes wrought by the end of the Pleistocene—or, at least, the current interglacial—is the focus of this chapter.

The key characteristic of the cultures of the early Holocene is adaptive change, reflected in the following features:

CHRONICLE

- In most places the archaeological record shows that human groups quickly shifted their subsistence focus as the animals and plants on which they previously had relied became extinct or unavailable in their home regions.
- Commonly, the post-Pleistocene subsistence base changed from megafauna to smaller animals, fish, shellfish, and birds, and included a greater reliance on plant foods previously absent or rare during glacial conditions.
- In some regions, rather than a broadening, the subsistence shift involved more intensive exploitation of some uniquely productive elements in the food quest. More intense exploitation means there was a focus on a small number of highly productive resources in those areas where such resources existed, for example, wild cereal grasses in the Middle East.
- In some areas, the focus on certain abundant resources encouraged a shift from a purely nomadic existence to a more sedentary one. (We will

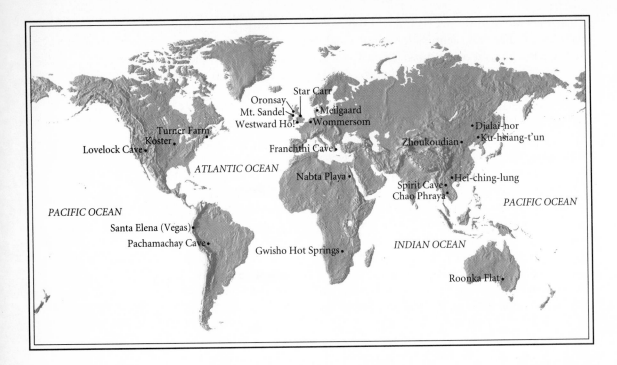

MAP 11.1

Sites of the early post-Pleistocene.

see that in some propitious regions, the intensification of the food quest and the shift from a nomadic to a sedentary way of life set the stage for a revolutionary change in the relationship between people and the foods on which they subsisted: a move from food collecting to food production, to be discussed in Chapter 12.)

• Various groups responded in unique ways to their newly established, heterogeneous conditions, producing far more cultural diversity, even within relatively circumscribed regions, than seen across vast geographical expanses during the Pleistocene.

The discussion will now turn to how various world regions reflected these cultural changes. Unfortunately, while vast regions during the Paleolithic can be readily characterized in terms of cultural adaptations, that cannot be done for the cultures of the Holocene. After the Pleistocene, the cultural situation becomes far more complicated, and an increasing number of distinct adaptations evolved in many different regions. The picture is so complex that only a brief description of some of the best known adaptations to life "after the ice" will be presented (Map 11.1).

EUROPE

A warming trend can be deduced from the pollen record of Europe for the period after 16,000 years ago. This trend was sufficient to render even Scan-

FIGURE 11.1

As this map of the coastline of Europe during the early Holocene shows, broad areas that were dry land 9,500 years ago are today under the sea. (Courtesy T. Douglas Price)

dinavia ice-free just 3,000 years later, by about 13,000 B.P. This warming was interrupted at least once by a shift back to glacial conditions. This so-called **Younger Dryas** stadial lasted only from 11,000 to 10,000 years ago but may still have caused human groups to abandon much of northwestern Europe during the period; there is a gap in archaeological evidence for human occupation of the north at this time. The Younger Dryas was, nevertheless, a relatively minor deviation from a trend that would result in near-modern conditions across much of Europe by 8,500 B.P. (Gamble 1986; T. D. Price 1991; C. Smith 1992). Sea level was rising, too, breaking the connection between Great Britain and the continent by 8,000 years ago and establishing modern coastlines relatively soon thereafter (Figure 11.1; Megaw and Simpson 1979; C. Smith 1992).

Though the northernmost reaches of the continent retained their Arctic-like characteristics, the Pleistocene tundra and its suite of large game animals, including woolly mammoth and rhinoceros, wild cattle, horse, and reindeer, was gone over most of Europe after 9,000 years ago. The cold-loving grasses and sedges of the tundra on which those large herbivores subsisted were replaced first by birch and pine trees and later by elm and oak to the south. The gregarious megafauna whose huge migratory herds were accommodated by the treeless expanse of the tundra could not exist in or migrate through the expanding, dense woodlands. These large animals were replaced by smaller, less mobile, forest-dwelling animal species, including red deer, roe deer, and wild pig, along with even smaller fur-bearing animals such as marten, beaver, otter, and wolf (T. D. Price 1991). As archaeologist T. Douglas Price (1991:190) points out, the key characteristic of the environment of Holocene Europe when compared to that of the Pleistocene is its vast array of plants and animals available for exploitation. Thus, the most salient feature of the food resource base of post-Pleistocene Europe is its diversity.

It is to the extremely diverse mixture of plants and animals establishing themselves in post-Pleistocene Europe that human groups adjusted themselves. This diversity, both within and between regions, helps to explain the cultural record of Europe after the ice. The European **Mesolithic**—the cultural period that follows the Paleolithic in Europe and precedes the appearance of farming cultures—is marked by many of the features of post-Pleistocene cultures (see earlier list).

Mesolithic Subsistence Patterns

Archaeologist Christopher Meiklejohn (1978) points out the greater diversity of species exploited by Mesolithic Europeans when compared to their Paleolithic forebears. In a survey of seven Mesolithic sites in Great Britain and France, eleven different large-animal species were reported, with an average of four different species at each site (Meiklejohn 1978:67). Upper Paleolithic sites in northern Europe commonly have only a single large mammal species represented.

Sites of the **Maglemosian** culture of the Mesolithic exemplify the broadening of the subsistence quest as well as the spread of a sedentary way of life made possible by the establishment of productive Holocene habitats. Maglemosian people built sizeable semipermanent villages on the margins of large, post-Pleistocene lakes in northern Europe (see the Case Study Close-Up section).

The Irish site of Mount Sandel shows evidence of the use of seasonally available resources that together span the entire year, beginning 7,500 years ago (T. D. Price 1987:250). This, along with the size of the substantial residential structures [circular buildings about 6 m (20 ft) in diameter], argues for a degree of permanence of occupation not seen previously.

In the cold climate of post-Pleistocene northern Europe, hunting appears to have been the most significant element in the subsistence quest. Mesolithic sites ordinarily produce a wide array of animal food species, including red deer, roe deer, elk, wild ox, wild sheep, goat, pig, and rabbit. Small fur-bearing mammals such as wolf, fox, badger, beaver, marten, squirrel, and hare were used by these Mesolithic people, almost certainly for their warm pelts.

Charred seeds provide evidence for the significance of plant foods in the Mesolithic diet. Hazelnut shells are commonly found in Mesolithic sites in Northern Europe, and the hazelnut and other nut foods, along with water lily and wild apple, probably made a significant seasonal contribution to the diet (T. D. Price 1987). At Mesolithic sites in southern France, a wider array of plant food remains have been recovered, including vetch, lentils, and chick-peas (T. D. Price 1987).

Although rising post-Pleistocene sea levels have inundated most Mesolithic coastal sites, and many ancient lakes have become dry land (see Figure 11.1), there still is evidence of the extensive use of lake and coastal resources during the Mesolithic. Modern dredging in the English Channel and the North Sea to facilitate ship traffic has brought up Mesolithic bone and antler artifacts from sites now located many meters underwater (T. D. Price 1987). Where local topography has preserved the ancient coast, Mesolithic sites are numerous. Excavation of such sites has shown an extensive reliance on coastal resources. Of greatest significance was the pike, a saltwater fish that enters inland channels and inlets to spawn. But the bones of cod, ling, perch, breem, eel, and haddock have also been recovered (G. Clark 1980). Marine mammals are also found in Mesolithic contexts. Species that were hunted include ringed, harp, and grey seals. The remains of hunted or beached whales and porpoises are also found. Fifty-five different bird species have been found in Mesolithic sites. For example, at Mount Sandel in Ireland, the remains of duck, pigeon, dove, grouse, goshawk, and capercaillie were excavated (T. D. Price 1987:248).

Shellfish also made an important contribution to the diet in coastal localities. For example, at the Danish site of Meilgaard, a shell midden was found with a volume of 2,000 m^3 (21,000 ft^3) made up of millions of mollusk shells (Bailey 1978). In Portugal, coastal middens consisting primarily of mollusk shell are common for the period after 7,400 B.P. Mesolithic shell middens dot the Island of Oronsay, 30 km (20 mi) off the west coast of Scotland (Mellars 1978). Crab and limpet shells, along with the bones of seal, fish, and thirty species of birds, were found among the food remains (T. D. Price 1987). At Westward Ho! in north Devon, England, Mesolithic kitchen middens of oyster, winkle, mussel, and limpet shells have been dated to more than 6,500 years ago (T. D. Price 1987).

Diversity and Regionalization

Regionalization is another process seen clearly in European Mesolithic sites. While a single lithic tradition characterizes the Middle Paleolithic across much of Europe, and while only a few geographically demarcated, different, but related traditions are present there in the Upper Paleolithic, the Mesolithic period in Europe is marked by a far more diverse cultural pattern.

For example, the **Hamburgian** cultural tradition of the northern European Upper Paleolithic was quite homogenous throughout northern Europe. Whereas at most three geographically separate and distinct stone-tool traditions within the Hamburgian have been recognized, archaeologist T. Douglas Price (1991:199) counts at least fifteen different regional stone-toolmaking patterns by the end of the Mesolithic.

Cultural regions of the European Upper Paleolithic—as determined by the geographical extent of archaeological sites where similar tool styles and types are found—have been estimated to encompass as much as 100,000 km² (42,250 mi²). During the Mesolithic, defining cultural regions or territories the same way results in the identification of a far greater number of much smaller territories, more on the order of 1,000 km² (422.5 mi²) each (T. D. Price 1991:200).

It seems clear that various groups are settling into their own distinct regions in Europe after the Pleistocene, evolving their own adaptations to their unique set of local postglacial environmental conditions, developing their own tool assemblages and their own distinctive patterns of subsistence and settlement.

Trade in the European Mesolithic

Mesolithic trade networks expanded, but in a pattern different from that established during the Upper Paleolithic (T. D. Price 1987). While trading networks actually extended over longer distances in the Upper Paleolithic (see Chapter 9), trade during the Mesolithic was more intraregional. Lithic raw materials were exchanged in greater amounts, but trading was generally restricted to within their smaller cultural regions. In other words, materials didn't move as far, but more of it was moving through the more geographically restricted regional systems.

For example, obsidian from the Mediterranean island of Melos is found abundantly in Mesolithic levels of Franchthi Cave on the Greek mainland. English Portland chert was traded, but only within England and not more than 240 km (160 mi) from its source. Brown quartzite from Wommersom in Belgium and the southern Netherlands has been found spread across a restricted area in northern Europe, at Mesolithic sites no more than 120 km (78 mi) from the source (G. Clark 1980), and almost always within an area about 250 km by 200 km (160 mi by 130 mi) (Figure 11.2; T. D. Price 1991:200).

Innovation in the Mesolithic

The European Mesolithic was also a time of great innovation. Early evidence of the manufacture of canoes is dated to the Mesolithic. The use of bow and

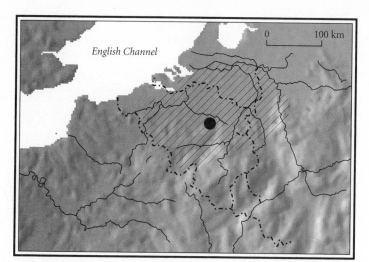

FIGURE 11.2
Map showing the distribution of Wommersom quartzite (shaded area) during the Mesolithic. The black circle marks the source of the stone.
(Courtesy T. Douglas Price)

arrow may predate the Mesolithic, going back perhaps more than 15,000 years to the Upper Paleolithic. The earliest evidence for the use of the bow in Europe, however, dates to between 8,000 B.P. and 9,000 B.P. in northern Europe. Also, the bones of wolflike animals have been found at Star Carr (see the Case Study Close-Up section), dating to before 7,000 years ago. These animals had not been used for food; and based on their relatively small size and the crowded nature of their teeth, they seem to be removed from a purely wild state. In fact, the wolflike bones at Star Carr and many other Mesolithic sites are examples of domesticated wolves—that is, dogs (G. Clark 1980).

NORTH AMERICA

Though the post-Pleistocene prehistory of the New World is distinct from that of the Old World, parallel patterns are apparent in the human response to the end of the Ice Age in both hemispheres. As in Europe, with deglaciation and the extinction of large herbivores that accompanied the end of the Pleistocene, the archaeological record bears witness to a dramatic shift in culture in North America after 10,000 years ago. Whether purely a result of climate change, overhunting, or some combination of the two (see Chapter 10), the massive disappearance of large game animals necessitated dramatic changes in the cultures of the Native Americans of the early post-Pleistocene.

New World prehistorians have recognized the great cultural changes that accompanied the end of the Pleistocene by bestowing a different name on the cultures of this period. Just as in Europe, the Upper Paleolithic is followed by the Mesolithic, in America the Paleoindian period is followed by the **Archaic,** lasting from about 9,000 to 3,000 years ago. The Archaic represents a com-

FIGURE 11.3

Lake Forest Archaic people exploited the shores of the Great Lakes and other large inland bodies of water (Lake Michigan is shown here). Chipped stone spearpoints are typical artifacts of this culture. (Artifact drawings from *A Typology and Nomenclature for New York State Projectile Points* by William A. Ritchie, 1971; reprinted with the permission of the New York State Museum and Science Service; photo by K. L. Feder)

plex era of the establishment of specific adaptations to the different climatic and environmental regimes that became established across North America.

Regionalism in the New World Archaic

Archaic cultures of North America traditionally have been divided geographically, as adaptations to the post-Pleistocene Arctic, the Desert Archaic of the Great Basin, the Southwestern Archaic, the Eastern Archaic, Central Archaic, and Western Archaic (Willey 1966). In other words, various prehistoric people, all descendant from the same Paleoindian ancestors, began following their own adaptive pathways in the face of the new conditions being established at the end of the Pleistocene.

Even this geographic breakdown masks the diversity within these regions. As in Europe, regionalization is the hallmark of the post-Pleistocene of North America. For example, archaeologist Dean Snow (1980), in his synthesis work on the archaeology of New England and New York State, further breaks down the Archaic cultures based on region, subsistence focus, and other behavioral characteristics. Snow describes a **Lake Forest Archaic** tradition (northern New England west of Maine and in western New York), whose apparent focus was the unique conditions of the areas adjacent to the Great Lakes and the lake region of western New England. The material culture shows a heavy reliance on **lacustrine** (lake) resources, with a settlement pattern of home bases on lake shores occupied in the spring, and seasonal winter and summer hunting in the uplands surrounding the lakes (Figure 11.3).

FIGURE 11.4

The Maritime Archaic people developed an adaptation that focused on resources of the Atlantic coast (the southern coast of Maine is shown here). Ground-stone artifacts are typical of this culture. (Artifact drawing from C. C. Willoughby's *Antiquities of the New England Indians,* 1935; photo by K. L. Feder)

Snow's **Maritime Archaic** is situated on New England's north Atlantic coast—primarily in Maine but also extending north into New Brunswick. Sites like Turner Farm in Maine, dating to 4,600 years ago, show a clear subsistence focus on sea resources. Bone fishhooks, net weights and plummets, and faunal remains indicate that fish was a major component of the diet; even pelagic (open ocean as opposed to coastal) creatures like swordfish were hunted from open boats in the deep sea. Human burials were filled with finely crafted objects like long slate knives and carvings of whales and dolphins (Figure 11.4). The human remains were powdered with red ochre (a mineral), giving the name "the Red Paint People" to these Archaic inhabitants of coastal Maine. The rich maritime resources allowed for sedentary coastal home bases.

Snow also defines a **Mast Forest Archaic** for most of southern New England. The term "mast" refers to the acorns and other nut foods from trees (hickory, beechnut, chestnut, walnut) that accumulate on the ground of the forest and serve as food for animals. These Mast Forest Indians focused on the rich resources of the river-drained woodlands of New England. They hunted deer and trapped small animals, fished in the rivers using nets and weirs as well as hooks and lines, collected acorn, hickory, walnut, and chestnut in the fall, and the seeds, leaves, and roots of wild plants in the spring (Figure 11.5).

While deep-sea fishing and mammal hunting in New England seems to have been the exclusive province of the Maritime Archaic tradition, the use of shore resources was not confined to them. The Mast Forest Archaic also has a coastal component, with a heavy reliance on shellfish like oyster, scal-

FIGURE 11.5

The Mast Forest Archaic cultural pattern is centered in the thickly wooded valleys of southern New England (a Connecticut woodland is shown here). Chipped-stone spearpoints are typical of Mast Forest Archaic artifacts. (Artifact drawings from *A Typology and Nomenclature for New York State Projectile Points* by William A. Ritchie, 1971; reprinted with the permission of the New York State Museum and Science Service; photo by K. L. Feder)

lop, soft-shell clam, and quahog. Before development in shoreline communities destroyed them, large shellfish middens were common in Mast Forest Archaic coastal sites in Connecticut and Massachusetts.

The same pattern of cultural regionalization in the Archaic is repeated elsewhere in North America. Piñon nuts were a major component of the diet throughout much of the desert west. The Archaic occupation of the desert shows a subsistence focus on desert lakes that are now dry, low-lying areas called sinks. For example, at Lovelock Cave, in Nevada, coprolites provide direct evidence on the diet of its Archaic inhabitants. The cave was located near a desert lake (now the dry Humbolt Sink). Virtually all of the food remains retrieved from the preserved human feces from the cave came from the lake and its immediate environs (Heizer and Napton 1970) and included duck, mudhen, chub fish, and plant foods like cattail and wetland grasses.

In the Arctic, the resources of the coast were heavily exploited by the Holocene inhabitants, with evidence of seal, sea lion, walrus, and puffin as major elements in the diet. In the far west, nut foods became key elements in the diet, establishing a subsistence pattern that would continue into the historic period.

Koster: Emblem of the Archaic

Perhaps no site in the American Midwest exemplifies better the Archaic period than the Koster site in Illinois (Struever and Holton 1979). Adjacent to the Illinois River, the site is the location of a series of villages dated from soon after the end of the Pleistocene. The inhabitants of all periods exploited the rich and seasonally varied habitat. In fact, the environs of the site were so economically rich from the standpoint of subsistence that as early as 7,000 years ago the inhabitants were cutting down sizeable trees and constructing permanent houses. This is far earlier than the permanent villages that appear in most of ancient North America, usually only after the introduction of an agricultural way of life.

The Archaic people of Koster hunted deer, small mammals, and migratory fowl, including ducks and geese. The carbonized seeds of wild smartweed, sunflower, goosefoot, pigweed, and marsh elder (see the discussion of the domestication of these crops in Chapter 12) were found at the site and were major contributors to the diet. Fish and freshwater shellfish were collected in the river, and nut foods such as hickory, hazelnut, and acorn were harvested seasonally in the uplands around the river valley. Ground nuts, wild duck potatoes, cattail shoots, pecans, pawpaws, persimmons, and sassafras root round out the broad subsistence base at Koster.

A Diverse Set of Adaptations

The focus on locally available foods and the development of highly specialized and localized economies is the most characteristic feature of the Archaic in North America. This is reflected in the foods eaten, the types of settlements people lived in, and the material culture seen in archaeological excavations. No longer is a single artifact style with a small number of regional and temporal variants the rule, as it was with the fluted-point tradition during Paleoindian times. We now see a complex, diverse pattern of stone-tool technologies spread across North America, much as was seen in the European Mesolithic, a pattern discernible across virtually all of the inhabited world in the post-Pleistocene.

ASIA

The Asian Mesolithic is less well known than that of Europe, but what is known follows the pattern established there. Kwang-Chih Chang's (1986) synthesis work on the archaeology of China describes different Mesolithic adaptations to China's distinct post-Pleistocene habitats. He begins by dividing the country geographically and culturally into north and south. In the north, Chang recognizes two major Mesolithic groupings on the basis of stone tools: a blade-and-flake industry in the forests of Manchuria, and a microblade industry in the riverine and lake habitats that constituted oases in the deserts of Mongolia (Figure 11.6).

The microblade manufacturers inhabited regions of Mongolia analogous to that of the Desert Archaic culture of North America in that their sites are on the margins of dry, shallow depressions that were small lakes during early post-Pleistocene times. Spears and arrow points are few at these sites, probably indicating the marginality of hunting in the north. The most common faunal

FIGURE 11.6

Artifacts from the post-Pleistocene culture in Manchuria, northern China. (From *The Archaeology of Ancient China* by K. C. Chang, Yale University Press, with permission)

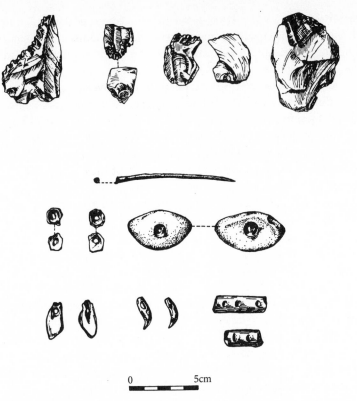

0   5cm

remain is ostrich shell fragments, and people almost certainly relied on the fish available in the lakes around which they settled.

Evidence at sites like Djalai-nor and Ku-hsiang-t'un, in the woodlands of Manchuria, indicates that hunting was more important than in the lakeside habitations. Spearpoints are more common, as are bone and antler tools. At sites like the Upper Cave at Zhoukoudian, a Mesolithic occupation of north China near where *Homo erectus* remains were discovered (see Chapter 6), the faunal remains of wapiti (elk) and ostrich have been found. While these were hunted for food, smaller mammals like badger, fox, wildcat, and tiger were hunted for their thick, warm fur and their teeth, which the Mesolithic occupants of the Upper Cave site perforated to make items of personal adornment. Zhoukoudian is located some distance from the Chinese coast, yet also found in abundance in the Upper Cave Mesolithic deposits were the remains of marine shellfish, which were traded for and then used to manufacture beads and other nonutilitarian items found at the site.

In southern China, another distinct set of Mesolithic adaptations evolved in response to the end-of-Pleistocene conditions. Environmental change was not as dramatic here, and there is great continuity with the Upper Paleolithic cultures of the region. The tradition of making stone tools from chipped pebbles called **Hoabinhian** marks the southern Chinese Mesolithic. Sites such as Hei-ching-lung imply a subsistence base that included wapiti, wild cattle, other small game, mollusks, and wild plant foods.

A similar pattern of regionalization can be seen further south in mainland southeast Asia (Higham 1989). Along with a great diversity of archaeological cultures dated to the Mesolithic, also seen is an increasingly sedentary way of life in some particularly rich areas. The broad range of foods available in Thailand at the Spirit Cave site, occupied more than 7,500 years ago, apparently allowed for a settling into and focusing on the territory immediately surrounding the cave. The Khong stream at the base of the cliff face where the cave was located provided fish and freshwater crab. The surrounding forest provided otter, several monkey species (including langur and macaque), bamboo rat, badger, porcupine, and the sambar and pig deer, the bones of which have all been found in the Spirit Cave excavations (Gorman 1972). Along with animal foods, the remains of 22 genera of plants have been recovered in the cave, including bamboo, betel nut (a stimulant), butternut, and assorted tropical fruits (Higham 1989:53).

Spirit Cave and other upland sites in north Thailand not only share their own unique set of adaptations, but also exhibit the same pattern seen in many other ecologically distinct regions of southeast Asia: the Red River Delta region of northern Vietnam, the Vietnamese coast, the Chao Phraya plains of southern Thailand, and the Gulf of Siam coast. Each region has produced vastly different yet contemporaneous archaeological cultures dating to the Mesolithic. In each case, local people developed distinctive adaptations to their own, rather narrowly circumscribed regions. In this way, the Asian cultures of the Mesolithic exhibit the same pattern seen in Europe and North America: cultural diversity evolving as a result of the developing ecological diversity of the post-Pleistocene.

AUSTRALIA

As a result of its geography, Australia experienced no drastic environmental changes at the end of the Pleistocene. This is not to say that there were no impacts. A drying in the southeast of the country resulted in the disappearance of most inland lakes by 16,000 B.P. The northern coast, on the other hand, saw an increase in rainfall as storm tracks changed. But because there had been no extensive glaciation in Australia during the Pleistocene, we find no deglaciation and attendant warming like that seen in northern Europe and North America.

Perhaps most significantly, worldwide rising sea level at the end of the Pleistocene reconfigured the Australian coastline. By 12,000 B.P., the land connection between Australia and Tasmania was breached; by 8,000 B.P., the

FIGURE 11.7

Stone hatchets and flaked adzes from the post-Pleistocene culture of Australia. (From *A Prehistory of Australia, New Guinea, and Sahul* by J. Peter White and James F. O'Connell, Academic Press, with permission)

cm

bridge between New Guinea and Australia was inundated; and by 6,000 years ago, modern sea levels were reached and the modern configuration of the coast largely was achieved (see Figure 10.2; J. White and O'Connell 1982).

Without the kinds of major environmental changes seen in Europe and North America at the end of the Pleistocene, we also fail to see in Australia the kinds of major cultural changes that characterize the Holocene on those continents. Again, things don't remain static. For example, ground stone hatchets and flaked stone adzes make their appearance about this time (Figure 11.7). The Australian "small-tool tradition," with its blades, burins, and bifacial projectile points, dated to a bit before 5,000 years ago and as much as 7,000 years ago, represents another addition to the Holocene archaeological record. These small tools are often made of nonlocal raw materials and may indicate an increase in trade between groups living great distances from one another.

The inhabitants of Australia seem to have maintained a relatively stable subsistence adaptation through the Late Pleistocene, Holocene, and even into the modern era. While shellfish were collected as much as 30,000 years ago at Lake Mungo (see Chapter 10), marine shellfish became a major component of the diet of Australia's coastal people only after 8,000 years ago, around the time that the modern coastal configuration was established. Large shell middens dating especially to after 6,000 B.P. are common along the temperate southeast coast and to a lesser degree on the tropical north coast. Shellfish seems not to have been a significant food source along the southwest coast at any time in Australia's history; there are no shell middens, and ethnographic groups in the area were not reported to have been much interested in shellfish (White and O'Connell 1982).

The major period of cultural change in Holocene Australia dates to the period beginning about 5,000 years ago. In their synthesis of Australian prehistory, J. Peter White and James F. O'Connell (1982:104–105) point out that at about this time the dingo, a wild dog (a nonmarsupial introduced to Australia by human settlers) tamed for hunting, is seen in archaeological contexts for the first time. Also, macrozamia, an otherwise poisonous plant whose underground stem, when properly prepared, produces an edible starch, becomes an important food source. There is also a substantial increase in site density in the eastern Australian highlands, made possible by the broadening of the subsistence quest to include new food sources and the development of new cooking techniques in southeast Australia, marked by the appearance after 4,500 years ago of a new style of hearth made from pieces of termite nest.

A few sites, Roonka Flat being the most impressive, exhibit evidence of an elaboration of burial ritual in the Holocene. Of the eighty-two burials located at this site, most date to recent times, but twelve can be assigned to the period between 4,000 and 7,000 years ago. A few of these were shaft tombs, vertical interments of the deceased. Most of the Roonka Flat burials contained grave goods, including the lower jaws of animals (with drilled holes for suspension), drilled shells, and bone pins. A few adults were buried with the bones of human infants.

Australia is huge, and has been occupied for 50,000 years. On the one hand, its material culture is easier to analyze than that of Europe, Asia, or North America because it is both more homogeneous and stable through time. On the other hand, there is a level of diversity apparent in subsistence data that more clearly follows the post-Pleistocene pattern seen in the rest of the world. As J. White and O'Connell (1982) maintain, the post-Pleistocene archaeological record of Australia reflects the significance of highly localized environmental factors in molding a settlement/subsistence pattern. Coastal, upland, desert, lake, and riverine foci all became established in different parts of the country. In that sense, Australia after the Pleistocene exhibits a pattern common to that seen in the rest of the world.

SOUTH AMERICA

As Karen Olsen Bruhns (1994) points out in her synthesis of South American prehistory, the end of the Pleistocene is marked by a subsistence shift from a specialized focus on big-game hunting to a broader base. However, not all new adaptations involved a broadening of the subsistence base. In some areas with a restricted community of edible plants and animals, human groups became highly specialized in exploiting individual species or a small number of species. For example, with the extinction of mastodon, horse, glyptodon (giant armadillo), megatherium (giant ground sloth), and many other Pleistocene species, some human groups who previously had at least partially relied on the hunting of these animals, shifted focus to the single set of large game animals remaining after the Pleistocene—**camelids.** The South American camels included the wild guanaco, llama, and vicuña. For example, at Pachamachay Cave in the Peruvian Andes, a subsistence focus on vicuña hunting developed after 9,000 years ago (Bruhns 1994).

Elsewhere, a broadening of the subsistence quest is apparent. The Vegas complex, located in the Santa Elena Peninsula of Ecuador, shows an early (late Paleoindian) evolution of a maritime subsistence focus. This shift is ultimately seen in the coastal desert from northern Peru to southern Chile, where archaeological evidence shows early post-Pleistocene groups heavily exploiting resources like mollusks. This maritime, or **littoral,** tradition is seen, if a bit later, in coastal Colombia and Venezuela and also along the Caribbean Atlantic coasts of South America. Hunting remained important in some areas; some of the coastal sites are located near tar pits, natural traps where animals could have been killed once mired in the thick natural petroleum deposits. But maritime resources seem to have become most important to those living near the coast in post-Pleistocene South America. Some places even show signs of a population movement away from the interior and toward the coast. These post-Pleistocene coastal sites tend to be larger than earlier sites, more permanent, and with more elaborate burials. A sedentary way of life on the coast, made possible by the rich and reliable resources of the sea, seems to have set the stage, at least in part, for the great cultural changes that were to occur in South America (see Chapters 12 and 14).

AFRICA

Like Australia, the African continent was not affected as severely by climate change at the end of the Pleistocene as were Europe, Asia, and the Americas. Africa was not glaciated, and suffered much less of the extinction of large mammals. And the kind of regionalization seen on the other continents in the early post-Pleistocene is seen in Africa in an earlier period. As indicated by archaeologist David W. Phillipson in his synthesis of African prehistory, the period of 100,000–8,000 years ago is characterized by the movement away from "broad cultural uniformity" and "towards the establishment of distinct regional traditions" (1993:60).

Typical among the regional cultures was that of the **Iberomaurusians** of northwest Africa (Klein 1993). At about 16,000 B.P. they inhabited the coastal plain and interior of what is today Tunisia and Morocco. They made small stone blade artifacts used as scraping and piercing tools—the former for scraping animal hides in clothing manufacture and the latter as arrow points or spearpoints for hunting. The animals that were the core of their subsistence strategy included wild cattle, gazelle, hartebeest, and Barbary sheep. Also important in their coastal habitat were marine mollusks, including snails. Though no plant food remains have been found in Iberomaurusian sites, grinding stones and digging stick weights indicate some reliance on seeds, nuts, and roots.

Change accompanies the end of the Pleistocene, but there is no great cultural upheaval in Africa. After 10,000 years ago in northwest Africa, the Iberomaurusian culture is replaced by another, called **Capsian;** as Richard Klein (1993) points out, this may have involved an actual migration of new people into the area, where they replaced the older inhabitants. Capsian subsistence is not very different from that of the preceding Iberomaurusians. They continued to hunt wild sheep, collect shellfish and snails, dig for roots, and grind seeds and nuts. The Capsians set very small **microlith** blades into wooden or bone handles. These tools appear to have been used to harvest wild stands of grains; the microliths themselves exhibit a diagnostic kind of wear or polish called "sickle sheen" from repeated use in cutting the stalks of tall, grasslike plants.

The use of microlithic **backed blades** is all but ubiquitous in Holocene Africa. During the early post-Pleistocene of southern Africa, microlithic industries predominate at coastal locales where preservation is high—in dry caves and waterlogged sites like Gwisho Hot Springs in Zambia, a broad array of artifacts was recovered, including bows and arrows, digging sticks, bark trays, and bags and clothing of leather. Plant foods were important in the diet

FIGURE 11.8
Naturalistic engraving of a rhinoceros found in southern Africa and dating to the post-Pleistocene. (From *African Archaeology* by David W. Phillipson, Cambridge University Press, with permission)

FIGURE 11.9
Rock paintings from southern Africa interpreted as representing two shamans in a trance. (From *African Archaeology* by David W. Phillipson, Cambridge University Press, with permission)

within a seasonal round that saw winter settlement of the coast and summers spent inland.

South Africa also saw a proliferation of artwork, with an abundance of naturalistic rock paintings depicting animals and people (Figure 11.8). As Phillipson (1993:77) points out, the paintings almost certainly had a ritual significance. The eland—a large antelope—is depicted most frequently, but it is not the animal most commonly represented in the faunal assemblage at archaeological sites dated to the same period. Historically, however, the eland played an important role in the religions of some southern African people, and its abundance in ancient rock paintings may indicate that the ritual importance of the eland has a long history. Also, some of the paintings show people in positions and contexts that were common in historical times and related to trance. Again, as Phillipson (1993:77) points out, early Holocene rock paintings of people bent over or in a crouched position, often with blood apparently flowing from their noses, match the descriptions of trance experience of the San people living in southern Africa. The San describe their trances as riding on the backs of snakes, and people riding on the backs of enormous serpents or snakes are also found in the rock paintings (Figure 11.9).

Central, eastern, and western Africa also have produced archaeological evidence of microlithic tool industries as well as diversity and regionalization of subsistence and settlement. In east Africa, on the shores of Lake Turkana, where so many key finds have been made related to human physical evolution (see Chapters 5 and 6), evidence of a specialized fishing adaptation has been recovered. In the dense forests of west Africa, a culture with a nonmicrolithic tool assemblage has been identified. Large stone hoes and axes predominate, with little evidence of hunting equipment. Subsistence may have been based on the abundant plant foods of the forest.

Africa too is marked by an explosion of cultural diversity as people became more specifically adapted to their own particular regions in the early Holocene. The stage is now set, here as elsewhere, for a revolution in human subsistence.

ISSUES AND DEBATES

WAS THE MESOLITHIC ONLY A "PRELUDE"?

For many scholars, the period immediately following the Pleistocene is not as intriguing as the periods before or a few thousand years after. It has not commanded as much attention in publications, for instance. Graham Clark's (1980) classic work on the European Mesolithic, *Mesolithic Prelude,* implies, by its very title, that the significance of this period rests not so much in what transpired, but in what it led to: the Neolithic (see Chapter 12). Archaeologist T. Douglas Price (1987:227) points out that for many scientists, at least until fairly recently, the Mesolithic was marked by cultural "impoverishment." Remains were sparse, the artwork was unimpressive, and the period seemed less interesting than the more romantic Upper Paleolithic (with its images of bands of big-game-hunting artists) and less important than the Neolithic, with the inception of a sedentary, "civilized," farming way of life.

As Price points out, this view is no longer tenable. The Mesolithic in Europe—in fact, the early post-Pleistocene of much of the world—was a vital period during which human groups responded to one of the greatest environmental challenges humanity had yet faced: the extinction of many large mammalian species that were unable to adapt to the changes of the early Holocene. Yet humanity thrived by fairly quickly developing many varied cultural adaptations to the changing conditions. While food resources, including shellfish, small mammals, and wild grains, were available to many groups in the Pleistocene, those who relied on big game had little reason to exploit these other possibilities. The end of the Pleistocene and the scaling back and even extinction of many of these big-game resources changed all that.

Wherever we look in the Old and New Worlds, human groups rose to the challenge of drastically changing environmental conditions, each in its own way. The ability of culture, with its enormous flexibility, to respond to such changes is the hallmark of our species and a reason for its great success—

both then and now. Being able to invent, virtually instantly, new strategies for survival rather than having to wait for nature somehow to "come up with" a new adaptation puts humanity at a tremendous advantage relative to other animal species. For human groups at the end of the Pleistocene, the only limitations were those of the imagination. And based on the diversity of the responses, this was hardly any limitation at all.

The post-Pleistocene also was the crucible in which was forged the adaptations that would lead to subsistence strategies that make modern life possible. It is hard to argue now with the characterization of the Mesolithic—and it could be applied to post-Pleistocene cultures the world over—by Russian archaeologist G. I. Mathyushin (G. Clark 1980:6; T. D. Price 1987:229) as "the most important epoch in history."

CASE STUDY CLOSE-UP

The site of Star Carr is perhaps the best known of the Maglemosian Mesolithic sites because of its fine state of preservation and its exemplary excavation by British archaeologist J. G. D. Clark (1971). The site has been reinterpreted since the publication of Clark's research, and many of his specific conclusions have been questioned (T. D. Price 1982, 1987; T. D. Price and Feinman 1993). Nevertheless, all agree that Star Carr provides a richly detailed image of life in the Mesolithic of Western Europe.

The main occupation area of this 9,500-year-old settlement was probably in a high, dry area on a peninsula extending into a now-dry lake, and probably in an area destroyed before the site was excavated. Luckily, an extensive array of artifacts was lost in or discarded into the lake by the site's inhabitants. First encased in mud and later covered with peat, many organic artifacts at the site—including bone, antler, and even wood—preserved remarkably well, and Clark's meticulous excavation resulted in their recovery. Some 17,000 flint artifacts were found, along with an array of antler spearpoints, animal bones, a wooden paddle, and birch bark, in an excavation that covered 350 m^2 (3,780 ft^2).

The faunal assemblage at the site indicates that the inhabitants hunted red deer, roe deer, elk, ox, and pig. Since deer shed and grow their antlers at fixed intervals during the year, the presence or absence of antlers on the skulls of hunted animals, as well as the stage of antler development, can inform us concerning the season or seasons during which the site was inhabited. In an analysis of the antlers and skulls, it was shown that Star Carr was occupied most intensively in the summer, though evidence exists for a year-round human presence (T. D. Price and Feinman 1993:171).

Smaller mammals also were used by the inhabitants: The bones of fur-bearing animals such as fox, wolf, badger, beaver, and hare were found at the site. The inhabitants also ate birds: The bones of duck, mergansers, grebes, and cranes were recovered. Surprisingly, despite the excellent level of preservation, no fish bones were found, perhaps indicating the inhabitants' lack of interest in that particular lake resource. Also, though the lakeside was home

FIGURE 11.10

Sample of barbed antler harpoons from the Mesolithic site of Star Carr in England. (From *The Excavation at Star Carr* by J. G. D. Clark, Cambridge University Press, with permission)

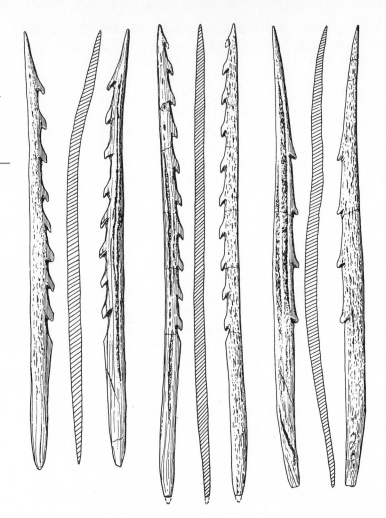

to a wide variety of plants, no direct evidence was collected at the site for the use of plant foods.

One category of tools found at the site could have been used for digging for roots—the elk antler **mattocks.** Flat sections of connected skull and antler were used as the digging blade, and a large hole was drilled through the base of the blade, into which a wooden handle was fastened. One of the mattocks found had a charred remnant of the wooden handle in place.

At Star Carr, the evidence points to the reliance on hunting for subsistence. Along with the faunal remains is substantial artifactual evidence. Most of the stone artifacts were manufactured on flakes removed from cores. Functionally, they comprise a hunter's tool kit with various cutting and scraping tools used in butchering and hide preparation. Though there are no stone spearpoints as such, an extensive assemblage of finely made antler and bone

FIGURE 11.11
Artist's conception of life at Star Carr, 9,500 years ago. (From *Ancient Britain* by James Dyer, B. T. Batsford Limited, with permission. Tracey Croft, artist)

barbed points exists: The stone burins were used to craft the antler and bone into tools. These antler and bone points are vicious-looking weapons, each with many sharp, down-pointing barbs (Figure 11.10). Once in an animal, they could not fall out or be pulled out without serious damage to the creature. These were highly effective hunting tools.

Star Carr provides a rich picture of life in the Mesolithic (Figure 11.11). The preservation of so much organic material allows for a detailed look at the subsistence of this group of post-Pleistocene people. Though it is difficult to generalize about Mesolithic culture precisely because it represents a period of such great diversity, one impression left by Star Carr probably can be widely applied: The inhabitants exploited a broad range of resources in their subsistence quest. In this sense, the people of Star Carr are models of the Mesolithic adaptation.

As a result of the common assumption that the early post-Pleistocene is a culturally uninteresting period, there are fewer places to visit that relate directly to this time in human antiquity. It is true that post-Pleistocene, pre-Neolithic sites produce less visually exciting artifacts and, therefore, are of less interest to casual tourists. You will find information on the pre-Neolithic in any museum that presents material on the origins of agriculture, at least as context for a display on the revolution in food production.

VISITING THE PAST

Perhaps one of the most impressive sites you can visit is that of Koster in Kampsville, Illinois. The Kampsville complex of research buildings is at the hub of an ambitious archaeology project that has identified thousands of sites in the area. The Koster site is the centerpiece of the work that has been conducted there. Though the Koster excavation itself has long been filled in, you'll find an on-site museum with displays focusing on the site.

SUMMARY

The common thread running through this chapter has been post-Pleistocene adaptation. Wherever we have looked in Europe, Asia, North and South America, Australia, or Africa we have seen the same trend. After about 12,000 B.P., human beings were faced with fundamental changes in the Pleistocene environments to which they had become adapted. Land covered in ice became exposed, temperatures rose, and some areas became drier, others wetter. Land connections were breached, and coastal configurations rapidly changed. Animals on which some humans subsisted became extinct, and new, different animals took their place. Plants became available that were useful for food, in the form of nuts, seeds, fruits, leaves, or roots.

People were faced with many options in the rapidly changing post-Pleistocene world. Some broadened the subsistence quest to include a wide variety of plant and animal resources. Some intensified the subsistence quest, focusing on a single resource or very few particularly productive resources. Some human groups became increasingly sedentary as they adapted to rich Holocene environments. As a result of the diversity of the post-Pleistocene resource base, cultural diversity increased exponentially, with myriad cultures proliferating, each thriving in its own territory.

Some settlements became more permanent, and population grew. In a number of cases, the food quest was intensified further still as groups attempted to increase the productivity of the resources on which they depended. This intensification set the stage for what will be discussed in Chapter 12: the revolution in food production.

TO LEARN MORE

There are some excellent sources on regional post-Pleistocene adaptations. For Europe, T. Douglas Price's (1987) "The Mesolithic of Western Europe" in the *Journal of World Prehistory* is a good place to start. For North America, see Brian Fagan's (1991a) text, *Ancient North America*. Another good book is Stuart Struever and Felicia Holton's (1979) *Koster: Americans in Search of Their Prehistoric Past*, which is aimed at a popular audience; see especially the chapter titled "A Day at Koster in 3500 B.C." An excellent source on this and other periods for South America is Karen Olsen Bruhns' (1994) *Ancient South America.* For the post-Pleistocene cultures of Australia, as for the rest of Australian prehistory, there is the venerable *A Prehistory of Australia, New Guinea, and Sahul* by J. Peter White and James F. O'Connell (1982). For Asia, the works by Kwang-Chih Chang (1986), *The Archaeology of Ancient China,* as well as by Charles Higham (1989), *The Archaeology of Mainland Southeast Asia,* have considerable discussions of the post-Pleistocene. For Africa, see David W. Phillipson's (1993) *African Archaeology.*

KEY TERMS

interglacials
interstadials
Younger Dryas
Mesolithic
Maglemosian
Hamburgian
Archaic

Lake Forest Archaic
lacustrine
Maritime Archaic
Mast Forest Archaic
Hoabinhian
camelid
littoral

Iberomaurusians
Capsian
microlith
backed blade
mattock

12

The Neolithic

ROOTS OF A REVOLUTION IN SUBSISTENCE AND SOCIETY

CHAPTER OVERVIEW

The Neolithic period represents a revolution in subsistence. Beginning about 12,000 years ago, some human groups began not just foraging for food, but actually producing it. Many different people began a slow process of artificial selection, tending plants and taming animals, allowing only those with characteristics desirable from a human subsistence standpoint to survive and propagate.

By 2,000 years ago, most human groups had adopted food production as their primary subsistence strategy.

CHRONOLOGY OF DOMESTICATION	12	11	10	9
Southwest Asia		sheep, barley, dog	wheat, lentils	goat, dog, cattle
Mesoamerica				
Africa				
East Asia			pig	
Europe				cattle
North America				
South America				

Thousands of years ago

8	7	6	5	4	3	2	1
			camel				
			maize	beans, squash, chili peppers			
sorghum	millet						
	chickpea, barley, lentil, wheat, sheep, goat, cattle		yams				
chicken, dog	rice						
millet, pig							
wheat, barley, legumes, sheep, goat, dog		millet, lentils					
			squash	sumpweed	smartweed, knotweed, maygrass, little barley, goosefoot	maize	
			sunflower				
	llama, alpaca		beans, chili peppers, ulluco, potato, manioc, cotton, quinoa	oca, maca, yacon, jicama, arracacha, maize			

Twentieth-century anthropologists are not the first to ponder the human past and to imagine how humanity has changed and evolved over the millennia. Many people, often through myth or legend, have tried to explain their own past and to chronicle major changes they realize must have occurred in their societies over time.

Consider, for example, the ancient Chinese legend of Shen Nung, first written down close to 3,000 years ago (Chang 1968). According to this legend, Shen Nung was a great hero who gave the people of China the tools necessary for the development of their civilization, including the knowledge of plant cultivation: "The ancient people ate meat of animals and birds. At the time of Shen Nung, there were so many people that the animals and birds became inadequate for people's wants, and therefore Shen Nung taught the people how to cultivate. . . . At the time of Shen Nung, millet rained down from Heaven. Shen Nung collected the grains and cultivated them" (Chang 1968:79).

The legend of Shen Nung represents a self-conscious attempt by the Chinese to explain what they understood as a fundamental change in their culture in past times—a shift from hunting and gathering to the cultivation of crops. Shen Nung gave the people the knowledge to plant, tend, and harvest crops, which, in turn, provided additional food. This rationale for the origins of agriculture actually sounds quite modern: the growth of human population beyond what hunting and gathering can support. We will see in this chapter's Issues and Debates that some twentieth-century anthropologists have suggested much the same cause.

Like the Chinese of 2,500 years ago, twentieth-century anthropologists also recognize the significance of agriculture in making modern life possible, and realize that humanity has not always had the knowledge of cultivation and animal husbandry. Like them, we seek to understand how and why we became agricultural. Our explanations do not rely on myth, but on scientific investigation of a period after the Pleistocene in many parts of the world when human groups began to change their relationship with their resource base. At that time a revolutionary change occurred. We call that revolution the **Neolithic.**

CHRONICLE

For most of human history, people have relied for their subsistence on **foraging**—hunting, fishing, and collecting wild plant foods. Myriad combinations of hunting, trapping, line and net fishing, collecting shellfish, digging for roots, harvesting wild grains, collecting seeds, nuts, and fruits, and so on have served to provide human groups with food for subsistence. Some groups had a broad resource base; others focused on a few highly productive resources. Some human groups were nomadic, continually traveling to wherever food could be found; others were more sedentary, staying in one place where a particularly abundant and constant food source was available. Some groups in some regions adhered to a schedule of movement that coincided with seasonal changes in resource availability; other groups in other regions followed a less varied schedule, doing much the same work and relying on the same set of food sources year-round.

What all these groups had in common, regardless of the particular plants or animals they relied on for food, was that those food sources were wild. For more than 99% of human prehistory, people have relied exclusively on the wild foods that nature provides (Figure 12.1). Only very recently have human groups begun actively to encourage the survival of certain wild plants or animals and to manipulate them so as to alter them from their ancestral state.

HUMANS TAKING THE PLACE OF NATURE: ARTIFICIAL SELECTION

Though we refer to the shift from foraging to farming as a revolution, that term may be misleading. In fact, settled agricultural life represents not so much a rapid revolution, but a point along a lengthy continuum of change. As archaeologist Naomi Miller (1992) lays out that continuum, it begins with foraging for wild foods and continues through a lengthy period of tending and encouraging plants or animals that are genetically identical to their wild relatives. In some instances, this may lead to manipulation of the reproduction of economically important plants or animals through **artificial selection,** that is, the directed evolution of new species possessing characteristics deemed beneficial to human beings. At this stage, human beings (in a manner analogous to natural selection as defined by Charles Darwin—see Chapter 2) select for propagation only those individuals within a plant or animal species that possess some natural endowments useful to people. In describing the "art" of artificial selection, Darwin pointed out: "One of the most remarkable features in our domesticated races is that we see in them adaptations, not indeed to the animal's or plant's own good, but to man's use or fancy" (1952:47).

So, both at the origins of agriculture and in our modern systems, humans protect and encourage only those individual plants that produce more or larger seeds, only those animals that exhibit less aggression and produce the most meat, milk, or wool, or only those trees that bear larger fruits. Selected individual animals in a wild species may be corralled and protected from predators. Certain individual plants within a wild species may be watered or weeded or planted near the village and then fenced in to prevent animals from eating them.

After many generations of such treatment, and as people have an increased opportunity to even more carefully select for propagation plants or animals with desirable characteristics, the cultivated plants and animals no longer resemble their wild ancestors or neighbors. They have been so altered through artificial selection that, again in a manner analogous to natural selection, they

FIGURE 12.1

The San people of the Kalahari are one of the very few foraging groups that survived into the twentieth century. (R. Lee/ Anthro-Photo)

can no longer be considered the same species. They have, in essence, coevolved with their human overseers, no longer changing under entirely natural conditions, but under the conditions established by people (Rindos 1984). Such plants and animals are said to be domesticated. Under extreme conditions of domestication, they cannot survive without human beings to attend to their needs and to propagate them. They are no longer adapted to a natural world but, rather, to a culturally constructed world of agriculture and animal husbandry. And in every case, the prehistoric record is clear: Wherever such a "revolution" occurred, it transpired over thousands of years. The following discussion documents such a process for the Near East, Mesoamerica, Asia, Africa, Europe, North America, and South America.

THE DOMESTICATION OF PLANTS AND ANIMALS

The **domestication** of plants and animals occurred in several world areas beginning after the end of the Pleistocene. There were two distinct contexts in which domestication occurred: "pristine" (or "primary") and "secondary" (Cowan and Watson 1992). As defined by C. Wesley Cowan and Patty Jo Watson in their edited volume *The Origins of Agriculture,* pristine situations are those in which the ancient culture engaged independently in a process that led to the domestication of locally available plants or animals. In a pristine situation, domesticated crops and animals are slowly added to a broader foraging subsistence base. Domesticates at first are a minor, supplementary component of the diet and become increasingly important as continuing refinements in the selected characteristics improve the quality of the food source for human exploitation. We will see that this process of independent, pristine agricultural development

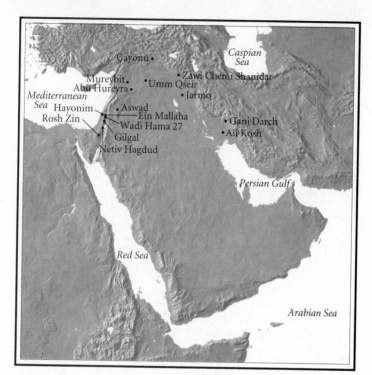

MAP 12.1
Archaeological sites in the Middle East where evidence of early food production has been found.

occurred in the Near East, Mexico, eastern North America, South America, Africa south of the Sahara, and East Asia.

Secondary conditions are those in which a local group adopts the already-domesticated plants and/or animals of another group. In some cases, the indigenous local adaptation was that of foraging for wild plants and animals, and a set of foreign domesticates supplemented and then ultimately replaced the local wild plant foods. This is the pattern seen in the archaeological record of Neolithic Europe and in the American Southwest. In other instances, the local economy was already using indigenous domesticates, which were then replaced by a set of superior (in yield, nutrition, and other features) plant and/or animal foods introduced from the outside. This was the process in eastern North America and parts of Africa.

THE NEAR EAST

Late Pleistocene people in the Near East, in what is now parts of Iran, Iraq, Israel, Jordan, Lebanon, Syria, and Turkey, exhibit a long period of intensive use of wild **cereal** grasses, especially wheat and barley (Map 12.1; Henry 1989; Maisels 1990; N. Miller 1992). Beginning along the Mediterranean and arcing first to the northeast and then down to the southeast, this area, today marked

FIGURE 12.2

The Fertile Crescent in the Near East provided rich habitats for Late Pleistocene and Early Holocene hunter/gatherers where the wild ancestors of some of the earliest domesticated crops grew.

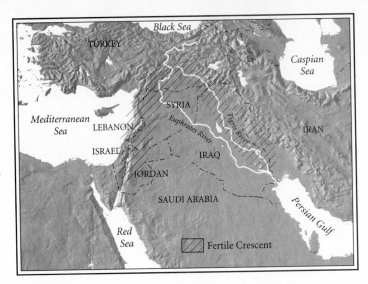

by highly productive agricultural lands, is referred to as the **Fertile Crescent** (Figure 12.2).

Late Pleistocene Foragers in the Near East

There are a number of distinct preagricultural societies in this general area, defined on the basis of differing stone tool industries, settlement patterns, and subsistence bases (Henry 1989). The **Geometric Kebaran,** beginning at about 14,500 B.P. and lasting until 12,500 years ago, is located in the moist Mediterranean woodlands of the central **Levant,** southward into the margins of the Negev and Sinai Deserts, and across southern Jordan. The contemporary Late Pleistocene **Mushabian** culture is located to the south in the steppe and arid zones of what today are the cores of the Negev and Sinai Deserts. The later **Natufian,** dating from about 13,000 to 9,800 B.P. is located in the Mediterranean woodland zone, part of the same area as the Kebaran from which it almost certainly developed. Farther north, in the foothills of the Zagros Mountains in Turkey, are the pre-Neolithic cultures of the **Zarzian** and **Karim Shahirian.**

As archaeologist Donald O. Henry (1989) indicates, the Mushabian sites seem to reflect the remains of small groups of highly mobile **simple foragers** with no particular focus on or commitment to any one food resource. Sites are small and impermanent, with direct evidence of the hunting of wild goats and gazelle. Dating to the same period as the Mushabian sites to the south, Kebaran sites vary more in size and complexity, indicating a pattern of population aggregation to take advantage of rich and seasonally available resources, particularly the wild cereal and nut foods available in the lowlands during spring and summer.

FIGURE 12.3

In Kenya, this traditional harvest, in which women use sickles, is probably quite similar to how wheat was harvested thousands of years ago in the Near East, where it was first domesticated. (Food and Agriculture Organization, United Nations, photo by Peyton Johnson)

The Origins of a Sedentary Life: The Natufian

It is during the Natufian, at about 13,000 years ago, that we see a dramatic shift in subsistence from simple to **complex foraging** based on plant foods. In complex foraging, subsistence is focused on a few rich resources. These are collected intensively and stored, both requiring and allowing for more sedentary, denser human populations. This pattern is reflected in the archaeological record of the Natufian by the appearance of grinding stones, food storage pits, pits for roasting plant foods, and microblades of flint exhibiting sickle polish. The stone blades exhibit a sheen or polish that has been shown through replicative experiment to be the result of their use in cutting cereal plant stalks like those of wheat, barley, millet, and sorghum (Unger-Hamilton 1989; Figure 12.3).

Kernels and stalks of wild wheat and barley have been found at many Natufian sites. For example, at Mureybit and Abu Hureyra, in Syria, wild einkorn wheat and vetch (a **legume**—a plant that produces pods with seeds) have been found in roasting pits dated to more than 11,000 years ago and as much as 13,000 years ago. These sites are located about 100 km (65 mi) from where wheat grows wild today. This may be an indication of intentional movement of the wild plant into a new territory by people consciously attempting to increase its geographical range. Carbonized kernels of wild barley, lentils, chickpeas, and field peas have been recovered at Wadi Hama 27 in Jordan, dated to 12,000 B.P.

Indirect evidence of the use of wild cereals by late Pleistocene people in the Near East includes heavy wear on human teeth (P. Smith 1972). This probably

315

resulted from the ingestion of stone particles that became mixed into the meal or flour when wild cereals were processed with stone grinding tools. An increase in the strontium level of human bones seen at these sites may be the result of an increase in the use of cereal grains at this time; high levels of strontium are found in these cereals (P. Smith, Bar-Yosef, and Sillen 1985).

The intensive collection and storage of wild cereals necessitates a more sedentary way of life because the food source stays put and needs to be monitored regularly for the best time to harvest. At the same time, the abundant and dependable wild cereals, legumes, and nut foods allow for a sedentary life. As a result, Natufian sites exhibit a far more complex and sophisticated architectural pattern than do the Mushabian or Kebaran. Whereas Mushabian and Geometric Kebaran sites generally are small and impermanent, preagricultural Natufian sites show the distinctive architecture of permanent villages. At Ein Mallaha, Hayonim Cave, and Rosh Zin in Israel, the remains of substantial houses with stone foundations ranging in diameter 2–9 m (about 6–29 ft) have been found (Henry 1989:211–212). Similarly substantial and permanent structures are known from Mureybet in Syria, where the preferred building materials were clay and wood, and Abu Hureyra in Syria, where the houses were built down into the earth. The amount of labor needed to build such domiciles is a clear indication that they were intended for long-term use.

Material culture, too, is far more complex and sophisticated at Natufian sites than at Mushabian or Kebaran sites. Bone, tooth, and shell beads and pendants are commonly found in burials. Dentalium shells, which were a favorite raw material, were available—often at great distances from the Natufian sites where found. Along with such items of personal adornment, other works of art have been recovered from Natufian sites, primarily carved stone statuettes of animals and people (Figure 12.4).

The First Agriculturalists

This focus on wild cereals beginning about 13,000 years ago resulted in what was probably the earliest domestication of plants in the world. Late Natufian and Karim Shahirian sites provide evidence of very early steps down the pathway of domestication sometime around 11,000 years ago. At Netiv Hagdud and Gilgal in Israel and at Ganj Dareh in Iran, barley kernels have been recovered that have been identified as an early domesticated version of that cereal. The size and morphology of the kernels distinguish them from wild barley, and they show features present in the domesticated grain. At Aswad in Syria and Çayönü in Turkey, domesticated wheats known as **emmer** and **einkorn** have been dated to more than 10,000 B.P. At both sites, lentils may also have been cultivated: At Aswad, 55% of the seeds of food plants recovered were from cultivated peas and lentils (N. Miller 1992:48).

The evolution of dependence on domesticated plants can be traced at the site of Ali Kosh in southwestern Iran: During the Bus Mordeh phase at

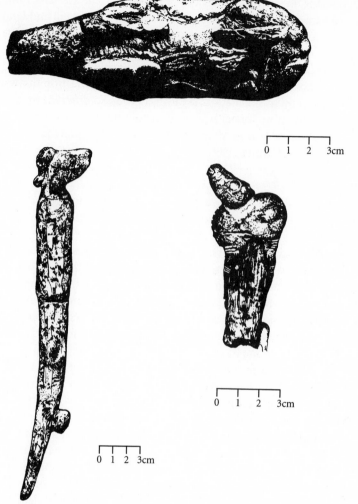

FIGURE 12.4

Natufian artwork: a carved animal (top) and two carved sickle hafts. (From *From Foraging to Agriculture: The Levant at the End of the Ice Age* by Donald O. Henry, University of Pennsylvania Press, with permission)

Ali Kosh, dated to more than 10,000 B.P., more than 29,000 seeds were recovered. The vast majority were from wild legumes and grasses, and only 10% were from domesticated emmer wheat and barley (Hole, Flannery, and Neely 1969:343). In the later Ali Kosh phase, 40% of the seeds were from domesticated emmer wheat; in the subsequent Mohammed Jaffar phase, the seeds of legumes rise to prominence.

In the Zagros Mountains, the site of Zawi Chemi Shanidar has produced a substantial faunal assemblage of sheep bones dated to 10,600 B.P. (G. Wright 1971). The population structure of the archaeological sample of the sheep is unlike what would be derived from a group of hunted animals. Almost all were slaughtered when young. This kind of consistency in the population profile of an animal species implies a level of control over the animals usually possible only under conditions of corralling. The animals, though genetically the same as those roaming wild, were kept, controlled, and tended by people. This incipient stage in domestication enabled the human overseers to dispose of (and eat) those animals with undesirable characteristics and to allow only those with attractive features to survive and reproduce more generations like them. This led to intensive and rapid selection that soon altered the captive animal population, creating a group so different from the wild population that it no longer was of the same species. This can be seen in changes in the bones of now-domesticated sheep and goats in the Near East after 10,000 B.P. (Gilbert 1989).

A Model of the Shift to a Food-Producing Way of Life in Southwest Asia

Archaeologist Donald O. Henry (1989) has proposed an explanation for what happened in the Natufian period in the Near East that led to the origins of agriculture: When Natufians abandoned a mobile pattern of simple foraging and adopted a complex foraging strategy, they produced an inherently unstable subsistence system. Whereas simple foragers faced with a food shortage can move to where food is more abundant, complex foragers (who have adopted a sedentary mode to exploit locally abundant wild plant foods) can, under the right circumstances with the right kinds of plants, artificially raise the "resource ceiling" (Henry 1989:4) of their territory by tending and encouraging economically important wild crops. In other words, complex foragers respond to a food shortage by beginning artificial selection.

In Henry's model, the Natufian pattern of complex foraging that focused on wild cereals and nuts expanded geographically when the Mediterranean woodlands, where wild cereals were particularly abundant, expanded as the Pleistocene waned and as conditions became wetter. But by 11,000 years ago, conditions changed for the worse: By 10,500 B.P. the Mediterranean woodlands that had sustained an increasing Natufian population had shrunk to half their size at the beginning of the Natufian. Having committed their subsistence energies to wild cereals whose abundance was declining, the Natufians responded by more actively encouraging those plants. This included tending the plants, as well as artificially selecting those that had beneficial characteristics. These were the first shots fired in the Neolithic revolution.

MESOAMERICA

Mesoamerica includes most of the modern nations located south of the United States and north of South America (including Mexico, Guatemala, Belize, El Salvador, the western regions of Honduras and Nicaragua, and northwestern Costa Rica). This area contributed many valuable agricultural crops

MAP 12.2

Archaeological sites in Mesoamerica where evidence of early food production has been found.

FIGURE 12.5

View of the Tehuacán Valley in central Mexico, where the earliest evidence of domestication in the New World has been recovered, dating to after 5,000 years ago. (© Robert S. Peabody Museum of Archaeology, Phillips Academy, Andover, Mass. All rights reserved. Photo by R. S. MacNeish and Paul Manglesdorf)

to the world, none more important than maize (corn), beans, and squash, the triumvirate of plants that provided the subsistence base for indigenous New World civilizations (see Chapter 14). The shift to an agricultural mode of subsistence has been documented in only a few sites: Guilá Naquitz Cave (Flannery 1986), Tamaulipas, and Tehuacán (MacNeish 1964, 1967). The Western Hemisphere's earliest evidence for the domestication of plants has been found in Mesoamerica (Map 12.2). Recent analysis dates the first New World domesticates to about 4700 B.P. (J. Long et al. 1989; Fritz 1994).

The Tehuacán Valley

One of the best-known sequences of domestication in the world comes from a dry highland valley in Mexico (Figure 12.5). The **Tehuacán** valley project was conducted in 1961–64 by archaeologist Richard MacNeish and an international team of fifty scholars from many disciplines (MacNeish 1964, 1967). The project resulted in a sequence of archaeological cultures spanning the period from 12,000 to 500 years ago, from the late Pleistocene to the period of initial European contact (De Tapia 1992).

The Cultural Sequence at Tehuacán

MacNeish defined a series of stages, or periods, in the valley based on evidence gathered from a series of occupied caves. He began the sequence with the **Ajuereado phase,** dated from 12,000 to 9,000 years ago. Recovered food remains indicate that hunting was of primary significance in the seasons when the caves were occupied. Sites were small and impermanent, leading MacNeish to suggest that small family groups—**microbands** of fewer than ten people each—wandered the valley, primarily hunting antelope and jackrabbit. Other, smaller fauna, such as turtles, rodents, gophers, and birds, were utilized, as were wild plant foods including avocado, foxtail grass, and amaranth, a grain (see Figure 12.7).

Toward the end of the Ajuereado phase, in the waning years of the Pleistocene, the Tehuacán valley experienced a period of drying that eliminated some of the resources on which local groups depended. In MacNeish's view, the increased aridity led to a decrease in the importance of hunting and an increased reliance on wild plant foods. This can clearly be seen in the subsequent **El Riego phase,** dated from 9,000 to 7,000 years ago. Strong evidence for an increasing focus on wild plants at this time can be seen in the preserved remains of wild squash, beans, chili peppers, amaranth, and avocado. In MacNeish's construct, the previous pattern of year-round nomadic microbands had been replaced during El Riego times with a more complex settlement system that included dry season fall/winter microbands but added larger macrobands during the wetter spring and summer months.

The settlement pattern of seasonal shifting from micro- to macrobands is continued in the **Coxcatlán phase,** dated from 7,000–5,400 B.P. The reliance on wild plant foods continued among those living in the caves. Later, in the **Abejas phase** (5,400–4,300 B.P.), an increasingly sedentary pattern of central-based bands was established. Larger, semipermanent villages or home bases were settled, though a geographically broad strategy of wild-food collection continued. During this phase domesticated plants first contributed to the diet; squash and maize date to this period in the valley.

Much less is known about the **Purrón phase** (4,300–3,500 B.P.) than about previous or subsequent phases. Pottery was used for the first time by the inhabitants of the valley, but little else is known. In the following **Ajalpán phase,** dating from 3,500 to 2,850 years ago, diet was based on foraging for wild foods as well as on domesticated maize, beans, and squash. Ajalpán settlements continued to grow, and the degree of sedentism increased from the previous phase. Simple irrigation canals were built to water crops, a clear indi-

cation of the importance placed on agriculture and further confirmation of the abandonment of a nomadic way of life (construction of canals represents a long-term commitment to stay in one place).

Dating the Shift to Agriculture at Tehuacán

In MacNeish's original analysis of the Tehuacán materials, the maize remains (Figure 12.6) were dated indirectly. Carbon dating is a destructive process, and the world's oldest maize specimens were deemed too valuable to sacrifice for dating purposes. Of necessity, MacNeish derived dates from more abundant (and less precious) additional organic remains and then associated those radiocarbon dates with maize remains found in the same layers. By this method MacNeish concluded that the oldest domesticated maize was about 7,000 years old, originating in the beginning of the Coxcatlán phase in the valley.

Unfortunately, caves like the ones MacNeish excavated can present the archaeologist with stratigraphy that is notoriously difficult to interpret. Especially in caves that have been used repeatedly over long periods, it is always possible that younger materials have worked their way down into deeper, older soil layers (for example, by burrowing animals or by people digging into the soil). So the validity of the dates derived for the maize has been a problem. Luckily, the recent introduction of **accelerator mass spectrometry (AMS)** dating (a form of radiocarbon dating) allows for the use (and destruction) of miniscule samples. As a result, twelve of the Tehuacán maize samples have now been dated directly. These direct dates, universally more recent than MacNeish's original determinations (A. Long et al. 1989; Fritz 1994), place the oldest maize to about 4,700 B.P., though some of the material may be a bit older (Fritz 1994).

As Gayle Fritz (1994) points out, this marks the earliest firm evidence so far for the domestication of plants in the New World. However, though quite different from modern corn, the Tehuacán maize cannot have been the first domesticated version of that plant. The oldest examples from Tehuacán are only an inch or two long, with eight rows of six to nine kernels each. But even these oldest, tiny cobs from Tehuacán exhibit a morphology that is entirely inappropriate for life in the wild. The kernels of this maize had been held tightly in place by long **glumes** (the casings in which individual kernels are enclosed). It took a human hand to remove the kernels from the glumes for eating or planting; the kernels would not have fallen out on their own and so the crop could no longer have survived in the wild. Human beings must have already selected for this characteristic before the date of the Tehuacán corn, perhaps because it made the early maize easier to harvest and to process without losing kernels. Older, even more primitive maize almost certainly will be discovered, bringing us back further toward the origin of its domestication in Mesoamerica. (Neolithic Portfolio, Color Plate 13.)

The Shift to Domesticated Foods Among the People of Tehuacán

The original analysis of dietary change through time at Tehuacán was based in part on the analysis of food remains in preserved fecal specimens recovered in archaeological strata in the excavated caves. A total of 116 preserved human fecal deposits were recovered in the valley. E. O. Callen (1967) was able to derive dietary percentages from the Tehuacán deposits. Unfortunately, those percentages necessarily reflect just a few meals of individual people, so Callen's statistics cannot be assumed to represent their diets over the long term. Moreover, if the caves were occupied only part of the year, then paleofeces and food remains recovered in middens or hearths reflect only those foods eaten when the caves were occupied. Since the caves were occupied during those seasons when wild plants were the subsistence focus, it stands to reason that the remains of wild plants would predominate in the archaeological record (Farnsworth et al. 1985:110), even if during the rest of the year other foods made significant contributions to the diet.

There is a way around this problem. An analysis of carbon isotopes has been successfully conducted on bones from twelve of the human skeletons recovered at Tehuacán, allowing for the reconstruction of the general diet of the inhabitants (Farnsworth et al. 1985). As discussed in Chapter 4, uptake of the ^{13}C isotope differs among plant groups. Those following the C4 photosynthesis pathway—chiefly grasses and sedges—use proportionally more ^{13}C than those following the CAM pathway—mostly succulents—which, in turn, use more than those following the C3 pathway—most trees, herbs, and shrubs. Animals (this includes people) incorporate into their bones proportions of ^{13}C that reflect the proportions in the plant foods they eat (or the proportions in the animals they eat, which reflect the proportions in the plant foods the animals eat). Since the carbon isotopes present in an individual's bones are the product of a lifetime's diet, seasonal changes or recent meals have little effect.

The isotope analysis of the Tehuacán material shows a clear jump in the reliance on C4 and/or CAM pathway plants early in the Tehuacán sequence and then little change thereafter. Because succulents are unlikely to sustain a human population, C4 plants were probably paramount. Therefore, tropical grasses must have been mainstays of the diet of the people who produced the archaeological sites in the Tehuacán Valley. Based on the isotope analysis, their overall diet (meaning, their reliance on C4 plants) did not change much for several millennia.

Combining MacNeish's reconstruction with the isotope data, the inhabitants of the valley appear to have gone through a long period of increasing sedentism before adopting an agricultural way of life. This lengthy period of dietary reliance on C4-pathway tropical grasses—including, perhaps, the wild progenitor of maize, **teosinte** (see Figure 12.19)—is similar to the situation seen in the Near East. Farnsworth and colleagues (1985:112) suggest that an extended period of reliance on wild plants and increasing sedentism in Tehuacán was "a Mesoamerican equivalent of the Natufian."

A Model of the Shift to a Food-Producing Way of Life in Mesoamerica

Kent Flannery (1968) has proposed a detailed explanation for the shift to an agricultural mode in Mesoamerica: The subsistence systems of Late Pleistocene Mesoamerica were inherently stable. The seasonally restricted availability of certain resources and scheduling preferences for some resources over others available at the same time of year maintained a stable system in which no one resource was so intensively exploited that its abundance was threatened. Such a system can be said to be in "equilibrium."

In Flannery's view, however stable such a system might have been, it was susceptible to even a minor change in general conditions. For example, a mutation in teosinte that produced more easily harvested plants (see this chapter's Issues and Debates section) might have rendered this previously minor wild food more attractive. To take advantage of this more desirable form of teosinte, other elements in the intricately balanced system may have been shifted. To encourage the growth of the new teosinte/wild maize, the settlement pattern may have changed to allow more time in those places where teosinte grew, to encourage the new form. But this could only have been accomplished by changing the entire system of seasonal movement and scheduling. A pattern of larger and more sedentary groups may have developed to take advantage of the new teosinte. Overall population would have increased, necessitating a

FIGURE 12.7

Agriculture established a new equilibrium for subsistence systems in Mesoamerica. Left: In this traditional agricultural field in modern Mexico, the farmer is harvesting amaranth that is growing among the corn plants. Right: The same process is seen in an image from a Spanish source dating to the sixteenth century. (Left: Courtesy Dan Early)

continual refinement through artificial selection of the new crop, to feed more mouths. Microbands would become macrobands, seasonal encampments semipermanent and then permanent villages.

In this way, the initial, casual, and almost accidental step of intensifying the exploitation of a crop could have thrown the entire system out of balance. The initial minor deviation from the established equilibrium would have become amplified as the culture tried to reestablish a new status quo. Other resources would have had to be granted less attention, resulting in the need to intensify further the use of the new crop. But intensification would have required a greater degree of sedentism, which would have meant even less time or opportunity for other resources. In Flannery's view, the intensification of the use of a particular food species can be the first step to the inevitable destruction of the subsistence system and the establishment of an entirely new equilibrium based on agriculture (Figure 12.7).

AFRICA

It cannot be said that there was a single agricultural revolution in Africa, or even that there was a single point of origin for the African shift to a domesticated food base. Africa is enormous and has a broad range of climates and environments and a wide range of plant and animal communities. Myriad hunting-and-gathering cultures developed in Africa during postglacial times, each adapting in its own way to its region. And many different food-producing

324

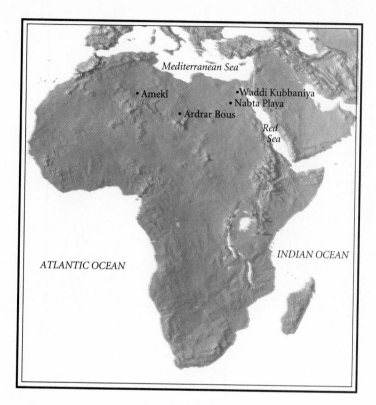

Mediterranean Sea

• Ameki

•Waddi Kubbaniya
• Nabta Playa

• Ardrar Bous

Red
Sea

ATLANTIC OCEAN

INDIAN OCEAN

MAP 12.3
*Archaeological sites in
Africa where evidence of
early food production has
been found.*

cultures developed in the African Neolithic, each devising its own adaptation
through food production of the available plants and animals (Map 12.3).

Neolithic Culture Complexes in Africa

Jack Harlan (1992) defines three distinct archaeological culture "complexes"
of the African Neolithic: Savanna, Forest Margin, and Ethiopian. Savanna
complex sites, located in the dry interior of central Africa, exhibit a reliance
on pearl millet, a plant known for its resistance to drought. Watermelon was
another important crop, not so much for its nutritive value, but for its ability
to store water and therefore to serve as a source of liquid. In the wetter, broad-
leaved savanna, sorghum and African rice played major roles in subsistence.
Other savanna plants contributing to the food quest were fonio (a cereal), Bam-
bara ground-nut, and kenaf, roselle, and tossa jute, all used as herbs in cooking.

In Harlan's Forest Margin complex, the focus is on forest resources combined with reliance on products of the savanna. Akee apples, Guinea millet,
and colas formed a part of the subsistence base. Oil palm and cowpea also were
important. Historically, the cultivation of yams, which grew wild on the forest
edge, was one of the most important contributors to subsistence. Finally, in

FIGURE 12.8

Sorghum, used in the United States primarily to produce animal feed, has been an important food crop historically, particularly in Africa, where it was domesticated as early as 8,000 years ago. (Food and Agriculture Organization, United Nations, photo by J. Chevalier)

Harlan's Ethiopian complex, finger millet, tef (a cereal), enset (a relative of the banana), and noog (which produces an edible oil) were significant.

A Chronology of Food Production

The African reliance on wild plants extends well back into the Late Pleistocene. At the Egyptian site of Waddi Kubbaniya, charred tubers of wild nutgrass have been dated to the period 18,000–17,000 years ago (Wendorf, Schild, and Close 1989; Wendorf et al. 1979). Heavily worn grindstones at the site were probably used to process the fat, starchy roots into flour. Stone blades inset into wooden or bone handles that served as sickles used in harvesting wild grains and the grinding stones necessary to process the grains into flour are both dated to 15,000–11,000 years ago in southern Egypt in a culture called the Qadan (Phillipson 1993).

An 8,000-year-old site in the Sahara Desert of southern Egypt, Nabta Playa, supplies further evidence of early Holocene subsistence in Africa. Researchers excavated one storage pit, fourteen hearths, and 122 cooking features (Wendorf et al. 1992). They recovered thousands of seeds representing forty different species of wild plants. Among the plants represented in the archaeological sample were sorghum and a number of varieties of millet (a grain crop). There are hundreds of varieties of sorghum; many produce edible grains, and others produce a sweet molasses or syrup. Millet and sorghum are commonly grown in modern, indigenous African agricultural systems (Figure 12.8). In fact, though not well known outside the semiarid tropics, millet and sorghum are the primary sources of protein in certain regions.

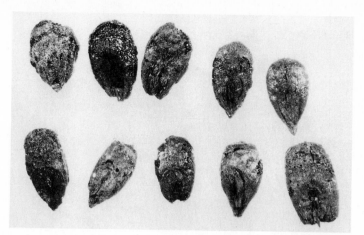

FIGURE 12.9

Charred seeds recovered from Nabta Playa. Among the forty or so plants identified in the archaeological sample were those of sorghum, in what has been identified chemically as an incipient stage of domestication. (Courtesy Dr. Krystyna Wasylikowa)

Also found in the storage and cooking features at Nabta Playa were the remains of various legumes, fruits, tubers, and nut foods. There is even some suggestion that the sorghum at least was in an incipient stage of domestication at this site (Figure 12.9). To the eye, the sorghum looks like the wild plant, but the chemistry of the fats within the seeds is more like that of the modern domesticate. The identification of the sorghum from the site as a domesticate on this basis, however, is still far from clear. Nevertheless, as the site researchers point out, it is a "short step" (Wendorf et al. 1992:724) from the intensive use of sorghum and other wild plants to their domestication.

The earliest clear evidence of a shift from foraging to food production in Africa dates to about 7,000 years ago, in an area that today is the Sahara Desert. A wet period, or **pluvial,** began about 8,000 B.P., and lakes dotted areas that today are desert. Faunal evidence indicates that **pastoralists** raising sheep, goats, and cattle proliferated throughout the Sahara during this wet period. A thousand years later, by 7,000 B.P., early agriculturalists were living along the Nile River in Egypt, raising sheep, goats, and cattle, and planting barley, emmer, lentil, and chickpea for food and flax for linen. The wild ancestors of domesticated sheep and goats are not native to Africa. These animals can be traced to the Middle East and Europe, where they lived in the wild and where domesticated versions appeared earlier than in Africa. Some of the crops were likewise introduced from the outside, but some may have been the result of indigenous experimentation. Also, though it has long been assumed that domesticated cattle moved into Africa from southwest Asia, where they are a thousand years older, recent DNA analysis supports the idea that Africans independently domesticated their indigenous wild cattle at this time (Zimmer 1994).

Neolithic Cultures South of the Sahara

In Africa south of the Sahara, another set of largely independent agricultural revolutions took place, focusing on entirely indigenous tropical crops. Vari-

FIGURE 12.10

Though a mainstay of agriculture in modern Asia, rice was not the first crop domesticated on that continent. (Top: *Preparation of the seed bed for rice sowing.*) *Even long after its domestication about 7,000 years ago, rice remained a minor component of the diet. Today, along with wheat and corn, it is one of humanity's primary foods.* (Bottom: *a modern rice paddy.*) (Both photographs, Food and Agriculture Organization, United Nations; *top:* photo by F. Botts, *bottom:* photo by Banoun/Caracciolo)

ous millets (pearl, foxtail, finger, bullrush, broomcorn) were domesticated in tropical Africa. Domesticated pearl millet has been found dating to as early as 6,500 years ago—for example, at the Ameki site (Harlan 1992). Early sorghum domestication is seen at the Adrar Bous site dating to 4,000 B.P. Yams, African rice, tef, fonio, groundnuts, ensete, and noog are among other, entirely indigenous crops that were domesticated in sub-Saharan Africa in antiquity—all of which are unknown in the rest of the Neolithic world.

MAP 12.4

Archaeological sites in East Asia where evidence of early food production has been found.

EAST ASIA

Most of us in the western world think of rice as the agricultural food base of Asian peoples (Figure 12.10). As pointed out by archaeologist Gary Crawford (1992:8), however, there actually are 284 separate taxa of domesticated plants and animals known to have been used in east Asia, and rice actually turns up rather late in the sequence.

Chronology of Food Production in China

The earliest evidence of plant or animal domestication in China from the Zengpiyan Cave site in Guilan dates to the period after 10,300 B.P. (Map 12.4). A large proportion (85%) of the animal bones are those of young pigs, less than two years of age (Chang 1986:102–103). As was the case at Zawi Chemi Shanidar in Iraq, this may indicate that the animals were not being hunted in the wild, but were kept and tended. That the canine teeth are smaller than in a wild pig population may be explained by the artificial selection for the propagation of less dangerous animals with smaller teeth.

In northern China, the earliest Neolithic culture currently recognized is the **Peiligang,** as represented by sites such as Cishan, Peiligang, Laoguantai, Dadiwan, and Lixiatsun (Chang 1986). Dating to between 8,500 and 7,000 years ago, the Peiligang culture is centered in the deciduous forest zone of northern China. The evidence shows clearly that Peiligang sites do not represent the first steps toward settled life based on agriculture; Peiligang sites are already well-established farming villages, with hunting, fishing, and the gathering of wild plants also contributing to the food quest. Cultigens include foxtail millet, broomcorn millet, and Chinese cabbage. Domesticated animals include pig, dog, and chicken.

The better-known, later Neolithic culture of China is called the **Yang-shao.** Typified by the Ban Po site near Xian, Yang-shao sites are five times larger than Peiligang sites, and the villages are not arranged as haphazardly; they appear to have been planned out before construction. Crops of the Yang-shao include foxtail millet, Chinese cabbage, and, for the first time in China, rice, though still a minor component of the diet. The earliest domesticated rice in China has been identified at the Hemudu site on the Yangtze River just south of Shanghai, with a radiocarbon date of 7,000 B.P. (Crawford 1992:25).

The proportion of carbon isotopes in the human bones recovered at Yang-shao sites has been interpreted as indicating that nearly three-fifths of the diet was supplied by millet (An 1989). The various millets are grasses producing a large quantity of small seeds in long spikes. The seeds are ground into a flour and used in porridge and bread.

Food Production in Southeast and Northeast Asia

The situation is not as clear in the rest of east Asia. Spirit Cave in northeast Thailand (mentioned in Chapter 11) shows a clear reliance by about 12,000 B.P. on foods that were to become an integral part of the agricultural economies of later Neolithic peoples, including soybean, almond, cucumber, and water chestnut (Gorman 1972). A possibly early form of domesticated rice—at least rice that has been altered only slightly from its wild form—has been identified at Non Nok Tha in Thailand, dating to 5,500 B.P. (Chang 1986). Indisputable evidence for domesticates in southeast Asia come from excavations in the Chao Phraya valley in northeast Thailand at sites dated to about 5,000 years ago (Higham 1989:80). The hunting and gathering of wild foods, along with the cultivation of rice, was the basis of this economy.

Data for Korea are sparse. Soils are very acidic, and few organic remains have been recovered in early archaeological contexts. We do know that by 3,000 B.P., domesticated millet was used in a mixed economy that included hunting, fishing, gathering, and agriculture (Nelson 1993). Some archaeological evidence, in the form of increased sedentism, suggests that farming may have begun a couple of thousand years earlier.

There is far more information for Japan, but the sequence is not clear. The Late Pleistocene/Early Holocene Jomon culture had a foraging subsistence base, with an emphasis on resources of the sea. This productive resource

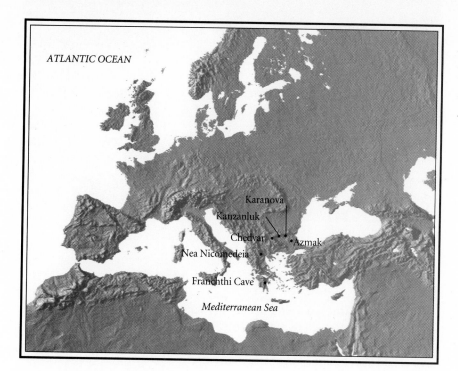

base allowed for a sedentary settlement pattern, with dense populations, elaborate material culture, and some large, semipermanent villages at more than 10,000 years ago. Evidence of domesticates, including rice, soybean, adzuki bean, buckwheat, and pear, does not appear at Jomon sites but appears in the later Yayoi culture, dated to about 2,400 B.P.

EUROPE

Europe is a diverse continent with a complex prehistory. As for a shift to an agricultural mode of subsistence, it can be argued that, as for Africa, there was not one revolution but several (Whittle 1985). As archaeologist Robin Dennell (1992) indicates, a series of parallel shifts to domesticated plants and animals occurred in southeast Europe, central Europe, along the northern margin of the Mediterranean, in the Alps, along the Atlantic coast, and in eastern and northeastern Europe. These agricultural revolutions, though not entirely independent of one another, occurred at different times, involved different crop and animal species, and had varying degrees of success (Map 12.5).

FIGURE 12.11

At Franchthi Cave in Greece wild oats, barley, peas, and lentils were eaten by the inhabitants more than 8,000 years ago. (Courtesy Thomas W. Jacobsen)

The Shift to Agriculture in Southeast Europe

The earliest evidence of a shift toward agricultural life comes from southeast Europe. As seen elsewhere in the world, this shift is prefaced by an extended period during which the subsistence focus was on the wild ancestors of crops that would later become important domesticates. For example, Franchthi Cave in Greece (Figure 12.11) contains evidence of the exploitation of wild oats, barley, peas, and lentils by 13,000 years ago (Hansen 1981). Pear and pistachio also appear to have been used during the early occupation of the cave.

By about 7,500 years ago, the focus on wild plants seems to have evolved into at least a partial reliance on domesticated crops. At Nea Nicomedeia, also in Greece, levels dated to this time produced evidence of domesticated varieties of wheat, barley, and legumes (Whittle 1985). Similar evidence was found at the sites of Azmak, Karanovo I, Chevdar, and Kazanluk in Bulgaria, where wheat, lentils, and grass-pea seem to have been the most important food crops (Dennell 1992:77).

The Shift to Agriculture in Western Europe

Throughout the rest of Europe, the shift to agriculture seems to have taken place later than in the southeast. For example, sites in the Swiss Alps exhibiting a reliance on domesticated crops, including emmer and bread wheat, lentils, peas, and millet, date to after 5,500 B.P. In the central European, early Neolithic culture called **Linienbandkeramik (LBK),** a subsistence base that included emmer, barley, and pulses (grainlike legumes) has been traced back to about 6,500 B.P. Along the Atlantic coast, in Great Britain, France, and Spain, evidence of the use of domesticates (a similar mixture of cereals and legumes) dates to no more than about 6,000 years ago.

For the most part, the Neolithic of Europe appears to have been imported from the south and east. Virtually all of the crops important in the European Neolithic, including einkorn, barley, bean, vetch, and lentils, are demonstrably Near Eastern in origin; there is little or no evidence for the existence of wild forms in Europe. The first appearance of these crops is in their domesticated form in the cultural contexts of archaeological sites dating to after 8,000 years ago. Often, these domesticated food sources seem to have been superimposed on an earlier, indigenous Mesolithic subsistence pattern (see Chapter 11) based on hunting animals and gathering acorns and hazel nuts (Dennell 1992). Certain crops—oats and some legumes—were probably domesticated independently by Europeans, but evidence so far indicates that this occurred rather late in the Neolithic, after Near Eastern domesticates had already entered (via migrating farmers) and become important parts of the food base.

NORTH AMERICA

One of the most enduring images of the Indians of eastern North America is that of the natives helping the Pilgrims of seventeenth-century Plymouth, in Massachusetts, to survive their first winter in the New World. They brought the European settlers corn, beans, and squash and taught them how to plant and prepare these native agricultural foods.

Indeed, most historical native cultures in North America that were agricultural were dependent on these three crops. As we have seen earlier in this chapter, however, the wild ancestors of two of these crops—maize and beans—were tropically adapted plants, certainly not native to New England or the rest of North America. These crops were introduced into those areas north of Mexico in some unknown way (trade, migration, indirect contact?).

It is clear, however, that when maize penetrated the eastern woodlands of native America sometime after 1,800 years ago, it did not replace an indigenous system of foraging for wild foods. Instead, maize initially supplemented an aboriginal pattern of hunting, collecting wild plants, and cultivating native squash and locally available seed plants. An independent, "pristine" pattern of indigenous domestication was established at about 4,000 B.P., more than 2,000 years *before* the initial appearance of maize in the east (B. D. Smith 1989, 1992, 1995).

Indigenous Domestication North of Mexico

The primary native crops domesticated by the Indians of the eastern woodlands were sunflower, sumpweed (also known as marsh elder), goosefoot (also called lamb's-quarter), and pigweed—all producers of starchy or oil-rich

FIGURE 12.12

A modern, many-headed form of sunflower. The sunflower was domesticated by the native inhabitants of eastern North America by about 4,200 years ago, at least 2,400 years before the introduction of Mesoamerican cultigens. (K. L. Feder)

seeds (Figure 12.12; Map 12.6). At Napoleon Hollow in Illinois, for example, charred sumpweed seeds retrieved from a 4,000-year-old archaeological deposit are uniformly larger (by almost a third) than the seeds of wild sumpweed (Ford 1985). The oldest evidence of domesticated sunflower has been dated to 4,265 B.P., at the Hayes site in central Tennessee, where the seeds are substantially larger than those of wild varieties (B. D. Smith 1995:191). Goosefoot seeds from Newt Kash Hollow and Cloudsplitter Rockshelter in Kentucky, though not larger, do have significantly thinner seed coats than wild plants. This is most likely the result of intentional human selection for plants that produced seeds with inedible coverings that were thinner and therefore easier to penetrate and remove. Both sites have been dated to about 3,400 B.P.

Squash was domesticated in Mesoamerica as part of a triad of agricultural crops that also included maize and beans. Though squash was long thought to have moved into North America from Mexico, archaeological evidence now indicates that it was domesticated independently in eastern North America as well. Squash seeds recovered at the Phillips Spring site in Missouri, dating to 4,500–4,300 B.P., are significantly larger than their modern wild counterparts (B. D. Smith 1995). The date for the site places squash domestication in eastern North America at about the time of the domestication of some of the seed crops mentioned earlier, further supporting a picture of a broad indigenous agricultural revolution in the east, two millennia before the introduction of maize.

The degree of reliance on these native domesticates is difficult to determine. One important source of quantitative information comes from Salts Cave in Kentucky, dated to between 2,600 and 2,200 B.P. In the 119 paleofeces found in the cave, domesticated goosefoot, sunflower, and marsh elder seeds make up nearly two-thirds of the undigested food remains recovered (goosefoot 25%, sunflower 25%, marsh elder 14%; Yarnell 1974, 1977).

Farming communities based on these native domesticates proliferated in the eastern woodlands, specifically in the American Midwest and Midsouth, between 3,000 and 1,700 years ago. Along with goosefoot, pigweed, marsh elder, and sunflower, other crops that were used included knotweed, maygrass, squash, and a little barley. As B. D. Smith (1992) indicates, the representation of the remains of these plants varies across the Midwest and Midsouth during this period. Their overall significance varied in different times and places as these domesticates became incorporated into a "mosaic of regionally variable . . . food production systems" (B. D. Smith 1992:109).

The Appearance of Maize in the Eastern Woodlands

Maize begins to turn up in the archaeological record by about 1,800 B.P.; some of the earliest evidence in North America for use of this most significant New World domesticate has been found at the Icehouse Bottom site in eastern Tennessee, with a radiocarbon date of 1,775 B.P. (Chapman and Crites 1987). The Holding site, east of St. Louis, also has produced maize and may be slightly

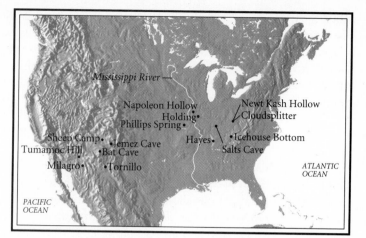

MAP 12.6

Archaeological sites in North America where evidence of early food production has been found.

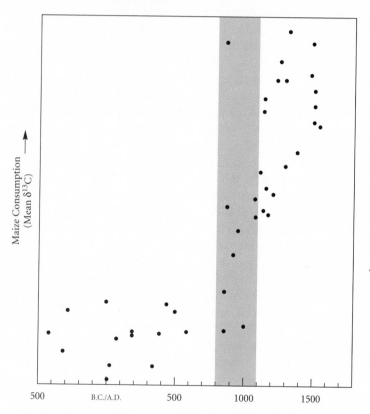

FIGURE 12.13

The dramatic jump in the level of ^{13}C concentration in the bones of prehistoric Native Americans around A.D. *1000 is taken to indicate an increase in the reliance on maize agriculture in eastern North America.* (From *The Emergence of Agriculture* by Bruce Smith. Copyright © 1995 by Scientific American Library. Used with the permission of W. H. Freeman and Company)

older (B. D. Smith 1995:191). For close to 1,000 years, however, maize continued to be a minor component of a broad subsistence system that still included hunting, fishing, collecting wild plants, and cultivating native seed crops. Analysis of human bone carbon isotope chemistry clearly shows the shift away from C3 and toward C4 pathway plants just before A.D. 1,000 (Figure 12.13).

All of the wild and indigenously domesticated crops of eastern North America are C3 plants; maize, however, is a C4 plant. This shift occurred about 1,000 years ago—sometime between A.D. 900–1,000—when maize took its place in North America at the core of the subsistence system, enabling the evolution of the most complex archaeological culture of North America, the Mississippian temple mound builders of the Midwest and Southeast (see Chapter 15).

The American Southwest

Unlike the situation in eastern North America, there is little evidence in the Southwest for the development of agricultural economies before the introduction of the Mesoamerican domesticates of maize, beans, and squash. These crops moved in and became part of the subsistence base of people who had not practiced agriculture previously.

AMS dates on maize from Bat Cave in western New Mexico and Tornillo Rockshelter in the southern part of that state show the crop to have been present by about 3,200 B.P. (B. D. Smith 1995:202–203). A growing list of other sites shows the appearance of maize by 3,000 years ago or soon thereafter—for example, Milagro in Arizona, and Tumamoc Hill and Jemez Cave in New Mexico (Minnis 1992). As Bruce Smith (1995) points out, it was during the four-century span between 3,200 and 2,800 B.P. that maize fully penetrated the American Southwest. Domesticated squash has been dated to about the same period [at Sheep Camp Shelter (Simmons 1986)], and beans appear to have come in 200 or 300 years later.

Though maize, squash, and beans originated as Mesoamerican crops, no Mexican artifacts or lifeways came north along with them. There was no movement of Mexican farmers northward, just the movement of the idea of domestication and the crops themselves, perhaps through trade. Most everything else in Southwest culture—their tools, pots, habitations—remained more or less the same. Mesoamerican crops simply were grafted onto already existing lifeways. These new foods required only minor cultural adjustments, and the native people continued to exploit the wild plants and animals they always had.

Archaeologist Alan Simmons (1986:83–84) suggested that maize was initially a secondary and supplemental resource for otherwise nonagricultural people in the Southwest. Maize would have been planted in late spring and early summer and harvested in the late fall for use as a "survival food" in the leaner winter months. A little bit of extra work in preparing the soil and planting the crops provided extra food and perhaps greater subsistence stability. Archaeologist Paul Minnis (1992:122) calls it "casual agriculture."

This pattern was successful, continuing essentially unchanged for more than a thousand years. It is only around 2,000 B.P. that Southwestern cultures begin to shift their subsistence drastically, relying ever more completely on domesticated crops.

SOUTH AMERICA

South America, like Africa, is enormous and contains a broad range of habitats with their attendant diverse plant and animal communities. As in Africa, this geographic expanse and biological diversity means human groups evolved many different regional cultural adaptations. And again, there was not just a single agricultural revolution in South America, but several (Map 12.7).

Three Regional Neolithics

Archaeologist Deborah Pearsall (1992) divides the South American Neolithic into three physiographic areas: low altitude, mid-altitude, and high altitude. Different plants growing wild in each of these divisions became the basis for distinct agricultural revolutions, with some crops from individual areas expanding into the others.

MAP 12.7
Archaeological sites in South America where evidence of early food production has been found.

After about 10,000 B.P. in South America, the system of foraging for wild
foods developed by Paleoindians was replaced by a more diverse and regionally specialized series of subsistence systems. In the Andes, hunters shifted
from megafauna to small post-Pleistocene game like deer and camelids (guanaco and vicuña). Elsewhere, subsistence shifted to a reliance on the abundant
root crops of both the lowlands and the highlands; there is evidence in Chile
for the use of a wild species of potato at Monte Verde by about 10,000 years
ago (see Chapter 10 for a discussion of the earliest occupation of that site).

The timing of the appearance of domesticates in South America is still
unclear, and AMS dating has not yet been widely applied, so the plant remains themselves have not been dated directly. Some researchers argue for an
early agricultural revolution dating back to close to 10,000 years ago, but the
evidence so far presented has been equivocal.

There is evidence of the domestication of common beans and chili peppers
at Guitarrero Cave in highland Peru by 5,000 years ago (located in Pearsall's
mid-altitude division) (Kaplan, Lynch, and Smith 1973; Lynch et al. 1985).
Also interpreted as an early domesticate at this site is the root crop ulluco, a
source of brightly colored, carbohydrate-rich **tubers.** Ulluco is still popular
as a delicacy in parts of South America. Dating to about the same time, in
Holocene South America, is Tres Ventanas Cave. The inhabitants were eating
domesticated potato, manioc (the root crop from which tapioca is made),
and other root crops.

Domesticated squash and gourds were recovered at Ayacucho Cave. Also at
this site is some of the earliest evidence for the domestication of an extremely
important crop in the agriculture of South America: quinoa (Figure 12.14).
Quinoa is a species of the genus *Chenopodium.* North American goosefoot is
another species in this genus. The earliest evidence of domesticated quinoa
comes from Panaulauca Cave in Peru. Quinoa seeds with thinner seed coats

than wild specimens have been dated there to between 4,000 and 5,000 B.P. (B. D. Smith 1995:173). Quinoa plants produce particularly nutritious seeds, with a mix of amino acids superior to the better-known grains (see the Issues and Debates section). In some areas of South America, particularly the higher altitudes, quinoa exceeded maize in agricultural importance (McCamant 1992). Only the potato was more important in the diet of the inhabitants of high-altitude South America.

Cold-loving, high-altitude-adapted domesticated root crops, especially the potato, were the staples of much of upland South America. The potato, today a major component of European cuisine, was certainly South America's most significant agricultural contribution to Europe. Other important root crops, today unknown to most North Americans, also played important roles in the diet of ancient South America (Vietmeyer 1992). Oca, second in importance only to the potato, produced nutritious tubers at altitudes up to 13,500 ft. The turniplike maca was cultivated at elevations of 14,000 ft, making it the only domesticated food crop able to be grown at that altitude. Other high-altitude roots domesticated and relied on as sources of food in the South American uplands were yacon, the legume jícama, ulluco, and arracacha. The 500-year-old Inca culture (to be discussed in Chapter 14) which occupied large portions of the western highlands of South America, relied more heavily on root crops than any of the world's ancient civilizations.

In lowland South America, domestication followed its own, largely separate path. At Chilca Caves, evidence has been recovered of domesticated manioc and sweet potato. Also at Chilca Caves is domesticated jícama, beans, and bottle gourds.

Though maize became a significant element of South American subsistence, it appears late in the sequence, probably after 4,000 B.P. [B. D. Smith (1995:159) suggests a date of 3,200 B.P.]. The first evidence of maize in South America was found at the Vegas site on the Ecuadorian coast. Though most archaeologists believe that maize was domesticated in Mesoamerica and diffused from there into South America, where it was adopted by cultures already practicing agriculture with their own, native crops, that conclusion is not unanimous. As Karen Bruhns (1994) points out, we simply do not know the ancient geographical extent of teosinte. This wild ancestor of maize may have grown in South America, where local people could have carried out the same selective process as their northern neighbors. In any event, maize did not become an essential part of the diet in South America until well after 4,000 B.P.

Animal Domestication in South America

Unlike the Old World, where domesticated animals were a major part of human diets, animal husbandry played a relatively minor role in the New World. Among the few New World species that were successfully domesticated were the guinea pig (used as a food), the turkey, the dog, and the Muscovy duck.

FIGURE 12.15

Llamas and alpacas were the only large animal species domesticated in the New World. Llamas, like this one, were used as beasts of burden and for food. (Food and Agriculture Organization, United Nations, photo by F. Mattioli)

By far the most significant animal domestication in the New World was in South America (Kent 1987).

As mentioned earlier, the wild camelid species, the guanaco and vicuña, were exploited by post-Pleistocene hunters in western South America. In the central Andes, camelids became increasingly important in the diet, replacing deer as the subsistence focus sometime after 8,000 years ago. Though why this shift occurred remains unclear, the ratio of camelid to deer bones increases dramatically as wild camels were exploited more intensively.

Vicuñas and guanacos are herd animals, with rigid dominance hierarchies. Their pattern of living in social groups and adhering to social hierarchies, along with their territoriality, rendered them attractive candidates for herding, controlling, taming, and then domesticating. Humans, placing themselves in the position of the most dominant members of the herd, could have exerted control over herds of wild camelids within their defined territory. Through artificial selection for animals more amenable to carrying heavy burdens and for animals that produced more meat and thicker wool, ancient South Americans produced the domesticated llama (as beasts of burden and for meat) and alpaca (for their wool and meat; Figure 12.15). Earliest evidence for this domestication has been found at Pachamachay and Lauricocha Caves in Peru, dating to as much as 6,500 B.P. (Wing 1977).

Cotton

As was the case in the Near East, where flax was domesticated for use as a fiber at about 7,000 B.P., a nonfood domesticate became an important element in the agricultural complex of South America. Domesticated cotton has been recovered at Ayacucho Cave dating to just after 5,000 years ago.

Cotton has also been recovered at the El Paraíso site on the Peruvian coast, a large and permanent settlement that has been dated to between 3,800 and 3,500 B.P. (Quilter et al. 1991). Eight or nine large complexes of rooms, covering a broad area, demarcate the site. Evidence found there suggests a mixed and broad subsistence base. Remains of domesticated food crops were recovered, including squash, chili pepper, common and lima bean, jícama root, and fruits, especially guava. At least of equal importance in the food quest were the rich natural resources of the coast, including anchovies, mussels, and clams. Wild plant foods also contributed to the subsistence base.

Remains of domesticated cotton were far more abundant at the site than any of the domesticated foods. Cotton fiber was a major raw material for the production of fishing nets and lines as well as cloth. The authors of the El Paraíso report maintain that the growth of this site is attributable to its location, perfect for the growing of cotton. Later, cotton became a major fiber for use in textiles of many cultures in South America.

HOW WAS DOMESTICATION ACCOMPLISHED?

ISSUES AND DEBATES

In the domestication of plants and animals, human beings take the place of nature in the selection process. We can examine how this may have occurred for a number of different crops: wheat, North American seed crops, maize, and beans.

The Domestication of Wheat

The **rachis** of wild wheat—the area of attachment of the individual kernels of wheat—becomes quite brittle when the wheat ripens. A brittle rachis is a distinct advantage in nature. It promotes seed dispersal, which, in turn, promotes the growth of more wheat plants in the following growing season. When the kernels are ripe, a brittle rachis can be shattered by the wind, a rain storm, or even an animal walking through a field (Figure 12.16).

Within any community of wild wheat plants today are individual plants that possess a combination of mutant genes for rachis form that results in a tougher, less brittle seed spike. Under conditions of natural selection, such forms are always in the minority, and they are at a clear disadvantage in terms of propagation: Their seeds are far less likely to disperse into the surrounding soil (see Figure 12.16).

When humans enter the picture, however, the nature of selection changes drastically. Though preferred under wild conditions, a brittle rachis is *disadvantageous* for humans harvesting a wild crop, especially for those using a sickle to cut the plants off at the base. The impact of the tool is likely to shatter a brittle rachis, widely disperse the seeds, and make harvesting quite time-consuming.

FIGURE 12.16

Seed heads of wild and domesticated varieties of einkorn and emmer wheat.

EINKORN   EMMER

wild   domesticated   wild   domesticated

FIGURE 12.17

One of the many modern forms of wheat. (Food and Agriculture Organization, United Nations, photo by the Kenya Information Office)

Either by accident or by design—and likely a combination of the two—when humans harvested wild wheat, a greater proportion of the mutant plants with a tough rachis were brought back to the village. Most of the seeds of the more abundant plants with brittle connections simply fell off and did not make it back to the settlement. Again either by accident or by design, more of the seeds of tough-rachis plants carrying the genetic instructions for that tough rachis became planted near human habitations. In this way, human beings changed fundamentally the process of selection, replacing a natural context for a human context to which the plants adapted (Figure 12.17).

Seed Bed Selection in Eastern North America

The indigenous domestication that occurred in eastern North America beginning about 4,000 years ago is another example of ancient domestication. Archaeologist Bruce Smith (1992:106) suggests the following scenario: The ancient inhabitants of eastern North America had developed a subsistence strategy that included wild sunflower, goosefoot, marsh elder, and pigweed. In an attempt to increase their harvest of these wild plants, Native Americans could have encouraged their growth by intentionally planting them in spring seedbeds near semipermanent villages (the site of Koster discussed in Chapter 11 is an example).

Like all people who rely on wild plants, the ancient Indians of eastern North America had a detailed knowledge of the characteristics of those plants and knew full well that seeds produce plants. They also were aware of the conditions necessary for the plants to flourish in their seedbeds. Just like modern gardeners tending domesticated crops, ancient people would have tended these spring seedbeds carefully. There would have been a high level of

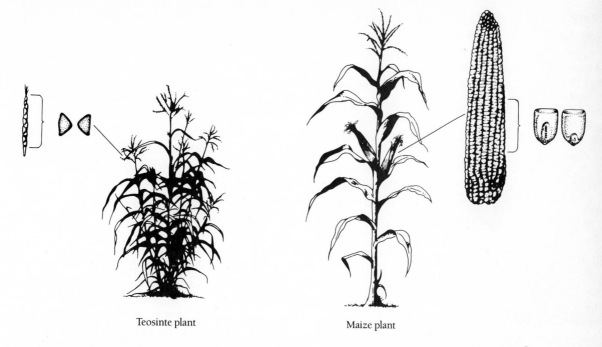

Teosinte plant

Maize plant

FIGURE 12.18
*Teosinte plant, spike, and
seeds and maize plant, cob,
and kernels.*

unintentional artificial selection for plants that produced larger seeds: Where the endosperm is larger, food reserves for growth are greater and the plant grows faster. Slower-growing plants are normally weeded out of a patch to provide room for the larger and faster-growing varieties. In the same way, seeds with thinner seed coats sprout more quickly, again giving the young plants a jump on the competition in the seedbed. Later-germinating (thicker seed coats), slower-growing (smaller seeds) plants are at a distinct selective disadvantage under the culturally controlled conditions of a seedbed. Generations of encouraging the growth of those plants that produced larger seeds with thinner seed coats because they grew more quickly created plants that produced seeds with more food and that were easier to process into flour. And this process resulted in plants that had been so intensively manipulated by human action that they no longer resembled their wild antecedents. They had been, in fact, domesticated.

From Teosinte to Maize

Wild maize, or teosinte, in some respects resembles the corn plant with which we are familiar. In fact, primitive varieties of maize are nearly identical to teosinte in cell form and genetic structure (Galinat 1992). However, teosinte produces not large cobs with rows of plump kernels, but small seed spikes, each with a brittle rachis and tiny, thickly encased seeds (Figure 12.18).

FIGURE 12.19

Teosinte is the wild ancestor of maize. This is a modern variety (Zea mays parviglumis), *from the Rio Balsas in Mexico, which may be the form from which domesticated maize is descended.*
(Courtesy of Dolores Piperno, Smithsonian Tropical Research Institute)

Teosinte seeds are nutritious and were exploited by ancient Mesoamericans. With their brittle rachis, however, they must have been difficult to harvest effectively, and with their thick glumes, or seed cases, they were equally difficult to process into an edible form.

Luckily, just a few genes control those features. Recent genetic analysis has shown that probably only about five genes control the physical characteristics that distinguish maize from teosinte (Raloff 1993), and maizelike teosinte mutants are produced in wild populations (Beadle 1977). These mutants yield naked seeds and possess a tougher rachis than regular teosinte, features that are not advantageous in the wild but are preferred by humans. We also know that a single mutation on one teosinte chromosome doubles the number of rows of kernels, and another alters the standard pattern of single spikelets to paired, again greatly increasing seed yield (Galinat 1992). Still another mutation enlarges the individual kernels.

As maize researcher Walton C. Galinat (1992) points out, ancient users of teosinte would have recognized the desirable characteristics of some of the mutant forms of that plant. In the wild, these rare forms would remain rare, since cross-pollination would be occurring with the overwhelming abundance of nonmutant forms. By isolating the mutants, however, ancient Mesoamericans could have ensured that plants with rare features, maladaptive in nature but desirable for humans, cross-bred only with mutants with the same or other desirable characteristics. As Galinat indicates, though ancient people lacked our knowledge of genetics, their powers of observation of the world around them were probably far better than our own—including, perhaps especially, the plant life on which they depended for survival. Applying the knowledge derived from such observation, they could have domesticated maize rather quickly. Genetic analysis of the hundreds of varieties of maize and the many different kinds of wild teosinte has been conducted by plant biologist John Doebley. He has identified one particular teosinte subgroup that, based on its genetic makeup, could be the common ancestor of the many varieties of the domesticated crop: a race of teosinte that grows along the Balsas River in Mexico (Raloff 1993) (Figure 12.19).

Beans

Wild beans grow in twisted pods that become brittle when ripe, and the beans themselves are rather impermeable. People selected for mutant beans with straight, limp, nonshattering pods for easier harvesting, and for more permeable varieties, which reduced the time needed for soaking in water before they could be cooked (Kaplan 1981; Kaplan and Kaplan 1992; De Tapia 1992). This process may have been repeated several times in Mesoamerica and South America, ultimately providing the world with four separate domesticated bean species: common, lima and sievas, scarlet runner, and tepary beans, and the many varieties of these various species, including kidney, lima, pinto, wax, and navy (Kaplan and Kaplan 1992:61; another commonly eaten bean, fava, is an Old World domesticate).

The Nature of Artificial Selection

Charles Darwin, who used artificial selection in agriculture as an analogy for natural selection in the wild, phrased it appropriately when, referring to horticulturists' ability to produce a spectacular array of plants and animals for human use, he stated: "The art is simple, and as far as the final result is concerned, has been followed almost unconsciously. It has consisted in always cultivating the best-known variety, sowing its seeds, and, when a slightly better variety chanced to appear, selecting it, and so onwards" (Diamond 1994:106). Much the same was true during the early post-Pleistocene.

WHY AGRICULTURE?

Many hypotheses have been put forth to explain why, more or less simultaneously, people the world over adopted an agricultural subsistence system. As archaeologist Mark Cohen (1977) has pointed out, under different environmental conditions, and focusing on many kinds of plant and animal resources, most of the world's people, between 11,000 and 2,000 years ago, either developed a domesticated food base independently or adopted the agricultural pattern of their neighbors. In other words, a 9,000-year revolution occurred that supplanted a pattern of foraging that had been successful for the hominid family for 4 million years.

That such a revolution took place is obvious. That there must have been some compelling human need behind it seems reasonable. What is not obvious, however, is *why* this shift took place at all.

Environmental Change

An environmental cause has often been suggested for this shift: The extinction at the end of the Pleistocene of plant and animal species on which some human groups depended for subsistence stimulated the development of agriculture to replace these extinct food sources. Environmental change is also at the root of British prehistorian V. Gordon Childe's (1942, 1951, 1953) "oasis hypothesis": Increasing post-Pleistocene aridity in the Near East forced surviving plants, animals, and people to congregate around permanent water sources. People became more knowledgeable about the wild species now in close proximity to them and slowly tamed and molded the species to fill their needs.

Cultural Evolution

Other researchers have proposed that agriculture developed as the result of cultural evolution. This "readiness hypothesis," championed by archaeologist Robert Braidwood (1960, 1975), assumes that human groups accumulated knowledge about the wild plants and animals on which they depended, and then discovered ways to increase the reliability, productivity, and usefulness of those species through selective breeding.

Population Growth

Some have suggested that domestication resulted from the need to increase productivity to feed a growing population. In his provocative book, *The Food Crisis in Prehistory,* archaeologist Mark Cohen (1977) argues that only an over-riding necessity could have induced human groups to shift to a subsistence pattern that involved fundamentally altering their way of life and adopting a far more labor-intensive pattern. Hunter/gatherers are known to work relatively short hours for their subsistence, especially compared to agriculturalists. The !Kung San people living in the Kalahari Desert in southern Africa, one of the least hospitable places on earth, work just twenty hours a week in subsistence activities (see Figure 12.1; Lee 1979). In Cohen's view, only the pressing need to feed an increasing number of mouths could compel people to abandon a more leisurely mode.

An Accident

Others maintain that the domestication of plants and animals was not accomplished through conscious choice to improve the subsistence base, but instead because human beings naturally alter the habitats they exploit. Humans change natural conditions simply by returning to the same place to collect foods seasonally, by killing or weeding out economically useless species, by disturbing the soil, by concentrating garbage, by moving plants or animals into areas outside of natural habitats, and by clearing out vegetation for villages (E. Anderson 1956). In this way people unintentionally create better conditions for individual members of species that fortuitously thrive in a human-dominated and culturally altered and manipulated habitat. Species adapt to these new conditions while humans, in turn, culturally adapt to take full advantage of these species, all in a process that archaeologist David Rindos (1984) calls "co-evolution."

Summary

There probably was no single "prime cause" for the development of agriculture in all the places that it occurred. Perhaps there was no one "Neolithic revolution," but many, each with its own explanation. As archaeologist Donald O.

Henry (1989:236) points out, "given the complex ecological relationships that governed the transition from forager to food-producer," complexity and diversity in explaining these transitions is to be expected.

However, significant patterns do exist in the record. A sedentary settlement pattern (evidenced by substantial and permanent architectural forms) *precedes* the appearance of domesticated foods. In other words, in the Late Pleistocene/ Early Holocene, some human groups began to settle into regions so plentiful in food resources that people could stay in one place for much of the year and collect enough food to survive and even thrive. Population might grow exponentially as the sedentary life may lower infant mortality and extends the length of life. During a long period of population growth, the food quest would be intensified to feed the growing number of mouths. One step in this intensification would be to artificially raise the productivity of the nearby wild plants by creating conditions that increase the yield of food: clearing forest, planting seedbeds, weeding, fencing in. At this point, the plant selection process changes: Whereas before plants were adapting to natural conditions, now they are adapting to artificial conditions produced by the cultural manipulation of the environment. This is the first step toward domestication and, ultimately, a way of life dependent entirely on food production.

THE REMARKABLY MODERN CUISINE OF THE ANCIENT WORLD

You have probably tried and perhaps eat often the "ethnic" foods of different cultures that are widely available in the modern world. Virtually every city in North America has restaurants specializing in many kinds of foods: Chinese and Japanese food with their rice-based dishes; Mexican cuisine with its corn flour tortillas and tacos and beans; Middle Eastern food with wheat flour pita bread; Greek food with lamb; German food with beef and pork; the Native American turkey we eat on Thanksgiving; and so on—all part of our modern diet.

All of these foods—rice, wheat, potato, corn, beef, chicken, pork, turkey— form the basis for the diet of the world's burgeoning human population at the end of the twentieth century. And all were domesticated in antiquity. In fact, it is difficult to come up with any economically significant modern food sources that were not part of the food base thousands of years ago during the Neolithic. Two exceptions are strawberries (not domesticated until the Middle Ages) and pecans (not domesticated until 1846) (Diamond 1994).

So, although we may think of ancient people as primitive, we have them to thank for virtually all the foods we rely on today. We have refined the work of the ancients by improving yield, increasing drought resistance, and accelerating ripening. But we have not added significantly to the inventory of domesticates. Statistics on 1986 worldwide yields of modern agriculture show this to be the case (Table 12.1). Most of the crops in Table 12.1 were discussed in this chapter. Wheat, corn, rice, potato, manioc, sweet potato, barley, sorghum,

TABLE 12.1
Agricultural Yields Worldwide, 1986

CROP	MILLION METRIC TONS	CROP	MILLION METRIC TONS
Sugar cane	932	Apple	40
Wheat	536	Coconut	39
Corn	481	Cabbage	38
Rice	476	Rye	32
Potato	309	Millet	31
Sugar beet	286	Watermelon	28
Barley	180	Yam	27
Manioc	137	Onion	25
Sweet potato	110	Sunflower	21
Soybean	95	Rape	20
Sorghum	71	Bean (dry)	15
Banana and plantain	68	Pea (dry)	14
Grape	67	Mango	14
Tomato	60	Avocado	10
Oat	48	Pineapple	10
Orange	41	Olive	9

From Heiser (1990:63)

and soybean are among the top modern crops and all are ancient in origin (Heiser 1990:63). Sugar cane surpasses their yields, but this is misleading because its weight is exaggerated as a result of water content.

NEOLITHIC NUTRITION

Some of the plant foods domesticated by Neolithic people are high in protein. For example, on a scale comparing relative protein content of various foods (Table 12.2), where eggs represent a perfect score of 100 for their rich and complete complement of amino acids, wheat rates a 44, rice a 57, and maize a 41. Compare this to beef's 69, chicken's 64, and fish's 70.

There is a serious problem, however, with relying on the cereals for protein: As Table 12.2 also shows, neither wheat, rice, nor maize provides complete proteins, for each lacks at least one of the eight essential amino acids necessary to sustain human life (isoleucine, leucine, lysine, methionine,

TABLE 12.2
Amino Acid Content of Various Foods

	AMINO ACID[a]								
FOOD	ISO-LEUCINE	LEUCINE	LYSINE	METHI-ONINE	PHENYL-ALANINE	THREO-NINE	TRYPTO-PHAN	VALINE	PROTEIN SCORE[b]
Hen's egg	393	551	436	210	358	320	93	428	100
Beef	301	507	556	169	275	287	70	313	69
Cow's milk	295	596	487	157	336	278	88	362	60
Chicken	334	460	497	157	250	248	64	318	64
Fish	299	480	569	179	245	286	70	382	70
Corn	230	783	167	120	305	225	44	303	41
Wheat	204	417	179	94	282	183	68	276	44
Rice	238	514	237	145	322	244	78	344	57
Bean	262	476	450	66	326	248	63	287	34
Soybean	284	486	399	79	309	241	80	300	47
Potato	236	377	299	81	251	235	103	292	34
Manioc	175	247	259	83	156	165	72	204	41
Coconut	244	419	220	120	283	212	68	339	55

From Heiser (1990:31)

[a]*Measured in milligrams per gram of nitrogen.*

[b]*Each food's protein content is scored relative to that of the hen's egg, which, as the highest in protein, is given a score of 100.*

phenylalanine, threonine, tryptophan, and valine). Wheat, rice, and maize, though high in protein, are each deficient in lysine. Quinoa, a significant South American domesticate, offers a more complete complement of amino acids, including lysine.

Remarkably, in the Near East, the Far East, and Mesoamerica, where wheat, rice, and maize, respectively, became the basis for a way of life, people also domesticated other wild crops that, though even less complete than wheat, rice, or maize in the amino acids they contain, are rich in lysine (Heiser 1990). In the Near East it was a suite of legumes—including lentil, chickpea, and peas—that provided the amino acid missing in wheat. In the Far East, lentils provided the lysine missing in rice. In Mesoamerica, beans supplied the missing protein component.

So, without any knowledge of nutrition or biochemistry, prehistoric people in different parts of the world domesticated a range of plants that together provided the essential amino acids needed for them to survive and prosper.

WAS AGRICULTURE THE "WORST MISTAKE IN THE HISTORY OF THE HUMAN RACE"?

Scientist Jared Diamond (1987a) labeled agriculture the "worst mistake in the history of the human race" in the title of a provocative essay. His interesting idea is backed up by some impressive archaeological evidence. Clearly, agriculture can provide more food than can most foraging systems, and in a wide variety of habitats. In terms of caloric output, when agriculture works, it wins, hands down. At the same time we have just seen that many of the world's ancient agricultural systems produced crops that complemented each other in amino acid content. So theoretically, not only does agriculture produce lots of food for lots of mouths, it gives a mixture of foods that together provide a healthy diet. Unfortunately, the evidence shows that this system often did not work very well.

Mark Cohen and George Armelagos (1984) have summarized the evidence for the prevalence of paleopathology—ancient disease—coincident with the origins of agriculture in North, Central, and South America, the eastern Mediterranean, western Europe, the Middle East, southern Asia, and Nubia. When comparing parameters of health as revealed by prehistoric skeletons, in most instances older hunter/gatherer groups exhibited higher levels of health and nutrition than did the farmers who succeeded them. Specifically, there were higher levels of infection in farmers than in previous foragers in the same regions. Some early farming populations show increases in tubercular infections (Buikstra 1984); others show higher levels of gastrointestinal infections (seen in a survey of mummified humans in South America; Allison 1984). Many more farming groups show higher rates of infections of uncertain origin. Of course, agriculture itself doesn't cause disease; it merely establishes the conditions conducive for disease to spread: large, dense, sedentary populations.

Ironically, chronic malnutrition seems to be another major problem that accompanied the shift to an agricultural way of life. While many people may stereotype hunter/gatherers as living hand-to-mouth, where every meal might be their last for some time, in most of the studies Cohen and Armelagos summarize, farmers show more evidence of malnutrition than do their foraging forebears. Nutritionally based anemia (as evidenced by porosity of the skull) was found to be more severe in a number of farming groups in the American Midwest. Other evidence for poorer nutrition among some farming groups included an overall decline in stature. Episodes of severe malnutrition among farmers was further indicated by more incidences of enamel hypoplasia (see the discussion in Chapter 7 regarding the Neandertals and this condition).

Perhaps most remarkable of all, for the majority of cases reported in a symposium Cohen and Armelagos organized on this issue, where age at death was calculated for the archaeological samples, hunter/gatherers lived longer than did the farmers in the same regions. They conclude: "Taken as a whole, these indicators fairly clearly suggest an overall decline in the quality—and probably in the length—of human life associated with the adoption of agriculture" (1984:594).

Another rather nasty result of a shift to an agricultural way of life seems to have been the institutionalization of warfare and violence. Direct evidence of personal violence is rare in Pleistocene archaeological contexts. Few skeletons exhibit traumatic wounds that might have resulted from interpersonal violence. In the Neolithic, however, such evidence becomes far more common within a context not of just one person killing another, but of whole groups taking up arms against their neighbors. Perhaps the problems inherent in an agricultural way of life and the always-present potential for a collapse of the subsistence base are at the heart of this phenomenon. Agriculture, though potentially of enormous benefit, is a fragile basis for subsistence. It allows for the existence of large and dense populations so long as it works; but when it doesn't work, there are a lot of hungry people. And when the neighbors of starving people have food, the hungry may become violent.

Maybe agriculture wasn't a mistake, but it had a fundamental drawback: Though it allowed more people to live, many did not live as well as their hunter/gatherer ancestors.

IMPLICATIONS OF THE NEOLITHIC: THE ROOTS OF SOCIAL COMPLEXITY

For most of human history, we have foraged for food. Small nomadic groups could easily supply the necessities for their families. No one needed more, and providing for more than one's needs made little sense. The organization of such societies could be rather simple, revolving around age and sex categories. Such societies likely were largely **egalitarian;** beyond the usual distinctions based on age and sex, virtually all people had equivalent rights, status, and access to resources.

Archaeologist Donald Henry (1989) suggests that the combination of a rich habitat and sedentism led to a dramatic increase in human population. In his view, nomadic, simple foragers have a relatively low level of fertility. Their high-protein, low-carbohydrate diets produce low proportions of body fat commonly associated with low fertility in women. High physical activity and long periods of nursing common among recent simple foragers also probably contributed to low levels of female fertility.

In Henry's view, the shift to complex foraging and a more sedentary existence would have contributed to higher fertility levels. A diet higher in wild cereals produces proportionally more body fat, leading to higher fertility among women. Cereals produce easily digested foods that would have supplemented and then replaced mother's milk as a primary food for older infants. Since lactation is a natural dampener of fertility, earlier weaning would

FIGURE 12.20

Excavations at Umm Qseir.

(Courtesy Frank Hole)

have resulted in closer spacing of births and the potential for a greater number of live births for each woman. A more sedentary existence may also have lowered infant mortality and perhaps increased longevity among the aged. These more vulnerable members of society could safely stay in a fixed village rather than be forced regularly to move great distances as part of a nomadic existence with its greater risk of accident and trauma.

All of this may have resulted in a trend of increasing size of some local human populations in the Holocene. Given sufficient time, even in very rich habitats, human population size can reach **carrying capacity:** the maximum population an area can sustain within the context of a given subsistence system. And human population growth is like a runaway train: Once it picks up speed, it is difficult to control. So even after reaching an area's carrying capacity, Holocene human populations probably continued to grow in food-rich regions, overshooting the ability of the territory to feed the population, again within the context of the same subsistence strategy. In some areas, small changes in climate or minor changes in plant characteristics may have further destabilized local economies.

One possible response to surpassing the carrying capacity of a region is for a group to exploit adjoining land. However, good land may itself be limited—for example, to within the confines of a river valley. Where neighbors are in the same position, having filled up all the available desirable habitat in their home territories, expansion also is problematic. Impinging on the neighbors' territory can lead to conflict, especially when they too are up against the capacity of the land to provide enough food.

Another option is to stay put but shift and intensify the food quest in the same territory. The impulse to produce more food to feed a growing population was satisfied in some areas by the development of more complex subsistence strategies involving intensive labor and requiring more cooperation and greater coordination of increasing numbers of people. This resulted in a change in the social and economic equations that defined those societies. Hierarchies that did not exist in earlier foraging groups but that were helpful in structuring cooperative labor and in organizing more complex technologies probably became entrenched, even before domestication and agriculture, as pre-Neolithic societies reacted to population increase.

The results of this strategy of intensification of the exploitation of wild foods were, at least in some regions, even better than the participants could have anticipated. Not only were people able to increase their wild food base enough to feed a larger population, they actually were able to produce a food surplus by artificially selecting for propagation the most productive individuals in their wild food species. This food surplus changed the social and economic equations yet again, setting the stage for a dramatic increase in complexity in some human societies. The results of this increase are the focus of the next chapter.

The revolution that is the focus of this chapter was not an event, but a slow process that only gradually changed the fundamental way people made a living. Analysis of this shift in the Khabur Basin in northeastern Syria is a perfect example (Zeder 1994a,b).

CASE STUDY CLOSE-UP

The area had been only sparsely occupied before 12,000 years ago. Beginning about 10,000 years ago, villages began turning up in the archaeological record with a subsistence base that included a variety of early domesticates, including wheat, lentils, peas, and beans. The bones of domesticated sheep and goats were found in early levels of these settlements, with pig and cattle remains showing up later.

A detailed analysis of one site in the Khabur Basin, Umm Qseir, clearly shows the evolutionary nature of the shift from foraging to farming (Figure 12.20). For example, after 8,000 B.P., domesticated sheep, goat, and pig contributed to the diet in the settlement. But the Neolithic residents of Umm Qseir had not abandoned their earlier pattern of hunting and gathering. More than half the animal remains recovered at the site were of wild animals— gazelle, deer, wild cattle, hare, turtles, wild ass, birds, and freshwater clams (Zeder 1994b:5).

The use of both wild and domesticated sources of food seems to reflect a seasonal rhythm at Umm Qseir. Most animal species have a mating season, and, combined with a fairly consistent gestational period for each species, most of the offspring are born within a narrow period of time during the year. Since the age of death of a juvenile animal can be estimated based on tooth eruption and bone development, archaeologists can often determine the time of year an animal was killed. In other words, if the young of a particular species tend to be born in the early spring, and many of the younger animals at a site were slaughtered in their fifteenth month of life, just count fifteen months from early spring to determine when they were slaughtered. In this hypothetical example, they were killed in the summer.

Pigs were slaughtered most commonly at Umm Qseir between August and October. The ages of sheep and goats killed at the site corresponds to this same period, which actually extended until January. This is the arid summer and early rainy season, precisely when wild resources would have been at their leanest. So domestication did not supplant foraging in the subsistence system at Umm Qseir. Instead, domestication allowed for the permanent occupation of an area rich with seasonally available wild foods, even during seasons when those wild foods were not plentiful.

As archaeologist Melinda Zeder (1994b) points out, here and elsewhere the Neolithic was not a period during which all people marched down the path to a purely agricultural mode of subsistence. For a long time, domestication complemented foraging but did not replace it. Only much later did agriculture and animal husbandry become the primary sources of food for most of the world's people, setting the stage for the period of time to be described in Chapters 13 and 14.

 **VISITING THE PAST**

The Chinese site of Ban Po is highlighted in an exhibit built at the site in Shaanxi. Many artifacts unearthed at the site are on display, including tools for tilling the soil (stone spades and hoes) and ceramic jars for storing food. Particularly informative is the array of recovered food remains on display. Clearly the people of Ban Po had a diverse economy; on display are the remains of chestnuts, hazelnuts, hackberries, pine nuts, snails, antelopes, pigs, foxes, cattle, and many species of fish that have been found. Domesticated millet, Chinese cabbage, and leaf mustard were also found. Part of the excavated site has been preserved at the museum, and visitors can also see reconstructed houses or "cottages."

Many other sites dating to after the food-producing revolution do not contain any direct evidence of the dramatic shift in human subsistence. But each such site is an object lesson in the enormous impacts of that revolution: the degree of sedentism implied, the size of the resident population, the specialization of labor, social stratification, the construction of monuments.

SUMMARY

Beginning sometime after 12,000 years ago, and in a number of world areas, the archaeological record shows a subtle, barely perceptible shift in how people supplied their subsistence needs. Whereas humans previously had fed themselves, like all other animals, by foraging for wild foods, some groups began intentionally encouraging the growth of particular plants (by turning over soil, planting seeds, weeding, thinning out, and in other ways tending them) and herding and selectively culling herds of animals. Human beings replaced nature as the selective force operating on certain species. This "artificial selection" encouraged the growth of those individuals within plant and animal species that were not necessarily well adapted to a life in the wild but that had characteristics advantageous to their human caretakers. Over many generations of selection, human beings in the Near East, Europe, eastern Asia, Africa, and North and South America developed new species that were the product not of natural processes, but of cultural requirements. This was the Neolithic Revolution, which, while slow, would revolutionize the way people made a living and how they lived—and how we live in the modern world.

TO LEARN MORE

A useful volume covering all of the major centers of plant and animal domestication in antiquity is *The Origins of Agriculture: An International Perspective,* edited by archaeologists C. Wesley Cowan and Patty Jo Watson (1992). It contains papers originally presented at a 1985 symposium of the American Association for the Advancement of Science. For the most up-to-date coverage of Old World domestication from a geneticist's point of view, see Daniel Zohary and Maria Hopf's (1993) *Domestication of Plants in the Old World.* This virtual encyclopedia features a crop-by-crop discussion of all of the important Old World domesticates. Archaeologist Bruce Smith's (1995) excellent synthesis entitled *The Emergence of Agriculture* presents a comparative survey of domestication around the world. A detailed treatment of the origins of agriculture in the Near East is Donald O. Henry's (1989) *From Foraging to Agriculture: The Levant at the End of the Ice Age.* Useful summaries of New World domestication can be found in *Chilies to Chocolate: Food the Americas Gave the World,* edited by Nelson Foster and Linda S. Cordell (1992). For a concise piece on domestication, read Jared Diamond's "How to Tame a Wild Plant," in the September 1994 issue of *Discover* magazine. The health impacts of the agricultural revolution are discussed in A. H. Goodman and George Armelagos's (1985) "Disease and Death at Dr. Dickson's Mound" in *Natural History* magazine.

KEY TERMS

Neolithic
foraging
artificial selection
domestication
cereal
Fertile Crescent
Geometric Kebaran
Levant
Mushabian
Natufian
Zarzian
Karim Shahirian
simple foragers
complex foraging

legume
emmer
einkorn
Tehuacán
Ajuerdo phase
microbands
El Riego phase
Coxcatlán phase
Abejas phase
Purrón phase
Ajalpán phase
accelerator mass
    spectrometry (AMS)
glume

teosinte
pluvial
pastoralists
Peiligang
Yang-shao
Linienbandkeramik
    (LBK)
tubers
rachis
egalitarian
carrying capacity

13

An Explosion of Complexity

THE FLOWERING OF CIVILIZATION IN THE OLD WORLD

CHAPTER OVERVIEW

Under many circumstances, agriculture allows for the production of a food surplus. A food surplus set the stage for the development of differential access to wealth, and with the concentration of wealth came social and political power.

"Civilization"—including monumental edifices, elaborate burials, large armies, full-time artisans, and so forth—developed in some parts of the Old World as fewer people were needed in the subsistence quest and as rulers attempted to legitimize and reinforce their position of power wealth. Mesopotamia, Egypt, the Indus Valley, Shang, and Minoan Crete are examples of the first civilizations in the Old World.

	10	9.5	9	8.5	8
West Asia	Umm Dabaghiyah		Jericho		Çatal Hüyük
					Hassuna
Egypt					
Sudan					
South Asia					
China					
Crete				First settlemer

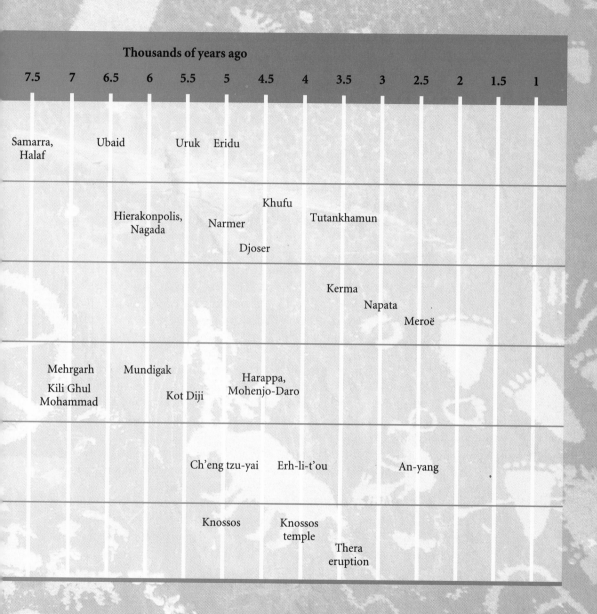

Thousands of years ago

| 7.5 | 7 | 6.5 | 6 | 5.5 | 5 | 4.5 | 4 | 3.5 | 3 | 2.5 | 2 | 1.5 | 1 |

Samarra, Halaf

Ubaid

Uruk   Eridu

Hierakonpolis, Nagada

Narmer

Khufu

Djoser

Tutankhamun

Kerma

Napata

Meroë

Mehrgarh

Mundigak

Kili Ghul Mohammad

Kot Diji

Harappa, Mohenjo-Daro

Ch'eng tzu-yai

Erh-li-t'ou

An-yang

Knossos

Knossos temple

Thera eruption

By the summer of 1922, the earl of Carnarvon had all but run out of patience. For fifteen years, he had provided financial support for the work of archaeologist Howard Carter, who was digging in Egypt in the Valley of the Kings—the royal burial ground, or "necropolis," outside of the ancient Egyptian capital of Thebes. In all that time, Carter had found little to interest Carnarvon or to enhance his benefactor's reputation as a sponsor of significant Egyptian archaeology.

Wealthy Europeans had provided the financial backing for much of the archaeology conducted in Egypt and in the Middle East in the nineteenth and early twentieth centuries. Funding significant excavations was a prestigious enterprise, and many wealthy individuals wished to be associated with the recovery of fabulous archaeological treasure.

In the peculiar practice of archaeological colonialism rampant throughout the eighteenth, nineteenth, and early twentieth centuries, wealthy Europeans purchased excavation "concessions" from foreign governments and then paid archaeologists to conduct investigations. Such excavation concessions, put bluntly, were the equivalent of mining permits. The objects recovered by foreign archaeologists in places like Egypt, Iraq, and Syria in the Old World and Mexico and Peru in the New World were not considered to belong to the nation in which the materials were found, but to the individual who had purchased the right to dig and who had funded the excavations. In most cases, these benefactors had contracts with their archaeologists detailing how artifacts were to be distributed on their recovery. Sponsors commonly dispersed their portion to other wealthy friends and to museums, enhancing their reputations as supporters of important research; at the same time they were divesting nations of their cultural heritage and rendering analysis of significant archaeological sites all but impossible.

In the summer of 1922 Carter had returned to England to see Carnarvon. Without any significant discoveries after fifteen years, without any glory to bask in, without any archaeological treasures to distribute, Carnarvon had decided to cut off Carter's support, and he informed Carter that this would be the final season he would fund archaeological research in the valley. Dejected, Carter returned to Egypt and commenced what he presumed would be his last digging for Carnarvon.

Carter knew there was not much time. His fieldwork season began in early November and he would be forced to quit by mid-December, when the tourist season began. Excavation in the tiny piece of ground still unexamined by Carter—the only such piece left in the excavation concession purchased by Carnarvon from the Egyptian government—would block the entrance to the tomb of Pharaoh Rameses VI, the valley's most popular visitor destination.

Carter began work on November 1, 1922, and within three days his Egyptian workers had discovered the beginning of a staircase leading down into the ground. The staircase was slowly cleared of rock; at the bottom was a sealed door bearing the official symbol of the royal burial ground: jackals, symbolically protecting the king's tomb. It seemed possible that Carter at last had found a sealed tomb of an Egyptian king.

Carter was cautiously optimistic, but there had been false starts and false hopes before. Believing that this was his last chance, Carter took a gamble and telegrammed Carnarvon in England: "At last have made wonderful discovery in the Valley. A magnificent tomb with seals intact. Recovered same for your arrival: congratulations" (Fagan 1994:205). Carter suggested that the earl travel to Egypt to witness the opening of what Carter fervently hoped was an unplundered tomb.

After a difficult trip, Carnarvon arrived, with his daughter. Carter provided a viewing area for Carnarvon and his daughter where, protected from the relentless Egyptian sun by an umbrella, they watched while workers opened the door at the bottom of the staircase. But instead of the hoped-for tomb, beyond the door was a rubble-filled corridor carved in the rock. Disappointed but intrigued, the workers began the laborious process of removing the rock and debris from the corridor, which extended an excruciating twenty-five feet. At the end lay yet another door.

The cleared second doorway stood before Carter and Carnarvon on November 26, a little more than two weeks before Carnarvon's patience and money—and Carter's time—were to run out. Carter drilled a hole through the door. Beyond was clearly an open space, a subterranean room. Carter widened the drilled hole just enough so he could put his head, one arm, and a candle through. Carter's own words to describe what he saw are some of the most famous in all archaeology:

> At first I could see nothing, the hot air escaping from the chamber causing the candle flame to flicker. But presently, as my eyes grew accustomed to the light, details of the room within emerged slowly from the mist, strange animals, statues, and gold—everywhere the glint of gold. For the moment—an eternity it must have seemed to the others standing by—I was struck dumb with amazement, and when Lord Carnarvon, unable to stand the suspense any longer, inquired anxiously, "Can you see anything?" it was all I could do to get out the words, "Yes, wonderful things!" (Buckley 1976:13).

Thus began the excavation of the fabulous tomb of the Egyptian "boy king," Tutankhamun (Figure 13.1). Though a relatively minor figure in Egyptian history, having served as pharaoh as a child from 1334 B.C. to 1325 B.C., Tutankhamun was to become the most famous of all ancient Egypt's rulers. His tomb had gone largely untouched since his death, and the spectacular array of burial goods in the tomb were to excite people everywhere (see the Civilization Portfolio, Color Plate 16).

The splendor of the tomb of Tutankhamun is emblematic of the focus of this chapter—the rise of what we commonly call **civilization.** The world over, a

CHAPTER SITES

EAST ASIA
An-Yang
Ch'eng tzu-yai
Erh-li-t'ou
Hsi-pei-kang
Hsiao-t'un
Ssu-tun
T'a-ssu

WEST ASIA
Çatal Hüyük
Choga Mami
Eridu
Halaf
Hassuna
Jericho
Samarra
Tell-es-Sawwan
Ubaid
Umm Dabaghiyah
Ur
Uruk
'Usaila
Yarim Tepe

INDIA/PAKISTAN
Amri
Anjira
Chanhu-Daro
Dhoraji
Gumla
Harappa
Judeirjo-Daro
Kalibangan
Kili Ghul Muhammad
Kot Diji
Lothal
Mehrgarh
Mohenjo-Daro
Mundigak
Rana Ghundai
Rhaman Dheri
Sandhanawala
Siah-damb
Tarakai Qila

FIGURE 13.1

The gold mask that covered the face of the boy king Tutankhamun as it was found by Howard Carter. (Photography by Egyptian Expedition, The Metropolitan Museum of Art)

series of Neolithic cultures, initially characterized by relatively small, permanent farming villages, as described in Chapter 12, experienced a remarkable growth and elaboration of material culture and social organization, eventually leading to societies led by pharaohs, kings, and emperors who built great temples and pyramids, fought wars, and ruled huge geographical expanses. How these cultures evolved, and what made elaborate tombs like Tutankhamun's possible (perhaps even necessary), is the focus of the next two chapters; the Old World in this chapter and the New World in Chapter 14.

This geographic breakdown between chapters does not imply any fundamental difference between what transpired in the two hemispheres. In both regions, state societies evolved from previous food-producing societies. Though what we are here identifying as civilization appeared earlier in the

Old World, neither hemisphere had a monopoly on complexity. Furthermore, the civilizations in the New World were not the result of contact with the Old World. The discussion of the evolution of complexity, as well as the definition of civilization presented in this chapter's Chronicle, apply equally to developments in the Old World and in the New World.

CHRONICLE

The shift to food production in the Neolithic constituted a revolution in subsistence. It also produced a revolution in society itself. A new social pattern developed to organize the labor required by the intensification of the food quest, and the production of a food surplus was enabled by the domestication of plants and animals. In essence, a food surplus served as the basis for a revolution in social, economic, and political complexity whose impacts continue to define the modern world system. Indeed, the modern world begins with the Neolithic.

A REVOLUTION IN SUBSISTENCE, A REVOLUTION IN SOCIETY

Society becomes more complex when the labor of many must be organized—to prepare seedbeds, to clear forests, to control water, to build animal corrals—to meet the requirements of a growing population. Certain individuals, as a result of their competence or charisma, are given the authority to organize these group or communal activities. These individuals are able to organize the labor, assign tasks, divide responsibilities, direct actions, and oversee duties. Through their skills to persuade, bargain, marshall group opinion, cajole, and even simply by the force of their will, they can get things done. They are invested not so much with power—there are no laws, police force, or army to coerce others to heed their directions—but with authority. They are good at organizing labor, keeping people happy, and successfully conducting projects that people recognize are for the good of the group. In Melanesia, such individuals are called "Big Men"; in anthropology that term is applied to individuals in any culture who perform such functions (Service 1975). When there are Big Men and some others below them who fill a limited number of specific roles in the society—in essence, people of higher status with differential access to resources—such a group is no longer egalitarian. Anthropologist Morton Fried (1967) labels these groups **rank societies.** Rather than everyone being more or less equal, there are a few sociopolitical "ranks" filled by a relatively small number of people.

A Neolithic Base for Big Men

In some post-Pleistocene settings, the extra work involved in the application of new, more intensive subsistence strategies, as organized by these newly developed leaders, substantially increased the food base. The additional labor invested in planting seedbeds, tending wild plants, or corralling wild animals created a new, cultural environment in which natural selection was supplanted by artificial selection. The result was domesticated plants and animals that eventually produced far more food than was actually needed to feed even the growing Holocene human population in some areas.

Those who could control the new food surplus—redistribute it, save it for times of need, or even own it—possessed, for perhaps the first time in human history, wealth and power. To be able to redistribute excess food, reward some and punish others, accumulate precious materials in trade, and distribute food—or withhold it—during lean times is to have power.

A food surplus poses the challenge of what to do with it all. To begin with, it needs to be stored. Village granaries are one solution, and their construction requires more communal labor. Once granaries are built and the grain is stored, the surplus must be protected from hungry animals, insects, and rot—not to mention greedy humans. So more communal projects are needed, more jobs are created for leaders to oversee, and there is more reinforcement for their position as leaders, so long as they are successful.

It is expensive to build storage facilities and to protect the food. So why bother? The most obvious reason is that a surplus can help tide people over during lean times—during nongrowing seasons or during slim harvests. Plus, a food surplus can be distributed to individuals or families who have contributed significantly to the group, as a reward for hard work. Also, a food surplus can be used as wealth to obtain other valuable goods; the surplus can be traded with the inhabitants of other regions for stone, metal, or other resources not locally available or accessible.

From Big Men to Chiefs

As long as such societies remain small, with Big Men managing only individual villages, the potential for complexity ordinarily is limited. As population grows, however, and as more importance is vested in the Big Man, that role may change. Anthropologist Elman Service (1975:71) refers to this as "the institutionalization of power": As the system expands geographically, group labor projects and the broader redistribution of food and other goods has a "politically integrative effect" (Service 1975:94). Social strata may develop, with the leader, or chief, and the chief's family at the top of the social pyramid. Chieftainship may be handed down from parent to child, further solidifying the position of the chief's family in the upper echelon of a stratified social system. A cadre of subordinate regional chiefs may also develop, each responsible for a local area, and all reporting to the head chief. Most everyone else makes up the broad base of the social pyramid of these **chiefdoms,** giving at least some of the surplus they produce to the chiefs.

ATLANTIC OCEAN

Stonehenge

A Neolithic Chiefdom

Chiefdoms, through organizing the labor of large numbers of people, can accomplish impressive material results. For example, the well-known monument of Stonehenge is perhaps the most impressive construction project of a chiefdom that developed in Neolithic Europe about 6,000 years ago (Map 13.1; Figure 13.2; Castleden 1987; Chippindale 1983). Thought by some archaeologists to be an astronomically based calendar, Stonehenge in southern England required an enormous amount of communal labor from a large workforce. The individual stones are huge: Each of the thirty uprights, or "sarsen stones," of the outside circle weighs about 24,000 kg (more than 50,000 lb). Several times harder than granite, these stones had to be quarried and then moved 40 km (25 mi) from their source. The stones of the trilithons—two uprights and one capstone—arranged in a horseshoe shape in the center are bigger still:

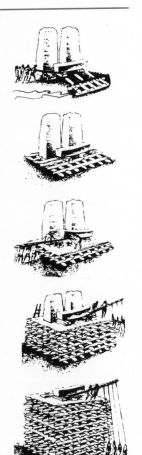

FIGURE 13.2

The monument of Stonehenge was probably constructed by a Neolithic chiefdom society.

FIGURE 13.3

Artist's conception of the raising of the stone lintels that topped the sarsens and trilithons of Stonehenge by using wooden platforms. (From C. Chippindale. 1983. *Stonehenge Complete.* London: Routledge)

Each of the uprights in the five trilithons stands more than 7 m (24 ft) high and weighs more than 45,000 kg (100,000 lb).

As impressive as this might sound, quarrying, moving, and erecting the enormous upright stones represents only a part of what the builders of Stonehenge accomplished. Joining all of the sarsens at the top in a continuous circle, and connecting each of the five pairs of uprights in the five trilithons, were lintel stones. In the sarsen circle, each lintel had to be shaped to exacting specifications, with the inside and outside surfaces accurately curved to form arcs of circles of two slightly different diameters. Tenons (bumps) were carved on the top of each upright to match mortises (depressions) in the bottom of each lintel; in this way, each lintel was held precisely in place and, at the same time, adjacent upright stones were connected to each other. Furthermore, each lintel stone, weighing more than 5,000 kg (12,000 lb), had to be raised up and placed on the tops of the uprights, probably by the sequenced construction of wooden cribbing around the upright stones to serve as a series of platforms on which the lintel would rest as it was levered up to a higher level (Figure 13.3).

The construction of Stonehenge clearly represents a prodigious effort by the members of an ancient chiefdom. As geographer and writer Rodney Castleden (1987) points out, there is no archaeological evidence of kings among the people who built Stonehenge, no splendid burials of absolute and godlike leaders. By about 5,500 B.P., there are some differentiated burials, and these have been interpreted as the interments of chiefs or Big Men.

COMPLEXITY'S FIRST TRACES IN THE OLD WORLD

Though certainly a dramatic indicator of the capacity of chiefs to mobilize labor, Stonehenge and the other stone monuments of the European Neolithic are not the earliest archaeological evidence for the kind of complexity found in chiefdom societies; some archaeological evidence for nonegalitarian societies turns up early in the Neolithic.

Jericho

Some of the earliest evidence of large-scale communal construction and social stratification in the world can be seen deep in the sequence at a few sites in west-

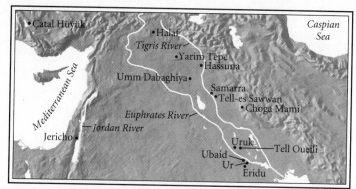

MAP 13.2

Archaeological sites in western Asia where evidence of the evolution of chiefdom and early state-level societies has been found.

FIGURE 13.4

The wall at Jericho, probably built by members of an ancient chiefdom society beginning some 9,000 years ago, is among the earliest archaeological evidence in the world for construction on a monumental scale.
(M. H. Feder)

ern Asia (Map 13.2). For example, the archaeological site of Jericho, in Israel, was a village with a number of distinct features that imply a movement away from the egalitarian pattern seen at other Neolithic sites (see Chapter 12). More than 9,000 years ago, the inhabitants of Jericho—later memorialized in the Old Testament of the Bible—built a massive stone wall around their community (Kenyon 1954). Made of dry-laid stone, the wall was 2 m (6½ ft) thick at the base, and nearly 7m (22 ft) high in places, with ramparts up to 9 m (30 ft) high (Figure 13.4). The construction of this wall required a level of coordination of labor not previously seen in the world.

Trade was an important element in the economy of early Jericho. Exotic raw materials, including Turkish obsidian, turquoise from the Sinai Peninsula, and cowrie shells from the Red Sea, are found at early levels of the site. The distribution of some of these exotic materials in human interments indicates a certain degree of social differentiation at Jericho: Whereas most burials were rather plain and undistinguished, one group of interments was set apart—

FIGURE 13.5

Çatal Hüyük was a large, complex settlement of more than 5,000 people by about 8,000 years ago. Its location near an important obsidian source may explain the size and complexity of the community at this early date.

(Drawing by Eliza McFadden, from *Plato Prehistorian* by Mary Settegast, published by the Rotenberg Press, 1986. Permission to reprint, courtesy of Rotenberg Press)

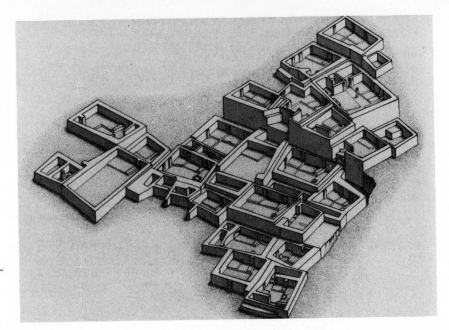

the skulls were coated with a mask of clay, and the exotic cowrie shells were set into the eye sockets.

Çatal Hüyük

At about 8,000 years ago, the site of Çatal Hüyük in Turkey covered an area three times as large as Jericho (Mellaart 1965; Todd 1976). About a thousand interconnected rooms honeycombed the settlement in blocks that cover the site (Figure 13.5). Most rooms are of a standard size: about 25 m² (264 ft²). Around forty of the excavated rooms produced no archaeological evidence of habitation, but appear instead to have been used for ceremonial purposes. These rooms have been labeled as shrines since they contain what seem to be images of fertility goddesses (some depicted as giving birth) as well as stylized bull heads carved into the walls. There also are painted depictions of leopards with women riding on their backs, birds, and headless human beings.

The site's population has been estimated at between 5,000 and 6,000. The large size and apparent complexity of Çatal Hüyük at this early date is probably related to its location adjacent to a major source of obsidian (volcanic glass) in the Konya Mountains. Konya obsidian is found widely distributed throughout southeastern Europe and western Asia via ancient trade networks; perhaps Big Men or chiefs managed or controlled the obsidian trade.

Jericho and Çatal Hüyük seem to presage a change that was to occur on a larger scale in a number of other world regions. In these places, the evidence is more dramatic that a fundamental change in social systems has been made and that such change had accelerated. This can be seen most clearly to the east, in the land between the rivers: Mesopotamia.

THE EVOLUTION OF THE STATE

"Civilization"—one of those problematic terms found in everyday speech as well as the parlance of archaeology—is easier to recognize than to define. Certainly, when we visit or see images of Egyptian pyramids or Mesopotamian temples (in this chapter) or ancient Maya cities or the palaces of the Inca (in Chapter 14), we know we are in the presence of the complex phenomenon called "civilization." But how can we formally define what we recognize intuitively?

Many social scientists avoid using the designation "civilization" altogether, preferring the term **state,** a reference to the political character of such societies. A state is both quantitatively and qualitatively different from a chiefdom. States ordinarily are bigger and their material accomplishments more impressive. But they are more than simply big, impressive chiefdoms; states are true class societies, often rigidly stratified into social levels. The ruling class controls the populace not by consensus, but by coercion and force. A state possesses a true "government," which archaeologist Joseph Tainter defines as a "specialized decision-making organization with a monopoly of force, and with the power to draft for work, levy and collect taxes, and decree and enforce laws" (1988:26). The ruling class in a state society runs the government. "Civilization" is most often used to characterize the recognizable material results of the development of state societies. Since archaeologists deal most directly with such material consequences, this discussion will use the terms "state" and "civilization" interchangeably.

THE CHARACTER OF CIVILIZATION

The most obvious symbols of state societies are **monumental works.** The ruins of huge public buildings, tombs, temples, palaces, pyramids, and such are all the spoor of ancient civilizations. Works such as the Egyptian Sphinx, the Pyramid of the Sun at Teotihuacán in Mexico, the Citadel at Mohenjo-Daro in Pakistan, and the great ziggurat at Ur in Iraq are the features by which we recognize ancient civilizations (Civilization Portfolio, Color Plates 14–26).

Social Stratification

But the monumental works and fine art of ancient civilizations do not define those civilizations; they merely reflect more fundamental elements of them

Social stratification
Monumental works
Food surplus
Large, dense populations
Labor specialization
System of record keeping

FIGURE 13.6

The features by which we define a civilization or state society.

(Figure 13.6). Great pyramids, walls, palaces, irrigation networks, temples, and roads, as well as beautiful paintings, exquisite ceramics, gold statues, and fine linen—the "wonderful things" that Howard Carter saw in Tut's tomb—are the result of a socioeconomic system unique to civilization. **Social stratification** in a complex civilization is a division of society into levels, or strata, that one does not achieve, but into which one is born. It defines one's role in life, one's status, one's power (or degree of powerlessness)—in essence, one's destiny. Monuments and great art are only the material symbols of the power of members of the elite social strata in these societies.

Monumental Works

Great monuments and art, therefore, are made possible by the social system of the state. The rulers in state societies have the power to cause the construction of fabulous tombs filled with splendid works of art. They can conscript armies, collect taxes, and call up workforces. Without some degree of social stratification, these large-scale construction projects would have been impossible to organize and carry out.

At the same time, such power adds compelling support for the existence of the state. In complex civilizations, most people must believe there are individuals who can rightfully require their labor, time, and wealth. As archaeologist Joseph Tainter puts it, the early elites had to convince the great mass of society that their rule was legitimate—in other words, "proper and valid"—and that the political world, with a powerful elite commanding from on high and accumulating great wealth, was "as it should be" (Tainter 1988:27). And, as the old saying goes, "nothing succeeds like success"; an awe-inspiring pyramid or temple goes a long way toward convincing the populace that the ruler who commanded such a thing to be built actually is as powerful as purported, and that allegiance is due that ruler.

A pyramid, a great tomb, a huge palace, and other monuments become the material symbols of the power of the state, both for those living within such systems and for us in the modern world who study them. They provide, as Tainter characterizes it, "sacred legitimization" (1988:28) for the power of the elite, and they reflect "the need to establish and constantly reinforce legitimacy" (1988:27).

Food Surplus

Equally important, these monumental works were made possible by the enormous **food surpluses** these societies produced, freeing substantial portions of their large and dense populations to devote at least a part of their labor and time to the monuments' construction. Where all hands are needed in the subsistence quest, there can be no great public works; where there is an enormous surplus coupled with a social pattern including classes that can monopolize that surplus—as well as monopolize the surplus labor of those freed from subsistence duties—monumental works become a possibility.

Large, Dense Populations

Since without a sizeable labor pool such monuments could never be built, a large population is a requirement of such societies, again supported by the evolving ability of farmers to produce increasing amounts of food and by increasing the yield of the same acreage. Increasingly efficient agricultural systems allow for increasingly large and dense communities, sometimes culminating in the development of urban centers, in other words, the city.

Labor Specialization

With the **specialization of labor,** certain individuals can devote all their time to perfecting skills in sophisticated and time-consuming specialties, such as technology, engineering, the arts, and crafts. Without the devotion of a lifetime's work, the level of skill exhibited in the great works associated with early civilizations, like the "wonderful things" in King Tut's tomb, could not have been achieved. Specialists can exist only in a society where enough food can be produced to feed all those people engaged in full-time specialist pursuits and where the social system provides a rationale for their existence. Such specialists are needed only in a society that demands their work by and for certain powerful people of an even higher class.

Record Keeping

Without some **system of record keeping** by which the elite could keep track of food surpluses and labor and, in essence, control history by recording it in a manner beneficial to them, it is unlikely that the entire system supporting the civilization could ever have developed. In modern America, for instance, how well would the Internal Revenue Service function—and how well would the country work—if there were no way to record individual income and yearly tax contribution? On the other hand, a system of keeping records that can reinforce the legitimacy of the rule of the king—for instance, by demonstrating descent from previous rulers or even from the gods—is another important way the system justifies and maintains itself. As a result of the record keeping of civilizations, in this and the next two chapters we begin to breach the edge of history, reaching the end of the human story that is the focus of this book—that part of the human saga from the period before history.

THE GEOGRAPHY OF CIVILIZATIONS

Perhaps most remarkably, the balance of these features of the world's first civilizations evolved from an earlier Neolithic base not once, but several times, in both the Old and New Worlds: in at least southwest Asia, Egypt, the Indus Valley of Pakistan, eastern China, and on the island of Crete (all discussed in this chapter), and in Mesoamerica and Peru (discussed in the next chapter). These primary civilizations developed more or less independently, each following its own path. The next sections will present brief synopses of the evolution of each of the centers of early civilization in the Old World.

Mesopotamia: Land Between the Rivers

The waters of the Tigris and Euphrates Rivers begin their journey to the Persian Gulf as a series of small streams in the modern nations of Turkey, Syria, Iraq, and Iran. Flowing southeast, the twin rivers are separated across their lengths by no more than 200 km (130 mi) and commonly by less than 100 km (65 mi) until they meet and jointly flow into the Persian Gulf. Together their valleys demarcate the boundaries of the region called **Mesopotamia,** and they played a fundamental role in producing the flat expanse of fertile soil in which the seeds of the world's first civilization were planted (see Map 13.2).

Foundations of Mesopotamian Civilization.   To the north, in the eastern horn of the Fertile Crescent, Neolithic villages had evolved in the early post-Pleistocene; subsistence was based on wheat, barley, lentils, sheep, and goats (see Chapter 12). In northern Mesopotamia, this period is symbolized by the **Umm Dabaghiyah** culture. Sites are small and the economy was mixed: some wheat and barley was planted and sheep, goats, pigs, and cattle were raised (Lamberg-Karlovsky and Sabloff 1995). Equally important was the hunting of onager (wild ass); the bones of this animal made up more than two-thirds of the faunal assemblage at the site.

By about 8,000 years ago, a subtle acceleration toward civilization has been recognized in the archaeological record. The sites of Hassuna, Samarra, and Halaf, each exhibiting distinctive pottery and architecture, lend their names to a chronological succession of three distinct cultures (with substantial temporal overlap): **Hassunan, Samarran,** and **Halafian.**

Dating from 8,000 B.P. to 7,200 B.P., Hassunan sites are small, typically about 100 m (325 ft) in diameter, with populations estimated at a few hundred (Lamberg-Karlovsky and Sabloff 1995:96). These sites show clear evidence of the primacy of agriculture in the subsistence base. Yarim Tepe, for example, has evidence of the planting of einkorn, emmer, bread, and club wheat as well as barley, peas, and lentils (Merpert and Munchaev 1987). While hunting wild animals persisted at Yarim Tepe, as evidenced by the remains of fallow deer, gazelle, and onager, 82% of the bones recovered were from domesticated animals, including sheep, goat, pig, and especially cattle (Maisels 1990:112).

Hassunan sites exhibit a few hints of what was to come in Mesopotamia—multiroomed houses with courtyards, for example, at Yarim Tepe. But, as archaeologists C. C. Lamberg-Karlovsky and Jeremy Sabloff (1995:97–98) point out, overall, Hassunan sites reflect a pattern of "rustic simplicity"; architecture was simple and homogeneous, there is no evidence of temples or palaces, few precious or luxurious items have been found, and there is no evidence of high-status burials indicative of class differentiation.

The site of Samarra and others included in the Samarran culture are located farther south, deep into the floodplain of the Tigris. These sites date to after 7,500 B.P. Part of the diets of the inhabitants of Samarran sites included the resources offered by the river; archaeological evidence points to heavy use of fish and mussels. The inhabitants of the Samarran site of Tell-es Sawwan supplemented their diets by hunting gazelle and fallow deer, while they planted emmer and bread wheat, barley, and caper (a fruit-producing shrub; Helbaek 1965).

That agriculture was a significant part of the subsistence system at Samarra and related sites is itself informative. As pointed out by archaeologist Joan Oates (1973), rainfall is meager in the central section of Mesopotamia, and an agricultural way of life would have been difficult, in some places impossible, without irrigation canals. Evidence of such canal building has been found at the Samarran site of Choga Mami. Later, irrigation becomes an increasingly significant factor in the lives of those living between the two rivers.

Some evidence exists for developing complexity in Samarran sites, including large-scale works that would have required a level of cooperation and coordination of labor not previously seen. Tell-es Sawwan, for example, was surrounded by an enormous wall and a ditch. Samarra has a large, buttressed fortification wall. The graves at Tell-es Sawwan are more elaborate than those at Hassunan sites, and more greatly differentiated. While most burials are plain, some are filled with alabaster, turquoise, copper, greenstone, obsidian, carnelian (a lustrous reddish-brown stone), and shell-bead necklaces and bracelets, implying an increasing gulf between members of the society, since turquoise, carnelian, and obsidian are not locally available and must have been traded for (Lamberg-Karlovsky and Sabloff 1995).

A new architectural feature is seen at this site. After about 7,400 B.P., the inhabitants constructed T-shaped buildings used to house the community's grain. As Lamberg-Karlovsky and Sabloff (1995:100–101) discuss, the communal storage of grain suggests a pooling of labor both in farming and in the construction of the building where the grain was stored. This portends what will happen a few centuries later, farther south into Mesopotamia.

Halafian sites, dating from 7,500 B.P. to 6,700 B.P., are not as well known as those of Hassuna or Samarra. Almost certainly the inhabitants were farmers. The residential architecture was simple, but a new architectural form is seen:

nonresidential, round buildings (sometimes called **tholoi**). They seem initially to have served as communal storage buildings, like the T-shaped buildings of the Samarran culture. The round buildings at some sites also contained human burials along with ceremonial objects, leading some archaeologists to suggest that they also served as the burial places for important people.

These archaeological discoveries dated to the Mesopotamian Neolithic show a clear evolutionary pattern of increasing sophistication and complexity in architecture and material culture. Communal projects and high-status burials imply the existence of chiefdoms at this point in the development of these societies. The existence of communal storage/ceremonial structures by the middle of the eighth millennium B.P. is intriguing, perhaps foreshadowing the key role of the temple in the first true civilization, the Sumerian city-states.

Accelerating Change: The Ubaid.   It is not until after 6,300 B.P., in the broad floodplain to the south, that a great leap forward was taken by the early Meso-potamians. The culture of southern Mesopotamia during this period, called **Ubaid,** is reflected in the sites of Tell al-'Ubaid, Tell Oueili, Eridu, 'Usaila, and Ur.

Southern Mesopotamia is not an area in which the world's first civiliza-tion might be expected. It is a land of sand dunes and marshes, a semiarid plain surrounded by a double-river system prone to unpredictable, ferocious flooding. Agriculture based on rainfall is impossible outside of marsh edges—the region receives as little as 15 cm (6 in.) of rain per year (H. Crawford 1991:8). The construction of irrigation canals is an absolute necessity for farmers in southern Mesopotamia.

Beyond the rich floodplain soil, Mesopotamia has few other resources. As archaeologist Harriet Crawford (1991) points out, Mesopotamia has no stone or metal sources and few areas with enough trees to provide wood for construction. It is not surprising, therefore, that Ubaid sites appear rather suddenly in this area, with no evidence of previous development. Much of the area simply was not attractive to Neolithic farmers in the Middle East. Southern Mesopotamia was populated only after population growth, made possible by the settled life of the Neolithic, forced people to expand onto the floodplain and away from the areas immediately adjacent to watercourses, sometime after 6,300 years ago. Similarly, this area was populated only when the construction of a system of water control became technologically—and socially—feasible.

The Role of Irrigation.   According to archaeologist Charles Maisels (1990), though the floodplain of the Tigris-Euphrates system is not an easy habitat to exploit, the construction of irrigation canals to water fields in the summer and to drain them after the spring floods makes it enormously productive farmland. Canal construction requires a large population whose labor can be organized. At the same time, an effective irrigation system allows for the pro-duction of even more food to support a larger and denser population. Maisels proposes that the deciding factors in the development of complex societies in Mesopotamia were (1) the need to concentrate population along the arable lands by the rivers, (2) the need to develop a socioeconomic behavioral pattern to allow for the construction of canals, and (3) the ability to irrigate to produce a food surplus.

Power Invested in the Temple.　In Mesopotamia and elsewhere, there was no political or military structure in place to provide the designers, builders, supervisors, maintainers, and controllers of the irrigation networks. Early Neolithic cultures were probably egalitarian or rank societies. But in Mesopotamia, as elsewhere, one institution in society was set apart and had extraordinary powers even before social complexity increased: the temple. Religious shrines or temples date back to well before the Ubaid period in Mesopotamia. As already mentioned, the familiar T-shaped northern Mesopotamian temple can be seen in prototype in Samarran sites, and, perhaps, as a functional prototype in the Halafian round storage buildings, where they seem to have served both as communal granaries and as places of religious significance. In the view of archaeologists C. C. Lamberg-Karlovsky and Jeremy Sabloff (1995), when population grew and expanded onto the floodplain, where irrigation works were a necessity, a need developed for the evolution of an institution that could organize the labor necessary to build and maintain these works. In their view, the religious elite quickly filled the power vacuum and became the dominant political, social, and religious force in Mesopotamian society. In other words, priests became chiefs. Control of the irrigation networks led to power, and with power came the ability to control the enormous food surplus that the evolving system produced.

Mesopotamia's First Cities: The Uruk Period.　After 6,000 B.P., dramatic changes occurred in southern Mesopotamia; by 5,500 B.P., the world's first densely populated, urban settlements developed. The first such city was Uruk (also called Warka). By about 5,000 years ago, Uruk's population swelled to an estimated 10,000 people; by 4,700 B.P. it may have been four or five times that size. The growth of Uruk occurred, at least in part, through a population implosion. Archaeological evidence indicates that many of the smaller farming communities around Uruk were abandoned about 4,700 years ago, with their populations congregating in the growing urban center. This movement of population may have resulted from widespread warfare, which is supported by evidence at Uruk itself where defensive fortifications were built at this time.

Another site, Eridu, became an urban center soon after Uruk, with an estimated population of 5,000, a large, finely built temple, and a neighborhood of larger houses with more impressive material culture, belonging to the newly evolved elite (Figure 13.7). By the Early Dynastic Period of the Sumerian civilization, dated from 4,850 B.P. to 4,600 B.P., there were more than twenty urban centers, or **city-states**—each with its own temple and with territory consisting

FIGURE 13.7

Artist's conception of the temple at the early Mesopotamian city of Eridu at around 5,000 B.P. (From *Art of the Ancient Near East* by Seaton Lloyd, copyright © 1961, Thames and Hudson, page 259, Praeger Publishers, an imprint of Greenwood Publishing Group, Inc., Westport, CT. Reprinted with permission)

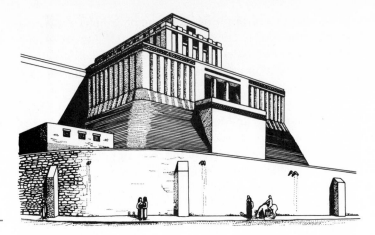

FIGURE 13.8

These clay tokens with impressed or incised symbols from the Middle East may represent the first evidence for a system of record keeping anywhere in the world. (Courtesy Départment des Antiquités Orientales, Musée du Louvre, Paris. Photograph courtesy of Denise Schmandt-Besserat)

of a four-tiered hierarchy of settlement types, including the city and its associated towns, villages, and hamlets (Civilization Portfolio, Color Plates 14 and 15; Adams and Nissen 1972).

The Beginning of the Written Record.   The first literate civilizations represent the beginning of history and, hence, the end of the focus of this book. Nevertheless, it is important to touch briefly on the origins of record keeping.

One of the most important works on the origins of writing in the Middle East, where writing appeared first, is by Denise Schmandt-Besserat (1992). She suggests that small baked-clay counters found in archaeological sites in the Middle East represent elements of an early system of record keeping for goods like bushels of wheat, sheep and goats, and jars of oil. These counters—called **tokens**—were made in sixteen basic shapes, mostly simple geometric forms, but also stylized animals and jars (Figure 13.8). Schmandt-Besserat examined a sample of over 8,000 tokens. The oldest date back as much as 10,000 years to early Neolithic cultures of the Middle East. Tokens have been found at Hassuna, Samarra, and Halaf.

Schmandt-Besserat (1992:163) describes the tokens as a method of "communication and data storage." In other words, the token form (and, later, markings incised in the tokens) represent a code, the first step in a record keeping system by which the Neolithic inhabitants of the Middle East could

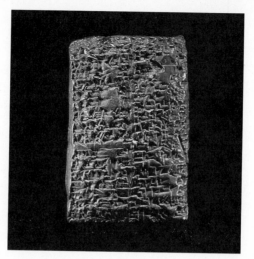

FIGURE 13.9
The cuneiform writing of Mesopotamia is the world's first written language.
(Lee Boltin, Boltin Picture Library)

keep track of valuable commodities like food, oil, and animals. Tokens have been found primarily in public buildings, as opposed to individual houses, and, importantly, in temples, implying their public function as well as the early connection between religion, the religious elite, and control of a food surplus. Thus, the tokens probably were used to keep track of food flowing into communal grain storage facilities or surplus food provided to the temple, perhaps as part of a tax or tithe.

Between 10,000 and 6,000 years ago, the tokens were plain; but after 6,000 B.P., tokens became increasingly more complex, with standardized designs incised into the clay. Also, tokens were stored in hollow clay balls called "envelopes" that also bore incised designs. Though initially used only to complement the information of the tokens themselves, the incised markings on the envelopes were to become the preferred medium of communication. It became simpler and more efficient to dispense with the tokens entirely and record information by making standardized impressions on clay tablets. These standardized impressions represented another code—in essence, the first written language, called **cuneiform** (Figure 13.9).

Schmandt-Besserat's view of the origins of a system of record keeping and, ultimately, record keeping through writing, meshes quite well with the reason suggested previously for why such a system was required by civilized societies. Knowledge is power, and the ability to control knowledge through a system of coded, permanent records provided those who knew the code and kept the records an enormous advantage in controlling first the economic system and ultimately the political and social systems. Those who keep the records know precisely what individuals have contributed food or wealth to the temple or the king—and know how much more is owed. A system of record keeping, usually but not universally through writing (see the discussion of the Inca in Chapter 14), played a major role, in Mesopotamia and elsewhere, in allowing the state to maintain its level of control.

Egypt of the Pharaohs

For most people, ancient Egypt uniquely illustrates the mystery and remarkable achievements of ancient civilization: the great pyramids at Gizeh, the enigmatic Sphinx, and the fabulous tombs filled with remarkable treasure (Civilization Portfolio, Color Plates 16–18). But achievements such as the pyramids (there were only about eighty of these monuments built) reflect the Egyptian civilization at its peak. The roots of Egyptian civilization lie in the earliest Neolithic cultures that developed in the Nile Valley (Map 13.3).

The Egyptian Neolithic.   The Egyptian Neolithic appears to be historically derivative. The crops and domesticated animals on which the Neolithic inhabitants subsisted were all used in southwest Asia at an earlier date (see Chapter 12). Between 7,000 and 5,000 years ago, a gradual shift to a Neolithic economy is seen along the Nile, the only region where a nonirrigation-based agriculture is possible in Egypt. At the sites of Merimde, Tasa, and Badari, wheat and barley appear to have been the most significant plant foods, domesticated flax provided fibers, and sheep, goats, cattle, and pigs were the primary sources of animal protein (Trigger 1983).

Sometime after 6,500 and at an accelerating rate after 5,500 B.P., a political coalescence began along the Nile among some of the early farming villages. The floodplain of the Nile demarcates the viable farmland in Egypt before the development of a sophisticated system of irrigation. The Nile runs through a desert, and small Neolithic villages developed along the river like pearls on a necklace.

Foundations of Civilization Along the Nile.   Perhaps as a result of increasing competition for the primary resource of good agricultural land, some well-positioned towns seem to have become what geographers call **central places—**places viewed by the local populace as locations of great spiritual and social power. We know of at least two of these incipient "states," by their "capitals": Nagada and Hierakonpolis.

Nagada predates Hierakonpolis, though the latter far exceeds the former in historical significance. At Nagada we see early evidence for the kind of social differentiation that is one of the defining features of civilization, in the form of sumptuous burials afforded a very small proportion of the population. By 5,500 B.P., it seems that Nagada controlled a large surrounding territory, and the power needed for that control was vested in a small group of people, a developing social elite whose status is symbolized—then and now—by their burial in elaborate tombs.

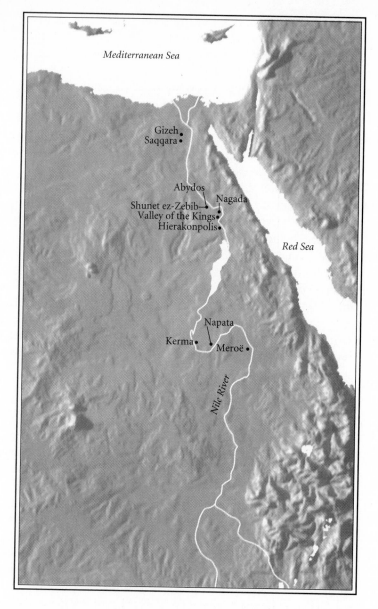

MAP 13.3

Archaeological sites in northern Africa where evidence of the evolution of chiefdom and early state-level societies has been found.

Hierakonpolis.   The evidence for the evolution of an increasingly complex society is far clearer at Hierakonpolis, largely due to the efforts of archaeologist Michael Hoffman (1979, 1983). Hierakonpolis began its history nearly 6,000 years ago as a small Neolithic village on the west bank of the Nile. This is now called the Nagada I, or Amratian, period of Egyptian prehistory. Pottery manufacture became a booming business at Hierakonpolis, and ceramics manufactured in its kilns are found up and down the Nile. While pottery likely originated as a small-scale, family-run affair, here it developed into a specialized craft, along with a class of "pottery barons." The burials of these people were larger and far more elaborate than the interments of the rest of society. Brick-lined tombs cut into the bedrock mark the final resting places of the growing class of pottery makers.

After 5,500 B.P., during Nagada II, or Gerzean, times, irrigation canals were constructed, probably in response to a change in the local climate. A dry period began, possibly resulting from local deforestation, which, in turn, resulted from the need to fuel the pottery kilns. The tombs of a developing elite became larger; some include a square stone building called a **mastaba** built on top of a subterranean brick-lined or rock-cut tomb.

As population along the Nile grew and as competition for resources increased, previously minor arguments or perceived injustices among and between neighboring towns grew into full-scale battles for control of the precious land base. The period after 5,100 B.P. is marked by the abandonment of small villages located around the central places of Nagada and Hierakonpolis. The populations of the small towns seem to have moved into the larger settlements, making them substantially larger and more complex. Fortifications around Nagada and Hierakonpolis were built and expanded at this time, and the burials of the growing elite became increasingly elaborate (Kemp 1977). At Hierakonpolis, for example, Tomb 100 is brick-lined, is much larger than previous tombs, and has wall paintings depicting the deceased as a ruler.

First Pharaoh.   A king list exists from the New Kingdom (1,540 B.C.–1,070 B.C.) containing the names of about 300 pharaohs (Kemp 1991:23). The list, now called the Royal Canon of Turin for the Italian museum where it is housed, apparently was a virtually complete enumeration of Egyptian rulers up to that time, providing the duration of their reigns, sometimes to the exact numbers of years, months, and days. This list traces back Egyptian kingship 958 years, to the rule of the first historically known pharaoh, Menes, who united Lower (northern) and Upper (southern) Egypt (since the Nile runs from south to north, the upper region of the river—its source—lies to the south, and its lower section—the delta—is in the north). Under the leadership of Menes, a single political entity was created that was to become one of the most remarkable of the early civilizations.

A plaque celebrating the unification of Egypt and the ascension of the first pharaoh was discovered at Hierakonpolis. On one side a man is depicted with a mace or baton raised as if about to strike a kneeling enemy soldier (Figure 13.10). The standing man is wearing a crown that we know from later writing to be the symbol of leadership of Upper Egypt. On the opposite side of the plaque, the same man is depicted wearing a crown that includes the symbol of kingship of Lower Egypt. We can read his name on the object: Narmer. In all likelihood, Narmer is another name for Menes (who is also called the Scorpion), positioned in the king list as the first pharaoh of a unified Egyptian state. Narmer's ascension to the throne of Egypt occurred about 5,100 B.P.

FIGURE 13.10

The Narmer Palette of Hierakonpolis depicts symbolically the unification of Upper and Lower Egypt under the leadership of Narmer, the first pharaoh, in about 5,100 B.P. (Giraudon/Art Resource, N.Y.)

This all sets the stage for developments in Egypt that, again, cross over the boundary between prehistory and history, and pass beyond the scope of this book. When the royal cemetery at Abydos is examined, royal tombs far beyond anything seen at Hierakonpolis are encountered. For example, the Shunet ez-Zebib, built almost 5,000 years ago, is an enormous burial enclosure surrounded by a monumental wall measuring about 125 m (404 ft) in length and 65 m (210 ft) in width, with walls more than 5 m (16 ft) thick and 11 m (36 ft) high (Kemp 1991:53). The exterior of the wall is decorated to give a paneled effect. Soon after the Shunet ez-Zebib was built, the burial tomb of the pharaoh Djoser was constructed at Saqqara (Figure 13.11). Built 4,600 years ago, Djoser's tomb is a stepped pyramid, a stone construction on a scale much larger than anything built previously in ancient Egypt. Ultimately, pharaohs commanded the labor of hundreds of thousands of workers and were buried in spectacular fashion, though only a fraction were buried in pyramid tombs that today are emblematic of ancient Egypt (Civilization Portfolio, Color Plate 18).

After the period of pyramid construction had long passed, a young boy ascended to the throne during a period of great turbulence. He ruled as pha-

FIGURE 13.11

The form of the stepped pyramid at Saqqara, built to memorialize the Egyptian pharaoh Djoser in about 4,600 B.P., was based on earlier mastaba tombs of Egypt's elite. (M. H. Feder)

raoh for ten years, from age 9 to age 19, when he died. His name was Tutankhamun, and his splendid burial will probably stand forever as a symbol of ancient Egypt; it also served as a metaphor for ancient civilization in the Prelude of this chapter.

Other African Civilizations.　Ancient Egypt's influence reached far from its center in northeasternmost Africa, perhaps most significantly to the south, to the ancient civilizations of **Nubia.** Initially inspired by the colossus to the north, Nubia developed its own uniquely African early civilization (see Map 13.3). The Egyptians called the land to the south **Kush.** If you travel south past the so-called first cataract near Aswan in modern Egypt (the first extensive rapids encountered along the Nile from north to south) into the modern nation of Sudan and continue to the sixth cataract, north of the Sudanese city of Khartoum, you have traversed the territory of ancient Nubia (O'Connor 1993).

Ancient Nubian civilization developed, at least initially, in response to the impact of the great civilization of Egypt just downstream. But ancient Egyptian civilization was not merely imported upstream, nor do we see Egyptian culture grafted wholesale onto an indigenous population's culture. Rather, developments to the north seem to have inspired the evolution, not of only a pale reflection of ancient Egyptian civilization, but of what archaeologist David O'Connor (1993) characterizes as a distinct civilization that was "Egypt's rival" in ancient Africa.

Dating to more than 3,500 years ago, the civilization of Kerma represents the first indigenous complex civilization in Africa south of the ancient Egyptian nation (Connah 1987). Kerma itself is located on the east bank of the Nile, south of the third cataract in Sudan. The site has been called "the earliest city in Africa outside of Egypt" (O'Connor 1993:50). The center of Kerma covered 15–25 acres and was surrounded by a huge wall 10 m (33 ft) high. Its fortifications included monumental towers called **deffufa** constructed of mud-brick; the western deffufa, of solid brick, is 52 m (170 ft) long and 27 m (88 ft) wide. Today it stands more than 19 m (57 ft) high, and was even taller in antiquity.

To the east of the city was a large cemetery, marked by enormous tumuli—earth mounds marking the graves of the elite—averaging 88 m (288 ft) in diameter (O'Connor 1993:54). These graves bear witness to the degree of social stratification in that society. The elite were placed on finely made wooden beds, some encased in gold, and well-crafted items were entombed with them for their enjoyment in the afterlife: bronze swords, bronze razors, fine clothing of leather, ostrich feather fans, and large quantities of pottery. The most impressive grave in the cemetery belongs to Tumulus X, an obviously important ruler of Kerma, surrounded by the sacrificed remains of close to 400 retainers (322 actual remains were found, but the burial was disturbed and more burials were probably interred with the primary grave).

After 2,800 B.P., the influence of Kerma faded and another Nubian kingdom arose. Called Napata, it was centered just downstream of the fourth cataract. It probably developed when Egypt's reach to the south weakened. Social stratification is evidenced at the cemeteries of El Kurru, Jebel Barkal, and Nuri, where the elite were buried in tombs topped with small pyramids reminiscent of ancient Egypt yet clearly of local construction. The main population center of the Napata polity was the large town of Sanam.

Perhaps the best known of the ancient Nubian cultures is that of Meroë. The Meroitic civilization dates from 2,500 B.P. to 2,200 B.P. and is the most complex and the most urban of the ancient civilizations south of Egypt (Connah 1987). The city of Meroë was a large settlement covering an area of about 0.75 km² (0.3 mi²). The center of the settlement consisted of a maze of monumental structures made of mud-brick and faced with fired brick. These buildings appear to have been palaces, meeting halls, temples, and residences for nobility and their workers. The central area of Meroë was surrounded by a monumental wall of mud-brick.

An enormous graveyard containing 600 simple interments of common people has been excavated to the east of the city. This can be compared to the graveyard farther to the east, called North Cemetery, where the tombs of Meroitic nobility were located, with small, stone pyramids built on top (Figure 13.12).

Clearly the civilizations of Nubia were at least partially indigenous developments with a heavy influence from the north. Contact with Egypt may have been the catalyst that set local people on the road to great social complexity and technological sophistication. Once initiated, however, Nubians evolved their own, distinct version of civilization.

The Indus Valley Civilization

Though it has generated less interest as well as less archaeology than either Mesopotamia or ancient Egypt, the Indus Valley civilization of the enormous

FIGURE 13.12

The pyramids of the rulers of Meroë, an African civilization, are located to the south of pharaonic Egypt and date to between 2,500 and 2,200 B.P. (© Marc and Evelyne Bernheim 1980, all rights reserved, Woodfin Camp and Associates)

cities of Harappa and Mohenjo-Daro deserves recognition as another primary Old World civilization (Allchin and Allchin 1982; Fairservis 1975; Possehl 1980).

The Indus civilization has been known to scholars in the West only since its two largest cities were first excavated in the early 1920s. The roots of the culture are barely known, with only a small handful of pre-Indus sites excavated. Though like Mesopotamia and ancient Egypt in other respects, the Indus culture had a written language that is, as yet, largely undeciphered. There are close to 4,000 preserved samples of Indus writing, but only a few of the individual signs have been interpreted (Parpola 1993). Until the Indus Valley script is deciphered, the people of the Indus cannot speak directly to us in the way that ancient Mesopotamians and Egyptians can.

Neolithic Cultures. Despite this lack of evidence, the remaining data indicate Neolithic roots for the Indus civilization that can be traced to the hills of Baluchistan (in modern Pakistan; Map 13.4). One site excavated in the uplands is Kili Ghul Muhammad, covering a small area 90 m (292 ft) by 55 m (178 ft). The structures at the site were mud-brick, and subsistence included the raising of sheep, goats, and oxen (Allchin and Allchin 1982). The only radiocarbon dates for Kili Ghul Muhammad date to between 6,100 B.P. and 6,400 B.P., though these were not derived from the earliest levels at the site, which probably date to a thousand or more years earlier than the dated levels. Another site in the Baluchistan Hills is Rana Ghundai. The houses, again, were of mud-brick, and here, too, sheep and goats were important for subsistence, along with cattle and ass.

Moving east, out of the uplands and closer to the Indus River, is the site of Mehrgarh, first occupied by about 8,000 B.P. Its location at the zone of transi-

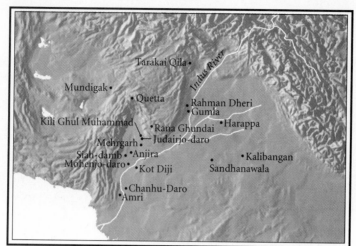

MAP 13.4
Archaeological sites in India, Pakistan, and Afghanistan where evidence of the evolution of chiefdom and early state-level societies has been found.

tion between the uplands to the west and the floodplain to the east is important in our investigation of the Indus Valley civilization. The Indus is a treacherous river characterized by devastating and unpredictable flooding. Unlike the situation in Egypt or Mesopotamia, early Neolithic sites are not found along the river. As archaeologists Bridget Allchin and Raymond Allchin point out, the realization on the part of local inhabitants of the rich agricultural soil the Indus system had to offer, coupled with their development of flood control and protection technology, allowed for the evolution of "an entirely new way of life" (1982:105). A transition took place at this time at the site of Mehrgarh, from small, simple farming villages such as those at Kili Ghul Muhammad, Rana Ghundai, Anjira, and Siah-damb to the urban civilization represented at Mohenjo-Daro and Harappa.

By 7,100 B.P. the inhabitants of Mehrgarh were practicing a mixed farming economy—the earliest evidence for a sedentary, agricultural way of life on the Indian subcontinent. They planted wheat, barley, and dates and raised domesticated cattle and water buffalo. Mehrgarh also has produced the earliest evidence in Asia of the domestication of cotton.

By a little before 7,000 years ago, Mehrgarh was no longer a simple Neolithic village. It boasts a rather sophisticated architecture that included the use of mud-brick to produce a substantial and permanent settlement. The village had a number of domestic units—probably the homes of individual families—containing six, and sometimes nine rooms. Some separate structures appear to have been public granaries. Exotic materials found in burials at the site include conch shell from the Arabian Sea, lapis lazuli from Badakshan, and turquoise from Turkmenia; these source areas are located as far as 500 km (325 mi) from the settlement.

Trade and competition—perhaps with attendant warfare—appears to have been important to the growth of larger and increasingly complex sites in Baluchistan after 6,000 years ago. One site, Mundigak, is located on a well-known historical trade route between the Near East and south Asia that apparently was first established at this time. Mundigak was surrounded by enormous defensive walls interrupted with bastions. These walls had a practical purpose; the village was twice destroyed and twice rebuilt during its occupation.

All these Neolithic sites west of the Indus provide a glimpse of the earliest stages of development of the Indus Valley civilization. They all exhibit a reliance on a diverse agricultural base of locally developed crops and animals and show a notable reliance on trade with points as distant as the Arabian Sea and central Asia. They share an architectural form of substantial and planned-out mud-brick houses. And they show a shift through time from the uplands of Baluchistan to the floodplain of the Indus itself. This shift is clearly seen in the archaeological record by about 5,500 B.P.

Flood Control and Civilization in the Indus Valley.   This shift was the key to the development of civilization in this part of the world. It was made possible by the development of flood control and protection technology: Villages were protected from the periodic rampages of the Indus by being built partly on artificial mounds above the floodwaters and by being surrounded by monumental walls high enough to protect from both enemies and the floodwaters.

Kot Diji is located on the rich floodplain about 32 km (20 mi) east of the Indus River, immediately adjacent to one of its ancient flood channels (Figure 13.13). The village is surrounded by a huge wall with a limestone rubble foundation and a mud-brick superstructure plus bastions 5 m (16 ft) high. This wall almost certainly served for defense not only against human enemies but also against the natural enemy of the floodwaters of the Indus. To the northeast is another large village, Kalibangan. Here too, a massive mud-brick wall surrounds the settlement. Other substantial, walled villages on the Indus floodplain, dating to the period after 5,500 B.P., include the sites of Amri, Gumla, Rhaman Dheri, and Tarakai Qila.

Cultural Convergence.   An interesting feature of these settlements is the degree of what Allchin and Allchin refer to as "cultural convergence" (1982:163). Whereas each of the previous Neolithic sites in Baluchistan exhibited its own artifact styles in pottery and items of adornment, as people began moving out onto the floodplain of the Indus, a certain uniformity appears, indicating a greater level of cultural and perhaps political unification. Most significantly, a common image of a horned buffalo head begins appearing on pottery throughout the area at many of the sites mentioned. Also, terra-cotta statues of women, following a standardized style, appear at many of the sites dating to this period; some archaeologists have dubbed these "mother goddesses," implying a degree of religious unification as well (Allchin and Allchin 1982:163).

A few of these floodplain settlements began an exponential increase in size sometime after 4,500 years ago, culminating in their crossing the boundary between town and true city. Though several Indus Valley settlements qualify as cities in size and complexity—among them the sites of Kalibangan, Chanhu-Daro, Judeirjo-Daro, Sandhanawala, and Dhoraji—two settlements stand out as representing the pinnacle of urban development: the ancient cities of Mohenjo-Daro, in the southern reaches of the Indus, and Harappa, to the north, on the now-dry channel of the Ravi River, tributary of the Indus.

Cities of the Indus.   During what specialists refer to as the "mature Harappan period" lasting for 500 years, from 4,500 B.P. to 4,000 B.P. (Possehl 1980:5), Mohenjo-Daro and Harappa developed into complex urban centers. These cities had planned neighborhoods following a rectangular grid pattern, a sophisticated drainage system (most individual homes in Mohenjo-Daro and Harappa had indoor bathrooms connected by drains to a citywide sewage system), communal granaries, bath houses, "citadels" consisting of great structures of unclear function (palaces, temples, granaries, perhaps) built atop artificial mounds, and populations of more than 35,000 people in each community (Figure 13.14 and Civilization Portfolio, Color Plate 19).

Hundreds of smaller farming villages were aligned with these two great cities, which together were the central places of a cultural entity that encompassed almost 770,000 km^2 (more than 300,000 mi^2) of territory (Possehl 1980:2). Even beyond the Indus Valley itself, large frontier settlements show the same material culture and written language. For example, the site of Lothal, located to the east of the Indus, still exhibits many of the architectural characteristics as well as the spatial layout of Mohenjo-Daro and Harappa, albeit on a smaller scale.

The degree of planning that went into Indus Valley urban sites is unmatched among the earliest civilizations. Mohenjo-Daro, Harappa, and Kalibangan follow virtually identical plans (see Figure 13.14). In these three cases, a citadel was built up on a platform of mud-brick on the western margin of

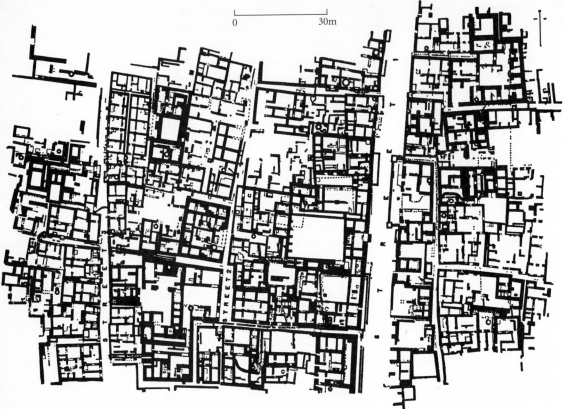

FIGURE 13.14

This map of Mohenjo-Daro exhibits the planned nature of the city, with its major avenues, parallel and perpendicular streets, and regularly sized buildings and rooms. (From M. Wheeler 1968. *The Indus Civilization.* New York: Cambridge University Press. Reprinted with permission of the publisher)

the city. The citadel was surrounded by large public buildings, including bath houses and granaries, and this "upper city" was encompassed by a monumental wall. In each case, the vast expanse of the city making up the residential area where tens of thousands of people lived was spread out to the east of the citadel. The lower city likewise was surrounded by a great wall. In all three cases it is clear that the cities did not grow simply by accretion, blocks of residences added haphazardly as needed in response to population growth. Instead, they show a pattern of forethought in their construction—broad main thoroughfares separated by secondary streets, which in turn were separated by narrow passageways leading to individual residences. Most of the roads were laid out in an often precise grid of parallel and perpendicular pathways. And the houses themselves were constructed with mud-bricks that are so regular that their makers, much like modern brickyards, must have adhered to established standards of size and form.

The dwellings in the lower cities of Indus urban centers range widely in size, from single-room apartments to mansions with dozens of rooms and enclosed courtyards. The size and elaborateness of some residences almost certainly bespeaks vast differences in the wealth and status of the individuals who lived in them. Neighborhoods of craft specialists have been identified at Mohenjo-Daro and Harappa. Certain sections of each city were blocked out for metal workers, potters, cloth makers, bakers, stone workers, and bead makers and can be defined archaeologically according to the tools of their various trades that have been found restricted to their respective neighborhoods. Other areas of the cities appear to have been the residences of scribes, priests, administrators, and traders (Allchin and Allchin 1982:185).

Indus Valley cities were also trading centers into which exotic and undoubtedly expensive raw materials flowed and in which finely finished goods were produced. Gold, copper, lead, lapis lazuli, turquoise, alabaster, amethyst, agate, chalcedony, and carnelian were brought into the city, often originating at sources many hundreds of kilometers distant (Allchin and Allchin 1982:186). Also, some trade was carried out between these Indus Valley cities and the city-states of ancient Mesopotamia. Harappan **seals** have been found in Mesopotamia; a small number of Mesopotamian **cylinder seals** have been found in Indus Valley sites. The island of Bahrain, in the Persian Gulf, served as a central point in this intercivilization trade network. In other words, more than 4,000 years ago Mesopotamia and the Indus Valley were part of an international trading network.

The Civilization of Ancient China

The roots of Chinese civilization can be traced back to the Yang-shao culture discussed in Chapter 12. Yang-shao sites are small, and subsistence was based on the cultivation of millet and, only later, rice (Map 13.5).

The Lung-shan Culture.   Chinese archaeologists perceive a change in Yang-shao sometime after 5,000 B.P. and define a new culture, the **Lung-shan,** as replacing Yang-shao. Rice became the dominant cultigen, and sites are larger and more permanent. A number of new features distinguish Lung-shan sites from earlier Yang-shao and presage the development of early Chinese complex civilizations. For example, at the Lung-shan site of Ch'eng tzu-yai, the village was enclosed by a monumental wall of stamped earth. The Chinese term for the stamped-earth or pounded-earth construction technique is **hang-t'u.** The hang-t'u technique was used frequently in later periods in Chinese history to make house walls as well as defensive structures.

The wall at Ch'eng tzu-yai is enormous and required a large labor force far beyond what previous cultures were able to gather. The wall is measured at 390 m (1,300 ft) by 450 m (1,500 ft), is 9 m (29 ft) wide at the top and 6 m (19 ft) high (Chang 1986:248).

The cemetery at the site reveals another significant element of civilization: status differentiation, as reflected in highly differentiated burials. Archaeologist K. C. Chang (1986) notes the existence of a four-tiered burial hierarchy. There are large elaborate graves at the site, with high-status tombs where the deceased were interred in wooden caskets and accompanied by fine

MAP 13.5

Archaeological sites in China where evidence of the evolution of chiefdom and early state-level societies has been found.

ceramics. In the same cemetery are narrow burial pits barely large enough to place a human body, with no casket or grave goods. A typical stratified society has far fewer members of the elite than of the peasant classes. As reflected in the burial statistics, Ch'eng tzu-yai had 5 upper-class burials, 11 second-class, 17 third-class, and 54 fourth- or low-class burials (Chang 1986:249).

This compares to the socioeconomic class structure at the enormous later Neolithic cemetery at T'a-ssu. Of the excavated graves there, 9 were judged to be upper class, 80 belonged to a middle tier, and 610 were plain, lower-class interments (Chang 1986:277). Some of the upper-class burials dating to this same period contained an incredible array of rare items exhibiting a high level of artistic sophistication. For example, a young man buried at the site of Ssu-tun was interred with 57 intricate, finely carved jade rings and jade tubes (called *ts'ung*).

Along with monumental village walls, which later became a common feature of Chinese civilization, and status-differentiated burials, the period from 5,000 to 4,000 years ago in China is marked by a number of other features that represent key elements in the earliest Chinese civilization. The increasing use of metal, especially copper, and the earliest use of bronze is evidenced during this time. Historian Jacques Gernet (1987) suggests that the sophisticated kilns—capable of producing very high, constant temperatures—used in the Chinese Neolithic to produce the fine ceramics that mark even the early years of that period helped the rapid advancement in metallurgy that marks Chinese civilization. In Gernet's view, the ability to manufacture bronze weapons was a key element in the evolution of Chinese civilization (the development of bronze metallurgy and the rise of China's first civilization do indeed overlap temporally). Gernet proposes that power was invested in those who controlled bronze production, and walled cities evolved as a result of competition and warfare.

A number of other identifiable hallmarks of later Chinese civilization appear at this time, between 5,000 and 4,000 years ago. The jade tubes and the practice of **scapulimancy**—divining by interpreting the patterns produced by heating animal shoulder blades in a fire—become geographically widespread, indicating a spatially broad sphere of interaction and the initial unification of people into first a religiously defined and ultimately a politically drawn entity. This is reminiscent of the "cultural convergence" seen in the Indus Valley immediately prior to the development of civilization there. In Chapter 14 we will see much the same process at work again in Mesoamerica and South America.

This is also the period when evidence of violence on a scale not previously seen in Chinese prehistory is present. Monumental village walls with ramparts, as well as the skeletal evidence of trauma, imply that warfare has already established itself during Lung-shan times.

Acceleration Toward Civilization.   The culmination of these early developments can be seen at the site of Erh-li-t'ou, dated to about 3,800 B.P. The site is an order of magnitude bigger than anything seen previously, covering an area of 2.5 km (1.6 mi) by 1.5 km (a little less than 1 mi). Bronze artifacts are common at the site, as are jade tubes. Some of the bronzes were utilitarian tools, including knives, chisels, axes, adzes, arrowheads, and other weapons. Many of the bronze artifacts were ceremonial or ornamental, including disks, fancy drinking vessels, and musical instruments.

There are large, impressive burials at Erh-li-t'ou, and some members of what we can confidently call the wealthy, elite class were buried in lacquered coffins. A unique feature of Erh-li-t'ou are the remains of two palaces. Far larger than any of the residences at the site, one palace was about 100 m (325 ft) on a side, the second somewhat smaller. The walls of both palaces consisted of thick berms of stamped earth.

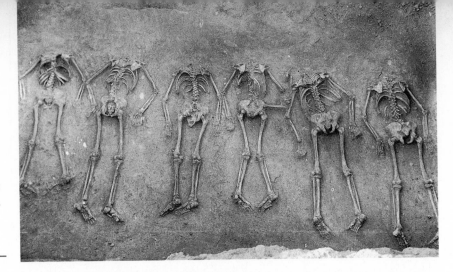

FIGURE 13.15

The burial remains of be-headed people who were sacrificed in ceremonies surrounding the death of a member of the royal class of the Shang civilization in China. (Courtesy of the Institute of History and Philology, Academia Sinica, Taiwan)

MAP 13.6

Archaeological sites in Crete where evidence of the evolution of chiefdom and early state-level societies has been found.

The Shang Civilization.   The site of Erh-li-t'ou was a precursor to the early florescence of Chinese civilization as represented by the Shang Dynasty. The Shang was China's first true urban civilization. For example, the modern city of An-yang is the site of the ancient city of Yin, a Shang capital city ruled by a succession of twelve kings beginning about 2,400 years ago.

Great tombs of the rulers residing at Yin have been found at the sites of Hsiao-t'un and Hsi-pei-kang. These enormous royal interments must have involved the labor of thousands of peasants. The graves are cruciform—in the shape of a cross. The king or emperor was buried in the center of the cross, with long, broad access ramps leading to the burial itself. The deceased noble-man or noblewoman was placed in an elaborate wooden coffin, surrounded by the symbols of rank and wealth that differentiated him or her from the rest of society: jade, bronze, and ceramic artifacts, and even chariots and sacrificed horses (Civilization Portfolio, Color Plate 20). Along the access ramps to the royal gravesite were found the remains of dozens of humans sacrificed to accompany their leader into the afterlife, decapitated and laid out neatly in rows along the rampways (Figure 13.15).

It is with the Shang that we enter the historical period of China's past. A written language containing more than 5,000 characters, only a fraction of which have been translated, has been found at Shang sites. Shang set the stage for all subsequent Chinese civilization. At least symbolically, the Chinese emperors who ruled well into the twentieth century were the inheritors of a culture that can be traced back to the time of the first dynasty of the Shang civilization.

Minoan Crete

The island of Crete is a tiny jewel in the eastern Mediterranean (Map 13.6). It is long and narrow, less than 250 km (152 mi) from east to west and no more than 56 km (35 mi) from north to south. Its entire area is barely 8,260 km^2 (3,189 mi^2), equaling the combined area of the two smallest states in the United States: Rhode Island and Delaware.

FIGURE 13.16

The temple at Knossos on Crete is the most impressive, though by no means the only, material evidence of the monumental architecture of the ancient Minoan civilization. (© Fritz Henle 1974/Photo Researchers, Inc.)

Since it is an island far from the mainland, Crete was occupied relatively late in prehistory. It was reachable only with the development in the Mediterranean of seaworthy boats and people with navigational skills. The oldest occupation of the island dates only to 8,000 B.P.; it was uninhabited by human beings before that time. Yet on this small island, Europe's first great civilization was to develop.

The Rediscovery of Minoan Crete.   In the 1890s, archaeologist Sir Arthur Evans discovered the remains of what he labeled the **Minoan** civilization on Crete (A. Evans 1921–1936). Evans had been inspired in his search by the Greek myth of King Minos of Crete, who kept a terrible half-human, half-bull monster called the Minotaur deep in the recesses of a tortuous labyrinth. Until the twentieth century, King Minos and his civilization were assumed by many people to be mythological. But some thinkers felt that the Greek myths reflected historical truths in at least some of their particulars. In perhaps the best-known example, archaeologist Heinrich Schliemann found the real Troy—assumed by many people to be the product of the imagination of ancient Greek writer Homer—by taking Homer literally in his description of that ancient city and its location. Likewise, Evans took seriously the core of the story of King Minos and a great civilization on Crete contemporary with or even older than that of ancient Greece.

Evans first visited Crete in 1894, and almost immediately he recognized the great archaeological potential of a hillside at **Knossos** on the north-central part of the island. Eventually, Evans was able to purchase the site. In 1900 he initiated excavations and quickly discovered the spectacular remains of a great palace or temple [Figure 13.16; see the chapter titled "Arthur Evans and the Minoans" in Brian Fagan's (1994) *Quest for the Past: Great Discoveries in Archaeology*]. This seemed to be the remains of the city of King Minos as described by the ancient Greeks. The temple was built on an artificial mound 7 m (22 ft) high, composed of the piled-up remains of ten successive building levels of Neolithic housing dating back to 8,000 B.P. (J. D. Evans 1968).

Who Were the Minoans?   The settlers of Crete were people from the mainland of southeastern Europe and southwestern Asia, probably from Greece and Anatolia (Renfrew 1972, 1979). Though initially discovered by chance, Crete soon was intentionally settled by people in the eighth millennium B.P. who brought their Neolithic food base with them. Archaeological excavation of Neolithic Crete reveals the presence of emmer and bread wheat, along with sheep, goats, pigs, and cattle, none of which are native to the island (Warren 1987). The Neolithic population grew and a number of farming villages dotted the island in the millennia following its initial settlement.

Geographically, Crete was quite fortuitously positioned at a crossroads for people sailing between southeastern Europe and the ancient civilizations of the Middle East and ancient Egypt. An influx of wealth from ancient trade between the peoples of three continents seems to have spurred a period of increasing complexity on Crete. The island itself provided perfect conditions for growing olives, and the olive oil produced on Crete and traded throughout the Mediterranean brought even more wealth to the island. A burst of development, centered at the site of Knossos, occurred at about 5,000 B.P., beginning with the importation of bronze from the mainland. By about 3,880 B.P., the first monumental edifice, the temple discovered and initially excavated by Evans, was constructed at the site of Knossos. The building consisted of a maze-like jumble of rooms, chambers, halls, and corridors. This main temple at Knossos is, in fact, called the "Labyrinth," a reference to the myth of King Minos' labyrinth with the Minotaur at its core (Castleden 1990a).

Though fed by trade and contact with older, established civilizations in Africa and the Middle East, civilization on Minoan Crete does not represent the transplantation of an alien culture. Crete benefited from its location, and the ideas and wealth that passed through the island certainly acted as a catalyst in the development of Minoan civilization. But, as archaeologist Colin Renfrew (1979) points out, Minoan Crete by and large involves an indigenous, European development of civilized life, traceable to a complexity that had been evolving in the Aegean for a thousand years.

The Temple at Knossos.   At its peak the temple at Knossos would cover an area of 20,000 m^2 (210,000 ft^2, or about 5 acres) and contain about 1,000 separate rooms. The temple included a central courtyard with a pillar-lined hallway, a huge number of storage rooms, a ceremonial bath, and grand staircases leading to upper levels—some parts of the temple had three or four stories. The walls of some of the living quarters and large halls were covered with magnificent frescoes of dolphins and especially bulls. The artistic depiction of bulls in ceremonial settings may be connected to the Greek story of the Minotaur. Where the Minoans depicted themselves in these paintings, we see a graceful and athletic people (Figure 13.17).

One set of rooms has been interpreted as the living quarters of the nobility of Knossos, replete with thrones, bathrooms, and a sophisticated drainage

system for waste water. The monumental proportions and complexity of the temple at Knossos are a clear indication of developing complexity in social, political, and economic spheres of the community. Further evidence of Minoan civilization is seen in the form of writing—so-called Linear A, as yet undeciphered. The existence of a record-keeping system is diagnostic of a civilization; the complex economic transactions at the heart of state society—taxes, for example—must be kept track of. The social "tax" of army service or labor conscription that allows the elite of a civilized society to build their great monuments and to protect their position of privilege also requires a system of record keeping.

Developments on Crete were halted, if only temporarily, by a catastrophic earthquake that all but destroyed the temple at Knossos at 3,650 B.P. Another impressive temple on Crete, at the site of Phaistos, was also damaged at this time. That temple later was destroyed utterly in a fire. Remarkably, however, this served only to spur further development on Crete in what is called the **New Temple Period.** Apparently, the wealth still pouring into the island was sufficient to overcome the effects of this natural disaster.

This peak in Minoan civilization occurred during the period 3,650–3,420 B.P. The temple of Knossos was rebuilt and became even larger and more impressive. Paintings and statuettes indicate a developing religion focused on goddesses and priestesses. There is little evidence of the kind of conspicuous consumption that marks ancient Egypt or Mesopotamia; there are no overwhelmingly ornate burials of an elite at Knossos or elsewhere on Crete. Small rural farming villages continued to supply their food surplus to support the temples located at Knossos and elsewhere. Large towns developed, each with its own temple and residential areas; Knossos was the largest and most impressive of these, but it was not the only one. At its peak, the population of Knossos and its surrounding "suburbs" was close to 100,000 (Marinatos 1972:709), making it the largest concentration of people anywhere in the ancient world up to that time.

The Eruption on Thera.   This pattern of evolving complexity was brought to a halt by another, even more devastating natural catastrophe. Around 3,420 B.P. (perhaps a bit earlier) there was a cataclysmic volcanic eruption on the island today called Santorini (the ancient Greeks called it Thera; before that it was Kalliste), 120 km (72 mi) north of Crete. Though it cannot be said that the explosion on Thera immediately destroyed Minoan civilization, it certainly had a major impact on the island nation (Marinatos 1972). The eruption itself, accompanied by severe earthquakes, badly damaged many settlements on Crete. The explosive force of Thera has been judged to have been four times as powerful as the volcanic eruption of Krakatoa in the Dutch East Indies in 1883 (Marinatos 1972:718), which killed 36,000 people.

Even more devastating were the great waves, or tsunamis, produced by the eruption of Thera. Nearly 100 m (300 ft) high, and traveling at the remarkable speed of 320 km (200 mi) an hour, these waves wiped out Minoan port settlements on the north coast of Crete, including Katsambas, Amnisos, Agii, and Theodhori, and inflicted enormous damage to the ports of Kytaiton, Kydonia, and Mallia (Castleden 1990b:33).

The Minoan civilization developed and flourished, at least in part, as a result of trade; the loss of ports through which trade items passed and the probable destruction of the Minoan fleet of trading vessels must have had a devastating impact on the Minoan economy. But ports can be rebuilt, ships replaced, and damaged temples repaired. Perhaps of even greater significance for the Minoans over the long term was the fallout of poisonous white ash, some 20–30 cm (8–12 in.) deep, following the explosive eruption on Thera. This all but destroyed the agricultural economy on Crete for a time, though Crete was not damaged as badly as Thera, itself home to a Minoan outpost that was totally destroyed in the eruption. The impact of the volcanic eruption on Thera was so widespread and catastrophic, it may have become legend later on in the Mediterranean world; some scholars have argued that Thera was the model for Plato's description of the Lost Continent of Atlantis (see Feder 1996 and Stiebing 1984).

The Minoans were able to survive after Thera's eruption. As historian William Stiebing (1984) points out, there is plenty of evidence of destruction on Crete coinciding with the eruption of Thera, but equally plentiful evidence of repair work afterwards. There is new evidence of construction of Minoan structures on top of the volcanic deposit soon after the eruption (Bower 1990). But the Minoans never fully recovered from the devastation following the eruption on Thera. It weakened them sufficiently so that soon after, they were conquered by a developing civilization on mainland Greece, the **Mycenaeans,** the precursors of the ancient, historical Greeks. From there the Minoans passed into legend until Sir Arthur Evans' archaeological investigation at Knossos at the outset of the twentieth century.

Many issues and debates concerning the evolution of the world's earliest civilizations revolve around two broad questions: (1) Why did state societies develop? and (2) Why do civilized societies collapse? An attempt to answer the first question will be made here, though the discussion applies also to the New World civilizations described in Chapter 14. The second question is dealt with in Chapter 14, though that discussion, too, applies equally to the Old World civilizations described in this chapter.

ISSUES AND DEBATES

WHY DID STATE SOCIETIES DEVELOP?

Living as we do in the modern version of a civilized, complex, state society, we may take it for granted that such a condition is intrinsically superior to other, perhaps simpler lifeways. After all, our complex civilization affords us our materially rich lives and provides us with opportunities to follow our own paths—including the pursuit of education.

But there is another perspective to consider, especially when dealing with early civilizations. Complex state societies offer to only a very small proportion of the population the "perks" so many of us expect. Historian Jacques Gernet, in discussing the development of civilization in ancient China, points out that the archaeological evidence for most of the people whose work propped up the state organization shows "the existence of a peasantry whose culture and tools (stone knives and wooden spades with curved handles) do not seem to have been very different from those of the Neolithic Age" (1987:44). Such was the case for all of the early civilizations discussed.

Especially in these older civilizations, most people worked harder than did people who lived in simpler Neolithic villages, and they gave up much of the control they had over their lives. Most people were needed to produce a surplus, part of which they turned over to the temple or the army or the state bureaucracy. The peasants, who made up the greatest proportion of the population in such societies, also provided labor for the state and often sons for military service—and possible death in foreign wars. Finally, as mentioned earlier in this chapter, simpler Neolithic societies probably were largely egalitarian, and most people had the same amount of wealth and about as much control over their lives as everyone else. With social stratification and the attendant evolution of an elite class or classes of kings, noblemen and noblewomen, generals, and specialists, most people became second- or third-class citizens of a much larger political entity; archaeologist Thomas Patterson (1993:ix) characterizes the rulers of state societies as "bullies." Considering these factors, asking why civilization developed seems reasonable.

Conflict Models

Archaeologist Jonathan Haas (1982) divides explanations for the evolution of the complex civilization into the categories "conflict" and "integration." Conflict-based explanations [Tainter (1988) calls them "internal conflict" models] propose that complex civilizations evolved as a way to reduce, control, and mediate conflict among people living in a society. The conflict theorists include Lewis Henry Morgan (1877) and Friedrich Engels (1891), archaeologist V. Gordon Childe (1951), and anthropologists Leslie White (1959) and Morton Fried (1967).

Conflict theories, though diverse, have a number of fundamental propositions in common: Civilization is viewed as the outcome of a series of steps that began with the development of an agricultural economy by Neolithic people. In certain areas during the Neolithic, a substantial food surplus was possible. The production of a surplus by an individual or family resulted in surplus, privately owned wealth. Some people got richer than others as a result of their larger surpluses. This, in turn, led to differences in status and ultimately to conflict between developing social classes. According to Joseph Tainter (1988:33), conflict theorists view the evolution of civilization and the state as the result of "divided interests" leading to domination and exploitation. An organizational solution to these conflicts arose in the form of a bureaucracy that served to validate the existence of social classes and at the same time served to mediate conflicts that arose between them.

Thus, according to the various conflict theories, agriculture leads to surplus, which leads to wealth, which produces different socioeconomic classes within Neolithic societies. With socioeconomic differentiation comes the need to develop institutions that suppress or mediate conflict between the newborn socioeconomic classes, often by sanctifying the newly evolved nonegalitarian social system. Symbols are needed to justify this new system ritually, and great works of art and architecture are produced. Thus do the social and material trappings of the state appear in the cultural evolutionary record.

Archaeologist V. Gordon Childe (1951) provides an even more explicit conflict-based explanation for the development of early civilizations. Childe also viewed the food surplus made possible by agriculture as central to the evolution of these civilizations. In his view, such a surplus was used by the inhabitants of agriculturally rich but otherwise resource-poor regions to trade for needed raw materials like metal, wood, and stone. To carry out such wide-scale trade most efficiently, some people would abandon the subsistence focus of the majority and become full-time specialist traders or administrators of that trade. From Childe's perspective, the need to produce ever-larger surpluses to obtain more trade goods encouraged the use of more intensive agricultural technologies, especially the construction of irrigation canals. The existence of these canals puts more and more power in the hands of those who control them; the water supply can be turned off to those who are not sufficiently cooperative or compliant to the will of the developing administrative elite. Ultimately, between increasing trade and increasingly complex and labor-intensive irrigation projects, a centralized bureaucracy develops. Though such a "class" may have developed initially only to give everyone the needed raw materials unavailable locally, it ultimately changed dramatically, monopolizing this excess wealth for its own use and aggrandizement.

Integration Models

Theories of state development that rely on models of integration rather than conflict have been proposed by thinkers as diverse as sociologist Herbert Spencer (1967), anthropologists Elman Service (1975) and Robert Carniero (1970), and historian Karl Wittfogel (1957). Integration theories, also, have a set of core propositions: Integration theories [Joseph Tainter (1988:32) divides them into "managerial" and "external conflict" models] see civilization as evolving from the need for increasingly complex integrative mechanisms in increasingly complex situations (Haas 1982:73). As Tainter (1988) points out, from the integrationist perspective, as the need developed to mobilize large and diverse populations to work together for the good of society, social institutions developed to expedite and at the same time justify, rationalize, codify, legitimize, and sanctify these activities.

From the integrationist perspective, most members of civilizations benefit both directly and indirectly from the complex, stratified social system. To be sure, a few people benefit much more than the masses. These benefits— great palaces, spectacular tombs, luxurious lifestyles—are viewed as the price paid by society as a whole for the benefits that accrue to everyone as a result of the key social roles played by the elite.

For example, in the view of historian Karl Wittfogel (1957) in his "hydraulic hypothesis," irrigation works played a pivotal role in the development of civilization. The sedentary and secure lifeway made possible by agriculture fostered the growth of human population and the size of some local populations increased significantly. With growth came the need to produce greater amounts of food to feed an increasing number of mouths. This stimulated the need to increase the productivity of existing farmland and to expand the acreage under cultivation. Along the floodplains of large rivers, this was made possible by the construction of sometimes enormous, complex, and costly (in labor investment) irrigation networks. Such waterworks required not just new technology, but new social and political institutions to organize and coordinate the labor necessary for their construction and maintenance. Consider, for example, the amount of labor, as well as the level of coordination, necessitated by the construction of Mesopotamian canals, some of which were up to 40 km (26 mi) long. Of necessity, power was vested in a class of managers who could call up and oversee the labor. Specialist groups who could design irrigation systems were needed. The same social and political apparatus used to organize labor to build canals could also help build defensive works around settlements as competition for land increased. Surplus labor could also be used to construct great homes and tombs for the members of the developing elite class; these material trappings of power were powerful symbols that served to legitimize the role of the elite class, further increasing the ability of these people to control the peasants.

Anthropologist Robert Carniero (1970) has suggested another avenue by which Neolithic societies may have crossed the threshold to civilization. Carniero cites the apparent ubiquity of evidence for warfare in the world's early civilizations (many of the examples in this chapter show archaeological evidence of the construction of defensive walls and other fortifications). He views this common thread as significant in the development of complex societies.

Though Carniero's use of warfare might seem to imply that his is a conflict-based model for the evolution of the state, in fact his model fits under the integrative approach [Tainter's (1988:32) "external conflict" subset of the integrative model]. In Carniero's view, in certain areas agricultural communities developed where their territories were inherently "circumscribed"—that is, geographically or socially restricted, surrounded either by unproductive farmland or productive land already inhabited by another group or groups of people. In such a scenario, once a group's home territory is filled up with a growing population, a rational option is to expand into the surrounding viable farmland or into the next group's territory by taking over their land through wars of conquest. The conquered group then becomes integrated into a larger political entity as second-class citizens. In this way, a system of social stratification develops. Social and political institutions must develop to incorporate these people into a growing political unit, symbols of power evolve, legitimizing the control of the victors over the vanquished, and the seeds of civilized life are sown.

Many Paths to Civilization

None of the hypotheses proposed to explain the evolution of the world's first civilizations can be applied universally. There was no unilinear sequence of development reflected in all the cases discussed in this chapter. Not all civilizations responded to the same pressures, not all societies passed through the same sequence of steps.

In some cases (Egypt, Indus Valley, Lowland Mesoamerica), rich farmland coupled with the lack of other important resources were key to the evolution of civilization. Social complexity developed in these regions partly because they could produce a food surplus and because they needed to create an effective system of trade. In other regions (early developments at Çatal Hüyük, discussed in this chapter, and places like Cerros in the Yucatán, and in Chavin de Huantár in South America discussed in Chapter 14), a rich resource base may have produced nodes of great surplus wealth and a developing social complexity. In some regions, the need to create enormous irrigation networks may have stimulated the growth of social institutions that led to social stratification. In some cases, social stratification and early state institutions may have already existed, but a quantum leap in their power may have occurred with the kind of social control made possible by the reliance on irrigation technology. In other regions, the need for large-scale defensive works may have resulted in the same kinds of changes in society (for example, in Mesopotamia, China, and the Indus Valley).

It seems there were many different pathways leading to societies we today recognize archaeologically as possessing the requisite features of what we have defined as civilization. Many cultural evolutionary roads have led to essentially the same place, and it is likely that not one, but some—possibly all—of the explanations offered here can help us understand the process in each of the areas discussed. It also is likely that quite different combinations of these explanations can be differentially useful in explaining what transpired in the world's first civilizations.

Ultimately, the Neolithic shift to a settled way of life based on food production may have, under certain circumstances, not only fostered the development of civilization, but rendered it inevitable. As Egyptologist Barry Kemp has put it: "It is as justifiable to look for 'causes' which slowed down the process in some parts of the world as it is to search for those which allowed its rapid passage in others" (1991:32).

The image presented in the frescoes of Knossos evokes a charming, peaceful people. Graceful and athletic men and women are shown marching and dancing, some are performing acrobatic movements, some are even leaping over charging bulls—images of a vibrant, lively culture.

CASE STUDY CLOSE-UP

But there is a darker side to the archaeology of Knossos, one of death and horror. In two separate instances, archaeologists have discovered what they believe to be clear evidence of the practice of human sacrifice among the ancient Minoans.

In the first instance, Greek archaeologists Yannis Sakellarakis and Efi Sapouna-Sakellaraki (1981) were excavating a small temple near the town of Arkhanes, about 7 km (4 mi) from Knossos. The temple had been destroyed by the earthquakes that hit Crete in 3,650 B.P. The excavators initially thought they had found the remains of four people killed when the temple collapsed during the quake. On closer examination, however, it turned out that only three had been victims of the earthquake; the fourth had been ritually killed by his comrades, his blood drained from his body, apparently in a last and desperate act to propitiate the angry gods causing the earth to shake the great temples of Crete to their foundations.

The body of the sacrifice victim was found on a platform used for animal sacrifice, common among the Minoans. Near the platform was a trough for catching the blood of the victim for use in ceremonies that followed the ritual killing. Near the altar was found a bronze knife for killing animals—ordinarily of the nonhuman kind—being offered up to the gods. Based on the forensic analysis of the skeleton, it appears that the human had been a healthy, strapping eighteen-year-old male. Though he died in the collapsed temple, his death was not the result of trauma. The cause of his death had been blood loss. His body was being drained of blood at the time of the destruction of the temple. Unfortunately, his ritual death did little to alter the fates of his friends or the fates of the people of Crete the day the temples collapsed 3,650 years ago.

An even more gruesome scene has been reconstructed by archaeologist Peter Warren (1984). Excavating at Knossos itself, in layers dating to the next great natural destruction inflicted on Minoan Crete—the eruption of Thera—Warren found the remains of two young children, an eight-year-old and an eleven-year-old, along with those of a slaughtered sheep, in a room of the temple at Knossos.

The children's bones show them to have been in good health before their deaths, without any pathologies or sign of disease. Furthermore, there is no evidence of trauma in the form of blows from a weapon; these children were not murdered in a fit of violence, nor were they killed in some sort of battle. Knife cut marks on their small bones are clear evidence of the stripping away of the flesh from their bodies, again much like the evidence for animal sacrifice seen at Minoan sites. Large vessels in the room where the children's bones were found contained shells, the remains of edible snails, and young human phalanges (finger or toe bones) and a human vertebra with a knife cut. Peter Warren interprets this evidence as implying that, not only were the children killed as part of a sacrifice, but their flesh was eaten as part of a practice of ritual cannibalism.

The grisly evidence of human sacrifice among the Minoans is quite uncommon. Such killing appears to have been a reaction to extreme circumstances. It is probably not coincidental that the evidence for these two sets of ritual human sacrifices are dated to periods of greatest challenge to Minoan Crete, the devastating earthquakes of 3,650 B.P. and the volcanic eruption of Thera at 3,420 B.P. It bears witness to the terrible steps a people may resort to in their desperate attempt to avert a natural catastrophe whose ultimate effects they may have only dimly recognized.

VISITING THE PAST

Because civilizations produced great works of art as well as monumental and durable works of architecture, many sites have been made readily accessible for tourism, and myriad opportunities exist for you to visit the past of these societies. Most standard tour guides will include information about visiting such sites. There even is a travel agency in New York City called Archaeological Tours that offers a wide selection of packages to various destinations related to the world's earliest civilizations, including Egypt, China, Peru, Mexico, Guatemala, and the Middle East.

Unfortunately, modern political uncertainties and conflicts make visiting some of the most important and impressive sites of ancient civilizations problematical or even downright dangerous. As with all foreign travel, it is wise for U.S. citizens to contact the State Department for information on travel advisories.

Currently, Mesopotamia, located in southern Iraq, is not available for visitation, and political unrest in Peru and some terrorism in Egypt has been directed toward tourists. On the other hand, problems are not all that common, and thousands of tourists safely flock to the pyramids, King Tut's tomb, the Sphinx, and other sites in Egypt. Though attacks on tourists get quite a bit of publicity, some of our own urban areas are probably at least as dangerous as many foreign destinations. Harappa and Mohenjo-Daro are open for tourist inspection, though it is probably wise to visit them with a group. While Shang material is somewhat limited, later periods in Chinese history are well documented by museums and sites. The most impressive of these sites almost certainly is Xian, where an elite burial containing a virtual army of 6,000 life-size clay sculptures of soldiers can be seen in their original place of burial.

The temple at Knossos on Crete is today a major tourist destination for Mediterranean cruise ships. Earlier in this century, Sir Arthur Evans reconstructed part of the temple, repairing and replacing columns and restoring some of the beautiful frescoes. Though such work is often controversial, some of Evans' reconstructions are probably fairly accurate and afford the casual visitor the unique opportunity to view at least some of the rooms in the temple as they appeared to the inhabitants more than 3,600 years ago. The museum at Herakleion, Crete, houses most of the impressive artifacts recovered at Knossos and other Minoan sites. In the United States, the University of Pennsylvania Museum in Philadelphia has an extensive collection of Minoan objects.

Computer technology provides another avenue for visiting the past. Though not a substitute for a real visit, perhaps a "virtual visit" can suffice until time, finances, and circumstance allow you to see the real thing. There currently are a number of fine CD-ROMs focusing on ancient cities and civilizations. These disks include detailed text, maps, narrated color slide shows, movies, and animations. The Royal Geographical Society has produced a helpful electronic guide called *The Egyptian Pyramids.* Sumeria Publishing and *Scientific American* have produced a disk entitled *Exploring Ancient Cities* that includes a section on Minoan Crete. Microsoft has recently released a CD-ROM, called *Ancient Lands,* focusing on ancient civilizations. Interlaced with 1,000 color and black-and-white images, animations, videos, a detailed text, and haunting music, *Voyage in Egypt: A Virtual Journey Through Ancient Egypt* is another entertaining and informative CD-ROM. The number of these CD-ROMs is increasing rapidly; by the time you read this, many more will be available.

For those with access to the Internet (Ceramics@uconnvm.uconn.edu) and the Worldwide Web (http://spirit.lib.uconn.edu/HTML/archnet.html), the University of Connecticut offers an exciting resource called ARCHNET. ARCHNET is a storehouse of on-line archaeological information, including virtual visits to archaeological sites and museums. By way of your computer, you can visit museums and sites, examine artifacts, view videos, and read text about the places you are visiting electronically.

Though it currently does not come close to providing the emotional impact of actual visit, multimedia CD-ROMs and services like ARCHNET put the archaeological world at your fingertips. Virtual visits are an inexpensive and convenient way to expand your archaeological horizons.

SUMMARY

The Neolithic set the stage for the development of sedentary farming villages in various places in the Old World. In a select few regions, there was an acceleration of cultural complexity with the development of a stratified social system that controlled the excess wealth made possible through the ability to produce an agricultural food surplus. Social elites developed as part of a reorganization of society that allowed for orderly and systematic trade, the construction of irrigation canals to increase the food base, and the construction of monumental defensive fortifications. In these same regions, the new way of organizing and controlling human labor was utilized by the developing elite to construct less practical, monumental works, such as temples, palaces, and mortuary features such as pyramids. This kind of monumental construction, today diagnostic of ancient civilizations, was both cause and effect of the new social dynamic of the world's first civilizations. Large, impressive monuments served as dramatic evidence of the power of the elite, and symbolized and reified this power at the same time that it magnified it.

In the Old World, the processes that led to the kinds of societies we are calling civilization occurred in Mesopotamia in the Middle East, in the Nile Valley of Egypt and the Sudan, in the Indus Valley of Pakistan, in eastern China, and in southeastern Europe on the Island of Crete.

TO LEARN MORE

To learn more about the discovery of King Tut's tomb, see Brian Fagan's (1994) chapter on Howard Carter and Tutankhamun in his book *Quest for the Past: Great Discoveries in Archaeology*. *Ancient Civilizations* by C. C. Lamberg-Karlovsky and Jeremy Sabloff (1995) is a thorough investigation of the origins of civilization in the Middle East, the Indus Valley, and Mesoamerica. Thomas C. Patterson's (1993) *Archaeology: The Historical Development of*

Civilizations is another good source. For a theoretical discussion of the origins of civilization, see Jonathan Haas' (1982) *The Evolution of the Prehistoric State.* Joseph Tainter's (1988) *The Collapse of Complex Societies* contains a brief and useful discussion of the origins of civilization.

To learn more about the florescence of any of the early civilizations mentioned in this chapter, the sources previously mentioned where each culture is covered are your best bet. In particular, for Mesopotamia, see Harriet Crawford's (1991) *Sumer and the Sumerians* and J. N. Postgate's (1992) *Early Mesopotamia: Society and Economy at the Dawn of History.* If you are interested in the civilization of Egypt, see Barry Kemp's (1991) *Ancient Egypt.* John Romer's (1984) *Ancient Lives: Daily Life in Egypt of the Pharaohs* presents a fascinating account of ordinary occurrences in the lives of ancient Egyptians. For a detailed chronology of the reigns of each of the pharaohs, see Peter A. Clayton's (1994) *Chronicle of the Pharaohs.* You can explore Indus Valley civilization in Bridget Allchin and Raymond Allchin's (1982) *The Rise of Civilization in India and Pakistan.* K. C. Chang's (1986) synthesis work *The Archaeology of Ancient China* is the best source on the Shang. Geographer Rodney Castleden's (1990b) *Minoans: Life in Bronze Age Crete* is a well-written, nontechnical presentation of the prehistory and history of the Minoan civilization. The CD-ROMs mentioned in the Visiting the Past section are filled with information in the form of text and visuals, and provide an interesting and often entertaining way to obtain more information about some of the early civilizations discussed in this chapter.

KEY TERMS

civilization	Hassunan	Kush
rank societies	Samarran	deffufa
chiefdom	Halafian	seal
state	tholoi	cylinder seal
monumental works	Ubaid	Lung-shan
social stratification	city-state	hang-t'u
food surplus	tokens	scapulimancy
specialization of labor	cuneiform	Minoan
system of record keeping	central place	Knossos
Mesopotamia	mastaba	New Temple Period
Umm Dabaghiyah	Nubia	Mycenaeans

14

An Explosion of Complexity

THE FLOWERING OF CIVILIZATION IN THE NEW WORLD

CHAPTER OVERVIEW

Under many circumstances, agriculture allows for the production of a food surplus. A food surplus set the stage for the development of differential access to wealth, and with the concentration of wealth came social and political power.

"Civilization"—including monumental edifices, elaborate burials, large armies, full-time artisans, and so forth—developed in some parts of the New World as fewer people were needed in the subsistence quest and as rulers attempted to legitimize and reinforce their position of power wealth. Highland and Lowland Mesoamerica, and western South America saw the development of the first civilizations in the New World.

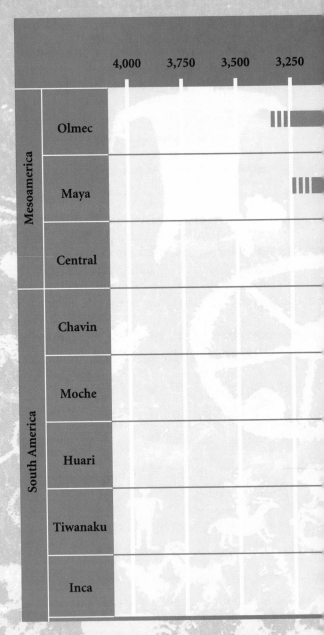

		4,000	3,750	3,500	3,250
Mesoamerica	Olmec				|||
	Maya				|||
	Central				
South America	Chavin				
	Moche				
	Huari				
	Tiwanaku				
	Inca				

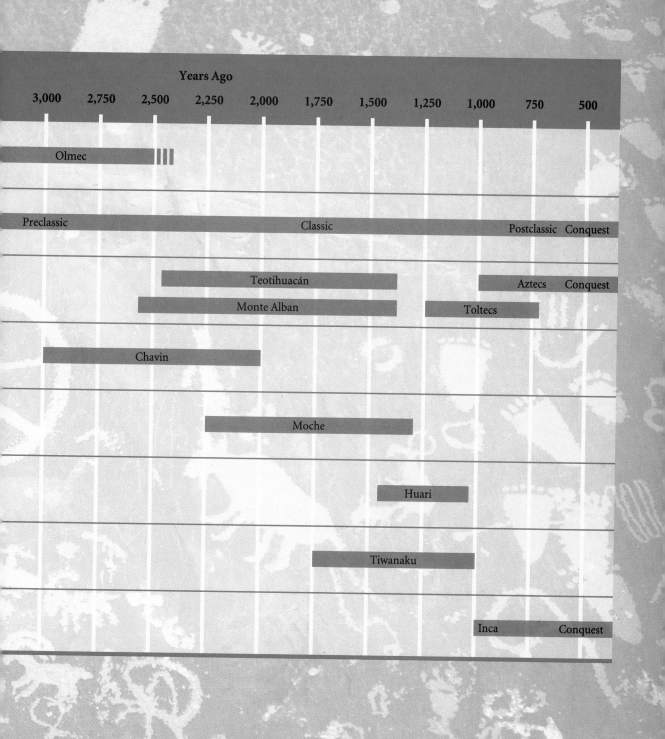

Years Ago

3,000   2,750   2,500   2,250   2,000   1,750   1,500   1,250   1,000   750   500

Olmec

Preclassic   Classic   Postclassic Conquest

Teotihuacán   Aztecs   Conquest

Monte Alban   Toltecs

Chavin

Moche

Huari

Tiwanaku

Inca   Conquest

Pacal the Great was only three years older than Tutankhamun when he ascended to the throne of a great nation. His reign, however, was to last far longer than that of the Egyptian boy-king, and he was to have a far greater impact on the history of his people. [Pacal's story as related here is taken largely from *A Forest of Kings: The Untold Story of the Ancient Maya* by Linda Schele and David Freidel (1990).]

Pacal became the ruler of a Maya state centered in the city of Palenque in Chiapas, Mexico, on our modern calendar date of July 29, A.D. 615. Though from a noble clan, Pacal the Great's father had not been king. Pacal's mother, however, Lady Zac-Kuk, was from a family of kings and served for three years as the ruler of Palenque, inheriting the throne from her uncle, who probably had no offspring of his own.

Since Maya descent was figured in the male line, it was unusual, but not unheard of, for Pacal to become king. That he did so is a testament to the power of his mother, who probably continued to wield great influence during the early years of her son's reign. It was not until after her death, in A.D. 640, that the now-thirty-seven-year-old Pacal became king in deed as well as law. He went on to initiate a vigorous campaign of construction that saw the completion of some of the most impressive temples and palaces built by an ancient civilization. The marvelous site of Palenque, visited by thousands of tourists each year, is largely the result of Pacal's leadership and that of his two sons.

Perhaps the greatest architectural achievement of Pacal's reign was the temple that would serve as his burial place (Figure 14.1). Not just a tomb, the Temple of the Inscriptions was intended to legitimize Pacal's kingship, even though his father had not been king, and to sanctify and confirm the legitimacy of the ascendance of his son, Kan-Xul II, to the kingship after Pacal's death. In an attempt to solidify his claim to the throne, as well as that of his sons, grandsons, and great-grandsons, Pacal had a detailed king list inscribed in the halls of the temple located atop his imposing burial pyramid. This king list elevated Pacal's mother to the status of a virtual goddess, comparable to the mother of the gods in Maya mythology. Just as the three central gods of Maya religion legitimately ascended to their "godship" through the divinity of their heavenly mother, the Temple of the Inscriptions seems to be asserting that Pacal too had legitimately ascended to his kingship through his earthly mother.

Pacal died on August 31, A.D. 683, at the age of 80, following a 67-year reign. In the ceremonies that marked the king's journey from this life to the next, his body was first brought up the steeply inclined stairway of the pyramid and into the temple at the apex. Next, it was carried down into the pyramid itself via a vaulted, internal stairway leading to the base (the pyramid had been constructed around and over the burial chamber).

At last, Pacal the Great, lord and king of Palenque, was laid to rest in a sarcophagus carved out of a single block of limestone. Pacal's face was covered by a mask bearing an obsidian, shell, and jade mosaic in the likeness of his own face. Pieces of jade, a stone of enormous significance to the Maya,

FIGURE 14.1

The Temple of the Inscriptions, at the Maya site of Palenque, is where Pacal the Great was buried.

(Barry D. Kass/Anthro-Photo)

were placed around the body. The lid that sealed the coffin, itself a work of art, depicts Pacal in his journey from life to death (Figure 14.2). Along the coffin's sides were carved the names of the kings that preceded Pacal, further emphasizing the legitimacy of his lineage's claim to the kingship of Palenque.

There Pacal rested until 1952, when his burial was discovered and the coffin lid raised. That his story can be told today, more than 1,300 years after he last looked out on his city in the jungle, is a testament to the ancient Maya. In building the Temple of the Inscriptions, in inscribing the king list on the temple walls, and in sealing the king in his limestone coffin, they ensured Pacal a measure of immortality.

As with Tutankhamun, the burial pyramid of Pacal confronts us with the monumental material and social consequences of the evolution of state societies. Pacal's tomb is clear evidence that complex, stratified societies such as those discussed in Chapter 13 evolved in the New World too. This chapter focuses on the ancient civilizations of Mesoamerica and South America.

MESOAMERICA

CHRONICLE

When Hernan Cortés entered the Aztec capital city of Tenochtitlán in central Mexico in A.D. 1521, he and his soldiers were astonished by what they saw. Laid out before them was a huge urban sprawl centered on two islands in the middle of an enormous lake. The islands were connected by numerous bridges and artificial causeways. The city these Spaniards saw and described was a teeming hub of people; modern estimates place the sixteenth-century population of Tenochtitlán at about 200,000 (R. E. Adams 1991; Sabloff 1989). Tenochtitlán clearly was a planned urban center with precisely

FIGURE 14.2

The lid of the sarcophagus of Pacal the Great depicts the ruler's journey to the afterlife. (Merle Greene Robertson copyright 1976)

laid-out streets demarcating neighborhoods and plazas. Enormous pyramids and temples defined the architectural style of the city, which was surrounded by a huge expanse of raised agricultural fields called **chinampas.**

The sixteenth-century Aztec civilization encountered by the Spanish conquistadors was the product of a long cultural evolution that began in the New World Neolithic. An agricultural economy based on the cultivation of corn,

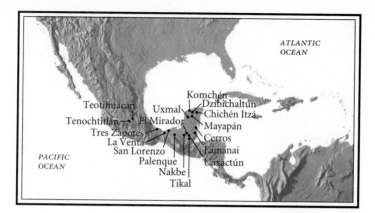

MAP 14.1
Archaeological sites in Mesoamerica where evidence of the evolution of chiefdom and early state-level societies has been found.

beans, squash, and a host of other domesticates was at the core of the development of social and political complexity that resulted in the New World civilizations of Mesoamerica (Map 14.1). This process began thousands of years before Cortés journeyed to the New World (see Chapter 12). But it was not until about 3,250 years ago that a new pattern emerged that seems to represent the development of the precursor of the civilized state in the region. This new pattern is called **Olmec** (Sharer and Grove 1989).

The Olmec

Small agricultural communities had been developing in Mesoamerica since 5,000 B.P. (see Chapter 12). It seems as though a geographically expansive pattern of small, egalitarian, independent farming villages located along the Gulf Coast tropical lowlands evolved into more intensively interconnected socially stratified chiefdoms by 3,250 years ago (Diehl 1989).

Population growth may partly explain how this happened. Some places in the lowlands offered particularly rich farm land. In the tropical lowlands of the Mexican Gulf Coast, the richest agricultural lands can be found along the natural levees produced by the rivers that flow through it. These rich regions attracted a relatively larger portion of the growing population.

Archaeologist Michael Coe (1968) has suggested that those families that controlled the most productive lands along the Gulf Coast could have produced agricultural surpluses that allowed them to amass wealth and, ultimately, power. These developing elites—perhaps initially Big Men and then chiefs—could mobilize the large regional populations to produce monumental works that might further legitimize their elevated social and economic status (Lowe 1989).

Those initially small farming villages that were located on the best lands became regionally significant as the residences of the developing elite. The sites of San Lorenzo and, soon thereafter, Tres Zapotes and La Venta became

FIGURE 14.3

This visage of an ancient Olmec chief was carved from an enormous solid block of basalt. (Michael Coe)

more than just villages; they became ceremonial centers where a unique constellation of art motifs and architectural patterns are seen. The motifs and patterns, called Olmec, include several common artistic and architectural elements: depictions of a half-human, half-jaguar god, the use of jade, iron ore mirrors, large earthen platforms, earthen pyramids, and huge basalt boulders carved into the likeness of human heads—perhaps actual depictions of some of the regional chiefs (Figure 14.3).

These features of Olmec indicate a growing ability to command and organize the labor of a large number of people, typical of chiefdom societies. The artificial platform constructed at San Lorenzo, for example, contained more than 2 million m^3 (75 million ft^3) of earth and is more than 32 m (105 ft) high. Many tons of basalt slabs were used to construct an elaborate drainage system, moving water away from the Olmec centers. The volcanic rock used to make the drainage conduits, as well as the carved heads weighing more than 18,000 kg (20 tons) each, was obtained from the Tuxtla Mountains, 95 km (60 mi) from these Olmec centers. The movement of this stone over such a great distance is another indicator of the ability of the Olmec chiefs to mobilize and manage the labor of a great mass of people.

Olmec settlements ultimately fall into one of three categories: (1) simple farming villages, (2) local centers with some evidence of monumental construction and elaborate artifacts, and (3) a handful of large ceremonial centers where archaeologists have found a qualitatively different level of monumental construction involving communal labor as well as fine craft work made of precious raw materials (Civilization Portfolio, Color Plates 21 and 22).

Olmec ceremonial centers were not urban in character—including San Lorenzo, Tres Zapotes, La Venta, and a few others where material evidence of the ability to harness a large pool of labor and to expend surplus wealth has been found. Population estimates for these largest Olmec sites are generally below a thousand. This includes the small elite class that inhabited residences placed on top of the raised earthen platforms and the larger group of people who served the needs of each center's elite. These sites were ceremonial centers where a unified religion, art style, and architectural pattern evolved. They probably relied on the labor of tens of thousands of people living in small farming villages and regional centers in the area surrounding each ceremonial center (R. E. Adams 1991:59).

Places like San Lorenzo began as settlements where rich farm land produced surplus wealth. This, in turn, enabled the development of chiefs who controlled the labor that produced the surplus. San Lorenzo and the other Olmec centers evolved into places where the controlling power of those chiefs was symbolized, reified, and magnified. Olmec can be interpreted as a common religious iconography—a standard set of visual images—that provided ideological and symbolic support for the sociopolitical system. The shared elements of Olmec religious iconography may have served to join the large populations living around the ceremonial centers into politically unified chiefdoms.

The spread of Olmec influence across a wide portion of Mesoamerica can be seen between 3,000 and 2,800 years ago. At this time, Olmec-like imagery appeared in El Salvador, Honduras, Costa Rica, Guatemala, and the highlands of Mexico (the Valley of Mexico and Oaxaca).

The Olmec were responsible for one more significant innovation: the earliest writing in the New World. At Tres Zapotes, a carved monument called a **stela** bearing a hieroglyphic inscription was found more than fifty years ago. The writing on the stela can be read because it used the same symbols as the Mayan language (Harris and Stearns 1992; and see the discussion that follows). Stela C at Tres Zapotes bears the date corresponding to our year 31 B.C.

Though Olmec cannot be viewed as the "mother culture" for all subsequent developments in Mesoamerica, it certainly set the stage for such historical civilizations as the Maya and the civilization centered at the city of Teotihuacán in central Mexico (see the Case Study Close-Up section), as well as the later Toltecs and Aztecs.

The Maya

To the south and east, in the tropical lowlands adjacent to those where the Olmec originated, perhaps the best-known and most interesting aboriginal

This platform structure, probably used for ceremonial or religious purposes, is in Dzibichaltún, in the north Yucatán. Dzibichaltún is an early example of a complex Maya settlement and ceremonial center. (K. L. Feder)

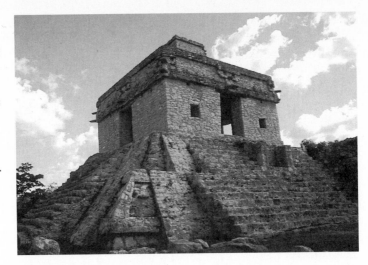

culture in the New World evolved (Coe 1993). Archaeologist Jeremy Sabloff (1994) summarizes the evidence for the evolution of Maya civilization in this way: In a region today located within the modern national borders of Guatemala, Belize, Honduras, and Mexico, originating perhaps in a small number of minor agricultural hamlets more than 2,800 and as much as 3,200 years ago, the Maya began their historical journey. By 2,300 B.P., some villages, like Nakbe, El Mirador, Lamanai, Cerros, and Tikal in the south and Dzibichaltún and Komchén in the north, had become local central places where the earliest evidence of public architecture has been found in the form of large stone platforms (Figure 14.4). Such structures likely were related to Maya religion, and these villages probably housed members of a religious elite and their attendants. Some geographically advantaged settlements (like Cerros, located on a bay by the mouth of a river) became trading centers where raw obsidian and jade and goods crafted from them, agricultural products like cotton and cacao, and perhaps fine ceramics were distributed, adding to the power of the developing religious elite (Sabloff 1994:115).

A productive agricultural system focusing on maize provided food for a growing population. Village population grew, and new villages were established during the period 2,600–2,300 B.P. As a result of this growth and an apparent movement of people from the countryside to the population centers, some of the Maya villages evolved into true urban settlements with large, dense populations.

As population grows, the amount of surplus that can be produced and concentrated in the hands of the elite also grows, as does their ability to solidify, sanctify, and symbolize that power. Monumental communal construction projects here, as in other early states, was both a cause and an effect of this process. The elite had the power to command the construction of monuments, and that construction, in turn, served to integrate people further into the political entity of the emerging state. At the same time, monuments provided tangible evidence of the power of the elite, further legitimizing their position of power and enabling them to command the construction of ever more impressive pyramids and temples.

The energy and resources needed to support the large urban centers and their sizeable elites grew, resulting in increased competition for resources and for people among the urban centers. Competition almost certainly led to serious conflicts and even warfare. There is evidence of extensive defensive earth embankments at some Maya cities, and Maya art has numerous depictions of military conflicts.

Agriculture probably intensified at this time. In some regions the Maya practiced slash-and-burn agriculture, in which forest land is cut and burned to produce fields that are abandoned after only a short period of use and allowed to grow over, to be used again after a period of agricultural dormancy. In some regions, however, a more energy-intensive agriculture was practiced, involving the construction of extensive ridged fields. The high ridges of land were built up in the fertile floodplain, high enough to remain dry even when the river flooded. Some Maya sites dating to this period show evidence of the construction of canals and even swamp reclamation projects.

The need for greater control of information in an increasingly complex cultural system may explain the development of a sophisticated system of writing and mathematics that the Maya derived from the Olmec (Coe 1992; Harris and Stearns 1992). In this civilization, the information deemed worthy of recording related not to accounting or economics, as was the case in Mesopotamia; Maya writing focused on their history, often emphasizing kingly succession (Schele and Freidel 1990). The desire and the ability to keep accurate records of time led the Maya to develop a highly accurate calendar based on sophisticated astronomical observations, particularly of the movements of the planets visible in the night sky (Aveni 1977).

All this coalesced by about 1,650 B.P. (A.D. 300) into what is called the Classic Maya civilization, with its spectacular sites, like Palenque, Tikal, and Uaxactún, and their temples, pyramids, and palaces (Sabloff 1994; Civilization Portfolio, Color Plate 23). Maya cities continued to grow. For example, by about 1,350 years ago, Tikal, in Belize, had a resident population of at least 40,000 and perhaps thousands more in the surrounding countryside. The site of Tikal also has produced evidence of city neighborhoods where particular craftspeople lived and produced their goods: stone tools, ceramics, and wooden implements. Maya burials, like Pacal's at Palenque, reflect the high status and great wealth of the upper classes.

Maya urban centers vied for scarce resources, and bloody wars were waged for control of trade, agricultural land, and the large populations living in the hinterlands. Here, the Maya enter history—a history they wrote themselves in their hieroglyphic language—with their stories of great hereditary rulers with evocative names (Flint-Sky-God, Great-Jaguar-Paw, Stormy-Sky, Lord Water) as well as of Pacal and his mother, Lady Zac-Kuk (Schele and Freidel 1990).

FIGURE 14.5

The pyramid known as El Castillo, or the Temple of the Feathered Serpent, is from the site of Chichén Itzá in the northern Yucatán. (K. L. Feder)

Later, after about A.D. 800, the great cities in the southern portion of the Maya realm stopped building temples and pyramids, and their populations declined dramatically. The geographical focus of the Maya then shifted to the north, where the great cities of Chichén Itzá and Uxmal developed, thrived, engaged in struggles for dominance, and ultimately collapsed (Figure 14.5; Civilization Portfolio, Color Plate 24). Between A.D. 1250 and A.D. 1450, the Maya city of Mayapán was the dominant political entity in the Yucatán, though a number of independent Maya states continued to thrive, outside of Mayapán's political reach. Warfare and politics led to the decline of Mayapán, and no single polity took its place. When the Spanish invaded the Yucatán in the sixteenth century A.D., the Maya world was vastly different than it had been just a few centuries previously, now a decentralized society with a scattered population. The construction of great monuments had all but ceased. There is no way of knowing what might have developed had the Spanish not invaded.

SOUTH AMERICA

As early as 8,000 years ago, a sedentary way of life was practiced by the inhabitants of the Peruvian coast. Though they still relied on foraging for subsistence, the rich resources of the coast, combined with productive inlands, allowed for a settled way of life (Map 14.2).

Neolithic Roots and Accelerating Complexity

Between 5,500 and 5,000 B.P., coastal villages increased in size and subsistence expanded to include domesticates such as gourds, squash, and kidney and lima beans (Pineda 1988). At this time at sites such as Huaca Prieta and Paracas, there is evidence of increasing social complexity. While most resi-

MAP 14.2

*Archaeological sites in west-
ern South America where
evidence of the evolution
of chiefdom and early state-
level societies has been
found.*

dential buildings at these sites are similar in size and form, certain structures
are larger and more ambitious than the others. Small pyramids and platforms
are in this category.

After 5,000 B.P., these specialized structures become increasingly large
and sophisticated. Large pyramids were built, dominating the sites of Ban-
durria, Rio Seco, and Aspero (Pineda 1988:76). There also is evidence at these
sites of a developing pattern of social stratification, in the form of differential
house size. For example, Aspero, a large site covering 12 hectares (30 acres),
has seven large and six smaller ceremonial mounds on top of which were
constructed small temples that contained human burials. Around the
mounds were open plazas and artificial terraces. A large resident population
exploited the rich resources of the coast.

By about 4,500 B.P., population growth in these coastal communities
forced expansion 10 or 20 km into the interior, where agriculture would have
been possible only with the construction of irrigation canals. This period is
also marked by a dramatic increase in the significance of cultigens in the diet

of the inhabitants. Maize, beans, gourds, squash, peanuts, avocado, and guava were all important food sources.

Though the precise process is not clear, it seems the development of irrigation technology, population growth, and movement into the interior was accompanied by social differentiation. Some villages, like Kotosh and Chavín de Huántar (which will be discussed in greater depth), were strategically located along natural trade routes between the coast to the west and the uplands to the east, and trade seems to have played an important role in the developing social complexity at these sites. The focus on monumental architecture associated with ceremonial structures like pyramids is a good indication that the newly evolved social and economic power, perhaps as a result of trade, was focused on a religious elite class who could control the increasingly complex economy.

While this pattern of development was restricted to the small, individual river valley systems that cross Peru, sociopolitical differentiation could not become too marked—there simply were not enough resources and wealth for the developing elites to monopolize to enable them to attain the status of Egyptian pharaohs or Mesopotamian city-state kings. This all changed after 3,000 B.P. Populations were growing, and their needs were expanding beyond the narrow confines of their own particular river valleys. In the view of archaeologist Tom Patterson (1993), contact and competition among the political entities within individual valleys was a significant factor in the development of Andean civilization.

Cultural Convergence: Chavin

About 3,000 years ago, an apparently unifying religion with a distinct and striking art style began to spread across the previously highly regionalized valleys. Called **Chavin** and initially centered at the site of Chavín de Huántar, like Olmec it seems to have served to bring together a large and geographically broad population under the banner of a single religious, if not political, entity (Burger 1992). Archaeologist Richard Burger (1988:111) calls Chavin an empire, but a "religious" empire, not a political one. The Chavin art style that accompanied the religion included the depiction of felines (possibly jaguars), birds of prey, snakes, the cayman (a South American crocodile), and the so-called Staff God—a presumed deity holding two rods (Figure 14.6). Accompanying Chavin artistic and religious expression were several technological innovations that served as unifying elements during this period of Peruvian prehistory. Beautiful and intricately woven textiles displaying common Chavin motifs were woven with the hairs of domesticated camelids. Across the broad and expanding region where Chavin motifs spread, hammered gold objects and three-dimensional objects made from joined sheets of gold are also found. Metallurgists creating Chavin motifs also used such production techniques as soldering and sweat-welding, plus the decoration technique

FIGURE 14.6
*Some of the distinctive
iconography of the Chavin
art style is shown here.*
(Gordon Willey)

of repoussé. Silver-gold alloys, a hallmark of South American metallurgy, are first seen in Chavin artifacts.

The site of Chavín de Huántar itself was strategically placed along a natural route of trade and transportation between the highland valleys, the Peruvian coast, and the interior tropical forest. As a result, it was probably a magnet for excess wealth generated by trade. A unifying art-religion would certainly have served to encourage this trade among previously diverse groups. As archaeologist Karen Olsen Bruhns (1994) indicates, the site began about 3,000 years ago as a ceremonial center with a small population of residents, serving at least in part to facilitate trade between disparate groups living in different habitats, newly combined through a common mode of religious expression. By a little after 2,500 B.P., however, the site had grown to become an urban center, one of the earliest in South America. By this time, the ceremonial center had become a bustling town, with a large, dense population spread out across 40 hectares (400,000 m², or 100 acres). Houses and neighborhoods were constructed according to a plan, a drainage system was in place, and there were temples and huge food storage facilities.

Perhaps as river valleys filled up with people, the need to obtain resources from outside these valleys increased. Places like Chavín de Huántar that were favorably located took advantage of this by regulating the trade that needed to pass through their territories. The Chavin art style, by spreading a common and unifying religion, initially served simply to facilitate trade among various groups. But it ultimately brought people closer together in all spheres, spreading technological innovations as well as new social patterns. Those people in a position to control trade and information as it flowed through this coalescing system became the first members of a differentiated class who lived in larger houses, and spent their time propitiating the Chavin gods and monopolizing certain key symbols of power in the developing civilization.

Moche

Chavin is simply one major step on the cultural evolutionary pathway taken in South America. About 1,700 years ago on Peru's northern coast, a culture called Moche developed, with stepped pyramids, hilltop forts, unique pottery styles, and fabulous burials. The so-called Moche Pyramid of the Sun (Huaca del Sol) is more than 41 m (135 ft) high, contains 130 million sun-dried bricks, and covers an area of 12.5 acres. In the village of Sípan, located about 150 km (95 mi) north of the Pyramid of the Sun, are the royal cemeteries of the Moche elite. Initially discovered and looted in 1986–87, Sípan caught the attention of the world when the thieves were captured by the police. The violated tomb led archaeologists to excavate in the cemetery. Several other spectacular unlooted tombs were found and excavated by professional archaeologists Walter Alva and Christopher Donnan (1993, 1994) (Civilization Portfolio, Color Plate 25).

The first excavated tomb, dating to about 1,660 years ago, was that of a man in his late thirties or early forties (Alva and Donnan 1994:29). In death he wore an elaborate feathered headdress, nose ornaments, and a beaded pectoral ornament (a chest covering). The tomb was filled with turquoise, copper, silver, and gold jewelry. At his right side lay a gold-and-silver scepter; on his left was a scepter of cast silver. Also accompanying this lord of the Moche were hundreds of pottery vessels, some quite elaborate and displaying human shapes; a number were in the form of warriors vanquishing their enemies. The chief resident of the grave did not make his voyage to the Moche version of heaven alone; he was buried with llamas, a dog, two men, three women, and a child. The additional males appear to have been sacrificed as part of the burial ceremony.

It is rare for archaeologists to encounter one such spectacular tomb in a lifetime. Walter Alva and Christopher Donnan were to find two more at the Moche royal cemetery at Sípan. The first, another royal, found in a plank coffin, was wearing a gilded copper headdress in the shape of an owl, with long, hanging bands representing the bird's feathered wings. The second burial was also richly appointed with gold, silver, and turquoise artifacts.

The royalty buried at Sípan appear to represent a class of warrior priests. Their clothing, ornamentation, and headdresses closely match artistic depictions from other Moche sites of great warriors. In those depictions, victorious warriors are being presented with the hands and feet of their enemies as trophies. Alva and Donnan discovered the remains of severed human hands and feet associated with the major burials at Sípan.

These royal Moche burials are emblematic of civilization. The ability to unify a large population, control their behavior, and exploit their labor and wealth made possible such sumptuous splendor in death for the Moche lords. The Moche were to be replaced by other civilizations in South America, including Tiwanaku and Huari, dated to after 1,400 B.P. Where Moche was confined to the Moche River valley, Tiwanaku and Huari covered far larger territories and continue the pattern seen in ancient South America of increasingly large empires (Conklin and Moseley 1988).

SOUTH AMERICAN EMPIRES

The capital of the Tiwanaku civilization was located in Bolivia, southeast of Lake Titicaca, at an elevation of 3,870 m (12,690 ft). The builders and sculptors of Tiwanaku are known for their massive monoliths crafted from single pieces of stone (Figure 14.7). The intricately carved Gateway of the Sun, the enormous Ponce Monolith of a Tiwanaku deity, and the Bennett Monolith, a huge sandstone depiction of a Tiwanaku god, are but a small part of the legacy of this civilization (Morris and von Hagen 1993). The amount of labor and the degree of specialization needed to produce these monuments, as well as the impressive architecture of the city of Tiwanaku itself, show just how pow-

FIGURE 14.7

The great gateway at Tiwanaku in South America is carved from a single slab of volcanic rock. (Feldman/Anthro-Photo)

erful ancient civilizations could become. The influence of Tiwanaku, and the subsequent Huari and then Chímu civilizations that followed it, extended across an enormous expanse of South America. These truly were empires, bringing under their control thousands of square kilometers and thousands of people. Together, they set the stage for the best-known of the South American civilizations, the Inca (Figure 14.8).

The Inca began as a small tribe living in the region of the modern city of Cuzco in Peru. Their military expansion began in the middle of the fifteenth century A.D. By A.D. 1500 they controlled an empire of close to 1 million km^2 (380,000 mi^2), extending along 4,000 km (2,500 mi) of South America's Pacific coast. The powerful Inca army subdued thousands of people spread across this broad area and incorporated them all into the Inca state. The Inca had no written language, but they developed a recording system that used knotted string called **quipu**. The story of the Inca brings us to the edge of history and the end of our discussion of South American civilization (Morris and von Hagen 1993).

ISSUES AND DEBATES

The world's first civilizations, as chronicled in this chapter and the preceding, had many features in common. They were all remarkable cultures that made spectacularly successful and complex adaptations to their environments. Yet they share something else, something that may indicate a fundamental instability in their adaptation: All of these civilizations collapsed.

FIGURE 14.8
The awesome setting of the Inca site of Machu Picchu is high in the Andes in Peru. (Stuart Franklin/ Magnum Photos)

WHY DO CIVILIZATIONS COLLAPSE?

Perhaps "collapsed" is not the best word to describe what happened to these first civilizations. Archaeologist George Cowgill (1988) points out that virtually all "collapsed" civilizations continued on in an attenuated form. In fact, many regained strength and power, only to "collapse" again, in a number of cycles. Cowgill (1988:256) considers "political fragmentation" a better term to describe what happened to these early state societies—and what, perhaps, eventually happens to them all. They don't really collapse, dry up, and blow away; they merely break up into smaller, often less centrally organized, politically simpler, autonomous entities. The term "collapse" will be used here because it is so ingrained in the archaeological literature and in popular parlance, but it will be used in the sense of Cowgill's idea of political fragmentation.

421

Anthropologists, archaeologists, and historians have long pondered the significance of the consistency of the ultimate collapse of civilized societies. Why do they collapse? And is collapse inevitable?

Cowgill (1988) suggests a number of reasons: These societies depend on tax revenues, and through time an increasing number of organizations obtain legal exemption from taxation while more and more citizens avoid taxes illegally. At the same time, expensive bureaucracies proliferate, marked by "increasing corruption, rigidity, incompetence, extravagance, and (perhaps) inefficiency" (Cowgill 1988:263). Citizens of complex state societies also have increasing expectations of services the state should be providing them. All of this sounds depressingly familiar, and does not bode well for our own, twentieth-century complex civilization.

Archaeologist Joseph Tainter (1988:89–90) has summarized the causes proposed for the collapse of civilizations.

Resource depletion   The large, dense populations associated with civilizations and their intensive exploitation of the environment leads to the depletion of key resources and ultimate collapse.

New resources   The discovery of new resources eliminates the need for the more complex and stratified social hierarchy of civilizations, and this leads to dissolution.

Catastrophes   Natural catastrophes such as hurricanes, earthquakes, and volcanic eruptions are the root cause of collapse.

Insufficient response to circumstances   As a result of their inherent complexity, civilizations become rigid in their adaptation, and their own inertia makes it difficult if not impossible to adapt quickly enough to respond to changes in external or internal conditions, resulting in collapse.

Other complex societies   Competition or conflict with other civilizations can lead to collapse.

Intruders   Attacks by a more mobile, more aggressive group of intruders can lead to collapse.

Mismanagement   The elite in a civilization may so abuse their power and direct so much of the surplus wealth and labor of their society to their own benefit that not enough is left to maintain the economic and political system, leading to collapse.

Economic nonviability   Civilizations require increasing amounts of labor and wealth to maintain themselves. As civilizations grow, the upper classes expand, and their need for surplus wealth increases. The overall costs of supporting the system with specialists, servants, slaves, soldiers, police, and so on grows at an increasing rate. Eventually, civilizations simply become top-heavy and economically nonviable. The increasing effort to maintain them produces diminishing returns. This leads to their collapse.

Just as there was no single explanation for the initial development of civilizations, there is no single explanation for their collapse. For example, the extensive use of irrigation, leading to salinization of previously rich farmland in southern Mesopotamia, may have decreased yields, contributing to collapse (H. Crawford 1991). However, this has been questioned by some researchers. M. A. Powell (1985) interprets the written record of the Sumerian civilization as showing that, though salinization presented a challenge to the farmers of Sumer, it was recognized and dealt with routinely.

As Tainter indicates, most of the explanations for why civilizations ultimately collapse beg the question. Environmental catastrophe, the presence of intruders, competition with other civilizations, and resource depletion as explanations still leave open the fundamental question: Why can't civilization adequately deal with or respond to such challenges?

For the cause of civilization's collapse, Tainter prefers his final explanation: economic nonviability. It is the broadest and most all-encompassing explanation and can be interpreted as covering virtually all of the others. Civilizations can and do respond to resource depletion, external threats, class warfare, mismanagement, and so on, but at an increasingly high cost. Eventually, even in the most complex and sophisticated of civilizations—and this includes our own, late twentieth-century Western culture—when the cost of complexity exceeds society's ability or willingness to bear it, that society collapses under its own weight. From our perspective this may seem like an awful prospect, but Tainter's outlook is useful here: "Collapse then is not intrinsically a catastrophe. It is a rational, economizing process that may well benefit much of the population" (1988:198).

**CASE STUDY
CLOSE-UP**

Teotihuacán was Mesoamerica's first urban civilization. The valley in which the city was located is a part of the Basin of Mexico. Though the area presented its inhabitants with rich agricultural soil, timber, and obsidian and other valuable lithic resources, rainfall is unpredictable and its high elevation (over 2,200 m, or 7,000 ft) produced a short growing season.

A detailed archaeological survey of the Basin of Mexico directed by archaeologist William Sanders (Sanders, Parsons, and Santley 1979) provides us with a chronology of settlement leading up to the dominance of the Teotihuacán urban center (Figure 14.9). Between 3,500 B.P. and 2,600 B.P., the basin was sparsely occupied by a people increasingly dependent on agriculture for their subsistence. Population grew dramatically after 2,600 B.P., and local villages were beginning to be drawn into broader polities, owing their allegiance and

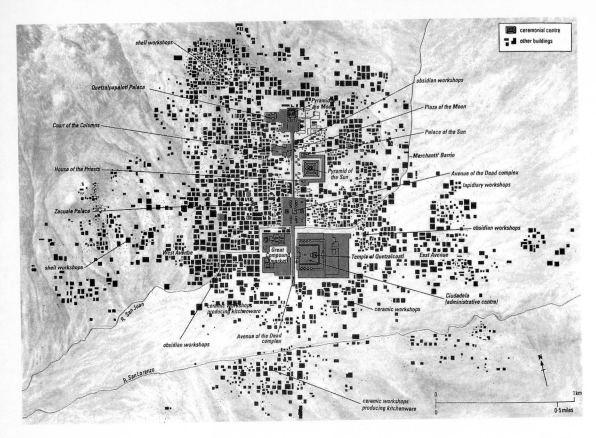

Legend:
- ceremonial centre
- other buildings

Labels on map: shell workshops, Quetzalpapalotl Palace, Court of the Columns, House of the Priests, Zacuala Palace, West Avenue, shell workshops, obsidian workshops, R. San Juan, ceramic workshops producing kitchenware, Avenue of the Dead complex, obsidian workshops, R. San Lorenzo, ceramic workshops producing kitchenware, Pyramid of the Moon, Pyramid of the Sun, Great Compound (market), Temple of Quetzalcoatl, East Avenue, ceramic workshops, obsidian workshops, Plaza of the Moon, Palace of the Sun, Merchants' Barrio, Avenue of the Dead complex, lapidary workshops, obsidian workshops, Ciudadela (administrative centre)

Scale: 0 — 1 km / 0 — 0·5 miles

FIGURE 14.9

Compare this site map of the ancient Mexican city of Teotihuacán with that of the Indus Valley city of Mohenjo-Daro in Pakistan (Figure 13.14). One city was in the Old World, one in the New World, but both were planned settlements and the capitals of vast ancient states. (Reproduced from *Past Worlds: The Times Atlas of Archaeology* by kind permission of Times Books Ltd., London)

labor to developing urban centers; for instance, the site of Cuicuilco had a population of a few thousand at this time.

Contemporary with Cuicuilco, Teotihuacán began its history as a small farming village, part of the developing settlement system of the Basin of Mexico. Its location afforded its inhabitants decided advantages over their neighbors: The village was adjacent to a significant source of obsidian, and the site straddles a major trade route to the south and east. The site is also well suited to irrigation-aided agriculture, and so was well-positioned when overall population growth in the Basin of Mexico strained the ability of simple agriculture to feed the increasing number of people living there.

By 2,100 B.P. there were a number of growing population centers, but all were secondary to Cuicuilco until a series of devastating volcanic eruptions effectively destroyed that site. In the ensuing struggle for dominance in the basin, Teotihuacán was victorious. The key to its success may have been a combination of location, resources, the great potential of irrigation, and the evolution of an elite class able to take advantage of this constellation of factors. As Lamberg-Karlovsky and Sabloff (1995) suggest, the growth of Teotihuacán may have been the result of all of these factors enhancing one another. To take advantage of its obsidian resource, miners of the stone, makers of tools, and full-time traders were needed. A greater emphasis on irrigation to produce more food freed more people to engage in specialties related to the obsidian trade. Enormous responsibility and attendant power and wealth rested in the hands of the elite, who controlled both trade and irrigation.

By 2,000 B.P. the city had a population of more than 60,000, and its urban character was fully established, with broad avenues, huge residential complexes, expansive plazas, and impressive pyramids. The Pyramid of the Sun (Civilization Portfolio, Color Plate 26), the centerpiece of the city, is a huge edifice with a volume of more than 1 million m³ (10 million ft³). Teotihuacán's population ultimately exceeded 125,000; by its peak at A.D. 600 the city had become a political capital for an empire of more than 500,000 people (Millon 1967, 1981).

My wife, my son Josh, then two and a half years old, and I traveled to the Yucatán Peninsula of Mexico in December, 1988. From our base in the old Spanish city of Mérida, we rented a Volkswagen minibus and toured the major Maya archaeological sites in the northern Yucatán. During our two-week tour, we were able to visit many fascinating places whose names bring to mind images of an ancient and alien culture: Chichén Itzá, Sayil, Labna, Xlapak, Dzibichaltún, Kabah, and Uxmal (pronounced "Oosh-mal").

VISITING THE PAST

Uxmal is located in the northern lowlands of the Yucatán in what is known as the Puuc region. The Maya produced a series of stunning architectural achievements at Uxmal. The site is dominated by the Pyramid of the Magician, a steep-sided, elliptical structure devoid of right angles (the corners of the pyramid are rounded) (Civilization Portfolio, Color Plate 24). A staircase brings the visitor to the top of the pyramid, where, as in most Maya pyramids, a magnificent and intricately designed ceremonial structure was built.

Uxmal, founded around A.D. 500, reached its zenith a few centuries later. It was an important administrative and religious center for the Maya. The massive and impressive structures of the site stand as a testament to the power of the state, to the ability of complex civilizations to command the labor, wealth, and allegiance of a large number of people. As such, it provides us with an appreciation for the ability of an elite to unify people into a single polity and to manipulate their labor as part of a complex social, economic, and political entity.

The sound and light show at the site was surprisingly well done. But the artificial light show, painting the ruins in shades of blue and red, could not compare with the light show nature had in store for us the next day. Standing at the ruin called the Palace of the Governors—it looks remarkably like a government office building, with a broad staircase and imposing facade—we looked down across the main section of the site, into the building called the Nunnery—four long structures surrounding a massive courtyard—into the ceremonial ball court, and, to the right, the wonderful Pyramid of the Magician. We were in awe of the city's alien beauty. Behind us the sun blazed brightly, illuminating the southern face of the pyramid with an eerie glow. To the north, behind the pyramid, the sky turned frighteningly dark as rain clouds moved in. Lightning sparked in the distance. It seemed as if the Maya gods were putting on a spectacular light show for those of us visiting the ancient city.

The city of Mérida in the Yucatán is well situated for the archaeological tourist. Tours of Uxmal and Chichén Itzá are offered by several agencies in Mérida. Chichén Itzá also makes a common side trip for people visiting the popular tourist spot of Cancún, on the east coast of the Yucatán. Tikal in Guatemala and Palenque in eastern Mexico are a little more difficult to get to, but many travel agencies offer tours to these sites. Archaeological Tours, mentioned earlier, has a number of packages to these and other Maya sites. In South America, political unrest notwithstanding, Machu Picchu is still a popular tourist destination.

SUMMARY

In the New World, just as in the Old World, farming societies developed that were able to produce a food surplus. This surplus enabled the development of social complexity and inequality. Societies exhibiting large-scale communal work, fine crafts, and social stratification developed sometime before 3,200 B.P. In Mesoamerica, a material culture and iconography called Olmec developed that included the depictions of a half-human, half-jaguar god, the use of jade, and iron ore mirrors; that constructed large earthen platforms and earthen pyramids; and that carved huge basalt boulders into the likeness of human heads.

By 3,000 years ago in South America, Chavin iconography developed, consisting of depictions of felines (possibly jaguars), birds of prey, snakes, the cayman (a South American crocodile), and the so-called Staff God—a presumed deity holding two rods.

Olmec and Chavin probably provided unifying religious symbolism for chiefdom societies. Both set the stage in their respective regions for the development of true state societies exhibiting the trappings of civilization (monumental works, social stratification, large, dense settlements, specialist classes, and a system of record keeping). The Maya, the complex pre-Aztec cultures of central Mexico, and the pre-Inca states of western South America developed independent of Old World civilizations.

TO LEARN MORE

Ancient Civilizations by C. C. Lamberg-Karlovsky and Jeremy Sabloff (1995) presents a thorough investigation of the origins of civilization in Mesoamerica (and the Middle East and Indus Valley). Thomas C. Patterson's

(1993) *Archaeology: The Historical Development of Civilizations* is as valuable for its discussion of New World civilization as it is for the Old World.

There is a wealth of good material on the Maya of Mesoamerica, in particular, Michael Coe's (1993) *The Maya*, Jeremy Sabloff's (1994) *The New Archaeology and the Ancient Maya*, and *A Forest of Kings* by Linda Schele and David Freidel (1990). For Teotihuacán and the civilizations of highland Mexico, see Richard E. Adams' (1991) *Prehistoric Mesoamerica*. For South America before the Inca, see Richard L. Burger's (1992) *Chavin and the Origins of Andean Civilization.* For the Inca, a wonderful source is the heavily illustrated *The Inka Empire and Its Andean Origins* by Craig Morris and Adriana von Hagen (1993). The Royal Geographic Society's CD-ROM *Inca Ruins* is another good source on the Inca.

Joseph Tainter's (1988) *The Collapse of Complex Societies* contains a detailed presentation on the collapse of such societies. The volume edited by Norman Yoffee and George Cowgill (1988), *The Collapse of Ancient States and Civilizations,* presents papers on the collapse of Mesopotamia, the Maya, Teotihuacán, Rome, and Chinese civilizations.

KEY TERMS

chinampas	stela	quipu
Olmec	Chavin	

15

Chiefs and Kings in Recent Prehistory

CHAPTER OVERVIEW

The world's first state societies had no exclusive right to or monopoly on cultural complexity. Other chiefdoms and state societies evolved in other parts of the world. Some of the same features seen in the world's earliest chiefdoms and civilizations turn up in later cultures—sometimes as a result of contact with other societies, sometimes as a result of their own independent invention. The Khmer civilization of southeast Asia, the complex state of Great Zimbabwe in southern Africa, the earthen pyramid builders of the American Midwest and Southeast, and the pueblo builders of the American Southwest are examples of these later complex states and chiefdoms.

	3,250	3,000	2,750	2,500
Mound Builders	Poverty Point			
American Southwest				
Khmer				
Zimbabwe				

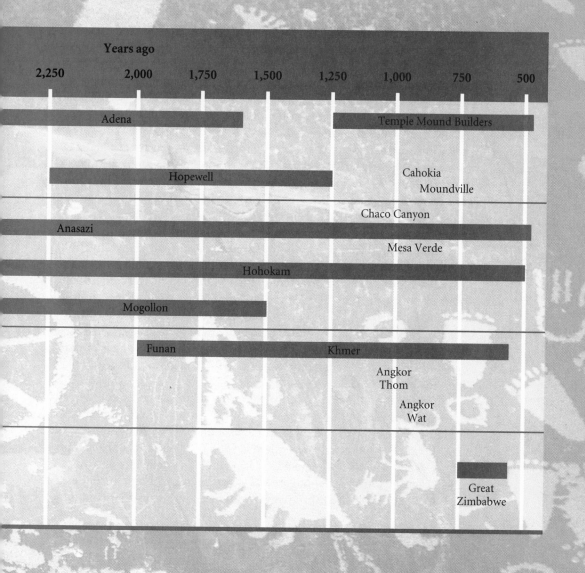

Years ago

| 2,250 | 2,000 | 1,750 | 1,500 | 1,250 | 1,000 | 750 | 500 |

Adena

Temple Mound Builders

Hopewell

Cahokia
Moundville

Chaco Canyon

Anasazi

Mesa Verde

Hohokam

Mogollon

Funan

Khmer

Angkor
Thom

Angkor
Wat

Great
Zimbabwe

For most of us the word "pyramid" conjures up images of the ancient Egyptian culture discussed in Chapter 13. Few people would think of Native Americans living in a place just east of the modern city of St. Louis. Yet there, and at dozens of other sites beginning more than a thousand years ago, a complex society built great truncated (flat-topped) pyramids, not of stone but of earth. In the ceremonial centers of the ancient Midwest and Southeast, we are confronted with a Native American chiefdom that produced some of the most impressive monumental works and the finest art seen in prehistoric North America (Map 15.1).

From atop the Monks Mound pyramid, thousands of acres of floodplain can be seen. The soil is rich and dark, the surrounding foliage thick and lush. It is called Monks Mound after the much later, historical inhabitants of a monastery built on an adjacent earthwork. Construction of this huge flat-topped pyramid in the settlement called Cahokia was begun more than 1,000 years ago by the native inhabitants of what is today East St. Louis in Illinois.

Monks Mound is impressive and represents a substantial investment of time and energy on the part of the settlement's inhabitants (Figure 15.1). The pyramidal mound of earth covers more than 94,000 m², or 16 acres. Its huge volume of earth (totaling 640,000 m³, or 22 million ft³) was moved, basketful by basketful, by a people with no animal power or mechanical contrivances. At its summit, the mound stands more than 30 m (100 ft) above the floodplain (Fowler 1989; Silverberg 1989). The huge pyramid served as a platform for the palace or temple that was the symbol of power of the political entity that was Cahokia.

From its summit, looking past the modern suburban landscape, we can try to imagine what the ancient town of Cahokia, with Monks Mound as its focal point, must have looked like at its peak, more than 700 years ago. In A.D. 1200, Cahokia was a dense settlement of 5,000, perhaps 10,000 people (Figure 15.2). [The highest estimates place Cahokia's population at closer to 30,000 (Fowler 1989:191), though most experts agree with the smaller estimate of 5,000.] In front of the great pyramid were other, smaller (but only

MAP 15.1

Archaeological sites in North America where evidence of the evolution of chiefdom-level societies has been found.

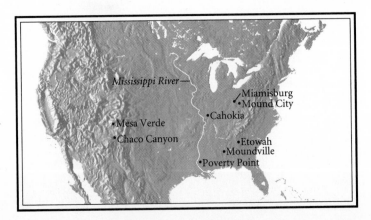

slightly less impressive) earthworks, demarcating an expansive plaza teeming with people. Scattered across the settlement were dozens of other pyramidal and conical mounds of earth, probably more than 100 total. To the west was an enormous circle of towering logs, the largest one located in the precise center of the monument. To the south was the burial of a great chief, laid to rest wearing a cape of 20,000 finely made mother-of-pearl beads, marked now by only a small earthen mound. In his tomb were more than 1,000 finely made arrow points, a copper tube, sheets of mica, shaped stones (called chunky stones), and the remains of people sacrificed as part of the ceremony surrounding his interment (Civilization Portfolio, Color Plate 27).

Surrounding the central part of the settlement, and protecting the homes of Cahokia's elite, was a log fence, or palisade, with bastions and watchtowers.

FIGURE 15.1

Monks Mound at Cahokia in East St. Louis served as the platform on which a chief's house or a temple was built. (K. L. Feder)

FIGURE 15.2

Artist's conception of Cahokia at its peak, around A.D. 1150. The dense, near-urban character of the settlement is clearly evident. (Cahokia Mounds State Historic Site. William R. Iseminger, artist. Reprinted with permission)

The wall of logs enclosed more than 200 acres, within which were eighteen separate earthen mounds, including Monks Mound. Consisting of an estimated 20,000 logs (and rebuilt three times), the huge stockade fence was as monumental a construction as Monks Mound itself.

Occupation debris from the sprawl of Cahokia's neighborhoods, suburbs, and satellite communities has been found by archaeologists across an area of 14 km² (5 mi²). As archaeologist Melvin Fowler points out: "Cahokia is unique. There is nothing else like it, either in size or complexity, representing Native American achievements within the boundaries of the United States" (1989:207).

Today, from the top of Monks Mound, we can ponder why people would have devoted their lives to the construction of this impressive, but otherwise apparently useless, monument. We can also look to the west and see the imposing Gateway Arch in downtown St. Louis, its polished steel surface gleaming in the distance. The arch, 630 ft tall and weighing nearly 17,000 tons, is a remarkable feat of engineering built between 1961 and 1966, along with an associated below-ground museum, and costing more than $11 million (Arteaga 1991).

The same question can be asked about the arch that was also posed for Monks Mound. Why would a people devote so much energy and wealth to the construction of such an impressive, but again merely symbolic, monument? As seen in the previous two chapters, such works are indicative of complex chiefdoms as well as of state societies—both ancient and modern. The monumental proportions of Monks Mound and many other earthen structures produced by the mound builders provide clear evidence of the power vested in the elite of an emerging, indigenous North American complex society.

CHRONICLE   The chiefdoms and civilizations discussed in Chapters 13 and 14 were the world's first. But the people who produced these societies had no monopoly on cultural complexity. This chapter will consider a number of specific, later cultural developments that can also be described as chiefdom and state levels of complexity. The discussion will not be all-inclusive. Instead, a small sample of the incredible diversity of such cultures will be presented: the Khmer civilization of southeast Asia, Greater Zimbabwe in Africa, the Mississippian-period mound builders of North America (of which the settlement at Cahokia is the primary example), and the recent prehistoric cultures of the American Southwest.

COMPLEXITY IN PREHISTORIC AMERICA
NORTH OF MEXICO

Images of Native Americans living in small, nomadic groups, hunting buffalo, and wearing warpaint have been standard fare in movies and on television. But such stereotyping masks the great diversity of cultures that Native Americans developed. Among the many cultural adaptations that evolved in

FIGURE 15.3
This enormous Adena burial mound in Miamisburg, Ohio, is the largest in that state, standing 21 m (68 ft) high. (K. L. Feder)

the New World, there were not only nomadic hunters, but also sedentary agricultural groups that created great chiefdoms. These chiefdoms included large populations and produced monumental works of architecture. Two areas in which such chiefdoms emerged are the Midwest/Southeast and the Southwest.

The Mound Builders of North America

The so-called "temple mound builders" of Cahokia and elsewhere were not the first Native Americans to produce monuments of earth. Beginning close to 5,000 years ago, some Archaic-period people (see Chapter 11) in the American South constructed earthen mounds. The Poverty Point site in Louisiana, dated to before 3,200 B.P., consists of a rather complex series of earth ridges (see Map 15.1).

Beginning close to 3,000 years ago and centered in the Ohio River Valley, people bearing a culture called **Adena** began constructing conical mounds in which a religious and perhaps economic and social elite were buried (Figure 15.3). Somewhat later, about 2,400 B.P., a different burial-mound-building group, the **Hopewell,** appeared with their own unique set of artifacts. The two traditions overlapped for about 200 years.

The settlements of both Adena and Hopewell people generally were small, consisting of tiny hamlets spread widely across much of southern and central Ohio and surrounding states to the south and west. Evidence for maize agriculture is scanty. Nevertheless, some of the burial mounds are quite impressive, covering several acres and rising to heights of 50 or 60 ft. They were constructed over the remains of either individuals or groups of people. Finely crafted goods, including ceramics, lithics, and stone pipes carved in the form of animals or even people, were present in the burials.

Adena and Hopewell burial mounds are impressive to see. Their construction must have required the labor of a large population living in the hinterlands around the burial sites—some of which, like Mound City in Chillicothe, Ohio, are the locations of large clusters of the mounds. The elite of Adena and Hopewell society were buried in these mounds. Adena and Hopewell are considered chiefdom societies.

The Mississippian Mound Builders

Later developments in the Mississippi River Valley and the American Southeast seem to represent a qualitatively different pattern. In fact, it now appears that these areas were the centers of an emerging Native American civilization— how far along that path is still a matter of debate. But certainly the major mound-builder sites were the central places of complex chiefdoms.

A cultural pattern evolved in the American Midwest and Southeast that included the construction of large ceremonial and population centers where the pooled labor of a sizeable surrounding population was called on by a religious elite to construct large truncated pyramids of earth. Cahokia was the largest and most impressive of these—and the only one with a resident population of a size and density that approaches an urban character (see Figures 15.1 and 15.2). There were many others, such as Etowah in Georgia and Moundville in Alabama, that, while smaller, less complex, and with fewer and smaller monumental earthworks, nevertheless present a fascinating picture of developing complexity and emerging civilization in the period after A.D. 1000.

The temple mound builders were able to maintain their society with a subsistence base primarily of maize and squash agriculture, with domesticated beans arriving relatively later, at about A.D. 1200. Rivers supplied fish, and the forests surrounding their habitations provided animal protein through hunting, as well as wild plant foods, including acorn and hickory nuts. Many of the larger, impressive sites—Cahokia in particular—were on the richest farm land. The enormous food surplus made possible by the agricultural use of these naturally rich "bottom lands," enabled the evolution of a class of priests and an attendant nobility and artisans. As seen again and again in Chapters 13 and 14 and now this chapter, the ability to produce a food surplus surely is at the root of the development of stratified, complex societies. The ability of a chief or king to control that surplus is the enabling factor in that leader's amassing of the wealth and power that allow or demand the other characteristics of complex societies (see Figure 13.6).

Cahokia

Archaeologist Timothy Pauketat (1994) has examined the evolution of Cahokia as a ceremonial and population center. His analysis showed that Cahokia was a central place in a three-tiered hierarchy of communities. Cahokia was at the apex of the sociopolitical pyramid, "a paramount center, a qualitatively different place" (Pauketat 1994:73). Beneath Cahokia was a second level of communities with a few small mounds, perhaps the villages of secondary chiefs. Pauketat (1994:76) counts as many as twenty-five mound sites in the area around Cahokia, at least some of which may have been part of the Cahokia polity. The bottom tier of sites includes numerous farmsteads in the surrounding hinterlands, inhabited by communities of people who probably supplied most of the food and labor needed to keep the chiefdom running.

The archaeological record at Cahokia shows that craft production was centralized at the site, with specialist artisans filling the demands of a powerful elite class for shell and bead pendant necklaces, copper ornaments, fire clay figurines, fine ceramics and lithics, and other materials made from exotic raw materials (Pauketat 1994:106). The exotic materials from distant sources that made their way into the hands of Cahokia's artisans include: copper from Illinois or possibly from as far away as Michigan; shell from the Gulf Coast; and galena (a lead mineral) from the eastern Ozarks (Pauketat 1994). The works of craft and art were produced for the elite class of Cahokians, who lived safely within the walls of the palisade and who were buried in the elaborate interments found at the site.

When the Spanish explorer Hernando de Soto and his contingent of more than 600 men traversed much of the American Southeast in the years 1539–1543, they encountered the direct descendants of the builders of the prehistoric temple-mound ceremonial centers (de la Vega 1988; Elvas 1611). They may actually have visited the site of Etowah during a late stage of its occupation. De Soto's chroniclers described a number of large settlements visited by the explorers whose populations they counted in the thousands. They also described agricultural fields stretching for miles. They even described the native practice of constructing earthen mounds, on which the chief's house sat.

Ironically, de Soto may have brought more than curiosity and greed with him. It has been suggested that he and his men unintentionally introduced infectious diseases to the Southeast (perhaps including smallpox) that the natives had not previously encountered and for which they therefore possessed no immunity (Brain 1980; Dobyns 1983; Ramenofsky 1987). Though some of the ceremonial centers had already been abandoned as a result of internal collapse—Cahokia among them—it is not certain that mound-builder society was destined for disintegration. It may have continued to develop, becoming increasingly complex and more recognizably a civilization. As Timothy Pauketat puts it when assessing the significance of the kind of social stratification and power evidenced in the archaeological record at Cahokia: "In other regions around the world similar conditions may have been necessary precursors to the rise of early states" (1994:6). But the accidental spread of lethal viruses may have diverted the trajectory of mound-builder culture, and we will never know what might have been.

FIGURE 15.4

A cluster of rooms in one of the so-called great houses at Chaco Canyon in north-western New Mexico. The largest Chaco great house, Pueblo Bonito, was built and occupied between A.D. 850 and A.D. 1150, contains more than 800 rooms, and is three stories high in places. (K. L. Feder)

The American Southwest

As mentioned in Chapter 12, the Mesoamerican domesticates maize and squash appear in the archaeological record of the American Southwest beginning about 3,200 years ago; beans came in a bit later (Wills 1988). These domesticates initially served to complement and supplement a highly productive foraging economy based on local wild crops.

It was not until about a thousand years later, at around 2,000 B.P., that maize-based agriculture replaced the traditional foraging subsistence system. A number of different cultural traditions based on agriculture then evolved in the prehistoric Southwest on the development of a new variety of maize, Maize de Ocho, that was better suited to the dry conditions and short growing season of this region. The best known of these cultures were the **Anasazi** in the four corners region (the broad area around the intersection of Arizona, New Mexico, Utah, and Colorado), the **Mogollon** in the uplands of New Mexico and northeastern Mexico, **Hohokam** in southern Arizona, and **Sinagua** in central Arizona (Cordell 1984; Willey 1966). These cultures vary in pottery styles, geography, and settlement patterns, but all relied to varying degrees on a subsistence base of maize, beans, and squash, and all lived a sedentary way of life (see Map 15.1).

All of the southwestern cultures just mentioned are known for their sometimes impressive architecture dating to after A.D. 500. Large **pueblos** were built of mud, stone, rubble, and combinations of these materials (Figure 15.4); remarkable "cliff-dwellings" were constructed—residences built into natural depressions in the faces of sheer cliffs (Figure 15.5; Civilization Portfolio, Color Plate 28).

Many sites in the Southwest dating to a bit before A.D. 1000 show large and dense populations living a highly successful way of life in a difficult environment. An impressive example is a cluster of large, multistoried structures built in Chaco Canyon in northwest New Mexico (see the Case Study Close-

FIGURE 15.5

Mesa Verde contains some of the most spectacular and monumental of the cliff dwellings. Cliff Palace is a remarkable town built into the side of a mountain.
(K. L. Feder)

Up section). They do not exhibit other features, described in Chapter 13, that are indicative of civilization or state societies. There is little evidence for the concentration of wealth, no sumptuous residences; in short, no evidence of the degree of social stratification seen in state societies. Nevertheless, the great houses of the ancient inhabitants of the Southwest provide an impressive lesson in the capacity of nonstate societies to organize the labor of a large population.

THE KHMER KINGDOM

Henri Mahout, having heard the stories of great temples in the jungle—great palaces "built by the gods," local people had told him—was determined to find out if there was any truth to the tales. Exploring the dense jungle near the town of Siam Reap in Cambodia in the 1860s, Mahout came upon the spectacular ruins of the ancient Khmer civilization and those of its immediate predecessors. His discovery brought to light the remains of what had been a remarkable world, previously unknown to Western historians and archaeologists (Map 15.2).

Mahout was to die in the jungle before he could announce the remarkable discovery to the world. However, he had kept a detailed diary of his research that was returned to his family in France after his death. When scholars read Mahout's account, it sparked a flurry of interest in and research on the Khmer civilization that has continued to this day, interrupted intermittently, most recently by the tragic Cambodian civil war.

Funan

The Khmer civilization developed from a local cultural base, but was inspired largely by contact with the outside world, in particular India and, later, China.

MAP 15.2

Archaeological sites in southeast Asia where evidence of the evolution of chiefdom and early state-level societies has been found.

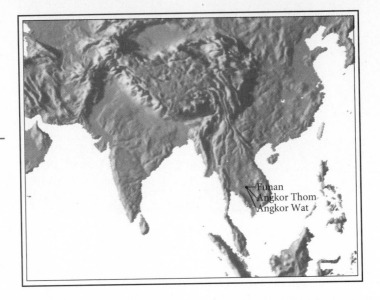

Funan
Angkor Thom
Angkor Wat

During the first century A.D., merchants from India established a mercantile community in what is today southern Cambodia. The merchants brought their customs with them, and local people adopted the Hindu religion of the Indian settlers. According to legend, the first settler of this community was a mythical Indian Brahmin (wise man) called Kambu, and the town he founded was called Kambuja (this is the source of the modern nation name Cambodia). Later records of the Chinese court that conducted trade with the merchants refer to this community as **Funan.** Funan is at the root of the southeast Asian civilization today called the **Khmer.**

The Khmer civilization is more recent than the Old World civilizations discussed in Chapter 13, but overlaps with the florescence of the Maya as well as some of the pre-Inca states of South America. It is "secondary" in the sense that it evolved in response to outside influences. Nevertheless, we can still see a pattern there that is found in the other examples discussed in this book. In southeast Asia, just as in the Indus Valley, China, lowland Mesoamerica, and South America, a common religious belief, reflected in a shared iconography that modern archaeologists can readily recognize, seems to have served to bring disparate groups under the umbrella of a common polity. Here, the Hindu religion brought in by the Indian traders provided the common bond. This common religion formed the basis of the Khmer civilization.

Funan had evolved from a merchant outpost community to a complex civilization by A.D. 500. Chinese texts that date to this period describe a rich nation with a wealthy nobility living in ornate wooden palaces, slaves serving the needs of the noble class, and an all-powerful king at the top of the social pyramid. These same texts detail a complex history of growth, of forming alliances, of decay and revitalization. They also speak of a royal marriage, combining the kingdoms of Funan and Chenla to the north. After this alliance was sealed in marriage, ties to India were broken, and a period of destruction ensued, with the area coming under the control of a kingdom centered on the island of Java.

The Khmer

Rapid changes were in the offing, however, after the ascension to the throne of a new king of Funan. King Jayavarman II, who ruled between A.D. 800 and 850, took a decaying civilization and initiated a period of expansion and construction that would lead to the monuments that so spark the imagination of modern scholars. With the appearance of Jayavarman II, Funan becomes known not by the name given it by its Chinese neighbors, but by the local name, Khmer.

Through the efforts of Jayavarman II, the Khmer polity became increasingly powerful again. He oversaw the construction of great canals and of sandstone, brick, and laterite (a hard, red soil) palaces or "pyramid-temples." These temples were built as homes of the gods and were conscious symbols of the king's power. The great temples housed not only statues of the various Hindu gods, but also the thousands of priests who attended to the needs of the gods in their palaces. The temples themselves were built on a plan that reflected Hindu beliefs. In Hinduism, the gods reside on the mythical Mount Meru. Khmer temples are built up on artificial platforms and have five towers; this is meant both to symbolize the location of Mount Meru and to represent its five peaks.

After the death of Jayavarman II, the expansion and growth he had initiated were continued. His successors built larger and increasingly spectacular pyramid-temples. By A.D. 944, the capital of the kingdom had been moved to Angkor by King Yasovarman I. At that time Angkor was largely a ceremonial center lived in only by the king, his noblemen and noblewomen, and the temple priests. By A.D. 980, however, Angkor had begun a period of rapid population growth. A full-fledged, walled city called Angkor Thom was built there, covering 15 km^2 (6 mi^2) and surrounded by a moat (Ciochon and James 1994).

The city itself was accessible by any of five huge bridges that crossed the moat. At the center of the city was an incredible, other-worldly temple called the **Bayon,** covered with sculpted images of Hindu gods, bas-reliefs, columns, and colonnades (Figure 15.6). Most of the buildings were made of sandstone. Millions of tons of this relatively soft rock (Ciochon and James 1994:40) were obtained from a huge quarry at Phnom Kulen, located 40 km (25 mi) to the northeast, from where it was floated on rafts or barges down the river to Angkor. Angkor Thom remained the capital of the Khmer kingdom until the thirteenth century (P. White 1986). Today, the ruins of the city mark the center of a 317 km^2 (124 mi^2) archaeological district littered with several hundred temples, palaces, and other monuments of the Khmer civilization.

FIGURE 15.6

The Bayon temple at Angkor Thom, built more than 1,000 years ago, is covered with sculpted images of Hindu gods, bas-reliefs, columns, and colonnades.
(© Adam Tanner/Comstock)

Angkor Wat

Angkor Wat, the most impressive and best-known Khmer temple, was constructed beginning in A.D. 1113 (Civilization Portfolio, Color Plate 29). It has been called the single largest religious structure ever built (Royal Geographical Society 1993a). The temple, with its towers, courtyards, plazas, and intricately carved walls, covers an area of 2.5 km^2 (1 mi^2). The tallest of its five intricately carved towers rises gracefully to a height of nearly 62 m (more than 200 ft). In the center of the temple complex is a tiny shrine housing the image of Vishnu, the Hindu god to which Angkor Wat is dedicated (Ciochon and James 1994). An outer gallery of Angkor Wat consists of eight enormous sculpted panels, together more than 800 m (nearly half a mile) long. Sculpted in bas-relief are hundreds of figures related to Hindu mythology, including the Hindu creation myth.

Along with the great temples, Khmer cities are marked by huge artificial reservoirs called **barrays.** The so-called Western Barray at Angkor Wat is 8 km

(5 mi) long and 2.25 km (1.25 mi) wide. It was carved out of the laterite that underlies the site. This quarried laterite may have been used in constructing the foundations of the monuments at Angkor. Allowed to fill with water after quarrying, these barrays then served as reservoirs for impounded rainwater for use in rice cultivation (Ciochon and James 1994:47–48).

The tumultuous history of the Khmer civilization came to an end in the fifteenth century A.D. Alien invaders regularly attacked Angkor, and it was abandoned in A.D. 1431. It experienced a renaissance of a sort late in the sixteenth century, only to be abandoned once again. Slowly the magnificent temples were swallowed by the jungle, where they lay hidden in the tropical forest until their rediscovery in the nineteenth century. They have inspired wonder and fascination ever since.

GREAT ZIMBABWE

For the Europeans who first encountered its ruins in southern Africa in the late nineteenth century, Great Zimbabwe was an enigma. Those first European visitors were impressed by the immensity of its construction and the fine quality of its masonry. Clearly, the people who had built the great walls and enclosures of Zimbabwe had been technologically sophisticated. Equally clearly, a complex social system must have been necessary to organize and oversee the labor needed to construct Great Zimbabwe. The first Europeans to investigate Zimbabwe found it inconceivable that local Africans had been responsible for building the site. Their racist assumption was that black Africans were incapable of such a complex undertaking. As archaeologist Graham Connah (1987:183) points out, the European colonizers of Africa sought to deny the indigenous people of that continent their rightful cultural heritage. Some Europeans even suggested that Zimbabwe was associated with Solomon's Temple in Jerusalem, implying that Zimbabwe had been built not by native Africans, but by interlopers from the Middle East.

Such nonsense persisted for more than a century. Even into the 1960s and 1970s, attempts were made to disassociate ancient Zimbabwe from the modern inhabitants of sub-Saharan Africa (see the discussion in Garlake 1973). But the archaeological record is clear on this point: The builders of Great Zimbabwe and many smaller sites of the same cultural tradition were the ancestors of the contemporary people of south-central Africa.

The Glory of Zimbabwe

Great Zimbabwe consists of an impressive set of stone structures demarcating the central, or elite, precinct of a large town or city (Figure 15.7). Great Zimbabwe is the largest of close to 200 settlements built in the same style in an area known geologically as the Zimbabwe Plateau. A greater number of

FIGURE 15.7

This stone tower, an example of the beautiful masonry used in Zimbabwe construction, is located within one of the enormous granite brick enclosures at the site. (© J. Laure 1991/ Woodfin Camp and Associates)

smaller sites in the area, without impressive stonework, probably represent the remains of outlying villages that were part of a large "formally organized state" (Connah 1987:199) dating to the period A.D. 1250–1450 (Map 15.3).

Zimbabwe-style architecture includes large, dry-laid stone walls made of rectangular granite "bricks." The walls are massive and broad, with bastions, stepped platforms, towers, and large monoliths (massive, upright, single stones) incorporated into their construction. Some wall sections are ornately designed, with the granite bricks laid in chevron and herringbone patterns. The monumental granite brick walls served as enclosures for a small part of the settlement, probably the elite of Zimbabwe society. Their homes were constructed of a high-quality clay, locally called *dagga*. The interiors of the large stone enclosures at Great Zimbabwe and other related sites are filled with the remains of densely packed dagga homes of the elite.

The two main structures at Great Zimbabwe—the Hill Ruin and the Great Enclosure—are the most imposing of the monuments built by these people. The Hill Ruin, the smaller of the two, has walls that stand 9 m (30 ft)

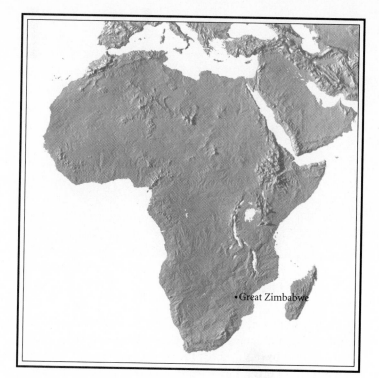

•Great Zimbabwe

high. The Hill Ruin actually consists of two separate enclosures connected by a narrow passageway walled in with granite bricks. The Great Enclosure is larger still, having an elliptical wall 244 m (800 ft) in circumference, 5 m (16 ft) thick, and 10 m (33 ft) tall enclosing a space of a maximum diameter of 90 m (300 ft; Figure 15.8). The masonry is the finest in ancient Africa outside of Egypt. Interior walls demarcate space within the Great Enclosure, and there is extensive evidence of dagga huts throughout.

The early archaeology at Great Zimbabwe centered on the great enclosures. Only recently have archaeologists turned their attention to the site surrounding the enclosures, where they have found the remains of extensive settlements of dagga huts. Population estimates vary, and it is as yet unclear whether Great Zimbabwe can be called a city. Nevertheless, there is a dense urban character to the community, and even the most conservative estimate puts Zimbabwe's population at about 5,000 adults. Some researchers gauge the total population of Great Zimbabwe to have been 18,000 at its peak (Connah 1987:184).

The Zimbabwe State

By one interpretation, Great Zimbabwe was the capital of a civilized state society, at the head of a hierarchy of smaller towns, with elites living in stone

FIGURE 15.8

The so-called Great Enclosure, one of the stone enclosures at Great Zimbabwe, consists of an imposing elliptical wall. (T. N. Huffman)

enclosures and small peasant villages without monumental stonework. Those living outside the enclosures and those living in smaller villages provided the necessary economic support for the sociopolitical system by growing surpluses of sorghum and millet and by raising sheep, goats, and cattle. The elite living in the enclosures were provided with food by the peasants. Archaeological faunal evidence implies that the elite had a diet different from that of the masses. At the Zimbabwe site of Manekweni, those living outside the enclosure were limited in their diet, with sheep and goat providing the bulk of their meat; those living inside the enclosure, though they produced no food, were provided with beef for their subsistence (Barker 1978).

The Zimbabwe elite appear to have derived and maintained their superior position through the wealth they were able to accumulate from trade. The Zimbabwe Plateau was a major source of gold prehistorically, and much of that gold was traded to the east coast of Africa.

Today the walls of Great Zimbabwe and related settlements are the most conspicuous evidence of the power of the elite of their society. It is likely that as trade in gold and other commodities enriched certain families on the Zimbabwe Plateau, those families became economically and socially distinguished from everybody else. The elites were able to have the enclosures constructed, setting them physically apart from the great mass of people and reinforcing the fact that they were economically and socially apart.

Today the silent walls speak volumes to the archaeologist and historian, indicating the enormous power vested in an elite within a chiefdom or state society to control the labor of the great mass of people. In this most obvious way, the great enclosures of Zimbabwe prove conclusively that their construction was made possible by the evolution of an indigenous African civilization similar in its essence to the older civilizations discussed in Chapters 13 and 14.

As mentioned earlier, the first Europeans to encounter the impressive ruins at Great Zimbabwe presumed that indigenous Africans were not capable of producing such sophisticated and complex architecture. The racism inherent in such an assumption should be clear. It should be assumed that an ancient city in Africa was built by Africans unless there is compelling evidence to the contrary.

> **ISSUES AND DEBATES**

Zimbabwe certainly was not the only instance in which Europeans were confronted by archaeological evidence that the ancestors of people they wished to believe were inferior had produced a sophisticated culture. The European response to Zimbabwe is part of a general pattern of European denial of civilized status to many of the non-European people they encountered in their explorations of the world in the fifteenth through nineteenth centuries. The story of the European reaction to the mound builders of North America is an extreme example of this form of racism.

THE MYTH OF THE MOUND BUILDERS

Robert Silverberg's (1989) *The Mound Builders* is a wonderful treatment of this sorry saga in American history (also see chapters in Feder 1996 and Williams 1991 for summaries of this issue). In the eighteenth and nineteenth centuries, European settlers of the North American continent were confronted with clear evidence—in the form of monumental works (the mounds themselves) as well as sophisticated artifacts found in and around the mounds—of the previous existence of an advanced, "civilized" culture in the heartland of the continent. Rather than conclude that the ancient native people of North America—the descendants of whom those European settlers were displacing and whose cultures they were destroying—had been responsible for the impressive achievements of the mound builders, they concocted a myth of a "vanished race." This vanished race, many Europeans believed, *not* the Indians, had built the mounds and manufactured the beautiful artifacts found in association with them. This myth was maintained despite the complete lack of evidence for the existence on this continent of anyone but the Indians and their ancestors, and despite the fact that historical records clearly described mound-building Indians living in dense settlements in the sixteenth century, before their populations were decimated by diseases introduced by European explorers and colonists (de la Vega 1988; Elvas 1611).

The controversy concerning the source of mound-builder culture was a vigorous one until recently. It was an issue of great concern to the Smithsonian Institution, which funded a number of investigations into the mound-builder question in the nineteenth century. Just around 100 years ago the federal Bureau of American Ethnology published Cyrus Thomas' (1894) voluminous work on the topic. During the course of his study, Thomas and his assistants examined 2,000 mound sites, collected over 40,000 artifacts, and examined countless historical documents and accounts. Not a shred of the evidence they examined supported the hypothesis of some vanished race of mound builders. Everything showed conclusively that the people who had built the mounds, produced the sophisticated material culture, and developed the complex society that left them behind had been the native people of North America. Stereotypes of primitive nomadic tribes of Native Americans were hard to break, but Cyrus Thomas did. It is remarkable to think that this issue was resolved barely 100 years ago. Today Cahokia is included on the World Heritage Site list, a United Nations honor roll of significant archaeological sites worldwide. Its inclusion honors the marvelous cultural achievements of the Native Americans who built it.

CASE STUDY CLOSE-UP

Chaco Canyon in northwestern New Mexico presents perhaps the most impressive of the Anasazi architectural achievements. Within just a few kilometers are about a dozen major prehistoric structures and many smaller buildings. Some of the structures built of stone brick are multistoried and have hundreds of individual rooms. Dating to about A.D. 1100, Pueblo Bonito is an extreme example: It is a single enormous building with over 800 rooms. Part of the structure was three stories high.

Chaco in particular, but other areas of the prehistoric Southwest as well, show extensive evidence of monumental architecture and social stratification implying a level of organization beyond that of simple egalitarian societies. Archaeologist Lynne Sebastian (1992) suggests an explanation for the development of this, at least as it relates to the Chaco Anasazi. She sees a shift in the settlement pattern in the area occurring between A.D. 700 and 900, from small, largely undifferentiated settlements to larger, more monumental construction. Sebastian feels that the excess labor available for these large construction projects resulted from a shift in subsistence strategies.

Possibly due to the Southwest's arid climate, so prone to periods of drought, farming was for a long time a mere supplement to the subsistence system. As population increased, however, there was a shift toward agriculture and greater sedentism. But herein a problem arose. Although in good years more mouths could be fed through agriculture, a greater reliance on farming brought with it the potential for greater disaster from a bad year with little rainfall and low crop yields. In Sebastian's (1992:100) opinion, the Anasazi strategy to cope with this problem was the overproduction of food in good years—the intentional production of a surplus through intensification of the agricultural system. The surplus could be stored for distribution in bad crop years. Indeed, there is a marked increase in storage area in Anasazi villages in the period A.D. 700–900. There is also evidence of the construction of water management facilities for the capture and distribution of rainwater, in other words, irrigation technology. In Sebastian's view, groups living in environmentally advantaged areas, like Chaco Canyon, were able to produce food surpluses through water management. In her model, large construction projects resulting in some of the impressive structures at Chaco had the goal of producing large storage areas for the food surplus.

FIGURE 15.9
Casa Rinconada, associated with the settlement of Pueblo Bonito, is one of the great kivas in Chaco Canyon, New Mexico.
(K. L. Feder)

The distribution of the surplus in bad years meant a large population was obliged to the people at Chaco who produced, stored, and distributed the food. In Sebastian's words, it is possible that "the great house residents were able to convert long-term patterns of power and obligation into permanent status and roles of leadership" (1992:123). She further suggests that they cemented and rationalized this power through Anasazi religion. People able to produce a large food surplus and then distribute it during lean times may have been thought to have supernatural connections. Sebastian relates this religious link to the mid-eleventh-century construction of great **kivas** at Chaco, structures of great religious significance in Anasazi and later cultures (Figure 15.9).

Roads were built connecting the main settlements in Chaco, an extensive trading network is evidenced by the use of exotic raw materials, and some of the material culture, especially the pottery, is quite elaborate and sophisticated. This exotic material was used in religious ceremonies, and some of it ended up in the burials of powerful people, probably further legitimizing their privileged position. When the overall climate improved between A.D. 1050 and 1130, the capacity for producing a food surplus increased, and the power of those to produce and control food grew even greater.

In the past twenty years, the nation of Cambodia (sometimes called Kampuchea) has been the scene of some of the most terrible, genocidal insanity of which our species is capable. For a long time, the Khmer temples discussed in this chapter were largely ignored by Cambodians, whose collective agony did not afford them the luxury of reflection on their distant past, and foreign scientists were not welcome or safe there. Anthropologist Russell Ciochon (Ciochon and James 1994) reports that when he visited Angkor Wat in 1989 (under the watchful eye of a heavily

VISITING THE PAST

armed contingent of government soldiers), the place was all but deserted. A more recent visit, in 1993, shows that the more stable current political situation has brought tourists back to the area. Just as this book was being finished, however, a tourist was killed in the area. Therefore it is recommended that the U.S. State Department be consulted before travel there. The travel company Archaeological Tours now offers a few travel packages that include visits to Angkor Wat. A "virtual visit" via CD-ROM is another, perhaps more practical option for many of us; see the disk *Angkor Wat* produced by the Royal Geographical Society (1993a).

The political situation in southern Africa since the dissolution of the apartheid governments of Rhodesia and South Africa has improved, though civil unrest is always a possibility because years of injustice and poverty are still being dealt with. The modern nation of Zimbabwe (formerly Rhodesia) was named for the African civilization discussed in this chapter. Tourist visits to Great Zimbabwe are possible.

I first visited Cahokia in 1976 while I was in nearby St. Louis for an archaeology conference. I had great trouble getting to the site at the time; nobody in the hotel had even heard of the place, much less knew how I might get there. Through sheer perseverance I made it to the site, where I found what was essentially an empty state park with a tiny, cinder-block museum. When I next visited the site to give a lecture in 1991, there was a splendid, multimillion-dollar museum that draws tens of thousands of visitors each year. Cahokia is a wonderful place. The mounds are impressive, as are the artifacts housed in the museum, and the museum's audiovisual presentation is informative and beautiful. If you are in the area, don't miss it! Etowah in Georgia and Moundville in Alabama are just two of the many additional fascinating mound-builder sites open to visitors. In Columbus, the Ohio Historical Society has a fine museum with an extensive display on Adena and Hopewell cultures.

Many of the most spectacular of the complex sites in the American Southwest are on federal land or Indian reservations and are readily accessible to even the casual tourist. Mesa Verde in southwestern Colorado offers probably the best views and walk-throughs of cliff dwellings (see Figure 15.5 and Civilization Portfolio, Color Plate 28). Chaco Canyon is accessible only via a dirt road, but it is well worth the bumpy trip. A series of pueblo structures, including the most monumental of the Anasazi architecture, are located within a short drive of each other. See David Grant Noble's (1981) *Ancient Ruins of the Southwest: An Archaeological Guide* for maps, descriptions of many of the most important sites in the Southwest, and a practical guide for visiting them.

Each of the cultures presented here, like those discussed in the previous two chapters, produced monumental structures and great works of art and craft. By visiting any one of them, you can achieve an appreciation for the power of the chiefdom and state societies to mobilize great numbers of people for communal projects and to produce social systems in which some are afforded the opportunity to devote their lives to the perfection of an artistic or scientific specialty.

SUMMARY

Processes set in motion in the early Neolithic led to the evolution of the world's first civilizations (discussed in Chapters 13 and 14) and continued to produce complex societies throughout the world. The cases discussed here of the Khmer civilization in Cambodia, the civilization of Great Zimbabwe in southern Africa, the pueblo builders of the American Southwest, and the mound builders of the American Midwest are but a sample of the various expressions of cultural complexity in the ancient world.

TO LEARN MORE

For the Khmer civilization of Cambodia, a very useful and detailed source is the CD-ROM *Angkor Wat* produced by the Royal Geographical Society (1993a) as part of their Electronic Guide series. For more general discussions—and lots of great photographs of the spectacular temples—see Peter White's (1986) "The Temples of Angkor: Ancient Glory in Stone," in *National Geographic,* and Russell Ciochon and Jamie James' (1994) "The Glory That Was Angkor," in *Archaeology* magazine.

P. S. Garlake's (1973) *Great Zimbabwe* is still an excellent source on this African civilization. The synthesis and overview of African civilizations entitled *African Civilization: Precolonial Cities and States in Tropical Africa, An Archaeological Perspective* by Graham Connah (1987) is another excellent source of information. For the mound builders at Cahokia and the history of their acceptance as an indigenous American civilization, see Robert Silverberg's (1989) *The Moundbuilders.* For details on Cahokia archaeology, see Melvin Fowler's (1989) *The Cahokia Atlas: A Historical Atlas of Cahokia Archaeology.* A new and extremely valuable book is Timothy Pauketat's (1994) *The Ascent of Chiefs,* a theoretical look at the evolution of a stratified social system at Cahokia. On the American Southwest, see Linda Cordell's (1984) *The Archaeology of the Southwest* and Lynn Sebastian's (1992) *The Chaco Anasazi.*

KEY TERMS

Funan	Anasazi	pueblo
Khmer	Mogollon	Adena
Bayon	Hohokam	Hopewell
barray	Sinagua	kiva

16
Evolutionary Epilogue

This book has chronicled our species' long and exciting journey as revealed through the scientific investigation of the period of time literally before history. Together we have traveled a pathway paved with the material remains of those who have passed here before us. Littering the trail have been their bones and their trash, their tools and their monuments. These are the things that have informed us of their story. And *their* story has been *our* story, the physical and cultural evolutionary history of all humankind. It is a tale yet unfolding, and of which we are all a part.

The Human Adaptation

As we have seen, 2.5 million years ago our human ancestors crossed an intellectual threshold that would forever determine the focus of the human adaptation. In our species' African nursery was born our unique reliance on *culture*—our ability to conceive strategies for survival intellectually, to implement those plans, and to teach our children, who, in turn, teach theirs. Using the intellectual potential conferred on us by our expanding brains, our *Homo habilis* ancestors initiated a pattern that has defined the hominid line. Though nature has not endowed us with great strength or speed, though we lack wings to fly and powerful jaws to bite, though our senses are muted in comparison with other species, we nevertheless have become a hugely successful species. What makes us unique and constitutes the foundation of our success is our intellectual capacity and the manifold cultural adaptations we have invented out of our creative imaginations. Our intelligence enables us to define our evolutionary destinies. We needn't wait for natural selection to slowly shift our adaptations to our environments. We change ourselves and simultaneously construct our environments, all in the time it takes to formulate a thought or to express an idea.

This process began when *Homo habilis* first visualized a sharp, durable edge within a dull, round rock. A few carefully placed, sharp blows with another stone, and the visualized edge became an actual one, capable of cutting, slicing, or chopping more effectively than any of the bodily "tools" nature had given us. In that instant our ancestors had evolved the equivalent of more powerful, piercing canine teeth, razor-sharp slicing claws, and rock-solid fists.

In a sense, all human history is based on the Oldowan stone-tool industry, and all human achievement has been but a series of variations on the theme established 2.5 million years ago on the African savanna. The Acheulean handaxe of *Homo erectus*, the Levallois and Mousterian industries associated with anatomically archaic varieties of our own species, *Homo sapiens*, and even cave paintings and barbed harpoons, domesticated plants and animals,

FIGURE 16.1

The space shuttle Columbia *blasts off on its maiden voyage, April 12, 1981.* (NASA)

socially stratified societies and walled cities—in fact, civilization itself—all these things are mere variations on the theme established in the Oldowan tools of the Lower Paleolithic. Throughout our stay on earth, human beings have perceived the need and possessed the intellectual capacity to develop new ways of gathering resources, manipulating the environment, recording and transmitting information, organizing labor—in essence, of living our lives. And cultural adaptation continues today to distinguish us from all other life on the planet.

From Stone Tools to Star Trek

Consider this example. On April 12, 1981, at 7:00 A.M., the first space shuttle, the *Columbia,* was successfully launched from pad 39A at the Kennedy Space Center, Cape Canaveral, Florida (Figure 16.1). It is probably not an exaggeration when writers describe this piece of U.S. space exploration hardware, this "artifact" of the late twentieth century, as the "single most complex machine ever built by man" (Melvyn Smith 1985:120). The shuttle orbiter weighed 75,000 kg (165,000 lb), had forty-nine rocket engines, four on-line computers and one backup, twenty-three antennas, sophisticated fuel cells to provide electrical energy for all the machinery on board, and millions of interworking, individual parts (all statistics from Gurney and Forte 1988). The entire shuttle, consisting of the delta-wing orbiter plus booster rockets, weighed 2 million kg (4.5 million lb).

At launch, the booster rocket engines developed 3 million kg (6.5 million lb) of thrust. In an achingly slow upward push against the powerful pull of the earth, the shuttle slipped through gravity's grasp and cleared the height of the 92 m (300 ft) launch tower in six seconds. At twelve minutes into its maiden voyage, the spacecraft was orbiting the earth. This first shuttle reached an altitude of 280 km (175 mi) (the standard altitude of commercial jets is 9.6 km, or 6 mi), traveling at 28,000 km per hour (17,500 mph) (a standard commercial jet cruises at under 960 km per hour, or 600 mph).

Though the *Columbia* carried no payload and circled the earth only thirty-six times in a little more than two days, its successful flight ushered in a new era of space exploration that included the deployment of satellites for investigating the earth, its weather patterns, its resource concentrations, and even the impacts of our own civilization on the ecological balance of the planet. The shuttle also enabled the launch of the defective Hubble space telescope—and its later in-space repair—that is adding immeasurably to our understanding of the universe. The shuttle paved the way for the regular and almost routine return to space.

Shuttle launches and safe returns are rarely front page news now. And although tragedies like the *Challenger* disaster have occurred, the shuttle program has also led to triumphs both small and large—of the human will to expand beyond our own planet. The space program represents some of the first faltering steps our species has taken to become not just inhabitants of the small planet that gave us life, but citizens of the infinite universe.

In all of our achievements in space, we have evolved literally beyond gravity. We have escaped the confines of our own planet, taking our environment with us. We have even walked on the surface of another world, to look back at our planet and recognize, perhaps for the first time in the history of our species, the fragility and the unity of our home (Figure 16.2).

All of these space accomplishments have taken place in little more than fifty years. The ability to live in space did not evolve. Human beings have done this entirely as a result of our ability to think. Given a few more generations, perhaps our children's children will be exploring farther into our universe and actually fulfilling the fictional promise of Captain James T. Kirk and Captain Jean-Luc Picard of the Starship(s) *Enterprise:* "to boldly go where no one has gone before."

Many Pathways

The heaviest Oldowan tools weigh little more than half a kilogram and took just a few blows with another rock to create. The space shuttle orbiter weighs 75,000 kg and took years to create from its millions of constituent parts. But

FIGURE 16.2

Space exploration, one of the truly monumental undertakings of our twentieth-century civilization, has provided a unique perspective for all of us inhabitants of the earth. (NASA)

the shuttle, as complex as it is, is simply a tool, a point along a continuum of complexity that began with Oldowan. The simple stone tool took our hominid ancestors where they had not gone before as surely as has the space shuttle, our computers, and all the other tools we have invented to allow us more effectively to feed ourselves, provide for our physical necessities, and explore the world and ourselves.

I am comparing Oldowan tools and the space shuttle because, though incredibly different in scale, they bespeak a common bond between our modern civilization and our ancient hominid forebears. But this implies no inevitable sequence of change, no inexorable "march of progress" from ancient hominids to Western society. When in this book we have looked back along our evolutionary pathway, we have seen that the pathway is, in actuality, made up of many intersecting and diverging avenues. There is no single highway of change leading inevitably to Western civilization, no necessary trail from stone tools to spacecraft. Our society represents merely one point along one of many possible pathways, one of many possible modes of adaptation, not better or more "evolved" than any others, and in no way an inevitable outcome of cultural evolution.

This is a difficult, but crucial, point to make. Many of us in the West view history as an endless upward spiral of material progress, an inevitable pathway of "improvement" of the human condition leading necessarily to us, to Western civilization. We also often view history as teaching moral lessons—history as a tale of good guys versus bad guys, with the good guys (that would be us) always coming out on top and their destiny being realized.

The belief that all of human prehistory and history followed a single, inevitable pathway—the perspective of **orthogenesis**—provides the philosophical underpinning for a hypothesis of **unilineal evolution** (see the discussion of cultural evolutionist Lewis Henry Morgan in Chapter 2). The view of the universality of cultural evolutionary sequences may be a popular one, but it is not the only view. The ancient Egyptians discussed in Chapter 13, for example, perceived history quite differently. As Egyptologist Barry Kemp (1991) points out, the Egyptians saw history not as a trajectory leading somewhere, but as a constant, ordered, linear series of transitions from pharaoh to pharaoh. History, for the ancient Egyptians, leads nowhere in particular, but proceeds along a constant line of kingship. When Egyptians wrote their own history, there was no search for meaning or pattern, no saga of a destiny fulfilled. For them, history simply was a list of kings, a succession of rulers.

Anthropologists view history differently. History for us is played out on an evolutionary stage where the only direction is that of change and adaptation. We view the ancient past neither as a continual parade of divine and semidivine leaders nor as a parable of the inevitability of material progress. We see a unique series of winding cultural pathways reflecting the myriad ways by which people adapted to their environment and constructed a way of life.

If a pattern leading to increasing technological complexity has been one of the cultural evolutionary pathways followed by our species and navigated in this book, it must be remembered that this has been neither the only nor the inevitable avenue traced by human beings. The trajectories seen in this book exhibit tremendous cultural diversity. Such diversity in the evolutionary pathways followed by human beings may be a key to our species' survival.

"Diversity" has become an American buzzword nowadays in an ongoing argument about what our nation has become and what it should be. Often, it refers to so-called racial diversity in neighborhoods, schools, and businesses. But I mean the term to signify variation on a broader geographic and temporal scale, a worldwide and "timewide" diversity of human cultural adaptation, from Arctic hunters to tropical rain forest horticulturists, from desert wanderers to seafaring islanders, from megalith-building farmers to grassland hunters, from urban nation states to tribal societies. It may take the collective wisdom of the cultures of all these people to ensure the survival of the species, ironically at the very time when cultural homogenization—the Westernization of the world—seems to be overtaking us.

I began this epilogue by likening the human story to a lengthy journey. Now, at last, in this book we have reached a milepost in our investigation. We have literally caught up with ourselves on the human evolutionary pathway; we have reached our present location on the trail. We can gaze back, as we have in this book, along the tortuous, serendipitous route and in the distance see, if only dimly, our ancient evolutionary ancestors. Ahead, we can imagine our species racing forward to some unknown, unfathomable point on the horizon of our future. Though the twists and turns will almost certainly bring us to a point that anthropologists have never even considered, we can all be certain of one thing: The journey will take us where no one has gone before.

KEY TERMS

orthogenesis
unilineal evolution

Glossary

Abejas phase The period of time in the **Tehuacán** Valley in highland Mexico from 5,400 to 4,300 B.P. Characterized by increased sedentism and the first appearance of domesticated maize, beans, and squash.

absolute date Any date where a year or range of years can be applied to a site or artifact, as opposed to a **relative date,** where only a chronological order can be established.

accelerator mass spectrometry (AMS) A technique in radiocarbon dating in which the actual number of ^{14}C atoms (or a proportion of them) is counted, as opposed to the traditional method which measures the amount of radioactivity given off by the sample.

Acheulean handaxe Symmetrical stone tool of the later Early Paleolithic. The bifacially flaked, teardrop-shaped all-purpose handaxe dates to as early as 1.4 million years ago in Africa. There, and after about 1.0 million years ago in Europe, the handaxe was manufactured by members of the species *Homo erectus.*

Act of Uniformity One of the statutes of the Clarendon Code, passed after the English Civil War of 1642–1651, intended to punish the Puritans and to purge them from the Church of England. It established the Book of Common Prayer—which the Puritans opposed—as the standard ecclesiastical work of the Church of England.

adaptation A mode or strategy for survival. An adaptation can be a physical characteristic; for example, the thick fur of a polar bear is a physical adaptation for life in the arctic. Adaptation can also be a cultural behavior; for instance, the material culture of the Inuit people (Eskimos), including harpoons, igloos, parkas, and dog sleds, are their invented, cultural adaptations to life under very cold environmental conditions.

adapted The state of being biologically designed or culturally prepared to survive in a given environment.

Adena A burial-mound-building culture centered in the Ohio River valley. Beginning about 3,000 years ago, this culture developed at the **chiefdom** level of sociopolitical integration, often building impressive tombs for their chiefs.

age-mortality profile In demographics, a graph showing the number or percentage of animals that reached each age category in a population. In a faunal sample, the age-mortality profile shows the percentage of animals that died or were killed in each age category.

Ajalpán phase The period of time in the **Tehuacán** Valley in highland Mexico from 3,500 to 2,850 B.P. Characterized by increased sedentism and increasing reliance on domesticated maize, beans, and squash, though still more than half of the diet consisted of wild foods.

Ajuerdo phase The period of time in the **Tehuacán** Valley in highland Mexico from 12,000 to 9,000 B.P. Human groups in the valley lived in small, nomadic microbands of fewer than ten people, subsisting on wild plant and animal foods.

altricial The condition of being born at an immature stage of development. The term originated in ornithology to describe bird species in which hatchlings are entirely dependent on one or both parents for all of their needs for an extended period. Used here to describe a similar circumstance in hominid species, both ancient and modern.

Anasazi A prehistoric culture centered in the Four Corners region of the American Southwest. The Anasazi sometimes constructed large and impressive structures that housed the population of the village.

anatomically modern *Homo sapiens* Human beings anatomically indistinguishable from those living today. They are found in the paleoanthropological record dating to more than 100,000 years ago.

anthropological linguistics The subfield of anthropology that studies language.

anthropology The study of humanity. A broad social science with varied foci on human biological and cultural adaptations, human origins, biological and cultural evolution, and modern cultures.

arboreal Life in the trees. Primates, for the most part (our species is a notable exception), exhibit an arboreal adaptation.

archaeologist A scientist who studies human beings through the analysis of the material remains of their behavior, that is, the artifacts they made and used and that have been preserved. Archaeologists often focus on human cultural evolution.

Archaic The chronological period in the New World that follows the **Paleoindian** period, begins at the end of the Pleistocene, and represents a period of cultural adaptation to the new, postglacial environment by Native Americans.

archaic *Homo sapiens* The extinct subspecies of humanity that shares much in common with modern *Homo sapiens* or **anatomically modern *Homo sapiens*** but that commonly retains primitive skeletal features and possesses a somewhat smaller mean cranial capacity than do modern people. The Neandertals are the best known archaic variety or subspecies of the human race. Also called **premodern *Homo sapiens.***

artifact Any object manufactured by a human being or human ancestor, but usually a portable object like a stone spearpoint or a clay pot, as distinguished from larger, more complex archaeological **features.**

artificial selection The process used in the **domestication** and refinement of plants and animals by which human beings select which members of a species will live and produce offspring. Humans make such decisions on the basis of their needs or desires concerning the form or behavior of the species, for example, plants that produce larger seeds, animals that produce woollier coats, or animals that produce more milk.

association The spatial relationships among archaeological **artifacts, ecofacts,** and **features.** Objects found in proximity to each other are said to be in association.

attritional profile An **age-mortality profile** in which most deaths in the sample occur in the "very young" and "very old age" categories and proportionally fewer deaths occur in the prime of life. Such a profile results when deaths are due to routine causes like disease and predation. Compare with **catastrophic profile.**

Aurignacian A lithic tool technology associated with anatomically modern human beings in Europe dating from 34,000–27,000 years ago. Includes long, narrow blade tools.

australopithecine Any member of the genus *Australopithecus,* including several species: *anamensis, afarensis, africanus, robustus, boisei,* and *aethiopicus.* The oldest members of the genus date back to at least 4.2 million years ago. The genus became extinct by 1 million years ago and was characterized by an ape-sized brain but also by the modern human behavioral trait of bipedal locomotion.

backed blade A stone blade tool in which one edge has been dulled, or "backed," so it can more readily be held in the hand during use.

barray Large reservoirs constructed by the ancient Khmer people in their elaborate ceremonial centers, like Angkor Wat and Angkor Thom. Initially resulting from sandstone quarrying for the construction materials for their temples, these large depressions filled with water and probably served as reservoirs.

basicranium The bones of the base of the cranium. Because the soft parts of hominid anatomy involved in the production of sound are connected to the base of the skull, the basicranium is a crucial part of the anatomy when assessing the ability of human ancestors to produce human speech.

Bayon The spectacular temple complex in the center of the ancient Khmer city of Angkor Thom that is covered with images of Hindu gods, bas-reliefs, columns, and colonnades.

Bering Land Bridge A broad piece of land, more than 1,500 km (1,000 mi) across, that connected northeastern Asia with northwestern North America during periods of sea level depression in the Pleistocene. People living in Asia walked east across the land bridge into the lands of the Western Hemisphere at least 15,000 years ago and possibly earlier.

bipedal locomotion The ability to walk on two feet. With a few notable exceptions (such as some large dinosaurs and birds), the hominids are the only creatures who habitually and efficiently walk on two feet.

blade A long, thin stone flake, commonly twice as long as it is wide, that represents an efficient use of stone, producing a high proportion of edge for the amount (weight) of stone used.

brachiation The ability to swing, arm over arm, through the trees.

brachiator An animal that has the ability of **brachiation.** Many primates are excellent brachiators. Among the apes, the various gibbons are unexcelled at brachiation.

burin A sharp and durable stone tool used in engraving to etch out thin slivers of antler or bone, which then were modified to make awls and needles.

C3 pathway The photosynthetic process employed by most trees, whereby a radioactive isotope of carbon—^{13}C—is differentially filtered out.

C4 pathway The photosynthetic process employed by most grasses and sedges, whereby a radioactive isotope of carbon—^{13}C—is more readily used than in plants that follow the **C3 pathway.**

calvarium The top part of a skull minus the lower jaw (mandible) and facial bones.

CAM pathway The photosynthetic pathway typical of succulent plants; uptakes ^{13}C at a level intermediate to that of the **C3 pathway** and the **C4 pathway.**

Cambrian Explosion The great proliferation of life forms seen in the paleontological record dating from about 600 million years ago.

camelid A large, ruminant animal, including bachtrian and dromedary camels in the Old World and llamas, alpacas, guanacos, and vicuñas in the New World.

Capsian A culture in northwestern Africa dating to after 10,000 years ago and characterized by hunting of wild sheep, collecting of shellfish and snails, and harvesting of wild grains.

carbon dating See **radiocarbon dating.**

carrying capacity The number of organisms a given region or habitat can support without degrading the environment.

catastrophic profile An **age-mortality profile** in which successively older age classes have fewer individuals. It is produced when a population is destroyed all at once, in other words, catastrophically.

catastrophist A person who believes that the current appearance of the earth can be explained best as having resulted from a series of natural catastrophes—for example, floods and volcanoes. Catastrophism was quite popular prior to the nineteenth century and lent support to the claim of a recent age for the earth.

central place As used in the field of cultural geography, the geographic focal point of a political entity. A large city or ceremonial center with religious structures often are central places for **states** or **chiefdoms.**

cereals Plants, especially grasses, that produce starchy grains. These were among the first domesticated foods produced during the **Neolithic.**

Châtelperronian A lithic technology that includes the use of blades and appears to be intermediate in form and time between **Mousterian** and **Aurignacian.** Associated with some late populations of Neandertals following contact with modern *Homo sapiens.*

Chavin A distinctive art style that developed in western South America beginning about 3,000 years ago. The religious iconography of Chavin seems to have served as a unifying influence, setting the stage for the later development of geographically broad empires.

chiefdom A level of sociopolitical integration more complex than the tribe but less complex than the **state.** The social system is ranked, not **egalitarian.** Individuals are placed in a hierarchy of power and prestige. Chiefdoms are less rigidly structured than state societies, and a chief's power is less than that of a king or a pharaoh.

chinampas Artificial islands in lakes and swamps produced by the Aztecs of central Mexico for intensive farming.

city-state A political entity characteristic of some early civilizations, especially in **Mesopotamia.** A central population center dominates the surrounding hinterlands. The wealth of the countryside flows into the city, where it is concentrated in the hands of the elite classes.

civilization As used here, cultures exhibiting social stratification, labor and craft specialization, a food surplus that supports a political and/or religious elite, monumental construction, and a system of record keeping.

cladistics A method of classification of living things based on the inferred pattern of evolutionary branching rather than current morphology. Any two or more species derived from a common ancestor are placed together in a **sister group,** regardless of their current dissimilarities.

Clovis A **fluted point** type of the Paleoindians. Large, laurel-leaf-shaped stone blades exhibiting a channel, or "flute" (as in a fluted column), on both faces to aid in hafting the stone point onto a wooden shaft. The channel begins at the base and generally extends from one-third to no more than one-half the length of the point. Clovis points date from about 11,500 to 10,000 B.P. (Compare to **Folsom.**)

complex foraging A system of hunting animals and gathering wild plants in which subsistence is focused on a few highly productive resources. These foods are collected and stored, allowing for a more sedentary settlement system. (Compare to **simple foragers.**)

Cordilleran The Pleistocene ice mass in North America centered in the Rocky Mountains.

core In stone tool manufacturing, the nucleus from which flakes or blades are removed. In manufacturing a core tool like an **Acheulean handaxe,** the stone nucleus becomes the tool. In a core-and-blade or core-and-flake technology, the core is merely the source for numerous sharp flakes that are then used as is or modified into tools.

cortex The exterior surface or rind of a **core,** usually removed in the process of stone tool manufacturing.

Coxcatlán phase The period of time in the **Tehuacán** Valley in highland Mexico from 7,000 to 5,400 B.P. that is characterized by a reliance on wild foods.

cranial suture The lines of connection between cranial bones, which appear as a squiggly line on both the interior and the exterior surfaces of the skull. Sutures progressively disappear with age and can be used to provide a general estimate for age at death.

cranium The bones of the head and face (excluding the lower jaw).

creationist One who believes that the universe, the earth, life, and humanity are the creation of an all-powerful god.

creation story A legend, myth, or folk tale intending to explain the origin of the universe, the earth, life, and humanity. Not intended as a scientific hypothesis, but, instead, an internally consistent, satisfying explanation for why we are here.

culture The invented, taught, and learned patterns of behavior of human groups. The extrasomatic (beyond the body or beyond the biological) means of adaptation of a human group.

cuneiform An early form of written records in Mesopotamia, involving the impression of standardized symbols on wet clay. Dating to close to 6,000 years ago, cuneiform is the earliest writing in the world.

cylinder seal Mesopotamian system of impressing symbolic notation onto wet clay with a marked cylinder.

deciduous dentition The baby teeth.

deffufa Monumental mud-brick towers built by the inhabitants of the ancient Nubian civilization of Kerma located south of the third cataract of the Nile in modern Sudan. Kerma dates to more than 3,500 years ago.

Denali Complex A lithic technology seen in the arctic and consisting of wedge-shaped cores, microblades, bifacial knives, and burins. Dating to about 10,000 years ago, several features of the Denali Complex are reminiscent of elements of older complexes in northeastern Asia, particularly that of Dyuktai Cave.

descent with modification The notion that each successive generation can be modified slightly through evolutionary processes; a fundamental feature of biological evolution.

diaphysis The shaft of a long bone. On either end of the diaphysis is an **epiphysis.**

diastema A gap between the teeth of both the mandible (lower jaw) and the maxilla (upper jaw). The large canine teeth of apes fit into the diastemas of their opposing jaws when those jaws are closed.

DNA (deoxyribonucleic acid) The genetic code; the genetic instructions for each life-form on the planet.

DNA hybridization Measuring the similarity between two different species by attempting to join halves of the genetic ladder, or double helix. Depending on how well the DNA of two different species bond together, genetic similarity can be assessed. Human beings and chimps, for example, exhibit about 99% identity in DNA hybridization.

domestication Through **artificial selection,** the production of new species of plants and animals that owe their existence to human intervention. Some domesticated species become so highly specialized to the demands of human beings that they can no longer survive and propagate without human assistance.

ecofact An element found in an archaeological context that exhibits human activity but that was not made by people and so is not, strictly speaking, an **artifact.** Burned wood in a fireplace, butchered animal bone in a trash pit, and charred seeds or nuts in a midden are all ecofacts.

egalitarian Social systems in which all members of the same age/sex category are equal in the sense that they all possess the same wealth, social standing, and political influence.

einkorn A variety of wheat, *Tripsicum monococcum,* that possesses hulled grains and was an important domesticate in the Neolithic. Today it is not a significant agricultural crop. (Compare to **emmer.**)

electron spin resonance dating A radiation-damage dating technique based on measurement of the buildup of electrons in crystalline materials. It can be applied to sites more than a few thousand years old. The upper limit of the technique is estimated to be more than 10 million years.

El Riego phase The period of time in the **Tehuacán** Valley in highland Mexico from 9,000 to 7,000 B.P. that was characterized by a subsistence focus on wild plants, including squash, beans, chili peppers, amaranth, and avocado. During this period, people traveled in microbands for part of the year but gathered in macrobands in the spring and summer months.

emmer A variety of wheat, *Tripsicum turgidum*, that became the primary stock of early agricultural wheat. It is the source of cultivated wheat in the modern world. (Compare to **einkorn**.)

empiricist An individual who subscribes to the scientific approach that emphasizes observation rather than speculation.

enamel hypoplasia A medical condition affecting the outside layers of teeth. Horizontal imperfections develop on the enamel in individuals who have experienced malnutrition during their early years.

encephalization The growth and development of the brain during the development of the individual.

endocast A mold of the brain produced naturally when sediment enters the skull and then mineralizes. Also produced artificially by coating the inside of the skull with a latex-based material. Endocasts can exhibit features of the exterior surface of the brain.

epiphyseal fusion The **epiphyses** of each long bone join to the **diaphysis** during physical maturation. The age of death of a juvenile individual can be assessed by reference to the degree of epiphyseal fusion exhibited.

epiphysis (pl., *epiphyses*) The long-bone endcap. The epiphyses join at the ends of the **diaphysis** of each long bone.

epistemology The study of knowledge; how you know what you know.

erosion The disintegration and transportation of geological material by wind, water, or ice.

ethnoarchaeology The archaeological study of a living group of people that often focuses on the processes by which human behavior becomes translated into the archaeological record.

ethnographer A cultural anthropologist who lives among a group of people or a cultural group and interacts with them daily, often for an extended period of time, observing their behavior.

ethnology The comparative study of culture. Ethnologists study human behavior cross-culturally, looking for similarities and differences in how people behave: how they raise their children, how they treat elders, how they organize their labor, and so forth.

evolution The systematic change through time of biological organisms or human cultural systems.

experimental replication The reproduction, under laboratory conditions, of facsimiles of archaeo-

logical artifacts. A process employed to analyze ancient technology.

faunal assemblage The animal bones found at a site and the species represented by those bones.

feature The combination of artifacts and/or ecofacts at a site, reflecting a location where some human activity took place. Features include fireplaces, middens, burials, cooking hearths, activity areas, and buildings. Also defined as nonportable, complex artifacts.

femur The upper leg bone.

Fertile Crescent A crescent-shaped region extending from the eastern Mediterranean coast of modern Israel, Lebanon, and Syria, north into the Zagros Mountains and then south toward the Persian Gulf (see Figure 12.2), marked by an abundance of wild cereal grain at the beginning of the **Holocene Epoch.** Not coincidentally, this region is where some of the world's first domestication of plants took place.

fire-cracked rock Rock that has been heated to a high temperature in, for example, a fireplace or hearth, and that has fractured as a result. Large quantities of fire-cracked rock in a given location are often diagnostic of an archaeological site.

fission-track dating A radiation-damage dating technique that measures the age of an artifact as a function of the amount of physical damage in the form of damage tracks left in a material by radioactive decay.

flake A stone fragment removed from a **core** by the blow of a **hammerstone,** antler baton, or pressure flaker. The flake can be discarded, used as is, or further modified for use as a specific tool.

fluted point Projectile point made by Paleoindians in the New World between 11,500 and 10,000 B.P. Exhibits a distinctive channel, or "flute" (as in a fluted column), on both faces. These channels aided in hafting the spearpoint onto its wooden shaft. The two major forms of fluted point are **Clovis** and **Folsom.**

Folsom A **fluted point** type of the Paleoindians. Generally smaller than **Clovis** points, Folsom points are also later in time, dating to after 11,000 B.P. Clovis points have been found in association with the bones of extinct elephants, whereas Folsom points have been found in association with the bones of bison. Folsom points are fluted, with the channels commonly extending nearly the entire length of the point.

food surplus The production of food beyond the needs of the producer and his or her family. A necessary concomitant of civilization, freeing entire classes of people from the subsistence quest and allowing for the existence of full-time rulers, soldiers, merchants, and priests.

foraging A subsistence system based on the collection of wild foods, including any combination of hunting wild game, gathering wild plants, fishing, and shellfish collecting.

foraminifera Microorganisms used in the study of ancient environments. By measuring the ratio of $^{16}O{:}^{18}O$ in foraminifera fossils, the amount of the earth's surface covered in ice at any given point in time can be indirectly determined.

Funan The name given to the earliest civilization in Southeast Asia, established in Cambodia during the first century A.D. by merchants from India.

gene flow The movement and exchange of genetic material among populations of a species through interbreeding.

Geometric Kebaran Pre-**Neolithic** culture in the Middle East, dating to the period 14,500–12,500 B.P. Located in the moist Mediterranean woodlands of the central **Levant** and extending into the margins of the Negev and Sinai Deserts and across southern Jordan, subsistence was based on **foraging.**

glacial Period of ice advance during the **Pleistocene Epoch.** Glacials generally last many thousands of years. Cold glacials were interrupted by equally long warmer periods called **interglacials.**

glacier A massive body of ice that, through a number of processes, can expand and move.

glume The case in which an individual cereal grain is enclosed.

gracile Lightly constructed, as referring to the overall appearance of a hominid skeleton. Modern humans are gracile, and when the term is applied to the fossils of extinct hominids it is in reference to their appearance relative to anatomically modern human beings. Bones that are more massive than those of modern humans are said to be **robust.**

grave goods Cultural materials placed into a grave, sometimes in a conscious attempt to provide the deceased with items it is believed are needed in the afterlife.

Gravettian Toolmaking tradition of the **Upper Paleolithic,** characterized by the production of small **blades** and denticulate knives. Dated from 27,000 to 21,000 B.P.

Halafian A culture in Mesopotamia dating from 7,500 to 6,700 B.P. Halafian sites generally are small farming villages.

half-life The amount of time it takes for half of the radioactive **isotope** in a given sample to decay into a stable form. The half-life of radiocarbon, for example, is 5,730 years, and that of radioactive potassium is 1.3 billion years.

Hamburgian A culture of the northern European **Upper Paleolithic.**

hammerstone In stone toolmaking, the lithic tool used in percussion flaking to remove flakes or blades from a core, or to detach additional flakes from flakes or blades.

hang-t'u The Chinese term for stamped or pounded and compacted earth used to make structures.

Harris lines Longitudinal cracks located at the ends of long bones; indicative of dietary stress during physical development.

Hassunan A culture in **Mesopotamia** dating from 8,000 to 7,200 B.P. that was characterized by small farming villages where subsistence was based on the growing of wheat, barley, peas, and lentils. Hunting supplemented the diet.

Hoabinhian Southeast Asian **Mesolithic** stone tool tradition based on the manufacture of tools from chipped pebbles.

Hohokam A culture in the American Southwest centered in southern Arizona. The Hohokam people constructed irrigation canals to water the fields in which they grew maize, beans, and squash.

Holocene Epoch The recent and current geological epoch. The Holocene followed the Pleistocene and represents a presumed break with glacial climates.

hominid Any creature believed to be in the direct human line, a member of the taxonomic family **Hominidae. Bipedal locomotion** is the single most salient characteristic of the hominids.

Hominidae The taxonomic family that contains human beings and all direct ancestors of humanity.

Hopewell Burial-mound-building culture centered in the Ohio River Valley. Beginning about 2,400 years ago, this culture developed at the **chiefdom** level of sociopolitical integration, sometimes building impressive tombs for their chiefs. Hopewell is generally later than **Adena.**

humerus The upper arm bone.

hypodigm All of the fossil specimens assigned to a species.

hypothesis A proposed explanation for some phenomenon that may be derived initially from empirical observation of the phenomenon by the process called induction. A hypothesis must be tested; predictions are deduced about what new data must be found if the hypothesis is to be supported. When data are found that contradict these predictions, the hypothesis is rejected or modified.

Iberomaurusians A culture in northwestern Africa dating to after 16,000 B.P. that inhabited the coastal plain and interior of modern Tunisia and Morocco. Subsistence was based on hunting wild cattle, gazelle, hartebeest, and Barbary sheep and collecting marine mollusks.

ice-free corridor (or **McKenzie corridor**) A proposed route of safe passage between the farthest-west extent of the **Laurentide** ice field and the farthest-east extent of the **Cordilleran** glacier. Paleoindians may have traveled down this corridor from the western arctic into the heartland of America.

ilium The upper blade of the pelvis.

impact wear Distinctive damage scars on stone tools that can be experimentally shown to have resulted from the tool's use as a projectile.

innominate The left or right side of the pelvis that consists of the **ilium,** the **ischium,** and the pubis.

in situ Literally "in place." Objects found at archaeological sites that are left in their precise place of discovery are said to be in situ.

interglacial A period during the **Pleistocene** when glacial ice melted and temperature ameliorated. Interglacials lasted for thousands of years, and were preceded and followed by **glacials.**

interstadial A short period during a glacial when glacial ice melted and temperature increased.

ischium The bottom rear portion of the **innominate** bone of the pelvis.

isotope A variety of an element's atomic form. Isotopes are distinguished by the number of neutrons in their atomic nuclei. Some isotopes are unstable and decay into other forms; these are said to be radioactive. Some radioactive isotopes can be used in dating paleontological or archaeological material.

Kabuh Formation A geological formation in Java dating to after 800,000 years ago that has been the source of several hominid fossils belonging to the species *Homo erectus.*

K/Ar dating Potassium/argon dating. The **half-life** of radioactive potassium has been measured as 1.3 billion years. Since potassium is an abundant element in the earth's crust and since Argon collects in rock solely as a result of the decay of radioactive potassium, this technique is widely applicable.

Karim Shahirian Pre-**Neolithic** culture located in the foothills of the Zagros Mountains in modern Turkey.

Khmer Local name given to the civilization of Southeast Asia dating to after A.D. 800. The great temple cities of Angkor Thom and Angkor Wat represent the culmination of this civilization at around A.D. 1000.

kiva A round structure used in religious ceremonies by Native American societies in the Southwest. Most kivas are relatively small, but so-called great kivas are enormous. Casa Rinconada in Chaco Canyon, for example, is nearly 20 m (63.5 ft) across.

knapper One who makes stone tools. *To knapp* is to make stone tools through the application of percussion and pressure.

Knossos An enormous and impressive site representing the culmination of Minoan civilization. The temple at Knossos was built beginning in 3,880 B.P. and at its height covered an area to about 20,000 m^2 and had 1,000 rooms built up to three stories and, in some sections, four stories.

knuckle walking The mode of locomotion employed by the great apes. When walking quadrupedally, these apes walk on the soles of their feet and on the second bones of their fingers.

Kush The Egyptian name for the land south of their territory. Kush began at the first cataract of the Nile in southern Egypt and extended to the sixth cataract, near the modern Sudanese city of Khartoum.

lacustrine Having to do with lakes.

Lake Forest Archaic An **Archaic** culture of eastern North America centered in, though not restricted to, the region of the Great Lakes. Lake Forest people exploited the food resources of the large lakes of eastern North America.

Lapita A pottery style known from the inhabited Pacific Islands. The movement of people from the western to the eastern Pacific can be traced by the presence and spread of Lapita pottery.

Laurentide The massive continental ice sheet of **Pleistocene** North America, centered in central northeastern Canada.

legume A large family of flowering plants, all of which produce fruits that grow in the form of a pod that splits along its seams when mature and opens to reveal the seeds. Garden peas, snap beans, lima beans, lentils, and chickpeas are all legumes domesticated during the **Neolithic.**

Levallois Stone tool technology involving the production of consistently shaped flakes from carefully prepared **cores.** Levallois technology is associated with archaic forms of *Homo sapiens.*

Levant The name applied to the areas along the eastern shore of the Mediterranean, including present-day Greece, Turkey, Syria, Lebanon, Israel, and Egypt.

Linienbandkeramik (LBK) An early **Neolithic** culture of central Europe dating to about 6,500 B.P. The subsistence base was domesticated **emmer** wheat, barley, and pulses.

littoral Related to the seashore.

logistical collecting A settlement-subsistence strategy that involves the movement of a group in a fixed seasonal round. The food collectors know when resources are available and where during the course of a year. They plan the movements of their settlements to coincide with the availability of food resources in their territory.

Lower Paleolithic Period from 2.5 million years ago to 250,000 years ago that encompasses the stone tool industries of *Homo habilis* and *Homo erectus.*

Lung-shan A Chinese culture that followed the **Neolithic Yang-shao.** Dated to 5,000 B.P., Lung-shan sites are larger, with evidence of substantial **hang-t'u** construction. Lung-shan cemeteries have produced clear evidence of a socioeconomically stratified society. Lung-shan laid the foundation for China's first complex state, the Shang.

Magdelanian Late Paleolithic culture in Europe dating from 16,000 to 11,000 B.P. Known from sites primarily in France and Spain, Magdelanian material culture included finely made barbed harpoons, carved decorative objects, and cave paintings.

Maglemosian An early Mesolithic culture of Europe adapted to a forest and lakeside environment. The famous site of Star Carr is a Maglemosian site.

mandible The lower jaw. (Compare to **maxilla.**)

Maritime Archaic An Archaic-period culture of northeastern North America centered along the coast of northern New England and the Canadian Maritime provinces. The subsistence focus was on the sea, fishing and hunting sea mammals. Burials with elaborate grave goods mark the Maritime Archaic.

mastaba Mud-brick structures built over the tombs of a developing elite in Egypt before the pharaohs. They became larger through time, were stacked on top of each other, and ultimately evolved into the pyramid tomb emblematic of ancient Egyptian civilization.

Mast Forest Archaic An Archaic-period culture of northeastern North America centered in central and southern New England. Subsistence focus was on the interior forest of New England, especially on the resources of the mast forest: nut foods such as acorn, hickory, chestnut, and walnut, and animals, especially deer.

mattock A digging tool with a working blade set at right angles to the handle. Antler mattocks have been found in European **Mesolithic** sites like Star Carr.

maxilla The upper jaw. (Compare to **mandible.**)

McKenzie corridor See **ice-free corridor.**

megafauna Very large animals; commonly used to describe the large, now-extinct herbivores of the Pleistocene world.

Melanesia Islands located north of New Guinea in the western Pacific.

Mesolithic The culture period after the Paleolithic and before the **Neolithic;** a period of the proliferation of many regional adaptations and an explosion of local cultural diversity.

Mesopotamia The land between the Tigris and Euphrates Rivers in modern Iraq. The world's first cities and complex civilization developed in Mesopotamia.

Messinian Event The late **Miocene** drying up of the Mediterranean Sea that resulted from massive growth in the antarctic ice sheet. This caused a massive drop in sea level worldwide that contributed to the shrinking of the forests of Europe and Africa, which resulted ultimately in a marked decrease in the number of ape species.

microbands Small cohabiting groups, commonly ten or fifteen people, who move together seasonally and nomadically.

microblade A very small stone blade, often with very sharp cutting edges. Groups of microblades often were set into wooden, bone, or antler handles.

microlith A very small stone tool.

Micronesia Small islands in the western Pacific, east of New Guinea.

Middle Paleolithic The Middle Stone Age, the period after the **Lower Paleolithic** and before the **Upper Paleolithic.** Covers the span from 250,000 to 40,000 years ago and includes the cultures of archaic and modern varieties of human beings.

Minoan The name given by Sir Arthur Evans to the early European civilization that evolved on the island of Crete. The temple at **Knossos** is the best-known manifestation of this culture.

Miocene Epoch The period of time from 25 million years ago to 5 million years ago. Forests were more extensive during the Miocene than they are today.

A broad array of arboreally adapted ape species thrived during this epoch; most became extinct at the end of the Miocene when the forests diminished in geographical extent.

mitochondrial DNA (mtDNA) Genetic material located in the mitochondria of cells. Analysis of mtDNA has proven useful in assessing evolutionary relationships among existing species.

mobiliary art Art that is portable. Mobiliary art made during the **Upper Paleolithic** includes **Venus figurines,** animal carvings, and geometrically incised bone and antler.

Mogollon A prehistoric culture located in the American Southwest, centered in the uplands of New Mexico and northeastern Mexico. The Mogollon people grew maize, beans, and squash, relying mostly on rainfall agriculture.

monumental works Large-scale communal construction projects characteristic of civilizations.

morphology Literally, the study of form. An analysis of the shape and form of skeletons or artifacts.

Mousterian The stone-tool tradition of the Neandertals and early anatomically modern human beings. A core-and-flake technology in which a series of different, standardized tool types were produced from stone flakes struck from cores.

musculoskeletal hypertrophy Great size and associated strength in the muscles and bones of a species or individual. Among recent human ancestors, the Neandertals exhibit an extreme level of musculoskeletal hypertrophy.

Mushabian Pre-**Neolithic** culture located in the steppe and arid zones of the Negev and Sinai Deserts in modern Israel and Egypt. Contemporary with the **Geometric Kebaran,** dating from 14,500 to 12,500 B.P.

Mycenaeans A southern European civilization that followed the **Minoans** and preceded the Greeks.

Natufian A Middle Eastern culture dated from 13,000 to 9,000 B.P., located in the Mediterranean woodland zone. The Natufian reliance on wild wheat and barley set the stage for the **Neolithic.**

natural selection The process proposed by Charles Darwin for how species evolve: Those individuals in a species that possess advantageous characteristics are more likely to survive and pass on those characteristics than are individuals that do not possess them.

Nenana Complex Perhaps the oldest stone tool complex identified in Alaska dating from 11,800 to 11,000 B.P. Predating the **Denali Complex,** Nenana includes bifacially flaked, unfluted spearpoints. Nenana bifaces are similar and perhaps related to tools made in eastern Russia about 14,000 years ago.

Neolithic The "New Stone Age." In the past, Neolithic was defined on the basis of the appearance of ground-stone tools as opposed to chipped-stone tools. Today, Neolithic refers to the period after 12,000 years ago when food-producing through the domestication of plants and animals replaced foraging as the dominant mode of subsistence.

neotony The apparent retention, in adults of one species, of juvenile physical characteristics of an evolutionarily related species. For example, physical features of adult human beings are similar to those of juvenile chimpanzees, which is an indication of our species neotony.

New Temple Period The culture period for **Minoan** Crete dating from 3,650 to 3,420 B.P. It followed a catastrophic earthquake that badly damaged the temple at **Knossos** and marks a florescence of Minoan culture.

niche The actual physical area occupied by an organism as well as its functional role in a community of organisms. Sometimes referred to as an organism's ecological address.

Nubia The territory south of the ancient Egyptian nation, primarily between the first and sixth cataracts of the Nile, from southern Egypt to Sudan. The ancient Egyptians called this area **Kush.**

nuclear DNA The genetic instructions contained in the nucleus of the cell that determine the biological makeup of the organism.

object piece In the manufacturing of stone tools, the stone that is being worked through the application of either percussion or pressure.

obsidian hydration A dating method based on the rate that a freshly exposed surface of obsidian begins to alter physically by chemically combining with water in the air or soil. The thickness of the hydration layer that develops in a given environment is a factor of time.

Occam's razor A fundamental rule in logical thinking: the principle that a person should not increase, beyond what is necessary, the number of assumptions required to explain anything. In logical thought, a person should not make more assumptions than the minimum needed.

occipital The area at the rear of the skull. In ancient hominids, the occipital area tends to be massive and **robust.** In anatomically modern human beings, the occipital tends to be smooth and **gracile.**

Oldowan The earliest stone tools, simple chopping tools and sharp flakes, dated to 2.4 million years ago that were probably made by *Homo habilis*. Some evidence suggests they may also have been produced by *Australopithecus robustus (Paranthropus)*.

Olmec An ancient culture of lowland Mesoamerica dating to 3,200 years ago. The Olmec produced a number of large ceremonial centers where they produced great earthworks, finely carved jade sculptures, and massive basalt carvings of human heads. The religious iconography of Olmec art seems to have served as a unifying element in ancient Mesoamerica.

opportunistic foragers Groups that follow a subsistence pattern in which they take advantage of whatever resources become available without much patterning or planning in advance.

orthogenesis The invalid notion of a predestined and progressive pattern of evolutionary change.

osteological Related to bones.

osteological comparative collection A bone library; a collection of bones used as models to aid in identifying the bones (species, sex, anatomical part) recovered in a paleontological or archaeological excavation.

paleoanthropologist An anthropologist who focuses on the physical evolution of our species, studying the skeletal remains and cultures of ancient hominids.

Paleo-Arctic tradition Stone-tool tradition in the arctic dating to the period before 9,000 years ago. The technology involved the production of **microblades** detached from **wedge-shaped cores.**

Paleoindian The period and culture in the New World dating from about 11,800 B.P. to about 10,000 B.P. **Fluted points** are the most distinctive element in the Paleoindian stone **tool kit.** Paleoindians hunted the late Pleistocene megafauna of the New World. Many archaeologists believe the Paleoindians were the first human settlers of the New World.

paleomagnetic dating A dating method based on the movement of the earth's magnetic poles.

paleopathological Related to ancient disease, trauma, or dietary deficiency.

paleopathology The study of ancient disease, trauma, or dietary deficiency, of which hominid skeletons often bear evidence.

paradigm Overarching perspective; essential view and assumptions about how the world—or some part of it—functions or operates. Evolution is a paradigm of biology.

parietal art Art on the walls of a cave, like the cave paintings of the **Upper Paleolithic.**

pastoralists People who raise and tend livestock, such as sheep or cattle, as the focus of their subsistence.

Peiligang Earliest **Neolithic** culture in northern China, with well-established farming villages dating to 8,500–7,000 years ago.

permanent dentition The adult, or permanent, teeth. Adult humans, apes, and Old World monkeys have thirty-two permanent teeth: sixteen in the **mandible** and sixteen in the **maxilla.**

petroglyph A design etched into a rock face. Darker, weathered rock surface is removed, creating a design or pattern by exposing lighter-colored rock beneath.

phylogeny The evolutionary history of a species of organism.

phylum (pl., *phyla*) The taxonomic level under "kingdom." Divides animal life into those with a backbone (Phylum Chordata) and those without.

Pleistocene Epoch The geological epoch beginning about 1.6 million years ago and ending about 10,000 years ago. It was marked by a succession of colder periods, or **glacials,** interrupted by warmer periods, or **interglacials.**

pluvial A period of increased rainfall in areas far south of large glacial masses during the **Pleistocene.**

polymerase chain reaction (PCR) A genetic engineering technique used to increase the quantity of DNA in a sample.

Polynesia Islands of the central and eastern Pacific; they are volcanic in origin.

pongid A member of the taxonomic family **Pongidae;** an ape.

Pongidae The taxonomic family that includes all of the apes.

postcranial Referring to the skeleton, all of the bones below the cranium.

preform A partially worked **core, flake,** or **blade.** In a preform, the first general steps have been made in producing a tool.

premodern *Homo sapiens* An extinct subspecies of humanity that shares much in common with modern *Homo sapiens* or **anatomically modern *Homo sapiens*** but that commonly retains primitive skeletal features and possesses a smaller mean cranial capacity than modern people. The Neandertals are the best-known archaic variety or subspecies of the human race. Also called **archaic *Homo sapiens.***

primate A member of the taxonomic order Primates: prosimians, monkeys, and apes. An animal with grasping hands and feet, stereoscopic vision, and a relatively large brain (in proportion to body size). Most, but not all, primates have nails instead of claws, tails, and an arboreal adaptation.

primatologist A person who studies primates.

prognathous Having a forward-thrusting lower face. Apes are prognathous, as are extinct hominids. Anatomically modern human beings tend to have flat, nonprognathous faces.

pubic symphysis The point of articulation between the two pubic bones of the pelvis. Changes in the appearance of the pubic symphysis occur fairly regularly during an individual's life and so can be used to determine the age of death.

pueblo Apartment-house-type structure of the ancient, and some modern, inhabitants of the American Southwest, that were constructed of adobe brick, rubble, and shaped stone.

punctuated equilibrium A mode of evolution in which long periods of stasis, or equilibrium, in a species are interrupted by short, relatively rapid bursts (punctuations) of great change, producing a new species.

Purron phase The period of time in the **Tehuacán** Valley in highland Mexico from 4,300 to 3,500 B.P. Little is known about this period in terms of subsistence. Pottery was used for the first time by valley inhabitants.

quadruped Any animal that habitually walks on four feet. Most animals, including most primates, are quadrupeds.

quipu A record-keeping system of the Inca in which a series of knotted strings were used as mnemonic devices to help record keepers keep track of information.

rank societies Societies characterized by a few sociopolitical levels filled by a relatively small number of people.

rachis The area of attachment between seeds and other seeds or between seeds and other parts of the plant. A brittle rachis is an adaptive feature under natural conditions, but, since it makes harvesting more difficult, it is selected against by humans through **artificial selection.**

radiocarbon dating **Radiometric** dating technique based on the decay of a radioactive isotope of carbon: ^{14}C, or radiocarbon. Carbon dating can be applied to virtually anything that was once part of a living organism, within a range from about 300 to 40,000 years ago. Also called **carbon dating.**

radiometric Referring to any dating technique based on the measurement of radioactive decay.

relative date A date that places a fossil or an archaeological site or artifact in a sequence with other specimens, but does not allow for the assignment of an age in terms of years or even a range of years. (Compare to **absolute date.**)

remote sensing A procedure that allows for the discovery of archaeological sites or artifacts without digging and that may include aerial photography and a number of technologies that allow for scanning below ground without disturbing the soil (proton magnetometry, electrical resistivity survey).

robust A term applied to skeletal features that are heavily built.

sagittal crest A ridge of bone that runs along the top of the skull from front to back and that provides added surface area for the attachment of powerful temporalis muscles that attach to the jaws. Male gorillas and some ancient hominid fossils possess a sagittal crest.

Sahul The land mass of "Greater Australia," including Australia proper, New Guinea, and Tasmania. During periods of **glacial** maxima in the **Pleistocene,** these three islands were combined in the single land mass of Sahul.

Samarran **Neolithic** culture of southern **Mesopotamia** dating to after 7,500 years ago. Samarran sites are located on the floodplain of the Tigris and Euphrates Rivers. There is evidence of communal works, including the construction of irrigation canals, fortification walls, and communal grain storage structures.

savanna Grasslands. The replacement of the Miocene forests of Africa with savannas set the stage for the evolution of an upright primate adapted for life under conditions of flat, open expanses and few trees.

scapulimancy A process of divining the future, popular in ancient China, in which the scapulae (shoulder blades) of animals are burned and the pattern of burning and breakage is "read" by a diviner.

seal A carved or molded symbol (on a ring, stamp, or cylinder) that was impressed into soft clay to leave one's official mark. Used in early **Mesopotamia** as a system of record keeping. (See also **cylinder seal.**)

settlement pattern The location, size, function, and seasonality of the various communities or activity areas within a given cultural system. The pattern of land use.

sexual dimorphism Differences in the form and size of the two sexes. Among most primates, the male tends to be larger and physically more powerful than the female.

simple foragers Hunters and gatherers with no particular focus on or commitment to any one food source.

Sinagua Literally "without water," refers to a prehistoric culture group in the American Southwest, specially in central Arizona.

sister group A term from the cladistic approach to classification. A group of two or more different species presumed to have a common ancestor that led to no other species.

site A place where people lived and/or worked and where the physical evidence of their existence, in the form of **artifacts, ecofacts,** and **features,** can be or has been recovered.

social stratification A pattern of social integration in which individuals are placed into a hierarchy of social levels. The presence of a hierarchy of differences in status and wealth in a society.

social system A system coordinating activities and interrelationships among individuals living in a group. Includes rules of kinship, descent, marriage, division of labor, and the definition of the roles, rights, and responsibilities of members of the group.

Solutrean The stone toolmaking tradition of the European **Upper Paleolithic** dating from 21,000 to 16,000 B.P. Solutrean bifaces include exquisitely made, symmetrical, leaf-shaped projectile points.

spear-thrower A tool used to increase the range and accuracy of the hand-thrown spear. It is a straight rod or board with a hook at one end that articulates with the end of the spear and effectively increases the length of the arm of the individual throwing the spear.

specialization of labor A cultural pattern in which some individuals can focus all or most of their labors on some specialty: metal working, pottery manufacturing, stone working, weaving, architectural design, and so on. By specializing, these individuals can become quite proficient at their craft, art, or science. The specialization of labor is characteristic of complex civilizations.

stadial A short period of increased glaciation. Stadials can occur either during **glacials** or **interglacials** and are separated by **interstadials.**

state A class society, often rigidly stratified into social levels. The ruling class controls the populace not by consensus but by coercion and force. The rulers in a state society have the powers to levy and collect taxes, to establish and enforce laws, and to conscript people to do the work of the state.

stela (pl., *stelae*) A column on which images or written messages have been inscribed. The Maya of Mesoamerica left a large number of stelae.

stratigraphic (stratigraphy) Related to the geological or cultural layer in which something has been found. Stratigraphic layering represents a relative sequence of geological time and/or cultural chronology.

striking platform Part of a stone **core** or worked **flake** that presents an area where the desired flake can be removed when struck with a **hammerstone** or antler hammer.

subsistence The material necessary to sustain life: water, food, clothing, shelter. Here it usually refers to the quest for food.

Sunda (or **Sundaland**) The combined land mass of the modern islands of Java, Sumatra, Bali, and Borneo. These islands became a single, continuous land mass during periods of glaciation and attendant lowered sea level during the **Pleistocene.**

supraorbital torus A continuous, projecting ridge of bone above and across the eye orbits. Commonly seen in modern apes and in ancient hominids, it is lacking in anatomically modern human beings, though less conspicuous brow ridges are present in some individuals.

system of record keeping Any symbolic system that usually, but not always, involves some form of writing for keeping track of economic transactions, historical events, religious rules, and the like. A fundamental need in complex civilizations.

taphonomic Referring to how materials become part of the paleontological or archaeological record.

taphonomy The study of how materials become part of the paleontological or archaeological record.

taxonomy A systematic classification based on similarities and differences among the items being classified. Organisms, artifacts, or even whole cultures can be classified in this way.

Tehuacán A valley in central highland Mexico that was the focus of a multidisciplinary research project that produced important archaeological data concerning the domestication of plants in the New World, particularly the **domestication** of maize and squash.

teosinte The wild ancestor of domesticated maize; grew and grows wild throughout the American tropics. The mutation of a very few teosinte genes changes the spikey stem, with its small, encased seeds, into a cob with a larger number of bigger, naked kernels.

test pit A hole or boring into soil in the search for archaeological evidence. In some parts of the world, a pattern of test pits spread out across an area is a primary method by which archaeological sites are searched for and by which the spatial distribution of buried materials at a site is first identified.

thermoluminescence A trapped-charge, radiation-damage technique for dating archaeological objects. Energy produced by natural radiation in soil becomes stored in nearby objects. The amount of stored energy is a function of the background radiation level (which can be measured) and time. Once the level of background radiation at a particular place is known, how much has accumulated in an archaeological object can be measured, and from that the age of the object (how long it has been accumulating the energy) can be determined.

tholoi A new architectural form seen at **Halafian** sites in **Mesopotamia** dating to after 7,500 years ago. Tholoi appear to have been communal storage facilities for **Neolithic** people, and may also have served as burial chambers for a growing class of socioeconomically important individuals.

three-age system The chronological breakdown of the history of human culture into a Stone Age, a Bronze Age, and an Iron Age, developed in 1836 by J. C. Thomsen as part of a guidebook for the archaeological collections at the Danish National Museum.

tibia The larger of the two long bones making up the lower leg; the shin bone.

tokens Small geometric shapes of clay, some bearing impressed symbols, dating back to 8,000 years ago in the Middle East that appear to represent an early system of record keeping that led ultimately to a system of writing.

tool kit A set of tools used together in performing a single task (for example, a butchering tool kit for dismembering an animal carcass). A tool kit can also refer to the entire range of tools used at a particular site or during a given time period or produced by a particular group of hominids.

trace element analysis Determining the geographic source of the materials used by an ancient people through the analysis of small, or trace, concentrations of elements or chemicals in those raw materials. The levels measured in archaeological artifacts are compared to the levels present in various possible sources. Where the concentrations in an artifact and a source closely match, it is suggested that the prehistoric people obtained the raw material from that source.

tuber A relatively short, fleshy, usually underground stem of a plant, often rich in starch and carbohydrates. Tubers have long contributed to the human food quest.

turnover-pulse A term coined by Elisabeth Vrba to refer to periods of significant environmental change that produce rapid and significant change in plant and animal species leading either to extinction or rapid evolution.

Ubaid The name given to the culture of southern **Mesopotamia** at 6,300 B.P. Irrigation canals constructed by the Ubaidic people made agriculture possible, and larger settlements grew up in the Mesopotamian floodplain at this time. Evidence of the growing power of the religious elite is seen at Ubaidic sites, with wealth becoming concentrated in the temples.

ulna One of the bones of the forearm. The ulna is the more interior bone, closer to the body, while the radius is the more exterior bone (on the thumb side).

Umm Dabaghiyah A **Neolithic** culture in northern **Mesopotamia** dating to more than 8,000 years ago and characterized by a subsistence base of wheat, barley, sheep, and goats. Hunting was still important, and their settlements were small.

uniformitarianism The belief that the appearance of the earth could be understood as resulting from the slow action of known processes over a very long period of time. This belief, first championed in the late eighteenth and early nineteenth centuries, allowed for a great age of the earth.

unilineal evolution All cultures pass through the same stages of development. It is usually asserted that some cultures may become stuck at a given stage. This concept is no longer widely accepted.

Upper Paleolithic The final phase of the Paleolithic, dating to after 40,000 years ago and associated with anatomically modern human beings in Europe.

Venus figurines **Upper Paleolithic** sculptures of females, often, but not always, with exaggerated secondary sexual characteristics. They have been found in geographic clusters in western, central, and eastern Europe, usually dated to the narrow time span between 25,000 and 23,000 years ago.

Wallacea The name given to the sea over the **Wallace Trench.**

Wallace Trench An undersea chasm located between New Guinea/Australia and Java/Borneo and nearly 7,500 m (25,000 ft) deep. It was not breached during periods of lowered Pleistocene sea levels, so population movement from southeast Asia to **Sahul** was accomplished, of necessity, via water.

wear patterns Characteristic and diagnostic traces of damage or polish left on stone tools as a result of their use. Analysis of wear patterns can often tell the researcher how a tool was used and on what material.

weathering The decomposition and disintegration of rock, usually at or near the earth's surface.

wedge-shaped cores **Cores** shaped like wedges from which blades are struck; found as part of the **Paleo-Arctic tradition** in northeastern Asia and also found as part of the **Denali Complex** in the American arctic.

Yang-shao An early **Neolithic** culture of China, dating to about 7,000 B.P. Yang-shao settlements appear to have been planned out. Subsistence was based on the cultivation of foxtail millet. Domesticated rice, though a minor dietary component, appears in China for the first time at these sites.

Younger Dryas The name given in Europe to a **stadial** that lasted between 11,000 and 10,000 years ago. Though a relatively short interlude of renewed glacial expansion during a general warming trend at the end of the **Pleistocene,** the Younger Dryas may have been severe enough to have caused the temporary abandonment by humans of much of northwest Europe.

Zarzian A pre-**Neolithic** culture identified in the foothills of the Zagros Mountains in Turkey.

References

Adams, R. E. W. 1991. *Prehistoric Mesoamerica.* Norman: University of Oklahoma Press.

Adams, R. McC., and H. J. Nissen. 1972. *The Uruk Countryside.* Chicago: University of Chicago Press.

Adovasio, J. M., J. Donahue, and R. Stuckenrath. 1990. The Meadowcroft Rockshelter radiocarbon chronology—1975–1990. *American Antiquity* 55:348–353.

———. 1992. Never say never again: Some thoughts on could haves and might have beens. *American Antiquity* 57:527–530.

Adovasio, J. M., J. D. Gunn, J. Donahue, R. Stuckenrath, J. Guilday, and K. Lord. 1979–80a. Meadowcroft Rockshelter—Retrospect 1977: Part 1. *North American Archaeologist* 1(1):3–44.

Adovasio, J. M., J. D. Gunn, J. Donahue, R. Stuckenrath, J. Guilday, K. Lord, and K. Volman. 1979–80b. Meadowcroft Rockshelter—Retrospect 1977: Part 2. *North American Archaeologist* 1(2):99–138.

Agenbroad, L. D. 1988. Clovis people: The human factor in the Pleistocene megafauna extinction question. In *Americans Before Columbus: Ice-Age Origins,* edited by R. C. Carlisle, 63–74. Ethnology Monographs, Vol. 12. Pittsburgh, Pa.: University of Pittsburgh.

Aiello, L. C. 1993. The fossil evidence for modern human origins in Africa: A revised view. *American Anthropologist* 95:73–96.

———. 1994. Variable but singular. *Nature* 368:399–400.

Allchin, B., and R. Allchin. 1982. *The Rise of Civilization in India and Pakistan.* Cambridge: Cambridge University Press.

Allison, M. J. 1984. Paleopathology in Peruvian and Chilean populations. In *Paleopathology at the Origins of Agriculture,* edited by M. N. Cohen and G. J. Armelagos, 515–529. New York: Academic Press.

Allsworth-Jones, P. 1990. The Szeletian and the stratigraphic succession in central Europe and adjacent areas: Main trends, recent results and problems for resolution. In *The Emergence of Modern Humans: An Archaeological Perspective,* edited by P. Mellars, 160–242. Ithaca, N.Y.: Cornell University Press.

Alva, W., and C. B. Donnan. 1993. *Royal Tombs of Sipán.* Los Angeles: Fowler Museum of Culture History.

———. 1994. Tales from a Peruvian Crypt. *Natural History* 103(5):26–34.

An Zhimin. 1989. Prehistoric agriculture in China. In *Foraging and Farming,* edited by D. R. Harris and G. C. Hillman, 643–649. London: Unwin Hyman.

Anderson, D. 1990. The Paleoindian colonization of eastern North America. *Research in Economic Anthropology* (supplement) 5:163–216.

Anderson, D. D. 1968. A stone age campsite at the gateway to America. *Scientific American* 218(6):24–33.

———. 1970. Microblade traditions in northwestern Alaska. *Arctic Anthropology* 7(2):2–16.

Anderson, E. 1956. Man as a maker of new plants and new plant communities. In *Man's Role in Changing the Face of the Earth,* Vol. 2, edited by W. L. Thomas, 767–777. Chicago: University of Chicago Press.

Andrews, Peter. 1985. Species diversity and diet in monkeys and apes during the Miocene. In *Primate Evolution and Human Origins,* edited by R. Ciochon and J. Fleagle, 194–204. Menlo Park, Calif.: Benjamin/Cummings.

Andrews, Peter, and Chris Stringer. 1989. *Human Evolution: An Illustrated Guide.* Cambridge: Cambridge University Press.

Andrews, Philip. 1984. An alternative interpretation of characters used to define *Homo erectus. Courier Forschungsinstitut Seckenberg* 69:167–175.

Ardrey, R. 1961. *African Genesis: A Personal Investigation into the Animal Origins and Nature of Man.* New York: Dell.

Arensburg, B., L. A. Schepartz, A. M. Tillier, B. Vandermeersch, and Yoel Rak. 1990. A reappraisal of the anatomical basis for speech in Middle Paleolithic hominids. *American Journal of Physical Anthropology* 83:137–146.

Arnheim, R. 1956. *Art and Visual Perception: A Psychology of the Creative Eye.* London: Faber and Faber.

Arsuaga, J.-L., I. Martinez, A. Garcia, J.-M. Carretero, and E. Carbonell. 1993. Three new human skulls from the Sima de los Huesos Middle Pleistocene site in Sierra de Atapuerca, Spain. *Nature* 362:534–537.

Arteaga, R. F. 1991. *Building of the Arch.* St. Louis, Mo.: Jefferson National Expansion Historical Association.

Asfaw, B., Y. Beyene, G. Suwa, R. Walter, T. White, G. WoldeGabriel, and T. Yemane. 1992. The earliest Acheulean from Konso-Gardula. *Nature* 360: 732–735.

Ashmore, W., and R. J. Sharer. 1996. *Discovering Our Past: A Brief Introduction to Archaeology*, 2d ed. Mountain View, Calif.: Mayfield.

Aveni, A., ed. 1977. *Native American Astronomy*. Austin: University of Texas Press.

Bahn, P. G. 1994. *Homo erectus* in Europe. *Archaeology* 47:25.

Bailey, G. N. 1978. Shell middens as indicators of postglacial economies: A territorial perspective. In *The Early Postglacial Settlement of Northern Europe: An Ecological Perspective*, edited by P. Mellars, 37–63. Pittsburgh, Pa.: University of Pittsburgh Press.

Barbetti, M., and H. Allen. 1972. Prehistoric man at Lake Mungo, Australia, by 32,000 years B.P. *Nature* 240:46–48.

Barker, G. 1978. Economic models for the Manekweni Zimbabwe, Mozambique. *Azania* 13:71–100.

Barlow, N., ed. 1958. *The Autobiography of Charles Darwin*. London: Collins.

Bartstra, G. J., S. Soegondho, and A. V. D. Wijk. 1988. Ngandong Man: Age and artifacts. *Journal of Human Evolution* 17:325–337.

Bar-Yosef, O. 1980. Prehistory of the Levant. *Annual Review of Anthropology* 9:101–133.

Bar-Yosef, O., B. Vandermeersch, B. Arensburg, A. Belfer-Cohen, P. Goldberg, H. Laville, L. Meignen, Y. Rak, J. D. Speth, E. Tchernov, A-M. Tillier and S. Weiner. 1992. The excavations in Kebara Cave, Mt. Carmel. *Current Anthropology* 33:497–534.

Beadle, G. 1977. The origin of *Zea mays*. In *The Origins of Agriculture*, edited by C. A. Reed, 615–635. The Hague: Mouton.

Beaumont, P., H. de Villiers, and J. C. Vogel. 1978. Modern man in sub-Saharan Africa prior to 49,000 B.P.: A review and evaluation with particular reference to Border Cave. *South African Journal of Science* 74:409–419.

Bednarik, R. G. 1993. Oldest dated rock art in the world. *International Newsletter on Rock Art* (4): 5–6.

Begun, D. R. 1992. Miocene fossil hominids and the chimp-human clade. *Science* 257:1929–1933.

Begun, D. R., and A. Walker. 1993. The endocast. In *The Nariokotome* Homo erectus *Skeleton*, edited by A. Walker and R. Leakey, 326–358. Cambridge: Harvard University Press.

Belfer-Cohen, A., and E. Hovers. 1992. In the eye of the beholder: Mousterian and Natufian burials in the Levant. *Current Anthropology* 33:463–471.

Ben-Itzhak, S., P. Smith, and R. A. Bloom. 1988. Radiographic study of the humerus in Neandertals and *Homo sapiens sapiens*. *American Journal of Physical Anthropology* 77:231–242.

Binford, L. 1978. *Nunamiut Ethnoarchaeology*. New York: Academic Press.

———. 1984. *Faunal Remains from Klasies River Mouth*. New York: Academic Press.

———. 1987a. *Bones: Ancient Men and Modern Myths*. New York: Academic Press.

———. 1987b. Were there elephant hunters at Torralba? In *The Evolution of Human Hunting*, edited by M. H. Nitecki and D. V. Nitecki, 47–105. New York: Plenum Press.

Binford, L., and S. Binford. 1966. A preliminary analysis of functional variability in the Mousterian of Levallois facies. *American Anthropologist* 68: 239–295.

Binford, L., and Chuan Kun Ho. 1985. Taphonomy at a distance: Zhoukoudian, "The Cave Home of Beijing Man." *Current Anthropology* 26:413–443.

Binford, L., and N. M. Stone. 1986. Zhoukoudian: A closer look. *Current Anthropology* 27:453–476.

Binford, S. 1968. Variability and change in the Near Eastern Mousterian of Levallois facies. In *New Perspectives in Archaeology*, edited by L. Binford and S. Binford, 49–60. Chicago: Aldine.

Birdsell, J. H. 1977. The recalibration of a paradigm for the first peopling of Greater Australia. In *Sunda and Sahul: Prehistoric Studies in Southeast Asia, Melanesia, and Australia*, edited by J. Allen, J. Golson, and R. Jones, 113–167. New York: Academic Press.

Bischoff, J. L., N. Soler, J. Maroto, and R. Julià. 1989. Abrupt Mousterian/Aurignacian boundary at c. 40 ka bp: Accelerator ^{14}C dates from l'Arbreda Cave (Catalunya, Spain). *Journal of Archaeological Science* 16:563–576.

Blumenschine, R. J. 1987. Characteristics of an early hominid scavenging niche. *Current Anthropology* 28:383–407.

———. 1989. A landscape taphonomic model of the scale of prehistoric scavenging opportunities. *Journal of Human Evolution* 18:345–371.

Blumenschine, R. J., and F. T. Masao. 1991. Living sites at Olduvai Gorge, Tanzania? Preliminary landscape archaeology results in the basal Bed II lake margin zone. *Journal of Human Evolution* 21:451–462.

Boaz, N. 1992. First steps into the human dawn. *Earth* (March):38–43.

Bonnichsen, R., and K. L. Turnmire, eds. 1991. *Clovis: Origins and Adaptations*. Corvallis, Ore.: Center for the Study of the First Americans.

Bordes, F. 1961. Mousterian cultures in France. *Science* 134:803–810.

———. 1972. *A Tale of Two Caves.* New York: Harper and Row.

Bordes, F., and J. Labrot. 1967. La stratigraphie du gisement de Roc de Combe et ses implications. *Bulletin de la Société Préhistorique Française* 64:15–28.

Borziyak, I. A. 1993. Subsistence practices of Late Paleolithic groups along the Dnestr River and its tributaries. In *From Kostenki to Clovis: Upper Paleolithic–Paleoindian Adaptations,* edited by O. Soffer and N. Preslov, 67–84. New York: Plenum.

Boule, M., and H. V. Vallois. 1923. *Fossil Men.* New York: Dryden Press.

Bowdler, S. 1974. Pleistocene date for man in Tasmania. *Nature* 252:697–698.

———. 1977. The coastal colonization of Australia. In *Sunda and Sahul: Prehistoric Studies in Southeast Asia, Melanesia, and Australia,* edited by J. Allen, J. Golson, and R. Jones, 205–246. New York: Academic Press.

———. 1990. Peopling Australasia: The "Coastal Colonization" hypothesis re-examined. In *The Emergence of Modern Humans: An Archaeological Perspective,* edited by P. Mellars, 327–343. Ithaca, N.Y.: Cornell University Press.

Bower, B. 1989. Talk of ages. *Science News* 136:24–26.

———. 1990. Minoan culture survived volcanic eruption. *Science News* 137:22.

———. 1992a. Early hominid's diet expands. *Science News* 141:253.

———. 1992b. *Erectus* unhinged. *Science News* 141:408–409, 411.

———. 1993a. Ancient American site identified in Alaska. *Science News* 143:215.

———. 1993b. Fossil jaw offers clue to human ancestry. *Science News* 144:277.

———. 1993c. Fossil may extend antiquity of human line. *Science News* 144:134.

———. 1993d. Lucy's new kin take a powerful stand. *Science News* 144:324.

———. 1994a. Asian hominids make a much earlier entrance. *Science News* 145:150.

———. 1994b. Neandertal tot enters human-origins debate. *Science News* 145:5.

———. 1994c. Siberian site cedes stone-age surprise. *Science News* 145:84.

———. 1994d. Savannas leave signs of slow takeover. *Science News* 145:38.

———. 1995. Human genetic origins go nuclear. *Science News* 148:52.

Bowlby, J. 1990. *Charles Darwin: A New Life.* New York: Norton.

Bowler, J. M., R. Jones, H. Allen, and A. G. Thorne. 1970. Pleistocene human remains from Australia: A living site and human cremation from Lake Mungo, western New South Wales. *World Archaeology* 2:39–60.

Bowler, J. M., A. G. Thorne, and H. A. Polach. 1972. Pleistocene man in Australia: Age and significance of the Lake Mungo skeleton. *Nature* 240:48–50.

Bowring, S. A., J. P. Grotzinger, C. E. Isachsen, A. H. Kroll, S. M. Pelechaty, and P. Kolosov. 1993. Calibrating rates of early Cambrian evolution. *Science* 261:1293–1298.

Braidwood, R. 1960. The agricultural revolution. *Science* 203:130–148.

———. 1975. *Prehistoric Men.* Glenview, Ill.: Scott, Foresman.

Brain, J. P. 1980. *Tunica Treasure.* Peabody Museum of Archaeology and Ethnology Papers 71. Cambridge, Mass.: The Museum.

Bräuer, G. 1984. A craniological approach to the origin of anatomically modern *Homo sapiens.* In *The Origins of Modern Humans: A World Survey of the Fossil Evidence,* edited by F. H. Smith and F. Spencer, 327–410. New York: Liss.

———. 1992. Africa's place in the evolution of *Homo sapiens.* In *Continuity or Replacement: Controversies in* Homo sapiens *Evolution,* edited by G. Bräuer and F. Smith, 83–98. Rotterdam: Balkema.

Bräuer, G., H. J. Deacon, and F. Zipfel. 1992. Comments on the new maxillary finds from Klasies River Mouth, South Africa. *Journal of Human Evolution* 23:419–422.

Bräuer, G., and E. Mbua. 1992. *Homo erectus* features used in cladistics and their variability in Asian and African hominids. *Journal of Human Evolution* 22:79–108.

Bräuer, G., and K. W. Rimbach. 1990. Late archaic and modern *Homo sapiens* from Europe, Africa, and Southwest Asia: Craniometric comparisons and phylogenetic implications. *Journal of Human Evolution* 19:789–807.

Brennan, M. U. 1991. Health and Disease in the Middle and Upper Paleolithic of Southwestern France: A Bioarchaeological Study. Ph.D. diss., New York University.

Brice, W. R. 1982. Bishop Ussher, John Lightfoot, and the age of creation. *Journal of Geological Education* 30:18–24.

Brooks, A. S., and B. Wood. 1990. The Chinese side of the story. *Nature* 344:288–289.

Brown, F., J. Harris, R. Leakey, and A. Walker. 1985. Early *Homo erectus* skeleton from west Lake Turkana, Kenya. *Nature* 316:788–792.

Brown, M. 1990. *The Search for Eve.* New York: Harper and Row.

Bruhns, K. O. 1994. *Ancient South America.* Cambridge World Archaeology. Cambridge: Cambridge University Press.

Bryan, A. L., ed. 1978. *Early Man in America from a Circum-Pacific Perspective.* Edmonton, Canada: Archaeological Researches International.

Buikstra, J. E. 1984. The lower Illinois River region: A prehistoric context for the study of ancient diet and health. In *Paleopathology at the Origins of Agriculture,* edited by M. N. Cohen and G. J. Armelagos, 215–234. New York: Academic Press.

Buckley, T. 1976. The discovery of Tutankhamun's tomb. In *The Treasures of Tutankhamun,* edited by K. S. Gilbert, J. K. Holt, and S. Hudson, 9–18. New York: Metropolitan Museum of Art.

Bunn, H., and E. Kroll. 1986. Systematic butchery by Plio-Pleistocene hominids at Olduvai Gorge, Tanzania. *Current Anthropology* 27:431–452.

Burger, R. L. 1988. Unity and heterogeneity within the Chavin Horizon. In *Peruvian Prehistory,* edited by R. W. Keatinge, 99–144. Cambridge: Cambridge University Press.

————. 1992. *Chavin and the Origins of Andean Civilization.* New York: Thames and Hudson.

Burnet, Reverend T. 1680. *Sacred Theory of the Earth.* London.

Burns, J. A. 1990. Paleontological perspectives on the ice-free corridor. In *Megafauna and Man: Discovery of America's Heartland,* edited by L. D. Agenbroad, J. I. Mead, and L. W. Nelson, 61–66. Hot Springs, S.D.: The Mammoth Site of Hot Springs and Northern Arizona University.

Butzer, K. 1991. An Old World perspective on potential mid-Wisconsin settlement of the Americas. In *The First Americans: Search and Research,* edited by T. D. Dillehay and D. J. Meltzer, 137–156. Boca Raton, Fla.: CRC Press.

Calder, N. 1983. *Timescale.* New York: Viking.

Callen, E. O. 1967. Analysis of the Tehuacan coprolites. In *Prehistory of the Tehuacan Valley,* Vol. 1—*Environment and Subsistence,* edited by D. Byers, 261–289. Austin: University of Texas Press.

Cann, R. L. 1992. A mitochondrial perspective on replacement or continuity in human evolution. In *Continuity or Replacement: Controversies in* Homo

sapiens *Evolution,* edited by G. Bräuer and F. Smith, 65–73. Rotterdam: Balkema.

Cann, R., O. Richards, and J. K. Lum. 1994. Mitochondrial DNA and human evolution: Our one lucky mother. In *Origins of Anatomically Modern Humans,* edited by M. H. Nitecki and D. V. Nitecki, 135–148. New York: Plenum.

Cann, R., M. Stoneking, and A. Wilson. 1987. Mitochondrial DNA and evolution. *Nature* 325:31–36.

Carbonell, E., J. M. Bermúdez de Castro, J. L. Arsuaga, J. C. Diez, A. Rosas, G. Cuenca-Bescós, R. Sala, M. Mosquera, and X. P. Rodriguez. 1995. Lower Pleistocene hominids and artifacts from Atapuerca-TD 6 (Spain). *Science* 269:826–830.

Carlisle, R. C., and J. M. Adovasio, eds. 1984. *Meadowcroft: Collected Papers on the Archaeology of Meadowcroft Rockshelter and the Cross Creek Drainage.* Pittsburgh: Department of Anthropology, University of Pittsburgh.

Carniero, R. 1970. A theory of the origin of the state. *Science* 169:733–738.

Caspari, R., and M. H. Wolpoff. 1991. The morphological affinities of the Klasies River Mouth skeletal remains. *American Journal of Physical Anthropology* 81:203.

Castleden, R. 1987. *The Stonehenge People: An Exploration of Life in Neolithic Britain 4700–2000 B.C.* London: Routledge.

Castleden, R. 1990a. *The Knossos Labyrinth.* London: Routledge.

————. 1990b. *Minoans: Life in Bronze Age Crete.* London: Routledge.

Catto, N., and C. Mandryk. 1990. Geology of the postulated ice-free corridor. In *Megafauna and Man: Discovery of America's Heartland,* edited by L. D. Agenbroad, J. I. Mead, and L. W. Nelson, 80–85. Hot Springs, S.D.: The Mammoth Site of Hot Springs and Northern Arizona University.

Cerling, T., Yang Wang, and J. Quade. 1993. Expansion of C4 ecosystems as an indicator of global ecological change in the late Miocene. *Nature* 361:344–345.

Chamberlain, A. T. 1991. A chronological framework for human origins. *World Archaeology* 23(2):137–146.

Chang, K. C. 1968. *The Archaeology of Ancient China.* 2nd ed. New Haven, Conn.: Yale University Press.

————. 1986. *The Archaeology of Ancient China.* 4th ed. New Haven, Conn.: Yale University Press.

Chapman, J., and G. D. Crites. 1987. Evidence for early maize (*Zea mays*) from Icehouse Bottom Site, Tennessee. *American Antiquity* 52:318–329.

Chard, C. 1974. *Northeast Asia in Prehistory.* Madison: University of Wisconsin Press.

Charteris, J., J. C. Wall, and J. W. Nottrodt. 1981. Functional reconstruction of gait from the Pliocene hominid footprints at Laetoli, northern Tanzania. *Nature* 290:496–498.

Chase, P. G. 1991. Symbols and Paleolithic artifacts: Style, standardization, and the imposition of arbitrary form. *Journal of Anthropological Archaeology* 10:193–214.

Chase, P. G., and H. L. Dibble. 1987. Middle Paleolithic symbolism: A review of current evidence and interpretations. *Journal of Anthropological Archaeology* 6:263–296.

Chen Tiemei, Yang Quan, and Wu En. 1994. Antiquity of *Homo sapiens* in China. *Nature* 368:55–56.

Chen Tiemei and Zhang Yinyun. 1991. Paleolithic chronology and possible coexistence of *Homo erectus* and *Homo sapiens* in China. *World Archaeology* 23(2):147–154.

Cherry, J. F. 1987. Island origins: The early prehistoric Cyclades. In *Origins: The Roots of European Civilization,* edited by B. Cunliffe, 16–29. Chicago: Dorsey Press.

Childe, V. G. 1942. *What Happened in History.* Baltimore: Pelican Books.

———. 1951. *Man Makes Himself.* New York: Mentor Books.

———. 1953. *New Light on the Most Ancient East.* New York: Norton.

Chippindale, C. 1983. *Stonehenge Complete.* Ithaca, N.Y.: Cornell University Press.

Churchill, S. E., and E. Trinkaus. 1990. Neandertal scapular glenoid morphology. *American Journal of Physical Anthropology* 83:147–160.

Ciochon, R., and R. Corruccini, eds. 1983. *New Interpretations of Ape and Human Ancestry.* New York: Plenum.

Ciochon, R., and J. James. 1994. The glory that was Angkor. *Archaeology* 47(2):38–49.

Clark, G. 1980. *Mesolithic Prelude.* Edinburgh: University of Edinburgh Press.

Clark, J. G. D. 1971. *Excavation at Star Carr.* Cambridge: Cambridge University Press.

Clarke, R. J. 1990. The Ndutu cranium and the origin of *Homo sapiens. Journal of Human Evolution* 19:699–736.

Clayton, P. A. 1994. *Chronicle of the Pharaohs: The Reign-by-Reign Record of the Rulers and Dynasties of Ancient Egypt.* London: Thames and Hudson.

Coe, M. 1968. *America's First Civilization.* New York: Van Nostrand.

———. 1992. *Breaking the Maya Code.* New York: Thames and Hudson.

———. 1993. *The Maya.* New York: Thames and Hudson.

Cohen, M. 1977. *The Food Crisis in Prehistory.* New Haven, Conn.: Yale University Press.

Cohen, M., and G. J. Armelagos. 1984. Paleopathology at the origins of agriculture: Editors' summation. In *Paleopathology at the Origins of Agriculture,* edited by M. N. Cohen and G. J. Armelagos, 585–601. New York: Academic Press.

Coltorti, M., M. Cremaschi, M. C. Delitala, D. Esu, M. Fornaseri, A. McPherron, M. Nicoletti, R. van Otterloo, C. Peretto, B. Sala, V. Schmidt, and J. Sevink. 1982. Reversed magnetic polarity in an early Paleolithic site in central Italy. *Nature* 300:173–176.

Conkey, M. 1978. Style and information in cultural evolution: Towards a predictive model for the Paleolithic. In *Social Archaeology: Beyond Subsistence and Dating,* edited by C. Redman, M. J. Berman, E. V. Curtin, W. T. Langhorne, N. M. Versaggi, and J. C. Wanser, 61–85. New York: Academic Press.

———. 1980. The identification of prehistoric hunter-gatherer aggregation sites: The case of Altamira. *Current Anthropology* 21:609–630.

———. 1981. A century of Paleolithic cave art. *Archaeology* 34(4):20–28.

Conklin, W. J., and M. Moseley. 1988. The patterns of art and power in the Early Intermediate period. In *Peruvian Prehistory,* edited by R. W. Keatinge, 145–163. Cambridge: Cambridge University Press.

Connah, G. 1987. *African Civilization: Precolonial Cities and States in Tropical Africa, an Archaeological Perspective.* Cambridge: Cambridge University Press.

Connolly, B., and R. Anderson. 1987. *First Contact: New Guinea's Highlander Encounter with the Outside World.* New York: Viking.

Constable, G. 1973. *The Neanderthals.* New York: Time-Life Books.

Cook, J., C. B. Stringer, A. P. Currant, H. P. Schwarz, and A. G. Wintle. 1982. A review of the chronology of the European Middle Pleistocene hominid record. *Yearbook of Physical Anthropology* 25:19–65.

Cordell, L. 1984. *The Archaeology of the Southwest.* New York: Academic Press.

Cosgrove, R., J. Allen, and B. Marshall. 1990. Paleoecology and Pleistocene human occupation in south central Tasmania. *Antiquity* 64:59–78.

Cowan, C. W., and P. J. Watson, eds. 1992. *The Origins of Agriculture: An International Perspective.* Washington, D.C.: Smithsonian Institution Press.

———. 1992. Some concluding remarks. In *The Origins of Agriculture: An International Perspective,* edited by C. W. Cowan and P. J. Watson, 207–212. Washington, D.C.: Smithsonian Institution Press.

Cowgill, G. L. 1988. Onward and upward with collapse. In *The Collapse of Ancient States and Civilizations,* edited by N. Yoffe and G. L. Cowgill, 244–276. Tucson: University of Arizona Press.

Crawford, G. W. 1992. Prehistoric plant domestication in East Asia. In *The Origins of Agriculture: An International Perspective,* edited by C. W. Cowan and P. J. Watson, 7–38. Washington, D.C.: Smithsonian Institution Press.

Crawford, H. 1991. *Sumer and the Sumerians.* New York: Cambridge University Press.

Crelin, E. S. 1987. *The Human Vocal Tract: Anatomy, Function, Development, and Evolution.* New York: Vantage Press.

Cummins, J., ed. 1992. *The Voyage of Christopher Columbus: Columbus' Own Journal of Discovery.* New York: St. Martin's Press.

Dalrymple, G. B., and M. A. Lanphere. 1969. *Potassium-Argon Dating: Principles, Techniques, and Applications to Geochronology.* San Francisco: W. H. Freeman.

Daniel, G., and C. Renfrew. 1988. *The Idea of Prehistory.* Edinburgh: Edinburgh University Press.

Darwin, C. 1845. *Journal of Researches into the Natural History and Geology of the Countries Visited During the Voyage of H.M.S. Beagle Round the World.* 2d ed. London: John Murray.

———. 1952. *The Origin of Species by Means of Natural Selection.* 1859 edition. Great Books of the Western World 49. Chicago: Encyclopaedia Britannica.

Dawson, C., and A. S. Woodward. 1913. On the discovery of a Paleolithic human skull and mandible in a flint-bearing gravel overlying the Wealdon (Hastings Beds) of Piltdown, Fletching (Sussex). *Quarterly Journal of the Geological Society* 69:117–151.

Day, M. 1986. *Guide to Fossil Man.* Chicago: University of Chicago Press.

Day, M., and E. H. Wickens. 1980. Laetoli Pliocene hominid footprints and bipedalism. *Nature* 286: 385–387.

Deacon, H. J., and R. Shuurman. 1992. The origins of modern people: The evidence from Klasies River. In *Continuity or Replacement: Controversies in* Homo

sapiens *Evolution,* edited by G. Bräuer and F. Smith, 121–130. Rotterdam: Balkema.

Dean, M. C., C. B. Stringer, and T. G. Bromage. 1986. Age at death of the Neandertal child from Devil's Tower, Gibraltar, and the implications for students of general growth and development in Neandertals. *American Journal of Physical Anthropology* 70: 301–309.

de Camp, L. S. 1970. *Lost Continents: The Atlantis Theme in History, Science, and Literature.* New York: Dover Books.

de la Vega, G. 1988. *The Florida of the Inca.* 1605 edition. Translated by John Varner and Jeannette Varner. Austin: University of Texas Press.

de Lumley, H. 1969. A Paleolithic camp at Nice. *Scientific American* 220(5):42–50.

Dennell, R. 1986. Needles and spear-throwers. *Natural History* 95(10):70–78.

———. 1992. The origins of crop agriculture in Europe. In *The Origins of Agriculture: An International Perspective,* edited by C. W. Cowan and P. J. Watson, 71–100. Washington, D.C.: Smithsonian Institution Press.

De Tapia, E. McC. 1992. The origins of agriculture in Mesoamerica and South America. In *The Origins of Agriculture: An International Perspective,* edited by C. W. Cowan and P. J. Watson, 143–171. Washington, D.C.: Smithsonian Institution Press.

Dettwyler, K. A. 1991. Can paleopathology provide evidence for "compassion"? *American Journal of Physical Anthropology* 84:375–384.

Diamond, J. 1987a. How do flightless mammals colonize oceanic islands? *Nature* 327:324.

———. 1987b. The worst mistake in the history of the human race. *Discover* 8:50–60.

———. 1994. How to tame a wild plant. *Discover* 15: 100–106.

Dibble, H. 1987. The interpretation of Middle Paleolithic scraper morphology. *American Antiquity* 52: 108–118.

Dickson, D. B. 1990. *The Dawn of Belief: Religion in the Upper Paleolithic of Southwestern Europe.* Tucson: University of Arizona Press.

Diehl, R. A. 1989. Olmec archaeology: What we know and what we wish we knew. In *Regional Perspectives on the Olmec,* edited by R. J. Sharer and D. C. Grove, 17–32. New York: Cambridge University Press.

Dikov, N. N. 1978. Ancestors of Paleoindians and proto-Eskimo-Aleuts in the Paleolithic of Kamchatka. In *Early Man in America from a Circum-*

Pacific Perspective, edited by A. L. Bryan, 68–69. Edmonton, Canada: Archaeological Researches International.

Dikov, N. N., and E. E. Titov. 1984. Problems of the stratification and periodization of the Ushki sites. *Arctic Anthropology* 21(2):69–80.

DiLeo, J. H. 1970. *Young Children and Their Drawings.* New York: Brunner/Mazel.

Dillehay, T. D. 1987. By the banks of the Chinchihuapi. *Natural History* 96(4):8–12.

———. 1989. *Monte Verde: A Late Pleistocene Settlement in Chile.* Vol. 1, *Paleoenvironment and Site Context.* Washington, D.C.: Smithsonian Institution Press.

Dillehay, T. D., and M. B. Collins. 1988. Early cultural evidence from Monte Verde in Chile. *Nature* 332: 150–152.

Dincauze, D. 1981. The Meadowcroft papers (Adovasio, Gunn, Donahue, Stuckenrath, Gilday, Lord, Volman, Haynes, and Mead). *Quarterly Review of Archaeology* 2:3–4.

———. 1984. An archaeo-logical evaluation of the case for pre-Clovis occupations. In *Advances in World Archaeology,* edited by F. Wendorf and A. Close. Vol. 3:275–323. New York: Academic Press.

———. 1993. Fluted points in the eastern forests. In *From Kostenki to Clovis: Upper Paleolithic–Paleoindian Adaptations,* edited by O. Soffer and N. Preslov, 279–292. New York: Plenum.

Dobyns, H. 1983. *Their Numbers Became Thinned.* Knoxville: University of Tennessee Press.

Donnelly, I. 1881. *Atlantis: The Antediluvian World.* 1971 ed. New York: Harper.

Doran, D. M. 1993. Comparative locomotor behavior of chimpanzees and bonobos: The influence of morphology on locomotion. *American Journal of Physical Anthropology* 91:83–98.

Dorit, R. L., Hiroshi Akashi, and W. Gilbert. 1995. Absence of polymorphism at the *ZFY* locus on the human Y chromosome. *Science* 268:1183–1185.

Dubois, E. 1894. *Pithecanthropus erectus.* Eine Menschenähnliche Übergangsform Aus Java. Batavia, Germany: Landersdruckerei.

Duhard, J-P. 1993. Upper Paleolithic figures as a reflection of human morphology and social organization. *Antiquity* 67:83–91.

Eldredge, N., and S. J. Gould. 1972. Punctuated equilibrium: An alternative to phyletic gradualism. In *Models in Paleobiology,* edited by T. S. Schopf, 82–115. San Francisco: Freeman, Cooper.

Elvas, Gentleman of. 1611. *The Discovery and Conquest of Tierra Florida by Don Ferdinando de Soto and Six Hundred Spaniards, his Followers.* New York: Burt Franklin.

Engels, F. 1891. *The Origins of the Family, Private Property, and the State.* Chicago: Kerr.

Evans, A. 1921–1936. *Palace of Minos.* 4 vols. Oxford: Oxford University Press.

Evans, J. D. 1968. Neolithic Knossos: The growth of a settlement. *Proceedings of the Prehistoric Society* 37(2):95–117.

Excoffier, L., and A. Langaney. 1989. Origin and differentiation of human mitochondrial DNA. *American Journal of Human Genetics* 44:73–85.

Fagan, B. M. 1991a. *Ancient North America: The Archaeology of a Continent.* London: Thames and Hudson.

———. 1991b. *Archaeology: A Brief Introduction.* 4th ed. New York: HarperCollins.

———. 1991c. *In the Beginning: An Introduction to Archaeology.* 7th ed. New York: HarperCollins.

———. 1994. *Quest for the Past: Great Discoveries in Archaeology.* Prospect Heights, Ill.: Waveland Press.

Fairservis, W. 1975. *The Roots of India.* Chicago: University of Chicago Press.

Falk, D. 1983. A reconsideration of the endocast of *Proconsul africanus:* Implications for primate brain evolution. In *New Interpretations of Ape and Human Ancestry,* edited by R. L. Ciochon and R. S. Corruccini, 239–248. New York: Plenum.

———. 1984. The petrified brain. In *Natural History* 93(9):36–39.

Farnsworth, P., J. E. Brady, M. J. DeNiro, and R. S. MacNeish. 1985. A re-evaluation of the isotopic and archaeological reconstruction of diet in the Tehuacán Valley. *American Antiquity* 50:102–116.

Feder, K. L. 1996. *Frauds, Myths, and Mysteries: Science and Pseudoscience in Archaeology,* 2d ed. Mountain View, Calif.: Mayfield.

———. 1994a. The Spanish *Entrada:* A model for assessing claims of pre-Columbian contact between the Old and New Worlds. *North American Archaeologist* 15(2):147–166.

———. 1994b. *A Village of Outcasts: Historical Archaeology and Documentary Research at the Lighthouse Site.* Mountain View, Calif.: Mayfield.

Feibel, C. S., F. H. Brown, and I. McDougal. 1989. Stratigraphic context of fossil hominids from the Omo Group deposits: Northern Turkana Basin, Kenya and Ethiopia. *American Journal of Physical Anthropology* 78:595–622.

Fischman, J. 1992. Hard evidence. *Discover* 13:44–51.

Fladmark, K. 1979. Routes: Alternate migration corridors for early man in North America. *American Antiquity* 44:55–69.

———. 1986. Getting one's Berings. *Natural History* 95(11):8–10, 14, 16–19.

Flannery, K. 1968. Archaeological systems theory and early Mesoamerica. In *Anthropological Archaeology in the Americas,* edited by B. Meggars, 67–87. Washington, D.C.: Anthropological Society of Washington.

———, ed. 1986. *Guilá Naquitz: Archaic Foraging and Early Agriculture in Oaxaca, Mexico.* New York: Academic Press.

Fleagle, J. 1988. *Primate Adaptation and Evolution.* New York: Academic Press.

Flint, R. F. 1971. *Glacial and Quarternary Geology.* New York: Wiley.

Flood, J. 1990. *Archaeology of the Dreamtime: The Story of Prehistoric Australia and Its People.* New Haven, Conn.: Yale University Press.

Foley, R. A., and P. C. Lee. 1989. Finite social space, evolutionary pathways, and reconstructing hominid behavior. *Science* 243:901–906.

Ford, R. 1985. Patterns of prehistoric food production in North America. In *Prehistoric Food Production in North America,* edited by R. Ford, 341–364. Anthropological Papers. Vol. 75. Ann Arbor: Museum of Anthropology, University of Michigan.

Fossey, D. 1983. *Gorillas in the Mist.* New York: Houghton Mifflin.

Foster, N., and L. S. Cordell, eds. 1992. *Chilies to Chocolate: Food the Americas Gave the World.* Tucson: University of Arizona Press.

Fowler, M. 1989. *The Cahokia Atlas: A Historical Atlas of Cahokia Archaeology.* Studies in Illinois Archaeology 6. Springfield, Ill.: Illinois Historic Preservation Agency.

Franciscus, R. G., and E. Trinkaus. 1988. Nasal morphology and the emergence of *Homo erectus. American Journal of Physical Anthropology* 75:517–527.

Frayer, D. W. 1992. Neanderthal features in post-Neanderthal Europeans. In *Continuity or Replacement: Controversies in* Homo sapiens *Evolution,* edited by G. Bräuer and F. Smith, 179–188. Rotterdam: Balkema.

Frayer, D. W., M. H. Wolpoff, A. G. Thorne, F. H. Smith, and G. G. Pope. 1993. Theories of modern human origins: The paleontological test. *American Anthropologist* 95:14–50.

Freeman, L. 1973. The significance of mammalian faunas from Paleolithic occupations of Cantabrian Spain. *American Antiquity* 38:3–44.

Frere, J. 1800. Account of flint weapons discovered in Hoxne in Suffolk. *Archaeologia* 13:204–205.

Fried, M. H. 1967. *The Evolution of Political Society.* New York: Random House.

Freud, S. 1976. *Introductory Lectures on Psychology.* Translated by J. Strachey. Harmondsworth, Middlesex: Penguin Books.

Frison, G. 1974a. Archaeology of the Casper site. In *The Casper Site: A Hell Gap Bison Kill on the High Plains,* edited by G. C. Frison, 1–112. New York: Academic Press.

———, ed. 1974b. *The Casper Site: A Hell Gap Bison Kill on the High Plains.* New York: Academic Press.

Fritz, G. 1994. Are the first American farmers getting younger? *Current Anthropology* 35(3):305–309.

Galanopoulos, A. G., and E. Bacon. 1969. *Atlantis: The Truth Behind the Legend.* Indianapolis: Bobbs-Merrill.

Galinat, W. C. 1992. Maize: Gift from America's first people. In *Chilies to Chocolate: Food the Americas Gave the World,* edited by N. Foster and L. S. Cordell, 47–60. Tucson: University of Arizona Press.

Gamble, C. 1982. Interaction and alliance in Paleolithic society. *Man* 17:92–107.

———. 1986. *The Paleolithic Settlement of Europe.* Cambridge: Cambridge University Press.

Gardner, H. 1980. *Artful Scribbles: The Significance of Children's Drawings.* New York: Basic Books.

Gargett, R. H. 1989. The evidence for Neandertal burial. *Current Anthropology* 30:157–177.

Garlake, P. S. 1973. *Great Zimbabwe.* London: Thames and Hudson.

Garn, S. M., A. B. Lewis, K. Koski, and D. Polachesk. 1958. The sex difference in tooth calcification. *Journal of Dental Research* 37:561–567.

Gernet, J. 1987. *A History of Chinese Civilization.* Cambridge: Cambridge University Press.

Gero, J., and M. Conkey, eds. 1990. *Engendering Archaeology.* Cambridge, England: Basil Blackwell.

Gibbons, A. 1992. Hungarian fossils stir debate on ape and human origins. *Science* 257:1864–1865.

———. 1993. Geneticists trace the DNA trail of the first Americans. *Science* 259:312–313.

Gifford-Gonzalez, D. 1993. You can hide, but you can't run: Representation of women's work in illustrations of Paleolithic life. *Visual Anthropology Review* 9(1):23–41.

Gilbert, A. S. 1989. Microscopic bone structure in wild and domestic animals: A reappraisal. In *Early Animal Domestication and Its Cultural Context,* edited by P. J. Crabtree, D. Campana, and K. Ryan, 46–86. Philadelphia: Museum Applied Science Center, University of Pennsylvania.

Gingerich, P. D. 1986. *Plesiadapis* and the delineation of the order Primates. In *Major Topics in Primate and Human Evolution,* edited by B. Wood, L. Martin, and P. Andrews, 32–46. Cambridge: Cambridge University Press.

Gish, D. 1972. *Evolution: The Fossils Say No.* San Diego: Creation Life Publishers.

Glob, P. V. 1969. *The Bog People.* New York: Ballantine Books.

Glover, I. C. 1993. Tools and cultures in Late Paleolithic southeast Asia. In *The First Humans: Human Origins and History to 10,000 B.C.,* edited by G. Burenhult, 128–130. San Francisco: HarperSanFrancisco.

Goebel, T., R. Powers, and N. Bigelow. 1991. The Nenana Complex of Alaska and Clovis origins. In *Clovis: Origins and Adaptations,* edited by R. Bonnichsen and K. L. Turnmire, 49–79. Corvallis, Ore.: Peopling of the Americas. Center for the Study of the First Americans.

Goodall, J. 1971. *In the Shadow of Man.* Boston: Houghton Mifflin.

———. 1986. *The Chimpanzees of Gombe: Patterns of Behavior.* Cambridge, Mass.: Belknap Press.

———. 1990. *Through a Window: My Thirty Years with the Chimpanzees of Gombe.* Boston: Houghton Mifflin.

Goodman, A. H., and G. Armelagos. 1985. Disease and death at Dr. Dickson's mound. In *Natural History* 94(9):12–18.

Gorman, C. 1972. Excavations at Spirit Cave, North Thailand: Some interim impressions. *Asian Perspectives* 13:79–107.

Gould, S. J. 1977a. The child as man's real father. In *Ever Since Darwin: Reflections in Natural History,* edited by S. J. Gould, 63–69. New York: Norton.

———. 1977b. Human babies as embryos. In *Ever Since Darwin,* 70–75. New York: Norton.

———. 1984. Human equality is a contingent fact of history. *Natural History* 93(11):26–33.

———. 1988. A novel notion of Neanderthal. *Natural History* 97(6):16–21.

———. 1991. Fall in the house of Ussher. *Natural History* 100(11):12, 14–16, 18–21.

———. 1994. Lucy on the earth in stasis. *Natural History* 103(9):12, 14, 16, 18–20.

Gowlett, J. 1984. Mental abilities of early man. In *Hominid Evolution and Community Ecology,* edited by R. Foley, 169–192. London: Academic Press.

———. 1986. Culture and conceptualisation. The Oldowan-Acheulean gradient. In *Stone Age Prehistory: Studies in Memory of Charles McBurney,* edited by G. N. Bailey and P. Callow, 243–260. Cambridge: Cambridge University Press.

Gramly, R. M. 1982. *The Vail Site: A Palaeo-Indian Encampment in Maine.* Bulletin of the Buffalo Society of Natural Sciences 30. Buffalo, N.Y.: Buffalo Society of Natural Sciences.

———. 1993. *The Richey Clovis Cache.* Buffalo, N.Y.: Persimmon Press.

Grayson, D. K. 1983. *The Establishment of Human Antiquity.* New York: Academic Press.

———. 1987. Death by natural causes. *Natural History* 96(5):8, 10, 12–13.

———. 1991. Late Pleistocene mammalian extinction in North America: Taxonomy, chronology, and explanations. *Journal of World Prehistory* 5(3):193–231.

Greenberg, J., C. G. Turner, II, and S. L. Zegura. 1986. The settlement of the Americas: A comparison of linguistic, dental, and genetic evidence. *Current Anthropology* 27(5):477–494.

Greene, J. C. 1959. *The Death of Adam: Evolution and Its Impact on Western Thought.* Ames: Iowa State University Press.

Grimaldi, D. 1993. Forever in amber. *Natural History* 102(6):59–61.

Grine, F. E. 1987. The diet of South African australopithecines based on a study of dental microwear. *L'Anthropologie* 91:467–482.

———. 1993. Australopithecine taxonomy and phylogeny: Historical background and recent interpretation. In *The Human Evolution Sourcebook,* edited by R. L. Ciochon and J. G. Fleagle, 198–210. Englewood Cliffs, N.J.: Prentice Hall.

Groube, L., J. Chappell, J. Muke, and D. Price. 1986. A 40,000-year-old human occupation site at Huon Peninsula, Papua New Guinea. *Nature* 324:453–455.

Grove, J. 1988. *The Little Ice Age.* London: Methuen.

Groves, C. P. 1989. A regional approach to the problem of the origin of modern humans in Australasia. In *The Human Revolution: Behavioural and Biological Perspectives in the Origins of Modern Humans,* edited by P. Mellars and C. Stringer, 274–285. Princeton, N.J.: Princeton University Press.

Grün, R. 1989. Electron spin resonance (ESR) dating. *Quaternary International* 1:65–109.

———. 1993. Electron spin resonance dating in paleoanthropology. *Evolutionary Anthropology* 2(5): 172–181.

Grün, R., P. B. Beaumont, and C. B. Stringer. 1990. ESR dating evidence for early modern humans at Border Cave in South Africa. *Nature* 344:537–539.

Grün, R., N. J. Shackleton, and H. J. Deacon. 1990. Electron-spin-resonance dating of tooth enamel from Klasies River Mouth cave. *Current Anthropology* 31(4):427–432.

Grün, R., and C. B. Stringer. 1991. Electron spin resonance dating and the evolution of modern humans. *Archaeometry* 33:153–199.

Gurney, G., and J. Forte. 1988. *Space Shuttle Log: The First 25 Flights.* Blue Ridge Summit, Pa.: Aero.

Guthrie, R. D. 1990. Late Pleistocene faunal revolution—New perspective on the extinction debate. In *Megafauna and Man: Discovery of America's Heartland,* edited by L. D. Agenbroad, J. I. Mead, and L. W. Nelson, 42–53. Hot Springs, S.D.: The Mammoth Site of Hot Springs and Northern Arizona University.

Haas, J. 1982. *The Evolution of the Prehistoric State.* New York: Columbia University.

Habgood, P. J. 1992. The origin of anatomically modern humans in east Asia. In *Continuity or Replacement: Controversies in* Homo sapiens *Evolution,* edited by G. Bräuer and F. Smith, 273–287. Rotterdam: Balkema.

Hager, L. D. 1994. "Fashioning the Primitive: 100 Years of Looking at Neandertals, Looking at Us." Paper presented at the annual meeting of the Society for American Archaeology, Anaheim, Ca.

Halvorson, J. 1987. Art for art's sake in the Paleolithic. *Current Anthropology* 28:63–71.

Hansen, J. M. 1981. *The Paleoethnobotany of Franchthi Cave, Greece.* Bloomington: Indiana University Press.

Harlan, J. 1992. Indigenous African Agriculture. In *The Origins of Agriculture: An International Perspective,* edited by C. W. Cowan and P. J. Watson, 59–70. Washington, D.C.: Smithsonian Institution Press.

Harris, J. F., and S. K. Stearns. 1992. *Understanding Maya Inscriptions.* Philadelphia: The University Museum, University of Pennsylvania.

Harrold, F. B. 1980. A comparative analysis of Eurasian Palaeolithic burials. *World Archaeology* 12: 195–211.

———. 1989. Mousterian, Chatelperronian, and Early Aurignacian in Western Europe: Continuity or discontinuity? In *The Human Revolution: Behavioural and Biological Perspectives in the Origins of Modern Humans,* edited by P. Mellars and C. Stringer, 677–713. Princeton, N.J.: Princeton University Press.

———. 1992. Paleolithic archaeology, ancient behavior, and the transition to modern *Homo.* In *Continuity or Replacement: Controversies in* Homo sapiens *Evolution,* edited by G. Bräuer and F. Smith, 219–230. Rotterdam: Balkema.

Haury, E. W., E. B. Sayles, and W. W. Wasley. 1959. The Lehner Mammoth site, southeastern Arizona. *American Antiquity* 25:2–30.

Hay, R. L., and M. Leakey. 1982. The fossil footprints of Laetoli. *Scientific American* 246(2):50–57.

Haynes, C. V. 1964. Fluted projectile points: Their age and dispersion. *Science* 145:1408–1413.

———. 1969. The earliest Americans. *Science* 166: 709–715.

———. 1980a. The Clovis culture. *Canadian Journal of Anthropology* 1:115–121.

———. 1980b. Paleoindian charcoal from Meadowcroft Rockshelter: Is contamination a problem? *American Antiquity* 45:582–587.

———. 1982. Were Clovis progenitors in Beringia? In *Paleoecology of Beringia,* edited by D. M. Hopkins, J. V. Matthews, Jr., C. E. Schweger, and S. B. Young, 383–398. New York: Academic Press.

———. 1987. Clovis origins update. *The Kiva* 52(2): 83–93.

———. 1992. Contributions of radiocarbon dating to the geochronology of the peopling of the New World. In *Radiocarbon Dating After Four Decades: An Interdisciplinary Perspective,* edited by R. R. Taylor, A. Long, and R. S. Kra, 355–374. New York: Springer-Verlag.

Hedges, S. B., S. Kumar, K. Tamura, and M. Stoneking. 1992. Human origins and analysis of mitochondrial DNA sequences. *Science* 255:737–739.

Heiser, Jr., C. B. 1990. *Seed to Civilization: The Story of Food.* Cambridge: Harvard University Press.

Heizer, R. F., and L. K. Napton. 1970. Archaeology as seen from Lovelock Cave, Nevada. *University of California Research Facility Contributions* 10(1).

Helbaek, H. 1965. Early Hassunan vegetable food at Tell-es Sawwan near Samarra. *Sumer* 20:45–48.

Henning, G. J., W. Herr, E. Weber, and N. I. Xirotiris. 1981. ESR-dating of the fossil hominid cranium from Petralona Cave, Greece. *Nature* 292:533–536.

Henry, D. O. 1989. *From Foraging to Agriculture: The Levant at the End of the Ice Age.* Philadelphia: University of Pennsylvania Press.

Higham, C. 1989. *The Archaeology of Mainland South-east Asia.* Cambridge: Cambridge University Press.

Higuchi, R., B. Bowman, M. Freiberger, O. A. Ryder, and A. C. Wilson. 1984. DNA sequences from the quagga, an extinct member of the horse family. *Nature* 312:282–284.

Hill, A., and S. Ward. 1988. Origin of the Hominidae: The record of African large Hominoid evolution between 14 My and 4 My. *Yearbook of Physical Anthropology* 31:49–83.

Hill, A., S. Ward, and B. Brown. 1992. Anatomy and age of the Lothagam mandible. *Journal of Human Evolution* 22:439–451.

Hill, A., S. Ward, A. Deino, G. Curtis, and R. Drake. 1992. Earliest *Homo. Nature* 355:719–722.

Hoffman, M. A. 1979. *Egypt Before the Pharaohs: The Prehistoric Foundations of Egyptian Civilization.* New York: Alfred A. Knopf.

———. 1983. Where nations began. *Science '83* 4(8):42–51.

Hole, F., K. Flannery, and J. A. Neely. 1969. *Prehistory and Human Ecology of the Deh Luran Plain: An Early Village Sequence from Khuzistan, Iran.* Ann Arbor: University of Michigan Press.

Holloway, R. 1980. Indonesian "Solo" (Ngandong) endocranial reconstructions: Preliminary observations and comparisons with Neandertal and *Homo erectus* groups. *American Journal of Physical Anthropology* 53:285–295.

———. 1981. The Indonesian *Homo erectus* brain endocasts revisited. *American Journal of Physical Anthropology* 55:503–521.

Hopkins, D. M. 1982. Aspects of the paleogeography of Beringia during the Late Pleistocene. In *Paleoecology of Beringia,* edited by D. M. Hopkins, J. V. Matthews, Jr., C. E. Schweger, and S. B. Young, 3–28. New York: Academic Press.

Hoppe, K. 1992. Antiquity of oldest American confirmed. *Science News* 142:334.

Huddleston, L. 1967. *Origins of the American Indians: European Concepts 1492–1729.* Austin: University of Texas Press.

Hughes, R. 1995. Behold the Stone Age. *Time* 145:52–57, 60, 62.

Hutchins, R. M., ed. 1952. *The Dialogues of Plato.* Chicago: William Benton/Encyclopedia Britannica.

Hutton, J. 1959. *Theory of the Earth: With Proofs and Illustrations.* 1795 edition, 2 vols. Weinheim, Germany: H. R. Engelmann (J. Cramer) and Wheldon & Wesley.

Ikeya, M. 1982. Petralona Cave dating controversy: Response to Henning et al. *Nature* 299:281.

Irwin, G. 1993. *The Prehistoric Exploration and Colonisation of the Pacific.* Cambridge: Cambridge University Press.

Irwin, G., S. H. Bickler, and P. Quirke. 1990. Voyaging by canoe and computer experiments in the settlement of the Pacific. *Antiquity* 64:34–50.

Isaac, G. 1977. *Olorgesailie: Archaeological Studies of a Middle Pleistocene Lake Basin in Kenya.* Chicago: University of Chicago Press.

James, S. R. 1989. Hominid use of fire in the Lower and Middle Pleistocene. *Current Anthropology* 30(1): 1–26.

Janus, C., and W. Brashler. 1975. *The Search for Peking Man.* New York: Macmillan.

Jelinek, A. J. 1992. Perspectives from the Old World on the habitation of the New. *American Antiquity* 57:345–347.

———. 1994. Hominids, energy, environment, and behavior in the Late Pleistocene. In *Origins of Anatomically Modern Humans,* edited by M. Nitecki and D. Nitecki, 67–92. New York: Plenum.

Jian Guan, and J. A. Rice. 1990. The dragon bones of Tongxin. *Natural History* 99(9):60–67.

Jochim, M. 1983. Paleolithic cave art in ecological perspective. In *Hunter-Gatherer Economy in Prehistory: A European Perspective,* edited by G. Bailey, 212–219. Cambridge: Cambridge University Press.

Johanson, D. 1993. A skull to chew on. *Natural History* 102(5):52–53.

Johanson, D., and M. Edey. 1982. *Lucy: The Beginnings of Humankind.* New York: Warner Books.

Johanson, D., L. Johanson, and B. Edgar. 1994. *Ancestors: In Search of Human Origins.* New York: Villard.

Johanson, D. C., F. T. Masao, G. G. Eck, T. D. White, R. C. Walter, W. H. Kinbel, B. Asfaw, P. Manega, P. Ndessokia, and G. Suwa. 1987. New partial skeleton of *homo habilis* from Olduvai Gorge, Tanzania. *Nature* 327:205–209.

Johanson, D., and J. Shreeve. 1989. *Lucy's Child: The Discovery of a Human Ancestor.* New York: William Morrow.

Johnson, E. 1991. Late Pleistocene cultural occupation on the southern plains. In *Clovis: Origins and Adaptations,* edited by R. Bonnichsen and K. L. Turnmire, 215–236. Corvallis, Ore.: Center for the Study of the First Americans.

Jones, R. 1987. Pleistocene life in the dead heart of Australia. *Nature* 328:666.

———. 1989. East of Wallace's Line: Issues and problems in the colonisation of the Australian continent. In *The Human Revolution: Behavioural and*

Biological Perspectives in the Origins of Modern Humans, edited by P. Mellars and C. Stringer, 741–782. Princeton, N.J.: Princeton University Press.

———. 1992. The human colonisation of the Australian continent. In *Continuity or Replacement: Controversies in* Homo sapiens *Evolution,* edited by G. Bräuer and F. Smith, 289–301. Rotterdam: Balkema.

Jordaan, H. V. F. 1976. Newborn adult brain ratios in hominid evolution. *American Journal of Physical Anthropology* 44:271–278.

Kano, T. 1990. The bonobo's peaceable kingdom. *Natural History* 99(11):62–71.

Kaplan, L. 1981. What is the origin of the common bean? *Economic Botany* 35:241–254.

Kaplan, L., and Lucille N. Kaplan. 1992. Beans of the Americas. In *Chilies to Chocolate: Food the Americas Gave the World,* edited by N. Foster and L. S. Cordell, 61–79. Tucson: University of Arizona Press.

Kaplan, L., T. F. Lynch, and C. E. S. Smith Jr. 1973. Early cultivated beans (*Phaseolus vulgaris*) from an intermontane Peruvian valley. *Science* 179:76–77.

Kappelman, J. 1993. The attraction of paleomagnetism. *Evolutionary Anthropology* 2(3):89–99.

Keeley, L. 1980. *Experimental Determination of Stone Tool Use: A Microwear Analysis.* Chicago: University of Chicago Press.

Keeley, L., and N. Toth. 1981. Microwear polishes on early stone tools from Koobi Fora, Kenya. *Nature* 293:464–465.

Kemp, B. 1977. The early development of towns in Egypt. *Antiquity* 51:185–199.

———. 1991. *Ancient Egypt.* New York: Routledge.

Kennedy, K. A. R., A. Sonakia, J. Chiment, and K. K. Verma. 1991. Is the Narmada hominid an Indian *Homo erectus? American Journal of Physical Anthropology* 86:475–496.

Kent, J. 1987. The most ancient south: A review of the domestication of the South American camelids. In *Studies in the Neolithic and Urban Revolutions,* edited by L. Manzanilla, 169–184. BAR International Series. Vol. 349. Oxford, England: British Archaeological Review.

Kenyon, K. 1954. Ancient Jericho. *Scientific American* 190(4):76–82.

Kiernan, K., R. Jones, and D. Ranson. 1983. New evidence from Fraser Cave for glacial age man in southwest Tasmania. *Nature* 301:28–32.

Kimbel, W. H., D. C. Johanson, and Y. Rak. 1994. The first skull and other new discoveries of *Australopithecus afarensis* at Hadar, Ethiopia. *Nature* 368: 449–451.

Kirch, P. V. 1984. *The Evolution of Polynesian Chiefdoms.* Cambridge: Cambridge University Press.

Klein, R. G. 1969. *Man and Culture in the Late Pleistocene: A Case Study.* San Francisco: Chandler.

———. 1976. The mammalian fauna of the Klasies River Mouth sites, Southern Cape Province, South Africa. *South African Archaeological Bulletin* 31: 75–98.

———. 1977. The ecology of early man in Southern Africa. *Science* 197:115–126.

———. 1982. Age (mortality) profiles as a means of distinguishing hunted species from scavenged ones in Stone Age archaeological sites. *Paleobiology* 8: 151–158.

———. 1983. The Stone Age prehistory of southern Africa. *Annual Review of Anthropology* 12:25–48.

———. 1987. Reconstructing how early people exploited animals: Problems and prospects. In *The Evolution of Human Hunting,* edited by M. H. Nitecki and D. V. Nitecki, 11–45. New York: Plenum.

———. 1989. *The Human Career: Human Biological and Cultural Origins.* Chicago: University of Chicago Press.

———. 1992. The archaeology of modern human origins. *Evolutionary Anthropology* 1(1):5–14.

———. 1993. Hunter-gatherers and farmers in Africa: The transformation of a continent. In *People of the Stone Age: Hunter-gatherers and Early Farmers,* edited by G. Burenhult, 39–47, 50–55. San Francisco: HarperSanFrancisco.

———. 1994. The problem of modern human origins. In *Origins of Anatomically Modern Humans,* edited by M. Nitecki and D. Nitecki, 3–17. New York: Plenum.

Knecht, H., A. Pike-Tay, and R. White. 1993. Introduction. In *Before Lascaux: The Complex Record of the Early Upper Paleolithic,* edited by H. Knecht, A. Pike-Tay, and R. White, 1–4. Boca Raton, Fla.: CRC Press.

Kramer, A. 1991. Modern human origins in Australasia: Replacement or evolution? *American Journal of Physical Anthropology* 86:455–473.

———. 1993. Human taxonomic diversity in the Pleistocene: Does *Homo erectus* represent multiple hominid species? *American Journal of Physical Anthropology* 91:161–171.

Krogman, W. M. 1962. *The Human Skeleton in Forensic Medicine.* Springfield, Ill.: Charles C. Thomas.

Krotova, A. A., and N. G. Belan. 1993. Amvrosievka: A unique Upper Paleolithic site in eastern Europe.

In *From Kostenki to Clovis: Upper Paleolithic–Paleo-indian Adaptations,* edited by O. Soffer and N. Preslov, 125–142. New York: Plenum.

Kurtén, B. 1976. *The Cave Bear Story: Life and Death of a Vanished Animal.* New York: Columbia University Press.

———. 1980. *Dance of the Tiger.* New York: Pantheon.

Lahr, M. M., and R. A. Foley. 1992. Discriminant analysis of five traits used in the multiregional model of modern human origins. *American Journal of Physical Anthropology* (Supplement) 14:104.

Laitman, J., and R. C. Heimbuch. 1984. The basicranium and upper respiratory system of African *Homo erectus* and early *Homo sapiens. American Journal of Physical Anthropology* 63:180.

Lamberg-Karlovsky, C. C., and J. A. Sabloff. 1995. *Ancient Civilizations: The Near East and Mesoamerica.* 2d ed. Prospect Heights, Ill.: Waveland Press.

Jia Lanpo and Huang Weiwen. 1990. *The Story of Peking Man.* New York: Oxford University Press.

Leakey, L. S. B., P. V. Tobias, and J. R. Napier. 1964. A new species of the genus *Homo* from Olduvai Gorge. *Nature* 202:7–9.

Leakey, M. 1971. *Olduvai Gorge 3.* Cambridge: Cambridge University Press.

Leakey, M., and R. Hay. 1979. Pliocene footprints in the Laetoli Beds at Laetoli, northern Tanzania. *Nature* 278:317–323.

Leakey, M. G., C. S. Feibel, I. McDougall, and A. Walker. 1995. New four-million-year-old hominid species from Kanapoi and Allia Bay, Kenya. *Nature* 376:565–571.

Leakey, R., and R. Lewin. 1992. *Origins Reconsidered: In Search of What Makes Us Human.* New York: Doubleday.

Leakey, R., and A. Walker. 1985a. A fossil skeleton 1,600,000 years old: *Homo erectus* unearthed. *National Geographic* 168(5):624–629.

———. 1985b. Further hominids from the Plio-Pleistocene of Koobi Fora, Kenya. *American Journal of Physical Anthropology* 64:135–163.

Lee, R. 1979. *The !Kung San: Men, Women, and Work in a Foraging Society.* Cambridge: Cambridge University Press.

LeGuin, U. K. 1972. *The Word for World Is Forest.* New York: Berkley Medallion.

Leigh, S. R. 1992. Cranial capacity evolution in *Homo erectus* and early *Homo sapiens. American Journal of Physical Anthropology* 87:1–13.

Leroi-Gourhan, A. 1968. The evolution of Paleolithic art. *Scientific American* 218(2):58–70.

———. 1982. *The Dawn of European Art: An Introduction to Paleolithic Cave Painting.* Cambridge: Cambridge University Press.

Lewin, R. 1987. *Bones of Contention: Controversies in the Search for Human Origins.* New York: Simon and Schuster.

Li Tianyuan, and D. A. Etler. 1992. New Middle Pleistocene hominid crania from Yunxian in China. *Nature* 357:404–407.

Lieberman, P. 1984. *The Biology and Evolution of Language.* Cambridge: Harvard University Press.

———. 1992. On Neanderthal speech and Neanderthal extinction. *Current Anthropology* 33:409–410.

Lieberman, P., E. Crelin, and D. H. Klatt. 1972. Phonetic ability and related anatomy of the newborn and adult human, Neanderthal Man, and the chimpanzee. *American Anthropologist* 74:287–307.

Lieberman, P., J. T. Laitman, J. S. Reidenberg, and P. J. Gannon. 1992. The anatomy, physiology, acoustics, and perception of speech: Essential elements in analysis of the evolution of human speech. *Journal of Human Evolution* 23:447–467.

Linden, E. 1992. A curious kinship: Apes and humans. *National Geographic* 181(3):2–45.

Long, A., B. Benz, J. Donahue, A. Jull, and L. Toolin. 1989. First direct AMS dates on early maize from Tehuacán, Mexico. *Radiocarbon* 31:1035–1040.

Long, J. C., A. Chakravarti, C. D. Boehm, S. Antonarakis, and H. H. Kazazian. 1990. Phylogeny of Human β-globin haplotypes and its implications for recent human evolution. *American Journal of Physical Anthropology* 81:113–130.

Lovejoy, O. C. 1981. The origin of man. *Science* 211: 341–350.

———. 1984. The natural detective. *Natural History* 93(10):24–28.

———. 1988. Evolution of human walking. *Scientific American* 259(5):118–125.

Lovejoy, O. C., K. G. Heiple, and A. Burnstein. 1973. The gait of *Australopithecus. American Journal of Physical Anthropology* 38:757–780.

Lovejoy, O. C., and E. Trinkaus. 1980. Strength and robusticity of the Neandertal tibia. *American Journal of Physical Anthropology* 53:465–470.

Lowe, G. W. 1989. The heartland Olmec: Evolution of material culture. In *Regional Perspectives on the Olmec,* edited by R. J. Sharer and D. C. Grove, 33–67. New York: Cambridge University Press.

Lu Zun'e. 1987. Cracking the evolutionary puzzle: Jinniushan Man. *China Pictorial* 4:34–45.

Luce, J. V. 1969. *Lost Atlantis: New Light on an Old Legend.* New York: McGraw-Hill.

Lundelius Jr., E. L. 1988. What happened to the mammoth? The climatic model. In *Americans Before Columbus: Ice-Age Origins,* edited by R. C. Carlisle, 75–82. Ethnology Monographs, vol. 12. Pittsburgh, Pa.: University of Pittsburgh.

Lyell, C. 1863. *The Geological Evidences of the Antiquity of Man.* London: Murray.

———. 1990. *Principles of Geology, Being an Attempt to Explain the Former Changes of the Earth's Surface, by Reference to Causes Now in Operation.* 1830 edition 2 vols. Chicago: University of Chicago Press.

Lynch, T. F. 1990. Glacial-age man in South America? A critical review. *American Antiquity* 55:12–36.

Lynch, T. F., R. Gillespie, J. A. J. Gowlett, and R. E. M. Hedges. 1985. Chronology of Guitarrero Cave, Peru. *Science* 229:864–867.

MacDonald, G. F. 1985. *Debert: A Paleo-Indian Site in Central Nova Scotia.* Buffalo, N.Y.: Persimmon Press.

MacNeish, R. S. 1964. Ancient Mesoamerican civilization. *Science* 143:531–537.

———. 1967. An interdisciplinary approach to an archaeological problem. In *Prehistory of the Tehuacan Valley.* Vol. 1, *Environment and Subsistence,* edited by D. Beyers, 14–23. Austin: University of Texas Press.

Magnusson, M., and H. Paulsson. 1965. *The Vinland Sagas.* New York: Penguin.

Maisels, C. K. 1990. *The Emergence of Civilization: From Hunting and Gathering to Agriculture, Cities, and the State in the Near East.* New York: Routledge.

Malthus, T. R. 1798. *Essay on the Principle of Population.* London: J. Murray.

Mandryk, C. A. 1990. Could humans survive the ice-free corridor?: Late-glacial vegetation and climate in west central Alberta. In *Megafauna and Man: Discovery of America's Heartland,* edited by L. D. Agenbroad, J. I. Mead, and L. W. Nelson, 67–79. Hot Springs, S.D.: The Mammoth Site of Hot Springs and Northern Arizona University.

Marinatos, S. 1972. Thera: Key to the riddle of Minos. *National Geographic* 141(5):702–726.

Marks, A. E. 1990. The Middle and Upper Paleolithic of the Near East and the Nile Valley: The problem of cultural transformations. In *The Emergence of Modern Humans: An Archaeological Perspective,* edited by P. Mellars, 56–80. Ithaca, N.Y.: Cornell University Press.

———. 1993. The early Upper Paleolithic: The view from the Levant. In *Before Lascaux: The Complex Record of the Early Upper Paleolithic,* edited by H. Knecht, A. Pike-Tay, and R. White, 5–21. Boca Raton, Fla.: CRC Press.

Marshack, A. 1972. Upper Paleolithic notation and symbol. *Science* 178:817–828.

———. 1976. Some implications of the Paleolithic symbolic evidence for the origin of language. *Current Anthropology* 17:274–282.

Martin, P. S. 1967. Prehistoric overkill. In *Pleistocene Extinctions: The Search for a Cause,* edited by P. S. Martin and H. E. Wright, 75–120. New Haven, Conn.: Yale University Press.

———. 1973. The discovery of America. *Science* 179: 969–974.

———. 1982. The pattern and meaning of holarctic mammoth extinction. In *Paleoecology of Beringia,* edited by D. M. Hopkins, J. V. Matthews, Jr., C. E. Schweger, and S. B. Young, 399–408. New York: Academic Press.

———. 1987. Clovisia the beautiful. *Natural History* 96:10–13.

Martin, P. S., and J. E. Guilday. 1967. A bestiary for Pleistocene biologists. In *Pleistocene Extinctions: The Search for a Cause,* edited by P. S. Martin and H. E. Wright, 1–62. New Haven, Conn.: Yale University Press.

Martin, P. S., and H. E. Wright, eds. 1967. *Pleistocene Extinctions: The Search for a Cause.* New Haven, Conn.: Yale University Press.

Martin, R. D. 1989. Evolution of the brain in early hominids. *Ossa* 14:49–62.

———. 1990. *Primate Origins and Evolution: A Phylogenetic Reconstruction.* Princeton, N.J.: Princeton University Press.

———. 1993. Primate origins: Plugging the gaps. *Nature* 363:223–234.

McCamant, J. F. 1992. Quinoa's roundabout journey to world use. In *Chilies to Chocolate: Food the Americas Gave the World,* edited by N. Foster and L. S. Cordell, 123–141. Tucson: University of Arizona Press.

McDermott, F., R. Grün, C. B. Stringer, and C. J. Hawkesworth. 1993. Mass-spectrometric U-series dates for Israeli Neanderthal/early modern hominid sites. *Nature* 363:252–255.

McHenry, H. M. 1991. Sexual dimorphism in *Australopithecus afarensis. Journal of Human Evolution* 20:21–32.

———. 1992. Body size and proportions in early hominids. *American Journal of Physical Anthropology* 87:407–431.

Megaw, J. V. S., and D. D. A. Simpson, eds. 1979. *Introduction to British Prehistory.* Leicester, England: Leicester University Press.

Mehringer, P. J., and F. F. Foit Jr. 1990. Volcanic ash dating of the Clovis cache at East Wenatchee, Washington. *National Geographic Research* 6(4):495–503.

Meikeljohn, C. 1978. Ecological aspects of population size and growth in late glacial and early postglacial northwestern Europe. In *The Early Postglacial Settlement of Northern Europe: An Ecological Perspective,* edited by P. Mellars, 65–79. Pittsburgh, Pa.: University of Pittsburgh Press.

Mellaart, J. 1965. *Earliest Civilizations of the Near East.* London: Thames and Hudson.

Mellars, P. 1978. Excavation and economic analysis of Mesolithic shell middens on the island of Oronsay (Inner Hebrides). In *The Early Postglacial Settlement of Northern Europe: An Ecological Perspective,* edited by P. Mellars, 371–396. Pittsburgh, Pa.: University of Pittsburgh Press.

———, ed. 1990. *The Emergence of Modern Humans: An Archaeological Perspective.* Ithaca, N.Y.: Cornell University Press.

Meltzer, D. J. 1989. Why don't we know when the first people came to North America? *American Antiquity* 54:471–490.

———. 1993a. Is there a Clovis adaptation? In *From Kostenki to Clovis: Upper Paleolithic–Paleoindian Adaptations,* edited by O. Soffer and N. Preslov, 293–310. New York: Plenum.

———. 1993b. Pleistocene peopling of the Americas. *Evolutionary Anthropology* 1(5):157–169.

———. 1993c. *Search for the First Americans.* Smithsonian: Exploring the Ancient World. Washington, D.C.: Smithsonian Books.

Mercier, N., H. Valladas, J-L. Joron, J-L. Reyss, F. Léveque, and B. Vandermeersch. 1991. Thermoluminescence dating of the late Neanderthal remains from Saint-Césaire. *Nature* 351:737–739.

Merpert, N. Y., and R. M. Munchaev. 1987. The earliest levels at Yarim Tepe I and Yarim Tepe II in northern Iraq. *Iraq* 49:1–36.

Miller, J. A. 1991. Does brain size variability provide evidence of multiple species in *Homo habilis*? *American Journal of Physical Anthropology* 84:385–398.

Miller, N. 1992. The origins of plant cultivation in the Near East. In *The Origins of Agriculture: An International Perspective,* edited by C. W. Cowan and P. J. Watson, 39–58. Washington, D.C.: Smithsonian Institution Press.

Millon, R. 1967. Teotihuacán. *Scientific American* 216:38–49.

———. 1981. Teotihuacán: City, state, and civilization. In *Supplement to the Handbook of Middle American Indians,* Vol. 1, edited by J. Sabloff, 198–243. Austin: University of Texas Press.

Minnis, P. E. 1992. Earliest plant cultivation in the desert borderlands of North America. In *The Origins of Agriculture: An International Perspective,* edited by C. W. Cowan and P. J. Watson, 121–141. Washington, D.C.: Smithsonian Institution Press.

Moeller, R. 1980. *6LF21: A Paleo-Indian Site in Western Connecticut.* Washington, Conn.: American Indian Archaeological Institute.

Molnar, S., and I. M. Molnar. 1985. The incidence of enamel hypoplasia among the Krapina Neandertals. *American Anthropologist* 87:536–549.

Monastersky, R. 1994a. Staggering through the ice ages. *Science News* 146:74–75.

———. 1994b. How stable is the current climate? *Science News* 146:75.

———. 1994c. Dinosaur DNA: Is the race finally over? *Science News* 146:324.

Moorrees, M. A., E. A. Fanning, and E. E. Hunt. 1963. Age variation of formation stages for ten permanent teeth. *Journal of Dental Research* 42:1490–1502.

Morgan, L. H. 1877. *Ancient Society.* 1964 edition. Cambridge, Mass.: Belknap Press.

Morgan, M., J. Kingston, and B. Marino. 1994. Carbon isotope evidence for the emergence of C4 plants in the Neogene from Pakistan and Kenya. *Nature* 367:162–165.

Morlan, R. E. 1970. Wedge-shaped core technology in northern North America. *Arctic Anthropology* 7(2):17–37.

Morris, C., and A. von Hagen. 1993. *The Inka Empire and Its Andean Origins.* New York: American Museum of Natural History.

Morris, H. 1974. *The Troubled Waters of Evolution.* San Diego: Creation Life Publishers.

Moser, S. 1992. The visual language of archaeology: A case study of the Neanderthals. *Antiquity* 66:831–844.

Mosimann, J. E., and P. S. Martin. 1975. Simulating overkill by Paleoindians. *American Scientist* 63:305–315.

Mowat, F. 1987. *Woman in the Mists.* New York: Warner Books.

Müller-Beck, H. 1967. On migrations of hunters across the Bering Land Bridge in the Upper Pleistocene.

In *The Bering Land Bridge,* edited by D. M. Hopkins, 373–408. Stanford, Calif.: Stanford University Press.

Napier, J. R., and P. H. Napier. 1967. *A Handbook of Living Primates.* New York: Academic Press.

Nelson, S. M. 1993. *The Archaeology of Korea.* Cambridge: Cambridge University Press.

Newcomer, M. 1971. Some quantitative experiments in handaxe manufacture. *World Archaeology* 3:85–94.

Nichols, J. 1990. Linguistic diversity and the first settlement of the New World. *Language* 66:475–521.

Noble, D. G. 1981. *Ancient Ruins of the Southwest: An Archaeological Guide.* Flagstaff, Ariz.: Northland Press.

O'Brien, P. 1984. What was the Acheulean hand ax? *Natural History* 93(7):20–23.

O'Connor, D. 1993. *Ancient Nubia: Egypt's Rival in Africa.* Philadelphia: University Museum, University of Pennsylvania.

Oates, J. 1973. The background and development of early farming communities in Mesopotamia and the Zagros. *Proceedings of the Prehistoric Society (London)* 39:147–181.

Oglivie, M. D., B. K. Curran, and E. Trinkaus. 1989. Incidence and patterning of dental enamel hypoplasia among the Neandertals. *American Journal of Physical Anthropology* 79:25–41.

Ohnuma, K., and C. A. Bergman. 1990. A technological analysis of the Upper Paleolithic levels (XXV–VI) of Ksar Akil. In *The Emergence of Modern Humans: An Archaeological Perspective,* edited by P. Mellars, 91–138. Ithaca, N.Y.: Cornell University Press.

Oliva, M. 1993. The Aurignacian in Moravia. In *Before Lascaux: The Complex Record of the Early Upper Paleolithic,* edited by H. Knecht, A. Pike-Tay, and R. White, 37–55. Boca Raton, Fla.: CRC Press.

Ovey, C., ed. 1964. *The Swanscombe Skull: A Survey of Research on a Pleistocene Site.* Occasional Paper 20. London: Royal Anthropological Institute of Great Britain and Ireland.

Owen, R. C. 1984. The Americas: The case against an Ice-Age human population. In *The Origins of Modern Humans: A World Survey of the Fossil Evidence,* edited by F. H. Smith and F. Spencer, 517–564. New York: Alam R. Liss.

Pääbo, S. 1985. Molecular cloning of ancient Egyptian mummy DNA. *Nature* 314:644–645.

———. 1989. Ancient DNA. *Proceedings of the National Academy of Sciences* 86:1939–1943.

Pääbo, S., J. A. Gifford, and A. C. Wilson. 1988. Mitochondrial sequences from a 7,000-year-old brain. *Nucleic Acids Research* 16:9775–9787.

Pääbo, S., R. G. Higuchi, and A. C. Wilson. 1989. Ancient DNA and the polymerase chain reaction. *Journal of Biological Chemistry* 264(17):9709–9712.

Parpola, A. 1993. *Deciphering the Indus Script.* Cambridge: Cambridge University Press.

Patterson, T. C. 1993. *Archaeology: The Historical Development of Civilizations.* Englewood Cliffs, N.J.: Prentice Hall.

Pauketat, T. R. 1994. *The Ascent of Chiefs: Cahokia and Mississippian Politics in Native America.* Tuscaloosa: University of Alabama Press.

PBS. 1980. Other People's Garbage. *Odyssey.* Television Documentary. PBS.

Pearsall, D. 1992. The origins of plant cultivation in South America. In *The Origins of Agriculture: An International Perspective,* edited by C. W. Cowan and P. J. Watson, 173–205. Washington, D.C.: Smithsonian Institution Press.

Pearson, R. 1978. *Climate and Evolution.* New York: Academic Press.

Pelligrino, C. 1991. *Unearthing Atlantis: An Archaeological Odyssey.* New York: Random House.

Pfeiffer, J. E. 1982. *The Creative Explosion: An Inquiry into the Origins of Art and Religion.* New York: Harper and Row.

Phillipson, D. W. 1993. *African Archaeology.* 2nd ed. Cambridge: Cambridge University Press.

Piaget, J., and B. Inhelder. 1969. *The Psychology of the Child.* London: Routledge and Kegan Paul.

Pickford, M. 1983. Sequence and environments of the lower and middle Miocene hominoids of western Kenya. In *New Interpretations of Ape and Human Ancestry,* edited by R. L. Ciochon, and R. S. Coruccini, 421–439. New York: Plenum Press.

Pineda, R. F. 1988. The late Preceramic and Initial Period. In *Peruvian Prehistory,* edited by R. W. Keatinge, 67–96. Cambridge: Cambridge University Press.

Pope, G. G. 1992. Craniofacial evidence for the origin of modern humans in China. *Yearbook of Physical Anthropology* 35:243–298.

Possehl, G. L. 1980. *Indus Civilization in Saurashtra.* Delhi, India: B. R. Publishing.

Postgate, J. N. 1992. *Early Mesopotamia: Society and Economy at the Dawn of History.* New York: Routledge.

Potts, R., and P. Shipman. 1981. Cutmarks made by stone tools on bones from Olduvai Gorge, Tanzania. *Nature* 291:577–580.

Poulianos, A. N. 1971–72. Petralona: A Middle Pleistocene cave in Greece. *Archaeology* 24/25:6–11.

Powell, M. A. 1985. Salt, seed, and yields in Sumerian agriculture: A critique of the theory of progressive salinisation. *Zeitschrift für Assyriologie* 75(1):7–38.

Powers, W. R., and T. D. Hamilton. 1978. Dry Creek: A Late Pleistocene human occupation in central Alaska. In *Early Man in America from a Circum-Pacific Perspective,* edited by A. L. Bryan, 72–77. Edmonton, Canada: Archaeological Researches International.

Powers, W. R., and J. F. Hoffecker. 1989. Late Pleistocene settlement in the Nenana Valley, central Alaska. *American Antiquity* 54:263–287.

Prentice, M. L., and G. H. Denton. 1988. The deep-sea oxygen isotope record, the global ice sheet system and hominid evolution. In *Evolutionary History of the Robust Australopithecines,* edited by F. E. Grine, 383–403. New York: Aldine de Gruyter.

Price, A. G., ed. 1971. *The Explorations of Captain James Cook in the Pacific: As Told by Selections of His Own Journals 1768–1779.* New York: Dover.

Price, T. D. 1982. Willow tales and dog smoke. *Quarterly Review of Archaeology* 3(1):4–8.

———. 1987. The Mesolithic of western Europe. *Journal of World Prehistory* 1:225–305.

———. 1991. The view from Europe: Concepts and questions about terminal Pleistocene societies. In *The First Americans: Search and Research,* edited by T. D. Dillehay and D. J. Meltzer, 185–208. Boca Raton, Fla.: CRC Press.

Price, T. D., and G. M. Feinman. 1993. *Images of the Past.* Mountain View, Calif.: Mayfield.

Quilter, J., Bernardino Ojeda E., D. M. Pearsall, D. H. Sandweiss, J. G. Jones, and E. S. Wing. 1991. Subsistence economy of El Paraíso, an early Peruvian site. *Science* 251:277–283.

Rak, Y. 1990. On the differences between two pelvises of Mousterian context from the Qafzeh and Kebara Caves, Israel. *American Journal of Physical Anthropology* 81:323–332.

Raloff, J. 1993. Corn's slow path to stardom. *Science News* 143:248–250.

Ramenofsky, A. F. 1987. *Vectors of Death.* Albuquerque: University of New Mexico Press.

Rathje, W. L. 1970. Praise the gods and pass the metates: A hypothesis of the development of lowland rainforest civilizations in Mesoamerica. In *Contemporary Archaeology,* edited by M. P. Leone, 365–392. Carbondale: University of Illinois Press.

Raven, C. E. 1950. *John Ray, Naturalist: His Life and Works.* London: Cambridge University Press.

Ray, J. 1974. *The Wisdom of God Manifested in the Works of the Creation.* 1691 ed. New York: Georg Olms Verlag.

Renfrew, C. 1972. *The Emergence of Civilization.* London: Methuen.

———. 1979. *Before Civilization: The Radiocarbon Revolution and Prehistoric Europe.* Cambridge: Cambridge University Press.

Renfrew, C., and P. Bahn. 1991. *Archaeology: Theories, Methods, and Practice.* New York: Thames and Hudson.

Rice, P. 1981. Prehistoric Venuses: Symbols of motherhood or womanhood? *Journal of Anthropological Research* 37:402–414.

Rice, P., and A. Paterson. 1985. Cave art and bones: Exploring the interrelationships. *American Anthropologist* 87:94–100.

———. 1986. Validating the cave art–archaeofaunal relationship in Cantabrian Spain. *American Anthropologist* 88:658–667.

———. 1988. Anthropomorphs in cave art: An empirical assessment. *American Anthropologist* 90:664–774.

Rightmire, G. P. 1979a. Cranial remains of *Homo erectus* from Beds II and IV, Olduvai Gorge, Tanzania. *American Journal of Physical Anthropology* 51:99–116.

———. 1979b. Implications of Border Cave skeletal remains for later Pleistocene evolution. *Current Anthropology* 20:23–35.

———. 1981. Patterns in the evolution of *Homo erectus. Paleobiology* 7(2):241–246.

———. 1984. *Homo sapiens* in sub-Saharan Africa. In *The Origins of Modern Humans: A World Survey of the Fossil Evidence,* edited by F. H. Smith and F. Spencer, 295–326. New York: Liss.

———. 1985. The tempo of change in the evolution of mid-Pleistocene *Homo.* In *Ancestors: The Hard Evidence,* edited by E. Delson, 255–264. New York: Liss.

———. 1990. *The Evolution of* Homo erectus: *Comparative Anatomical Studies of an Extinct Human Species.* New York: Cambridge University Press.

———. 1991. The dispersal of *Homo erectus* from Africa and the emergence of more modern humans. *Journal of Anthropological Research* 47:177–191.

Rightmire, G. P., and H. Deacon. 1991. Comparative studies of late Pleistocene human remains from Klasies River Mouth, South Africa. *Journal of Human Evolution* 20:131–156.

Rindos, D. 1984. *The Origins of Agriculture: An Evolutionary Perspective.* New York: Academic Press.

Roberts, D. 1993. The Ice Man: Voyager from the Copper Age. *National Geographic* 183(6):36–67.

Roberts, R. G., R. Jones, and M. A. Smith. 1990. Thermoluminescence dating of a 50,000-year-old human occupation site in northern Australia. *Nature* 345:153–156.

Rogan, P. K., and J. J. Salvo. 1990. Molecular genetics of pre-Columbian South American mummies. *UCLA Symposium in Molecular Evolution* 122:223–234.

Romer, J. 1984. *Ancient Lives: Daily Life in Egypt of the Pharaohs.* New York: Holt, Rinehart and Winston.

Rose, M. D. 1983. Miocene hominoid postcranial morphology: Monkey-like, ape-like, neither, or both? In *New Interpretations of Ape and Human Ancestry,* edited by R. L. Ciochon and R. S. Corruccini, 405–420. New York: Plenum.

Rose, Mark. 1993. Early skull found in Java. *Archaeology* 46(5):18.

Rose, Mark. 1995. The last Neandertals. *Archaeology* 48(5):12–13.

Rosenberg, K. R. 1992. The evolution of modern human childbirth. *Yearbook of Physical Anthropology* 35:89–124.

Ross, A., and D. Robins. 1989. *The Life and Death of a Druid Prince: The Story of Lindow Man, An Archaeological Sensation.* New York: Summit Books.

Ross, P. E. 1991. Mutt and Jeff: Did Cro-Magnons and Neanderthals co-exist? *Scientific American* 265(3): 40–48.

Royal Geographical Society. 1993a. *Angkor Wat.* San Francisco: InterOptica. CD-ROM.

Royal Geographical Society. 1993b. *The Egyptian Pyramids.* San Francisco: InterOptica. CD-ROM.

Royal Geographical Society. 1993c. *Inca Ruins.* San Francisco: InterOptica. CD-ROM.

Ruff, C. B. 1993. Climatic adaptation and hominid evolution: The thermoregulatory imperative. *Evolutionary Anthropology* 2(2):53–60.

Ruff, C. B., E. Trinkaus, A. Walker, and C. S. Larsen. 1993. Postcranial robusticity in *Homo.* I: Temporal trends and mechanical interpretation. *American Journal of Physical Anthropology* 91:21–53.

Ruspoli, M. 1986. *The Cave of Lascaux: The Final Photographs.* New York: Henry N. Abrams.

Sabloff, J. 1989. *The Cities of Ancient Mexico: Reconstructing a Lost World.* New York: Thames and Hudson.

———. 1994. *The New Archaeology and the Ancient Maya.* New York: Scientific American Library.

Sakellarakis, Y., and E. Sapouna-Sakellaraki. 1981. Drama of death in a Minoan temple. *National Geographic* 159(2):205–222.

Sanders, W., J. R. Parsons, and R. Santley. 1979. *The Basin of Mexico: The Cultural Ecology of a Civilization.* New York: Academic Press.

Santa Luca, A. P. 1980. The Ngandong fossil hominids: A comparative study of a Far Eastern *Homo erectus* group. *Yale University Publications in Anthropology* 78:1–175.

Saunders, J. J. 1977. Lehner Ranch revisited. *The Museum Journal* 17:48–64.

Savage, D. E., and D. E. Russell. 1983. *Mammalian Paleofaunas of the World.* Reading, Mass.: Addison-Wesley.

Scala Archives. 1994. *Voyage in Egypt: A Virtual Journey Through Ancient Egypt.* Acta-Emme. CD-ROM.

Schele, L., and D. Freidel. 1990. *A Forest of Kings: The Untold Story of the Ancient Maya.* New York: Quill/William Morrow.

Schick, K. D., and N. Toth. 1993. *Making Silent Stones Speak: Human Evolution and the Dawn of Technology.* New York: Simon and Schuster.

Schmandt-Besserat, D. 1992. *Before Writing: From Counting to Cuneiform.* 2 vols. Austin: University of Texas Press.

Schrenk, F., T. Bromage, C. Betzler, U. Ring, and Y. Juwayayi. 1993. Oldest *Homo* and Pliocene biogeography of the Malawi Rift. *Nature* 365:833–836.

Scientific American. 1994. *Exploring Ancient Cities: Sumeria.* San Francisco. CD-ROM.

Sebastian, L. 1992. *The Chaco Anasazi: Sociopolitical Evolution in the Prehistoric Southwest.* Cambridge: Cambridge University Press.

Service, E. R. 1975. *The Origins of the State and Civilization.* New York: W. W. Norton.

Shackleton, N., and N. Opdyke. 1973. Oxygen isotope and paleomagnetic stratigraphy of equatorial Pacific core V28-238: Oxygen isotope temperatures and ice volumes on a 10^5 and 10^6 year scale. *Quaternary Research* 3:39–55.

———. 1977. Oxygen-isotope and paleomagnetic stratigraphy of Pacific core V28-239 Late Pliocene and latest Pleistocene. In *Investigation of Late Quaternary Paleoceanography and Paleoclimatology,* vol. 145, edited by R. M. Cline and J. Hays, 449–464. New York: Geological Society of America.

Shackleton, N., J. Backman, H. Zimmerman, D. V. Dent, M. A. Hall, D. G. Roberts, D. Schnitker, J. G. Baldauf, A. Despraires, R. Homrighausen, P. Huddleston, J. B. Keene, A. J. Kaltenback, K. A. O. Krumsiek, A. C. Morton, J. W. Murray, and J. Westberg-Smith. 1984. Oxygen isotope calibration of the onset of ice-rafting and history of glaciation in the North Atlantic region. *Nature* 307:620–623.

Shapiro, H. L. 1974. *Peking Man.* New York: Simon and Schuster.

Sharer, R., and W. Ashmore. 1993. *Archaeology: Discovering Our Past.* 2nd ed. Mountain View, Calif.: Mayfield.

Sharer, R., and D. Grove. 1989. *Regional Perspectives on the Olmec.* New York: Cambridge University Press.

Shea, J. J. 1988. Spear points from the Middle Paleolithic of the Levant. *Journal of Field Archaeology* 15: 441–450.

———. 1989. A functional study of the lithic industries associated with hominid fossils in Kebara and Qafzeh Caves, Israel. In *The Human Revolution: Behavioral and Biological Perspectives in the Origins of Modern Humans,* edited by P. Mellars and C. Stringer, 611–625. Princeton, N.J.: Princeton University Press.

———. 1990. A further note on Mousterian spear points. *Journal of Field Archaeology* 17:111–114.

———. 1992. Lithic microwear analysis in archaeology. *Evolutionary Anthropology* 1(4):143–150.

———. 1993. Lithic use-wear evidence for hunting by Neandertals and early modern humans from the Levantine Mousterian. In *Hunting and Animal Exploitation in the Later Paleolithic and Mesolithic of Eurasia,* Archaeological Papers, vol. 4, edited by G. L. Peterkin, H. M. Bricker, and P. Mellars, 189–197. Washington, D.C.: American Anthropological Association.

———. 1994. Hunting technology in the Middle Paleolithic/Middle Stone Age: An interregional perspective. Paper presented at the Society for American Archaeology, Anaheim, California.

Shipman, P. 1983. Early hominid lifestyle: Hunting and gathering or foraging and scavenging. In *Animals and Archaeology.* International Series 163, vol. 1, edited by J. Clietton-Brock and C. Grigson, 31–49. London: British Archaeological Association.

———. 1984. Scavenger hunt. *Natural History* 93(4): 20–27.

———. 1986. Scavenging or hunting in early hominids: Theoretical framework and tests. *American Anthropologist* 88:27–43.

———. 1990. Old Masters. *Discover* 11:60–65.

Shipman, P., and J. Rose. 1983. Evidence of butchery and hominid activities at Torralba and Ambrona: An evaluation using microscopic techniques. *Journal of Archaeological Science* 10:465–474.

Shreeve, J. 1993. As the old world turns. *Discover* 14(1): 24–28.

Shutler Jr., R., ed. 1983. *Early Man in the New World.* Beverly Hills, Calif.: Sage Publications.

Sibley, C. G., and J. E. Ahlquist. 1984. The phylogeny of the hominoid primates, as indicated by DNA-DNA hybridization. *Journal of Molecular Evolution* 20:2–15.

Sillen, A., and C. K. Brain. 1990. Old flame. *Natural History* 99(4):6–10.

Silverberg, R. 1989. *The Moundbuilders.* Athens: Ohio University Press.

Simek, J. F. 1992. Neanderthal cognition and the Middle to Upper Paleolithic transition. In *Continuity or Replacement: Controversies in* Homo sapiens *Evolution,* edited by G. Bräuer and F. Smith, 231–246. Rotterdam: Balkema.

Simmons, A. H. 1986. New evidence for the early use of cultigens in the American Southwest. *American Antiquity* 51:73–89.

Singer, R., and J. Wymer. 1982. *The Middle Stone Age at Klasies River Mouth in South Africa.* Chicago: University of Chicago Press.

Sjøvold, T. 1992. The Stone Age iceman from the Alps: The find and the current status of investigation. *Evolutionary Anthropology* 1(4):117–124.

Skelton, R. R., and H. M. McHenry. 1992. Evolutionary relationships among early hominids. *Journal of Human Evolution* 23:309–349.

Smith, B. D. 1989. Origins of agriculture in eastern North America. *Science* 246:1566–1570.

———. 1992. Prehistoric plant husbandry in eastern North America. In *The Origins of Agriculture: An International Perspective,* edited by C. W. Cowan and P. J. Watson, 101–119. Washington, D.C.: Smithsonian Institution Press.

———. 1995. *The Emergence of Agriculture.* New York: Scientific American Library.

Smith, B. H. 1993. The physiological age of KNM-WT 15000. In *The Nariokotome* Homo erectus *Skeleton,* edited by A. Walker and R. Leakey, 195–220. Cambridge: Harvard University Press.

Smith, C. 1992. *Late Stone Age Hunters of the British Isles.* London: Routledge.

Smith, F. H. 1991. The Neandertals: Evolutionary dead-ends or ancestors of modern people? *Journal of Anthropological Research* 47(2):219–238.

———. 1992. The role of continuity in modern human origins. In *Continuity or Replacement: Controversies in* Homo sapiens *Evolution,* edited by G. Bräuer and F. Smith, 145–158. Rotterdam: Balkema.

———. 1994. Samples, species, and speculations in the study of modern human origins. In *Origins of*

Anatomically Modern Humans, edited by M. Nitecki and D. Nitecki, 227–252. New York: Plenum.

Smith, F. H., A. B. Falsetti, and S. M. Donnelly. 1989. Modern human origins. *Yearbook of Physical Anthropology* 32:35–68.

Smith, G. E. 1927. *Essays on the Evolution of Man.* London: Oxford University Press.

Smith, M. A. 1987. Pleistocene occupation in arid Central Australia. *Nature* 328:710–711.

Smith, Melvyn. 1985. *An Illustrated History of the Space Shuttle.* Newbury Park, Calif.: Haynes.

Smith, P. 1972. Diet and attrition in the Natufians. *American Journal of Physical Anthropology* 37: 233–238.

Smith, P., O. Bar-Yosef, and A. Sillen. 1985. Archaeological and skeletal evidence for dietary change during the Late Pleistocene/Early Holocene in the Levant. In *Paleopathology at the Origin of Agriculture,* edited by M. N. Cohen and G. J. Armelagos, 101–130. New York: Academic Press.

Snow, D. 1980. *The Archaeology of New England.* New York: Academic Press.

Soffer, O. 1992. Social transformations at the Middle to Upper Paleolithic transition. In *Continuity or Replacement: Controversies in* Homo sapiens *Evolution,* edited by G. Bräuer and F. Smith, 247–259. Rotterdam: Balkema.

———. 1993. Upper-Paleolithic adaptations in central and eastern Europe and man–mammoth interactions. In *From Kostenki to Clovis: Upper Paleolithic–Paleoindian Adaptations,* edited by O. Soffer and N. Preslov, 31–50. New York: Plenum.

———. 1994. Ancestral lifeways in Eurasia: The Middle and Upper Paleolithic record. In *Origins of Anatomically Modern Humans,* edited by M. Nitecki and D. Nitecki, 101–119. New York: Plenum.

Solecki, R. 1971. *Shanidar: The First Flower People.* New York: Knopf.

Spencer, H. 1967. *The Evolution of Society.* Chicago: University of Chicago Press.

Spencer-Wood, S. 1991. Toward an archaeology of materialistic domestic reform. In *The Archaeology of Inequality,* edited by R. H. McGuire and R. Paynter, 231–286. Cambridge, Mass.: Basil Blackwell.

Spindler, K. 1994. *The Man in the Ice.* New York: Harmony Books.

Stafford Jr., T. W. 1990. Late Pleistocene megafauna extinctions and the Clovis culture: Absolute ages based on accelerator ^{14}C dating of skeletal remains. In *Megafauna and Man: Discovery of America's Heartland,* edited by L. D. Agenbroad, J. I. Mead, and L. W. Nelson, 118–122. Hot Springs, S.D.: The Mammoth Site of Hot Springs and Northern Arizona University.

Stern, J. T., and R. L. Susman. 1983. The locomotor anatomy of *Australopithecus afarensis. American Journal of Physical Anthropology* 60:279–317.

Stiebing Jr., W. H. 1984. *Ancient Astronauts, Cosmic Collisions, and Other Popular Theories About Man's Past.* Buffalo, N.Y.: Prometheus Press.

———. 1993. *Uncovering the Past: A History of Archaeology.* New York: Oxford University Press.

Stiles, D. 1991. Early hominid behaviour and culture tradition: Raw material studies in Bed II, Olduvai Gorge. *The African Archaeological Review* 9:1–19.

Stipp, J. J., J. H. A. Chappell, and I. McDougall. 1967. K/Ar age estimate of the Pliocene–Pleistocene boundary in New Zealand. *American Journal of Science* 265:462–474.

Stone, A. C., and M. Stoneking. 1993. Ancient DNA from a pre-Columbian Amerindian population. *American Journal of Physical Anthropology* 92:463–471.

Stoneking, M. 1993. DNA and recent human evolution. *Evolutionary Anthropology* 2(2):60–73.

Straus, L. G. 1989. Age of the modern Europeans. *Nature* 342:476–477.

Stringer, C. B. 1981. The dating of European Middle Pleistocene hominids and the existence of *Homo erectus* in Europe. *Anthropologie* 19(1):3–14.

———. 1988. The dates of Eden. *Nature* 331:565–566.

———. 1990. The emergence of modern humans. *Scientific American* 263(6):98–104.

———. 1992a. Replacement, continuity, and the origin of *Homo sapiens.* In *Continuity or Replacement: Controversies in* Homo sapiens *Evolution,* edited by G. Bräuer and F. Smith, 9–24. Rotterdam: Balkema.

———. 1992b. Reconstructing recent human evolution. *Philosophical Transactions of the Royal Society of London (B)* 337:217–224.

———. 1993. Secrets of the pit of the bones. *Nature* 362:501–502.

———. 1994. Out of Africa: A personal history. In *Origins of Anatomically Modern Humans,* edited by M. Nitecki and D. Nitecki, 149–174. New York: Plenum.

Stringer, C. B., and P. Andrews. 1988. Genetic and fossil evidence for the origin of modern humans. *Science* 239:1263–1268.

Stringer, C. B., and C. Gamble. 1993. *In Search of the Neanderthals.* New York: Thames and Hudson.

Stringer, C. B., and R. Grün. 1991. Time for the last Neandertals. *Nature* 351:701–702.

Stringer, C. B., R. Grün, H. P. Schwarcz, and P. Goldberg. 1989. ESR dates for the hominid burial site of Es Skhul in Israel. *Nature* 338:756–758.

Struever, S., and F. A. Holton. 1979. *Koster: Americans in Search of Their Prehistoric Past.* Garden City, N.Y.: Anchor Press/Doubleday.

Stuart, G. E. 1972. Who were the mound builders? *National Geographic* 142(6):782–810.

Susman, R. L. 1994. Fossil evidence for early hominid tool use. *Science* 265:1570–1573.

Susman, R. L., J. T. Stern, and W. L. Jungers. 1984. Arboreality and bipedality in the Hadar hominids. *Folia Primatologica* 43:113–156.

Svoboda, J. 1993. The complex origin of the Upper Paleolithic in the Czech and Slovak Republics. In *Before Lascaux: The Complex Record of the Early Upper Paleolithic,* edited by H. Knecht, A. Pike-Tay, and R. White, 23–36. Boca Raton, Fla.: CRC Press.

Swisher, C. C., G. H. Curtis, T. Jacob, A. G. Getty, A. Suprijo, and Widiasmoro. 1994. Age of the earliest known hominids in Java, Indonesia. *Science* 263: 1118–1121.

Szabo, B., and D. Collins. 1975. Ages of fossil bones from British interglacial sites. *Nature* 254:680–682.

Szalay, F., and E. Delson. 1979. *Evolutionary History of the Primates.* New York: Academic Press.

Tague, R. G. 1992. Sexual dimorphism in the human bony pelvis, with a consideration of the Neandertal pelvis from Kebara Cave, Israel. *American Journal of Physical Anthropology* 88:1–21.

Tague, R. G., and C. O. Lovejoy. 1986. The obstetric pelvis of A.L. 288-1 (Lucy). *Journal of Human Evolution* 15:237–255.

Tainter, J. 1988. *The Collapse of Complex Societies.* New York: Cambridge University Press.

Tankersley, K. B., and C. A. Munson. 1992. Comments on the Meadowcroft Rockshelter radiocarbon chronology and the recognition of coal contaminants. *American Antiquity* 57:321–326.

Tanner, N. 1981. *On Becoming Human.* Cambridge: Cambridge University Press.

Taylor, R. E. 1991. Frameworks for dating the Late Pleistocene peopling of the Americas. In *The First Americans: Search and Research,* edited by T. D. Dillehay and D. J. Meltzer, 77–111. Boca Raton, Fla.: CRC Press.

Templeton, A. R. 1992. Human origins and analysis of mitochondrial DNA sequences. *Science* 255:737.

———. 1993. The "Eve" hypothesis: A genetic critique and reanalysis. *American Anthropologist* 95: 51–72.

Terrell, J. 1986. *Prehistory in the Pacific Islands.* Cambridge: Cambridge University Press.

Thomas, C. 1894. *Report on the Mound Explorations of the Bureau of American Ethnology.* Washington, D.C.: Smithsonian Institution.

Thomas, D. H. 1989. *Archaeology.* 2nd ed. Chicago: Holt, Rinehart and Winston.

———. 1991. *Archaeology: Down to Earth.* New York: Harcourt Brace Jovanovich.

Thomas, G. V., and A. M. J. Silk. 1990. *An Introduction to the Psychology of Children's Drawings.* New York: New York University Press.

Thorne, A. G. 1977. Separation or reconciliation? Biological clues to the development of Australian society. In *Sunda and Sahul: Prehistoric Studies in Southeast Asia, Melanesia, and Australia,* edited by J. Allen, J. Golson, and R. Jones, 187–204. New York: Academic Press.

Thorne, A. G., and M. H. Wolpoff. 1992. The multiregional evolution of humans. *Scientific American* 266(4):76–83.

Tierney, J., L. Wright, and K. Springen. 1988. The search for Adam and Eve. *Newsweek* (Jan. 11): 46–52.

Tobias, P. V. 1991. *Olduvai Gorge IV: The Skulls, Endocasts, and Teeth of* Homo habilis. Cambridge: Cambridge University Press.

Todd, I. A. 1976. *Çatal Hüyük in Perspective.* Menlo Park, Calif.: Benjamin/Cummings.

Toth, N. 1985. The Oldowan reassessed: A close look at early stone artifacts. *Journal of Archaeological Science* 2:101–120.

———. 1991. The material record. In *The First Americans: Search and Research,* edited by T. D. Dillehay and D. J. Meltzer, 53–76. Boca Raton, Fla.: CRC Press.

Trigger, B. G. 1983. The rise of Egyptian civilization. In *Ancient Egypt: A Social History,* edited by B. G. Trigger, B. J. Kemp, D. O'Connor, and A. B. Lloyd, 1–70. New York: Cambridge University Press.

Trinkaus, E. 1983a. Neandertal postcrania and the adaptive shift to modern humans. In *The Mousterian Legacy,* 165–200. Oxford, England: British Archaeological Reports, International Series, vol. 164.

———. 1983b. *The Shanidar Neandertals.* New York: Academic Press.

———. 1984. Neandertal pubic morphology and gestation length. *Current Anthropology* 25:509–514.

———. 1985. Pathology and the posture of the La Chappelle-aux-Saints Neandertal. *American Journal of Physical Anthropology* 15:193–218.

———. 1986. The Neandertals and modern human origins. *Annual Review of Anthropology* 15:193–218.

———. 1989. The Upper Pleistocene transition. In *The Emergence of Modern Humans: Biocultural Adaptations in the Later Pleistocene,* edited by E. Trinkaus, 42–46. Cambridge: Cambridge University Press.

Trinkaus, E., and P. Shipman. 1993. *The Neandertals: Changing Images of Mankind.* New York: Knopf.

Trinkaus, E., and D. D. Thompson. 1987. Femoral diaphyseal histophometric age determinators for the Shanidar 3, 4, 5, and 6 Neandertals and Neandertal longevity. *American Journal of Physical Anthropology* 72:123–129.

Trinkaus, E., and I. Villemeur. 1991. Mechanical advantages of the Neandertal thumb in flexion: A test of a hypothesis. *American Journal of Physical Anthropology* 84:249–260.

Turner, A. 1992. Large carnivores and earliest European hominids: Changing determinants of resource availability during the Lower and Middle Pleistocene. *Journal of Human Evolution* 22:109–126.

Turner, A., and A. Chamberlain. 1989. Speciation, morphological change and the status of African *Homo erectus. Journal of Human Evolution* 18:115–130.

Tyler, E. 1865. *Researches into the Early History of Mankind and the Development of Civilization.* London: J. Murray.

———. 1871. *Primitive Culture: Researches into the Development of Mythology, Philosophy, Religion, Language, Art, and Custom.* London: J. Murray.

Unger-Hamilton, R. 1989. The epi-Paleolithic southern Levant and the origins of cultivation. *Current Anthropology* 30:88–103.

Valdes, V. C., and J. L. Bischoff. 1989. Accelerator ^{14}C dates for Early Upper Paleolithic (Basal Aurignacian) at El Castillo Cave (Spain). *Journal of Archaeological Science* 16:577–584.

Valladas, H., J. L. Reyss, J. L. Joron, G. Valladas, O. Bar-Yosef, and B. Vandermeersch. 1988. Thermoluminescence dating of Mousterian "Proto-Cro-Magnon" remains from Israel and the origin of modern man. *Nature* 331:614–616.

Van Peer, P., and P. M. Vermeersch. 1990. Middle to Upper Paleolithic transition: The evidence for the Nile Valley. In *The Emergence of Modern Humans: An Archaeological Perspective,* edited by P. Mellars, 139–159. Ithaca, N.Y.: Cornell University Press.

Van Riper, A. B. 1993. *Men Among the Mammoths: Victorian Science and the Discovery of Human Prehistory.* Chicago: University of Chicago Press.

Vercors. 1953. *You Shall Know Them.* Translated by Rita Barisse. Boston: Little, Brown and Company.

Vietmeyer, N. 1992. Forgotten roots of the Incas. In *Chilies to Chocolate: Food the Americas Gave the World,* edited by N. Foster and L. S. Cordell, 95–104. Tucson: University of Arizona Press.

Vigilant, L., M. Stoneking, H. Hardpending, K. Hawkes, and A. Wilson. 1991. African populations and the evolution of human mitochondrial DNA. *Science* 253:1503–1508.

Villa, P. 1990. Torralba and Aridos: Elephant exploitation in Middle Pleistocene Spain. *Journal of Human Evolution* 19:299–309.

Vrba, E. 1985. Ecological and adaptive changes associated with early hominid evolution. In *Ancestors: The Hard Evidence,* edited by E. Delson, 63–71. New York: Liss.

———. 1988. Late Pliocene climatic events and hominid evolution. In *The Evolutionary History of the "Robust" Australopithecines,* edited by F. E. Grine, 405–426. New York: Aldine de Gruyter.

———. 1993. The pulse that produced us. *Natural History* 102(5):47–51.

Walker, A., and R. Leakey, eds. 1993. *The Nariokotome* Homo erectus *Skeleton.* Cambridge: Harvard University Press.

Walker, A., R. E. Leakey, J. M. Harris, and F. H. Brown. 1986. 2.5 Myr *Australopithecus boisei* from west of Lake Turkana, Kenya. *Nature* 322:517–522.

Walker, A., and M. Pickford. 1983. New post-cranial fossils of *Proconsul africanus* and *Proconsul nyanzae.* In *New Interpretations of Ape and Human Ancestry,* edited by R. L. Ciochon and R. S. Corruccini, 325–352. New York: Plenum.

Wallace, D. C., K. Garrison, and W. C. Knowler. 1985. Dramatic founder effects in Amerindian mitochrondrial DNAs. *American Journal of Physical Anthropology* 68:149–155.

Ward, S. C., and D. R. Pilbeam. 1983. Maxillofacial morphology of Miocene hominoids from Africa and Indo-Pakistan. In *New Interpretations of Ape and Human Ancestry,* edited by R. L. Ciochon and R. S. Corruccini, 211–238. New York: Plenum.

Warren, P. 1984. Knossos: New excavations and discoveries. *Archaeology* 37(4):48–55.

———. 1987. Crete: The Minoans and their gods. In *Origins: The Roots of European Civilization,* edited by B. Cunliffe, 30–41. Chicago: Dorsey Press.

Weaver, K. 1985. The search for our ancestors. *National Geographic* 168(5):560–623.

Weidenreich, F. 1943. The skull of *Sinanthropus pekinensis:* A comparative study on a primitive hominid skull. *Paleontologica Sinica* New Series, D:10.

Wendorf, F., A. E. Close, R. Schild, K. Wasylikowa, R. A. Housley, J. R. Harlan, and H. Królik. 1992. Saharan exploitation of plants 8,000 years B.P. *Nature* 359:721–724.

Wendorf, F., R. Schild, and A. Close. 1989. *Loaves and Fishes: The Prehistory of Waddi Kubbaniya.* Dallas, Tex.: Department of Anthropology, Southern Methodist University.

Wendorf, F., R. Schild, N. El Hadidi, A. Close, M. Kobusiewicz, H. Wieckowska, B. Issawa, and H. Hass. 1979. Use of barley in the Egyptian Late Paleolithic. *Science* 205:1341–1347.

Wendt, W. E. 1976. Art mobilier from the Apollo 11 Cave, South West Africa: Africa's oldest dated works of art. *South African Archaeological Bulletin* 31:5–11.

West, F. H. 1967. The Donnelly Ridge site and the definition of an early core-and-blade complex in central Alaska. *American Antiquity* 32:360–382.

———. 1975. Dating the Denali complex. *Arctic Anthropology* 11(1):76–81.

———. 1981. *The Archaeology of Beringia.* New York: Columbia University Press.

Wheat, J. B. 1972. *The Olsen-Chubbuck Site: A Paleo-Indian Bison Kill.* Salt Lake City, Utah: Memoir of the Society for American Archaeology 26.

Wheeler, P. E. 1991. The thermoregulatory advantages of hominid bipedalism in open equatorial environments: The contribution of increased convective heat loss and cutaneous evaporative cooling. *Journal of Human Evolution* 21:107–115.

Whiston, W. 1696. *A New Theory of the Earth.* London.

White, J. P. 1993. The settlement of ancient Australia. In *The First Humans: Human Origins and History to 10,000 B.C.,* edited by G. Burenhult, 147–151, 153–157, 160–165. San Francisco: HarperSanFrancisco.

White, J. P., and J. F. O'Connell. 1982. *A Prehistory of Australia, New Guinea, and Sahul.* New York: Academic Press.

White, L. 1959. *The Evolution of Culture: Civilization to the Fall of Rome.* New York: McGraw-Hill.

White, P. W. 1986. The Temples of Angkor: Ancient glory in stone. *National Geographic* 161(5): 552–589.

White, R. 1982. Rethinking the Middle/Upper Paleolithic transition. *Current Anthropology* 23:169–192.

———. 1986. *Dark Caves, Bright Visions: Life in Ice Age Europe.* New York: American Museum of Natural History.

———. 1993. Technological and social dimensions of "Aurignacian-age" body ornaments across Europe. In *Before Lascaux: The Complex Record of the Early Upper Paleolithic,* edited by H. Knecht, A. Pike-Tay, and R. White, 277–299. Boca Raton, Fla.: CRC Press.

White, T. 1980. Evolutionary implications of Pliocene hominid footprints. *Science* 208:175–176.

White, T., and P. A. Folkens. 1991. *Human Osteology.* San Diego: Academic Press.

White, T., and G. Suwa. 1987. Hominid footprints at Laetoli: Facts and interpretations. *American Journal of Physical Anthropology* 72:485–514.

White, T., G. Suwa, and B. Asfaw. 1994. *Australopithecus ramidus,* a new species of early hominid from Aramis, Ethiopia. *Nature* 371:306–312.

Whitley, D. S., and R. I. Dorn. 1993. New perspectives on the Clovis vs. pre-Clovis controversy. *American Antiquity* 58:626–647.

Whittle, A. 1985. *Neolithic Europe: A Survey.* Cambridge: Cambridge University Press.

Willey, G. R. 1966. "North and Middle America," Volume 1 of *An Introduction to American Archaeology.* Englewood Cliffs, N.J.: Prentice Hall.

Williams, S. 1991. *Fantastic Archaeology: The Wild Side of North American Prehistory.* Philadelphia: University of Pennsylvania Press.

Willis, D. 1989. *The Hominid Gang: Behind the Scenes in the Search for Human Origins.* New York: Viking.

Wills, W. H. 1988. *Early Prehistoric Agriculture in the American Southwest.* Santa Fe, N.M.: School of American Research.

Wilmsen, E. 1974. *Lindenmeier: A Pleistocene Hunting Society.* New York: Harper and Row.

Wilson, A. C., and R. L. Cann. 1992. The recent African genesis of humans. *Scientific American* 266(4): 68–73.

Wing, E. 1977. Animal domestication in the Andes. In *Origins of Agriculture,* edited by C. A. Reed, 837–860. The Hague: Mouton.

Wittfogel, K. 1957. *Oriental Despotism: A Comparative Study of Total Power.* New Haven, Conn.: Yale University Press.

Wolpoff, M. H. 1984. Evolution in *Homo erectus:* The question of stasis. *Paleobiology* 10(4):389–406.

———. 1989a. Multiregional evolution: The fossil alternative to Eden. In *The Human Revolution: Behavioral and Biological Perspectives in the Origins of Modern Humans,* edited by P. Mellars and C. Stringer, 62–108. Princeton, N.J.: Princeton University Press.

———. 1989b. The place of the Neandertals in human evolution. In *The Emergence of Modern Humans: Biocultural Adaptations in the Later Pleistocene,* edited by E. Trinkaus, 97–141. Cambridge: Cambridge University Press.

———. 1992. Theories of modern human origins. In *Continuity or Replacement: Controversies in* Homo sapiens *Evolution,* edited by G. Bräuer and F. Smith, 25–64. Rotterdam: Balkema.

Wolpoff, M. H., and R. Caspari. 1991. Metric analysis of the skeletal material from Klasies River Mouth, Republic of South Africa. *American Journal of Physical Anthropology* 81:319.

Wolpoff, M. H., A. G. Thorne, F. H. Smith, D. W. Frayer, and G. G. Pope. 1994. Multiregional evolution: A worldwide source for modern human populations. In *Origins of Anatomically Modern Humans,* edited by M. Nitecki and D. Nitecki, 175–199. New York: Plenum.

Wolpoff, M. H., X. Z. Wu, A. G. Thorne. 1984. Modern *Homo sapiens* origins: A general theory of hominid evolution involving the fossil evidence from East Asia. In *The Origins of Modern Humans: A World Survey of the Fossil Evidence,* edited by F. H. Smith and F. Spencer, 411–484. New York: Liss.

Woo Ju-kang (Wu Rukang). 1966. The skull of Lantian Man. *Current Anthropology* 7(1):83–86.

Wood, Bernard. 1992a. Early hominid species and speciation. *Journal of Human Evolution* 22:351–365.

Wood, Bernard. 1992b. Origin and evolution of the genus *Homo. Nature* 355:783–790.

Wright, G. 1971. Origins of food production in southwestern Asia: A survey of current ideas. *Current Anthropology* 12:447–477.

Wright, H. E. Jr., 1991. Environmental conditions for Paleoindian immigration. In *The First Americans: Search and Research,* edited by T. D. Dillehay and D. J. Meltzer, 113–135. Boca Raton, Fla.: CRC Press.

Wu Rukang (Woo Ju-kang) and Xingren Dong. 1982. Preliminary study of *Homo erectus* remains from Hexian, Anhui. *Acta Anthropological Sinica* 1(1): 2–13.

Yarnell, R. 1974. Plant food and cultivation of the Salts Caverns. In *Archaeology of the Mammoth Cave Area,* edited by P. J. Watson, 113–122. Orlando, Fla.: Academic Press.

———. 1977. Native plant husbandry north of Mexico. In *Origins of Agriculture,* edited by C. A. Reed, 861–878. The Hague: Mouton.

Yellen, J. E., A. S. Brooks, E. Cornelissen, M. J. Mehlman, and K. Stewart. 1995. A Middle Stone Age worked-bone industry from Katanda, Upper Semliki Valley, Zaire. *Science* 268:553–556.

Yi Seonbonk and G. Clark. 1985. The "Dyuktai Culture" and New World origins. *Current Anthropology* 26:1–13.

Yoffee, N., and G. L. Cowgill, eds. 1988. *The Collapse of Ancient States and Civilizations.* Tucson: University of Arizona Press.

Zeder, M. A. 1994a. After the revolution: Post-Neolithic subsistence in northern Mesopotamia. *American Anthropologist* 96:97–126.

———. 1994b. New perspectives on agricultural origins in the ancient Near East. *AnthroNotes* 16(2):1–7.

Zihlman, A. 1979. Gathering and the hominid adaptation. In *Female Hierarchies,* edited by L. Tiger and H. M. Fowler. Chicago: Beresford Book Service.

Zimmer, C. 1994. Cows were in the air. *Discover* 15:29.

Zohary, D., and M. Hopf, 1993. *Domestication of Plants in the Old World.* Oxford, England: Oxford Scientific Publications/Clarendon Press.

Zubrow, E. 1989. The demographic modeling of Neanderthal extinction. In *The Human Revolution: Behavioral and Biological Perspectives in the Origins of Modern Humans,* edited by P. Mellars and C. Stringer, 212–231. Princeton, N.J.: Princeton University Press.

Index